PAGE
42

ON THE
ROAD

YOUR COMPLETE DESTINATION GUIDE
In-depth reviews, detailed listings
and insider tips

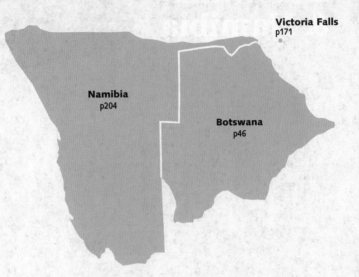

Victoria Falls
p171

Namibia
p204

Botswana
p46

THIS EDITION WRITTEN AND RESEARCHED BY

Alan Murphy
Anthony Ham, Trent Holden, Kate Morgan

welcome to Botswana & Namibia

Wildlife Watching

Botswana is one of Africa's great safari destinations. There are more elephants here than in any other country on the planet. But whether it's elephants, lions, leopards, hyenas, rhinos, buffaloes, antelopes or myriad other species, the numbers and variety in Botswana will quickly overwhelm your digital camera. In Namibia the series of waterholes around Etosha Pan attract astounding numbers of animals especially in the dry season, making wildlife watching as simple as parking your car, putting your feet up and letting the animals come to you. And if that's not up-close-and-personal enough, what about the chance to track highly endangered black rhinos... on foot?

Landscape

The landscapes of Namibia and Botswana will sometimes leave you wondering if you have arrived on another planet. That mighty gash hacked out of the earth's surface at Fish River Canyon is one of the great natural sights on the continent. Lonely desert roads expose you to a wilderness that will clear your mind and work its way into your soul. Humongous slabs of flat-topped granite rise out of mists of windblown sand and swirling dust – the effect is ethereal with the granite appearing to float above the ground. As the road

Ever wanted to experience the raw, wild heart of Africa? Teeming with wildlife and lush with extraordinary landscapes, Botswana and Namibia unfurl African dreams.

(left) A towering sand dune in Sossusvlei (p297)
(below) A belligerent hippo in the Okavango Delta (p88)

snakes into the distant horizon you may just feel as though you are driving through a coffee-table book of landscapes.

Ancient Culture

The ancestors of the San, an ancient people who have direct links back to the Stone Age, left behind extraordinary records in the form of rock paintings dotted throughout the region. The Tsodilo Hills, Botswana's only Unesco World Heritage Site, showcase the pictorial record of this prehistoric culture, as do extensive galleries of rock art in Namibia. Also, in Namibia, opportunities to interact with local cultures in the north include meeting the Himba of the Kaokoveld (a Herero subgroup that were a part of the early Bantu migrations). Here the women are famous for smearing themselves with a fragrant mixture of ochre, butter and bush herbs, which dyes their skin a burnt-orange hue.

Adventure Activities

Namibia is Southern Africa's headquarters for adrenaline-pumping fun. Fling yourself out of a plane and float back to earth, hurl yourself down a sand dune, surf the breakers on the Atlantic coast or head off into a desert sunset atop a camel. There are many ways to ensure that a visit to this region lives with you long after the desert sands recede into the distance.

❯ Botswana & Namibia

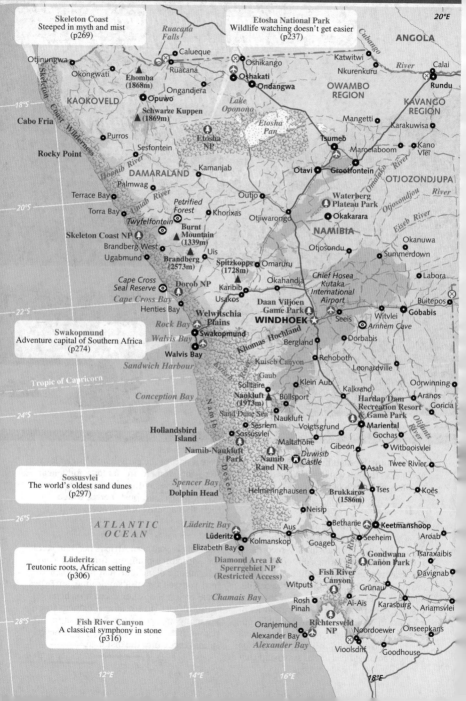

Skeleton Coast
Steeped in myth and mist
(p269)

Etosha National Park
Wildlife watching doesn't get easier
(p237)

20°E

ANGOLA

Swakopmund
Adventure capital of Southern Africa
(p274)

Sossusvlei
The world's oldest sand dunes
(p297)

Lüderitz
Teutonic roots, African setting
(p306)

Fish River Canyon
A classical symphony in stone
(p316)

Ruacana Falls · Calueque · Katwitwi · Nkurenkuru · River · Calai · Rundu

Otjinungwa · Okongwati · Ehomba (1868m) · Ruacana · Oshikango · Oshakati · Ondangwa · KAVANGO REGION · Karakuwisa

Opuwo · Ongandjera · Oshakati · OWAMBO REGION · Mangetti · Kano Vlei

KAOKOVELD · Schwarze Kuppen (1869m) · Lake Oponono · Etosha Pan · Tsumeb · Maroelaboom

Cabo Fria · Purros · Sesfontein · Etosha NP · Kamanjab · Otavi · Grootfontein · OTJOZONDJUPA

Rocky Point · Hoanib River · DAMARALAND · Otjiwarongo · Okanuwa

Palmwag · Outjo · Waterberg Plateau Park · Okakarara · Summerdown

Terrace Bay · Uniab River · Petrified Forest · Khorixas · Okakarara · Labora

Torra Bay · Twyfelfontein · Burnt Mountain (1339m) · Otjiwarongo · NAMIBIA · Otjosondu

Skeleton Coast NP · Brandberg West · Uis · Otjosondu

Ugabmund · Brandberg (2573m) · Spitzkoppe (1728m) · Omaruru · Chief Hosea Kutaka International Airport · Buitepos

Cape Cross Seal Reserve · Dorob NP · Karibib · Okahandja · Gobabis

Cape Cross Bay · Usakos · Daan Viljoen Game Park · Seeis · Witvlei · Arnhem Cave

Henties Bay · Welwitschia Plains · WINDHOEK · Dorbabis

Rock Bay · Swakopmund · Khomas Hochland · Bergland · Rehoboth · Leonardville

Walvis Bay · Kuiseb Canyon · Gaub · Klein Aub · Kalkrand · Oorwinning

Sandwich Harbour · Solitaire · Büllsport · Aranos · Goricia

Tropic of Capricorn · Naukluft (1973m) · Hardap Dam Recreation Resort & Game Park · Mariental · Gochas · Witbooisvlei

Conception Bay · Sand Dune Sea · Naukluft · Voigtsgrund · Gibeon · Twee Rivier

Hollandsbird Island · Sesriem · Sossusvlei · Maltahöhe · Asab

Namib-Naukluft Park · Namib Rand NR · Duwisib Castle

Spencer Bay · Helmeringhausen · Brukkaros (1586m) · Tses · Koës

Dolphin Head · Neisip

A T L A N T I C   O C E A N · Bethanie · Keetmanshoop · Aroab

Lüderitz Bay · Aus · Seeheim · Tsaraxaibis

Lüderitz · Kolmanskop · Goageb · Gondwana Cañon Park · Davignab

Elizabeth Bay · Diamond Area 1 & Sperrgebiet NP (Restricted Access) · Fish River Canyon · Grünau · Karasburg · Ariamsvlei

Chamais Bay · Witputs · Rosh Pinah · Ai-Ais · Karasburg · Onseepkans

Oranjemund · Richtersveld NP · Noordoewer · Goodhouse

Alexander Bay · Vioolsdrif

12°E · 14°E · 16°E · 18°E

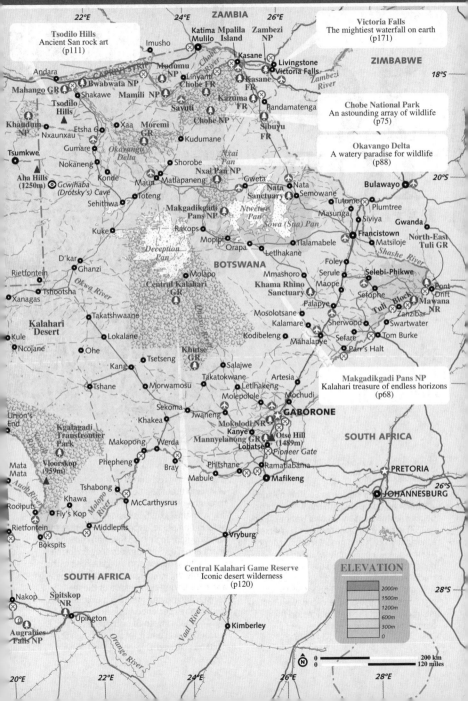

Tsodilo Hills
Ancient San rock art
(p111)

Victoria Falls
The mightiest waterfall on earth
(p171)

Chobe National Park
An astounding array of wildlife
(p75)

Okavango Delta
A watery paradise for wildlife
(p88)

Makgadikgadi Pans NP
Kalahari treasure of endless horizons
(p68)

Central Kalahari Game Reserve
Iconic desert wilderness
(p120)

ZAMBIA
ZIMBABWE
BOTSWANA
SOUTH AFRICA
SOUTH AFRICA
Kalahari Desert

22°E 24°E 26°E 28°E
18°S
20°S
26°S
28°S

ELEVATION

2000m
1500m
1200m
600m
300m
0

200 km
120 miles

Imusho
Katima Mulilo
Mpalila Island
Zambezi NP
Kasane
Livingstone
Victoria Falls
Andara
Mudumu NP
Linyanti
Chobe FR
Kasane FR
Bwabwata NP
Mahango GR
Shakawe
Mamili NP
Savuti
Kazuma FR
Pandamatenga
Tsodilo Hills
Chobe NP
Sibuyu FR
Khaudum NP
Nxaunxau
Etsha 6
Xaa
Moremi GR
Kudumane
Tsumkwe
Gumare
Okavango Delta
Shorobe
Nxai Pan
Bulawayo
Nokaneng
Matlapaneng
Nxai Pan NP
Gweta
Nata
Aha Hills (1250m)
Gcwihaba (Drotsky's) Cave
Maun
Nata Sanctuary
Semowane
Tutume
Plumtree
Sehithwa
Toteng
Ntwetwe Pan
Masunga
Siviya
Gwanda
Kuke
Makgadikgadi Pans NP
Rakops
Sowa (Sua) Pan
Francistown
Matsiloje
North-East Tuli GR
Mopipi
Orapa
Tlalamabele
Shashe River
D'kar
Deception Pan
Letlhakane
Foley
Rietfontein
Ghanzi
Molapo
Mmashoro
Serule
Selebi-Phikwe
Tshootsha
Central Kalahari GR
Khama Rhino Sanctuary
Maope
Sefophe
Pont Drift
Xanagas
Kalamare
Palapye
Mawana NR
Takatshwaane
Mosolotsane
Sherwood
Swartwater
Zanzibar
Tuli Block
Kule
Lokalane
Kodibeleng
Sefare
Tom Burke
Ncojane
Ohe
Mahalapye
Tsetseng
Khutse GR
Parr's Halt
Kang
Salajwe
Takatokwane
Artesia
Tshane
Morwamosu
Letlhakeng
Mochudi
Makgadikgadi Pans NP
Union's End
Sekoma
Molepolole
GABORONE
Khakea
Jwaneng
Mokolodi NR
Kgalagadi Transfrontier Park
Makopong
Werda
Kanye
Otse Hill (1489m)
SOUTH AFRICA
Vloorskop (959m)
Phepheng
Bray
Mannyelanong GR
Lobatse
Pioneer Gate
Mata Mata
Phitshane
Ramatlabama
Auob River
Tshabong
Mabule
Mafikeng
PRETORIA
Rooiputs
Khawa
Fly's Kop
McCarthysrus
Molopo River
JOHANNESBURG
Rietfontein
Middlepits
Bokspits
Vryburg
Nakop
Spitskop NR
Upington
Kimberley
Augrabies Falls NP
Orange River
Vaal River

Zambezi River
Okwa River
Okwa River
Auob River

N

16 TOP EXPERIENCES

Etosha National Park (Namibia)

1 There are few places in Southern Africa that can compete with the wildlife prospects in extraordinary Etosha National Park (p237). A network of waterholes dispersed among the bush and grasslands surrounding the pan – a blindingly white, flat, saline desert that stretches into the horizon – attracts enormous congregations of animals. A single waterhole can render thousands of sightings over the course of a day – Etosha is simply one of the best places on the planet for watching wildlife.

Sossusvlei (Namibia)

2 Towering red dunes of incredibly fine sand that feels soft when it trickles through your fingers and changes indelibly with the light, Sossusvlei (p297) is an astounding place, especially given that the sands originated in the Kalahari millions of years ago. The Sossusvlei valley is dotted with hulking dunes and interspersed with unearthly dry *vleis* (low, open landscapes), and clambering up the face of these constantly moving giants is a uniquely Namibian experience. You survey the seemingly endless swath of nothingness that surrounds you and it feels as though time itself has slowed. Dry *vlei* and red dunes, Sossusvlei

Okavango Delta (Botswana)

3 The Okavango (p88) is an astonishing, beautiful, wild place. Home to wildlife spectacles of rare power and drama, the delta changes with the seasons as flood waters ebb and flow, creating islands, river channels and pathways for animals that move this way and that at the waters' behest. Exclusive and remote lodges are an Okavango speciality but self-drivers can find outstanding campsites in the heart of the Okavango's Moremi Game Reserve. No visit to the delta is complete without drifting through the waters in a traditional *mokoro* (dugout canoe).

Fish River Canyon (Namibia)

4 This enormous gash in the surface of the planet in the south of Namibia is an almost implausible landscape. Seen most clearly in the morning, Fish River Canyon (p316) is desolate, immense and seemingly carved into the earth by a master builder. The exposed rock and lack of plant life is quite startling and trying to take pictures is soon replaced with thoughtful reflection and a quiet sense of awe. Its rounded edges and sharp corners create a symphony in stone of gigantic and imposing proportions.

PATRICIO ROBLES GIL / GETTY IMAGES ©

DANITA DELIMONT / GETTY IMAGES ©

PATRICK DIEUDONNE / GETTY IMAGES ©

Chobe National Park (Botswana)

5 There are more elephants in Chobe – tens of thousands of them – than anywhere else on earth. And these are big elephants, *really* big. Then there are the iconic landscapes of Savuti, with its elephant-eating lions; or Linyanti, one of the best places on the continent to see the highly endangered African wild dog; or the Chobe Riverfront, where most of Africa's charismatic megafauna comes to drink. Put all of this together and it's easy to see why Chobe National Park (p75) ranks among the elite of African safari destinations.

Lüderitz (Namibia)

6 Namibia is a country that defies African stereotypes and this is perhaps nowhere more true than in the historic colonial town of Lüderitz (p306). Straddling the icy South Atlantic and the blazing-hot Namib Desert, this bizarre mini-Deutschland is seemingly stuck in a time warp. After walking its streets, and sitting down to a plate of sausages and sauerkraut with an authentic Weiss beer, you'll survey the German art nouveau architecture, check the map again and shake your head in disbelief.

San Rock Art (Botswana)

7 The Tsodilo Hills (p113), Botswana's only Unesco World Heritage Site, are sometimes referred to as the 'Louvre of the Desert'. More than 4000 ancient paintings, many dating back thousands of years, adorn the caves and cliffs of these picturesque mountains, which remain a sacred site for the San people. Expertly rendered in ochre-hued natural pigments, the paintings are at once beautiful and an invaluable chronology of the evolving relationship between human beings and the natural world. And such is their remoteness that you might just have them all to yourself.

The San People

8 In both Botswana and Namibia opportunities exist to interact with the San people – the original inhabitants of Southern Africa whose presence stretches back as much as 20,000 years. Lying at the edge of the Kalahari in Namibia, Otjozondjupa (p254) is part of the traditional homeland of the Ju/'hoansi San. In Tsumkwe you can arrange everything from bush walks to hunting safaris. In Botswana chances to interact with these modern-day descendants of all our ancestors – in a way that can benefit the local community – exist in villages such as D'kar (p119).

Adventure Activities

9 Namibia is fast becoming the headquarters of adventure sports in the region. If you want to jump out of a plane, hurtle down the face of a sand dune in the world's oldest desert, or live out your *Lawrence of Arabia*–inspired fantasies on the back of a camel, you're in the right place. A uniquely African activity is black rhino tracking – on foot – through wild bushland with a couple of trackers, a guide and a lot of caution. Sandboarding near Swakopmund

IAN MURPHY / GETTY IMAGES ©

CRAIG PERSHOUSE / GETTY IMAGES ©

THORSTEN MILSE / ROBERT HARDING WORLD IMAGERY / CORBIS ©

Victoria Falls

10 The largest, most beautiful and simply the greatest waterfall in the world. As iconic to Africa as 'Dr Livingstone I presume', thunderous Victoria Falls (p171) will blow your mind and soak your shirt. It's the sheer scale of the falls that is its most impressive feature. A million litres of water a second are funnelled over the 108m drop, creating a plume of spray that can be seen for kilometres. When you're in Southern Africa this really is a sight that you should move heaven and earth to see.
Victoria Falls National Park, Zimbabwe

Swakopmund (Namibia)

11 Easily Namibia's finest urban scene, swanky Swakopmund (p274) is a feast of German art nouveau architecture, with its seaside promenades, half-timbered homes and colonial-era buildings. Stuck out on the South Atlantic coast and surrounded by desert, it feels like a movie set. Let loose on a skydive, horse ride or sandboard down a 300m dune because you are in the adventure capital of the region. 'Swakop' pulls off the backpacker scene and the clinking-wine-glass set equally, so you'll find your niche here. Hohenzollern Building, Swakopmund

Skeleton Coast (Namibia)

12 Travel in this part of Namibia, a treacherous stretch of the coast where many ships have become graveyards, is the stuff of road-journey dreams. It's a murky region with rocky and sandy coastal shallows, where rolling fogs and swirling sandstorms encapsulate its ghostly, isolated and untamed feel. The Skeleton Coast (p269) is among the most remote and inaccessible areas in the vast country of Namibia. And it's here in this wilderness that you can put your favourite music on, sit back and let reality meet your imagination.

13

ROGER DE LA HARPE / GETTY IMAGES ©

14

DAVE HAMMAN / GETTY IMAGES ©

Makgadikgadi Pans National Park (Botswana)

13 Part of the world's largest network of salt pans, the endless horizons of Makgadikgadi (p74) are one of the Kalahari's least-known treasures. It is here, during the rainy season, that zebras migrate en masse, in one of the great wildlife migrations in a continent of many. During the dry season wildlife draws near to the rejuvenated Boteti River in similarly epic numbers. And across the pans, remote islands of baobabs rise up from the salt like evocations of some ancient African oasis. Rock formations on Kubu Island, Sowa Pan, Makgadikgadi Pans National Park

Central Kalahari Game Reserve (Botswana)

14 There is something about the Kalahari (p116). Perhaps it owes its unmistakable gravitas to a name that carries more than a whiff of African magic. Or perhaps it is the sheer vastness of this desert, Africa's largest protected wilderness area. The presence of black-maned Kalahari lions doesn't hurt either. Whatever the reason, this is not your average desert, home instead to ancient river valleys, light woodland and surprising concentrations of wildlife around its extensive network of salt pans. And then there is the silence of the Kalahari night...

SHAEN ADEY / GETTY IMAGES ©

DAVID CAYLESS / GETTY IMAGES ©

Camping out on Safari

15 There's nothing quite like it for sharpening your senses and heightening your awareness of Africa. Sleeping under the stars is a soulful experience and the antithesis of the modern world's clamour – an infinity of stars, the crackle of the campfire, the immensity of the African night. But it's not for the faint-hearted, with wind whistling in the guy ropes, the not-so-distant roar of a lion, and the knowledge that only flimsy canvas separates you from an angry hippo. Campsite on the Orange River, |Ai- |Ais Richtersveld Transfrontier Park

The Himba/Herero

16 The rich culture of Namibia is best experienced in the varied communities of its Herero population (numbering approximately 120,000), of which the Himba of the Kaokoveld are a subgroup. The characteristic Herero women's dress is derived from that of Victorian-era German missionaries and consists of an enormous crinoline worn over a series of petticoats, with a horn-shaped hat or headdress. In contrast, Himba women are famous for smearing themselves with a fragrant mixture of ochre, butter and bush herbs, which dyes their skin a burnt-orange hue. Himba mother and child

need to know

See also each destination's opening pages

Currency
» Namibian dollars (N$)
» Botswana pula (P)

When to Go

Desert, dry climate

Rundu
GO Jun–Nov

• **Tsumeb**
GO May–Oct

• **Windhoek**
GO Apr–Nov

•
Swakopmund
GO Apr–May, Oct–Dec

Luderitz •
GO Apr–Oct

High Season
(May-Oct)

» Dry season, warm clear days, hotter in September to October in Botswana.

» Best time for wildlife watching as animals congregate around waterholes.

» Sandstorms in Swakopmund and Walvis Bay June to August.

Shoulder Season
(Nov & Apr)

» A good time with fewer tourists and good wildlife viewing.

» The 'little rains' come in Namibia in November.

» By April the floodwaters have reached the upper Delta in Botswana.

Low Season
(Dec-Mar)

» The rainy season, many tracks impassable but fewer tourists.

» The parks can be lush with new-season growth.

» From December to March it's roasting and some long hiking trails are closed.

Your Daily Budget

Budget up to US$50

» Dorm beds and campsites: US$10-20

» Use combis (minibuses) to get around between major towns

» Namibia is more budget-friendly than Botswana

» Do a supermarket shop before visiting national parks

Midrange US$50-100

» Guesthouse, B&B or hotel double: US$60-80

» Namibia has more options than Botswana

» Shop around for the best 4WD deal – options vary considerably

Top end over US$100

» Lodge and camps: US$100 plus

» Best eating is in the cities, larger towns and upmarket lodges

» Tours widely available

Language

» English

Visas

» Not required for most nationalities visiting Namibia; visitors to Botswana require a visa but they are free for many nationalities.

Mobile Phones

» Local SIM cards can be used in Australian and European phones. Wide swathes of both countries (especially Namibia) not covered by the mobile network.

Driving

» Drive on the left; steering wheel is on the right side of the car, as in the UK and Australia.

Websites

» **Botswana Tourism** (www.botswanatourism.co.bw) Department of Tourism website.

» **Cardboard Box Travel Shop** (www.namibian.org) Namibia's best adventure-travel agency.

» **Lonely Planet** (www.lonelyplanet.com) Destination information, hotel bookings, traveller forum and more.

» **Namibia Wildlife Resorts** (www.namibiawildliferesorts.com) Info and booking service for Namibia's national parks.

Money

» ATMs widely available in larger towns and cities.

» Credit cards widely accepted in most shops, restaurants and hotels (but not all petrol stations).

» Travellers cheques can be cashed at most banks and exchange offices.

» US$ the best currency to carry, although GBP and South African rand also widely accepted.

Don't Leave Home Without

» Binoculars and a field guide.

» Mosquito repellent, net and prophylaxis.

» Neutral-coloured clothing for safari.

» Small beanbag for steadying camera .

» Tracks4Africa paper and GPS maps.

» Travel insurance.

» Wind and waterproof jacket.

» Yellow fever vaccination certificate.

» An adaptor for electrical appliances.

» A Leatherman-style multipurpose tool and a compass.

Arriving in Southern Africa

» **OR Tambo International Airport, Johannesburg**
The main gateway to the region with regular flights to Windhoek and Gaborone.

» **Chief Hosea Kutako International Airport, Windhoek**
Taxis – N$300.

» **Sir Seretse Khama International Airport, Gaborone**
Taxis – rarely turn up at the airport (P70 to the centre).
Courtesy minibuses are operated by the top-end hotels for their guests; non-guests may be able to hitch a ride.

Driving in Remote Areas

Careful preparations for any remote trips in Botswana and Namibia are required. You will need a robust 4WD vehicle, and enough supplies to see you through the journey – this includes enough food and water for the entire trip. You should also travel in a convoy of at least two vehicles. Carry several spare tyres for each vehicle, a tyre iron, a good puncture-repair kit and a range of vehicle spares, as well as twice as much petrol as the distances would suggest. For navigation, use a compass, or preferably a global positioning system (GPS). Relevant topographic sheets are also extremely helpful. Avoid camping in shady and inviting riverbeds, as large animals often use them as thoroughfares, and even when there's not a cloud in the sky, flash floods can roar down them with alarming force.

if you like...

Fly-In Safaris

Botswana is Southern Africa's top-end safari destination, and many tour operators specialise in fly-in safaris or include a fly-in element in their itineraries. It can be the only way to reach remote areas in Namibia such as the north of the Skeleton Coast.

Okavango Delta Particularly popular, the luxury lodges operating these services are some of Africa's most exclusive (p103)

Moremi Game Reserve The only officially protected area within the delta, so plenty of wildlife; several truly decadent lodges (p103)

Chobe National Park Lodges here boast panoramic views across the Chobe River with herds of elephants easily seen from the grounds of your accommodation (p75)

Tuli Block A swath of freehold farmland in Botswana's east supports luxury lodges operating fly-in safaris to this unique landscape and rich concentrations of wildlife (p66)

Skeleton Coast Wilderness Area Remote, wild and virtually inaccessible unless you're willing to fly in (p273)

Rock Art

The rock art of these countries is both an extraordinary chronology of an ancient people and a startling artistic form that is a link to our ancient ancestors. Dotted around in hills and caves, these are magical, sacred works of art.

Tsodilo Hills Revered by the San, this 'desert Louvre' is one of Botswana's premier sites for this pictorial form of San chronology and includes the fascinating 'zebra painting' (p111)

Twyfelfontein One of Africa's most extensive galleries of rock art (p262)

The Brandberg Fire Mountain is an extraordinarily beautiful slab of granite, containing the famous 'White Lady of the Brandberg' among a treasure chest of ancient rock paintings (p260)

National Museum of Namibia Excellent rock-art display with some great reproductions; ideal to visit before seeing rock-art sites (p209)

Birdwatching

Botswana is a birding utopia with almost 600 species recorded. Namibia's best birdlife is concentrated in the lush Caprivi Strip. Species include the delta's famous African skimmers, bee-eaters, lilac-breasted rollers, pygmy geese, goshawks, several species of vultures and African fish eagles.

Okavango Panhandle A narrow strip of swampland that extends for about 100km to the Namibian border, the area is known for its fine birdwatching (p108)

Chobe Riverfront There is extraordinary variety in the birdlife along the riverfront and overhead there's a good chance of spotting African fish eagles (p81)

Nata Bird Sanctuary A quarter of Botswana's birds call the sanctuary home and it's covered in a sea of pink flamingos, and other migratory birds, during the rains (p68)

Caprivi Strip Mahango Game Reserve and Mamili National Park present Namibia's best birdwatching opportunities. Mamili has recorded more than 430 species (p248)

Walvis Bay Lesser and greater flamingos flock in large numbers to pools along the Namib Desert coast, particularly around Walvis Bay and Lüderitz (p286)

MARTIN HARVEY / GETTY IMAGES ©

» Gunn's Camp (p101), Okovango Delta

Adventure Sports

Adventure sports thrive in Namibia with most enthusiasts zeroing in on the Atlantic coast. Here you can sandboard an ancient desert, throw yourself out of a plane, surf the Atlantic or go horse riding into a blazing sunset.

Swakopmund Namibia and indeed Southern Africa's capital of adventure sports, this is adrenaline-junkie heaven (p274)

Rhino Tracking Following black rhinos through the bush may not be considered a traditional adventure sport, but when it's on foot... (p265)

Quad Biking Opportunities exist in both countries, although in Botswana it is generally limited to top-end lodges (eg in Makgadikgadi Pans)

Scenic Flights Namibia's coastline, especially the Skeleton Coast, or the Okavango Delta in Botswana, offer the chance of light-aircraft or helicopter flights over jaw-dropping scenery

Trekking Multi-day hiking opportunities exist throughout the region, although many are closed out of season

Watching Wildlife

Some of the best wildlife watching on the continent is at your fingertips here. Unique wildlife opportunities include tracking black rhinos in the wild, and catching a glimpse of some of the world's remaining African wild dog population.

Chobe National Park Often noted as one of Africa's best parks for watching wildlife. Accessible and with a great variety of animals including dense elephant populations (p75)

Etosha National Park Another destination that showcases incredible wildlife numbers and accessibility with animals crowding around easily seen waterholes (p237)

Okavango Delta One of the world's largest inland river deltas, the waters come and go, sustaining vast quantities of wildlife (p88)

Makgadikgadi Pans National Park The largest network of salt pans in the world, Nxai Pans has a reputation for cheetah sightings (p74)

Landscapes

One of the best things about driving yourself is the incredible array of landscapes you encounter: from swirling desert sands and slabs of ancient granite mountains, to rock-strewn moonscapes, bush and grass savannahs and life-giving water playgrounds with well-vegetated islands.

Southern Namibia In the desolate southern Namib are pastel-coloured mountains 'floating' in swirling mists of sand and dust like a mirage

Etosha Pan Stand out on the pan and survey an empty saline nothingness that bursts into life after the rains; and just behind is an artist's palette of African savannah (p237)

Okavango Delta As desert turns into fertile land the ebb and flow of Mother Nature on the landscape is more apparent here, one of the world's largest inland river deltas, than anywhere in the region (p88)

Northwestern Namibia Some of the region's most incredible landscapes imaginable include the Skeleton Coast and the Kaokoveld with its wide-open vistas and lonely desert roads (p258)

If you like ... movie sets, Namibia in particular is a popular destination, recently hosting the *Mad Max 4* crew just outside of Henties Bay.

Deserts

Deserts here are smothered in superlatives such as 'oldest desert in the world' and 'the largest volume of sand of any desert on earth' but it's the colours, the naked space and the rhythm of hot and cold that most visitors will remember.

The Kalahari The 'land of thirst', a dry, parched land imbued with mesmerising colour, is a primeval landscape made up of stone, thorns and brush (p116)

Kgalagadi Transfrontier Park One of the largest and most pristine arid wilderness areas on the continent. The only place in Botswana where you'll see shifting sand, this is true desert (p126)

Namib Desert One of the oldest and driest ecosystems on earth with a landscape that is constantly changing – known for its iconic sand dunes shaped by the wind, while colours shift with the changing light (p290)

National Parks

Often protecting remarkable landscapes, ecosystems and populations of African animals, the region's parks are the reason most visitors are here. The scale of many parks is immense and the range of activities they offer well organised.

Namibia's National Parks Etosha has an extraordinary landscape that combines a vast dried saline pan with rich bush and grassland that supports astonishing diversity and numbers of wildlife. The Khaudum National Park is largely undeveloped and a real wilderness adventure. The Caprivi Strip plays host to a number of parks that scrape the edge of Botswana's Okavango Delta (p342)

Botswana's National Parks The wildlife-rich Chobe has some of the best wildlife viewing in Southern Africa. Moremi Game Reserve shelters a healthy population of very rare wild dogs. The Makgadikgadi and Nxai Pans National Parks play host to herds of wildebeest, zebra and other hoofed mammals and one of the largest migrations on earth (p151)

Off-Road Driving

There's plenty to challenge 4WD enthusiasts who like to get off-road. In many remote places age-old tracks (in perilous condition after the rains) are the only way to navigate through the African wilderness.

Central Kalahari Game Reserve An off-roader's dream; if you're after solitude, desertscapes and the echo of lions roaring in the night, this enormous heart of the African wilderness could become your favourite (p120)

The Kaokoveld One of the last true wildernesses in Southern Africa, the remote and beguiling Kaokoveld is crisscrossed by sandy tracks laid down decades ago – this is a serious off-road challenge (p265)

Khaudum National Park With virtually no signage, and navigation dependent on GPS coordinates and topographic maps, Khaudum is a wildlife and off-road adventure (p247

Makgadikgadi Pans If the notion of exploring 12,000 sq km of disorientating salt pans is your idea of an adventure, then calibrate your GPS and head straight here (p68)

» Meerkat, Makgadikgadi Pans (p68)

Architecture

An ensemble of European architecture, particularly the remarkably rich collection of German art nouveau buildings found in Namibia, is often a shock to first-time visitors. In Botswana visitors may stumble across a colonial vestige harking back to the early 1900s.

Lüderitz There is an absurdity to this town littered with German colonial relics wedged between the desert and the rollers of the south Atlantic – it's just ludicrous...(p306)

Swakopmund This is where Namibia's German heritage shines, with its seaside promenades, half-timbered homes and colonial-era buildings (p274)

Windhoek There are a few streets in the capital where colonial styling still radiates. Neo-baroque cathedral spires, as well as a few seemingly misplaced German castles, punctuate the skyline (p205)

Botswana Traditional Batswana architecture is compact and beautiful and blends well with the landscape. Mochudi is a village where visitors can see classic Botswanan architecture (p58)

Hiking

A great way to experience the magic of the region is to hear the crunch of the earth beneath your boots. Some of Southern Africa's great hikes are here and multi-day treks really enable you to immerse yourself in this ancient landscape.

Fish River Canyon The best – and really one of the only – ways to get a feel for this massive gash in the earth is to embark on a challenging five-day hike along the valley floor (p316)

Kgalagadi Transfrontier Park A remote corner of Botswana, the park offers some challenging multi-day hikes along wilderness tracks (p126

Waterberg Plateau Park Four-day guided and unguided trails are available through some pristine wilderness landscape with the possibility of some rare wildlife sightings (p231)

month by month

March

A big month for festivals in the region; the rains are still around but the sizzling temperatures are coming to an end.

Mbapira/Enjando Street Festival

Windhoek's biggest street party occurs in March every year. It's also a good excuse for people to dress in extravagant ethnic clothes that bring the streets to life.

Maitisong Festival

Held in Gaborone over one week in March and/or April, this festival (www.maitisong.org) is the highlight of the Botswana calendar for lovers of local and regional music, dance and drama. The festival features an outdoor programme that takes place on several stages throughout the capital.

Independence Day

On 21 March, this Namibian national day is celebrated in grand style, with a parade and sports events. Many can still recall the day that Namibia wrestled control of its own affairs off South Africa in 1990.

Ditshwanelo Human Rights Film Festival

A series of screenings on various human-rights subjects are held at the AV Centre, Maru a Pula School, during this festival (www.ditshwanelo.org.bw), and guest speakers are invited to talk about their experiences.

April

The end of the low season – parks have new growth, the rains are finishing and the temperatures are becoming more pleasant but tourist numbers are still down.

Windhoek Karnival (WIKA)

Established in 1953 by a small group of German immigrants, Windhoek's April Karnival (www.windhoek-karneval.com) is now one of the highlights of Namibia's cultural calendar, culminating in the Royal Ball.

Maun Festival

A two-day celebration with plenty of music, parades, poetry, theatre, craftwork, dance and food; visual arts also feature. The festival, held in Maun, raises funds for local schools while commemorating northwestern Botswana's rich cultural roots.

May

Beginning of the dry season and a great time to visit before high season proper; a couple of very interesting festivals showcase both cinema and traditional culture.

Wild Cinema Festival

This film festival is just a few years old but proving popular. It showcases the work of local and South African talent at cinemas throughout Windhoek.

Tjilenje (Ngwao Boswa) Cultural Festival

Celebrations during this festival are rural, taking place in Nlapkhwane (northeastern Botswana) and include traditional Tswana dancing, games and yummy homemade cooking.

July

High season is beginning to crank up. Expect warm, clear days and ideal conditions (apart from coastal Namibia where sandstorms can be a problem).

President's Day
Folk flock home to their villages to celebrate this holiday on the third weekend of July. It features the usual festival antics – dancing, singing and speeches.

August

Wildlife watching is at its best as water sources become limited in the parks; and August has some festivals dedicated to both bushman culture and important historical events.

Kuru Dance Festival
Another worthwhile cultural festival, held near D'kar in the Kalahari Desert, when all aspects of traditional bushman culture are on display. Traditional dancing and local music feature throughout the three days of the festival.

Maherero Day
This is one of Namibia's largest festivals, falling on the weekend nearest 26 August. Dressed in traditional garb, the Red Flag Herero people gather in Okahandja for a memorial service to commemorate their chiefs killed in the Khoikhoi and German wars.

September

Temperatures are rising in Botswana but it's still a popular time for travel to the region and tourist numbers are high. Windhoek puts on some great celebrations.

/AE//Gams Arts Festival
Windhoek's main arts festival is held in September, and includes troupes of dancers, musicians, poets and performers all competing for various prizes. The best of Namibian food is also on show.

Windhoek Show
In late September or early October the city holds this show (www.windhoekshow.na), with its roots in agriculture, on the showgrounds near the corner of Jan Jonker and Centaurus Sts. Historically the event stretches back to 1899.

Domboshaba Festival of Culture & History
Held near the Domboshaba ruins in Botswana, this cultural celebration pays homage to a period 1000 years ago when the Kalanga inhabited the valleys around Limpopo. Kalanga dance features as does choral music, crafts and traditional foods.

October

The end of high season, with the rains around the corner, but Windhoek is a magnet for beer drinkers and it's a popular time, especially for German tourists.

Oktoberfest
Windhoek stages its own Oktoberfest – an orgy of food, drink and merrymaking in an event that showcases the best in German beer, usually drunk at tables set up inside large marquees. There's plenty of traditional German dress on display too.

Orange Youth Cup
Every year Botswana's top youth football teams get together for a showdown. Unearthing talent is a prime goal of the tournament and it could provide a break for some talented youngsters.

itineraries

Whether you've got six days or 60, these itineraries provide a starting point for the trip of a lifetime. Want more inspiration? Head online to lonelyplanet. com/thorntree to chat with other travellers.

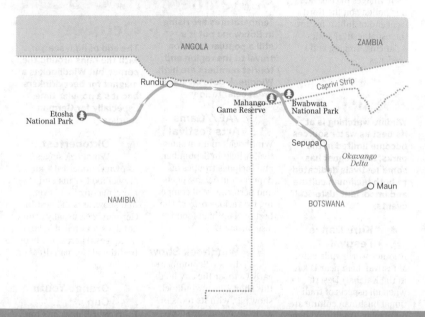

10 days
A Taste of the North

> From **Etosha National Park**, home to some of the best wildlife viewing in Southern Africa, depart via the Von Lindequist Gate in the east and head northeast to steamy **Rundu** on the Angolan border, via Grootfontein. Spend a day lazing in one of the river side lodges on the banks of the Okavango River and then track east into the Caprivi Strip to **Bwabwata National Park** and the **Mahango Game Reserve**, which attract large groups of elephants and herd animals. Head south through the reserve to the Mahango-Mohembo border post, where formalities are straightforward, and cross into Botswana. From here you can track down the western side of the Okavango Panhandle and down to **Sepupa**. For a taste of the delta to come, you can organise a *mokoro* (dugout canoe) trip here or go fishing – it's a good place for a break before the serious business of wildlife watching starts further into the delta. When you're ready to begin your delta adventure head southeast to **Maun**, the main gateway to the Okavango Delta, with some good accommodation options. The road is sealed all the way.

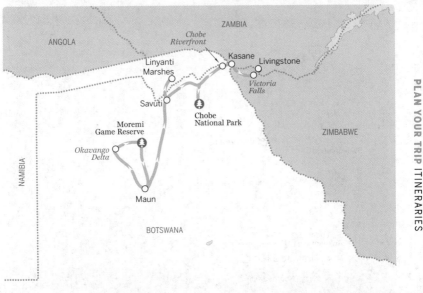

Three Weeks
Essential Botswana & Victoria Falls

For most of this trip, you will have to be completely self-sufficient and fully confident in your navigation and survival skills. For the less adventurous, tour operators in Maun are happy to help you organise a custom safari.

Starting in **Maun**, the classic staging point for all Botswanan safaris, you can stock up on supplies before heading out to the **Okavango Delta**, either by *mokoro* or charter plane. If you're pinching your pennies, there's no shortage of budget camping trips to choose from, though it's certainly worth stretching your budget to allow for a few nights in one of the safari-chic tented camps in the wildlife-rich **Moremi Game Reserve** (try Chief's Island if you can afford it). Containing some of the densest concentrations of wildlife on the continent, Moremi is also the only protected area of the delta.

The next stage of your bush travel is a 4WD expedition through **Chobe National Park** (known for its huge populations of massive elephants). Stop at **Savuti**, where most megafauna are resident, and which is particularly well known for sightings of predators; **Linyanti Marshes**, an extensive wetland with opportunities to see elephants, lions, wild dogs, cheetahs and leopards; and the **Chobe Riverfront**, which is the most accessible part of Chobe and has the largest wildlife concentration in the park. Whether you travel by private vehicle or tour bus, the overland route through Chobe is one of the country's most spectacular and wildlife-rich journeys.

Make another supply stop in the border town of **Kasane**, at the meeting point of four countries – Botswana, Zambia, Namibia and Zimbabwe – and it's time to cross the border to visit the world-famous **Victoria Falls**. The falls are the seventh natural wonder of the world and a visit reveals nature at its most inspiring. Whether you base yourself in **Livingstone**, Zambia or **Victoria Falls**, Zimbabwe, it's worth exploring life on both sides of the Zambezi River. And of course, if you've got a bit of cash burning a hole in your pocket, there's no shortage of pulse-raising activities to help you get a quick adrenaline fix. Try a micro flight over the falls for a unique perspective of this watery wonder.

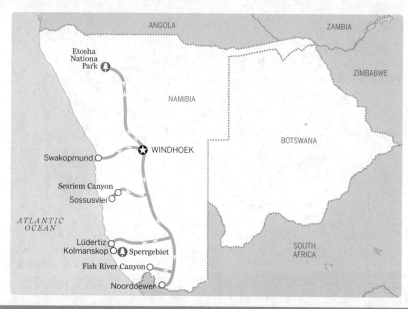

Essential Namibia

This enormous itinerary meanders more than 2500km, from dusty bushveld to dramatic canyons. It combines a good dose of culture with death-defying activities, and all of it is accessible with a 2WD vehicle. There are also decent, if slow, public-transport links.

Before striking off into the desert, spend a couple of days getting your bearings in the lovely capital of **Windhoek**, which still bears architectural traces of its German colonial history. Ideally with a rental car loaded with plenty of supplies and a few friends, make a beeline north for **Etosha National Park**, one of the finest safari parks on the continent. It is possible to actually drive out onto the pan with its white saline floor stretching as far as you can see into the horizon.

Although you're going to have to backtrack, you can quickly bypass Windhoek en route to seaside **Swakopmund**, where you can take your holiday up a notch in a flurry of exciting activities, including dune boarding and quad biking. Back on the main road south, keep the heart beating during a scramble up the massive barchan dune fields of **Sossusvlei** and/or a trek through **Sesriem Canyon**. The ever-shifting dunes of the Namib Desert are particularly worth gazing upon at sunrise when their colourful hues dance over the landscape.

Continuing the canyon theme, head south for **Fish River Canyon**, a geological wonder of monumental proportions that is one of Africa's hidden highlights. If you've packed sturdy hiking boots you could embark on a multi-day hike along the canyon floor. From Fish River Canyon, detour west to marvel at the German anachronism that is **Lüderitz**. Sausages washed down with German beer are a prerequisite before embarking on your explorations. Nearby, you can stop off at the diamond-mining ghost town of **Kolmanskop** and explore the overwhelming emptiness of the **Sperrgebiet**.

Finish things off in **Noordoewer**, which sits astride the Orange River and is the starting point for white-water rafting through some wild canyon country. Alternatively, head across the South African border to cosmopolitan Cape Town, which you can enjoy for a week or a weekend before setting off on the next adventure.

» (above) Christuskirche, Windhoek's best-recognised landmark (p205)
» (left) Rafts on the banks of the Orange River (p346)

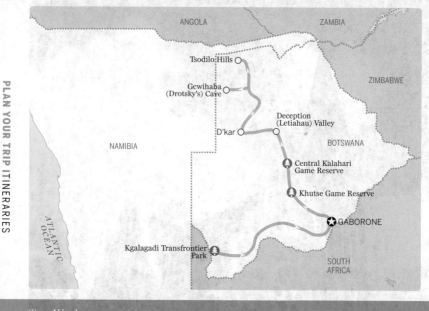

ANGOLA

ZAMBIA

ZIMBABWE

Tsodilo Hills

Gcwihaba (Drotsky's) Cave

Deception (Letiahau) Valley

D'kar

NAMIBIA

BOTSWANA

Central Kalahari Game Reserve

Khutse Game Reserve

ATLANTIC OCEAN

GABORONE

Kgalagadi Transfrontier Park

SOUTH AFRICA

Two Weeks
Secrets of the Kalahari

If you're looking to leave the khaki-clad tourist crowds behind, this off-the-beaten-track option in Botswana takes you straight through the heart of the Kalahari. If you're starting in Johannesburg, head west for the border, where you can cross at Bokspits to enter the enormous **Kgalagadi Transfrontier Park**. The park is one of the only spots in the Kalahari where you can see shifting sand dunes, though the undisputed highlight is its pristine wilderness and low tourist volume. The Kalahari of your imagination, it's noted for its wildlife watching, being home to large numbers of springboks, gemsboks, eland and wildebeest as well as predators, including lions, cheetahs, leopards, wild dogs, jackals and hyenas. If you like birdwatching then you're in for a treat here too.

From here, head east towards Gaborone and then loop back to enter the southern gates of the utterly wild **Khutse Game Reserve**. Here are well-maintained trails and around 60 pans that once made up the largest inland lake on the continent. Leopard and lion sightings are possible wildlife highlights. From here, traverse north through some exciting 4WD territory into the adjoining **Central Kalahari Game Reserve**, where you can navigate one of the continent's most prominent topographical features. It's about the size of Denmark, so there's plenty of scope for losing yourself in Africa's raw heart. Before leaving, spend a night or two in **Deception (Letiahau) Valley**, renowned for its rare brown hyenas. Although wildlife densities are significantly lower than in Chobe or the Okavango Delta, so are the numbers of safari vehicles.

Heading north, you'll pass through **D'kar**, where you can pick up some beautiful San crafts. If you're here in August immerse yourself in traditional bushman culture at the Kuru Dance Festival. Then press on for the remote **Gcwihaba (Drotsky's) Cave**, renowned for its 10m-long stalagmites and stalactites, as well as Commerson's leaf-nosed bats. Finally, at the furthermost tip of the country, you'll come to the mystical **Tsodilo Hills**, which are a treasure chest of painted rock art that continue to be revered by local communities. The beautiful colours of these remote hills are striking but it's the 4000-plus prehistoric rock paintings throughout the hills that most people are here to see.

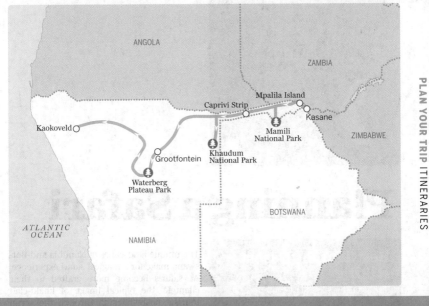

Two Weeks
Caprivi to Kaokoveld

This is not an itinerary for the faint-hearted. Many places in Namibia give you a vague sense that you've reached the end of the earth, but some of the destinations in this itinerary really are otherworldly. Getting to them, too, presents a major challenge that definitely requires determination as well as a fair bit of cash.

To do this trip as a continuous journey, you're best off starting from **Kasane** in Botswana. From here, you can charter a plane or boat to **Mpalila Island**, a luxuriously remote retreat stranded in the middle of the Zambezi. It's where Zimbabwe, Botswana, Namibia and Zambia intersect. From here, head into Namibia's Caprivi Strip and visit the mini-Okavango of the **Mamili National Park** where the rains bring a delta-like feel to the forested islands that contain some of Namibia's best birdwatching. Drive from here to the untamed wilderness that is **Khaudum National Park**, a serious adventure destination. Here, wandering sandy tracks lure visitors through bushlands and across valleys where African wild dogs can be seen – the only place in Namibia with that particular boast. There are also large numbers of herd animals, including roan antelopes and a bird diversity that will thrill twitchers.

From Khaudum the road will take you south through **Grootfontein**, from where it's worth making a short detour to the **Waterberg Plateau Park**. The park is famous as a haven of endangered species like sable, roan and white and black rhinos, some of which you may be lucky enough to spot along one of the well-marked hiking trails. It's an unusual place in that it feels a little like a lost world on top of the plateau with its pristine bushy landscapes – take advantage of the hides at the waterholes for your best chance to spot wildlife.

North of Grootfontein the road takes you into Namibia's cultural heartland, the Owambo region, from where you can access the remote and mysterious **Kaokoveld**, homeland to the Himba – a culturally rich tribal group that has retained its striking appearance and dress – and one of the most inaccessible areas of the country.

Planning a Safari

Best Tips for Desert Hiking

Rise before the sun and hike until the heat becomes oppressive. Rest through the heat of midday and begin again after about 3pm. During warmer months, time your hike with the full moon, allowing you to hike at night.

Best Places to Spot Wild Dogs

In Moremi Game Reserve (in the Okavango Delta) – one of the few healthy wild dog populations in Africa.
In Namibia head for the wild Khaudum National Park.

Best Destinations for a Safari

In Botswana, the Okavango Delta and Chobe National Park; in Namibia, Etosha National Park.

Best Tips for a Self-Drive Safari

If you haven't driven in Africa before, go with someone who has.
Take a satellite phone – easy and relatively inexpensive to hire

The unique landscapes of Namibia and Botswana make for a magical safari experience. As safaris become more crafted to their clientele, the typical image of khaki-clad tourists bushwhacking through the scrub becomes more obsolete. These days a safari can incorporate anything from ballooning over the undulating dunes of the Namib to scooting along the lush channels of the Okavango in a traditional *mokoro* (dugout canoe). Horse-riding, trekking, birding, fishing, night drives and camel safaris are all on the agenda. The typical safari is now a highly sophisticated experience that reconnects with that vital sense of adventure.

Wildlife watching tops the region's list of attractions and forms the basis of most safaris, and little wonder. Etosha National Park in Namibia and Botswana's Okavango Delta and Chobe National Park (among others) are packed with animals – in fact you'll find the greatest density and variety of wildlife in Southern Africa, and some of the best wildlife watching on the continent. The evocative topography is just the icing on the cake.

It's good to keep in mind that although there are safaris catering to most budgets, a Botswanan, and to a lesser degree Namibian, safari can be expensive. Certainly most safari experiences are skewed towards the top end of the market in Botswana.

This chapter provides an overview of the factors to consider when planning a safari. There is a lot more to choose from at the higher end of the price spectrum, where ambience, safari style and the operator's overall focus are important considerations. However, good, reliable budget operators can also be found in both countries.

Planning Your Trip

Choosing an Operator

A good operator is the single most important variable for your safari, and it's worth spending time thoroughly researching those you're considering. At the budget level in particular, you may find operators who cut corners so be careful to go with a reputable outfit. There are many high-quality companies that have excellent track records. Operators recommended in this guidebook enjoyed a good reputation at the time of research, as do many others that couldn't be listed due to space considerations. However, we can't emphasise enough the need to check on the current situation with all of the listed companies and any others you may hear about.

Do some legwork (the internet is a good start) before coming to Botswana or Namibia. Get personal recommendations, and once in the region, talk with as many people as you can who have recently returned from a safari or trek with the company you're considering.

Be sceptical of price quotes that sound too good to be true, and don't rush into any deals, no matter how good they sound.

Also, take the time to go through the itinerary in detail, confirming what is expected and planned for each stage of the trip. Be sure that the number of wildlife drives per day and all other specifics appear in the written contract, as well as the starting and ending dates and approximate times.

Safari Style

While price can be a major determining factor in safari planning, there are other considerations that are just as important.

» **Ambience** Will you be staying in or near the park? (If you stay well outside the park, you'll miss the good early-morning and evening wildlife-viewing hours.) Are the surroundings atmospheric? Will you be in a large lodge or an intimate private camp?

» **Equipment** Mediocre vehicles and equipment can significantly detract from the overall experience. In remote areas, lack of quality equipment or vehicles and appropriate back-up arrangements can be a safety risk.

» **Access & activities** If you don't relish the idea of spending hours on bumpy roads, consider parks and lodges where you can fly in. To get out of the vehicle and into the bush, target areas offering walking and boat safaris.

» **Guides** A good driver/guide can make or break your safari.

» **Community commitment** Look for operators that do more than just give lip service to ecotourism principles, and that have a genuine, long-standing commitment to the communities where they work. In addition to being more culturally responsible, they'll also be able to give you a more authentic and enjoyable experience.

» **Setting the agenda** Some drivers feel that they have to whisk you from one good 'sighting' to the next. If you prefer to stay in one strategic place for a while to experience the environment and see what comes by, discuss this with your driver. Going off in wild pursuit of the Big Five means you'll miss the more subtle aspects of your surroundings.

» **Less is more** If you'll be teaming up with others to make a group, find out how many people will be in your vehicle, and try to meet your travelling companions before setting off.

» **Special interests** If birdwatching or other special interests are important, arrange a private safari with a specialised operator.

When to Go

Getting around is easier in the dry season (May to October), and in many parks this is when animals are easier to find around waterholes and rivers. Foliage is also less dense, making wildlife spotting simpler. However, as the dry season corresponds in part with the high-travel season, lodges and camps in some areas get crowded and accommodation prices are at a premium.

Apart from these general considerations, the ideal time to make a safari very much depends on which parks and reserves you want to visit and your particular interests. For example, the wet season is the best time for birdwatching in many areas, although some places may be inaccessible during the rains. Wildlife concentrations also vary markedly, depending on the season. See the country chapters for more information.

ARIADNE VAN ZANDBERGEN / GETTY IMAGES ©

MARTIN HARVEY / GETTY IMAGES ©

1. Naukluft Mountains (p293)
Rising from gravel plains, the mountains are bound by gorges, caves and springs.

2. Okovango Delta (p88)
A *mokoro* (dugout canoe) is poled along the shallow delta in the Ngamiland district.

3. Cheetah-Watching
The cheetah can reach speeds of up to 112km/h, but must rest for 30 minutes between hunts.

4. Damaraland (p260)
Laced with rivers and springs, Damaraland is one of Southern Africa's last 'unofficial' wildlife areas.

MANIR RICHARD / GETTY IMAGES ©

A BEGINNER'S GUIDE TO TRACKING WILDLIFE

Visitors to Africa are always amazed at the apparent ease with which professional guides locate and spot wildlife. While most of us can't hope to replicate their skills in a brief visit, a few pointers can hone your approach.

» **Time of day** This is possibly the most important factor for determining animal movements and behaviours. Dawn and dusk tend to be the most productive periods for mammals and many birds. They're the coolest parts of the day, and also produce the richest light for photographs. Although the middle of the day is usually too hot for much action, this is when some antelopes feel less vulnerable at a watering hole, and when raptors and reptiles are most obvious.

» **Weather** Prevailing conditions can greatly affect your wildlife-viewing experience. For example, high winds may drive herbivores and birds into cover, so concentrate your search in sheltered areas. Summer thunderstorms are often followed by a flurry of activity as insect colonies and frogs emerge, followed by their predators. Overcast or cool days may prolong activity such as hunting by normally crepuscular predators, and extremely cold winter nights force nocturnal species to stay active at dawn.

» **Water** Most animals drink daily when water is available, so water sources are worthwhile places to invest time, particularly in the dry season. Predators and very large herbivores tend to drink early in the day or at dusk, while antelopes tend to drink from the early morning to midday. On the coast, receding tides are usually followed by the appearance of wading birds and detritus feeders such as crabs.

» **Food sources** Knowing what the different species eat will help you to decide where to spend most of your time. A flowering aloe might not hold much interest at first glance, but knowing that it is irresistible to many species of sunbirds might change your mind. Fruiting trees attract monkeys, while herds of herbivores with their young are a predator's dessert cart.

» **Habitat** Knowing which habitats are preferred by each species is a good beginning, but just as important is knowing where to look in those habitats. Animals aren't merely randomly dispersed within their favoured habitats. Instead, they seek out specific sites to shelter – hollows, trees, caves and high points on plains. Many predators use open grasslands but also gravitate towards available cover, such as large trees, thickets or even grass tussocks. 'Ecotones' – where one habitat merges into another – can be particularly productive because species from both habitats overlap.

» **Tracks and signs** Even when you don't see animals, they leave many signs of their presence. Spoor (tracks), scat (droppings), pellets, nests, scrapes and scent marks provide information about wildlife, and may even help to locate it. Check dirt and sand roads when driving – it won't take long for you to recognise interesting spoor. Elephant footprints are unmistakable and large predator tracks are fairly obvious. Also, many wild cats and dogs use roads to hunt, so look for where the tracks leave the road – often they mark the point where they began a stalk or sought out a nearby bush for shade.

» **Equipment** Probably the most important piece of equipment you can have is a good pair of binoculars. These help you not only to spot wildlife but also to correctly identify it (this is essential for birding). Binoculars are also useful for viewing species and behaviours where close approaches are impossible. Field guides, which are pocket-sized books that depict mammals, birds, flowers etc of a specific area with photos or colour illustrations, are also invaluable. These guides also provide important identification pointers and a distribution map for each species.

UP CLOSE & PERSONAL

The threat of attack by wild animals is rare, but compliance with a number of guidelines will further diminish the chances of an unwelcome encounter. The five most dangerous animals are the Big Five: lions, leopards, buffalos, elephants and rhinos.

» Always sleep inside a tent and be sure to zip it up completely. If you hear a large animal outside, lie still even if it brushes against the tent.

» Never pitch a tent in an open area along a riverbank as this is probably a hippo run.

» When camping, don't keep fresh fruit (especially oranges) in your tent, because they can attract elephants.

» If you encounter a lone buffalo, a lion (especially a lioness) or an elephant that detects your presence, back away slowly and quietly.

» Do not run away from a lion. If you respond like a prey species, the lion will react accordingly.

» Elephant cows with calves should be avoided, and do not approach any elephant with visible injuries.

» When travelling in a boat watch for signs of hippos and steer well away from them.

» When a hippo feels threatened, it heads for water – don't be in its way!

» Visitors should take care not to swim in rivers or waterholes where crocs or hippos are present. Always use extreme caution when tramping along any river or shoreline.

» Be aware that hyenas are also potentially dangerous, although they're normally just after your food.

Types of Safari

Fly-In Safaris

If the world is your oyster, then the sheer sexiness of taking off in a little six-seater aircraft to nip across to the next remote safari camp or designer lodge is a must. It also means you'll be able to maximise your time and cover a selection of parks and reserves to give yourself an idea of the fantastic variety of landscapes on offer.

The biggest temptation will be to cram too much into your itinerary, leaving you rushing from place to place. Be advised, it's always better to give yourself at least three days in each camp or lodge in order to really avail yourself of the various activities on offer.

While a fly-in safari is never cheap, they are all-inclusive and what you pay should cover the cost of your flight transfers as well as meals, drinks and activities in each camp. Obviously, this all takes some planning and the earlier you can book a fly-in safari the better – many operators advise on at least six to eight months' notice if you want to pick and choose where you stay.

Fly-in safaris are particularly popular, and sometimes a necessity, in the delta region of Botswana. Given the country's profile as a top-end safari destination, many tour operators specialise in fly-in safaris or include a fly-in element in their itineraries.

Mobile Safaris

Most visitors to Botswana and Namibia will experience some sort of organised mobile safari – ranging from an all-hands-on-deck 'participation safari', where you might be expected to chip in with camp chores and supply your own sleeping bag and drinks, all the way up to top-class, privately guided trips.

As trips at the lower end of the budget scale can vary enormously in quality it pays to canvass opinion for good local operators. This can be done on Lonely Planet's Thorn Tree forum (http://thorntree.lonelyplanet.com), or by chatting to other travellers on the ground. Failing this, don't hesitate to ask lots of questions of your tour operator and make your priorities and budget clear from the start.

Maun is Botswana's mobile-safari HQ, while most safaris in Namibia will need to be booked out of Windhoek. For those booking through overseas tour operators, try to give as much notice as possible, especially if

WILD DRIVING & CAMPING IN BOTSWANA & NAMIBIA

These are road-tested tips to help you plan a safe and successful 4WD expedition.

» Invest in a good Global Positioning System (GPS). You should always be able to identify your location on a map, though, even if you're navigating with a GPS. We found the Tracks4Africa program to be the best.

» Stock up on emergency provisions, even on main highways. Fill up whenever you pass a station. For long expeditions, carry the requisite amount of fuel in metal jerry cans or reserve tanks (off-road driving burns nearly twice as much fuel as highway driving). Carry 5L of water per person per day, as well as a plenty of high-calorie, non-perishable emergency food items.

» You should have a tow rope, a shovel, an extra fan belt, vehicle fluids, spark plugs, bailing wire, jump leads, fuses, hoses, a good jack and a wooden plank (to use as a base in sand and salt), several spare tyres and a pump. A good Swiss Army knife or Leatherman and a roll of gaffer tape can save your vehicle's life in a pinch.

» Essential camping equipment includes a waterproof tent, a three-season sleeping bag (or a warmer bag in the winter), a ground mat, fire-starting supplies, firewood, a basic first-aid kit and a torch (flashlight) with extra batteries.

» Natural water sources are vital to local people, stock and wildlife, so please don't use clear streams, springs or waterholes for washing yourself or your gear. Similarly, avoid camping near springs or waterholes lest you frighten the animals and inadvertently prevent them from drinking. You should always ask permission before entering or camping near a settlement. Remember that other travellers will pass through the region long after you've gone, so, for the sake of future tourism, please be considerate and respect the local environment and culture.

» Avoid camping in shady and inviting riverbeds, as large animals often use them as thoroughfares, and even when there's not a cloud in the sky, flash floods can roar down them with alarming force. In the interests of the delicate landscape and flora, keep to obvious vehicle tracks; in this dry climate, damage caused by off-road driving may be visible for hundreds of years to come.

» Sand tracks are least likely to bog vehicles in the cool mornings and evenings, when air spaces between sand grains are smaller. Move as quickly as possible and keep the revs up, but avoid sudden acceleration. Shift down gears before deep sandy patches or the vehicle may stall and bog.

you want to travel in the high season. This will give you a better chance of booking the camps and lodges of your choice.

Overland Safaris

Given the costs and complex logistics of arranging a big safari, many budget travellers opt for a ride on an overland expedition, run by specialists like **Africa in Focus** (www.africa-in-focus.com) and **Dragoman** (www.dragoman.com). Most of these expeditions are multicountry affairs with Namibia and Botswana featuring as part of a longer itinerary starting in either Cape Town (South Africa) or Nairobi (Kenya) and covering a combination of countries including Namibia, Botswana, Zimbabwe, Zambia, Malawi and Tanzania.

The subject of overlanding often raises passionate debate among travellers. For some the massive trucks and concentrated numbers of travellers herded together are everything that's wrong with travel. They take exception to the practice of rumbling into tiny villages to 'gawk' at the locals and then roaring off to party hard in hostels and bush camps throughout the host countries. Often the dynamic of travelling in such large groups (15 to 20 people at least) creates a surprising insularity, resulting in a rather reduced experience of the countries you're travelling through.

For others, the overland truck presents an excellent way to get around on a budget and see a variety of parks and reserves while meeting up with people from different walks of life. Whatever your view, bear in

» When negotiating a straight course through rutted sand, allow the vehicle to wander along the path of least resistance. Anticipate corners and turn the wheel slightly earlier than you would on a solid surface – this allows the vehicle to skid round smoothly – then accelerate gently out of the turn.

» Driving in the Kalahari is often through high grass, and the seeds it disperses can quickly foul radiators and cause overheating; this is a problem especially near the end of the dry season. If the temperature gauge begins to climb, remove as much plant material as you can from the grille.

» Keep your tyre pressure slightly lower than on sealed roads, but don't forget to reinflate upon returning to the tarmac.

» Avoid travelling at night, when dust and distance may create confusing mirages.

» Keep to local speed limits.

» Follow ruts made by other vehicles.

» If the road is corrugated, gradually increase your speed until you find the correct speed – it'll be obvious when the rattling stops.

» If you have a tyre blowout, do not hit the brakes or you'll lose control and the car will roll. Instead, steer straight ahead as best you can, and let the car slow itself down before you bring it to a complete stop.

» In rainy weather, gravel roads can turn to quagmires and desert washes may fill with water. If you're uncertain, get out and check the depth, and only cross when it's safe for the type of vehicle you're driving.

» Always be on the lookout for animals.

» Avoid swerving sharply or braking suddenly on a gravel road or you risk losing control of the vehicle. If the rear wheels begin to skid, steer gently in the direction of the skid until you regain control. If the front wheels skid, take a firm hand on the wheel and steer in the opposite direction of the skid.

» In dusty conditions, switch on your headlights so you can be seen more easily.

» Overtaking can be extremely dangerous because your view may be obscured by dust kicked up by the car ahead. Flash your high beams at the driver in front to indicate that you want to overtake. If someone behind you flashes their lights, move as far to the left as possible.

mind that you're unlikely to get the best out of any particular African country by racing through on an inflexible itinerary.

The classic overland route through Namibia and Botswana takes in Fish River Canyon, Sossusvlei, Etosha National Park, Swakopmund, the Skeleton Coast, the Caprivi Strip, the Okavango Delta, Chobe National Park and goes on to Victoria Falls in Zimbabwe.

Self-Drive Safaris

It's possible to arrange an entire safari from scratch if you hire your own vehicle. This has several advantages over an organised safari, primarily total independence and being able to choose your travelling companions. However, as far as costs go, it's generally true to say that organising your own safari will cost nearly as much as going on a cheap organised safari. Also bear in mind that it's wise to make all your campsite bookings (and pay for them) in advance, which means that you'll need to stick to your itinerary.

Apart from the cost, vehicle breakdowns, accidents, security, weather conditions and local knowledge are also major issues. It's not just about hiring a 4WD, but having the confidence to travel through some pretty rough terrain and handle anything it throws at you. However, if all this doesn't put you off then it can be a great adventure.

Your greatest priority will be finding a properly equipped 4WD, including all the necessary tools you might need in case of a breakdown.

RENTING A 4WD IN SOUTH AFRICA

Renting in South Africa is almost invariably cheaper and more reliable than doing so in Botswana or Namibia, even accounting for the extra distance you'll need to drive just to get into those countries. While you could rent from one of the mainstream car rental agencies, there are some specialist 4WD operators that can set you up perfectly for almost any self-drive expedition into Botswana or Namibia. You may be able to arrange to pick up the vehicle in either country, but this will, of course, cost extra.

A good option for vehicle rental is **Explorer Safaris** (082-855 1574; www.explorer safaris.co.za; Johannesburg) in Johannesburg. All of their vehicles are two years old or less and are fitted with a fold-out camper, rooftop tent, gas cookers, a fridge and all necessary camping equipment. Rates range from R995 up to R1575 per day, depending on the vehicle and the duration of the rental period, plus petrol and insurance. Booked in conjunction with **Drive Botswana** (www.drivebotswana.com), it's an excellent overall package.

Other South African companies that rent 4WDs with camping equipment include:

Around About Cars (0860 422 4022; www.aroundaboutcars.com)

Britz (011-396 1860; www.britz.co.za)

Buffalo Campers (27-11 021 0385; www.buffalo.co.za)

Note: if you're planning a self-drive safari in northeastern Namibia or northern Botswana, you'll need to watch out for the wet season (December to March) when some tracks become completely submerged and driving is particularly risky.

You can find pretty much all the camping essentials you need in major supermarket chains, which have outlets throughout Botswana and Namibia. They stock everything from tents and sleeping bags to cooking equipment and fire lighters.

Walking & Hiking Safaris

At many national parks, you can arrange walks of two to three hours in the early morning or late afternoon, with the focus on watching animals rather than covering distance. Following the walk, you'll return to the main camp or lodge.

It's also possible in Namibia to arrange safaris on foot to track black rhinos in the wild. This presents a unique opportunity to see one of Africa's most endangered animals in the wild. Such a safari usually takes place on private concessions.

Horseriding Safaris

Riding on horseback is a unique way to experience the landscape and its wildlife – Botswana presents numerous opportunities to canter among herds of zebras and wilde-

beest. The horse-riding safaris in Botswana are highly rated and there are numerous operators. You'll need to be an experienced rider though, as most horse-riding safaris in Botswana don't take beginners – after all, you need to be able to get yourself out of trouble should you encounter it.

Local Tour Operators

Typically most visitors to Botswana and Namibia will book a safari with a specialist tour operator and many local operators do the bulk of their business this way. The recommendations here provide an overview of some of the best operators in Botswana and Namibia. Other agencies are listed throughout the guide.

Audi Camp Safaris (www.safaris-botswana. com) Specialises in budget mobile and *mokoro* trips. Safaris are practically all-inclusive but you have to bring your own sleeping bags and drinks. It also runs the friendly, no-frills Audi Camp.

Capricorn Safaris (www.capricornsafaris. com) One of the largest operators in Botswana with affiliations in Kenya and Tanzania. Focus on luxury tented safaris in all the main national parks. Note: groups can be quite large.

Desert & Delta Safaris (www.desertdelta. co.za) A top-notch tour operator with luxury camps and lodges located in Moremi, Chobe and the Okavango Delta. You can expect a uniformly high standard of service.

Drive Botswana (www.drivebotswana.com) Arranges 4WDs through Explorer Safaris in South Africa, but also organises a complete package itinerary, including maps, trip notes and bookings for campsites, all at no extra cost. We found the owner, Andy Raggett, to be outstanding and unfailingly professional.

Kaie Tours (www.kaietours.com) A Gaborone-based tour operator specialising in well-priced art and craft tours, hiking trails, overnight stays with local families and camping safaris in the Kalahari with San guides.

Mabaruli African Safaris (www.mabaruli. com) Based in Windhoek, this outfit offers cycling safaris as well as a tour that takes in Namibia (Etosha National Park), Botswana (Okavango Delta) and Zambia (Victoria Falls).

Masson Safaris (www.massonsafaris.com) A family-run outfit based in Botswana with over 25 years' experience in running mobile safaris.

Skeleton Coast Safaris (www.skeleton coastsafaris.com) Conducts four- to six-day fully catered expeditions that use a combination of aircraft and 4WD vehicles to explore this wonderfully remote coastal landscape, including shipwreck sites. Some of the safaris also take in other prime Namibian destinations such as Sossusvlei and Etosha.

Wild Attractions Expeditions & Safaris (www.africansecrets.net) This safari company runs out of Island Safari Lodge. Very big on bird-watching and *mokoro* trips, for which it uses local polers.

Wild Dog & Crazy Kudu Safaris (www. wilddog-safaris.com) This popular backpacker-orientated tour operator runs a variety of expeditions throughout Namibia.

Wilderness Safaris (www.wilderness-safaris. com) Wilderness Safaris manages an impressive array of luxury camps and lodges in Namibia, Botswana, Zimbabwe and further afield, and supports a number of commendable conservation and community projects.

regions at a glance

Before delving into some of the best landscapes, wildlife watching and cultural experiences on the continent, remember that together these countries make up a huge area, and even crossing between them overland requires careful planning. Chobe National Park and the Okavango Delta in Botswana are the two big wildlife regions, along with Etosha National Park in Namibia's north. Incredible landscapes just seem to pop up, but Namibia's north and the Kalahari are the stuff of legend, providing desertscapes, foggy coastline and flat-topped granite monoliths. Culturally, central Namibia delivers on German heritage while the north is the home of the Himba people. Both countries offer access to some of the best galleries of San rock art in Africa while the capitals, Windhoek and Gaborone, provide opportunities to delve deeper into the cultural fabric of the region.

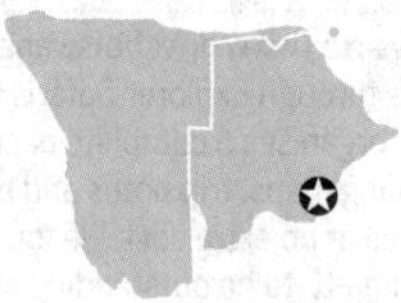

Gaborone

Wildlife ✓
Culture & Crafts ✓✓
Food ✓

City Parks
The nearby Mokolodi Nature Reserve (a few retired predators) and in-town Gaborone Game Reserve (herbivores and good bird-watching only) is the best Gaborone can muster. But the Department of Wildlife and National Parks office (for paying park fees and booking some campsites) may make Gaborone an important stop.

Botswana's Story
The National Museum and the Three Dikgosi (Chiefs) Monument both have a certain run-down charm, but Gaborone's thriving cultural life includes important arts projects and tours (and even an opera house) inspired by Alexander McCall Smith's *No.1 Ladies' Detective Agency.*

A Varied Plate
Perhaps more than anywhere else in the country, Gaborone is a great place to eat, with some excellent cafes, steakhouses and even a place serving impala stew.

p47

Eastern Botswana

Wildlife ✓✓
Landscapes ✓✓
Activities ✓✓

Tuli Block & Khama Rhino Sanctuary
The only real wildlife place here is Tuli Block, where you'll find healthy populations of big cats, elephants and other important species, while the Khama Rhino Sanctuary is Botswana's rhino ark.

Tswapong Hills
It's rare to find variety in Botswana's salt-pan-flat terrain, but the Tswapong Hills are a little-known pocket of dramatic canyons cutting deep into the hills that from a distance give no hint of the drama that lies within.

Hiking
Botswana is not known for its hiking possibilities, but the Tswapong Hills offer fine landscapes, some intriguing ruins and good birdwatching.

p59

Makgadikgadi & Nxai Pans

Landscapes ✓✓✓
Wildlife ✓✓✓
Lodges ✓✓

Salt Pans
The largest salt pans on earth offer up views where the horizon never seems to end, an extraordinary, humbling sight. In places the pans are interrupted by baobab islands, while the Boteti River is one of the great curiosities of Botswana's natural world.

Migrations
A zebra migration that may be the largest in Africa catches most of the attention but there are also flamingos in their massed hordes in the Nata Bird Sanctuary. The dry season's wildlife concentrations in the west around the Boteti River also rarely disappoint.

Luxury Lodges
Botswana's call to exclusivity is heard here, albeit on a smaller scale than the more famous Okavango or Chobe further north. There's a handful of remote and opulent lodges out on the pans here and a fine riverside option.

p68

Chobe National Park & Kasane

Wildlife ✓✓✓
Landscape ✓✓✓
Lodges & Campsites ✓✓✓

Elephants & the Rest
Chobe means elephants, big elephants, and more than 70,000 of them at last count. Elephants might get all the attention (rightly so, we might add), but there are also infamous lion prides, leopards, cheetahs and wild dogs, plus a full suite of antelopes to keep them all happy.

Rivers, Rocks & Marshes
Chobe Riverfront is classic safari country with land- and water-based possibilities as abundant as the wildlife. Savuti has some fabulous outcrops and the intriguing Savuti Channel to its name, while the marshes of Linyanti are like a mini Okavango Delta.

Chobe Digs
From remote lodges in Linyanti, Savuti and elsewhere to riverside campsites all across the park, Chobe's accommodation choices are brilliant and perfectly located for watching the park's epic wildlife shows.

p75

Okavango Delta

Landscape ✓✓✓
Wildlife ✓✓✓
Activities ✓✓✓

Water World
The Okavango is a signature African landscape, a terrain sculpted by the waters that rise and fall in time with the seasons, year after year. The combination of river, savannah, forest and all manner of variations on the themes offer a stirring backdrop of singular variety.

Greatest Wildlife Show on Earth
The Big Five have returned to the Okavango (although seeing rhinos would be a rare bonus), and the delta is otherwise like walking into the set of a wildlife documentary. The Okavango Panhandle is especially good for birdwatching.

Land, River & Sky
Scenic flights over this breathtaking world of water are a memorable way to explore; add to this *mokoro* (dugout canoe) expeditions, foot safaris and wildlife drives, and the delta's exploration possibilities are endless.

p88

Kalahari

Landscapes ✓✓✓
Wildlife ✓✓✓
Culture ✓✓

Desert
The Kalahari is a place of legend, an iconic landscape that calls to travellers to leave behind the modern world and seek out the desert's solitude. From the red dunes of the Kgalagadi to the grasslands of the fossilised river valleys, this is a desert unlike any other on earth.

Famous Lions
Big cats may be thinly spaced out across the desert, but they remain something of a Kalahari speciality. The renowned black-maned lions of the region remain one of the great sights, but there's plenty more to track down.

The San
The Kalahari is the ancestral homeland of the San, and although encounters with this ancient people are rare, many lodges and camps allow you to explore a small corner of the Kalahari with San guides, while D'kar is home to a fine San arts project.

p116

Windhoek

Architecture ✓
Shopping ✓✓
Cuisine ✓✓

Colonial Gems
Neo-baroque cathedral spires, as well as, oddly, a few German castles and some lovely 20th-century colonial shells, ensure Windhoek is worth a wander. Try walking Independence Ave and Fidel Castro St up to Christuskirche, the capital's best-known landmark.

Crafts & Curios
A stroll through Post St Mall reveals lots of wooden carvings, but the place to immerse yourself in weaving, crafts, antiques and all manner of artistic ventures is the Old Breweries Craft Market.

Foodie Fare
Whether you need a pasta hit or prefer your seafood cooked Angolan style, Windhoek surprises with its international cuisine offerings. German and Namibian fare is of course available, but there is much more on offer in the capital.

p205

Northern Namibia

Wildlife ✓✓✓
Off-roading ✓✓✓
Culture ✓✓

Etosha & the Waterberg
Wildlife watching reaches its pinnacle in Etosha National Park, where verdant bushland contains an extraordinary density and variety of wildlife. There are useful viewing hides to spot rare gems such as roan and sable antelope in the Waterberg.

Remote Reaches
The rawness of Africa can be experienced in the huge northern swathe of Namibia with a sturdy 4WD, navigational equipment, supplies and a sense of adventure. Places such as Damaraland, the Kaokoveld, the Skeleton Coast and the Caprivi Strip remove all obstacles between you and nature.

The Himba & the San
The Kaokoveld is the ancestral home of the Himba people, a culturally rich tribal group. The San are more difficult to encounter, but look out for their incredible rock art – especially around Damaraland – and duck into Otjozondjupa, where visits to San villages are possible.

p243

Central Namibia

Adventure Activities ✓✓✓
Atlantic Towns ✓✓
Desert ✓✓✓

Heart Stoppers
Namibia is Southern Africa's headquarters for adrenaline-pumping fun. Shoot down a dune on a sandboard, fling yourself out of an aircraft and float back to earth or go camel riding into a desert sunset. The stunning landscape is just the icing on the cake.

Urban Fun
Swakopmund is something of an enigma, a German colonial relic that may be crumbling into the desert except for the influx of tourists who pour in to enjoy its raft of activities, German-style ambience, cuisine and hospitality. Walvis Bay, just a short ride away, has a developing waterfront and some great restaurants.

Shifting Sands
Namib-Naukluft Park is one of the world's largest national parks – this is desert country and the swirling sand dunes here are mesmerising. The dunes – silent, constantly shifting, gently hued in colour and ageless – are a highlight of Namibia.

p273

Southern Namibia

Landscape ✓✓✓
Colonial Traces ✓✓
Canoeing ✓✓

Canyons & Desert Roads
The landscapes, from the moment you enter southern Namibia from South Africa, are stunning – granite monoliths rise from the plains through mists of windblown sand and dust. The enormous gash hacked out of the planet at Fish River Canyon should not be missed – this naked symphony in stone is truly awesome.

Lüderitz & Castles
Stuck between the Namib Desert and the wind-savaged Atlantic coast, defying both the elements and logic, the time-warp town of Lüderitz makes for a surreal colonial exploration. Charming hints of yesteryear, such as neo-baroque Duwisib Castle, poke their architecturally intriguing heads out of the surrounding desert.

Water Adventures
Noordoewer sits astride the Orange River, in the deep south of Namibia, and two outfits offer canoe and rafting trips that access wonderfully wild canyon country.

p300

> **Every listing is recommended by our authors, and their favourite places are listed first**

> **Look out for these icons:**

 Our author's top recommendation

A green or sustainable option

FREE No payment required

On the Road

Botswana

Botswana

📘27 / POP 2 MILLION

Includes »

Best for Wildlife Watching

» Chobe National Park (p75)
» Makgadikgadi Pans National Park (p74)
» Central Kalahari Game Reserve (p120)
» Tuli Block (p66)

Best of the Outdoors

» Mokoro trip, Okavango Delta (p99)
» Tsodilo Hills (p113)
» Kgalagadi Transfrontier Park (p126)
» Tswapong Hills (p63)
» Bush camping anywhere

Why Go?

Blessed with some of the greatest wildlife spectacles on earth, Botswana is one of *the* great safari destinations in Africa. There are more elephants in Botswana than any other country on earth, the big cats roam free and there's everything from endangered African wild dogs to aquatic antelopes, and from rhinos making a comeback to abundant birdlife at every turn.

This is also the land of the Okavango Delta and the Kalahari Desert, at once iconic African landscapes and vast stretches of wilderness. Put these landscapes together with the wildlife that inhabits them, and it's difficult to escape the conclusion that this is wild Africa at its best.

Botswana may rank among Africa's most exclusive destinations – accommodation prices at most lodges are once-in-a-lifetime propositions – but self-drive expeditions are also possible. And whichever way you visit, Botswana is a truly extraordinary place.

When to Go

Maun

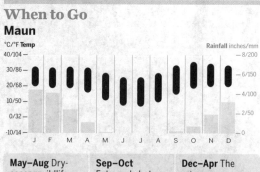

| May–Aug Dry-season wildlife concentrations around water-holes and generally fine weather | Sep–Oct Extremely hot temperatures and good dry-season wildlife watching | Dec–Apr The rainy season when many tracks are impassable but tourist numbers fewer |

GABORONE

POP 231,600 / ELEV 900M

Botswana's small capital may be the country's largest city, but it's a pretty low-key place. There aren't that many reasons to come here – it's a world of government ministries, shopping malls and a seemingly endless urban sprawl with outer neighbourhoods known as 'Phases' and 'Extensions' – which is why most travellers either fly to Maun, or cross overland elsewhere. It *can* be convenient if you're looking to make reservations for the small handful of government-run campsites, although that's unlikely to be reason enough to come here on its own. But if you do find yourself here, 'Gabs' has a handful of decent restaurants and good hotels.

The city is largely a modern creation, with little sense of history to provide interest. Indeed, ask a Motswana who was born and raised in Gaborone where they're from, and they may well tell you the name of a family village or cattle post they've never seen. And yet, while a local Motswana may not see Gaborone as a traditional family 'home', they do see it as the place where their future, and that of their nation, is forged. As such, it can be an interesting place to take the pulse of the nation.

History

Archaeological evidence suggests that the banks of the nearby Notwane River have been continuously occupied since at least the middle Stone Age. However, the first modern settlement, Moshaweng, was established in the late 1880s by Chief Gaborone of the Tlokwa clan. Early European explorers and missionaries named the settlement Gaborone's Village, which was then inevitably shortened to 'Gaborones' (the 's' was dropped in 1968).

In 1895 the South African diamond magnate Cecil Rhodes used Gaborone to launch the Jameson Raid, an unsuccessful rebellion against the Boers who controlled the gold mines near Johannesburg. Rhodes was forced to resign his post as prime minister of Cape Colony, and the raid served as the catalyst for the second Boer War (1899–1902).

In 1897 the railway between South Africa and Rhodesia (now Zimbabwe) passed 4km to the west of the village, and a tiny settlement known as Gaborone's Station soon appeared alongside the railway line. By 1966 the greater Gaborone area was home to fewer than 4000 inhabitants, but it was selected as the capital of independent Botswana due to its proximity to the railway line and its large water supply.

Although urban migration from elsewhere in Botswana has characterised much of Gabs' recent history, economic turmoil in Zimbabwe has sparked a wave of illegal immigration to Botswana's capital, further increasing the city's growth.

◎ Sights

Although there's little in the way of sights, the confluence of motivated embassy staff, NGO types and ambitious Batswana makes for a fairly full calendar of events that focuses on cultural and arts-related activities.

Gaborone Game Reserve   WILDLIFE RESERVE
(off Map p50; ☑318 4492; adult/child/vehicle P10/5/10; ☺6.30am-6.30pm) This reserve was established in 1988 by the Kalahari Conservation Society to give the Gaborone public an opportunity to view Botswana's wildlife in a natural and accessible location. Although the reserve is only 5 sq km, it's the third-busiest in the country and boasts wildebeest, eland, gemsboks, kudu, ostriches and warthogs. The birdlife, which includes kingfishers and hornbills, is particularly plentiful and easy to spot from observation areas. The reserve also has a few picnic sites, a game hide and a small visitor-education centre.

All roads in the reserve are accessible by 2WD; guided drives are not offered. The reserve is located about 1km east of Broadhurst Mall and can be accessed from Limpopo Dr.

FREE **National Museum & Art Gallery**   MUSEUM
(Map p53; ☑397 4616; 331 Independence Ave; ☺9am-6pm Tue-Fri, to 5pm Sat & Sun) If you come here with expectations reasonably lowered, you may enjoy this small, neglected museum. It's a good way to kill an hour if you're

IMPORTANT NUMBERS

Country code	☑267
Area codes	Botswana does not use area codes
International access codes	☑00
Emergency	☑999

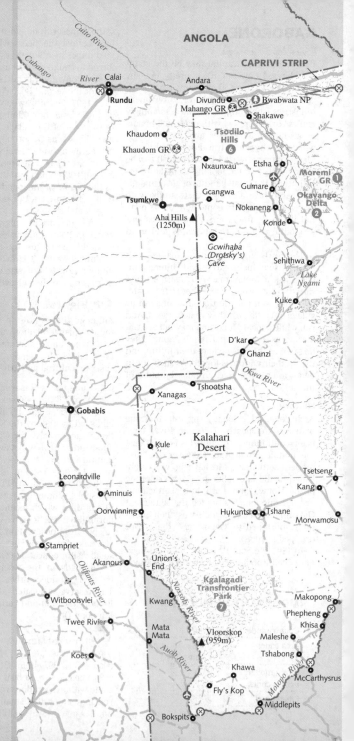

Botswana Highlights

1 Enjoy the ultimate safari at the **Moremi Game Reserve** (p103), with some of the best wildlife watching on earth

2 Glide gently through the vast, unspoiled wilderness of the **Okavango Delta** (p99) in a wooden *mokoro* (dugout canoe)

3 Get up close and personal with Africa's largest elephant herds at **Chobe National Park** (p75)

4 Look for black-maned lions in the heart of the Kalahari Desert at the **Central Kalahari Game Reserve** (p120)

5 Watch the wildlife gather by the banks of the Boteti River in **Makgadikgadi Pans National Park** (p74)

6 Leave the crowds behind and search for ancient rock art in the soulful and beautiful **Tsodilo Hills** (p113)

7 Explore the Kalahari's best dune scenery at **Kgalagadi Transfrontier Park** (p126), in Botswana's deep south

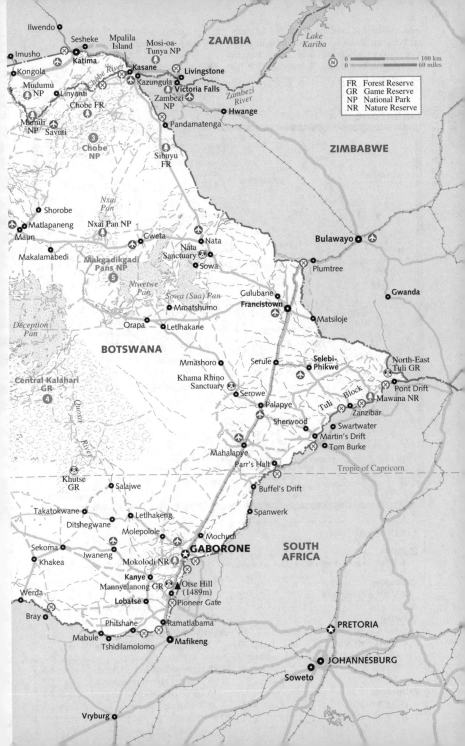

into taxidermy; exhibits of stuffed animals sit between those on precolonial and colonial history – it's curious how there is next to no mention of the San, Botswana's first inhabitants. In the art-gallery section, there's

a permanent collection of traditional and modern African and European art.

FREE **Three Dikgosi Monument** MONUMENT
(Map p50; ☑367 4616; btw Eastern & Western Commercial Sts; ⊙9am-6pm Tue-Fri, to 5pm Sat & Sun)

Gaborone

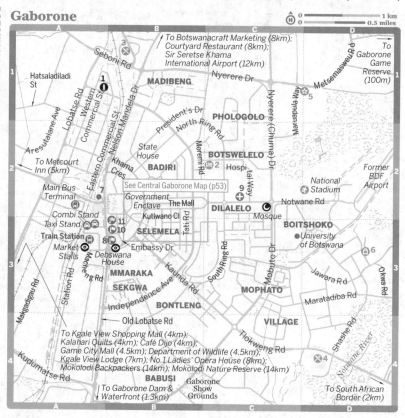

Gaborone

MAITISONG FESTIVAL

Botswana's largest performing-arts festival, the week-long Maitisong Festival is held in late March or early April. The festival features an outdoor programme of music, theatre, film and dance that takes place on several stages throughout the capital. There's also an indoor programme, held in the Maitisong Cultural Centre and in the Memorable Order of Tin Hats (MOTH) Hall; highlights include some of the top performing artists from around Africa.

Programmes to events are usually available in shopping malls and centres during the month leading up to the festival. Outdoor events are free; indoor events cost from P40 to P200. For P500 you can buy a ticket that provides access to everything on offer during the festival.

It's an interesting kind of history when your nationalist heroes are three guys who argued your country should *continue* to be a protectorate of Africa's biggest imperialist power, but welcome to Botswana. (It should be noted that, by helping to keep Botswana under the administration of the British Crown, the Batswana chiefs Bathoen, Khama II and Sebele prevented the country from coming under the control of Cecil Rhodes, who most likely would have been a far more exploitative administrator.)

The *dikgosi* (chiefs) are memorialised in imposing form at this large, badly placed (in the shadow of an office block) monument, which also includes panels featuring carvings of national virtues, including 'Botshabelo' (refuge), 'Bogaka' (heroism), 'Boitshoko' (endurance), 'Maikarabelo' (global responsibility) and 'Boipuso' (independence).

👉 Tours

If time is tight and you're a fan of Alexander McCall Smith's *No.1 Ladies' Detective Agency*, a couple of places run excellent themed tours.

Garcin Safaris   TOURS
(📞393 8190; www.garcinsafaris.com; 1-/2-day tours €126/402) Resident and Gaborone expert Marilyn Garcin does great tours of the city, including a *No.1 Ladies' Detective Agency*–focused jaunt. She also offers recommended safaris around Botswana.

Africa Insight   TOURS
(📞7265 4323; www.africainsight.com; half-/full-day tours P495/860) *No.1 Ladies' Detective Agency* tours endorsed by the author Alexander McCall-Smith himself, with more wide-ranging excursions also possible.

🎉 Festivals & Events

Check p161 for a list of public holidays, which are always cause for celebration in the capital. Details about these events are advertised in local English-language newspapers and in the What's On column of the *Botswana Advertiser*.

Maitisong Festival   PERFORMING ARTS
(www.maitisong.org) Established in 1987, the Maitisong Festival is the largest performing-arts festival in Botswana. It's held annually for seven days during the last week of March or the first week of April.

Traditional Dance Competition   DANCE
Held in late March.

🛏 Sleeping

With most foreign visitors heading straight for the north and bypassing the capital in the process, Gaborone primarily caters to domestic and business travellers. Even so, the city has a good range of accommodation to suit most budgets.

If you don't have a private car, it's recommended that you book your first night's accommodation before you arrive, as many places will provide an airport transfer. With hotels dotted all over the capital, hiring a taxi to find a hotel with an available room is an expensive headache.

TOP CHOICE Metcourt Inn   HOTEL $$
(📞363 7907; www.peermont.com; r from P720; ❄🛜) Located within the Grand Palm Resort complex and part of the reliable Peermont suite of hotels, this affordable business hotel has classy rooms with a hint of Afro-chic in the decor. If this is your first stop in Africa, you'll wonder what all the fuss is about. But if you've been out in the bush, it's heaven on

a midrange budget. Take Molepololole Rd from Nelson Mandela Dr then it's around 6km further on the left.

Mokolodi Backpackers
BACKPACKERS $

(off Map p50; ☑7716 8685; admin@backpackers. co.bw; campsites P95, dm/s P165/220, chalets P370-525; @☀) This great place around 14km south of the city centre is the only place with a real backpacker vibe around Gaborone. It has attractive chalets, and good campsites and dorms. It's an excellent alternative to staying in the city centre, and handy for the Mokolodi Nature Reserve, 1km away.

Motheo Apartments
APARTMENT $$

(Map p50; ☑318 1587; www.motheoapartments. co.bw; Moremi Rd, off Independence Ave; apt P420-820; ❄️🛜☀) Close to the Mall and National Museum, this well-run place has good self-catering apartments that are a nice alternative to the big business-style blocks that characterise so many other Gaborone hotels. The properties come with internet, DSTV and other mod cons, and are all self-catering.

Walmont Ambassador at the Grand Palm
HOTEL $$$

(☑363 7777; www.walmont.com; Molepolole Rd; r from P1755; ❄️🛜☀) Located 4km west of the city centre, this resolutely modern and polished hotel is situated in a Las Vegas–inspired mini city complete with restaurants, bars, casino, cinema and spa. You'll pay to stay, but it's worth it to be pampered.

Brackendene Lodge
HOTEL $$

(☑391 2886; www.brackendenelodge.com; Tati Rd; r from P250, s/d with bathroom & breakfast P420.50/458, with kitchen P433/473.40; ❄️🛜) The Brackendene is one of the better-value hotels in town. Rooms are simple but large and kitted out with TVs and air-con; there's a reasonably reliable wi-fi signal. It's quiet, but you're within walking distance of the Mall.

Kgale View Lodge
HOTEL $$

(off Map p50; ☑312 1755; www.kgaleviewlodge.com; Phase 4, Plot 222258; r from P550; ❄️🛜☀) This locally recommended B&B has friendly service, attractively decorated if simple rooms and a generally welcoming atmosphere. It's the sort of place that books up fast with return customers, so call ahead. The lodge is around 9km south of the city centre along the Old Lobatse Rd.

Cresta President Hotel
HOTEL $$$

(☑395 3631; www.crestahotels.com; The Mall; s/d US$171/192; ❄️🛜☀) The first luxury hotel in

the city overlooks the Mall in the heart of the city. It's modern and service is helpful, and while there are no surprises, that's a pleasant-enough surprise in itself.

🍴 Eating

Gabs has its fair share of good restaurants aimed at an expat market, although they're pretty spread out, especially in the far-flung shopping malls of the city. You'll also find numerous outlets of Western fast-food outlets, while the upmarket hotels are another good place to try.

For cheap African food, there are dozens of stalls near the bus station that sell plates of cheap traditional food, such as mealie pap (maize-meal porridge) and stew, as well as a few stands on the Mall during lunchtime.

If you're self-catering, there are well-stocked supermarkets in every mall and shopping centre.

⬆️ Courtyard Restaurant
TOP CHOICE
AFRICAN, INTERNATIONAL $$

(off Map p50; ☑392 2487; www.botswanacraft. bw; Western Bypass, off Airport Rd; mains P55-85; ⏰8am-4pm) In the garden area out the back of Botswanacraft, this tranquil spot serves up imaginative African cooking (including impala stew and guinea fowl pot) with other local staples making a rare appearance. It also serves a mean lamb curry, salads and sandwiches.

Bull & Bush Pub
INTERNATIONAL $$

(Map p50; ☑397 5070; www.bullandbush.net; off Nelson Mandela Dr; mains P85-110; ⏰noon-10.30pm Mon-Fri, to 11.30pm Sat & Sun) This long-standing Gaborone institution is deservedly popular with expats, tourists and locals alike. Though there's something on the menu for everyone, the Bull & Bush is renowned for its thick steaks and cold beers. It has some themed nights – Wednesday is BBQ night, Thursday is pizzas – while on any given night, the outdoor beer garden is buzzing with activity.

Beef Baron
STEAKHOUSE $$

(☑363 7777; Grand Palm Resort; mains P65-190; ⏰6.30-10.30pm Mon-Sat) With a name like this, there's no mystery about the menu, with Gaborone's finest cuts of Botswana beef served in upmarket surrounds. It's inside the Grand Palm Resort complex; walk through the lobby of the Walmont Ambassador and you're there. Reservations are recommended, especially on weekends. Part of the same complex, **Mokolwane's Restaurant** (buffet P199) has an excellent buffet.

Cafe Dijo CAFE **$**
(off Map p50; ☑315 0575; Old Lobatse Rd, Kgale View Shopping Mall; mains P62; ☺7am-4pm Mon-Fri, 9am-1pm Sat; 🛜) Next door to Kalahari Quilts in the Kgale View Shopping Mall, this classy but casual place is one of our favourite haunts in Gabs. The lunch specials include pepper steak pie, chicken tandoori wraps and light Thai-inflected dishes, followed up with Gaborone's best carrot cake. With free wi-fi and great coffee, you could easily spend hours here.

Linga Longa INTERNATIONAL **$$**
(Map p50; ☑370 0844; Riverwalk Mall; mains P48-126; ☺8am-11pm) This place is a vague cross between an American sports bar and a British pub, with a menu that begins with breakfast and moves on to steaks, curries and calamari rings.

Rodizio's STEAKHOUSE **$$$**
(Map p50; ☑392 4428; 1st fl, Riverwalk Mall; set menu from P175; ☺noon-3pm & 6-10.30pm Mon-Sat, 2-8pm Sun) Indulge the carnivore in you.

BOTSWANA GABORONE

Central Gaborone

Central Gaborone

◎ **Sights**
1 National Museum & Art Gallery D1

🛏 **Sleeping**
2 Brackendene Lodge C2
3 Cresta President Hotel.........................C2

🛍 **Shopping**
4 Botswana Book Centre B2

ℹ **Information**
5 Barclays Bank B2
  Beni Fama Bureau de Change ....(see 8)

6 Central Police Station............................C2
7 French Embassy.....................................C2
8 Moby Trek B2
9 South African Embassy.......................... B1
10 Standard Chartered Bank....................D2
11 Standard Chartered Bank....................B2
12 Tourist Office..C2
13 UK Embassy..B2
14 Zambian Embassy................................C2

🚍 **Transport**
15 Air Botswana.. B1

Part of a chain of Brazilian super meat houses/samba parties, Rodizio's is where waiters walk around with skewers of meat, and you hold up little flags indicating whether you want more or less. Gastrointestinal overload eventually occurs, but at least you die with a smile on your face and meat juice on your lips.

Equatorial Café
CAFE $

(Map p50; Riverwalk Mall; mains from P30; ☺7am-10pm Mon-Thu, to 11pm Fri & Sat) The best espressos in town are served here, along with fruit smoothies, falafel and gourmet sandwiches. It even has real bagels!

🍷 Drinking

When money is made in Botswana it tends to come to Gabs, which means there are a few places here to let off steam. Don't be surprised if some places charge a P50 cover on weekends.

Kalahari Cocktail Lounge
COCKTAIL BAR

(Grand Palm Resort; cocktails P49-60; ☺7am-late) This classy venue inside the Grand Palm Resort complex (it's behind reception in the Walmont Ambassador) does a small range of cocktails complemented by teas, coffees, smoothies and snacks. You may need to sidle up to the bar and wait for a table on weekend nights.

Bull & Bush Pub
PUB

(Map p50; www.bullandbush.net; Off Nelson Mandela Dr) This popular restaurant (p52) is also a centre for expat nightlife, where young (and some not-so-young) Gaborone denizens go to behave badly. The dance floor gets hot, the beer is cold and all in all this can be a hell of a fun place. Sundays are more mellow with live jazz.

☆ Entertainment

To find out what's going on in Gaborone and where, check the *Arts & Culture Review* lift-out in the *Mmegi/Reporter* newspaper, and the What's On section of the *Botswana Advertiser*. Another excellent resource is whatsoningabs.com.

As Gabs gets richer, nightclubs become more popular, although we're yet to find any that are popular enough to last more than a season or two. They tend to be a cross between enormous disco-ball funhouses and Southern African shebeens. Expect to pay around P50 cover on weekend nights.

Maitisong Cultural Centre
PERFORMING ARTS

(Map p50; ✆397 1809; http://maitisong.org; Maruapula Way; ☺ticket office 8.30am-1pm & 2-4.30pm Mon-Fri) Maitisong ('Place of Entertainment') puts on some excellent shows in its large theatre, with events ranging from Shakespearean plays to Batswana music most weeks. You'd be remiss not to check this spot out if you're in Gabs for longer than a few days.

No.1 Ladies' Opera House
PERFORMING ARTS

(off Map p50; ✆7291 4876; no1.operahouse@gmail .com; off Lobatse Rd; ☺ticket office 10.30am-3.30pm Tue-Fri, 9.30am-2pm Sat) Located a few kilometres south of Gaborone (take the Lobatse Rd and turn left at the satellite dishes), this collaboration between author Alexander McCall Smith and the local arts scene showcases Setswana singing, community theatre performances and even full-scale opera shows. There's also the cute Bean Bag Café (✆7702 0477; breakfast/lunch from P35/60; ☺9am-4pm Tue-Fri, to 3pm Sat & Sun) that does good coffee, cakes and light meals.

🛍 Shopping

Gaborone is home to a number of Western-style malls that contain bars, restaurants, shops, supermarkets, takeaways, banks, office parks and petrol stations. The main malls are the African Mall, Broadhurst Mall, Riverwalk Mall, Rail Park Mall, Game City Mall and South Ring Mall.

If you've time, some of the best handicrafts are available straight from the source at workshops in nearby Oodi, Gabane and Thamaga. Otherwise, Gaborone has a handful of outstanding shops selling high-quality crafts at fixed prices.

Botswanacraft Marketing
HANDICRAFTS

(off Map p50; ✆392 2487; www.botswanacraft. bw; Western Bypass, off Airport Rd; ☺8am-6pm Mon-Fri, to 5pm Sat, 9am-1pm Sun) Botswana's largest craft emporium sells traditional souvenirs, including pottery from Gabane and Thamaga, San jewellery and baskets from across the country, at fixed prices. It also has books, jewellery, carvings and textiles, but most of these are from elsewhere in Africa, from Mali to the Congo. There's also the good on-site Courtyard Restaurant (p52).

Kalahari Quilts
ARTS & CRAFTS

(off Map p50; ✆7261 8711; www.kalahariquilts. com; Unit 7A, Kgale Hill Shopping Mall; ☺9am-5pm Mon-Fri, to 2pm Sat) These stunning quilts are made by Batswana women, overseen by the engaging Jenny Healy, and are a genuinely unique craft to take home. Each one bears an individual imprint, although all do a good job at capturing the primary-colour-heavy palette that is this country's sensory assault. There's a lot more than quilts around – baby slings, cushion covers and the like are all for sale.

Exclusive Books BOOKS
(Map p50; ☑370 0130; Riverwalk Mall; ☺9am-5pm Mon-Fri, to 2pm Sat) Easily Gaborone's best bookshop, this large shop in the Riverwalk Mall has literature, nonfiction and travel books, with excellent sections focused on Africa.

Thapong Visual Arts Centre ARTS & CRAFTS
(Map p50; ☑316 1771; www.thapongartscentre.org. bw; Baratani Rd, The Village; ☺8am-5pm Mon-Fri, 9am-5pm Sat & Sun) A small gallery of modern and contemporary local work that should be a first stop for anyone interested in buying art that goes beyond the usual African wildlife stuff and wooden masks.

Botswana Book Centre BOOKS
(Map p53; The Mall; ☺8.30am-5pm Mon-Fri, to 12.30pm Sat) You wouldn't cross town for it, and like the Mall it inhabits it has a neglected air. But this bookshop is worth dropping into for its excellent range of international magazines, with quite a few newspapers thrown in as well.

ⓘ Information

Dangers & Annoyances

Gaborone is a generally safe city by African standards and it's certainly a welcome respite from the tension you feel on the streets of some South African cities. Crime does happen here – mostly pickpocketing and petty theft, with occasional muggings – although most visitors encounter no problems during their stay.

Even so, it pays to be careful. Always take cabs at night, especially if you're a woman or on your own. Use drivers recommended by hotels and try to keep their phone numbers, as some people have been robbed in unmarked cabs. The main Mall is fine to walk around in during the day but is probably best avoided after dark. Tsholofelo Park, just south of Gaborone Private Hospital, also warrants a wide berth. Try not to walk along public greenways, as they're both a traffic hazard and a likely target for muggers.

Traffic is becoming an increasing problem as more Batswana buy cars and start driving, often for the first time in their lives. Be extremely careful on the road during the last weekend of the month, when everyone gets paid and many people get drunk and get behind the wheel – a toxic combination.

Emergency
Ambulance (☑997)
Central Police Station (Map p53; ☑355 1161; Botswana Rd)
Fire Department (☑998)
Police (☑999)

Internet Access
Wireless (usually but not always free) is now almost standard in most Gaborone hotels. Otherwise, most internet cafes rarely last the distance.
Moby Trek (Map p53; 1st fl, Unit 24, Embassy Chambers, The Mall; per hr P10; ☺8am-7.30pm Mon-Fri, 9am-7.30pm Sat, 10am-7.30pm Sun)

Medical Services
Gaborone Hospital Dental Clinic (☑395 3777; Segoditshane Way) Part of the Gaborone Private Hospital.
Gaborone Private Hospital (☑300 1999; Segoditshane Way) For anything serious, head to this reasonably modern, but expensive, hospital, opposite Broadhurst Mall. The best facility in town.
Princess Marina Hospital (Map p50; ☑355 3221; Notwane Rd) Equipped to handle standard medical treatments and emergencies but shouldn't be your first choice for treatment.

Money
Major branches of Standard Chartered and Barclays banks have foreign-exchange facilities and ATMs, and offer cash advances. The few bureaus de change around the city offer quick service at slightly better rates than the banks, but they charge up to 2.75% commission.
American Express (1st fl, Riverside Mall; ☺9am-5pm Mon-Fri, to 1.30pm Sat)
Barclays Bank (Map p53; The Mall; ☺8.30am-3.30pm Mon-Fri, 8.15-10.45am Sat)
Beni Fama Bureau de Change (Map p53; 1st fl, Unit 25, Embassy Chambers, The Mall; ☺9am-5pm Mon-Fri, to 1pm Sat)
Standard Chartered Bank (Map p53; The Mall; ☺8.30am-3.30pm Mon-Fri, 8.15-11am Sat)
UAE Foreign Exchange (1st fl, Riverside Mall; ☺9am-5pm Mon-Fri, to 1.30pm Sat)

Post
Central Post Office (The Mall; ☺7.30am-noon & 2-4.30pm Mon-Fri, to 12.30pm Sat)

Tourist Information
Tourist Office (Map p53; ☑395 9455; www.botswanatourism.co.bw; Botswana Rd;

BORDER CROSSINGS: GABORONE

Gaborone's proximity to Johannesburg (280km away) makes it a popular entry/exit point for self-drivers travelling between Botswana and South Africa. The most direct route is through **Pioneer Gate** (Skilpadshek; ⊘6am-midnight), which connects Lobatse (Botswana) and Zeerust (South Africa).

Formalities on the Botswana side of the border are fairly straightforward – you'll be asked for your car's details and your vehicle may be searched for fresh meat and dairy products. On the South African side, things were a little chaotic when we visited but the new border post was nearing completion. Travellers entering and departing are rarely held up for long, although if your vehicle is registered in South Africa, make sure you have the paper from the rental company granting permission to take the car outside the country. If you're travelling via this route, allow longer than you expect as the succession of townships on the South African side of the border can slow you down considerably.

Other convenient border posts:

Tlokweng Gate (Kopfontein; 6am to midnight) Another busy crossing that can work for Johannesburg and is good for Madikwe Game Reserve.

Ramotswa (Swartkopfontein; 7am to 7pm) Less-frequented crossing that can also be used for Zeerust and Johannesburg.

Sikwane (Derdepoort; 6am to 7pm) For Madikwe Game Reserve.

Ramatlabama (6am to 10pm) Connects Gaborone and Johannesburg via Mafikeng.

⊘7.30am-6pm Mon-Fri, 8am-1pm Sat) Moderately useful collection of brochures; next to the Cresta President Hotel.

ⓘ Getting There & Away
Air

From **Sir Seretse Khama International Airport**, 14km northeast of the centre, **Air Botswana** (Map p53; ☑368 0900; www.airbotswana.co.bw; Matsitam Rd; ⊘9.30am-5pm Mon-Fri, 8.30-11.30am Sat) operates international services to Harare, Johannesburg and Lusaka, as well as domestic services.

DESTINATION	FARE (PULA)
Francistown	from 680
Kasane	from 1050
Maun	from 882

Bus

Please note that minibuses to Johannesburg drop you off in a pretty unsafe area near Park Station; try to have onward transport arranged *immediately* upon arrival.

Domestic buses leave from the main bus terminal. To reach Maun or Kasane, you'll need to change in Francistown. Buses operate according to roughly fixed schedules and minibuses leave when full.

DESTINATION	FARE (PULA)	DURATION (HR)
Francistown	60	6
Ghanzi	130	11
Kanye	18	2
Mochudi	12	1
Palapye	52	4
Serowe	57	5
Thamaga	8	1

ⓘ Getting Around
To/From the Airport

Taxis rarely turn up at the airport; if you do find one, you'll pay around P70 to the centre. The only reliable transport between the airport and town are the courtesy minibuses operated by the top-end hotels for their guests. If there's space, nonguests may talk the driver into a lift.

Another option is **AT&T Travel** (☑395 2640; airportres@at-t-travel.com; Queen's Rd; ⊘6.30am-9pm), which runs occasional private or shared airport shuttle services.

Car

Unless you're planning to stick to the sealed roads, it's difficult to see why you'd need to rent a car on arrival – if you're planning to rent a 4x4, you're better off doing so in South Africa or Namibia. For the record, most major international car rental companies have offices (which may not be staffed after 5pm) at the airport.

Combi

Packed white combis (minibuses), recognisable by their blue number plates, circulate according to set routes and cost P5. They pick up and drop off only at designated lay-bys marked 'bus/taxi stop'. The main city loop passes all the main shopping centres except the Riverwalk Mall and the Kgale View Shoping Mall, which are on the Tlokweng and Kgale routes respectively. Combis can be hailed either along major roads or from the combi stand.

Taxi

Taxis, which can be easily identified by their blue number plates, are surprisingly difficult to come by in Gabs. Very few cruise the streets looking for fares, and most seem to be parked around Botswana Rd. You're better off arranging one through your hotel. If you manage to get hold of one, fares (negotiable) are generally P40 to P75 per trip around the city.

Final Bravo Cabs (☎312 1785)
Speedy Cabs (☎390 0070)

AROUND GABORONE

Gaborone is surrounded by a few interesting day or half-day trips, although they're more if you find yourself at a loose end than fabulous attractions in their own right. Almost all can be visited using public transport or hired taxi, though you'll get around quicker if you have your own wheels.

North of Gaborone

MATSIENG ROCK CARVINGS

The Batswana regard the Matsieng Rock Carvings as one of the four 'creation sites'. According to legend, the footprint and rock carvings belonged to Matsieng, who marched out of a hole followed by wild and domestic animals. There is a small information board

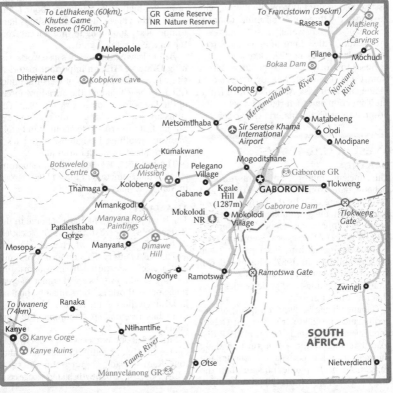

Around Gaborone

THE WEAVERS OF OODI

The village of Oodi is best known for the internationally acclaimed **Lentswe-la-Oodi Weavers** ([phone] 310 2268; [clock] 8am-4.30pm Mon-Fri, 10am-4.30pm Sat & Sun), a cooperative established in 1973 by Ulla and Peder Gowenius, two Swedes who hoped to provide an economic base for women from the villages of Oodi, Matebeleng and Modipane. At the workshop, wool is hand spun, then dyed using chemicals over an open fire (which creates over 600 colours) and finally woven into spontaneous patterns invented by individual artists. Most of the patterns depict African wildlife and aspects of rural life in Botswana. The women can also weave customised pieces based on individual pictures, drawings or stories if requested. By car, get on the highway from Gaborone towards Francistown, and take the turn-off for Oodi village. Follow signs for another 7.5km to the workshop. Any northbound bus from Gaborone can drop you off at the turn-off for Oodi, though you will have to walk or hitch the rest of the way.

at the gate and, on the other side of the fence from the car park, a tiny room with some explanations. The site lies at the end of a well-signposted 1km-long 2WD track that starts about 6km north of Pilane.

MOCHUDI

As evidenced by ruined stone walls in the hills, the charming village of Mochudi was first settled in the 1500s by the Kwena, who are one of the three most prominent lineage groups of the Batswana. In 1871, however, the Kgatla settled here after being forced from their lands by north-trekking Boers.

Buses to Mochudi (P15, one hour) depart from Gaborone when full. By car, head to Pilane and turn east. After 6km, turn left at the T-junction and then right just before the hospital to reach the historic village centre.

West of Gaborone

GABANE

The ancient hilltop settlements around Gabane date from between AD 800 and 1200, and were built by the early Bangologa people, who once inhabited this area. A more contemporary attraction is Pelegano Village ([phone] 394 7054; Gabane; [clock] workshop 8am-4.30pm Mon-Fri, craft shop 7.30am-1pm Sat, 2-4pm Sun), established in 1982. This wonderful artisan complex offers local crafts such as hand-fired ceramics and wine bottles recycled into dinner glasses.

Gabane village is 12km southwest of Mogoditshane and 23km from central Gaborone. Pelegano Village is 900m along a dirt road that starts at the second turn-off along the road from Mogoditshane – look for the Pelegano signs. By public transport, take the bus towards Kanye from Gaborone (P18, 25 minutes) and walk the last bit to Pelegano Village.

MANYANA

Manyana is famous for its Zimbabwean-style **rock paintings**, which date back over 2000 years and feature paintings of three giraffes, an elephant and several antelopes. The site is located on the southern extreme of an 8m-high rock overhang about 500m north of the village. Because the site is hard to find, it's a good idea to hire a local from the village to act as a guide.

Before leaving the area, it's also worth visiting **Dimawe Hill**, an important historical site where several groups of warriors under Chief Sechele I halted the invading forces of the Boers from South Africa in 1852. The ruins are scattered around the granite hills, not far from the roadside about 5km before Manyana. Nothing is signposted, but it's a pleasant place to wander around.

The bus (P15, 1½ hours) from Gaborone stops at the T-junction at the end of the road in Manyana village.

THAMAGA

The rural village of Thamaga is home to the **Botswelelo Centre** ([phone] 599 9220; Molepolole Rd; tours P5; [clock] 8am-5pm), which is also known as Thamaga Pottery. This nonprofit community project was started by missionaries in the 1970s and now sells a wide range of creations for good prices. Tours must be booked in advance. Buses run frequently from the main bus terminal in Gaborone (P12, one hour).

Situated about 5km east of the Botswelelo Centre in Mmankgodi, 2km off the Gaborone–Kanye road, **Bahurutshe Cultural Lodge** ([phone] 7241 9170; www.bahurutshelodge.com;

campsites/chalets P75/400) is an innovative cultural village, chalet complex and camping ground where visitors can very easily access the traditional elements of Batswana music, dance and cuisine. The comfy chalets really do up the African-hut thing, with cool stone, mud walls and rustic-smelling thatch enclosing you in the evening.

South of Gaborone

MOKOLODI NATURE RESERVE
This 3000-hectare private reserve (⌘316 1955; www.mokolodi.com; per vehicle per day P60, day/night game drives per person P140/200, giraffe/rhino tracking P490/590; ⊙7.30am-6pm, often closed Dec-Mar) was established in 1991 and is home to giraffes, elephants, zebras, baboons, warthogs, rhinos, hippos, kudu, impala, waterbucks and klipspringers. The reserve also protects a few retired cheetahs, leopards, honey badgers, jackals and hyenas, as well as over 300 species of birds.

Mokolodi also operates a research facility, a breeding centre for rare and endangered species, a community-education centre, and a sanctuary for orphaned, injured or confiscated birds and animals; it's also the base for Cheetah Conservation Botswana (www.cheetahbotswana.com). Among the activities on offer are rhino- and giraffe-tracking; check the website for details.

It is important to note that the entire reserve often closes during the rainy season (December to March) – phone ahead before you visit at this time. Visitors are permitted to drive their own vehicles around the reserve (you will need a 4WD in the rainy season), though guided tours by 4WD or on foot are available. If you're self-driving, pick up a map from the reception office.

🛏 Sleeping
Mokolodi Nature Reserve Campsite   CAMPGROUND **$$**
(campsite per adult/child P120/60, chalets P680-1240) Spending the night in the reserve is a refreshing and highly recommended alternative to staying in Gaborone. The campsites are secluded and well groomed, and feature *braai* (barbecue) pits, thatched bush showers (with steaming-hot water) and toilets. If you want to safari in style, there are also three- to eight-person chalets in the middle of the reserve; prices increase significantly on weekends. Advance bookings are necessary. If you don't have a vehicle, staff

can drive you to the campsite and accommodation areas for P10.

ℹ Getting There & Away
The entrance to the reserve is located 12km south of Gaborone. By public transport, take a bus to Lobatse and get off at the signposted turn-off. From there, it's a 1.5km walk to the entrance.

OTSE
The town of Otse (pronounced *oot*-see) is known for Otse Hill (1489m), Botswana's highest point, although the main attraction for travellers is the Mannyelanong Game Reserve (admission free; ⊙daylight hr Sep, Oct & Feb-Apr). This reserve is an important breeding centre for the endangered Cape Griffon vulture, which nests in the cliffs. (In case you were wondering, Mannyelanong means 'where vultures defecate' in Setswana.) Loud noises can scare the birds and cause chicks and eggs to fall from the nests, so please mind the fences and be careful not to speak too loudly.

Otse village is about 45km south of Gaborone. Any Lobatse-bound bus can drop you outside the game reserve (which is obvious from the cliffs and fence).

KANYE
Built around the base of Kanye Hill, the capital of the Bangwaketse people is home to the **Kanye Gorge**, where the entire population of the town once hid during a Ndebele raid in the 1880s. An easy 1.5km walk along the cliff face from the eastern end of Kanye Gorge will take you to **Kanye Ruins**, the remains of an early 18th-century stone-walled village.

Buses regularly travel between Gaborone and Kanye via Thamaga (P10, two hours). The bus station is 1.5km west of the main shopping centre.

EASTERN BOTSWANA

For the Batswana, this relatively densely populated land may be the most important part of Botswana; for travellers, this is largely an ignored area, a place to be bypassed on the way to Maun, Kasane and the Kalahari.

But the Batswana heartland is worth exploring, home as it is to Botswana's most important rhino sanctuary, to the ruins and dramatic landscapes of the Tswapong Hills, and to the Tuli Block, one of Botswana's most underrated wildlife destinations.

Eastern Botswana

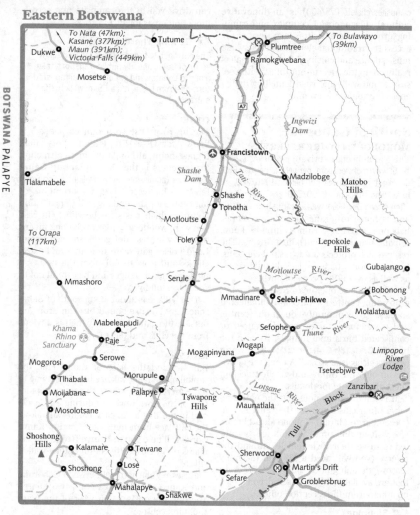

Palapye

POP 41,100

Palapye's original name was Phalatswe, which means 'many impala' in Sekgalagadi or 'large impala' in Setswana. To most Batswana, however, Palapye is known as the 'powerhouse of Botswana', due to the massive coal-burning power plant that was opened in nearby Morupule in 1986. Palapye's other claim to fame is that it's the birthplace of Festus Mogae, the country's former president. Most travellers only stop here to break up the long drive north.

🛏 Sleeping & Eating

Majestic Five Hotel   HOTEL $$$

(📞492 1222; www.majesticfive.co.bw; Hwy A1; d/f/ste from P1300/2100/2500; 🕸🛜🏊) A few kilometres south of the centre on the road to Gaborone, and opened in 2011, Palapye's newest hotel has well-appointed rooms and is overall the best deal in town. The evening buffet (P150 per person) is also Palapye's best place to eat.

Cresta Botsalo Hotel   HOTEL $$$

(📞492 0245; www.crestahotels.com; Hwy A1; r US$135; 🕸🛜🏊) This once-lovely place is liv-

gen Shopping Centre. From this shopping centre, shared taxis and combis also go to Serowe (P12, 30 minutes) and Orapa (P96, 4½ hours).

To Bulawayo (48km)

Gwanda

ZIMBABWE

Shashe River

Molema Bush Camp
Northern Tuli GR
Tuli Circle
Tuli Safari Lodge
Limpopo Valley Airport
Tuli GR
Limpopo River
Pont Drift
Mathathane
Soloman's Wall & Motloutse Ruins
Platjan
Wild at Tuli
Baines Drift
Alldays

Serowe

POP 57,600

The historically significant town of Serowe is worth a detour if you're in the area – ignore the modern town centre and instead spend time in two monuments to the past.

In 1902 Chief Khama III abandoned the Bangwato capital in Phalatswe and built Serowe on the ruins of an 11th-century village at the base of Thathaganyana Hill. Serowe was later immortalised by South African writer Bessie Head, who included the village in several of her works, including the renowned *Serowe – Village of the Rain Wind*. This book includes a chronicle of the Botswana Brigades Movement, which was established in 1965 at the Swaneng Hill Secondary School in Serowe and has since brought vocational education to many remote areas.

◉ Sights

FREE **Khama III Memorial Museum** MUSEUM
(☏463 0519; ◷8am-5pm Tue-Fri, 10am-4.30pm Sat) The Khama III Memorial Museum outlines the history of the Khama family, one of the most important dynasties in Southern Africa. The museum includes the personal effects of Chief Khama III and his descendants as well as various artefacts illustrating Serowe's history. There are also exhibits on African insects and snakes, San culture and temporary art displays. The museum is about 800m from the central shopping area on the road towards Orapa. Donations are welcome.

Royal Cemetery CEMETERY
Before leaving town, hike up to the top of Thathaganyana Hill where you'll find the Royal Cemetery, which contains the grave of Sir Seretse Khama, the founding father of modern Botswana, and Khama III; the latter is marked by a bronze duiker (a small antelope), which is the Bangwato totem. Be advised that police consider this a sensitive area, so visitors need to seek permission (and possibly obtain a guide) from the police station in the barracks house. To reach the police station, follow the road opposite the petrol station until you reach the *kgotla* (traditionally constructed Batswana

ing on past glories. Although marketing itself as a business hotel, the phones weren't working and the wireless signal was weak when we were here. If the bar's full, noise can also be a problem. Thankfully, the rooms remain excellent, with air-con, cable TV and comfy beds. The hotel is next to the Caltex petrol station, about 50m north of the junction along the highway.

ⓘ Getting There & Away

Buses along the route between Gaborone (P52, four hours) and Francistown (P30, two hours) pass through Palapye and stop at the chaotic En-

BOTSWANA SEROWE

community affairs hall), and the surrounding barracks; one of the buildings houses the police station.

🛏 Sleeping

Tshwaragano Hotel HOTEL $

(✒463 0377; www.tshwaraganohotel.com; chalets P240-260; ❄) This small but quaint hotel with chalet-style accommodation is built on the slopes of Thathaganyana Hill and boasts great views of the town. The attached bar-restaurant is usually the most hopping place in town – it's all relative. The hotel is above the shopping area on the road to Orapa.

Serowe Hotel HOTEL $$

(✒463 0234; www.serowehotel.com; s/d incl breakfast P575/695; ❄☀) The Serowe Hotel is a terrific hotel of the kind you don't expect to find in Serowe; it's 2km southeast of town on the road to Palapye. Comfortable and well-furnished rooms ensure a quiet night's sleep, and the laid-back outdoor bar is a good bet for a nightcap. The popular restaurant serves English fare as well as vegetarian meals.

ℹ Getting There & Away

Buses travel between Serowe and Gaborone (P62, four hours) about every hour. Alternatively, from Gabs catch a Francistown-bound bus, disembark at the turn-off to Serowe, and catch a shared taxi or combi to Serowe. Combis and shared taxis also depart for Orapa (P92, four hours) when full; this combi route passes by the entrance to the Khama Rhino Sanctuary.

Khama Rhino Sanctuary

With the rhinos all but disappeared from Botswana, the residents of Serowe banded together in the early 1990s to establish the 4300-hectare **Khama Rhino Sanctuary**

BORDER CROSSINGS: TULI BLOCK & EASTERN BOTSWANA

If you're looking for the fastest route between Johannesburg and northern Botswana, the busy border crossing at **Martin's Drift** (✒in South Africa 014-767 2929; Groblersbrug; ⊕6am-10pm) is your best bet. Entering Botswana, if you don't have any pula you will be allowed to step into Botswana territory to change money and then return; change no more than you need as exchange rates can be extremely poor. After completing all visa and customs formalities, your vehicle will be searched for fresh meat, fresh fruit and dairy products. Botswana petrol prices are generally lower than those in South Africa; there's a petrol station just inside the border on the road to Palapye. Going the other way, South African customs may search your car (they're looking for rhino horn), but most checks are fairly cursory.

If your destination inside Botswana is the Tuli Block, avoid Martin's Drift, for two reasons. First, Martin's Drift is generally known for being stricter in its customs searches. And secondly, the gravel road that shadows the border from Martin's Drift towards the Tuli Block was awfully corrugated when we last drove it. The small crossing of **Zanzibar** (✒263 0012; ⊕8am-4pm) is one option, although don't be caught out by its shorter opening hours.

Another possibility is the small post at **Platjan** (✒263 0001, in South Africa 014-767 2959; ⊕6am-6pm), which is best for the central Tuli area, and the southern sections of the Northern Tuli Game Reserve. If you're coming from Johannesburg, you travel via Alldays and there are three turn-offs to Platjan. The first two involve driving along dirt roads, while the third and best, 38km beyond Alldays along a tar road, involves around 20km along dirt roads. The crossing over the Limpopo River is via a low concrete bridge that can sometimes be impassable in the rainy season – ring ahead if you're unsure.

The final option, good also for the Northern Tuli Game Reserve, is **Pont Drift** (✒264 5260, in South Africa 015-575 9909; ⊕7.30am-4pm), although note that this border crossing usually requires a 4WD and can be closed when the river is too high. If you've prebooked your accommodation, you can leave your vehicle with the border police and then get a transfer by vehicle (if dry) or by cable car (if the river is flooded; P35) to your lodge. If you need to arrive after 4pm, a later crossing time can be negotiated, although you'll have to ring 48 hours in advance and pay a fee (usually P70 per person, plus extra for the officers who have stayed on to let you through).

(📞463 0713; www.khamarhinosanctuary.org.bw; adult/child P52/26, vehicle under/over 5 tonnes P63.40/190.20; ⊙7am-7pm). Today the sanctuary protects 40 white and four black rhinos; the sanctuary was not originally set up for black rhinos but when one wandered across the border from Zimbabwe it was the start of a beautiful relationship. Some rhinos have been released into the wild, especially in the Okavango Delta, joining imports from Botswana's regional neighbours. The sanctuary is also home to wildebeest, impala, ostriches, brown hyenas, leopards and over 230 bird species.

👁 Sights & Activities

The best time for spotting the rhinos is late afternoon or early morning, with Malema's Pan, Serwe Pan and the waterhole at the bird hide the most wildlife-rich areas of the sanctuary; these locations are clearly marked on the sanctuary map (P10) available at the park entrance.

The main roads within the sanctuary are normally accessible by 2WD in the dry season, though 4WD vehicles are required in the rainy season. The office at the entrance sells basic nonperishable foods, cold drinks and firewood.

Two-hour day/night **wildlife drives** (P462.70/633.90) can take up to four people. **Nature walks** (P200) and **rhino-tracking excursions** (P317) can also be arranged. You can also hire a guide to accompany your vehicle for P190.20.

🛏 Sleeping

Rhino Sanctuary Trust CAMPGROUND, CHALETS $ (campsite per adult/child P67.80/33.90, dm P317, chalets P469.10-710; 🏊) Shady campsites with *braai* pits are adjacent to clean toilets and (steaming-hot) showers, while there are also some six-person dorms. For a little more comfort, there are rustic four-person chalets and six-person A-frames; both have basic kitchen facilities and private bathrooms. There's also a restaurant, bar and a swimming pool. If you don't have a vehicle, staff can drive you to the campsite and accommodation areas for a nominal fee.

❶ Getting There & Away

The entrance gate to the sanctuary is 26km northwest of Serowe along the road to Orapa (turn left at the poorly signed T-junction about 5km northwest of Serowe). Khama is accessible by any bus or combi heading towards Orapa.

Tswapong Hills

East of Palapye, these boulder-strewn hills represent some of the most dramatic landforms in Botswana. Pleasing from a distance, up close the hills watch over intriguing ruins while steep-walled gorges drive deep into the rocky interior, sheltering oasislike picnic spots and important colonies of breeding Cape vultures close to the northern limit of their range, as well as other birdlife. Accessible from both north and south, it's a popular escape for local residents with nary a tourist in sight. You'll need your own wheels – public transport is practically nonexistent.

👁 Sights

Southern Tswapong Hills

The most interesting ruins in the region are scattered close to the southern Tswapong foothills.

Old Palapye (Phalatswe)   RUINS

About 20km southeast of Palapye amid low-lying scrub, thinly scattered stone walls mark the site of the former Bangwato capital. After the Christian Bangwato chief Khama III and his people arrived from Shoshong in 1889, Phalatswe was transformed from a stretch of desert to a settlement of 30,000 people. Spread over a large area and signposted along the main track, stone walls denote the town's former marketplace and other buildings. More intact is the impressive Old Palapye Church, a Gothic-style London Missionary Society church that was completed in 1894. When the Bangwato capital was moved to Serowe in 1902, Chief Khama sent a regiment to torch Phalatswe, but the church remained standing. Built from locally quarried red mud brick, it's one of Botswana's most striking ruins.

Motetane Gorge   CANYON

The walls of the Tswapong Hills are riven with deep canyons, and the east–west Motetane Gorge is the prettiest of them. The turnoff to the gorge is well signposted en route to the church and trails lead out from the small parking area. The trails in this area are littered with sacred ancestral sites, some of which are signposted. Watch for hyenas along the trails.

Northern Tswapong Hills

The region's most impressive rock formations are those on the northern side, and there are also community-run campsites and well-appointed chalets, making it more accessible for tourists.

Moremi Gorge   CANYON

(adult/child/vehicle P40/20/30) The approach to Moremi Gorge gives little hint of what lies ahead. Beyond the entrance gate, a track leads past campsites (per adult/child P70/35) with their cold-water ablutions blocks, to a parking area. From here, a trail leads into this vertiginous canyon. Apart from the sheer beauty of the site and the abundant birdlife (with Cape vultures wheeling overhead or perched at their nesting sites high on the cliffs), watch for small ancestral shrines in rocky clefts and the signposted boulder that fell to the valley floor on the day that Botswana's president Sir Seretse Khama died on 13 July 1980. Back near the site entrance, there are some lovely en-suite chalets (single/double P350/450) which opened in 2012; they have fine views towards the hills from their large balconies, with state-of-the-art Alva barbecues on hand.

ℹ Getting There & Away

To get to the southern side of the Tswapong Hills, take the A-1 south of Palapye for 8km, then the A-141, whereafter there are signs to Old Palapye (Phalatswe); there is a well-signposted turn-off after the village of Lecheng.

For northern Tswapong Hills, travel 20km north of Palapye along the A-1, then take the road signposted with a number of village names, including Tamasane and Kgagodi. Later, follow the signs to Moremi – the entrance to the gorge is around 3km beyond Moremi village.

Francistown

POP 99,000

Francistown is Botswana's second-largest city and an important regional centre – there's a fair chance you'll overnight here if you're on the way north coming from South Africa. There's a small museum, a handful of decent restaurants and plenty of supermarkets.

Unlike most Botswana cities, Francistown's history tells an interesting story. In 1867 Southern Africa's first gold rush was ignited when German Karl Mauch discovered gold along the Tati River. Two years later, a group of Australian miners along with Englishman Daniel Francis arrived on the scene in search of their stake. Although Francis headed for the newly discovered Kimberley diamond fields in 1870, he returned 10 years later to negotiate local mining rights with the Ndebele king Lobengula and laid out the town that now bears his name.

◉ Sights

FREE **Supa-Ngwao Museum**   MUSEUM

(☑ 240 3088; off New Maun Rd; ⊘8am-5pm Mon-Fri, 9am-5pm Sat) Housed in the 100-year-old Government Camp, the Supa-Ngwao Museum includes a prison and a police canteen, and has interesting small displays about local and regional culture and history (*supa-ngwao* means 'to show culture' in Setswana). The museum also hosts temporary art exhibitions and occasional special events. Donations are suggested.

🛏 Sleeping

TOP CHOICE **Woodlands**
Stop Over   CAMPGROUND, CHALET $$

(☑244 0131; www.woodlandscampingbots.com; campsite per person P83, s/d chalets P330/475, r from P685; ❄) A wonderfully tranquil place 10km north of town off the road to Maun, Woodlands is the pick of the places to stay around Francistown if you have your own wheels. The chalets are nicely appointed, the campsites a wonderful respite from dusty Botswana trails, and Anne and Mike are welcoming hosts.

Cresta Marang Gardens   HOTEL $$$

(☑241 3991; www.crestahotels.com; Old Gaborone Rd; s/d from US$144/169; ❄🐾🕸❄) One of the better hotels in the Cresta chain in Botswana, this excellent hotel has expansive grounds, standard rooms and some lovely thatched cottages on stilts.

Digger Inn   HOTEL $$

(☑244 0107; www.diggerinn.co.bw; St Patrick St, Village Mall; d/f P705/860; ❄🕸) At the northern end of the city centre, Diggers Inn is at once quiet, central and part of the most happening expat enclave (Village Mall) in the city. The rooms here are large, if a little careworn, and the decor evokes Francistown's mining heyday. Overall it's good value and a worthwhile alternative to the chain hotels.

Metcourt Inn   HOTEL $$

(☑241 1100; www.metcourt.com; Blue Jacket St; r from P770; ❄🕸) This outpost of the Metcourt chain offers extremely comfortable, well-priced and recently renovated three-star rooms. Which is just as well, as the location

Francistown

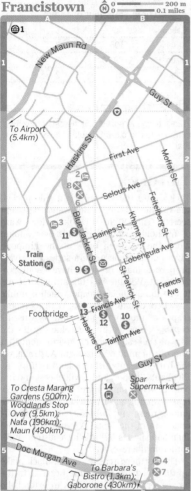

Francistown

◎ Sights
1 Supa-Ngwao Museum.........................A1

◎ Sleeping
2 Digger Inn...A2
3 Grand Lodge...A3
4 Metcourt Inn...B5

◎ Eating
5 Pie City..B3
6 Savanna...A2
7 Spur Steak Ranch...............................B5
8 Thorn Tree..A2

ⓘ Information
9 Barclays Bank......................................A3
10 First National Bank............................B4
11 FxA Bureau de Change.......................A3
Kokela Internet Café...................(see 6)
12 Standard Chartered Bank.................B4
Tourist Office...............................(see 2)

ⓘ Transport
13 Air Botswana..A4
14 Main Bus Terminal..............................B4

bank, this is an OK midrange option that feels like an old-school country motel. It's popular with locals and strikes a decent balance between rustic and roadside, although the pub can get a little rowdy if you're after a tranquil stay.

🍴 Eating

Self-caterers have a choice of several well-stocked supermarkets along Blue Jacket St. In addition to the Lonely Planet–reviewed options, you'll also find some local food stalls at the corner of Blue Jacket St and Selous Ave.

TOP CHOICE **Thorn Tree** CAFE $
(St Patrick St, Village Mall; mains P35-60; ⊙6am-3pm Mon-Sat; 🛜) An oasis of sophistication at the northern end of Francistown, Thorn Tree (no relation to Lonely Planet's famous online bulletin board) does burgers, salads, jacket potatoes, fresh fish and great coffee; the outdoor terrace is lovely. Highly recommended.

Barbara's Bistro INTERNATIONAL $$
(Francistown Sports Club; mains from P55; ⊙noon-2pm & 7-10pm Mon-Sat) Located in the eastern outskirts of town, this quaint, leafy spot is

(central but next to the busy road and over-looking rubbish-strewn fields at the back) is not Botswana's finest.

Grand Lodge HOTEL $
(☏241 2300; Blue Jacket St; s/d P275/350; ✳) This is an excellent choice if you want to stay in the city centre. Standard rooms wouldn't win a style award but they're elevated above the norm by the presence of air-con, cable TV, a fridge and a hotplate.

Tati River Lodge MOTEL $$
(☏240 6000; www.trl.co.bw; campsite per person P60, s/d from P594/709; ✳✳) On the river-

a good choice for a casual atmosphere and good international-style food.

Savanna INTERNATIONAL $$
(St Patrick St, 1st fl, Village Mall; mains P55-110; ☺10am-10pm Mon-Sat; ☎) Probably the pick of Francistown's sit-down restaurants, this place serves up the town's best steaks, but watch out also for the daily specials. The bar is also one of few expat haunts in town.

Pie City BAKERY $
(Blue Jacket St, Blue Jacket Mall; pies P8.75; ☺7am-7pm) For a quick bite, it's difficult to go past the flaky pastries on these pies; the chilli sausage roll is heavenly.

Spur Steak Ranch STEAKHOUSE $$
(Blue Jacket St; mains P60-120; ☺noon-10pm Mon-Sat; ☎) You've seen it before – an American-themed steakhouse in the heart of Africa with a menu that covers steaks and seafood. It's the sort of place your kids will love but you might cringe at.

ℹ Information
Internet
Kokela Internet Café (St Patrick St, Village Mall; per hr P12; ☺8am-5pm Mon-Sat)

Money
Barclays Bank (Blue Jacket St; ☺8.30am-3.30pm Mon-Fri, 8.15-10.45am Sat)
FxA Bureau de Change (Blue Jacket St; ☺8.30am-4.30pm Mon-Fri, to 12.30pm Sat)
Standard Chartered Bank (Blue Jacket St; ☺8.30am-3.30pm Mon-Fri, 8.15-11am Sat)

Medical Services
Nyangabgwe Hospital (☎211 1000, emergency ☎997)

Tourist Information
Tourist Office (☎244 0113; St Patrick St, Village Mall; ☺7.30am-6pm Mon-Fri, 9am-2pm Sat) Moderately useful for brochures.

ℹ Getting There & Away
Air
You can fly between Francistown and Gaborone with **Air Botswana** (☎241 2393; Francis Ave) for around P680; as always, these cheaper fares are available online, while buying a ticket at the office could cost upwards of P1000.

Bus & Combi
From the main bus terminal, located between the train line and Blue Jacket Plaza, buses and combis connect Francistown with the following destinations.

DESTINATION	FARE (PULA)	DURATION (HR)
Gaborone	60	6
Kasane	106	7
Maun	89.90	5
Nata	41	2

ℹ Getting Around
Francistown's airport is 5.5km west of the city centre. A taxi into town shouldn't cost more than P50.

Tuli Block
Tucked into the nation's right side pocket, the Tuli Block is one of Botswana's best-kept secrets. This 10km- to 20km-wide swath of freehold farmland extends over 300km along the northern bank of the Limpopo River and is made up of a series of private properties, many of which have a conservation bent. Wildlife is a big attraction here, but so too is the landscape, which is unlike anywhere else in Botswana. With its moonscapes of muddy oranges and browns, its kopjes overlooked by deep blue sky, it's the sort of Dalí-esque desert environment that puts one in mind of Arizona or Australia, yet the barren beauty belies a land rich in life. Elephants, hippos, kudu, wildebeest and impala as well as small numbers of lions, cheetahs, leopards and hyenas circle each other among rocks and kopjes scattered with artefacts from the Stone Age onwards. More than 350 species of birds have also been recorded in the reserve.

The northern reaches of the Block make up the Northern Tuli Game Reserve. In the longer term, there are plans to extend the reserve's boundaries south, and, even further into the future, join up with contiguous protected areas across the border in Zimbabwe. Once owned by the British South Africa Company (BSAC), the land was ceded to white settlers after the railway route was shifted to the northwest. However, much of the land proved to be unsuitable for agriculture and has since been developed for tourism. As such, the potential for this region is endless.

One advantage of visiting the Tuli Game Reserve is that entrance is free. Night drives (not permitted in government-controlled parks and reserves) are also allowed, so visitors can often see nocturnal creatures, such as aardwolves, aardvarks and leopards. The best time to visit is May to September, when animals congregate around permanent water sources.

Please note that the Tuli Block is private land, so visitors are not allowed to venture off the main roads or camp outside the official campsites and lodges. Also, exploring this region without a private vehicle is virtually impossible.

◉ Sights

The landscape in Tuli Block is defined by its unusual rock formations. It's all beautiful, but there are a couple worth seeking out. Both sights can be explored on foot, and are accessible from the road between Zanzibar and Pont Drift.

Solomon's Wall   NATURAL SIGHT
Tuli Block's most famous feature is Solomon's Wall, a 30m-high dolerite dyke cut naturally through the landscape on either side of the riverbed.

Motloutse Ruins   RUIN
Near Solomon's Wall are the Motloutse Ruins, a Great Zimbabwe–era stone village that belonged to the kingdom of Mwene Mutapa.

🛏 Sleeping

Reservations are strongly recommended at all of the Lonely Planet–reviewed places – most don't accept walk-in guests.

[TOP CHOICE] Wild at Tuli   TENTED CAMP $$$
(📞7211 3688; www.wildattuli.com; Kwa-Tuli Game Reserve; per person self-catering/full board P595/960) This fabulous camp on an island in a branch of the Limpopo River is run by respected conservationists Judi Gounaris and Dr Helena Fitchat, and they bring a winning combination of warmth and conservation knowledge to the experience. Meals are home-cooked and eaten around the communal table, the tents are extremely comfortable, and game drives on the 5000-hectare property (home to a full but often elusive complement of predators) are also included in the price. They'll even let you sleep in one of the hides overlooking a waterhole.

Tuli Safari Lodge   LODGE $$$
(📞264 5303; www.tulilodge.com; ste with full board P820-2410; ❄💻) In the Northern Tuli Game Reserve, this fine lodge is set in a riverine oasis and surrounded by red rock country that teems with wildlife. Although at the up-

per end of the scale for the Tuli Block, the rates are a bargain compared to other exclusive private reserves in the country and the standards are nonetheless high. Be sure to have a drink at the outdoor bar built around the base of a 500-year-old *nyala* tree. The game reserve is just beyond the Pont Drift border post. The rate includes game drives.

Mashatu Game Reserve   TENTED CAMP $$$
(📞in South Africa 011-442 2267; www.mashatu.com; chalet s/d US$660/880, luxury tent US$480/640; ❄💻) One of the largest private wildlife reserves in Southern Africa is renowned for its big cats and large elephant population. Accommodation is in enormous luxury suites decorated with impeccable taste in the main camp, while the tents are also beautifully turned out. The game reserve is close to the Pont Drift border post.

Limpopo River Lodge   TENTED CAMP $$
(📞7210 6098; www.limpoporiverlodge.co.za; campsite per person P118, chalets/rondavels per person from P343) Consisting of a number of riverside *rondavels* (round, traditional-style huts) and chalets, this comfortable lodge in the southern reaches of the Tuli Block is another good choice. The brick *rondavels* have thatch roofs and barbecue areas, and the wildlife ticks all the right boxes in the Tuli Block. Camping is also possible.

Molema Bush Camp   CAMPGROUND, CHALETS $$
(📞264 5303; www.molema.com; campsite per adult/child P95/60, chalets s/d P450/610) Run by the owners of Tuli Safari Lodge, this campground in the Northern Tuli Game Reserve is one of few real options for self-drive visitors hoping to camp. The sites are shady and have private ablution blocks, while the simple chalets are comfy and reasonably priced.

ℹ Getting There & Away

There are daily flights between Johannesburg and the Limpopo Valley Airport at Polokwane, which is convenient for the Mashatu Game Reserve and Tuli Safari Lodge; flights can sometimes be booked as part of a package with either reserve.

You'll need your own vehicle to reach the Tuli Block. Once there, most roads in the Tuli Block are negotiable by 2WD, though it can get rough in places over creek beds, which occasionally flood during the rainy season.

Until it has been upgraded, avoid the deeply corrugated gravel road that runs north and roughly parallel to the South African border from Sherwood and the Martin's Drift; far better if you're coming from South Africa to approach via the border posts of Platjan or Pont Drift. From elsewhere in Botswana, the lodges can be accessed from the west via the sealed road from Bobonong.

NORTHEASTERN BOTSWANA

Makgadikgadi & Nxai Pans

The elemental power of Botswana's landscapes are nowhere more obvious than in the country's north. Within striking distance of the water-drowned terrain of the Okavango Delta, Chobe River and Linyanti Marshes lies Makgadikgadi, the largest network of salt pans in the world. Here the country takes on a different hue, forsaking the blues and greens of the delta for the burnished oranges, shimmering whites and golden grasslands of this northern manifestation of the Kalahari Desert. It's as much an emptiness as a place, a land larger than Switzerland, mesmerising in scope and in beauty.

Two protected areas – Makgadikgadi Game Reserve and Nxai Pans National Park, separated only by the asphalted A3 – preserve large tracts of salt pans, palm forests, grasslands and savannah. Since both parks complement one another in enabling wildlife migrations, the two were established concurrently in the early 1970s and combined into a single park in the mid-1990s. Although they enclose only a fraction of the pan networks, the parks provide a convenient focal point for visiting; the horizonless

WORTH A TRIP

ELEPHANT SANDS

Some 52km north of Nata on the Nata–Kasane road, 2km down a sand road, Elephant Sands (☎7353 6473; www.elephantsands.com; campsites per person P60, s/d/f chalets P300/540/650) has simple thatch-roofed chalets and campsites that could do with a little more shade. Elephant sightings are almost guaranteed at the waterhole, and lions, jackals and a full suite of herbivores is possible on the game drives (P190) and bushwalks (P130).

pans of Nxai Pan have gained a reputation for cheetah sightings, while the return of waters to the Boteti River in the west has led to a wildlife bonanza of wildebeest, zebra and antelope species pursued by lions. But there are also some fabulous areas outside park boundaries, with iconic stands of baobab trees and beguiling landscapes.

There are camps deep in the pans to suit a range of budgets, with good accommodation choices also in the gateway towns of Nata and Gweta.

NATA
POP 7700

The dust-bowl town of Nata serves as the eastern gateway to the Makgadikgadi Pans, as well as an obligatory fuel stop if you're heading to either Kasane or Maun; the fuel situation in Gweta was uncertain at the time of research, making this an even more important place to fill up. As it has a collection of good places to stay far out of proportion to its size, it can be a good place to break up a long journey.

◉ Sights

Nata Bird Sanctuary   WILDLIFE RESERVE
(☎7154 4342; admission P55; ☺7am-7pm) This 230-sq-km community-run wildlife sanctuary was formed when local people voluntarily relocated 3500 cattle and established a network of tracks throughout the northeastern end of Sowa Pan.

Although the sanctuary protects antelopes, zebras, jackals, foxes, monkeys and squirrels, the principal draw is the large population of water birds. Over 165 species of birds have been recorded here, including kingfishers, carmine and blue-cheeked bee-eaters, martial and black-breasted eagles, and secretary and kori bustards. When the Nata River flows in the rainy season, the sanctuary also becomes a haven for Cape and Hottentot teals, white and pink-backed pelicans, and greater and lesser flamingos. Visitors should pick up a copy of the *Comprehensive Bird List & Introductory Guide* (P5) from reception at the entrance, although supplies often run short.

In the dry season (May to October), it's possible to drive around the sanctuary in a 2WD with high clearance, though it's best to enquire about the condition of the tracks in the sanctuary before entering. During the rainy season, however, a 4WD is essential.

The entrance to the sanctuary is 15km southeast of Nata.

🛏 Sleeping

Nata Lodge   LODGE $$

(📞620 0070; www.natalodge.com; campsite per adult/child P70/45, d luxury tents/chalets P635/800; ❄❄) The Nata Lodge has risen from the ashes (it burned down in 2008) with luxury wood-and-thatch chalets, stylish safari tents and a good campsite all set amidst a verdant oasis of monkey thorn, marula and *mokolane* palms. The attempts at incorporating San and desert artwork into the general vibe of the place are subtle yet effectively accomplished. Game drives into the pans start at P165 per person; cultural tours of Nata village (P115) are also organised, while dinner costs P140.

Northgate Lodge   LODGE $$

(📞621 1156; www.northgate.co.bw; s/d/f P555/636/945; ❄❄) In the heart of town next to the petrol stations, Northgate Lodge is more about breaking up the journey than finding a remote base for a few days. The rooms are pleasant enough and excellent value. Depending on your perspective, the location is either too busy or convenient, standing as it does at crossroads that lead to all corners of the country. We lean towards the former unless you're travelling by public transport, but make up your own mind.

Nata Bird Sanctuary
Campsite   CAMPGROUND $

(📞7154 4342; campsite per person/vehicle P35/15;) Nata Bird Sanctuary offers several serene and isolated campsites with clean pit toilets, *braai* pits and cold showers. All of the five campsites are accessible by 2WD if it hasn't been raining heavily. From the campsites, it's possible to access the pan on foot (7km), though you should bring a compass with you, even if you're only walking a few hundred metres into the pan.

ℹ Getting There & Away

Regular combis travelling en route to Kasane (P88, five hours), Francistown (P41, two hours) and Maun (P76, five hours) pass by the Northgate Lodge.

GWETA
POP 7000

Gweta is an obligatory fuel stop if you're heading to either Kasane or Maun, although be warned – its petrol station was closed for repairs when we passed through, so check before leaving Nata or Maun. The village itself is a dusty and laid-back crossroads on

---

THE PANS IN A NUTSHELL

The Sowa (Sua), Nxai and Ntwetwe Pans together make up the 12,000-sq-km Makgadikgadi Pans. While Salar de Unyuni in Bolivia is the biggest single pan in the world, the Makgadikgadi network of parched, white dry lakes is larger. Ancient lakeshore terraces reveal that the pans were once part of a 'superlake' of over 60,000 sq km that reached the Okavango and Chobe Rivers to the far north. However, less than 10,000 years ago, climatic changes caused the huge lake to evaporate, leaving only salt behind.

the edge of the pans, framed by bushveld and big skies. The name of the village is derived from the croaking sound made by large bullfrogs from the pans, which, incredibly, bury themselves in the sand until the rains provide sufficient water for them to emerge and mate.

🛏 Sleeping

Gweta has two excellent places to stay.

Planet Baobab   LODGE, CAMPGROUND $$

(📞in South Africa 011-447 1605; www.unchartedafrica.com; campsite per adult/child P68/45, d tents P450, s/d/q huts from P1010/1120/1760; 📶❄) About 4km east of Gweta, you'll see a huge concrete aardvark (no, you're not hallucinating) that marks the turn-off for Planet Baobab. This inventive lodge forsakes masks and wildlife pix, replaced by a great open-air bar-restaurant (meals P49 to P90) filled with vintage travel posters, metal seats covered in cow hide, beer-bottle chandeliers and the like. Outside, *rondavels* and chalets are scattered over the gravel, and staff contribute to a vibe as funky as it is friendly. Campers can pitch a tent beneath the shade of a baobab tree. It has an excellent range of activities and creative pan excursions of up to four nights.

Gweta Lodge   LODGE $$

(📞621 2220; www.gwetalodge.com; d safari tents P350, s/d/f P390/525/795; ❄📶❄) In the centre of town, Gweta Lodge is a friendly place that manages to combine mellow poolside Southern African colonial outpost (note the lithographs in the kitchen) with funky, end-of-the-world party place, and make it work.

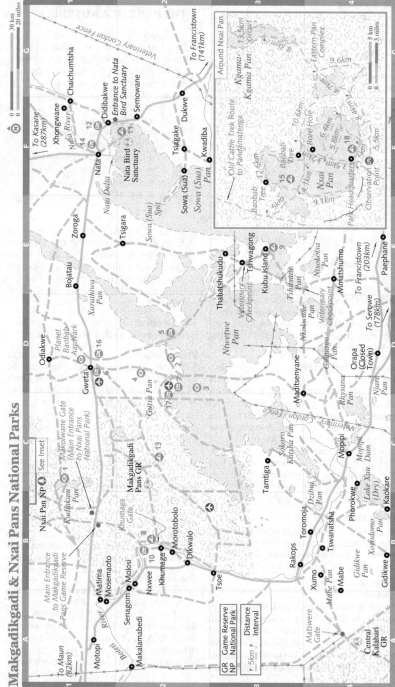

Makgadikgadi & Nxai Pans National Parks

The rooms are large and comfortable, and there are plans for an overhaul of the campsites. In addition to half-day/overnight tours of Ntwetwe Pan (P650/1200), the lodge offers activities like quad biking (P300) and walking tours of the village (P100). Lunch (P22 to P80) and dinner (P140) are served by the pool.

ⓘ Getting There & Away

Hourly combis travelling to Francistown (P44, three hours) and Maun (P47, four hours) pass along the main road.

SOWA PAN

Sowa (also spelt Sua) Pan is mostly a single sheet of salt-encrusted mud stretching across the lowest basin in northeastern Botswana. Sowa means 'salt' in the language of the San, who once mined the pan to sell salt to the Bakalanga. Today it is mined by the Sua Pan Soda Ash Company, which sells sodium carbonate for industrial manufacturing.

NATA DELTA

During the rainy season (November to May), huge flocks of water birds congregate at the Nata Delta, which is formed when the Nata River flows into the northern end of the Sowa Pan. When the rains are at their heaviest (December to February), the pan is covered with a thin film of water that reflects the sky and obliterates the horizon. The **Nata Bird Sanctuary** is the most easily accessible part of the delta.

SOWA SPIT

This long, slender protrusion extends into the heart of the pan and is the nexus of Botswana's lucrative soda-ash industry. Although security measures prevent public access to the plant, private vehicles can proceed as far as Sowa village on the pan's edge.

Views of the pan from the village are limited, though they're better if you're travelling through the area in a 4WD.

KUBU ISLAND

Along the southwestern edge of Sowa Pan is a ghostly, baobab-laden rock, entirely surrounded by a sea of salt. In Setswana, *kubu* means 'hippopotamus' (in ancient times this was a real island on a real lake inhabited by an abundance of hippos). It's not only the name that evokes a more fertile past – the fossilised shit of water birds that once perched here still adorns the boulders.

As unlikely as it may seem, given the current environment and climate, this desolate area may have been inhabited by people as recently as 500 years ago. On one shore lies an ancient crescent-shaped stone wall of unknown origin, which has yielded numerous artefacts, testament to those who lived here before the waters dried up (some think it served as a space in male initiation ceremonies).

The **island** (www.kubuisland.com) is now protected as a national monument, administered by the local Gaing-O-Community Trust.

⊨ Sleeping

Kubu Island Campsite   CAMPGROUND $
(☑7549 4669; www.kubuisland.com; Lekhubu, GPS: S20°53.460', E25°49.318'; campsite per adult/child P100/50) This sprawling campground has 14 sites and is one of Botswana's loveliest, with baobabs as a backdrop to most campsites, many of which have sweeping views of the pan. There are bucket showers and pit toilets. There was, however, a rumour that the campsite will be relocated away from the island due to concerns over the growing impact of tourism.

MAKGADIKGADI & NXAI PANS AT A GLANCE

Why Go?
Underrated wildlife watching, especially along the pretty Boteti River and the hallucinatory, horizonless landscape of the pans.

Gateway Towns
Gweta, Nata and (at a stretch) Maun.

Wildlife
Nxai Pans is one of the best places in Botswana for spotting cheetahs, while Makgadikgadi can be good for lions. There are dense concentrations of wildlife along the Boteti River in the dry season, with much wider dispersal during the wet when herbivores migrate east in large numbers.

Birds
Around 165 bird species inhabit the Nata Bird Sanctuary (beyond the parks but part of the same pan network) in the east; flamingos and pelicans arrive in numbers in the rainy season.

When to Go
Dry season (May to October) is best for driving on the pans, with big wildlife concentrations along the Boteti River later in the season. During the wet season, driving can be perilous but the zebra migration on the eastern pans can be quite a sight.

Moving Around
The lodges that surround the parks offer game drives; otherwise you'll need your own 4WD.

Budget Safaris
Few budget options but the campgrounds and lodges of Maun and Gweta may offer affordable excursions. For self-drivers, Khumaga, South Pan, Baines' Baobab and Kubu Island campsites are excellent.

Author Tip
Always ask about driving conditions before setting out onto the pans; failing to do so could ruin your trip.

❶ Getting There & Away
Access to Kubu Island involves negotiating a maze of grassy islets and salty bays. Increased traffic has now made the route considerably clearer, but drivers still need a 4WD and a compass or GPS equipment. The island can be difficult to reach after rains.

From the Nata–Maun highway, the track starts near Zoroga (GPS: S 20°10.029', E 25°56.898'), about 24km west of Nata. After about 72km, the village of Thabatshukudu (GPS: S 20°42.613', E 25°47.482') will appear on a low ridge. This track then skirts the western edge of a salt pan for 10.3km before passing through a veterinary checkpoint. Just under 2km further south, a track (17km) heads southeast to the northern end of Kubu.

From the Francistown–Rakops Rd, turn north at the junction for Letlhakane and proceed 25km until you reach Mmatshumo village. About 21km further north is a veterinary checkpoint. After another 7.5km, an 18km track heads northeast to the southern end of Kubu. This turn-off (GPS: S 20°56.012', E 25°40.032') is marked by a small cairn.

NTWETWE PAN
The Ntwetwe Pan was fed by the Boteti River until it was left permanently dry following the construction of the Mopipi Dam, which provides water for the diamond mines in Orapa. The waters may have returned to the river but Ntwetwe is now famous for its extraordinary lunar landscape, particularly the rocky outcrops, dunes, islets, channels and spits found along the western shore.

GREEN'S BAOBAB

On the Gweta–Orapa track, 27km south of Gweta, is **Green's Baobab** (GPS: S 20°25.543′, E 25°13.859′), which was inscribed by the 19th-century hunters and traders Joseph Green and Hendrik Matthys van Zyl, as well as other ruthless characters.

CHAPMAN'S BAOBAB

About 11km further south is the turn-off to the far more impressive **Chapman's Baobab** (GPS: S 20°29.392′, E 25°14.979′), which has a circumference of 25m and was historically used as a navigation beacon. It may also have been used as an early post office by passing explorers, traders and travellers, many of whom left inscriptions on its trunk.

GABATSADI ISLAND

The enormous crescent-shaped dune known as Gabatsadi Island has an expansive view from the crest that has managed to attract the likes of Prince Charles. (He went there to capture the indescribably lonely scene in watercolour, but the paints ran because it was so hot!) The island is just west of the Gweta–Orapa track, about 48km south of Gweta.

🛏 Sleeping

In a remote corner of Ntwetwe Pan, Uncharted Africa, the same company that manages Planet Baobab, operates three exclusive tented camps.

Accommodation at the camps is in classic 1940s East African–style canvas tents furnished with regal linens and romantically lit by paraffin lanterns. Buckets of hot water are delivered on request, though flush toilets are a welcome modern concession. The central 'mess tent' operates as a field museum where local guides and world-renowned experts deliver lectures and lead discussions on the area's flora and fauna. There's also a dining tent, a drinks tent and a separate tea tent where you can indulge in high tea while relaxing on Oriental rugs and cushions. Safari expeditions put you in touch with local meerkats, rare brown hyenas and San culture. Rates include full board, wildlife drives, bushwalks and a range of activities including quad bikes and horse-riding safaris.

Air fares cost around US$150 per person one way from Maun. Road transfer from Gweta costs around US$110 per person one way, and escorts (with your own 4WD) from Gweta cost US$165 per vehicle.

Camp Kalahari TENTED CAMP $$$
(☑in South Africa 011-447 1605; www.unchartedafrica.com; s/d US$704/1122; ❋)

San Camp TENTED CAMP $$$
(☑in South Africa 011-447 1605; www.unchartedafrica.com; s/d US$1425/2200; ❋) One of the most luxurious tented camps in Africa.

Jack's Camp TENTED CAMP $$$
(☑in South Africa 011-447 1605; www.unchartedafrica.com; s/d US$1596/2500; ❋) If you've got

DRIVING SAFELY ON THE PANS

Prospective drivers should keep in mind that salt pans can have a mesmerising effect, and even create a sense of unfettered freedom. Once you drive out onto the salt, remember that direction, connection, reason and common sense appear to dissolve. Although you may be tempted to speed off with wild abandon into the white and empty distance, exercise caution and restrain yourself. You should be aware of where you are at all times by using a map and compass (GPS units are not foolproof).

As a general rule, always follow the tracks of other drivers – these tracks are a good indication that the route is dry. In addition, never venture out onto the pans unless you're absolutely sure the salty surface and the clay beneath are dry. Foul-smelling salt means a wet and potentially dangerous pan, which is very similar in appearance and texture to wet concrete. When underlying clay becomes saturated, vehicles can break through the crust and become irretrievably bogged. If you do get bogged and have a winch, anchor the spare wheel or the jack – anything to which the winch may be attached – by digging a hole and planting if firmly in the clay. Hopefully, you'll be able to anchor it better than the pan has anchored the vehicle.

It is important to stress that to explore the pans properly and independently requires more of a 4WD expedition than a casual drive. Lost travellers are frequently rescued from the pans, and there have been a number of fatalities over the years. And remember: *never* underestimate the effect that the pans can have on your sense of direction.

SEASONS ON THE PANS

As everywhere in Botswana, seasons play an important role in determining what sort of experience you're likely to have here. In the dry season, from May to October, the great salt pans are long, low and white, curtained by an electric-blue sky and pulsing with an unstoppable glare. During the sizzling heat of the late winter (August), the stark pans take on a disorienting and ethereal austerity. Heat mirages destroy the senses as imaginary lakes shimmer and disappear, ostriches take flight, and stones turn to mountains and float in midair. But as the annual rains begin to fall in the late spring, depressions in the pans form temporary lakes and fringing grasses turn green with life. Herd animals arrive to partake of the bounty, while waterbirds flock to feed on algae and tiny crustaceans. A word of warning: wet pans make for difficult driving at this time.

some serious cash to burn, the highly recommended Jack's Camp is one of the most luxurious lodges in the whole of Africa.

MAKGADIKGADI PANS NATIONAL PARK

This 3900-sq-km park extends from the Boteti River in the west to the Ntwetwe Pan in the east. The return of water to the Boteti River in recent years has drawn plenty of wildlife, particularly in the dry season from May to October (including one of Southern Africa's most spectacular wildebeest and zebra migrations) when the river, even at low levels, is the only source of permanent water in the reserve.

🛏 Sleeping

Leroo-La-Tau LODGE $$$
(☎686 1559; www.desertdelta.com; per person Jan-Apr US$476, s/d May-Dec US$1113/1712; ☀) Luxury East African–style canvas tents with private verandahs overlooking the Boteti riverbed make for some of the best views in the Kalahari – sunset, when the animals come down to drink, is the time to nurse a sundowner on the verandah. The lodge is just across the river from the reserve but game drives yield excellent wildlife viewing. Otherwise, expect expansive rooms, wonderful facilities and professional service. Rates include full board, wildlife drives, bushwalks and a range of activities.

Khumaga Campsite CAMPGROUND $
(http://sklcamps.com; GPS: S 20°27.311; E 24°30.968'; campsite per adult/child US$50/25) The Khumaga Campsite sits high above the bank of the Boteti and is an attractive site with good shade, *braai* pits and an excellent ablutions block with flush toilets and (usually) hot showers. Some readers have complained of night-time noise from the village

across the river, but the last time we slept here all we could hear was a frog symphony.

Njuca Hills Campsite CAMPGROUND $
(GPS: S 20°25.807; E 24°52.395') Although closed due to a lack of water at the time of our visit, the Department of Wildlife, which administers the site, assured us that there were plans to reopen. It's quite a long way from the riverbank, offering a more remote experience than Khumaga Campsite.

❶ Getting There & Away

The main entrance to the national park is 141km west of Nata and 164km east of Maun. A 4WD is needed to drive around the park, and the road from the main gate to the Khumaga Campsite is deep sand.

There's another entrance close to Khumaga Campsite, but you'll need to cross the river on a pontoon ferry (per vehicle P120).

NXAI PANS NATIONAL PARK

This 2578-sq-km park lies on the old **Pandamatenga Trail**, which once connected a series of bore holes and was used until the 1960s for overland cattle drives. The grassy expanse of the park is interesting during the rains, when large animal herds migrate from the south and predators arrive to take advantage of the bounty, but it's also impressive when the land is dry and dust clouds migrate over the scrub and salt pans. The region is specked with umbrella acacias, and cheetah and elephant sightings are common.

BAINES' BAOBABS

In the south of the park are the famous **Baines' Baobabs** (GPS: S 20°06.726; E 24°46.136'), which were immortalised in paintings by the artist and adventurer Thomas Baines in 1862. Baines, a self-taught naturalist, artist and cartographer, had originally been a member of David Livingstone's expedition up the Zambezi but was mistakenly accused of theft by Livingstone's brother and forced to leave the party. Livingstone's brother later realised his mistake (but never publicly admitted it), yet Baines remained the subject of ridicule in Britain. Today, a comparison with Baines' paintings reveals that in almost 150 years, only one branch has broken off.

🛏 Sleeping

South Camp
CAMPGROUND $

(www.xomaesites.com; GPS: S 19°56.159', E 24°46.598'; campsite per adult/child P226/113) Around 37km from the park gate along a sandy track, South Camp has 10 sites clustered quite close together behind some trees at the edge of one of the pans. There's a good ablutions block with flush toilets and (usually hot) showers, as well as *braai* pits.

Baines' Baobab
CAMPGROUND $

(www.xomaesites.com; GPS: S 20°08.362', E 24°46.213'; campsite per adult/child P350/175) Just three sites sit close to the famed baobabs, a wonderfully evocative site once the day trippers go home. There are bucket showers and pit toilets.

Nxai Pan Camp
TENTED CAMP $$$

(🖊6861449; www.kwando.co.bw; s/dfromUS$620/ 880; 🏊) Eight rooms done up in a chic African-modern style curve in a crescent around an open plain; inside, smooth linens and indoor and outdoor showers do a good job of pushing the whole rustic-luxury vibe. From a large, polished deck, observers can watch elephants, zebras and cheetahs cross the grassland, or from the comfort of a pool, if you want to be really indulgent.

ℹ Getting There & Away

The entrance to the park is at Makolwane Gate, which is about 140km east of Maun and 60km west of Gweta. A 4WD is required to get around the national park.

Two tracks lead from the main track to Baines' Baobabs; when we visited, the longer, northernmost of the two was much easier to traverse, but ask at the park gate.

CHOBE NATIONAL PARK & KASANE

Chobe National Park is one of the great wildlife destinations of Africa. Famed for its massive elephants and enormous elephant population, Chobe, which encompasses nearly 11,000 sq km, is itself the size of a small country and an important epicentre of Botswana's safari industry. It was first set aside as a wildlife reserve in the 1930s and became Botswana's first national park in 1968.

Of the three major wildlife-watching areas of the park, **Chobe Riverfront** supports the largest wildlife concentration in the park. It's also the most accessible and lies within easy striking distance of the gateway town of Kasane. The extension of the sealed road from Kasane as far as Kachikau has brought the predator-rich **Linyanti Marshes** that much closer to civilisation without losing its remote Okavango feel. And soulful **Savuti**, which can be reached from Maun or Kasane, is almost the riverfront's match when it comes to wildlife and has a wonderfully remote feel; the miraculous return of waters to the Savuti Channel has restored the region to its former glory.

Whether you're self-driving and camping under the stars or flying into your luxury lodge, Chobe can be enjoyed by everyone.

Kasane & Around

POP 13,600

Kasane lies in a riverine woodland at the meeting point of four countries – Botswana, Zambia, Namibia and Zimbabwe – and the confluence of two major rivers, the Chobe and the Zambezi. It's also the northern gateway to Chobe National Park, and the jumping-off point for excursions to Victoria Falls. Although it's nowhere near as large or developed as Maun, there's certainly no shortage of lodges and safari companies, as well as petrol stations and supermarkets for those heading out into the wilds.

About 12km east of Kasane is the tiny settlement of **Kazungula**, which serves as the border crossing between Botswana and Zimbabwe, and the landing for the Kazungula ferry, which connects Botswana and Zambia.

◉ Sights

Kasane has little to detain you and most people use it as a base for visiting nearby Chobe National Park.

Caracal Biodiversity Centre
ZOO

(Map p78; 🖊6252392; www.caracal.info; Airport Rd; admission P35; ☉9am-5pm) Signposted as Biodiversity Centre, about halfway between the main highway and the Chobe Safari Lodge, this research and education centre rescues

Chobe National Park

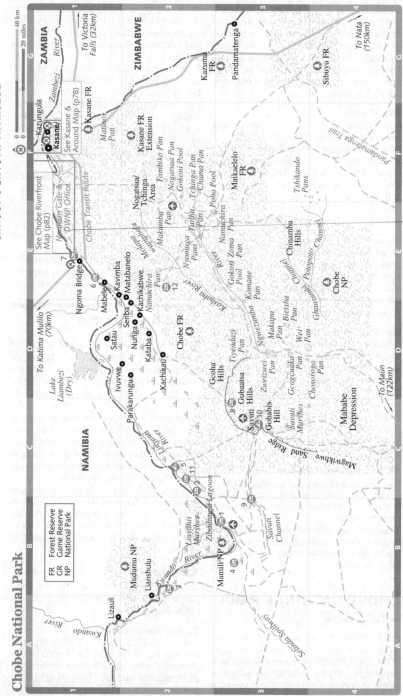

ZAMBIA

ZIMBABWE

NAMIBIA

Forest Reserve
Game Reserve
National Park

FR
GR
NP

Kwando River

Lizauli

Mudumu NP

Lianshulu

Kwando River

Linyanti
Marshes

Mamili NP

Zibadianja Lagoon

Savuti
Channel

Selinda Spillway

Magwikhwe Sand Ridge

Linyanti River

Parakarungu

Ivuvwe

Kachikau

Lake
Liambezi
(Dry)

To Katima Mulilo
(70km)

Ngoma Bridge

Mabele

Kavimba
Matabanelo

Seriba
Nunga

Kachikabwe

Satau

Kataba

Chobe FR

Namuchira

Gcoha
Hills

Gubaatsa
Hills

Gobabis
Hill

Savuti
Marshes

Gcagwakbe
Pan

Chosoroga
Pan

Wei
Pan

Mababe
Depression

To Maun
(122km)

Tiyendazi
Pan

Zwetzwei
Pan

Ngwezumba
River

Makapa
Pan

Bietsha
Pan

Kasinka River

Nyamga
Pans

Gokoni
Zoma
Pan

Komane
Pan

Gokoni
Pool

Potopoto Channel

Ghauwitsha Channel

Chinamba
Hills

Chobe
NP

Maikaelelo
FR

Tshikando
Pans

Poha Pool

Chuma Pool

Tchinga
Pan

Tebinga Pan

Gokoni Pool

Nogatsaa
Pan

Nogatsaa/
Tchinga
Area

Tambiko Pan

Makumba
Pan

Tuliba
Pan

Ncamasere

Namuchira

Nyomga
Pans

Njamutobo

Chobe Transit Route

See Chobe Riverfront
Map (p82)

Northern Gate &
DWNP Office

See Kasane &
Around Map (p78)

Kasane

Kazungula

Kazungula

Zambezi River

To Victoria
Falls (32km)

Kasane FR

Matino
Pan

Kasane FR
Extension

Kazuma
FR

Pandamatenga

Sibuyu FR

To Nata
(150km)

Pandamatenga Trail

7

6

Katima Mulilo

5

11

2

1

9

4

10

8

12

40 km
20 miles

0
0

Chobe National Park

small wildlife species, then rehabilitates some into the wild and keeps the rest. It has some birds, a mongoose or two, and a particularly large selection of snakes; if the latter give you frisson, this is the place to look at them through the glass.

🏃 Activities

Most lodges and campsites organise three-hour wildlife drives into Chobe National Park (from P195), three-hour boat trips along Chobe Riverfront (from P190) and full-day excursions to Victoria Falls (from P1250) across the border in Zimbabwe.

In addition to those outfits that operate out of the lodges, the following safari companies are among those that operate out of Kasane.

Kalahari Holiday Tours TOUR
(Map p78; ☑625 0880; www.kalaharichobe.com) Half-, full- and multiday safaris into Chobe.

Pangolin Photography Safaris TOUR
(Map p78; www.pangolinphoto.com; 3hr game drives or boat trips US$120) Photography tours along the Chobe Riverfront using the latest cameras with instruction thrown in; park fees cost extra.

Gecko TOUR
(Map p78; ☑625 2562; www.oldhousekasane.com) Canoe and fishing trips add variety to the usual game drives.

🛏 Sleeping

Kasane has good accommodation across a range of budgets, although it helps if you

have your own vehicle as some of the better places are some distance away from the town centre.

Chobe Safari Lodge LODGE $$$
(Map p78; ☑625 0336; www.chobesafarilodge.com; President Ave; campsite per adult/child P75/60, r P975-1175; ❋🏊) One of the more affordable upmarket lodges in Kasane (or Botswana for that matter), Chobe Safari is excellent value, especially if you're travelling with little ones, with family rooms and tents available. Understated but comfortable rooms are priced according to size and location, though all feature attractive mosquito-netted beds and modern furnishings.

⭐ **Senyati Safari**
Camp CAMPGROUND, CHALETS $$
(off Map p78; ☑7188 1306; www.senyatisafaricamp.com; off Kazungula-Nata Rd; campsite per adult/child from P115/63, s/d/f chalets P400/520/690; ❋🏊) Off the main highway south of Kasungula (the turn-off is well signposted 6.8km south of Kasungula, from where it's a further 1.6km off road), this wonderful spot has comfy chalets and some of northern Botswana's best campsites, each with their own ablutions block. The bar and some of the chalets overlook a waterhole where elephants congregate in large numbers nightly, and wild dogs have also been known to pass by for a drink. You'll need your own wheels to get here.

Old House GUESTHOUSE $$
(Map p78; ☑625 2562; www.oldhousekasane.com; President Ave; r P550-900; ❋🛜🏊) Close to the centre and with a lovely intimate feel, the Old House has lovely rooms adjacent to a quiet garden by the riverbank. The bar-restaurant is one of Kasane's best, and the rooms are stylish and comfortable without being overdone.

Kubu Lodge LODGE $$$
(Map p78; ☑625 0312; www.kubulodge.net; Kasane-Kazungula Rd; s/d US$255/310; ❋🏊) Located 9km east of Kasane, this riverside option lacks the stuffiness and formality found in most other top-end lodges but is their match for quality. Rustic wooden chalets are lovingly adorned with thick rugs and wicker furniture, and scattered around an impeccably manicured lawn dotted with fig trees.

Toro Safari Lodge LODGE, CAMPGROUND $$
(Map p78; ☑625 2694; www.torolodge.co.bw; off Kasane-Kazungula Rd; campsite per person P81, chalets from P671, apt P1003; ❋@🏊) Down a

Kasane & Around

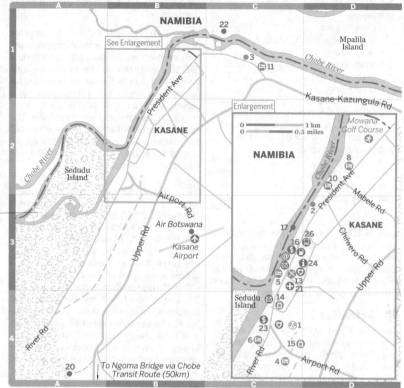

side road off the main Kasane–Kazungula road, this excellent place has campsites beneath maturing trees, comfortable chalets (some with river view) and attractive grounds that run along the riverbank.

Garden Lodge
LODGE **$$$**

(☑7164 6064; www.thegardenlodge.com; President Ave; s/d incl breakfast US$312/400; ☞☒) This simple but charming lodge is built around a tropical garden and features a number of well-furnished rooms that exude a homey atmosphere. It's a little more quirky than the average lodge in these parts, with hints of eccentricity that put it above the pack.

Elephant Valley Lodge
TENTED CAMP **$$$**

(☑in South Africa 011-781 1661; www.kubulodge.net; off Kasungula-Nata Rd; per person from US$430; ☒☒) Located not far south of Kasungula in a quiet forest location, this place has luxury safari tents, some of which are surrounded

by forest. There's also a waterhole where elephants come to drink, and the rates include meals and game drives.

Chobe Marina Lodge
LODGE **$$$**

(☑625 2221; www.chobemarinalodge.com; President Ave; s/d US$486/784; ☒☒) Occupying an attractive spot along the river, Chobe Marina Lodge is conveniently located in the centre of Kasane. The rooms blend African aesthetics and mod cons, and as a result are really rather lovely. Rates include all meals, activities, park fees and airport transfers.

Thebe River Camping
LODGE, CAMPGROUND **$$**

(☑625 0314; www.theberiversafaris.com; Kasane-Kazungula Rd; campsite per person P93, tent P396, tw/f P690/1000; ☒) Perched alongside the Chobe River, this leafy backpackers lodge is one of the more budget-friendly options in Kasane. Well-groomed campsites are located near *braai* pits and a modern ablution block

with steaming showers and flush toilets. There's also a thatched bar-restaurant that serves cheap food and cold beers – come night-time, if there is anything going on in Kasane, it's going on here.

✕ Eating

📍 Old House   INTERNATIONAL $$
(📞625 2562; www.oldhousekasane.com; President Ave; breakfast P45-60, light meals P30-60, mains P45-85) This open-air bar-restaurant close to the riverbank is every bit as good as the guesthouse it inhabits. The menu contains all the usual suspects such as burgers, toasted sandwiches, salads, steaks and pizzas, with fish and chips not forgotten either. There's also a kids menu.

Hot Bread Shop   BAKERY $
(Hunters' Africa Mall, off President Ave; ◷7.30am-7pm) If you're arriving from the bush and

craving freshly baked bread, look no further than this fine place up behind the Shell petrol station. It also does a few cakes and pastries.

Coffee & Curry INDIAN $
(Map p78; ☏625 2237; Shop 1AB, Hunters' Africa Mall, off President Ave; mains P45-70; ⊗9am-10pm Mon-Sat, 11am-9pm Sun) Just about everything (except African!) is served at this simple Indian-run place, with an especially good selection of curries and other Indian dishes, as well as a few pizzas and Southeast Asian–inspired dishes.

Spar Supermarket SUPERMARKET $
(Map p78; Hunters' Africa Mall, off President Ave; ⊗7.30am-7pm Mon-Fri, 8am-6pm Sat, 8am-5pm Sun) Kasane's best supermarket is right in the heart of town.

🛍 Shopping

African Easel Art Gallery HANDICRAFTS
(Map p78; ☏625 0828; President Ave, Audi Centre; ⊗8am-1pm & 2-5pm Mon-Fri, 8.30am-12.30pm Sat) An upmarket gallery exhibiting purchasable work by artists from Botswana, Namibia, Zambia and Zimbabwe, as well as woodcarvings from around the continent.

Chobe Women's Arts & Crafts HANDICRAFTS
(Map p78; Airport Rd; ⊗8am-5pm) This NGO-backed store sells locally woven baskets made by the women of the region. The women are often present, and are happy to demonstrate their weaving techniques.

Kingfisher Trading Co HANDICRAFTS
(Map p78; President Ave, Audi Centre; ⊗8am-5pm Mon-Fri, 8.30am-1pm Sat) A simple shop selling African curios at fixed (though reasonable)

CHOBE NATIONAL PARK AT A GLANCE

Why Go?
Chobe is one of Botswana's most accessible and varied parks. From the relative isolation of Savuti and Linyanti to the more easily accessed and busier Chobe Riverfront, this is one of Africa's best parks for watching wildlife.

Gateway Towns
Kasane (for Chobe Riverfront and Linyanti) or Maun (Savuti).

Wildlife
Chobe has tens of thousands of elephants and some of the largest elephant herds in Africa. Savuti is good for predators, Linyanti for hippos and possibly African wild dogs, and Chobe Riverfront for all of the above. Watch also for roan antelopes and the rare oribi antelopes.

Birds
Over 440 species of birds have been recorded here.

When to Go
The best time to visit Chobe is during the dry season (April to October), when wildlife congregates around permanent water sources. Try to avoid January to March, as getting around can be difficult during the rains (although this is peak season for flying into Savuti).

Moving Around
Unless you've joined a mobile safari, you'll need your own 4WD vehicle. Game trails are clearly marked, but at the time of writing there was particularly deep sand between Savuti and Linyanti, and between Linyanti and Kachikau where the sealed road begins.

Budget Safaris
Most lodges and many camps in Kasane offer two- to three-hour game drives or boat safaris to Chobe Riverfront for around P200 per person.

Author Tip
Be mindful of the decongestion strategy in Chobe Riverfront.

prices, as well as fishing gear and a small selection of wildlife books.

ℹ Information

Emergency

Chobe Private Clinic (Map p78; ✆625 1555; President Ave) Offers 24-hour emergency services.

Kasane Hospital (Map p78; ✆625 0333; President Ave) Public hospital on the main road.

Police Station (✆625 2444; President Ave; ☺24hr) On the main road.

Internet Access

Cape to Cairo Bureau de Change & Internet (Hunters' Africa Mall, off President Ave; per hr P40; ☺8.30am-5pm Mon-Fri, to 4.30pm Sat)

Chobe Post Office (Hunters' Africa Mall, off President Ave; per hr P40; ☺9am-5pm Mon-Fri, to noon Sat) Good connections.

Open Door Bureau de Change (President Ave; per hr P30; ☺8.30am-5pm Mon-Fri, to 4.30pm Sat)

Money

Barclays Bank (Map p78; Hunters' Africa Mall, off President Ave; ☺8.30am-3.30pm Mon-Fri, 8.15-10.45am Sat) Offers better exchange rates than the bureaux de change. Be sure to stock up on US dollars (post-1996) if you're heading to Zimbabwe.

Cape to Cairo Bureau de Change & Internet (Map p78; Hunters' Africa Mall, off President Ave; ☺8.30am-5pm Mon-Fri, to 4.30pm Sat) Charges 3% commission on cash, 4% on travellers cheques.

Open Door Bureau de Change (Map p78; President Ave; ☺8.30am-5pm Mon-Fri, to 4.30pm Sat) Next to Choppies Supermarket; charges 2% commission on cash, 3% on travellers cheques.

Tourist Information

Tourist Office (Map p78; ✆625 0555; Hunters' Africa Mall, off President Ave; ☺7.30am-6pm Mon-Fri, 9am-2pm Sat) Plenty of brochures for lodges and safari companies, and generally helpful, although you're better off visiting the park gate for information on Chobe National Park.

Department of Wildlife & National Parks (DWNP; Map p78; ✆625 0235; Sedudu Gate) This is the place to pay for your park permit and get information on visiting Chobe National Park.

ℹ Getting There & Away

Air

Air Botswana (✆625 0161; www.airbotswana. co.bw) connects Kasane to Maun (from P369)

and Gaborone (from P1050). Air Botswana has an office at Kasane airport, which is near the centre of town.

Bus & Combi

Combis heading to Francistown (P106, seven hours), Maun (P96, six hours) and Nata (P88, five hours) run when full from the Shell petrol station and bus terminal on Mabele Rd.

Car & Motorcycle

The direct route between Kasane and Maun is only accessible by 4WD, and may be almost impassable after heavy rains. Also remember that there is nowhere along the Kasane–Maun road to buy fuel, food or drinks, or to get vehicle repairs.

All other traffic between Kasane and Maun travels via Nata, a road which is, mercifully, being upgraded as we write.

ℹ Getting Around

Combis travel regularly between Kasane and Kazungula, and continue to the immigration posts for Zambia and Zimbabwe if requested. The standard fare for anywhere around Kasane and Kazungula is about P35.

Chobe Riverfront

The Chobe Riverfront rarely disappoints, with arguably Botswana's densest concentration of wildlife. Although animals are present along the riverfront year-round, the density of wildlife can be overwhelming during the dry season, especially during September and October. Whether you cruise along the river in a motorboat, or drive along the banks in a 4WD, you're almost guaranteed an up-close encounter with some of the largest elephant herds (and some of the largest elephants) on the continent.

Spend even a couple of hours along the riverfront and you'll likely see elephants, giraffes, hippos, lions and possibly the more elusive cheetahs and leopards along the banks. During the dry season (April to October), herds of antelopes, zebras, buffaloes and wildebeest also congregate along the river. The marshy river flood plain is also inhabited by Chobe's two trademark antelopes, namely the water-loving red lechwe and the increasingly rare puku. The latter has a face like a waterbuck but can be distinguished by its notched, inward-curving horns and its small, stocky build.

The birdlife along the riverfront is extraordinarily varied. Along the river, listen

Chobe Riverfront

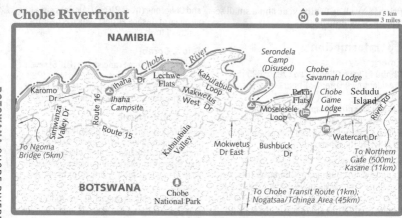

NAMIBIA

Chobe River

Karomo Dr • Ihaha Dr • Lechwe Flats • Kabulabula Loop • Makwetus West Dr

Serondela Camp (Disused) • Chobe Savannah Lodge

Puku Flats • Chobe Game Lodge • Sedudu Island

Simwanza Valley Dr • Route 16 • Ihaha Campsite • Route 15 • Kabulabula Valley

Moselesele Loop

River Rd

Watercart Dr

To Ngoma Bridge (5km)

Mokwetus Dr East • Bushbuck Dr

To Northern Gate (500m); Kasane (11km)

BOTSWANA   Chobe National Park

To Chobe Transit Route (1km); Nogatsaa/Tchinga Area (45km)

0 ——— 5 km
0 ——— 3 miles

for the screaming fish eagles overhead as they make precision dives for fish.

If you don't have your own wheels, any of the hotels and lodges in Kasane can help you organise a wildlife drive or boat cruise along the riverfront. Although the majority of travellers' experiences in Chobe are limited to riverfront wildlife drives and boat cruises, most people are more than satisfied with these tours. Two- to three-hour cruises and wildlife drives typically cost around P200, though you will also have to pay separate park fees. As always, shop around, compare prices and choose a trip that suits your needs.

🛏 Sleeping

If you're planning on independently venturing deeper into the national park, the first thing you must do is book your campsites prior to arrival in Chobe. If you don't have a reservation, SKL (which runs three campsites in the park) has an office right outside the Chobe Riverfront park entrance. Be warned, however, that in peak periods the campsites are booked out months in advance.

Ihaha Campsite   CAMPGROUND $
(kwalatesafari@gmail.com; GPS: S 17°50.487', E 24°52.754'; campsite per adult/child P260/130) Ihaha is the only campsite for self-drivers along the Chobe Riverfront – staying here gives you the run of the park without having to negotiate the decongestion strategy. The trees need more time to mature and shade can be in short supply at some of the sites. But the location is excellent – it's by the water's edge

about 27km from the Northern Gate. There's an ablutions block and *braai* areas.

Chobe Game Lodge   LODGE $$$
(☏ 625 1761, 625 0340; www.chobegamelodge.com; River Rd; per person Jan-Apr US$476, s/d May-Dec US$1113/1712; ☀) This highly praised safari lodge is one of Botswana's pinnacles of luxury. The lodge is constructed in the Moorish style and flaunts high arches, barrel-vaulted ceilings and tiled floors. The individually decorated rooms are elegant yet soothing, and some have views of the Chobe River and Namibian flood plains. Service is attentive and professional, and there's a good chance you'll spot herds of elephants along the riverfront as you walk around the hotel grounds. The lodge is located about 9km west of the Northern Gate.

Chobe Chilwero Lodge   LODGE $$$
(Map p78; ☏ in South Africa 011-438 4650; www.sanctuarylodges.com; Airport Rd; per person Jan-Apr US$620, May-Dec US$1055; ❄ 🛜 ☀) Chilwero means 'place of high view' in Setswana, and indeed this exclusive lodge boasts panoramic views across the Chobe River. Accommodation is in one of 15 elegant bungalows featuring romantic indoor and outdoor showers, private terraced gardens and colonial fixtures adorned with plush linens. The lodge is on expansive grounds that contain a pool, a spa, an outdoor bar and a well-reviewed gourmet restaurant.

Ngoma Safari Lodge   LODGE $$$
(☏ Zimbabwe 13 43211; www.ngomasafarilodge.com; s/d Jan-Apr US$495/990, May-Dec US$1031/1650; ❄ @ ☀) At the western end of the

Chobe Riverfront, close to the Ngoma Bridge border crossing between Botswana and Namibia, this lovely lodge is removed from the clamour close to Kasane. It offers eight stylishly appointed, river-facing suites with thatched roofs on a rise set back from the riverbank. Earth tones dominate the decor in the rooms and the service is everything you'd expect for the price.

Muchenje Safari Lodge   LODGE $$$
(☑620 0013; www.muchenje.com; per person Jan-Apr US$375, s/d May-Dec US$790/1190; ❄@☎) High on a hill overlooking the Chobe River at the western end of the Chobe Riverfront, Muchenje has 11 spacious rooms decorated in an attractive colonial style. There are vantage points over the riverbank from numerous points around the property, including each room's private verandah.

❶ Getting There & Away

From central Kasane, the Northern Gate is about 6km to the southwest. Unlike all other national parks operated by the DWNP, you do not need a campsite reservation to enter, though you will be expected to leave the park prior to closing if you do not have one. All tracks along the riverfront require a 4WD vehicle, and you will not be admitted into the park without one.

You can either exit the park via the Northern Gate by backtracking along the river or via the Ngoma Bridge Gate near the Namibian border. If you exit via Ngoma, you can return to Kasane via the Chobe transit route. (If you're simply bypassing Chobe en route to/from Namibia, you do not have to pay park fees to travel on this road.) Be advised that elephants frequently cross this road, so keep your speed down and do not drive at night.

BORDER CROSSINGS: KASANE & CHOBE

Kasane stands at a crossroads of countries, with Namibia, Zambia and Zimbabwe all within an hour's drive of the town centre.

Namibia
The **Ngoma Bridge–Kasane Gate** (open 6am to 6pm) lies 57km west of Kasane and is handy for Namibia's Caprivi Strip. As always, coming into Botswana your car will be searched for fresh meat, fresh fruit and dairy products (all of which will be confiscated if found), and you may be required to walk through a soda solution (and drive your car through the same) as part of measures to protect the country from foot-and-mouth disease. Otherwise, this is a relatively hassle-free border crossing.

Zambia
The **Kazungula–Mambova Gate** (6am to 8pm) requires a river crossing by ferry. Don't be put off by the extraordinary queue of trucks (some of which wait up to five days to cross this border) – drive to the front of the queue. Leaving or entering Botswana should pose no special problems (save for the usual customs searches and foot-and-mouth controls). For crossing into Zambia, we recommend hiring a local fixer (agree a fee up front, never hand over money until all formalities are completed, and get your fixer's mobile phone number and check that it works). It is possible to do it all on your own, but it will take longer and the paperwork required can be confusing. All fees into Zambia are paid in kwacha, apart from visa fee and road toll fee (US$48 for Botswana-registered vehicles, US$20 for Namibian or South African vehicles). Sample costs include ZMW30 council levy, ZMW150 carbon tax and ZMW182 third-party insurance.

Zimbabwe
The surprisingly quiet **Kazungula–Victoria Falls Gate** (6am to 6pm) advertises that the border is open until 10pm but we wouldn't count on it. The border is generally hassle-free. Those on day excursions to/from Victoria Falls will encounter few difficulties, while self-drivers can expect around two hours in total, with whispered requests for small 'gifts' common among customs officials on the Zimbabwean side. As long as your documents are in order and you're not in a hurry, be firm but calm and refuse all requests and you should be on your way in no time.

CHOBE RIVERFRONT (DE)CONGESTION

Chobe is one of few national parks in Botswana where you may enter as a day tripper without a confirmed lodge or campsite reservation. Before you celebrate, read on.

Chobe Riverfront's proliferation of lodges and the park's proximity to Kasane and its numerous hotels and lodges means that safari trails (more specifically the main trail along the riverbank) can become overwhelmed by vehicles. Perhaps in response to complaints from exclusive lodges within the park, the park and local authorities have instituted a controversial system aimed at reducing the number of vehicles during peak times. Under the strategy, tour operators are allowed to visit the park from dawn until 9am and from 2.30pm to sunset. Self-drivers and day trippers are left with the wholly unappealing hours of 9am to 2.30pm. That, at least, is the official position.

However, when we visited (self-driving) during a particularly busy period in late June 2012, we were allowed in at 3pm and allowed to stay until sunset. Confused? The park rangers openly acknowledged that the decongestion strategy is in a state of flux, and that they weren't enforcing the restrictions until further notice.

Our advice is to turn up at the Chobe Riverfront (Sedudu) gate of the park almost immediately after you arrive in Kasane to enable you to plan your visit. And unless you're in a convoy of vehicles, it's always worth trying to discuss the situation with the rangers at the gate if at first they refuse you entry.

Nogatsaa/Tchinga Area

The Nogatsaa/Tchinga area may lack the overwhelming numbers of animals found along the riverfront or in Savuti, but it still supports herds of buffaloes and elephants as well as reedbucks, gemsboks, roans and the rare oribi antelopes. Although Nogatsaa/Tchinga lacks a permanent source of water, the pans (sometimes called 'dams') present in the area store water for months after the rains have stopped.

The clay around this region is popularly known as 'black cotton', and it often defeats even the most rugged of 4WD vehicles. If you're planning on exploring the area in detail, it's best to first seek local advice, especially during the rainy season.

Savuti

Savuti, in the southwestern corner of Chobe National Park, is one of Africa's great safari destinations, its flat, wildlife-packed expanses awash with distinctly African colours and vistas. With the exception of rhinos, you'll find all of Africa's most charismatic megafauna in residence here or passing through, and the return of waters to the Savuti Channel has only added to this area's considerable appeal.

The area contains the remnants of the 'superlake' that once stretched across northern Botswana, although the modern landscape has a distinctive harsh and empty feel to it. Because of the roughness of the terrain and the difficulty in reaching the area, Savuti is an obligatory stop for all 4WD enthusiasts en route between Kasane and Maun. Although home to its share of elite lodges, there is also an excellent campsite for self-drivers.

◎ Sights

Savuti Marshes   NATURAL SIGHT
For decades since the early 1980s, this vast open area in southern Savuti consisted less of marshes than sweeping open plains, save for occasional inundations during the rainy season. But the area's name again makes sense with the return of water to the Savuti Channel. Once-dry tracks now disappear into standing water that draws predators and prey from all across the region. The marshes lie between the Savuti Channel and the main Savuti–Maun track. If the waters allow, we recommend the picnic spot as the perfect riverside place for lunch.

Leopard Rock   NATURAL SIGHT
The rocky monoliths that rise up from the Savuti sand provide more than welcome aesthetic relief amid the flat-as-flat plains of northern Botswana. The outcrops' caves, rocky clefts and sometimes dense undergrowth also represent ideal habitat for leopards. The southernmost of these monoliths (the first you come to if you're driving from Maun or Moremi Game Reserve) is known as Leopard Rock and sightings of the most

elusive of Africa's big cats are reasonably common here. A 1.6km-long sandy track encircles the rock.

Gobabis Hill   HILL
Another of the rocky monoliths, Gobabis Hill is home to several sets of 4000-year-old rock paintings of San origin. The best are the depictions of livestock halfway up to the summit on the south side of the rock; park at S 18°35.632', E 024°04.770', from where it's an easy 150m climb up to the paintings. Be careful, however; the area is a known haunt of leopards and we spent one blissful morning watching a pride of lions between the paintings and the Savuti Channel just 200m away. The paintings are signposted as 'Rock Paintings' off the main track and again at the parking place. The western edge of Gobabis Hill is guarded by a fine baobab, which is visible from the main track.

🛏 Sleeping

Savuti offers that typical Botswana juxtaposition of luxurious tented camps alongside simpler riverside campsites, in the process offering options at both extremes of the pricing spectrum.

Savuti Campsite   CAMPGROUND $
(sklcamps.com; GPS: S 18°34.014', E 24°03.905'; campsite per adult/child US$50/20) One of the best campsites in northern Botswana, five of the seven sites overlook the river – sites one to four could do with a little more shade but are otherwise lovely, while Paradise camp is our pick. The ablutions block has sit-down flush toilets, *braai* pits and showers (usually hot). Be careful of wandering baboons and elephants; the old Savuti Camp Site nearby was destroyed by thirsty elephants!

Camp Savuti   TENTED CAMP $$$
(http://sklcamps.com; s/d May-Dec full board US$500/700) Given a licence to run the public campsites, cheeky SKL has also taken on the big boys with some beautifully appointed canvas tents overlooking the Savuti Channel. Prices are a touch below the longer-established camps but the quality is pretty much on a par.

Savute Safari Lodge   LODGE $$$
(📞686 1559; www.desertdelta.com; per person Jan-Apr US$476, s/d May-Dec US$1113/1712) Next to the former site of the legendary Lloyd's Camp, this upmarket retreat consists of 12 contemporary thatched chalets in neutral

THE SAVUTI CHANNEL

Northern Botswana contains a bounty of odd hydrographic phenomena. For instance, the Selinda Spillway passes water back and forth between the Okavango Delta and Linyanti Marshes. Just as odd, when the Zambezi River is particularly high, the Chobe River goes ahead and reverses the direction of its flow, causing it to spill into the area around Lake Liambezi. Historically, there was also a channel between the Khwai River system in the Okavango Delta and the Savuti Marshes.

But the strangest phenomenon of all is probably the Savuti Channel, which links the Savuti Marshes with the Linyanti Marshes and – via the Selinda Spillway – the Okavango Delta. Most confounding is the seeming complete lack of rhyme or reason to the flow of the channel. At times, it will stop flowing for years at a stretch (eg from 1888 to 1957, 1966 to 1967 and 1982 until 2008). When flowing, the channel changes the entire ecosystem, creating an oasis that provides water for thirsty wildlife herds and acts as a magnet for a profusion of water birds. Between flows, the end of the channel recedes from the marshes back towards the Chobe River, while at other times the Savuti Marshes flood and expand; as a result, many of the trails shown on many maps were impassable at the time of research. What's more, the flow of the channel appears to be unrelated to the water level of the Linyanti–Chobe River system itself. In 1925, when the river experienced record flooding levels, the Savuti Channel remained dry.

According to the only feasible explanation thus far put forward, the phenomenon may be attributed to tectonics. The ongoing northward shift of the Zambezi River and the frequent low-intensity earthquakes in the region reveal that the underlying geology is tectonically unstable. The flow of the Savuti Channel must be governed by an imperceptible flexing of the surface crust. The minimum change required to open or close the channel would be at least 9m, and there's evidence that this has happened at least five times in the past 100 years.

SAVUTI: LION VERSUS ELEPHANT

Reports of lions preying on elephants have for decades emerged from the Botswana wilds, but because most attacks took place at night in national parks where night driving was prohibited, no one could say for sure. That was until the early 1990s when film-makers Dereck and Beverley Joubert finally captured on film one of wild Africa's most epic contests. The resulting documentary *Ultimate Enemies*, which was filmed in the Savuti region of Botswana's Chobe National Park, is as confronting as it is extraordinary.

Male lions weigh on average 190kg, while females weigh 126kg. Although there have been isolated cases of large lion prides killing rhinos or hippos, the preferred prey size of lions is on average around 350kg. Elephants, on the other hand, weigh between 4 and 6 tonnes. When lions kill elephants, it the largest predator-to-prey weight ratio known among terrestrial mammals. Taking place in the dry season of August to November (with a peak in October), the hunts observed by the Jouberts were only successful at night, and only when less than five elephants and 27 or more lions were present (the pride's overall size was 30). Surprisingly, no infant elephants were killed by lions, probably due to high levels of maternal vigilance and protection – most lions killed were between four and 11 years old.

Reports of lions attacking elephants have tapered off somewhat in recent years as the pride filmed by the Jouberts has divided and groups have gone their separate ways. But the reputation for strength and ferocity that these exploits have earned the lions of Savuti remains very much in place.

tones and with a fairly standard layout. The main safari lodge is home to a sitting lounge, an elegant dining room, a small library and a cocktail bar. There is also a breathtaking viewing deck where you can watch the sunset over the bush.

Savute Elephant Camp LODGE $$$
(☑bookings 068-686 0302; www.savuteelephant camp.com; s/d May-Dec full board US$1856/2650; ✳) The premier camp in Savuti is made up of 12 lavishly appointed East African–style linen tents on raised wooden platforms, complete with antique-replica furniture. The main tent houses a dining room, lounge and bar, and is next to a swimming pool that overlooks a pumped waterhole. For booking information, contact Orient-Express Safaris in Maun.

Savute Under Canvas TENTED CAMP $$$
(☑in South Africa 011-809 4300; www.savuteunder canvas.com; per person US$415-680) This cross between a tented camp and luxury mobile safari enables you to experience the freedom of camping (sites are moved every few days) with the exclusivity that comes with having a beautifully appointed tent, butler and excellent meals served in between your game drives. Tents have bathroom facilities, including hot bucket showers.

❶ Getting There & Away

Chartered flights use the airstrip several kilometres north of the lodges in Savuti. Check with your lodge regarding booking a flight.

Under optimum conditions, it's a four-hour slog from Sedudu Gate to Savuti, though be advised that this route is often unnavigable from January to March. Access is also possible from Maun or the Moremi Game Reserve via Mababe Gate, though the track is primarily clay and very tough going when wet. All of these routes require a 4WD vehicle.

Linyanti Marshes

In the northwest corner of Chobe National Park, the Linyanti River spreads into a 900-sq-km flooded plain that attracts stunning concentrations of wildlife during the dry season. On the Namibian side of the river, this well-watered wildlife paradise is protected by the Mudumu and Mamili National Parks, but apart from 7km of frontage along the northwestern edge of Chobe National Park, the Linyanti Marshes in Botswana are protected only by their remoteness.

Game trails run along the marsh shoreline and sightings of the marshes' stable populations of elephants, lions, wild dogs, cheetahs and leopards are fairly common, although you'll need to be patient, especially for big cats. Given that most of the luxury lodges are outside the national park, night drives are a highlight.

🛏 Sleeping

Linyanti Camp Site CAMPGROUND $
(http://sklcamps.com; GPS: S 18°16.228', E 23°56.163'; campsite per adult/child US$50/25) Most of the sites at this campground run by the excellent SKL sit on a shady and gentle rise just up from the water's edge, with good views of the marshes costing nothing extra. There are all the usual *braai* pits, hot showers, sit-down flush toilets and, in the dry season, lots of elephants and baboons. Expect hippos to make an awful lot of noise during the night.

Camp Linyanti TENTED CAMP $$$
(http://sklcamps.com; GPS: S 18°16.228', E 23°56.163'; s/d May-Dec full board US$500/700) Just as it has in Savuti, SKL has set up a luxury tented camp within earshot of the cheaper public sites. The camps are luxurious without being overdone, and with prices significantly less than their near neighbours they're well worth considering.

Three Baobabs TENTED CAMP $$$
(⌨7164 6064; www.threebaobabs.com; s/d US$470/620) Located on a 45-hectare private farm and run by the owners of the respected Garden Lodge in Kasane, Three Baobabs is wonderfully secluded (there are no signs, thereby keeping out the curious). The tents are spacious and beautifully turned out; the outdoor bathtubs are rather special. The lodge is 55km from Savuti, and 27km west of Kachikau.

Savuti Camp TENTED CAMP $$$
(⌨in South Africa 011-807 1800; www.wilderness-safaris.com; s/d Jan-Apr US$963/1416, May-Dec US$1473/2436; ❄❄) In wooded country and overlooking the water between Savuti and Linyanti, this wonderfully remote small camp has large and luxurious tents of the kind you'd expect from the upmarket Wilderness Safaris group. The perennial waterhole it overlooks attracts large concentrations of elephants and lions during the dry season.

Duma Tau TENTED CAMP $$$
(⌨in South Africa 011-807 1800; www.wilderness-safaris.com; s/d Jan-Apr US$1123/1736, May-Dec US$1588/2666; ❄❄) This 10-room camp was rebuilt completely in 2012 with a commitment to sustainability; all of the camp's power comes from solar energy and waste disposal is state of the art. The raised tents overlook the hippo-filled Zibadianja Lagoon from a mangosteen grove. The lagoon can be explored by boat when the water levels are high, or you can kick back in a luxury tent under thatch.

King's Pool Camp TENTED CAMP $$$
(⌨in South Africa 011-807 1800; www.wilderness-safaris.com; s/d Jan-Apr US$1495/2388, May-Dec US$2287/3972; ❄❄) Occupying a magical setting on a Linyanti River oxbow overlooking a lagoon, this nine-room camp is one of the most luxurious properties in Linyanti, with private plunge pools in the rooms and an overall stunning attention to detail and service. Accommodation at King's Pool is in private thatched chalets featuring indoor and outdoor showers. This place almost prides itself on being noisy – you will almost certainly be woken up by the nearby hippos, elephants, baboons and lions.

Lebala Camp TENTED CAMP $$$
(⌨686 1449; www.kwando.co.bw; per person Jan-Apr US$550, s/d May-Dec US$1350/2226) The name means 'open plains', which is what you get in terms of a view, along with dense game concentrations, a commitment to multiple game drives and excellent bushwalks. The grasslands eventually give way to the marshlands of Linyanti, which conceal abundant birdlife. The eight rooms, with open-air bathrooms, are large and, as you'd expect, supremely comfortable.

Lagoon Camp TENTED CAMP $$$
(⌨686 1449; www.kwando.co.bw; per person Jan-Apr US$550, s/d May-Dec US$1350/2226) Overlooking a lagoon (just to be different) is this series of luxury tents, which looks out over flood plains and river tracks thick with wild dogs, lions and buffaloes. Fishing trips and evening boat cruises are available. There are fine views from many vantage points, not least some of the free-standing bathtubs.

Selinda Camp TENTED CAMP $$$
(⌨in South Africa 011-807 1800; www.wilderness-safaris.com; s/d Jan-Apr US$963/1416, May-Dec US$1473/2436; ❄❄) This vintage-style East African nine-person camp is the simplest and most affordable of the four camps, though it is still luxurious by any stretch of the imagination.

❶ Getting There & Away

From the south, the track from Savuti is a hard slog of deep sand. The track running east towards Kachikau (where it meets the sealed road to Kasane) is only slightly better.

Most guests choose to fly into their camp on a chartered flight from Maun or Kasane.

OKAVANGO DELTA

Welcome to one of Africa's most iconic landscapes. There is something elemental about the Okavango Delta – the rising and falling of its waters, the daily drama of its wildlife encounters, its soundtrack of lions roaring, saw-throated leopard barks and the crazy whoop of a running hyena, the mysteries concealed by its papyrus reeds swaying gently in the evening breeze. Viewed from above on a scenic flight from Maun, the countless tributaries of the Okavango Delta can seem like an eagle's talon clutching at the country and not letting go. At ground level, the ghostly silhouettes of dead trees in the dry season give the delta a hint of the apocalypse.

The stirring counterpoint to the Kalahari Desert that consumes so much of Botswana is the Okavango Delta. The up-to-18,000-sq-km expansion and expiration of the Okavango River is Southern Africa's massive outpouring of fertility. Indeed, the contrast the Okavango presents compared to the rest of Botswana is one of her most beguiling aspects: here, in the heart of the thirst lands, is one of the world's largest inland river deltas, an unceasing web of water, rushing, standing, flooding, dying. And the waters do die. They never make it to the sea, soaking instead into the salt pans of central Botswana. But before they do, they sustain vast quantities of wildlife that shift with the seasons in this mother of waters.

The Okavango's fly-in luxury lodges make a strong claim to be Africa's most exclusive safari destinations. Fork out a fortune for nights spent deep in the inner delta and you're unlikely to regret it. And yet, it is possible to gain a delta foothold for those on a smaller budget through a combination of mobile safaris from Maun and self-driving to the campsites of the Moremi Game Reserve. Whichever way you travel, you'll take home so many experiences of a lifetime and the reason is simple: this is one of the most extraordinary places in Africa.

Maun
POP 65,700

As the main gateway to the Okavango Delta, Maun (pronounced 'mau-UUnn') is Botswana's primary tourism hub. With good accommodation and a reliably mad mix of bush pilots, tourists, campers, volunteers and luxury safari-philes, it's a decent enough base for a day or two, though it's earned something of a reputation for petty crime. The town itself has little going for it – it's strung out over kilometres with not much of a discernible centre – but some of the hotels and camps have lovely riverside vantage points.

◎ Sights

FREE **Nhabe Museum** MUSEUM
(☏686 1346; Sir Seretse Khama Rd; ◷9am-4.30pm Mon-Sat) This small and simple museum is housed in a historic building built by the British military in 1939 and used during WWII as a surveillance post keeping tabs on the German presence in Namibia. The museum offers a few displays about the history of the Ngamiland district (the subdistrict of northwestern Botswana where the Okavango Delta is located) and some temporary exhibitions of photography, basket weaving and art. Donations are welcome. The museum also houses the Bailey Arts Centre, which allows local artists to produce and sell baskets, screen prints, paintings and pottery, among other things.

Crocodile Farm ZOO
(☏686 4539; admission P25; ◷9am-4.30pm Mon-Sat) This community-run crocodile farm is basically all the encouragement you need to keep your hands and feet inside the *mokoro* while cruising through the delta. The farm is about 15km south of the Maun 'Mall'. To get there, just follow the road that runs by the Barclays Bank outside of town and you shouldn't miss it.

☞ Tours

Maun is brimful of travel agencies and safari companies, which can be a little daunting at first. If you take your time and keep a few simple rules in mind, you shouldn't have too many problems.

First of all, it helps to know that most delta lodges are affiliated with specific agencies, so it pays to shop around and talk to a few different tour operators. Second, if you're planning an extended trip into the delta or intend to stay at a luxury lodge, contact one or more recommended agencies or operators *before* you arrive if possible. While the cheaper lodges can usually accommodate guests at the drop of a hat, don't come to Maun and expect to jump on a plane to a safari lodge or embark on an overland safari the next day.

An excellent place to start (and perhaps even finish) is at Travel Wild (☑686 0822; www.travelwildbotswana.com; Mathiba I St), opposite the airport, which serves as a central booking and information office for lodges, safaris and other adventures. It can't provide you with direct bookings, but it also has great contacts with all local safari providers.

All of the Lonely Planet–reviewed operators can organise safaris into the delta and beyond.

African Animal Adventures　　　TOUR
(☑7230 1054; www.africananimaladventures.com) A highly recommended outfit that does horse safaris into the delta and the salt pans of Makgadikgadi. Can also be contacted through the Old Bridge Backpackers (p93) and Gweta Lodge (p69).

African Secrets　　　TOUR
(☑686 0300; www.africansecrets.net; Mathiba I St, Matlapaneng) This excellent operation is run out of the Island Safari Lodge.

Afro-Trek　　　TOUR
(☑686 2574; www.afro-trek.com; Shorobe Rd, Matlapaneng) This company specialises in mid-market safaris and is in the Sedia Hotel.

Audi Camp Safaris　　　TOUR
(☑686 0599; www.okavangocamp.com; Shorobe Rd, Matlapaneng) Well-run safaris into the delta and further afield out of the popular Audi Camp.

Crocodile Camp Safaris　　　TOUR
(☑686 0222; www.crocodilecamp.com; Shorobe Rd, Matlapaneng) This budget operator is at the Crocodile Camp.

Ker & Downey　　　TOUR
(☑686 0570; www.kerdowney.com; Mathiba I St, Maun) One of Africa's most exclusive tour operators, Ker & Downey is all about pampering and luxury lodges.

Naga Safaris　　　TOUR
(☑680 0587; www.nagasafaris.com) Custom-made, flexible itineraries make this operator stand out.

REGIONS OF THE OKAVANGO

The Okavango Delta is a complex and unique ecosystem but its scope can be daunting. It is, however, easier to plan a trip through the region than you might imagine, especially if you think of the delta as having four distinct areas.

» **Eastern Delta** This part of the delta is far more accessible, and therefore cheaper to reach, from Maun than the Inner Delta and Moremi. You can easily base yourself in Maun, and arrange a day trip by *mokoro* (dugout canoe) or an overnight bush-camping trip for far less than the cost of staying in (and getting to) a lodge in the Inner Delta or Moremi.

» **Inner Delta** The area west and north of Moremi is classic delta scenery where you can truly be seduced by the calming spell of the region. Accommodation is mostly in top-end luxury lodges, almost all of which are only accessible by expensive chartered flights.

» **Moremi Game Reserve** This region includes Chief's Island and the Moremi Tongue, and is one of the most popular destinations within the delta. The Moremi Game Reserve is the only officially protected area within the delta, so wildlife is plentiful. Moremi has a few campsites as well as several truly decadent lodges with prices to match. The reserve is accessible by 4WD from Maun or Chobe as well as by charter flight.

» **Okavango Panhandle** This swampy extension of the Inner Delta stretches northwest towards the Namibian border. Although this area does not offer the classic delta experience, it is growing in popularity due to its ease of accessibility bya public transport or 2WD. As a general rule, this is prime birdwatching and fishing terrain, rather than the domain of wildlife safaris.

Okavango Delta

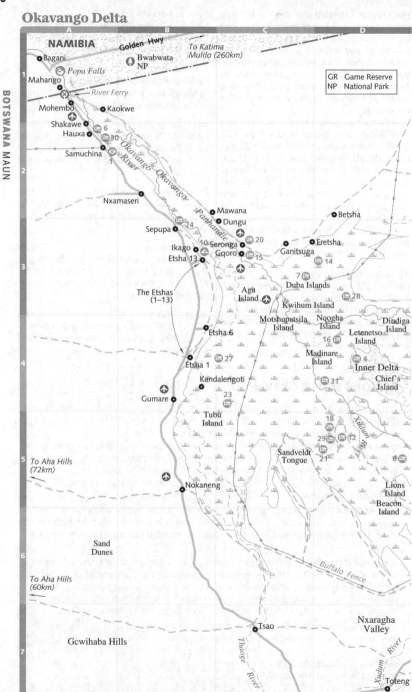

NAMIBIA

Golden Hwy

Bagani

Popa Falls

Bwabwata NP

To Katima Mulilo (260km)

Mahango

GR Game Reserve
NP National Park

River Ferry

Mohembo

Kaokwe

Shakawe

6

Hauxa

30

Samuchina

Okavango River

Okavango

Nxamaseri

Panhandle

Mawana

Dungu

Betsha

Sepupa

24

Ikago

40

Seronga

20

Etsha 13

Gqoro

15

Ganitsuga

Eretsha

14

7

Duba Islands

The Etshas (1–13)

Aga Island

Kwihum Island

28

Motshupatsila Island

Nqogha Island

Dindiga Island

Letenetso Island

Etsha 6

16

Madinare Island

4

Inner Delta

Chief's Island

Etsha 1

27

Kandalengoti

31

23

18

Gumare

Tubu Island

Xhum River

Sandveldt Tongue

29

12

21

8

To Aha Hills (72km)

Nokaneng

Lions Island

Beacon Island

Sand Dunes

Buffalo Fence

To Aha Hills (60km)

Gcwihaba Hills

Tsao

Nxaragha Valley

Thaoge River

Xudum River

Toteng

Okavango Delta

⦿ Sights

1 Krokavango Crocodile Farm A2

🛏 Sleeping

2 Baine's Camp E5	
3 Camp Okavango E4	
4 Chief's Camp D4	
5 Chitabe Camp F5	
Chitabe Lediba .... (see 5)	
6 Drotsky's Cabins A2	
7 Duba Plains C3	
8 Eagle Island Camp D5	
9 Footsteps E4	
10 Guma Lagoon Camp B3	
11 Gunn's Camp E5	
12 Kanana Camp D5	
13 Kwara Camp E4	
14 Mapula Lodge D3	
15 Mbiroba Camp C3	
16 Mombo Camp D4	
17 Moremi Crossing E5	
18 Nxabega Okavango Camp D5	
19 Oddball's E5	
20 Okavango Houseboats C3	
21 Pom Pom Camp D5	
22 Sandibe Safari Lodge E5	
23 Seba Camp C4	
24 Sepupa Swamp Stop B3	
25 Shinde Island Camp E4	
26 Stanley's Camp E6	
27 Tubu Tree Camp C4	
28 Vumbura Plains Camp D3	
29 Xaranna Camp D5	
30 Xaro Lodge A2	
31 Xigera Camp D4	
32 Xugana Island Lodge E3	

Nxuma Adventure Safaris   TOUR
(☏7646 2829; nxumu@hotmail.com) *Mokoro*
and other boat trips in the Okavango, as well
as San-guided walks; ask for Oscar.

Okavango River Lodge   TOUR
(☏686 3707; www.okavango-river-lodge.com;
Shorobe Rd, Matlapaneng) Reliable safaris run
out of the Okavango River Lodge.

Old Bridge Backpackers   TOUR
(☏686 2406; www.maun-backpackers.com;
Shorobe Rd, Matlapaneng) This experienced
budget operation is run from the Old Bridge
Backpackers and we're yet to hear a bad
word about them.

OKAVANGO DELTA AT A GLANCE

Why Go?
Quite simply, the Okavango is one of the greatest wildlife-watching destinations on earth, with a full complement of African megafauna and stunning scenery that changes with the seasons.

Gateway Towns
Maun.

Wildlife
A full complement of herbivores (including large elephant herds, numerous antelope species and a small number of recently introduced rhinos in the Inner Delta) inhabits the delta. Most commonly sighted are hippos, which are submerged throughout most of the day, only to emerge in the late afternoon and evening to graze on the riverbanks. Hippos are easily startled and prone to attack – keep your distance.

The delta also supports a stable population of predators, including lions, cheetahs, leopards and hyenas. At the canine end of the spectrum, Moremi is also home to 30% of the world's remaining African wild dogs.

Birds
The Okavango is a world-class birding destination, with charismatic species such as the African fish eagles, oft-heard Pel's fishing owl and an abundance of waterbird species. The Okavango Panhandle in particular is known for its birdwatching.

When to Go
Generally, the best time to visit the delta is from July to September, when the water levels are high and the weather is dry.

Tracks can get extremely muddy and trails are often washed out during and after the rains. From January to March, the Moremi Game Reserve can be inaccessible, even with a state-of-the-art 4WD. Bear in mind that several lodges close down for part or all of the rainy season. Mosquitoes are prevalent, especially in the wet season (November to March).

Moving Around
Unless you're staying at an upmarket lodge in which game drives are included, or have organised your visit on a mobile safari from Maun, you'll need your own fully equipped 4WD to get around. Boat trips are also an essential part of the Okavango experience.

Budget Safaris
Maun is the best place to join a mobile safari into the delta, although in most cases you'll waste precious time if you arrive in town without a reservation. One place that offers reliable and well-priced safaris is the Old Bridge Backpackers. The Eastern Delta's proximity to Maun makes it one of the more accessible regions of the delta.

Author Tip
Allocate as much time as you can to the delta, allowing you to experience a mix of iconic experiences, from exclusive fly-in lodges to *mokoro* trips and self-driving excursions.

Wild Lands Safaris   TOUR
(☎7230 2489; www.wildlandsafaris.com) A reliable operator with a good customer-service record and camping safaris to suit a range of budgets.

Wilderness Safaris   TOUR
(☎in South Africa 011-807 1800; www.wilderness safaris.com; Mathiba I St, Maun) Near the airport, this operator specialises in upmarket safaris.

Wilmot Safaris   TOUR
(☎686 2615; www.wilmotsafaris.com) Run by the legendary Lloyd Wilmot, who used to run Lloyd's Camp in Savuti, with adventurous mobile safaris.

SCENIC FLIGHTS

Flying over the delta in a light plane or helicopter is the experience of a lifetime. Yes, prices can be steep but the views are unforgettable.

To join a scenic flight you can either contact one of the following charter companies or simply ask at the front desk at your accommodation. But plan ahead, as it's unlikely that you'll be able to contact a charter company and join a scenic flight on the same day.

Per-hour prices for scenic flights in a three-/five-/seven-seater plane start at P2000/2650/3400, but shop around for the best quote. Prices vary according to the size of the plane and the number of passengers.

In most cases, a departure tax of P50 must be added per person to the quoted prices.

The offices for all air-charter companies in Maun are either in or next to the airport. Bring your passport with you when making a booking.

Delta Air   SCENIC FLIGHTS
(☑686 0044; synergy@info.bw; Mathiba I St) Near the Bushman Craft Shop inside the airport gate.

Helicopter Horizons   SCENIC FLIGHTS
(☑680 1186; www.helicopterhorizons.com; per person from US$110) A range of helicopter options, all with the passenger doors removed to aid photography.

Major Blue Air   SCENIC FLIGHTS
(☑686 5671; www.majorblueair.com; Mathiba I St)

Mack Air   SCENIC FLIGHTS
(☑686 0675; www.mackair.co.bw; Mathiba I St) Offers scenic flights; around the corner from Wilderness Safaris.

Moremi Air Services   SCENIC FLIGHTS
(☑686 3632; www.moremiair.com) In the airport terminal building.

Northern Air   SCENIC FLIGHTS
(☑686 0385; kerdowney.travel/northern_air; Mathiba I St) Part of the Ker & Downey office.

Wilderness Air   SCENIC FLIGHTS
(☑686 0778; www.sefofane.com) Part of Wilderness Safaris.

🛏 Sleeping

Most campsites, hotels and lodges – except Riley's – are in either Sedie or Matlapaneng.

The attraction of the latter is that the camps and lodges are quiet, secluded and pleasantly located along Thamalakane River. The downside is that they can be up to 10km from central Maun. Many are accessible by public transport, however, and most offer transfers to/from Maun daily, usually for a small fee. Most campsites, hotels and lodges also have a decent restaurant and bar.

Okavango River
Lodge   CAMPGROUND, CHALETS $
(☑686 3707; www.okavango-river-lodge.com; Matlapaneng; campsite per person P70, s/d/f chalets P250/330/400, s/d tents P150/280) This down-to-earth spot off Shorobe Rd has a lovely setting on the riverbank. The owners are friendly and unpretentious, and pride themselves on giving travellers useful (and independent) information on trips through the delta. Between this spot and the Old Bridge Backpackers, you'll find most of Maun's tourist and expat-oriented nightlife. On that note, we've got to give the owners credit for the excellent name of their boat: *Sir Rosis of the River*.

Island Safari Lodge   CAMPGROUND, CHALETS $$
(☑686 0300; www.africansecrets.net; Matlapaneng; campsite per person P60, s/d budget r P375/580, chalets up to P870; 🛜🏊) One of the original lodges in Maun, Island Safari Lodge is also still one of the best, with a range of accommodation that nicely spans different budgets. The campsites have ablutions blocks and give access to the lodge's pool, restaurant and bar. The budget rooms are run-down but well-priced, while the chalets are excellent value. It also runs a professional, well-established series of safaris; the riverside location is ideal on lazy Okavango afternoons and the restaurant is excellent.

🔝 **Old Bridge**
Backpackers   CAMPGROUND $
(☑686 2406; www.maun-backpackers.com; Hippo Pools, Old Matlapaneng Bridge; campsite per person P60, dm P155, s/d tents without bathroom P225/348, d tents with bathroom P505; @🏊) One of the great bolt holes on Southern African overland trails, 'the Bridge', as it's known, has a great bar-at-the-end-of-the-world kind of vibe. Bush pilots and backpackers chat each other up, families take a break from the rigours of life on the African road, and a semi-regular cast of drunks keeps the bar propped up. Accommodation ranges from dorms by

Maun

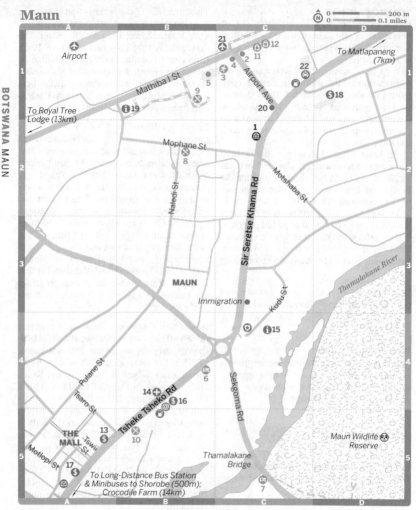

the riverbank, well-appointed campsites and some more-private tents to retreat to at day's end. A good range of *mokoro* trips and the like is on offer. In short, this is a place that understands travel and doesn't make you pay over the odds for it.

Audi Camp   CAMPGROUND **$$**
(📞686 0599; www.okavangocamp.com; Matlapaneng; campsite per person from P60, s/d tents without bathroom from P140/170, with bathroom P540/640; @⛱) Off Shorobe Rd, Audi Camp is a fantastic campsite that's become in-

creasingly popular with families, although independent overlanders will feel utterly welcome as well. Management is friendly and helpful, and there's a wide range of safari activities. The restaurant does a mean steak as well. If you don't have your own tent, the pre-erected tents, complete with fan, are a rustically luxurious option.

Maun Rest Camp   CAMPGROUND **$**
(📞686 3472; simonjoyce@info.bw; Shorobe Rd, Matlapaneng; campsite per person from P60, s/d tents P200/350) This no-frills rest camp off

Maun

Shorobe Rd is spotless and boasts what justifiably may be 'the cleanest ablution blocks in Maun'. The owners also pride themselves on turning away the overland truck and party crowd (there's no bar), so you can be assured of a quiet and undisturbed night's rest here.

Crocodile Camp   CAMPGROUND, CHALETS **$$**
(📞7560 6864; www.crocodilecamp.com; Matlapaneng; campsite per person P60, chalets per person incl breakfast P400; 🏊) 'Croc Camp' occupies a superb spot right on the river and is a quieter place for those not needing shots of presafari sambuca (not that it doesn't serve sambuca). Off Shorobe Rd, the campsite is excellent and secure, and there are also thatched riverside chalets with bathrooms.

Discovery Bed & Breakfast   B&B **$$**
(off Map p97; 📞7244 8298; www.discoverybedandbreakfast.com; Matlapaneng; s/d from P275/425; 🏊) Dutch-run Discovery does a cool job of creating an African-village vibe in the midst of Maun – the owners strive for and achieve 'affordable accommodation with a traditional touch'. The thatched, *rondavel*-style housing looks pretty bush from the outside and feels as posh as a nice hotel on the inside. A pretty garden connects the dusty grounds,

and there's a good communal fire pit for safari stories with fellow travellers.

Sedia Riverside Hotel   HOTEL **$$**
(📞686 2574; www.sediahotel.com; Shorobe Rd, Sedie; campsite per person P35, s/d P600/695, chalets P925-1250; ❄🏊) If you feel more comfortable in a hotel-style environment, the Sedia Hotel is a good option. This resort-like complex features an outdoor bar, a continental-inspired restaurant and a huge swimming pool. You can choose from a number of rooms and self-contained chalets, or simply pitch a tent and take advantage of all the hotel facilities.

Maun Lodge   LODGE **$$$**
(📞686 3939; www.maunlodge.com; Sekgoma Rd, Maun; s/d P1095/1260, chalets P941; ❄🏊) This upmarket option is just south of the town centre and boasts all the luxuries you'd expect at this price. It's certainly a comfortable option, though it's lacking in personality and atmosphere, especially if you're coming from (or going to) any of the luxury lodges in the delta.

Cresta Riley's Hotel   HOTEL **$$$**
(📞686 0204; www.crestahotels.com; Tsheke Tsheko Rd, Maun; s/d P1039/1444; ❄🛜🏊) Riley's is the only hotel or lodge in central Maun and

BOOKING A MOKORO TRIP

A day trip from Maun into the Eastern Delta usually includes a two- to three-hour return drive in a 4WD to the departure point, two to three hours in a *mokoro* (perhaps longer each day on a two- or three-day trip), and two to three hours' hiking. At the start of a *mokoro* trip, ask the poler what he has in mind, and agree to the length of time spent per day in the *mokoro*, out hiking and relaxing at the campsite – bear in mind that travelling by *mokoro* is tiring for the poler.

One of the most refreshing things about booking *mokoro* trips is the absence of touts wandering the streets of Maun. That's because all polers operating *mokoro* trips out of Maun are represented by the **Okavango Kopano Mokoro Community Trust** (☎686 4806; off Madhiba I St; ⏰8am-5pm Mon-Fri, to noon Sat). This trust sets daily rates for the polers (P180 per poler per day, plus a P55 daily membership fee for the trust) by which all safari operators have to abide.

In terms of pricing, catering is an important distinction. 'Self-catering' means you must bring your own food as well as cooking, sleeping and camping equipment. This option is a good way to shave a bit off the price, though most travellers prefer catered trips. It's also easier to get a lower price if you're booking as part of a group or are planning a multiday tour.

Finally, a few other things to remember:

» Ask the booking agency if you're expected to provide food for the poler (usually you're not, but polers appreciate any leftover cooked or uncooked food).

» Bring good walking shoes and long trousers for hiking, a hat, and plenty of sunscreen and water.

» Water from the delta (despite its unpleasant colour) can be drunk if boiled or purified.

» Most campsites are natural, so take out all litter and burn toilet paper.

» Bring warm clothes for the evening between about May and September.

» Wildlife can be dangerous, so make sure to never swim anywhere without checking with the poler first.

it has a long pedigree – this place has been here since before tourists began arriving, although it's barely recognisable these days, even more so since the Cresta chain made it one of its landmark properties. It offers comfortable rooms in a convenient setting in leafy grounds – just don't expect a lodge/wilderness experience.

Thamalakane Lodge LODGE **$$$**
(☎7250 6184; http://thamalakane.com; Shorobe Rd; chalets P1397-1929; ✳@☒) With a beautiful setting on a sun-drenched curve of the Thamalakane River, overlooking wading hippos and waving reeds, Thamalakane wins in the location, location, location stakes. But it's also got beautiful little chalets built of stone, stuffed with modern amenities and dressed up in safari-chic tones, and a kitchen cranking out some of the best food in Maun. The lodge is around 19km northeast of Maun off the road to Shorobe.

Royal Tree Lodge LODGE **$$$**
(Off Map p94; ☎680 0757; http://royaltreelodge. com; per person low season full board US$262, s/d high season from US$395/610; ✳@☒) This private farm-reserve, about 13km west of the airport, is a lovely luxury option that maintains a good crew of regular visitors. These returnees are probably impressed by the resident wandering giraffes, kudus and ostriches, the large, beautifully decked-out private cabins, and the utter sense of calm and quiet here far away from Maun's bustle.

✖ Eating & Drinking

Maun is not one of the culinary capitals of the world. That's not to say you can't get a decent meal – many of the camps have accomplished kitchens, particularly the Island Safari Lodge, Audi Camp and Thamalakane Lodge are all excellent. Away from the camps and lodges, good restaurants in the city centre are pretty thin on the ground. Otherwise, Maun has versions of every *peri-*

Matlapaneng

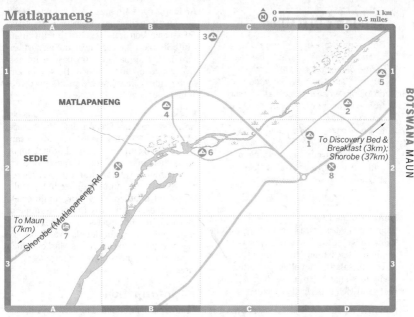

Matlapaneng

🟢 Activities, Courses & Tours
African Secrets ....(see 3)
Afro-Trek......................................(see 7)
Audi Camp Safaris........................(see 1)
Crocodile Camp Safaris...............(see 2)
Okavango River Lodge................(see 3)
Old Bridge Backpackers ....(see 6)

🛏 Sleeping
1 Audi Camp D2
2 Crocodile Camp D1
3 Island Safari Lodge...............................C1
4 Maun Rest Camp B1
5 Okavango River Lodge..........................D1
6 Old Bridge Backpackers C2
7 Sedia Riverside Hotel...........................A3

⊗ Eating
8 Motsana Arts Cafe.................................D2
9 Sports Bar & Restaurant B2

🔒 Shopping
Motsana ....(see 8)

peri-obsessed fast-food chain in Southern Africa.

Most lodges have their own bar, most of which are fairly sedate; if you're after a more overland and expat scene, try the Old Bridge Backpackers or Okavango River Lodge. Of the restaurants, Sports Bar has the best and liveliest bar. For a more African vibe, there are, of course, numerous *shebeen* (illegal drinking establishments) serving home-brewed sorghum beer to a local crowd; the staff at your hotel or lodge can point you in the right direction for this sort of off-licence fun.

Motsana Arts Cafe   CAFE $$
(www.motsana.com; Shorobe Rd, Matlapaneng; meals P45-60; ☺8am-8pm; 📶) Housed in an innovative new arts complex northeast of town on the road to Shorobe, this cool, casual and sophisticated cafe serves up burgers, salads, paninis, Cajun chicken with avocado and all-day breakfasts, with free wi-fi thrown in.

Hilary's   INTERNATIONAL $$
(off Mathiba I Rd, Maun; meals from P50; ☺8am-4pm Mon-Fri, 8.30am-noon Sat) This homey place offers a choice of wonderfully earthy meals, including homemade bread, baked potatoes, soups and sandwiches. It's ideal for vegetarians and anyone sick of greasy sausages and soggy chips. We're just sorry it doesn't open in the evenings.

SECURITY IN MAUN

Botswana is an extremely safe destination in which to travel, but as the centre of the country's tourism industry, Maun has not been without its problems. A rise in petty theft (usually from cars or campsites, but rarely with violence) may have diminished thanks to a police crackdown, but it still pays to be careful – don't leave valuables or bags in parked cars in the city centre and lock them away if you're sleeping in a tent at one of the campsites.

French Connection   FRENCH $$
(Mophane St, Maun; meals from P45; ☺8.30am-5pm Mon-Sat) Close to the airport but on a quieter backstreet, this fine little place serves up salads, baguettes and other light meals in a shady garden setting. The roast beef sandwich is perfectly executed.

Bon Arrivee   INTERNATIONAL $$
(Mathiba I St, Maun; meals P60-120; ☺8am-10pm) Pilot puns and flight-deck jokes are laid on very thick at this airport-themed place, which sits, of course, right across from the airport. The food is good – lots of pasta, steak and seafood – but don't come here an hour before your flight expecting a quick turnaround.

Sports Bar & Restaurant   INTERNATIONAL $$
(Shorobe Rd, Matlapaneng; meals P50-80; ☺5-10pm) Bucking the trend by only opening for dinner, Sports Bar does the usual pasta and pizza suspects with occasional curries and some excellent Botswana-bred steaks. When the kitchen closes, the place morphs into an expat-filled bar with music you can dance to on Fridays and Saturdays. You'll need a taxi (P40 from the city centre) or your own wheels to get here.

🛍 Shopping

Bushman Craft Shop   HANDICRAFTS
(Mathiba I St, Maun; ☺8am-5pm) Although it caters more to travellers who need a last-minute souvenir before catching a flight out of town, this small shop near the airport has a decent range of books, textiles and woodcarvings.

African Arts & Images   ARTS & CRAFTS
(www.juneliversedge.com; Mathiba I St, Maun; ☺9am-5pm Mon-Sat) Next to the Bushman Craft Shop on the road near the airport terminal, this upmarket shop has an impressive range of books about Botswana and high-quality photographic prints by owner June Liversedge.

Motsana   ARTS & CRAFTS
(www.motsana.com; Shorobe Rd, Matlapaneng; ☺8am-6pm; 🕾) This two-storey Moroccan-style building on the road to Shorobe, run by the owners of Audi Camp, is one of Botswana's more innovative cultural spaces. There's an arts cafe, numerous shops selling artfully conceived handicrafts, photographic prints and textiles, and a fairly full programme of movie nights, dance classes and live theatre – check the website for details. Watch out for the monthly Sunday Farmers Market, which usually takes place on the last Sunday of the month.

ℹ Information

If you're planning on spending a few days in Maun, pick up a copy of the *Ngami Times*, which is published every Friday.

Emergency

Delta Medical Centre (📞686 1411; www.deltamedicalcentre.org; Tsheke Tsheko Rd) Along the main road; this is the best medical facility in Maun. It offers a 24-hour emergency service.

Maun General Hospital (📞686 0661; Shorobe Rd) About 1km southwest of the town centre.

MedRescue (📞390 1601, 680 0598, 992; www.mri.co.bw) For evacuations in the bush.

Police Station (📞686 0223; Sir Seretse Khama Rd)

Internet Access

Many hotels now offer internet access, either in the form of wireless access or a publicly accessible computer. Most internet cafes come and go with unreliable regularity. Ask at the post office to see if it has joined other Botswana post offices in offering internet access.

Open Door Bureau de Change (Tsheke Tsheko Rd; per hr P30; ☺7.30am-6pm Mon-Fri, 8am-4pm Sat, 9am-4pm Sun)

Money

Barclays Bank (Tsheke Tsheko Rd; ☺8.30am-3.30pm Mon-Fri, 8.15-10.45am Sat) Has foreign-exchange facilities and offers better rates than the bureaux de change. Barclays charges 2.5% commission for cash/travellers cheques, but no commission for cash advances with Visa and MasterCard.

Open Door Bureau de Change (Tsheke Tsheko Rd; ⊘7.30am-6pm Mon-Fri, 8am-4pm Sat, 9am-4pm Sun)

Standard Chartered Bank (Tsheke Tsheko Rd; ⊘8.30am-3.30pm Mon-Fri, 8.15-11am Sat) Has foreign-exchange facilities and offers better rates than the bureaux de change. Standard Chartered charges 3% commission for cash and travellers cheques, but isn't as well set up as Barclays Bank.

Sunny Bureau de Change (Sir Seretse Khama Rd, Ngami Centre; ⊘8am-6pm) Although you will get less favourable exchange rates at the bureaux de change than at the banks, they are a convenient option if the lines at the banks are particularly long.

Post
Post Office (⊘9am-5pm Mon-Fri, 9am-noon Sat) Near the Mall.

Tourist Information
Department of Wildlife & National Parks (DWNP; ☑686 1265; Kudu St; ⊘7.30am-4.30pm Mon-Fri, 7.30am-12.45pm & 1.45-4.30pm Sat, 7.30am-12.45pm Sun) To pay national park entry fees and book park campsites not in private hands; it's in a separate compound behind the main department building and well signposted.

Tourist Office (☑686 1056; off Mathida I St; ⊘7.30am-6pm Mon-Fri, 9am-2pm Sat) Provides information on the town's many tour companies and lodges.

ℹ Getting There & Away
Air
Air Botswana (☑686 0391; www.airbotswana.co.bw) has flights to Gaborone (from P882) and Kasane (from P369). In addition to domestic flights, there are international flights between Maun and Johannesburg (South Africa), Victoria Falls (Zimbabwe) and Livingstone (Zambia).

Bus & Combi
The **bus station** (Tsheke Tsheko Rd) for long-distance buses and combis is southwest of the centre. For Gaborone, you'll need to change in Ghanzi or Francistown.

DESTINATION	FARE (PULA)	DURATION (HR)
D'kar	43	4
Francistown	89.90	5
Ghanzi	63	5
Gweta	47	4
Kasane	96	6
Nata	76	5
Shakawe	108	7

THE MOKORO EXPERIENCE

One of the best (and also cheapest) ways to experience the Okavango Delta is to glide across the waters in a *mokoro* (plural *mekoro*), a shallow-draft dugout canoe traditionally hewn from an ebony or a sausage-tree log. With encouragement from several international conservation groups, however, the Batswana have now begun to construct more *mekoro* from fibreglass. The rationale behind this is that ebony and sausage trees take over 100 years to grow while a *mokoro* only lasts for about five years.

A *mokoro* may appear precarious at first, but it is amazingly stable and ideally suited to the shallow delta waters. It can accommodate two passengers and some limited luggage, and is propelled by a poler who stands at the back of the canoe with a *ngashi*, a long pole made from the mogonono tree.

The quality of a *mokoro* trip often depends on the passengers' enthusiasm, the meshing of personalities and the skill of the poler. Most polers (but not all) speak at least some English and can identify plants, birds and animals, and explain the cultures and myths of the delta inhabitants. Unfortunately, polers are often shy and lack confidence, so you may have to ask a lot of questions to get the information.

How much you enjoy your trip will depend partly on your expectations. If you come in the spirit of immersing yourself in nature and slowing down to the pace of life here on the delta, you won't leave disappointed. It's important to stress, however, that you should not expect to see too much wildlife. From the *mokoro*, you'll certainly spot plenty of hippos and crocs, and antelopes and elephants are frequently sighted during hikes. However, the main attraction of a *mokoro* trip is the peace and serenity you'll feel as you glide along the shallow waters of the delta. If, however, your main interest is viewing wildlife, consider spending a night or two in the Moremi Game Reserve.

Car & Motorcycle

The direct route between Kasane and Maun is only accessible by 4WD, and may be almost impassable after heavy rains. Also remember that there is nowhere along the Kasane–Maun road to buy fuel, food or drinks, or to get vehicle repairs. All other traffic between Kasane and Maun travels via Nata, a road which is, mercifully, being upgraded as we write.

ⓘ Getting Around

To/From the Airport

Maun airport is close to the town centre, so taxis rarely bother hanging around the terminal when planes arrive. If you have prebooked accommodation at an upmarket hotel or lodge in Maun or the Okavango Delta, make sure it provides a (free) courtesy minibus. Otherwise, walk about 300m down Airport Rd to Sir Seretse Khama Rd and catch a combi (around P40 to P50 for the camps in the Matlapaneng or Sedie districts northeast of the city).

Car Rental

Renting a car in Maun can be hideously expensive and you'd want to have it arranged long before your arrival in town. It may sound obvious, but stipulate when making the booking that you plan to take the vehicle off-road. If you do arrive without a reservation, there are a number of car-rental agencies opposite the airport on Mathiba I St.

Combis & Taxis

Combis marked 'Maun Route 1' or 'Sedie Route 1' travel every few minutes during daylight hours between the station in town and a stop near Crocodile Camp in Matlapaneng. The standard fare for all local trips is P5.

Taxis also ply the main road and are the only form of public transport in the evening. They also hang around a stand along Pulane St in the town centre. A typical fare from central Maun to Matlapaneng is about P15/40 in a shared/private taxi. To preorder a taxi, ask your hotel or campsite for a recommendation.

Shorobe

Around 40km north of Maun along the road to Kasane, Moremi or Savuti, Shorobe has little to detain you. The main reason for stopping is to shop for traditional baskets at the **Shorobe Baskets Cooperative**. The cooperative draws together around 70 local women who produce Ngamiland-style baskets with beautiful and elaborate patterns. It's right next to the main road through town and signposted. If it's closed, ask around (at the nearby shop, for example) and someone should be able to track down the key.

ⓘ Getting There & Away

A small number of buses leave daily for Shorobe (P8, one hour) from the main bus station in Maun. If you're driving, the sealed road ends soon after Shorobe and is one of the most rutted, washboard roads in Botswana – pray that it has been upgraded by the time you arrive.

Eastern Delta

The Eastern Delta includes the wetlands between the southern boundary of Moremi Game Reserve and the buffalo fence that crosses the Boro and Santandadibe Rivers, north of Matlapaneng. If you're short of time and/or money, this part of the Okavango Delta remains an affordable and accessible option. From Maun, it is easy to arrange a day trip on a *mokoro* or a two- or three-night *mokoro* trip combined with bush camping.

🛏 Sleeping

Although most excursions through the Eastern Delta are budget trips that involve bush camping, there are a handful of upmarket lodges in the region if you're looking for a little luxury.

Chitabe Camp   TENTED CAMP $$$
(☏in South Africa 011-807 1800; www.wilderness-safaris.com; s/d low season US$1123/1736, high season US$1588/2666; ❄❂) Near the Santandadibe River, at the southern edge of Moremi Game Reserve, Chitabe is an island oasis (only accessible by boat or plane) renowned for the presence of African wild dogs and other iconic wildlife, including leopards, lions and cheetahs. Accommodation is in East African–style luxury tents, which have bathrooms and are built on wooden decks and sheltered beneath the shade of a lush canopy.

Chitabe Lediba   TENTED CAMP $$$
(☏in South Africa 011-807 1800; www.wilderness-safaris.com; s/d low season US$1123/1736, high season US$1588/2666; ❄❂) On the other side of the island from Chitabe Camp, and also run by Wilderness Safaris, Chitabe Lediba is the baby brother in the family. With only five tents, Chitabe Lediba has a warm and intimate atmosphere.

UNUSUAL DELTA MAMMALS

In the northeast corner of the delta, watch out for rare sitatungas – splay-hoofed swamp antelopes, which are particularly adept at manoeuvring over soft, saturated mud and soggy, mashed vegetation. When frightened, they submerge like hippos, leaving only their tiny nostrils above the surface.

Red *lechwes*, of which there are estimated to be between 30,000 and 60,000, are easily distinguished by their large rumps. In the shallow and still pools of the palm islands, reedbucks wade and graze on water plants, and the islands are also inhabited by large herds of impala.

Sandibe Safari Lodge　　　　LODGE **$$$**
(☑in South Africa 011-809 4300; www.andbeyond africa.com; per person low season US$570, high season US$1145; ✺) Understated elegance is the theme at this riverine forest retreat, which consists of eight ochre-washed chalets surrounded by thick bush and towering trees. Dinner is served by candlelight and lantern in the main adobe-walled compound, while the night's festivities revolve around a campfire in a scenic clearing next to the water.

❶ Getting There & Away

If you're either on a *mokoro* day trip or a multiday bush-camping expedition from Maun, you will be transported to/from the Eastern Delta by 4WD. Transport into the lodges is usually via charter flights (enquire with your lodge) and then *mokoro* or 4WD.

Inner Delta

Welcome to the heart of the Okavango, a world inaccessible by roads and inhabited by some of the richest wildlife concentrations on earth. Although budget trips are possible in some areas, the quintessential delta experience is staying in one of the fly-in luxury lodges – if you're going to make a splash with your money in Botswana, make it here.

Roughly defined, the Inner Delta occupies the areas west of Chief's Island and between Chief's Island and the base of the Okavango Panhandle. *Mokoro* trips through the Inner Delta are almost invariably arranged with licensed polers affiliated with specific lodges, and operate roughly between June and December, depending on water levels. To see the most wildlife, you will have to pay park fees to land on Chief's Island or other parts of Moremi Game Reserve. Also, be sure to advise the poler if you'd like to break the trip with bushwalks around the palm islands.

🛏 Sleeping

Oddball's　　　　TENTED CAMP **$$$**
(☑686 1154; www.oddballscamp.com; tents low season US$240, high season US$340) For years, Oddball's was a well-regarded budget lodge, but although it's still way below lodge prices elsewhere in the delta, we reckon it's asking too much considering you're still staying in budget dome tents. It occupies less-than-exciting woodland beside an airstrip, but is within walking distance of some classic delta scenery. There's a 30% single supplement for lone travellers.

Gunn's Camp　　　　TENTED CAMP **$$$**
(☑686 0023; www.gunns-camp.com; per person low season US$371, s/d high season US$672/1102) Gunn's is a beautiful option for those wanting the amenities of a high-end safari – expertly cooked meals, attentive service and wonderful views over its island location in the delta – with a more rugged sense of place. The elegant tented rooms are as comfy as you'll find anywhere, but there is more of a feeling of being engaged with the wilderness, what with the hippos, warthogs and even elephants that occasionally wander through the grounds. Compared with prices elsewhere, Gunn's represents fabulous value.

Kanana Camp　　　　TENTED CAMP **$$$**
(☑686 0375; www.kerdowneybotswana.com; per person low season US$495, s/d high season US$1050/1640) This classy retreat occupies a watery site in a maze of grass- and palm-covered islands. It's an excellent base for wildlife viewing by *mokoro* around Chief's Island or fishing in the surrounding waterways. Accommodation is in eight well-furnished linen tents that are shaded by towering riverine forest.

Mapula Lodge　　　　TENTED CAMP **$$$**
(☑686 3369; www.mapula-lodge.com; per person low season US$415, s/d high season

US$936/1440) Located on the fringe of the Moremi Game Reserve, this lodge has a style all its own. African hardwoods dominate the decor, with zinc bathtubs adding to a more rustic, *Out of Africa* feel without ever compromising on comfort. There's a 30% single supplement.

Moremi Crossing   TENTED CAMP $$$
(☏686 0023; www.moremicrossing.com; per person low season US$321, s/d high season US$567/892; ✈) Part of the well-regarded portfolio of Under One Botswana Sky, this well-priced collection of lovely chalets flanks a simply gorgeous (and enormous) thatched dining and bar area that overlooks a long flood plain where you can often see wandering giraffes and elephants. The camp is to be commended for pioneering a plumbing system that minimises environmental impact (it's also quite a feat of engineering – ask to see how it all works).

Pom Pom Camp   TENTED CAMP $$$
(☏686 4436; www.pompomcamp.com; per person low season US$456, s/d high season US$882/1512; ✈) This intimate camp was one of the original luxury retreats in the delta, though frequent renovations have kept it up to speed with recent properties. Six linen tents are skilfully placed around a scenic lagoon, which contributes to the tranquil and soothing atmosphere. For this price, some of the tents could be a little larger.

Nxabega Okavango Camp   TENTED CAMP $$$
(☏in South Africa 011-809 4300; www.andbeyond africa.com; per person low season from US$495, high season from US$1090; ✈) In a grove of ebony trees on the flats near the Boro River, this exquisitely designed tented camp has sweeping views of the delta flood plains. Ten tents with private verandahs surround an impressively built thatched lodge that oozes style and sophistication.

Xigera Camp   TENTED CAMP $$$
(☏686 0086; www.wilderness-safaris.com; s/d low season US$963/1416, high season US$1473/2436; ✈) Pronounced 'kee-*jera'*, this isolated spot is deep in the heart of the Inner Delta and renowned for its rich birdlife. The area surrounding the camp is permanent wetland, which gives Xigera a lush and tropical atmosphere. Accommodation is in eight hybrid tent-chalets that are well furnished and a creative departure from the traditional linen tent.

Tubu Tree Camp   TENTED CAMP $$$
(☏686 0086; www.wilderness-safaris.com; s/d low season US$1123/1736, high season US$1588/2666; ✈) Get your khaki and pith-helmet fix from the gorgeous tilted accommodation that hovers over this pretty little corner of the Okavango. Porches look out from your accommodation over one of the largest consistent dry areas of the delta, which often teems with a good variety of wildlife.

Duba Plains   TENTED CAMP $$$
(☏686 0086; www.wilderness-safaris.com; s/d low season US$963/1416, high season US$1473/2436; ✈) North of the Moremi Game Reserve, Duba Plains is one of the most remote camps in the delta. Both the intimate layout of the grounds (there are only six tents) and the virtual isolation of this part of the delta contribute to a unique wilderness experience.

Seba Camp   TENTED CAMP $$$
(☏686 0086; www.wilderness-safaris.com; s/d low season US$963/1416, high season US$1473/2436; ✈) Seba, the lovely Setswana word meaning whisper, is set in an equally lovely riverine forest. While it offers many of the same aristocratic offerings as other top-end safari lodges, what sets it apart is the emphasis on family service; unlike other properties, this one welcomes children. Youngsters (and oldsters) can pass their days watching researchers study nearby elephants that have been released into the wild from captivity.

Eagle Island Camp   TENTED CAMP $$$
(☏686 0302; www.orient-express.com; per person high season from US$900) Widely considered to be one of the most beautiful camps in the delta, Eagle Island occupies a fairly stunning concession deep in the waters. You'll be shacked up in silk-soft luxury tents and helicopter safaris are part of your stay, plus the usual range of wildlife drives, walks, lavish meals and the rest, you lucky thing.

Footsteps   TENTED CAMP $$$
(☏686 0375; www.kerdowneybotswana.com; per person low season US$495, s/d high season US$795/1260) This relatively new programme, run by Ker & Downey safaris, places an emphasis on walking and *mokoro* safaris across the delta flood plains. It's the sort of thing that rewards fit travellers, but with that said, the rest camps are still impressively posh – the theme is old Africa exploration, but we doubt Livingstone ever laid his bushy beard on the soft sheets K&D provides.

DELTA LODGES

The lodges of the Eastern Delta, Inner Delta and Moremi Game Reserve rank among the most exclusive and indulgent safari experiences in Africa.

Rates for staying in most lodges include accommodation or camping equipment, all meals and several activities or excursions, such as *mokoro* trips, nature walks and wildlife drives. The more-expensive places also include drinks (beer and wine only), and entry fees to Moremi Game Reserve. All rooms, chalets and tents have private bathrooms (unless stated otherwise).

Transfers (if required) by road, or more usually by air, from Maun are never included in normal daily rates, though they may be included in package deals. Most lodges and booking agencies deal exclusively with a particular Maun-based air-charter company, so your chances of finding other charter companies offering discounted fares to a certain lodge are negligible.

Most lodges have radically different rates for 'high season' (about July to October) and 'low season' (about November to June). Some places offer unadvertised discounted rates for 'shoulder seasons' (early March to mid-June and mid-October to late November), but you'll have to ask. The rates listed are always per person sharing a twin or double room. Single supplements are usually charged. Rates listed include all government taxes and service charges. Tips are always extra.

Most lodges offer substantial (but rarely published) discounts to citizens and residents of Botswana and to citizens of 'regional countries'; ie mainly South Africa and Namibia. Although tariffs are quoted in US dollars by the lodges, payment is possible in pula – but at a rate that suits the lodge. Payment by credit card may incur an additional surcharge, so check first with the lodge.

All lodges in the Eastern Delta, Inner Delta and Moremi Game Reserve must be prebooked, preferably before you arrive in Maun. Although each camp has a unique atmosphere and location, accommodation is usually in one of a handful of safari-chic linen tents or chalets, which surround a central mess tent where you can dine, socialise or unwind.

Vumbura Plains Camp   TENTED CAMP **$$$**
(✆686 0086; www.wilderness-safaris.com; s/d low season US$1495/2388, high season US$2287/3972; ☒) One of the flagship properties of Wilderness Safaris, this regally luxurious twin camp is on the Duba Plains at the transition zone between the savannahs and swamps north of the delta. As such, the wildlife viewing here is superlative, and the area is famous for attracting large buffalo herds. Accommodation is in either the six-tent Vumbura camp or the slightly smaller five-tent Little Vumbura, which occupies a nearby island.

ⓘ Getting There & Away

The only way into and out of the Inner Delta for most visitors is by air. This is an expensive extra, but the pain is alleviated if you look at it as two scenic flights. Chartered flights to the lodges typically cost about US$150 to US$200 return. A *mokoro* or 4WD vehicle will meet your plane and take you to the lodge.

Moremi Game Reserve

Moremi Game Reserve (sometimes called Moremi Wildlife Reserve), which covers one-third of the Okavango Delta, is home to some of the densest concentrations of wildlife in Africa. Best of all, it's one of the most accessible corners of the Okavango, with well-maintained trails and accommodation that ranges from luxury lodges to public campsites for self-drivers.

Moremi is also unusual because it's the only part of the Okavango Delta that is officially cordoned off for the preservation of wildlife. It was set aside as a reserve in 1963 when it became apparent that poaching was decimating wildlife populations. Named after the Batawana chief Moremi III, the reserve has been extended over the years and now encompasses almost 5000 sq km.

Moremi has a distinctly dual personality, with large areas of dry land rising between vast wetlands. The most prominent 'islands' are Chief's Island, accessible by

BOTSWANA MOREMI GAME RESERVE

Moremi Tongue

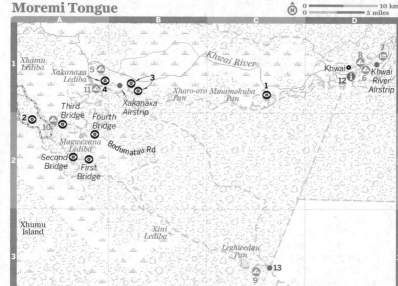

mokoro from the Inner Delta lodges, and Moremi Tongue at the eastern end of the reserve, which is mostly accessible by 4WD. Habitats in the reserve range from mopane woodland and thorn scrub to dry savannah, riparian woodland, grassland, flood plain, marsh, and permanent waterways, lagoons and islands.

With the recent reintroduction of the rhinos, Moremi is now home to the Big Five (lions, leopards, buffaloes, elephants and rhinos), and notably the largest population of red *lechwe* in the whole of Africa. The reserve also protects one of the largest remaining populations of endangered African wild dogs. Birding in Moremi is also incredibly varied and rich, and it's arguably the best place in Africa to view the rare and secretive Pel's fishing owl.

Entry fees to the reserve should be paid for in advance at the DWNP office in Maun, although they can be paid at the gate if you have no other choice. Self-drivers will, however, only be allowed entry to the reserve if they have a confirmed reservation at one of the four public campsites.

If you're coming from Maun, the reserve entrance is located at South (Maqwee) Gate, about 99km north of Maun via Shorobe. From Kasane and the east, a track links

Moremi Tongue

Sights
1	Dombo Hippo Pools	C1
2	Mboma Island	A2
3	Paradise Pools	B1
4	Xakanaxa Lediba	A1

Sleeping
5	Camp Moremi	A1
6	Khwai Camp Site	D1
7	Khwai River Lodge	D1
8	Sango Safari Camp	D1
9	South Gate Camp Site	C3
10	Third Bridge Camp Site	A2
11	Xakanaxa Camp	A1
	Xakanaxa Camp Site	(see 11)

Information
12	North (Khwai) Gate & Park Headquarters	D1
13	South (Maqwee) Gate	C3

Chobe National Park with the other gate at North (Khwai) Gate.

The village of Khwai has a couple of shops that sell basic supplies. Otherwise, petrol and supplies are only available in Kasane and Maun.

◉ Sights

Chief's Island   ISLAND
The largest island in the Okavango Delta, Chief's Island (70km long and 15km wide) is so named because it was once the sole hunting preserve of the local chief. Raised above the water level by tectonic activity in ancient times, it's here that so much of the delta's wildlife retreats as water levels rise. As such, the island is home to what could be the richest concentrations of wildlife in Botswana, and is the Okavango Delta as you always imagined it. The combination of reed-fringed waters, grasslands and light woodlands makes for game viewing that can feel like a BBC wildlife documentary brought to life. Not surprisingly, the island is home to some of the most exclusive lodges and tented camps in Africa.

Third Bridge   BRIDGE
Literally the third log bridge after entering the reserve at South Gate (although both First Bridge and Second Bridge were, at the time of writing, easy to bypass in the dry season along parallel tracks), this rustic and rather ramshackle bridge spans a reed-filled, tannin-coloured pool on the Sekiri River. The neighbouring campsite is one of our favourites in the Okavango. Don't even think of going for a swim here – it's a favourite haunt for crocs and hippos.

Mboma Island   ISLAND
The grassy savannah of this 100-sq-km island, a long extension of the Moremi Tongue, contrasts sharply with the surrounding landscapes and provides some excellent dry-season wildlife watching – cheetah, lion and buffalo sightings are reasonably common. The 32km sandy Mboma Loop starts about 2km west of Third Bridge and is a pleasant side trip. Boat trips from the Mboma Boat Station on the island's northwestern tip are highly recommended.

Xakanaxa Lediba   LAKE
With one of Africa's largest heronries, Xakanaxa Lediba (Xakanaxa Lagoon) is renowned as a birdwatchers' paradise. In addition to herons, potential sightings here include storks, egrets and ibises. The area also supports an array of wildlife and large numbers of fish. There are myriad trails around the Xakanaxa backwaters – the Shell Map of the Moremi Game Reserve is the most detailed resource.

Paradise Pools   LAKE
One of the loveliest corners of Moremi, the area known as Paradise Pools is as delightful as the name suggests. In the dry season, trails lead past forests of dead trees and along the perimeter of reed-filled swamps, while impala and other antelope species drink nervously at the receding shoreline of waterholes. When we were last here, there were lion and leopard sightings in the area.

Dombo Hippo Pools   LAKE
The drive between North Gate (including Khwai) and Xakanaxa Lediba follows one of Botswana's more scenic tracks, although the exact route changes with the years depending on flood levels. Worthwhile stops en route include Dombo Hippo Pool (about 14km southwest of North Gate), where hippos crowd along the shore. You can watch

BOTSWANA MOREMI GAME RESERVE

THE CARNIVORE CHAIN OF COMMAND

By far the largest African carnivore, the lion sits pretty much unchallenged at the top of the pecking order and is usually able to kill anything it can get hold of, including other predators. Adult lions usually only worry about other lions, though large hyena clans occasionally kill injured or adolescent lions, and they're certainly able to drive small prides from their kills.

Hyenas also trail after other predators in the hopes of getting a free meal. At Moremi, it's fairly common to see spotted hyena clans trailing African wild dogs on the hunt. Again, strength in numbers is a key factor: a few hyenas can lord over an entire pack of wild dogs, though a single hyena is easily harassed into retreating. Coincidentally, both hyena clans and wild-dog packs dominate leopards, but individuals do so at their peril as leopards will occasionally bring down a lone hyena or wild dog.

At the very bottom of the hierarchy is the world's fastest land predator, the cheetah. By sacrificing brute force for incredible speed, cheetahs are simply unable to overpower other predators. Nor can they afford the risk of injury and invariably give way to other super-predators, regardless of numbers.

WHEN TO VISIT MOREMI

The best time to see wildlife in Moremi is the late dry season (July to October), when animals are forced to congregate around permanent water sources, which are accessible to wildlife (and humans). September and October are optimum times for spotting wildlife and birdlife, but these are also the hottest two months. January and February are normally very wet, and as tracks in the reserve are mostly clay, they are frequently impassable during these months.

their shenanigans in relative safety from an elevated observation post.

🏃 Activities

Moremi is the launching point for some wonderful boat excursions into the delta. Although *mokoro* trips may be possible, most of what's on offer is in open-sided motor-propelled boats. More jetties spring up with each passing year, but at the time of writing there were two in the Xakanaxa area, with a further site at the Mboma boat station on Mboma Island. Prices start at P520/544/627 per hour for an eight-/12-/16-seater craft.

🛏 Sleeping

There are four public campsites in Moremi, but they're often booked well in advance, especially during South African school holidays (mid-April, July, September, and December to January) – book as early as possible. Each site has an ablutions block with sit-down flush toilets, running water (which needs to be boiled or purified for drinking), picnic tables and *braai* pits.

CHIEF'S ISLAND & AROUND

Stanley's Camp   TENTED CAMP **$$$**
(☑in South Africa 011-438 4650; www.sanctuary retreats.com; per person low season US$565, s/d high season US$1665/2220) Although less ostentatious than other lodges in Moremi, Stanley's, located near the Boro River near the southern end of Chief's Island, lacks the formality and pretence commonly found in this corner of the country. The eight tents are simple but spacious, and elephant sightings in particular are almost guaranteed in

the camp's vicinity, with wild dogs also a possibility.

Baine's Camp   TENTED CAMP **$$$**
(☑in South Africa 011-438 4650; www.sanctuary retreats.com; per person low season US$675, s/d high season US$2033/2710) Five elevated suites overlook a tree line that conceals (but not too much) great wildlife viewing in a shady, woodsy area of the delta close to the southern end of Chief's Island; the outdoor bathtubs are pure indulgence. There's a very private, world-in-its-infancy sense of fresh beauty in the place; you'd be forgiven for thinking a naked couple arguing over an apple were about to emerge from the landscape.

Chief's Camp   TENTED CAMP **$$$**
(☑in South Africa 011-438 4650; www.sanctuary retreats.com; per person low season US$995, s/d high season US$3053/4070) Considered by many to be one of the premier camps in the delta, Chief's blends into its marshy surroundings like a hunter in a duck blind. Except you're not trying to pot-shot wildlife here – just photograph or watch it from 12 pretty incredible luxury 'bush pavilions'.

Mombo Camp   TENTED CAMP **$$$**
(☑686 0086; www.wilderness-safaris.com; s/d low season US$2230/3430, high season US$3026/4862; ✈) Ask anyone in Botswana for the country's most exclusive camp and they're likely to nominate Mombo, situated (with its sister camp, Little Mombo) on the north-west corner of Chief's Island. The surrounding delta scenery is some of the finest in the Okavango and the wildlife watching is almost unrivalled. The rooms are enormous and the entire package – from the service to the comfort levels and attention to detail – never misses a beat.

THIRD BRIDGE, XAKANAXA & AROUND

Third Bridge Camp Site   CAMPGROUND **$**
(Map p104; www.xomaesites.com; Third Bridge; GPS: S19°14.340', E23°21.276'; per adult/child P226/113) The favourite campsite for many self-drivers in the region, Third Bridge has sites that are away from the main track – with a setting on the edge of a lagoon (watch out for hippos and crocs), it's a beautiful place to pitch for the night. As always, be wary of baboons and avoid camping on the bridge or sleeping in the open because wildlife – especially lions – uses the bridge as a thoroughfare.

Xakanaxa Camp Site — CAMPGROUND $

(Xakanaxa Lediba; Map p104; kwalatesafari@gmail.com; GPS: S19°10.991', E23°24.937'; campsite per adult/child P260/130) A favourite Moremi campground, Xakanaxa occupies a narrow strip of land surrounded by marshes and lagoons. It's no coincidence that many upmarket lodges are located nearby – the wildlife in the area can be prolific and campers are frequently woken during the night by elephants or serendaded by hippo grunts. But be warned: a young boy was tragically killed by hyenas here in 2000. Boat journeys onto the lagoon are also possible.

South Gate Camp Site — CAMPGROUND $

(Maqwee Camp Site; Map p104; kwalatesafari@gmail.com; GPS: S 19°25.526', E 23°38.654; campsite per adult/child P260/130) This campsite is reasonably developed but its distance from the main wildlife-watching areas would make this our last choice of the public campsites. Alternatively, it's a good option if you don't think you can reach Third Bridge or Xakanaxa by nightfall. Be careful not to leave any food lying about, as the baboons here are aggressive and ill-tempered.

Camp Moremi — TENTED CAMP $$$

(Map p104; ☑686 1559; www.desertdelta.com; per person low season US$476, s/d high season US$1113/1712; ☎) This long-standing wilderness retreat sits amid giant ebony trees next to Xakanaxa Lediba and is surrounded by wildlife-rich grasslands. Accommodation is in East African–style linen tents that are attractively furnished with wooden fixtures.

Moremi Under Canvas — TENTED CAMP $$$

(☑in South Africa 011-809 4314; www.moremiundercanvas.com; per person US$415-680) This cross between a tented camp and luxury mobile safari enables you to experience the freedom of camping (sites are moved every few days) with the exclusivity that comes with having a beautifully appointed tent, butler and excellent meals served in between your game drives. Tents have bathing facilities, including hot bucket showers.

Camp Okavango — TENTED CAMP $$$

(☑686 1559; www.desertdelta.com; per person low season US$476, s/d high season US$1113/1712; ☎) Set amid sausage and jackalberry trees on Nxaragha Island, just outside Moremi, this charming lodge is elegant, and the staff are famous for their meticulous attention to detail. If you want Okavango served up

with silver tea service, candelabras and fine china, this is the place for you.

Xugana Island Lodge — LODGE $$$

(☑686 1559; www.desertdelta.com; per person low season US$476, s/d high season US$1113/1712; ☎) Set on a pristine lagoon just north of Moremi, this lodge offers superb bird-watching and fishing. This area was historically frequented by San hunters, and Xugana means 'kneel down to drink' – a reference to the welcome sight of perennial water after a long hunt. Accommodation is in beautiful thatched chalets with modern furnishings.

Shinde Island Camp — TENTED CAMP $$$

(☑686 0375; www.kerdowneybotswana.com; per person low season US$495, s/d high season US$1265/1900) This lagoon-side camp sits just north of Moremi, between the savannah and the delta, and is one of the oldest camps in the delta. Eight linen tents surround a central lodge known for its class and formality.

Xakanaxa Camp — TENTED CAMP $$$

(Map p104; ☑in South Africa 011-463 3999; www.xakanaxa-camp.com; per person low season US$531, s/d high season from US$1301/1786) This camp, of longer standing than most, offers a pleasant mix of delta and savannah habitat, and teems with huge herds of elephants and other wildlife. However, it's most famous for its legendary birdwatching, especially along the shores of the nearby Xakanaxa Lediba. It's very good at providing the luxury safari experience.

KHWAI

Khwai Camp Site — CAMPGROUND $

(Map p104; http://sklcamps.com; GPS: S 19°10.359', E 23°45.122'; campsite per adult/child US$50/25) The campsites at this expansive campground are shady and well developed, with some lovely sites close to the riverbank; others are a little further inland. There's also an ablutions block and good wildlife watching in the area. In July 2012 there was a nonfatal leopard attack on a lone camper; always drive to the ablutions block from your campsite after dark. There are a couple of small shops in Khwai village on the other side of the river selling food and other supplies.

Khwai River Lodge — LODGE $$$

(Map p104; ☑686 1244; www.khwairiverlodge.com; per person high season from US$900) Perched on

THE BEST OF THE DELTA ON DVD

Dereck & Beverley Joubert, National Geographic 'Explorers in Residence', have spent almost 30 years visiting the Okavango Delta and documenting its wildlife, especially the big cats. The result is an extraordinary portfolio of DVDs that captures the spirit of the delta and the daily dramas of its wildlife. Jeremy Irons' narration on many of the stories adds gravitas, if any were needed.

The Last Lions (2011) Follows a lioness and her cubs as they struggle to survive around Duba Island in the heart of the delta (narrated by Jeremy Irons).

Living with Big Cats (2007) An intimate portrait of the filmmakers, the delta and the animals that take centre stage in their films.

Eye of the Leopard (2006) A remarkable chronicle of two years in the life of a leopard mother and her cub in the delta.

Ultimate Enemies (2003–06) Three-part series documenting the enduring rivalry of lions with buffaloes, hyenas and elephants.

the northern shores of the Khwai River, this opulent lodge overlooks the Moremi Game Reserve, and is frequently visited by large numbers of hippos and elephants. Accommodation is in 15 luxury tents that are larger and more extravagant than most upmarket hotel rooms.

Sango Safari Camp TENTED CAMP $$$
(Map p104; ☑683 0230; www.sangosafaricamp. com; per person low season US$295, high season US$540, without park fees & game drives US$235/425) On the north side of the Khwai River not far from the village, Sango's is somewhat less pretentious than some other Moremi camps but nonetheless maintains an air of quiet exclusivity. Hand-crafted furnishings are a nice touch, while game drives generally go where other lodges don't. It's also unusual in offering cheaper rates for those driving their own vehicles and not looking to join the game drives.

Kwara Camp TENTED CAMP $$$
(☑686 1449; www.kwando.co.bw; per person low season US$515, s/d high season US$1208/1818) This island camp lies in an area of subterranean springs that form pools that support enough fish to attract flocks of pelicans ('kwara' means 'where the pelicans feed'). These pools also attract heavy concentrations of wildlife, which is a major drawcard for the lodge. Although the place is luxurious, the atmosphere is informal and relaxed.

Xaranna Camp TENTED CAMP $$$
(☑in South Africa 011-809 4300; www.andbeyond africa.com; per person US$650-1150) With its own island, 25,000-hectare concession and just nine tents, Xaranna can feel like your

own personal paradise. As such, there's a lot of room for wildlife, which you can often see from the gorgeous tents that overlook a syrup-slow channel of the delta.

❶ Getting There & Away

Chartered flights (and/or 4WD) are usually the only way to reach the luxury lodges of Moremi.

If you're driving from Maun, take the sealed road to Shorobe, where the road turns into awfully corrugated gravel. Once inside the park, it's about 52km (two hours) from South Gate to Third Bridge along a reasonable track, en route passing through beautiful, wildlife-rich country. It's about 25km (one hour) from Third Bridge to Xakanaxa Lediba, and another 45km (1½ hours) from there to North Gate.

Check the road conditions with the DWNP offices in Gaborone or Maun, and/or with other drivers, before attempting to drive into Moremi during the wet season; some tracks can even be impassable well into the dry season.

Okavango Panhandle

The main attractions of the Okavango Panhandle, a narrow strip of swampland that extends for about 100km from Etsha 13 to the Namibian border, are birdwatching and fishing. You may see other wildlife but don't count on it, as it's more elusive and thinly spread.

A geological curiosity, the panhandle is the result of a 15km-wide geological fault that constricts the meandering river until it's released into the main delta. In the panhandle, the waters spread across the valley on either side to form vast reed beds and papyrus-choked lagoons. Here a cosmopolitan mix of people (Mbukushu, Yei, Tswana, Herero, European and San, as well as Angolan refugees) occupy clusters of fishing villages and extract their livelihoods from the rich waters.

As the rest of the delta grows more expensive, the Okavango Panhandle is booming as a result of local cooperatives that offer affordable accommodation and *mokoro* trips. Although it is arguably not the 'real delta', the panhandle is the main population centre in the region and the panhandle has permanent water year-round, which means it's always possible to organise a *mokoro* trip.

Along the road between Sehithwa and Shakawe, there are petrol stations in Sehithwa, Gumare, Etsha 6 and Shakawe, but fill up whenever you can as supplies can run dry. Shakawe has a supermarket and a Barclays ATM.

Sights

Krokavango Crocodile Farm ZOO
(7230 6200; willeroxl@gmail.com; adult/child P25/15; 8.30am-4pm Mon-Sat) It's difficult to know what to make of this place, which lies not far south of Drotsky's Cabins (the turn-off from the main Sehithwa–Shakawe road is at GPS S 18°26.363, E 21°53.114'). Partly a refuge for rescued crocodiles from the Okavango Panhandle (usually those that have acquired a taste for local livestock), it has some extraordinary specimens, including some up to 5m long. At the same time, it also breeds crocodiles for the lucrative crocodile-skin market (think purses, belts etc) and there are almost 8000 captive-bred crocs onsite. Feeding time is at 11am on Tuesdays and Fridays; there's a shop, and a visit to the farm is by guided tour.

Activities

The most popular leisure activity in the panhandle is **fishing**. Anglers from around the world flock here to hook tigerfish, pike,

barbel (catfish) and bream. Tigerfish season is from September to June, while barbel are present from mid-September to December.

Most lodges and campsites along the panhandle can arrange fishing trips, and hire out gear.

Sleeping

Panhandle camps are mostly in the midrange, and have until recently catered mainly for the sport-fishing crowd. However, this is changing along with the recent increase in travellers looking for affordable delta trips. Camping is also available at most lodges.

Sepupa Swamp Stop CAMPGROUND $$
(7567 0252; www.swampstop.com; Sepupa; campsite per person from P100, tents/chalets from P220/750;) This laid-back riverside campsite is secluded, handy to Sepupa village, very affordable and accessible (3km) from the Maun–Shakawe road. The lodge can arrange *mokoro* trips through the Okavango Polers Trust and transfers to Sepupa, as well as boat trips that start at P285/1725 per hour/day. Most *mokoro* trips from here require a boat transfer as the waters here are mostly too deep for poling.

Mbiroba Camp CAMPGROUND $
(687 6861; www.okavangodelta.co.bw; campsite per person P100, rondavels P175, chalets from P325) This camp is run by the Okavango Polers Trust and is the usual launching point for *mokoro* trips into the delta. Sadly, like so many community projects, the camp has gone downhill in recent years and the campsites, bar, traditional restaurant and two-storey chalets have all seen better days. Mbiroba is 3km from Seronga village.

Drotsky's Cabins LODGE & CAMPGROUND $$$
(683 0226; drotsky@botsnet.bw; campsite per person P125, chalets & A-frames from P1250;) This lovely, welcoming lodge lies beside a channel of the Okavango River, about 5km southeast of Shakawe and about 4km east

---

BORDER CROSSING: THE OKAVANGO PANHANDLE

The **Mohembo–Shakawe Gate** (6am to 6pm) is generally hassle-free, but remember when calculating the border post's opening hours that Namibia is one hour behind Botswana from late May to the end of August. As always, coming into Botswana your car will be searched for fresh meat, fresh fruit and dairy products (all of which will be confiscated if found), and you may be required to walk through a soda solution (and drive your car through the same) as part of measures to protect the country from foot-and-mouth disease.

of the main road. Set amid a thick riverine forest, it's very secluded, with fabulous bird-watching and fine views across the reeds and papyrus. The chalets have air-con; the A-frames are fan only. Boats can be rented and the bar-restaurant serves breakfast/lunch/dinner for P120/150/170. The campsite is similarly attractive and there's a boat to take you to the restaurant in the evening.

Xaro Lodge   LODGE $$$

(☏683 0226; xarolodge@info.bw; luxury tents P1250) Run by the son of the owners of Drotsky's Cabins, this lodge is remote – about 10km downstream from Drotsky's – but serene and extremely picturesque. Accommodation is in several clean and tidy 'luxury' tents that surround a modest bar-restaurant. The main activity at the lodge is fishing, though it also makes for a great retreat and there's good birdwatching in the vicinity. Boat transfers from Drotksy's Cabins cost P20 per person.

Guma Lagoon Camp   CAMPGROUND $$$

(☏687 4626; www.guma-lagoon.com; campsite per person P124, 2-person cabins P941) This lovely spot at the panhandle's lower end is a fantastic place. Each of the shady campsites has its own shower and toilet, and the tranquil setting continues with a lovely public area where you can order drinks and also use the kitchen. Most of the chalets overlook the water. It can also arrange all manner of excursions, from boat hire and fishing trips to night drives and three-day *mokoro* trips. If you're driving, the trail is well signposted

from Etsha 13. Transfer to or from Etsha13/Seronga costs P112/1232.

Okavango Houseboats   HOUSEBOATS $$$

(☏686 0802; www.okavangohouseboats.com; houseboats P6000) Floating down the river in one of these houseboats, which vaguely resemble Mississippi steamboats that got lost somewhere in Angola, gives a new, aquatic twist to the 'mobile safari' experience. The craft depart from Seronga, and should be booked well in advance. Expect some amazing birding and riverside wildlife viewing. The boats accommodate six to 20 people. Petrol and food costs extra – check the website for details.

❶ Getting There & Away

The road between Maun and Shakawe, via Sehithwa, is sealed (if potholed in places) and continues into Namibia. You'll need a 4WD for the tracks into most lodges and campsites; most will arrange pickups (for a fee) from the nearest town.

To reach Sepupa, catch a bus towards Shakawe from Maun, disembark at the turn-off to the village (P80, six hours) and hitch a lift or walk (about 3km) into Sepupa. To get to Seronga, there are several options: ask Sepupa Swamp Stop about a boat transfer (P215 per person, minimum of six people) or wait for the public boat (P50 per person, two hours), which leaves Sepupa more frequently in the afternoon. Alternatively, catch the bus all the way from Maun to Shakawe (P110, seven hours); jump on a combi (P8, 30 minutes) up to Mohembo; take the free car ferry (45 minutes, 6.30am to 6.30pm) across the river; and then hitch (which is usually

---

THE OKAVANGO POLERS TRUST

Established in 1998 by the people of Seronga, the Okavango Polers Trust (☏687 6861; www.okavangodelta.co.bw) provides cheaper and more accessible *mokoro* trips and accommodation for visitors. Since the collective is run entirely by the village, all profits are shared by the workers, invested into the trust and used to provide the community with better facilities. The trust directly employs nearly 100 people, including polers, dancers, cooks, managers and drivers. As no travel agency or safari operator is involved, the cooperative can afford to charge reasonable prices for *mokoro* trips. Although it's not uncommon to pay upwards of US$200 per day for a *mokoro* trip out of Maun, the trust charges around P750 per day for *two* people. Keep in mind, however, that you must self-cater (ie bring your own food, water and, if necessary, camping and cooking equipment).

There's no longer a daily bus from Mohembo to Seronga, but it's almost always possible to hitch from the free Okavango River ferry in Mohembo. Plan on paying about P20 for a lift. When they're operating, water taxis run along the Okavango between Sepupa Swamp Stop and Seronga (P50, two hours); transfers from the Seronga dock to Mbiroba Camp, 3km away, cost P200. Otherwise, Sepupa Swamp Stop can arrange boat transfers to Seronga starting from P1700 per boat.

THE ETSHA VILLAGES

During the early days of Angola's civil war, the Mbukushu people fled southwards and were granted refugee status in Botswana. In 1969 they organised themselves into 13 groups based on the clan and social structure they carried over from Angola. Each group proceeded to settle in a village 1km from the next, and were subsequently named Etsha 1, Etsha 2 and so on by the Botswana government.

Etsha 6, 3km east of the main road, is the largest of the villages strung along or just off the Sehithwa–Shakawe road. In the village you'll find the **House of the River People** (admission P10), a museum and cultural centre featuring the traditions and artistry of the Bayei, Mbukushu and San people of the Okavango region. The adjacent Okavango Basket Shop is an excellent place to buy Ngamiland baskets, pottery and carvings. Up to six daily combis between Maun and Shakawe stop in Etsha 6.

easy enough) along the good sandy road (accessible by 2WD) to Seronga. Otherwise, drive via Shakawe and Mohembo, or fly to Seronga from Maun – try **Mack Air** (www.mackair.co.bw).

NORTHWESTERN BOTSWANA

Tsodilo Hills & Around

The far northwest of Botswana, outside of the Okavango Delta, is a wild and remote border space of small towns and cattle posts separated by long, windy stretches of yellow grass and bleached thornbush. Elsewhere are marshy outflows wrapped in reeds, the latter used in the construction of some of the country's prettiest crafts. Scattered throughout are rocky outcroppings, the sides of their walls daubed with pigments and paintings from the San and their relatives.

Tourism infrastructure remains essentially undeveloped and very few visitors make it out here – you may have the 'desert Louvre' of the Tsodilo Hills, for example, almost completely to yourself.

LAKE NGAMI

Arriving at the shores of Lake Ngami in 1849, Dr David Livingstone witnessed a magnificent expanse of water teeming with animals and birdlife. However, for reasons not completely known, the lake disappeared entirely a few years later, reappearing briefly towards the end of the 19th century, a pattern that has continued.

Lake Ngami lacks an outflow and can only be filled by an overflow from the Okavango Delta down the Nhabe River. Following heavy rains in 1962, the lake reappeared

once more, covering an area of 250 sq km. Although the lake was present for nearly 20 years, it mysteriously disappeared again in 1982, only to reappear once more in 2000. Since then, heavy rains have kept the lake partially filled at various times, though it's anyone's guess when it will dry up again.

Following heavy rains, the lake attracts flocks of flamingos, ibises, pelicans, eagles, storks, terns, gulls and kingfishers. Although there is no accommodation around the lake, unofficial camping is possible along the lakeshore, though you will need to be entirely self-sufficient.

All (unsigned) tracks heading south from the sealed road between Toteng and Sehithwa lead to the lake.

GCWIHABA (DROTSKY'S) CAVE

In 1932 a group of San showed Gcwihaba (meaning 'hyena's hole') to a farmer named Martinus Drotsky, who humbly decided to name the cave after himself. Although Drotsky is most likely the first European to have explored the cave, legend has it that the fabulously wealthy Hendrik Matthys van Zyl stashed a portion of his fortune here in the late 1800s.

The interior of the cave is famous for its 10m-long stalagmites and stalactites, which were formed by dripping water that seeped through the ground and dissolved the dolomite rock. The cave is home to large colonies of Commerson's leaf-nosed bats (which have a wingspan of up to 60cm) and common slit-faced bats (distinguished by their long ears), which, although harmless, can make your expedition a hair-raising experience.

Gcwihaba (Drotsky's) Cave (GPS S 20°01.302', E 21°21.275') is not developed for tourism: the interior of the cave is completely dark, and there are no lights or route

Northwestern Botswana

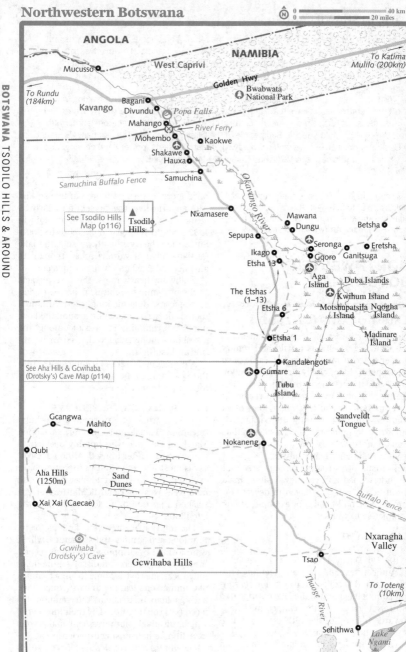

N 0 ——— 40 km
0 ——— 20 miles

ANGOLA

NAMIBIA

West Caprivi

Golden Hwy

To Katima Mulilo (200km)

Mucusso

Bwabwata National Park

To Rundu (184km)

Kavango

Bagani
Divundu
Popa Falls
Mahango
River Ferry
Mohembo
Kaokwe
Shakawe
Hauxa
Samuchina

Samuchina Buffalo Fence

See Tsodilo Hills Map (p116)
Tsodilo Hills

Okavango River

Nxamasere

Mawana
Dungu
Betsha

Sepupa
Seronga
Eretsha
Ikago
Gqoro
Ganitsuga
Etsha 13
Aga Island
Duba Islands
Kwihum Island
The Etshas (1–13)
Motshupatsila Island
Nqogha Island
Etsha 6
Madinare Island
Etsha 1

Kandalengoti

See Aha Hills & Gcwihaba (Drotsky's) Cave Map (p114)

Gumare
Tubu Island
Sandveldt Tongue

Gcangwa
Mahito

Qubi

Nokaneng

Aha Hills (1250m)
Sand Dunes

Xai Xai (Caecae)

Buffalo Fence

Gcwihaba (Drotsky's) Cave
Gcwihaba Hills

Nxaragha Valley

Tsao

Thaoge River

To Toteng (10km)

Sehithwa
Lake Ngami

To Ghanzi (162km)

markings. It is possible to walk (about 1km) through the cave from one entrance to the other, but venturing far inside the cave is only for those with proper lighting and some experience and confidence; carry with you several strong torches (flashlights), as well as emergency light sources such as matches and cigarette lighters. The main entrance is signposted from the end of the track, and is near a noticeboard. The cave is permanently open and there is no admission charge.

Unofficial camping is possible beneath the thorn trees.

❶ Getting There & Away
A fully equipped 4WD with high clearance is essential for visiting Gcwihaba (Drotsky's) Cave, which is signposted off the main Maun–Shakawe highway.

AHA HILLS
Straddling the Botswana–Namibia border, the 700-million-year-old limestone and dolomite Aha Hills rise 300m from the flat, thorny Kalahari scrub. Due to the almost total absence of water, there is an eerie dearth of animal life – there are few birds and only the occasional insect. However, the main attraction of the Aha Hills is their beguiling solitude and isolation. When night falls, the characteristic sounds of Southern Africa are conspicuously absent, though the resulting stillness is near perfect.

With precious few reliable maps, the Aha Hills present the perfect opportunity to put the guidebook down and explore a region that very few tourists visit. There are no facilities here, but unofficial camping is allowed within 100m of the main track. Basic supplies and drinkable bore water are available in the villages of Xai Xai and Gcangwa.

The hills are located about 33km south of Gcangwa and about 12km north of Xai Xai. Travelling onward, you can reach Gcwihaba (Drotsky's) Cave.

TSODILO HILLS
The Unesco World Heritage–listed Tsodilo Hills rise abruptly from the northwestern Kalahari, west of the Okavango Panhandle. Rare outposts of vertical variety in this extremely flat country, these lonely chunks of quartzite schist are dramatic and beautiful, distinguished by streaks of vivid natural hues – mauve, orange, yellow, turquoise and lavender. The hills are also a site of huge spiritual significance for the region's original inhabitants, the San. The major drawcards are more than 4000 prehistoric rock paintings spread over 200 sites throughout the hills.

Excavations of flaked stone tools indicate that Bantu people arrived as early as AD 500, but layers of superimposed rock paintings and other archaeological remnants suggest that ancestors of the San have been here for up to 30,000 years.

The Tsodilo Hills are now a national monument and under the auspices of the National Museum in Gaborone. All visitors must report to the headquarters at the Main (Rhino) Camp, about 2.5km north of the airstrip. Admission to the hills is free.

The best time to visit is during winter (April to October) as daytime temperatures

TSODILO LEGENDS
The Tsodilo Hills are imbued with myth, legend and spiritual significance for the original San inhabitants. Most significantly, the San believe the Tsodilo Hills are the site of the first Creation, and the Mbukushu claim that the gods lowered the people and their cattle onto Female Hill.

Four main chunks of rock make up the Tsodilo Hills – Male Hill, Female Hill, Child Hill and a distant hillock known as North Hill, which remained nameless until recently – and each of them has a story attached. According to one San legend, for example, Male Hill sent away North Hill (a wife of Male Hill) for being too argumentative. The hollows within some of the hills are also believed to represent animal footprints.

And visitors from the outside world are not immune to the Hills' magic. The Tsodilo Hills were the 'Slippery Hills' described by Sir Laurens van der Post in his 1958 classic The Lost World of the Kalahari. Hoping to make a documentary film of the hills, his cameras inexplicably jammed, his tape recorders ceased functioning and his group was attacked by swarms of bees on three consecutive mornings. When he learned that two members of his party had ignored a warning from his San guide by killing a warthog and steenbok while approaching the sacred hills, van der Post buried a note of apology beneath the panel of paintings that now bears his name.

Aha Hills & Gcwihaba (Drotsky's) Cave

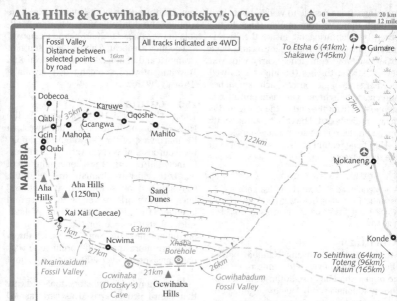

in the summertime can be excruciatingly hot. From December to February, watch out for bees.

Sights & Activities

The hills can be explored along any of five walking trails. Although there are some signposts, most trails require a guide (expect to pay around P50 to P60 for a two- to three-hour hike, or P100 per day), which can be arranged at the Main (Rhino) Camp. Early morning is the best time to walk the hills, followed by late afternoon.

There is a small, dusty **museum** (Map p116; admission free; ⊙daylight hours) with a small handful of ethnographic exhibits and wall-sized quotes about the rock art at Main (Rhino) Camp.

In addition to the following trails and paintings, one of the most fascinating paintings is the **zebra painting** (Map p116) on a small outcrop north of Female Hill. This stylised equine figure is now used as the logo of Botswana National Museum and Monuments.

Male Hill Trail
WALKING

On the northern face of Male Hill is a painting of a solitary male **lion** (Map p116). The summit of Male Hill is accessible along the Male Hill Trail by climbing from the hill's base near the male lion painting. The route is rough, rocky and plagued by false crests, but the view from the summit may well be the finest in the Kalahari.

Lion Trail
WALKING

Between Male and Female Hills, the Lion Trail crosses the flat valley between the hills and links the Male Hill Trail with another trail called the Rhino Trail. And therein lies the trail's main appeal, as it doesn't pass anything particularly interesting.

Rhino Trail
WALKING

From the Overland Camp Site, the steep and signposted Rhino Trail is probably the most interesting of the trails. It climbs past several distinctive paintings to a water pit where dragonflies and butterflies flit around a slimy green puddle. Near this site is an odd tree, once described to Laurens van der Post as the **Tree of True Knowledge** (Map p116) by the San guide who led him there. According to the guide, the greatest spirit knelt beside this fetid pool on the day of Creation. In the rocks beyond this pool are several 'hoof prints', which the Mbukushu believe were made by the cattle lowered onto the hill by the god Ngambe.

The Rhino Trail continues over the crest of a hill into a bizarre grassy valley flanked by peaks that seem a bit like an alternative universe. The route passes several rocky outcrops and rock paintings, and then descends into the prominent hollow in the southeastern side of Female Hill. Inside the hollow is a **rhino** (Map p116) painting, which also includes a 'forgery' of a buffalo that was created more recently. Directly across the hollow, one of the few Tsodilo paintings containing human figures depicts a dancing crowd of sexually excited male figures – Alec Campbell, the foremost expert on the hills and their paintings, has amusedly dubbed it the '**Dancing Penises**' (Map p116).

On the southeast corner of Female Hill, look for the amazing **whale** (Map p116) and penguin paintings that suggest an intriguing link between the early San and the Namibian coast. Around the corner and to the west, the **rhino** (Map p116) and giraffe painting portrays a rhino family and an authentic -looking giraffe.

Divuyu Trail   WALKING
An adjunct to the Rhino Trail, a short but hazardously rocky climb along what is sometimes called the Divuyu Trail leads to Laurens van der Post's **Panel** (Map p116), which contains eland and giraffes. This trail also leads to the **Divuyu Village Remains** (Map p116).

Cliff Trail   WALKING
Another route, the partially marked Cliff Trail, goes past the unassuming site known as the '**Origin of Sex**' (Map p116) painting, around the northern end of Female Hill and into a deep and mysterious hidden valley. This trail also passes an amazing natural **cistern** (Map p116) (in a rock grotto near the northwestern corner of Female Hill), which has held water year-round for as long as anyone can remember. The San believe that this natural tank is inhabited by a great serpent with twisted horns, so visitors should warn the occupant of their approach by tossing a small stone into the water. This impressive feature is also flanked by several rock paintings.

🛏 Sleeping
Unofficial camping is possible anywhere, but be wary of wild animals, and please be respectful of local people.

The main campsites are run by the National Museum and services are basic. You'll need to be self-sufficient to stay here, although very basic supplies are available at Mbukushu village, but it's best to carry in your own food.

Camping is free at all the sites, although you usually have to register at the Main Camp. The staff's presence rarely amounts to much more than an attendant on duty at the Main Camp. Other camps dotted around the area include **Malatso Camp** and **Makoba Woods Camp**.

FREE **Main (Rhino) Camp**   CAMPGROUND
(Map p116) Tsodilo Hills' main campsite has a simple ablutions block with sit-down toilets and cold-water showers; staff sometimes lock the block in the evening. The campsite is rarely full and it shouldn't be too hard to

---

TSODILO ROCK ART

The rock art of the Tsodilo Hills is at once sacred to the San and a stirring chronological record of the region's natural history rendered in pictorial form. The paintings here are usually known as 'finger paintings', and most were executed in ochre or red (obtained from hematite extracted from the local rocks) and then filled in with the same (or a lighter) colour. Around half of the paintings represent animals (giraffes, eland, cattle and rhinoceros are the most prevalent forms), with geometric patterns and human figures making up the rest. The older paintings, which are thought to date from the Later Stone Age to the Iron Age, are generally attributed to the San. However, it's fairly certain that the most recent works (usually rendered in white) were painted by 'copycat' Bantu artists. Interestingly, neither the San nor the Mbukushu accept responsibility for any of the works, maintaining that the paintings have been there longer than even legend can recall.

If you're looking for more detailed information on the hills, look for *Contested Images*, which contains a chapter on the Tsodilo Hills by Alec Campbell. For more on rock art in general (although it has a small section on the Tsodilo Hills), try *African Rock Art* by David Coulson and Alec Campbell. You could also contact the **Trust for African Rock Art** (TARA; www.africanrockart.org).

Tsodilo Hills

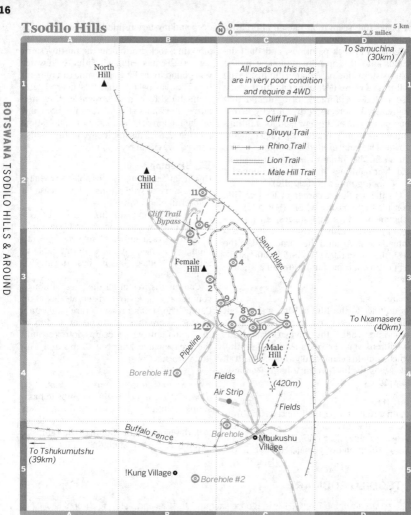

0   5 km
0   2.5 miles

To Samuchina
(30km)

All roads on this map
are in very poor condition
and require a 4WD

- - - - Cliff Trail
▫▫▫▫▫ Divuyu Trail
⊢—⊢—⊢ Rhino Trail
═══ Lion Trail
· · · · Male Hill Trail

North
Hill ▲

Child
Hill ▲

Cliff Trail
Bypass

11
6
3

Female
Hill ▲

4

2

9

8 1

7   5

12

10

Male
Hill ▲

Sand Ridge

To Nxamasere
(40km)

Pipeline

Borehole #1

Fields

Air Strip

(420m)

Fields

Buffalo Fence

Borehole

Mbukushu
Village

To Tshukumutshu
(39km)

!Kung Village ●   ◎ Borehole #2

find a shady corner, although the sites are close together and dusty rather than green. The camp is the closest to the main trail trailhead.

❶ Getting There & Away

CAR

Although numerous routes connect the Sehithwa–Shakawe road with the Tsodilo Hills, the good gravel track is the only one worth recommending. It's well signposted off the main road just south of Nxamasere village, and around 35km from the main road to the entrance to the site.

MOBILE SAFARIS

Although it might be possible to arrange a mobile safari to the Tsodilo Hills through one of the operators in Maun, you'll need a group to avoid skyrocketing costs.

KALAHARI

The parched alter ego of the Okavango Delta, the Kalahari is a primeval landscape, recalling in stone, thorns and brush the earliest memories of the human experience. This impression of a land where time began

Tsodilo Hills

finds voice in the hot winds and snap of thorn bush under a San tracker's feet in the Kalahari. It is the timeless roar of a Kalahari lion resonating across the still desert air. It is a valley that cuts through the desert's heart and follows the path left by ancient rivers that long ago disappeared into the dust.

The Tswana call this the Kgalagadi: Land of Thirst. And this is indeed dry, parched country. By some accounts, the Kalahari has the largest volume of sand of any desert on earth. Such statistics can be misleading – this is no desert of rolling sand dunes. But this is undoubtedly a land painted by a sand palette: blood and mud reds and bleached bone yellow; dust that bites you back as you taste it in the morning. But come the nights, this hard end of the colour wheel shifts into its cooler, sometimes white-cold shades: indigo nights that fade to deepest black, and blue stars ice-speckling the impossibly long horizon. Indeed, the local San insist that

here you can hear 'the stars in song' behind the dark.

The Kalahari's 1.2-million-sq-km basin stretches across parts of the Democratic Republic of the Congo, Angola, Zambia, Namibia, Botswana, Zimbabwe and South Africa, and in Botswana it also includes places like the Tsodilo Hills and Makgadikgadi Pans. But in this section here we focus on the chain of parks and small towns that cut through the centre and south of the country.

Ghanzi

POP 15,700

The 'capital of the Kalahari' isn't much more than a break in the dust. It may be difficult to understand how a town could prosper in such inhospitable terrain, but it helps that Ghanzi sits atop a 500km-long low limestone ridge containing vast amounts of artesian water. The town itself is a place of few attractions, but its appeal lies in its statistics – Ghanzi is 275km from Maun, 540km from Windhoek and 636km from Gaborone. Spend any time in the country's west and you're likely to spend some time here, whether to fill your petrol tank, stock up on supplies or get a good night's sleep.

Interestingly enough, the name 'Ghanzi' comes from the San word for a one-stringed musical instrument with a gourd soundbox, and *not* the Setswana word *gantsi* (flies), though this would arguably be more appropriate.

🛏 Sleeping & Eating

Most places can hook you up with wildlife drives, San cultural activities and the like. Interesting alternatives to staying in Ghanzi are the Dqãe Qare Game Farm (p120) in nearby D'kar and Grassland Safari Lodge (p120), 60km east.

BORDER CROSSING: NAMIBIA

The **Buitepost–Mamuno Gate** (7am to midnight) is convenient for travelling between Windhoek and Gaborone, the Kalahari or Maun. Like most such crossings, it is for the most part hassle-free, but remember when calculating the border post's opening hours that Namibia is one hour behind Botswana from late May until the end of August. As always, coming into Botswana your car will be searched for fresh meat, fresh fruit and dairy products (these will be confiscated if found), and you may be required to walk through a soda solution (and drive your car through the same) as part of measures to protect the country from foot-and-mouth disease.

There's a supermarket diagonally across the intersection from the Kalahari Arms Hotel

Thakadu Bush Camp

CAMPGROUND **$$**

(7212 0695; www.thakadubushcamp.com; campsite per person P70, s P455-595, d P615-770, s/d cottage with shared bathroom P220/290;) This popular campsite is a fun place to stop for a night or three, enjoying the boozy, friendly ambience and letting the stars soar overhead. There's a refreshing swimming pool on-site and a pub-style restaurant and bar. The rough access road is just passable to low-slung 2WD vehicles – use caution. The campsite is located 6km southwest of Ghanzi.

Kalahari Arms Hotel

HOTEL **$$**

(659 6298; www.kalahariarmshotel.com; Henry Jankie Dr; campsite per person P60, s/d P620/710;) This Ghanzi institution has modern (if slightly tired) rooms with air-con and cable TV, though the campsite is cramped and can be noisy. The rooms in *rondavels* in the garden by the pool are nicest and cost the same as other accommodation. The dining room at the Kalahari Arms is Ghanzi's only real restaurant. Although it's a bit pricey (mains from P60), the menu has all the usual suspects of steak, chips and pasta, and in Ghanzi you won't exactly be spoiled for choice.

Tautona Lodge

LODGE **$$**

(659 7499; www.tautonalodge.com; campsite per person P100, s/d P595/780, chalets from P700/860;) This reasonable lodge is 5km northeast of Ghanzi, and has expansive grounds featuring two swimming pools and a watering hole that is frequented by antelopes. Spacious rooms in Batswana-style thatched buildings have air-con and cable TV, and are decorated with traditional spreads, although they're more comfortable than luxurious. It also has a range of chalets and family suites.

Kalahari

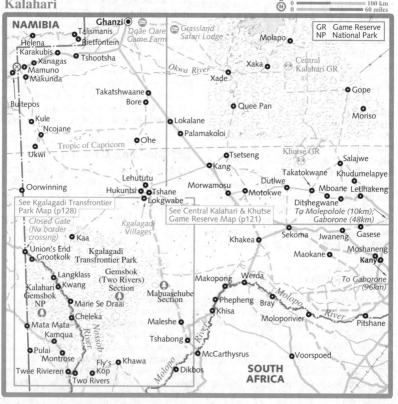

HENDRIK MATTHYS VAN ZYL

Since the 19th century, Ghanzi has served as a rest stop for traders and travellers crossing the Kalahari. Although the town has seen its fair share of odd characters, perhaps the most infamous (and ruthless) individual to pass through was a man by the name of Hendrik Matthys van Zyl.

During the 1860s and '70s, this former politician from the Transvaal in South Africa crossed the Kalahari on several occasions, trading munitions, shooting elephants and killing San along the way. From 1877 to 1878 Van Zyl based himself in the town of Ghanzi and proceeded to shoot more than 400 elephants, which yielded no less than 4 tonnes of ivory. With the proceeds from the ivory sales, Van Zyl built a two-storey mansion with stained-glass windows, filled it with imported furniture, and lived like a king in the poverty-stricken wilderness.

However, Van Zyl was suddenly and mysteriously killed in 1880, which gave rise to a series of legends surrounding the cause of his death. According to one tale, Van Zyl was murdered by a revenge-seeking San, possibly one of his own servants. Another tale claims that he was murdered by the Khoikhoi people in retaliation for past injustices. Shortly after his death, Van Zyl's wife, daughter and three sons disappeared to the Transvaal and were never heard of again.

Prior to his death, a rumour circulated that Van Zyl hid a large portion of his fortune in Gcwihaba (Drotsky's) Cave, although nothing has been recovered to date.

Ghanzi Trailblazers   CAMPGROUND $
(☑7210 2868; www.ghanzitrailblazers.co.bw; campsite per person from US$10, huts/chalets per person from US$20/40) This relaxed place offers guided walks with San guides, horse riding, Bushmen huts and simple motel-style rooms in chalets, as well as an OK campsite and communal dining area.

Tasty Chicken   INTERNATIONAL $
(Henry Jankie Dr; mains from P35) The local greasy spoon serves little more than fried chicken and chips, but in the remote Kalahari even that's something you might appreciate.

🛍 Shopping

Gantsi Craft   HANDICRAFTS
(☑659 6241; Henry Jankie Dr; ⊗8am-12.30pm & 2-5pm Mon-Fri, 8am-noon Sat) This cooperative was established in 1953 as a craft outlet and training centre for the San. It's an excellent place to shop for traditional San crafts, including hand-dyed textiles, decorated bags, leather aprons, bows and arrows, musical instruments and woven mats. Prices are 30% to 50% lower than in Maun or Gaborone, and all proceeds go to the local artists.

❶ Getting There & Away

From the bus terminal behind the BP petrol station along Kgosi Sebele Way, there are buses to Maun (P63, five hours, two daily) via D'Kar (P15, one hour), and to Gaborone (P130, 11 hours, three daily).

A combi leaves most mornings for the Namibian border at Mamuno (P35, three hours), but there are no cross-border services.

D'kar
POP 1670

This small village just north of Ghanzi is home to a large community of Ncoakhoe San who operate an art gallery, cultural centre and wildlife ranch under the auspices of the **Kuru Family of Organisations** (KFO; www.kuru.co.bw), an affiliated group of nongovernmental organisations (NGOs) working towards the empowerment of the indigenous peoples of Southern Africa.

◉ Sights

FREE **Kuru Art Project**   CRAFT
(☑659 6102; ⊗8am-12.30pm & 2-5pm Mon-Fri) This fabulous art project provides opportunities for local artists to create and sell paintings and other artwork; it's worth spending an hour or two leafing through the various folios of artworks. It's well signposted along D'kar's only road, close to the turn-off to the Ghanzi–Maun highway.

FREE **Museum**   CULTURAL CENTRE
(⊗8am-12.30pm & 2-5pm Mon-Fri) When we last visited, there were plans for this dusty little museum to be overhauled; in the meantime,

it's a modest affair with a few exhibits on San culture. It's almost next door to the Kuru Art Project.

🛏 Sleeping

Dqãe Qare Game Farm   CAMPGROUND **$$**
(📞7252 7321; www.dqae.org; campsite per person P60, San huts per person with/without half board P418/260, lodge rooms per person with/without half board P499/328) Dqãe Qare Game Farm is a 7500-hectare private reserve where visitors can participate in traditional activities organised by the local San community. There are guided bushwalks and plenty of opportunities to gain insights into traditional hunting and gathering techniques. Money spent at the farm is invested in the community. Although it's possible to drop by for an hour or two, spending a night either camping or in one of the San huts is a great opportunity to meet locals in a relaxed setting. The ranch is 15km southeast of D'kar and only accessible by 4WD. If you don't have a 4WD, contact the farm to arrange transport from D'kar/Ghanzi. These transfers cost P140/245 per four-passenger vehicle to the farm.

Grassland Safari Lodge   LODGE **$$$**
(📞7210 4270; www.grasslandlodge.com; s/d low season US$324/540, high season US$408/680) Unaffiliated with KFO but highly recommended by readers is Grassland Safari Lodge, located well off the beaten track, about 60km from the main Ghanzi–Maun road. This admirable lodge with its own waterhole runs a predator-protection programme that temporarily houses lions, cheetahs, leopards and wild dogs that are often shot by farmers protecting their livestock. It also conducts wildlife drives and horse safaris, and hosts excellent cultural activities with local San – Grassland's owner, Nelltjie Bowers, can speak the clicking Naro language. Contact the lodge in advance for directions to the property; it also offers transfers from D'kar for US$40 for two people.

Central Kalahari Game Reserve

The dry heart of the dry south of a dry continent, the Central Kalahari Game Reserve (CKGR) is epic in scale and, at all times, awe inspiring. If remoteness, desert silences and the sound of lions roaring in the night are your thing, this could become one of your favourite places in Africa.

Covering 52,000 sq km (about the size of Denmark), this is Africa's largest protected area. The CKGR is perhaps best known for Deception Valley, where Mark and Delia Owens studied brown hyenas and lions from 1974 to 1981, which is described in their book *Cry of the Kalahari*. Three similar fossil valleys – the Okwa, the Quoxo (Meratswe) and the Passarge – also bring topographical relief to the virtually featureless expanses, although the rivers ceased flowing more than 16,000 years ago.

Camping is only allowed at designated campsites, which must be booked in advance. You will not be permitted into the park without a campsite reservation.

The nearest reliable petrol supplies are located in Ghanzi, Maun and Rakops. Collecting firewood is banned in the CKGR, so bring your own.

☞ Tours

Most lodges and tour operators in Maun can organise mobile safaris around the CKGR. Trips can cost anywhere from US$150 to US$250 per day, though prices can vary greatly according to the season and the number of people in the party. It's easier to get a lower price if you're booking as part of a group.

🛏 Sleeping

There are campsites dotted around the reserve. Most lack facilities, but most campsites have a *braai* pit, bucket showers and a pit toilet. You'll need to be fully self-sufficient for water, food and petrol. The more expensive lodges within the CKGR are usually accessed via charter flight.

Kori Camp Site   CAMPGROUND **$**
(📞381 0774; dwnp@gov.bw; campsite per person P30) The four campsites known as Kori sit on the hill that rises gently from the western shoreline of Deception Valley. There's plenty of shade and some have partial views of the valley, making it a wonderful base.

Passarge Valley Camp Sites   CAMPGROUND **$**
(📞395 3360; www.bigfoottours.co.bw; campsite per adult/child P200/100) These three campsites have no facilities, but their location on the valley floor (some kilometres apart) is among the best in the Kalahari. Site No 2, under a shady stand of trees in the centre of the valley floor, is simply wonderful and the world is yours and yours alone.

Central Kalahari & Khutse Game Reserves

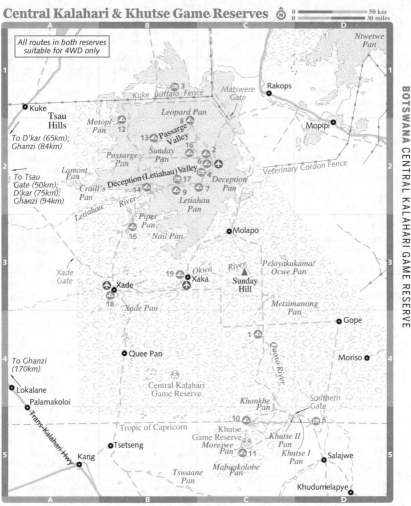

Central Kalahari & Khutse Game Reserves

Sleeping

1	Bape Camp Site	C4
2	Deception Valley Camp Site	C2
3	Deception Valley Lodge	B1
4	Kalahari Plains Camp	C2
5	Khutse Kalahari Lodge	D5
6	Kori Camp Site	C2
7	Lekhubu Camp Site	C2
8	Leopard Pan Camp Site	B2
9	Letiahau Pan Camp Site	B2
10	Molose Pan Camp Site	C5
11	Moreswe Pan Camp Site	C5
12	Motopi Camp Site	B2
13	Passarge Valley Camp Sites	B2
14	Phokoje Pan Camp Site	B2
15	Piper Pan Camp Site	B3
16	Sunday Pan Camp Site	B2
17	Tau Pan Camp	B2
18	Xade Campsite	B3
19	Xaka Campsite	B3

CENTRAL KALAHARI GAME RESERVE (CKGR) AT A GLANCE

Why Go?
The solitude of Southern Africa's largest desert, fine wildlife watching without the crowds and a sense of inhabiting one of the last great wilderness regions in Africa.

Gateway Towns
Ghanzi, Rakops and (at a stretch) Maun.

Wildlife
In the heart of the park, gemsboks, springboks and bat-eared foxes are common, as are lions, leopards, cheetahs, jackals and brown hyenas; wild dogs are also possible. Remember, however, that the desert environment ensures that wildlife densities are far smaller than in places like Chobe or Moremi but so too are the densities of safari vehicles – you need patience to see the wildlife here and the reward is that you might just have the wildlife all to yourself.

Birds
Birds are numerous around the ancient river valleys with sightings of larger species such as ostrich and kori bustard. The vivid crimson-breasted shrike is a common visitor to campsites.

When to Go
The park is most easily accessible during the dry season (May to September) when tracks are sandy but easily negotiated by 4WD vehicles. During the rainy season, tracks can be muddy and nearly impassable for inexperienced drivers; watch also for grass seeds clogging engines and searing temperatures in October.

Moving Around
Unless you're staying at an upmarket lodge in which game drives are included, or have organised your visit on a mobile safari from Maun, you'll need your own fully equipped 4WD to get around.

Budget Safaris
Maun is the best place to join a mobile safari into the CKGR, although in most cases you'll waste precious time if you arrive in town without a reservation.

Author Tips
Passarge Valley is far quieter than Deception Valley – we spent an entire afternoon driving along its length one July and saw not one other vehicle. Ask for the free photocopied map at the park's entrance gates. And finally, waterholes in some areas in the northern part of the reserve – Letiahau, Pipers, Sunday, Passarge and Motopi – are artificially pumped to provide water for animals and are good places to watch and wait.

Piper Pan Camp Site   CAMPGROUND **$**
(☑395 3360; www.bigfoottours.co.bw; campsite per adult/child P200/100) Slightly removed from the main circuit in the heart of the reserve, Piper Pan has a wonderfully remote feel and wildlife watching is good thanks to a waterhole next to the pans. The pans are 26km southwest off the main Letiahau track. Check the Bigfoot Tours website for GPS coordinates.

Motopi Camp Site   CAMPGROUND **$**
(☑395 3360; wwwbigfoottours.co.bw; campsite per adult/child P200/100) In the northwestern corner of the reserve, these three campsites are wonderfully isolated from the rest of the reserve. Nearby Motopi Pan is great for wildlife, and lions are common in the surrounding area – we spent hours with one pride here without seeing another vehicle. When we visited, the Tracks4Africa satellite-navigation program was incorrect for the three sites, which are some distance off the main track. While they're likely to have rectified that by the time you read this, just in case the GPS coordinates for the sites are: Campsite 1 (S 21°10.581', E 23°04.811'),

Campsite 2 (S 21°08.074', E 23°04.444') and Campsite 3 (S 21°09.927', E 23°06.097').

Deception Valley Lodge   LODGE $$$
(www.deceptionvalley.co.za; s/d Jun-Oct US$546/840, Nov-May US$458/704; 🐾) On the edge of the reserve, this exclusive bush retreat was designed to blend into the surrounding nature without detracting from its ambience. Soothing rooms blend Victorian and African design elements, and feature a private lounge and outdoor shower. The lodge is about 120km south of Maun, and the route is accessible to 2WD vehicles during the dry season.

Tau Pan Camp   LODGE $$$
(☑686 1449; www.kwando.co.bw; s/d from US$620/880; 🐾) The first camp to be opened within the CKGR, this solar-powered luxury lodge overlooks magnificent Tau Pan from a rugged sand ridge. Wildlife drives and San-led bushwalks are the order of the day, and neither disappoint, especially when the rains hit and this becomes one of Southern Africa's best wildlife-viewing locations. The

lodge maintains a strong eco sensibility throughout, and comes highly recommended by former guests.

Kalahari Plains Camp   TENTED CAMP $$$
(☑in South Africa 011-807 1800; www.wilderness-safaris.com; s/d mid-Jun–Oct US$756/1116, Nov-mid-Jun US$889/1382; ❄🐾) Run by the reliably luxurious Wilderness Safaris, these six posh, solar-powered tents are maintained in impeccable style in a gorgeous location near Deception Pass in the park's northeast. Black-maned Kalahari lions are common in the area, and the exclusive service plus total isolation makes for serious out-of-body travel joy.

ⓘ Getting There & Away

Airstrips (for chartered flights only) are located near Xade, Xaka and Deception Pan.

A 4WD is essential to get around the reserve, and a compass (or GPS equipment) and petrol reserves are also recommended. Several 4WD tracks lead into the CKGR, but not all are official entrances. Accessible gates:

THE SAN & THE CKGR

The Central Kalahari Game Reserve (CKGR) was originally established in 1961 as a private reservation for the San in order to protect them from the encroachments of the modern world and to protect their ancestral homelands. But the government of Botswana later changed its mind (primarily, critics say, because diamonds were found within the park's boundaries), and although the southern and western parts of the CKGR are still home to small populations of San, a recent wave of forced relocations has greatly reduced this population. The future of the San is now one of the biggest political hot potatoes for the current Botswanan government.

Nearly all of Botswana's and Namibia's San were relocated from their ancestral lands to new government settlements such as New Xade in the central Kalahari. In 2006 this resettlement programme earned the government a reprimand from the UN's Committee on the Elimination of Racial Discrimination. The Botswanan government maintains that its relocation policies have the San's best interests at heart. Development, education and modernisation are its buzzwords. The trouble is, many San actively rejected the government's version of modernisation if it meant giving up their ancestral lands and traditions.

After South Africa's highest court found in favour of the Richtersveld people (relatives of the San) of Northern Cape Province in 2003 – for the first time, the court recognised that indigenous people have both communal land ownership and mineral rights over their territory – the San of Botswana launched a similar appeal. The court case brought by the First People of the Kalahari (FPK) against the government's relocation policies was concluded in May 2006, and approximately 1000 San attached their names to the effort. During the proceedings many San tried to return home to the CKGR, but most were forced off the grounds of the reserve. In December 2006 the High Court ruled that the eviction of the San was 'unlawful and unconstitutional'. One justice went so far as to say that not allowing the San to hunt in their homeland 'was tantamount to condemning the residents of the CKGR to death by starvation'.

A few San have been allowed back into the reserve, although the government continues to drag its heels in fully implementing the court ruling.

Matswere Gate (GPS: S 21°09.047', E 24°00.445') The main gate, it's signposted off the tarmac B300 just northwest of Rakops.

Tsau Gate (GPS: S 21°00.081', E 24°47.845') In the reserve's far northwest and the most accessible gate from Maun.

Southern Gate (GPS: S 23°21.388', E 24°36.470') Along a track from Khutse Game Reserve.

Xade Gate The track to the gate starts near D'kar and is signposted.

Khutse Game Reserve

This 2500-sq-km reserve, which is an extension of the southern boundary of the Central Kalahari Game Reserve, is a popular weekend excursion for residents of Gaborone, but it's still deliciously remote and crowds are rare. It has all the attractions of the Kalahari, including good wildlife watching (although population densities are low), well-maintained trails and around 60 mineralised clay pans that once belonged to Africa's largest inland lake. Leopard and lion sightings in particular are possible.

The name Khutse, which means 'where one kneels to drink' in Sekwena (the local dialect of Setswana), indicates that the area once had water, though today the reserve experiences continual droughts.

Pick up the free photocopied map of the reserve from the park entrance. Camping in Khutse is only allowed at designated campsites. Although day trippers might be able to convince the park rangers to let you in for a look, officially you will not be permitted into

OTHER KALAHARI CAMPSITES

In addition to the campsites covered under the main sleeping heading, there are campsites at Deception Valley, Leopard Pan, Phokoje Pan, Xade, Bape and Xaka. These are all administered by (and hence bookable through) the Department of Wildlife and National Parks (p152).

Bigfoot Tours (395 3360; www.bigfoottours.co.bw; camping per adult/child P200/100) has additional campsites at Lekhubu, Letiahauand Sunday Pan.

the park without proof of a campsite reservation and it's a long road back to Gaborone if you don't have one.

The last reliable petrol supply is at Molepolole, although we were able to stock up at Lethlakeng. Food and drinks are available at Molepolole, Letlhakeng and (usually) Salajwe.

⊙ Sights

Khutse is at its best during spring and autumn, but try to avoid weekends and holidays (including South Africa's school holidays), as Khutse will be full of visitors.

Moreswe & Molose Pans

The pans at the western end of the reserve provide good wildlife watching thanks to the waterholes, one at each pan; the Moreswe waterhole was being repaired when we visited but there were still lions in the vicinity. Molose is busier, whereas Moreswe feels more remote. The most direct (but least interesting) trail from the reserve's entrance gate to Moreswe is 62km long, but the longer (72km) northern loop takes you past a series of pans and is much better for wildlife.

The Northern Pans

A series of pans – Galalabadimo, Sutswane, Khutse 2, Motailane, Tshilwane, Mahurushele, Sekushwe and Khwankwe – lines the main northern trail from the entrance gate all the way northwest to where the trails forge on north into the heart of the Kalahari. In fact, much of what is called Khutse, including the last three pans mentioned above, actually lies within the Central Kalahari Game Reserve, although it is administered as part of the Khutse Game Reserve.

🛏 Sleeping

Khutse boasts several superbly located campsites. In addition to the campsites reviewed by Lonely Planet, there are sites at Khutse, Mahurushele and Khankhe Pans. All are administered by Bigfoot Tours.

Moreswe Pan Campsite   CAMPGROUND $
(395 3360; www.bigfoottours.co.bw; campsite per adult/child P200/100) Our pick of the campsites in Khutse, these four sites far from civilisation are fine places to rest, and some have terrific, sweeping views over the pan, with the waterhole nearby. Each of the sites has a *braai* pit, bucket showers and a pit toilet. All three of the big cats are known

THE KALAHARI CONSERVATION SOCIETY

The Kalahari Conservation Society (KCS) is a non-governmental organisation (NGO) that was established in 1982 by former president of Botswana Sir Ketumile Masire. KCS was formed in recognition of the pressures on Botswana's wildlife and has spent the last three decades actively collaborating with other NGOs and government departments to help conserve the country's environment and natural resources. To date, the organisation has been involved in more than 50 conservation projects in the Kalahari, Chobe National Park, Moremi Game Reserve and the Okavango Delta.

The KCS aims to promote knowledge of Botswana's rich wildlife resources and its environment through education and publicity; to encourage, and sometimes finance, research into issues affecting these resources and their conservation; and to promote and support policies of conservation towards wildlife and its habitat. To achieve these objectives, the KCS relies on private donations, and memberships.

For more information, visit the website at www.kcs.org.bw.

to frequent the area. We stayed in site No 2 on our most recent visit and thought it one of the loveliest campsites in the country.

Molose Pan Campsite CAMPGROUND **$**
(☑395 3360; www.bigfoottours.co.bw; campsite per adult/child P200/100) Busier than the campsites at Moreswe (the four sites here are 24km closer to the entrance gate), these sites are nonetheless excellent, with a nearby waterhole maintained by the park authorities and open plains country offering good wildlife visibility.

Khutse Kalahari Lodge LODGE **$$**
(☑7197 2900; www.khutsekalaharilodge.com; r P750) Signposted off the main track from Letlhakeng to the Khutse entrance gate, this is the only lodge in the Khutse area. Rooms, now a little run-down, inhabit 24 attractively furnished *rondavels* and there's a cosy main dining area. Activities include game drives into the reserve and San-related experiences. You'll need a 4WD to reach the lodge.

❶ Getting There & Away

The entrance gate and park office are 210km from Gaborone. The road is sealed until Letlhakeng (109km from the park entrance), whereafter it's around 100km on a patchy gravel road to the turn-off to Kaudwane, then a sandy track for the last few kilometres to the park entrance. A 4WD vehicle is necessary for exploring the reserve.

Kang

POP 6560

The small settlement of Kang, 277km southeast of Ghanzi, sits at the turn-off to the Kgalagadi Transfrontier Park. As such, it's

an important crossroads town for those travelling between Namibia, South Africa and Botswana (at some places in town you can pay in the currencies of any of the three countries). Kang wouldn't win a beauty contest but it has a reliable petrol station as well as affordable places to eat and sleep.

🛏 Sleeping & Eating

Kang Ultra Stop MOTEL **$$**
(☑651 7294; www.kangultrastop.com; campsite per person from P40; r P390-560; ▣) At the main petrol station in town, Kang Ultra Stop aims to meet all of your needs in one. The motel-style rooms are simple but reasonably priced and well maintained, the restaurant (mains from P40) serves uninspiring but filling meals such as chicken schnitzel or pizza, and the petrol station has a general store and curio shop. There's also a bar that can get rowdy in the evenings.

Kang Echo Lodge MOTEL **$$**
(☑651 7094; www.echolodge.co.bw; r from P525) Similar in style to Kang Ultra Stop, Kang Echo Lodge has comfortable if uninspiring motel-style rooms that are set back a little from the highway. The Ultra Stop's facilities, including restaurant, are a short walk away.

Nkisi Guesthouse GUESTHOUSE **$$**
(☑651 7374; www.nkisiguesthouse.com; d/f from P520/650; ▣) The third of three places to stay clustered around the petrol station, Nkisi has a touch more style, with rooms sporting earthy colour schemes; some rooms are also suitable for families, with bunks in addition to double beds.

VILLAGES OF THE KGALAGADI

Hukuntsi, Tshane, Lokgwabe and Lehututu are collectively known as the Kgalagadi Villages, and were one of the most remote areas in Botswana prior to the paving of the road leading to Kang. For travellers, the villages serve as the jumping-off point for Kgalagadi Transfrontier Park.

The main commercial centre for the four villages, **Hukuntsi**, is a good place to fill up on petrol and stock up on supplies. Along the route from Hukuntsi to Tshatswa (about 60km to the southwest) are sparkling-white salt pans that fill with water during the rainy season and support large populations of gemsboks, ostriches and hartebeest. Hukuntsi is 114km southwest along a sealed road from Kang and 271km north of Tshabong along a sandy 4WD track.

Tshane is 12km east of Hukuntsi and has a colonial police station dating from the early 1900s.

Lokgwabe, which lies 11km south of Hukuntsi, was settled by the Nama leader Simon Kooper, who sought British protection in Bechuanaland after leading the 1904 Nama rebellion in Namibia. He was subsequently pursued across the Kalahari by German troops and 800 camels. German detritus, including empty tins of corned beef, still litters the route.

Named after the sound made by ground hornbills, **Lehututu**, located 10km northwest of Tshane, was once a major trading post but is now little more than a spot in the desert.

There are no hotels in the area. If you're camping, ask for permission and advice about a suitable campsite from the *kgosi* (chief) in any of the villages.

Kang Lodge　　　　　　　MOTEL $$
(☑651 8050; www.kanglodge.com; s/d/ste P330/ 510/550; ❈) Just out of town along the road to Gaborone, Kang Lodge is similar to other places in town, although lone travellers get a better deal here. There's an OK restaurant (mains from P40) attached.

❶ Getting There & Away

Buses between Ghanzi and Gaborone pass through Kang, although there's no public transport into the Kgalagadi Transfrontier Park – you'll need your own wheels or be prepared to hitch.

Kgalagadi Transfrontier Park

In 2000 the former Mabuasehube-Gemsbok National Park was combined with South Africa's former Kalahari Gemsbok National Park to create the new Kgalagadi Transfrontier Park. The result is a 28,400-sq-km binational park that is one of the largest and most pristine arid wilderness areas on the continent. The park is also the only place in Botswana where you'll see the shifting sand dunes that many mistakenly believe to be typical of the Kalahari. This is true desert; in the summer it can reach 45°C, and at night it can drop to -10°C.

Kgalagadi is home to large herds of springboks, gemsboks, eland and wildebeest, as well as a full complement of predators, including lions (one estimate puts the lion population of the park at around 450), cheetahs, leopards, wild dogs, jackals and hyenas. Over 250 bird species are present, including several endemic species of larks and bustards.

Camping in the park is only allowed at designated campsites and must be booked at the DWNP office in Gaborone or Maun. You will not be permitted into the Botswana side of the park without a campsite reservation.

The two main gates (where entry permits are bought) are at Twee Rivieren (South Africa) and Two Rivers (Botswana). To reach the Mabuasehube section, there are gates along the tracks from the south, north and east, but entry permits must be bought at the park headquarters (at Mpaathutlwa Pan). There is also a 4WD track from Tshatswa to the new northern gate of the Gemsbok (Two Rivers) Section at Kaa.

Campers staying at the Polentswa and Rooiputs campsites can pick up firewood at Two Rivers campsite (Botswana), while petrol and basic food supplies are available at Twee Rivieren (South Africa). There are also reliable petrol supplies at Hukuntsi, Jwaneng, Kang and Tshabong. Maps of the combined park are available at the gates at Two Rivers and Twee Rivieren.

◉ Sights

MABUASEHUBE SECTION

The Mabuasehube section of the park covers 1800 sq km, and focuses on the low red dunes around three major and several minor salt-pan complexes. The largest, Mabuasehube Pan, is used as a salt lick by migrating herds in late winter and early spring.

TWO RIVERS SECTION

Although you can now reach the Two Rivers section from either Kaa or Mabuasehube, access is still easiest from South Africa. The pools of rainwater that collect in the dry riverbeds of the Auob and Nossob Rivers provide the best opportunities for wildlife viewing in the park.

KALAHARI GEMSBOK NATIONAL PARK (SOUTH AFRICA)

This section is characterised by a semidesert landscape of Kalahari dunes, camelthorn-dotted grasslands and the dry beds of the Auob and Nossob Rivers. One advantage of visiting this side of the park is that many roads are accessible by 2WD.

🏃 Activities

There are several challenging wilderness tracks through this remote corner of Botswana. The **Nossob Eco Trail** is a four-day hike, entirely self-catered, that stops at basic campsites along the way. Hand-held radios are provided for the journey, which requires a minimum of two and a maximum of five vehicles. The cost per vehicle (maximum five occupants) is R1730. You must prebook through the DWNP (p152) in Gaborone.

The Swartbas Wilderness Trail (☏054-561 2000) is a two-day hiking track with basic camping facilities accessible by sturdy 4WD. It is closed from April to November.

🛏 Sleeping

All campsites in the Botswana sections of the park must be booked in advance through the DWNP (☏381 0774; dwnp@gov.bw; camping per person P30).

Bookings for huts and chalets on the South African side are recommended from June to September and during all weekends and public and school holidays. Contact the National Parks Board (☏South Africa 012-428 9111; www.sanparks.org).

MABUASEHUBE SECTION

There are rudimentary campsites at Lesholoago Pan, Khiding Pan, Mabuasehube Pan, Mpaathutlwa Pan, Monamodi Pan and

---

KGALAGADI TRANSFRONTIER PARK AT A GLANCE

Why Go?
This, at last, is the Kalahari of your imagination, with rolling red sand dunes, arid savannah and good wildlife watching.

Gateway Towns
Kang

Wildlife
The park is an important bastion of the Kalahari lion, with healthy populations of leopards, cheetahs, giraffes and gemsboks, among other species.

When to Go
The best time to visit is from December to May, although the park can be visited year-round.

Moving Around
You'll need your own 4WD vehicle for getting around the park, although some of the camps are accessible by 2WD.

Author Tip
Book your campsite as early as possible, especially if your visit coincides with South African school or public holidays.

Kgalagadi Transfrontier Park

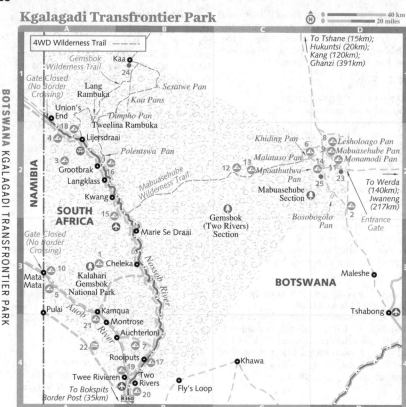

Kgalagadi Transfrontier Park

Bosobogolo Pan. Facilities are limited to pit latrines, but most have waterholes for viewing wildlife.

On the road between Mabuasehube and the Two Rivers section of the park you'll find Motopi 1 and Motopi 2 campsites. The former is 71km west of Mabuasehube (95km from Two Rivers), while Motopi 2 is 60km from Mabuasehube and 106km from Two Rivers.

TWO RIVERS SECTION

In the western area of the Botswana section of the park, campsites are found along the Nossob Valley at Two Rivers. Although within Botswana territory, these campsites must be accessed from the South African side of the border.

Two Rivers
CAMPGROUND $

(DWNP; ☎381 0774; dwnp@gov.bw; campsite per person P30) This site has cold showers and sit-down flush toilets and may be accessible from north of Bokspits in Botswana without having to go into South Africa first; check when making your booking.

Polentswa
CAMPGROUND $

(DWNP; ☎381 0774; dwnp@gov.bw; campsite per person P30) This simple campsite has shade and latrines but no running water.

Rooiputs
CAMPGROUND $

(DWNP; ☎381 0774; dwnp@gov.bw; campsite per person P30) A good site with shade and basic ablution blocks about 30km from Two Rivers.

Swart Pan
CAMPGROUND $

(DWNP; ☎381 0774; dwnp@gov.bw; campsite per person P30) A simple campsite.

KALAHARI GEMSBOK NATIONAL PARK

Huts and chalets are all equipped with bedding and cooking equipment. Each place has a shop that sells basic supplies, such as food, drinks (including alcohol) and usually petrol.

For information on the following camps, check out http://sanparks.org.za/parks/kgalagadi/tourism/accommodation.php.

Twee Rivieren
CAMPGROUND, CHALETS $$

(campsites R155-180, chalets R715-1040; ❋☎) The most accessible and popular rest camp on either side of the river, Twee Rivieren features a swimming pool and, unusually for this area, an outdoor bar-restaurant. Rustic chalets have modern amenities including air-con, hot showers and a full kitchen. This is the only one of the Kgalagadi camps to have 24-hour electricity and relatively strong mobile (cellphone) signal.

Nossob Rest Camp
CAMPGROUND, CHALETS $$

(campsites R180, chalets from R460, 2-/4-bed chalets R630/1275, 6-bed guesthouse R1040) This fairly basic rest camp is attractively situated alongside the Nossob River, just 3½ hours

from Twee Rivieren. There's generator electricity for 18 hours every day and the area is known for its predators.

Mata Mata Rest Camp
CAMPGROUND $$

(campsites R180, chalets from R615, 4-bed guesthouses R1040-1710; ☎) A pretty basic rest camp, Mata Mata sits alongside the scenic Auob River near the Namibian border and a 2½ hour drive from Twee Rivieren. There's generator electricity for 18 hours every day and giraffes are frequent camp visitors.

Bitterpan Wilderness Camp
CABIN $$$

(2-bed reed cabins R945) Getting out here requires coming through Nossob on a one-way 4WD-only route, but damn if these stilted tents hovering over a shimmering waterhole and within sight of red sand dunes aren't worth it for their sheer romance. The sense of isolation makes this the perfect Kalahari retreat.

Gharagab Wilderness Camp
CABIN $$$

(2-bed cabins R965) Blending into the wiry bush of the northern portion of the park, Gharagab is a dusty, surreally beautiful spot for watching sunsets over the local waterhole with sand dunes and thorn savannah all around. You'll need a 4WD to reach the camp, and accommodation is in log cabins with solar-powered electricity and hot water.

Grootolk Wilderness Camp
CABIN $$$

(2-bed cabins R1050) Only 20km from the Botswana–Namibia–South African border, and several eons from the modern world, these desert cabins are a desert escapist's dream. Usually accessible by 2WD vehicle, the camp is 2½ hours' drive from Nossob and six hours from Twee Rivieren.

Kielekranke Wilderness Camp
CABIN $$$

(2-bed cabins R1050) Another gorgeous set of tented cabins set deep within the Kalahari, Kielekranke has the usual self-catering kitchen with solar power. Check-in is at Twee Rivieren, 50km or 90 minutes away.

Urikaruus Wilderness Camp
CABIN $$$

(2-bed cabins R1050) A stilted camp hidden amid camelthorn trees that has good wildlife viewing near its dry riverbed and waterhole. The cabins are connected by an elevated walkway, and have kitchens and solar power. Check in at Twee Rivieren, 72km or two hours' drive away.

Kalahari Tented Camp　　　TENTED CAMP **$$$**
(tents R1070-1215) This series of 15 tents (including a honeymoon pitch – nice) perches over a waterhole in the dried-out Auob River, with stunning blood-red thirst lands all around. Basic supplies are available at Mata Mata Rest Camp, 3km away.

!Xaus Lodge　　　　　　LODGE **$$$**
(☑in South Africa 021-701 7860; www.xauslodge.co.za; s/d R4030/6200; ❄❃) If you're after a more luxurious experience, book a night in Kgalagadi's only upmarket lodge accommodation. Owned and operated by the local San community, the lodge is a dry, dreamy fantasy in ochre, decorated with wall hangings made by a local women's sewing collective and overlooking an evocative circular pan. The on-site pool feels a little much in these dry lands, but the San staff, cultural activities and excellent wildlife drives round out a wonderful package.

❶ Getting There & Away

Airstrips (for chartered flights only) are located at Ghanzi, Tshabong, Twee Rivieren and Nossob Camp.

The Two Rivers section is accessible from the south via Two Rivers and from the north via Kaa. Access to the Kalahari Gemsbok National Park is via Twee Rivieren. Both are about 53km north of the Bokspits border crossing. The border crossings to Namibia at Union's End and Mata Mata are closed because traffic disturbs the wildlife. Access to the Mabuasehube Section is possible from the south (via Tshabong), north (via Tshane) and east (via Werda).

UNDERSTAND BOTSWANA

Botswana Today

By any standards, Botswana's recent history is a lesson to other African countries. Instead of suffering from Africa's oft-seen resource curse, Botswana has used the ongoing windfall from its diamond mines to build a stable and, for the most part, egalitarian country, one whose economic growth rates have, for decades, been among the highest on earth. This is a place where things work, where education, health and environmental protection are government priorities. Even when faced with one of the most serious challenges confronting Africa in the 20th

century – HIV/AIDS – the government broke new ground in making antiretroviral treatment available to all.

For all such promising news, Botswana is far from perfect. The government's treatment of the indigenous San people remains a serious concern among human rights activists – in late 2010, Survival International called for a boycott of Botswanan diamonds, accusing the government of trying to force the San from their ancestral lands.

In the economic sphere, the country's dependence on diamonds is also a major concern when looking into Botswana's future; diamond production is expected to peak and then decline over the next 20 years. In 2012 the world's leading diamond producer began transferring its diamond-sorting operations from London to Botswana, an important step in granting Botswana a greater stake in the industry. Even so, the dependence on diamonds makes the economy vulnerable to a fluctuating world economy – when world demand contracted in 2009, so, too, did Botswana's economy (by almost 5%) for the first time in living memory; the industrial sector shrank by 30%. Impressive growth rates have since returned but the episode remains an important cautionary tale for the government. Unemployment stands officially at around 7.5%, but unofficially it could be closer to 40%.

Botswana's customary political stability – the Botswana Democratic Party (BDP) has ruled the country since independence – has been shaken a little in recent years, but only a little. A two-month strike over pay in 2011 was followed by defections from the ruling party, although some government members soon returned to the fold after the opposition failed to unify around a common platform. The BDP's hold on to power appears to be safe for a few years yet.

History
First Footprints

To understand Botswana, one must look deep into the past. Here, history extends back through the millennia to the earliest rumblings of humanity on the planet, when humans took their first footsteps on the savannahs of southern and eastern Africa. Developing rudimentary tools, these people hunted and gathered across the abundant plains, moving seasonally over grassland and scrub in and around the extensive wet-

THE UNHAPPIEST PLACE ON EARTH?

We've always found people in Botswana to be a pretty welcoming and cheerful lot, and their booming economy suggests that there is much for them to be happy about. But not everyone agrees. In 2012 the New Economics Foundation (www.neweconomics.org) surveyed people in 151 countries in order to create the latest version of its Happy Planet Index. Contrary to popular reporting in Botswana in the wake of the survey, the index doesn't measure people's day-to-day happiness. Instead, it reveals the efficiency with which countries convert their natural resources into long and happy lives for their citizens while maintaining a small ecological footprint. In other words, the countries that do well are those where people achieve long, happy lives without overstretching the earth's natural resources. Having languished in the lower regions since the index was created in 2006, in 2012 Botswana came in...*last*.

lands that once covered the north of the country.

By the Middle Stone Age, which lasted until 20,000 years ago, the Boskop, the primary human group in Southern Africa, had progressed into an organised hunting and gathering society. They are thought to be the ancestors of the modern-day San.

Archaeological evidence and rock art found in the Tsodilo Hills place these hunter-gatherers in shelters and caves throughout the region from around 17,000 BC. The paintings that gave expression to the natural world in which they lived attest to their increasing level of sophistication – clumsy stone tools gave way to bone, wood and, eventually, iron implements. Better tools meant more efficient hunting, which allowed time for further innovation, personal adornment and artistic pursuits such as the emerging craft of pottery.

Such progress prompted many of these hunter-gatherers to adopt a pastoral lifestyle – sowing crops and grazing livestock on the exposed pastures of the Okavango Delta and the Makgadikgadi lakes. Some migrated west into central Namibia, and by 70 BC some had even reached the Cape of Good Hope.

Settlement

Following the fragmented trail of ancient pottery, archaeologists and anthropologists have been able to piece together the complex, criss-crossing migration of different ethnic groups into Southern Africa. From AD 200 to 500, Bantu-speaking farmers began to appear on the southern landscape from the north and east. To begin with, relations between the San and Khoikhoi appear to have been cordial, and the groups mixed freely, traded and intermarried. After all,

there was much to learn from each other. The farmers brought with them new political systems, and superior agricultural and metalworking skills. At the Tswapong Hills, near Palapye, there's evidence of an early iron-smelting furnace that dates back to AD 190. One of the earliest and most powerful Bantu groups to settle in the region was the Sotho-Tswana, who consisted of three distinct entities: the Northern Basotho (or Pedi), who settled in the Transvaal of South Africa; the Southern Basotho of Lesotho; and the Western Basotho (or Batswana), who migrated north into Botswana.

Cattle herders began arriving from Zimbabwe around AD 600, and in the 13th century most of eastern Botswana came within the sphere of influence of Great Zimbabwe, one of Africa's most legendary ancient kingdoms. Between the 13th and 15th centuries, Great Zimbabwe incorporated many chiefdoms of northeastern Botswana, and the region was still part of Zimbabwe-based dynasties several hundred years later.

The only other significant migrations into Botswana were those of the Herero in the late 19th century. Faced with German aggression in Namibia, they fled eastwards, settling in the northwestern extremes of Botswana.

Rise of the Tswana

One of the most significant developments in Botswana's human history was the evolution of the three main branches of the Tswana ethnic group during the 14th century. It's a typical tale of family discord, where three brothers – Kwena, Ngwaketse and Ngwato – broke away from their father, Chief Malope, to establish their own followings in Molepolole, Kanye and Serowe respectively. Realistically, these fractures probably occurred

BOOKS ABOUT BOTSWANA HISTORY

History of Botswana (Thomas Tlou and Alec Campbell) Published in 1984 and essentially a school textbook, this is still one of the best resources on Botswana's past from the Stone Age to independence.

Missionary Travels (David Livingstone) Enjoy the drama of discovery in this evocative classic of travel literature. Janet Wagner Parsons' biography *The Livingstones at Kolobeng* is another good read.

Seretse Khama: 1921–1980 (N Parsons, W Henderson and T Tlou) The definitive biography of the country's first president.

Seretse and Ruth: Botswana's Love Story (Wilf and Trish Mbanga) An insider's account of one of the most dramatic love stories and political scandals of its time.

Building of a Nation: A History of Botswana from 1800 to 1910 (J Ramsay, B Morton and T Mgadla) Arguably the best account of Botswana's colonial history.

Botswana: The Road to Independence (P Fawcus and A Tilbury) An erudite history by two of Britain's most senior administrators during the protectorate period.

Diamonds, Dispossession and Democracy in Botswana (Kenneth Good) A searing critique of modern Botswana's rulers and its treatment of the San.

in response to drought and expanding populations eager to strike out in search of new pastures and arable land.

The Ngwato clan split further in the late 18th century, following a quarrel between Chief Khama I and his brother Tawana, who subsequently left Serowe and established his chiefdom in the area around Maun. The four major present-day Batswana groups – the Batawana, Bakwena, Bangwaketse and Bangwato – trace their ancestry to these splits and Botswana's demographic makeup owes much to the dispersal of the various groups.

The Difaqane

As people fanned out across Southern Africa, marking out their territories of trade and commerce, the peaceful fragmentation of the past became increasingly difficult. By the 1700s villages were no longer small, open affairs but fortified settlements situated on strategic, defensive hilltops. This antagonistic mood was exacerbated by the increasing trade in ivory, cattle and slaves, which prompted raids and counter-raids between powerful tribes eager to gain control over these lucrative resources.

The most prominent aggressor was the Zulu warlord Shaka, the new chief of the Zulu confederation. From his base in Natal he launched a series of ruthless campaigns aimed at forcibly amalgamating or destroying all tribes and settlements in his way. By 1830 the Bakwena and Bangwato areas had been overrun, and survivors had started the *difaqane* (literally 'the scattering' or exodus). In Shaka's wake came his equally ruthless Ndebele general, Mzilikazi, who continued to send raiding parties into the villages of Botswana and forced villagers to flee as far as Ghanzi and Tshane in the heart of the Kalahari. His troops also defeated the Bangwaketse, who fled into the desert, finally settling near Letlhakeng.

The Tswana states of Ngwaketse, Kwena and Ngwato were only reconstituted in the 1840s after the ravages of the *difaqane* had passed. Realising from their experience that their divided nation was vulnerable to attack, they began to regroup under the aegis of King Segkoma I.

These new states were then organised into wards under their own chiefs, who then paid tribute (based on labour and cattle) to the king. Botswana may have begun to unite, but the states were also highly competitive, vying with each other for the increasing trade in ivory and ostrich feathers being carried down new roads to the Cape Colony in the south. Those roads also brought Christian missionaries into Botswana for the first time and enabled the Boer trekkers to begin their migrations further north.

The Boers & the British

While Mzilikazi was wreaking havoc on the Batswana and missionaries were busy trying to convert the survivors to Christianity, the Boers were feeling pressured by their British neighbours in the Cape. The Boers were farmers from the eastern Cape in Southern Africa, the descendants of Dutch-speaking settlers. In 1836, around 20,000 Boers set out on the Great Trek across the Vaal River into Batswana and Zulu territory and proceeded to set up their own free state ruling the Transvaal – a move ratified by the British in the Sand River Convention of 1852. Effectively, this placed the Batswana under the rule of the so-called new South African Republic, and a period of rebellion and heavy-handed oppression ensued. Following heavy human and territorial losses, the Batswana chiefs petitioned the British government for protection from the Boers.

But Britain had its hands full in Southern Africa and was in no hurry to take on and support a country of uncertain profitability. Instead, it offered to act as arbitrator in the dispute. By 1877, however, animosity against the Boers had escalated to such a dangerous level that the British conceded and annexed the Transvaal – thereby starting the first Boer War. The war continued until the Pretoria Convention of 1881, when the British withdrew from the Transvaal in exchange for Boer allegiance to the British Crown.

With the British out of their way, the Boers once again looked northwards into Batswana territory. In 1882 the Boers managed to subdue the towns of Taung and Mafikeng, and proclaimed them the republics of Stellaland and Goshen. They might have gone much further had it not been for the annexation of South West Africa (modern-day Namibia) by the Germans in the 1890s.

With the potential threat of a German–Boer alliance across the Kalahari, which would have put paid to their dreams of expansion into mineral-rich Rhodesia (Zimbabwe), the British started to look seriously at the Batswana petitions for protection. In 1885 they proclaimed a protectorate over their Tswana allies, known as the British Crown Colony of Bechuanaland.

Cecil John Rhodes

British expansion in Southern Africa came in the form of a private venture under the auspices of the British South Africa Company (BSAC), owned by millionaire businessman Cecil John Rhodes.

By 1889 Rhodes already had a hand in the diamond-mining industry in Kimberley (South Africa), and he was convinced that other African countries had similar mineral deposits just waiting to be exploited. He aimed to do this through the land concessions that companies could obtain privately in order to colonise new land for the Crown. The system was easily exploited by Rhodes, who fraudulently obtained large tracts of land from local chiefs by passing off contracts as treaties. The British turned a blind eye, as they eventually hoped to transfer the entire Bechuanaland protectorate to the BSAC and relieve themselves of the expense of colonial administration.

Realising the implications of Rhodes' aspirations, three Batswana chiefs – Bathoen, Khama III and Sebele – accompanied by a sympathetic missionary, WC Willoughby, sailed to England to appeal directly to the British parliament for continued government control of Bechuanaland. Instead of taking action, the colonial minister, Joseph Chamberlain, advised them to contact Rhodes directly and work things out among themselves.

Naturally, Rhodes was immovable, so the delegation approached the London Missionary Society (LMS), which in turn took the matter to the British public. Fearing that the BSAC would allow alcohol in Bechuanaland, the LMS and other Christian groups backed the devoutly Christian Khama and his entourage. The British public in general felt that the Crown should be administering the empire, rather than the controversial Rhodes. Public pressure rose to such a level that the government was forced to concede to the chiefs. Chamberlain agreed to continue British administration of Bechuanaland, ceding only a small strip of the southeast (now known as the Tuli Block) to the BSAC for the construction of a railway line to Rhodesia.

Colonial Years

By 1899 Britain had decided it was time to consolidate the southern African states, and it declared war on the Transvaal. The Boers were overcome in 1902, and in 1910 the Union of South Africa was created.

By selling cattle, draught oxen and grain to the Europeans streaming north in search of farming land and minerals, Bechuanaland enjoyed an initial degree of economic independence. However, the construction of the railway through Bechuanaland to Rhodesia and a serious outbreak of foot-and-mouth disease in the 1890s destroyed the transit trade. This new economic vulnerability, combined with a series of droughts and the need to raise cash to pay British taxes, sent many Batswana to South Africa to look for work on farms and in mines. Up to 25% of Botswana's male population was abroad at any one time. This accelerated the breakdown of traditional land-use patterns and eroded the chiefs' powers.

The British government continued to regard the protectorate as a temporary expedient until it could be handed over to Rhodesia or the new Union of South Africa. Accordingly, investment and administrative development within the territory were kept to a bare minimum. Even when there were moves in the 1930s to reform administration or initiate agricultural and mining development, these were hotly disputed by leading Tswana chiefs, on the grounds that they would only enhance colonial control. So the territory remained divided into eight largely self-administering 'tribal' reserves and five white settler farm blocks, with the remainder classified as 'crown' (ie state) land. Similarly, the administrative capital, Mafikeng, which was situated outside the protectorate's border, in South Africa, remained where it was until 1964.

Independence

The extent to which the British subordinated Botswanan interests to those of South Africa during this period became clear in 1950. In a case that caused political controversy in Britain and across the empire, the British government banned Seretse Khama from the chieftainship of the Ngwato and exiled him for six years. This, as secret documents have since revealed, was in order to appease the South African government, that objected to Khama's marriage to a British woman at a time when racial segregation was enforced in South Africa.

This only increased growing political agitation, and throughout the 1950s and '60s Botswanan political parties started to surface and promote the idea of independence, at the precise historical moment when African colonies elsewhere were seeking their freedom. Following the Sharpeville Massacre in 1960, South African refugees Motsamai Mpho, of the African National Congress (ANC), and Philip Matante, a Johannesburg preacher affiliated with the Pan-Africanist Congress, joined with KT Motsete, a teacher from Malawi, to form the Bechuanaland

People's Party (BPP). Its immediate goal was independence.

In 1962 Seretse Khama and Kanye farmer Ketumile 'Quett' Masire formed the moderate Bechuanaland Democratic Party (BDP). The BDP formulated a schedule for independence, drawing on support from local chiefs such as Bathoen II of the Bangwaketse, and traditional Batswana. The BDP also called for the transfer of the capital into Botswana (ie from Mafikeng to Gaborone) and a new nonracial constitution.

The British gratefully accepted the BDP's peaceful plan for a transfer of power, and Khama was elected president when general elections were held in 1965. On 30 September 1966, the country – now called the Republic of Botswana – was granted full independence.

In contrast to the situation in so many other newly independent African states, Seretse Khama wisely steered Botswana through its first 14 years of independence. He guaranteed continued freehold over land held by white ranchers, and adopted a strictly neutral stance (at least until near the end of his presidency) towards South Africa and Rhodesia. The reason, of course, was Botswana's economic dependence on the giant to the south, but, that said, Khama refused to exchange ambassadors with South Africa and officially disapproved of apartheid in international circles.

Modern Politics

Sir Seretse Khama died in 1980 (not long after Zimbabwean independence), but his Botswana Democratic Party (BDP), formerly the Bechuanaland Democratic Party, continues to command a substantial majority in the Botswana parliament. Sir Ketumile 'Quett' Masire, who succeeded Khama as president from 1980 to 1998, followed the path laid down by his predecessor and continued to cautiously follow pro-Western policies.

Festus Mogae handed over the presidency to vice-president Ian Khama (son of Sir Seretse Khama) on 1 April 2008, and in the same year he won the prestigious Mo Ibrahim Prize for African Leadership, a US$5 million windfall aimed in part at rewarding good governance and those African leaders who voluntarily relinquish the reins of power. Whatever the international community thought of Mogae, his decision to make Khama president generated concern at home as Khama had not yet been

DIAMONDS: A COUNTRY'S BEST FRIEND

In the 1960s Botswana ranked as one of the world's poorest countries, with GDP per capita at less than US$200. Educational facilities were minimal, with less than 2% of the population having completed primary school and fewer than 100 students enrolled in university. In the entire country there was only one, 12km-long, sealed road.

Then, in 1967, everything changed with the discovery of diamonds at Orapa. Two other major mines followed at Letlhakane in 1977 and Jwaneng in 1982, making Botswana the world's leading producer of gem-quality stones – Botswana still extracts around one-quarter of the world's diamond supply. With the exception of the Lerala mine, opened in 2008, the country's diamond industry is run by Debswana, a joint venture between the Botswanan government and South African company De Beers.

Where other African countries have squandered the proceeds of bountiful natural resources or have descended into conflict in what has become known as the 'resource curse', Botswana has bucked the trend. The government has spread this wealth throughout Botswana's small population fairly equitably, and diamond dollars have been ploughed into infrastructure, education (adult literacy stands at 84.4%) and health. Private business has been allowed to grow and foreign investment has been welcomed. In 1994 Botswana became the first country in the world to graduate from the UN's Least Developed Country Status, a league table of development based around key economic, social and quality-of-life indicators. From 1966 to 2005 Botswana's economy grew faster than any other in the world. In 2011 Botswana ranked 32nd on Transparency International's Corruption Perception Index, the highest ranking of any country in Africa. In the same year, Botswana's GDP per capita was a respectable US$16,200, compared with US$500 in Zimbabwe, US$1600 in Zambia, US$7500 in Namibia and US$11,100 in South Africa.

Conscious of the need to develop alternative revenue streams, Botswana's government is desperately trying to diversify into manufacturing, light engineering, food processing and textiles. Tourism, too, is set to play a major role in the country's future, although the challenge remains to increase revenue without adversely affecting the environment and local communities.

elected as president. Since assuming power, Khama has cracked down on drinking, demanding earlier curfews at bars (sometimes enforced, sometimes not). In addition, Khama, a former commander of the Botswana Defence Force, has appointed military and law enforcement colleagues to government posts traditionally held by civilians, which has caused some concern in civil society. Nonetheless, the BDP with Khama at the helm easily won elections in October 2009.

People of Botswana

All citizens of Botswana – regardless of colour, ancestry or tribal affiliation – are known as Batswana (plural) or Motswana (singular). Almost everyone, including members of non-Tswana tribes, communicates via the lingua franca of Setswana, a native language, rather than the official language of English. Alongside language, education has played an important role in building a unified country, and the government proudly claims that its commitment of over 30% of its budget to education is the highest per capita in the world.

In Tswana, tribal groups are usually denoted by the prefix 'ba', which means 'the people of...'. Therefore, the Herero are known as Baherero, the Kgalagadi as Bakgalagadi, and so on. Botswana's eight major tribes (there are 26 tribal groups in all) are represented in the House of Chiefs.

Tswana

Botswana means 'land of the Tswana' and about 80% of the country's population claims Tswana heritage. The origins of the Tswana are simple enough. As land-owning agriculturalists, the Tswana ethnic group has clearly defined areas of influence. The Bangwato are centred on the Serowe area, the Bakwena in and around Molepolole, and the Bangwaketse near Kanye. A later split in the Bangwato resulted in a fourth group, the Batawana, who are concentrated near Maun in the northwest.

HIV/AIDS: A NATIONAL CATASTROPHE

While sub-Saharan Africa is home to roughly 11% of the world's population, it currently accounts for almost 67% of all estimated global HIV cases. Twenty-four of the world's most affected countries are in Africa, and Botswana's HIV prevalence places it second among them. According to UNAIDS and the World Health Organization, 24.8% of all adult Batswana are HIV positive, and women represent over half of those cases.

Botswana symbolises the tremendous challenge that HIV/AIDS poses to African development in the 21st century. It is blessed with sizeable diamond reserves that have fuelled rapid economic growth since independence and have raised incomes for thousands of its citizens to world-class standards. Yet almost 6000 people die of HIV/AIDS here every year and life expectancy (56.93 years for men, 54.51 years for women) is far lower than it should be in a country with Botswana's impressive economic profile; it's estimated that without the scourge of AIDS, life expectancy in Botswana would now be on a par with the USA. In 2001 former president Festus Mogae lamented that, unless the epidemic was reversed, his country faced 'blank extinction'. Some economic experts also fear that AIDS will make Botswana poorer by the day, as the virus tends to hit people in their most productive years.

In the midst of all the gloom, Botswana has taken some of the most admirable steps of any sub-Sahara African nation in reversing the damaging trends wrought by AIDS. In 2001 Botswana became the first African country to trial antiretroviral (ARV) drug therapy on a national scale, for which it earned international praise. And it is one of just a handful of countries worldwide that have committed to providing ARV treatment free to all of its HIV-positive citizens. In addition, it has committed itself to reversing the epidemic by 2016.

These policies are already bearing some fruit. Life expectancy has reached current levels from an appalling low of 35 years in 2005. In 2012 transmission of the disease from mother to child was down from between 20% and 40% to around 2%. Across Gaborone, you see billboards asking passers-by: 'Who is in YOUR sexual network?' But issues remain. Anecdotally, workers in medical nongovernmental organisations (NGOs) in Gaborone told us the prevalence of antiretrovirals has made some people less likely to practise safe sex.

To keep up with the effects of HIV/AIDS on sub-Saharan countries, log on to www. unaids.org, www.avert.org and www.who.int.

Known for being proud, conservative, resourceful and respectful, the Batswana have an ingrained feeling of national identity and an impressive belief in their country. Their history – a series of clever manoeuvres that meant they avoided the worst aspects of colonisation – has nurtured a confidence that is rare in postcolonial Africa.

The importance of the family in Batswana society has made the crisis caused by the HIV/AIDS pandemic particularly damaging. At last count, the country had more than 93,000 AIDS orphans, a staggering 4.5% of the population. How the country reacts to this breakdown of traditional family networks is one of the greatest challenges facing its people.

TRADITIONAL TSWANA CULTURE

In Batswana society, traditional culture acts as a sort of societal glue. Villages grew up around reliable water sources and developed into complex settlements with *kgosi* (chiefs) ultimately responsible for the affairs of the community. Respect for one's elders, firmly held religious beliefs, traditional gender roles and the tradition of the *kgotla* – a specially designated meeting place in each village where social and judicial affairs are discussed and dealt with – created a well-defined social structure with some stiff mores at its core. At a family level, in Batswana village life each family was entitled to land, and traditional homesteads were social places, consisting of communal eating places and separate huts for sleeping, sometimes for several family members.

Even today, as mudbrick architecture gives way to breeze blocks, and villages grow into busy towns and cities, most homes retain traditional features and life is still a very social affair. The atmosphere in family compounds is busy and convivial, although everything is done at a leisurely pace. Likewise, in shops and businesses people spend a huge amount of time greeting and agreeing with each other, and checking up on each other's welfare.

Historically, the Batswana are farmers and cattle herders. Cattle, and to a lesser extent goats and sheep, are still, in many ways, the measure of a family's status.

Bakalanga

Botswana's second-largest ethnic group, at around 11% of the population, the Bakalanga is another powerful land-owning group whose members are thought to descend from the Rozwi empire – the culture responsible for building Great Zimbabwe. In the colonial reshuffle, the Bakalanga were split in two and now some 75% of them live in western Zimbabwe. In Botswana, they are based mainly, although not exclusively, around Francistown.

Herero

The Herero probably originated from eastern or central Africa and migrated across the Okavango River into northeastern Namibia in the early 16th century. In 1884 the Germans took possession of German South West Africa (Namibia) and systematically appropriated Herero grazing lands. The ensuing conflict between the Germans and the Herero was to last for years, only ending in a calculated act of genocide that saw the remaining members of the tribe flee across the border into Botswana.

The refugees settled among the Batawana and were initially subjugated but eventually regained their herds and independence. These days the Herero are among the wealthiest herders in Botswana.

Basubiya & Wayeyi

The Basubiya, Wayeyi (Bayei) and Mbukushu are all riverine tribes scattered around the Chobe and Linyanti Rivers and across the Okavango Panhandle. Their histories and migrations are a textbook example of the ebb and flow of power and influence. For a long time, the Basubiya were the dominant force, pushing the Wayeyi away from the Chobe River and into the Okavango after a little spat over a lion skin, so tradition says. The Basubiya were agriculturists and as such proved easy prey for the growing Lozi empire (from modern Zambia), which in turn collapsed in 1865. They still live in the Chobe district.

Originally from the same areas in Namibia and Angola as the Mbukushu, the Wayeyi moved south from the Chobe River into the Okavango Delta in the mid-18th century to avoid the growing conflict with the Basubiya. They established themselves around Lake Ngami and eventually dispersed into the Okavango Delta. At the same time, the Bangwato (a Batswana offshoot) were pushing northwards and came into contact with the Wayeyi. Over time this relationship became a form of clientship, which many Wayeyi still feel resentful about today.

In 1948 and 1962 the Wayeyi made efforts to free themselves of Batswana rule, but neither attempt succeeded. In 1995 these efforts were renewed in a more concerted manner with the establishment of the Kamanakao Association, which aims to develop and protect Wayeyi culture and language. Following this, the Wayeyi decided to revive their chieftainship and on 24 April 1999 they elected Calvin Diile Kamanakao as Chief Kamanakao I and recommended him for inclusion in the House of Chiefs. The government rejected this proposal, so in 2001 the Wayeyi took the matter to the High Court, which passed judgment that chiefs elected by their own tribes should be admitted to the house. In 2008 the Wayeyi chief Shikati Fish Matepe Ozoo was appointed to the House of Chiefs by former president Festus Mogae. In the meantime, the UNHCR has pointed out that most Wayeyi children cannot speak their ancestral tongue, one of the keys to maintaining a distinct ethnic identity.

THE STATS

Botswana has one of the lowest population densities on earth: three people for every square kilometre which puts it on a par with Australia, Mauritania and Mongolia. An estimated 61% of people in Botswana live in urban settlements, mostly in eastern Botswana. Like most African countries, Botswana has an overwhelmingly young population, with an average age of 22.5 years, and one-third of the population under 14.

ETIQUETTE TIPS

Although there are a lot of rules of social etiquette within Batswana culture, foreigners are not expected to know or abide by most of them. Of course, you should maintain common sense – wearing shorts and T-shirts to church, for example, won't endear you to anyone. In general, you should always err on the side of modesty when interacting with locals. For instance, despite the way they dance at the club, Batswana traditional culture frowns on excessive public displays of affection between couples, married or not. Even public hand-holding is pretty rare. With that said, Batswana, who are used to riding in cramped combis (minibuses) and growing up in rural villages, may not have the same sense of personal space you possess, and might think nothing of resting a hand on your leg on a crowded bus.

Greetings are an important formality in Botswana and should not be overlooked. You tend to get better answers to your questions if you greet people with a friendly *'Dumela'*, followed by a *'rra'* (for men) and *'mma'* for women. It is also important to emphasise that a two-hand handshake (ie your left hand on your elbow while you shake) is preferable to a Western-style handshake. Putting your left hand on your elbow is also important when money is changing hands.

Because the national culture is so defined by hierarchy, it is not common for children to question or talk back to parents, or for underlings to contradict overlings. This shouldn't affect most visitors to the country, but it may explain why lodge or other employees are so deferential towards their bosses and sometimes unwilling to offer an opinion that may contradict their superiors.

Mbukushu

The Mbukushu (or Hambukushu), who now inhabit the Ngamiland area around the Okavango Delta, were originally refugees from the Caprivi Strip in northeastern Namibia. They were forced to flee south in the late 18th century after being dislodged by the forces of Chief Ngombela's Lozi empire. The Mbukushu carried on to southeastern Angola, just north of present-day Andara (Namibia). There, they encountered Portuguese and African traders, who began purchasing Mbukushu commoners from the tribal leadership to be used and resold as slaves. To escape, some Mbukushu headed back to the Okavango Panhandle, where they mixed and intermarried with the Batawana. Many remain in and around the villages of Shakawe and Sepupa.

San

The San are Botswana's first inhabitants: they were living in the Kalahari and Tsodilo Hills as far back as 30,000 years ago, as archaeological finds in the Kalahari have demonstrated. Some linguists even credit them with the invention of language. Unlike most other African countries, where the San have perished or disappeared through war and interbreeding, Botswana, along with Namibia, retains the remnants of its

San communities – barely 100,000 individuals in total, which may include many mixed San. Of these, around 60% live in Botswana (the !Kung, G//ana, G/wi and !xo being the largest groups), where they make up just 3% of Botswana's population, and 35% in Namibia (the Naro, !Xukwe, Hei//kom and Ju/'hoansi), with the remainder scattered throughout South Africa, Angola, Zimbabwe and Zambia.

For a window on the life of the San, join local hunter !Nqate in Craig and Damon Foster's film *The Great Dance*, an inspiring collaborative project that involved the local community at every stage of the filming and editing.

And a word on terminology: in Botswana you'll often hear the term 'Basarwa' being used to describe the San, but this is considered by the San to be pejorative as it literally means 'people of the sticks'.

THE PAST

Traditionally the San were nomadic hunter-gatherers who travelled in small family bands (usually between around 25 and 35 people) within well-defined territories. They had no chiefs or hierarchy of leadership and decisions were reached by group consensus. With no animals, crops or possessions, the San were highly mobile.

Everything that they needed for their daily existence they carried with them.

Initially, the San's social flexibility enabled them to evade conquest and control. But as other powerful tribes with big herds of livestock and farming ambitions moved into the area, inevitable disputes arose over the land. The San's wide-ranging, nomadic lifestyle (some territories extended over 1000 sq km) was utterly at odds with the settled world of the farmers and soon became a source of bitter conflict. This situation was rapidly accelerated by European colonists, who arrived in the area during the mid-17th century. The early Boers pursued an extermination campaign that lasted for 200 years and killed as many as 200,000 indigenous people. Such territorial disputes, combined with modern policies on wildlife conservation, have seen the San increasingly disenfranchised and dispossessed. What's more, in the modern world their disparate social structure has made it exceedingly difficult for them to organise pressure groups to defend their rights and land as other groups have done. Even so, they have enjoyed a measure of success in fighting their expulsion from the Central Kalahari Game Reserve.

THE FUTURE

Like so many indigenous peoples the world over, the San are largely impoverished. Many work on farms and cattle posts or live in squalid, handout-dependent and alcohol-plagued settlements centred on boreholes in western Botswana and northeastern Namibia, as debate rages around them as to their 'place' in modern African society. As such, the outlook for the San is uncertain.

Tourism provides some measure of economic opportunity for the San, who are often employed in Ghanzi- and Kalahari-based lodges as wildlife guides and trackers. But it is also argued that for this race to survive into the 21st century, they require not only self-sufficiency and international support but institutional support and recognition from within the Gaborone government.

For more on the San and the challenges they face in modern Botswana, contact the grassroots bodies such as SASI (South African San Institute; www.san.org.za) or Survival International (www.survivalinternational.org).

Religion

Batswana society is imbued with spirituality, whether that be Christianity or local indigenous belief systems. For most Batswana, religion is a vital part of life, substantiating human existence in the universe as well as providing a social framework.

Botswana's early tribal belief systems were primarily cults centred on ancestor worship. For the Batswana, this meant the worship of Modimo, a supreme being who created the world and represented the ancestors. Other ethnic groups may have differing cosmologies, but the majority of belief systems revolve around the worship of an omnipotent power (for the San it is N!odima and for the Herero it is Ndjambi) and the enactment of rituals to appease the ancestors, who are believed to play an active role in everyday life.

By the 19th century, Christian missionaries had begun to arrive, bringing with them an entirely new set of ideas that dislodged many indigenous traditions and practices. They established the first schools and as a result the Christian message began to spread.

Today about 30% of Batswana adhere to mainstream Christian faiths (the majority are either Catholic or Anglican), while around 60% adhere to the practices of the African Religion, an indigenous religion that integrates

THE HOUSE OF CHIEFS

Democracy may provide the basis for Botswana's political system, but the 35-member *Ntlo ya Dikgosi* (House of Chiefs) also plays an important symbolic role. A purely advisory body with no legislative or veto powers, the House of Chiefs has eight members who are hereditary chiefs from Botswana's major ethnic groups, 22 indirectly elected members who serve five-year terms (most are chiefs or subchiefs of other tribes) and five members who are appointed by the country's president. The House of Chiefs oversees all legislation that relates to tribal law, organisations and property, and must be consulted for any proposed constitutional changes. And although its legal power is limited, it would be a brave president who completely ignored the views of a body that represents significant elements of his constituency.

WOMEN IN BOTSWANA

If the statistics are to be believed, Botswana's women are clawing back admirably against centuries of inequality. Yes, only 7.9% of the country's parliamentarians are women, but 73.6% of adult women in Botswana have reached secondary school or higher (compared to 77.5% of men) and female participation in the labour force stands at 72.3% (compared with 80.9% among men). One of Botswana's Paramount Chiefs is a woman, and around half of the country's professional and technical workers are female.

But Botswana has a dark side and it's one that you'll rarely hear anyone speaking about. In a recent survey conducted by the **Women's International League for Peace and Freedom** (www.peacewomen.org), 86% of respondents rated violence against women as a community problem and 88% said it was on the increase. Over 60% saw severe beating as the most prevalent form of abuse; 47% identified rape. A third of respondents knew a woman who had fled her home due to violence.

Traditional culture is often cited as the 'excuse' for battering women, as traditional law permits men to 'chastise' their wives. Monica Tabengwa, director of Metlhaetsile Women's Information Centre, went on record saying, 'Most women expect to be battered and most men consider it their duty to batter'. Customary or traditional law has always regarded women as legal minors who require their husband's consent to buy or sell property and enter into legally binding contracts. That may be about to change after Botswana's High Court in 2012 overturned a customary law which prevented women from inheriting the family home, holding that the law ran counter to Botswana's constitution, which guarantees equal rights for men and women.

Botswana's current laws prohibit rape but do not recognise the concept of marital rape. The minimum sentence for rape is 10 years; the penalty increases to 15 years with corporal punishment if the offender is HIV positive, and to 20 years with corporal punishment if the offender knew they were HIV positive at the time of the rape.

Christian liturgy with the more ritualistic elements of traditional ancestor worship. It comprises a variety of churches (the Healing Church of Botswana, the Zionist Christian Church and the Apostolic Faith Mission), and is extremely popular in rural areas.

Arts & Crafts

Botswana's earliest artists were the San, who painted the world they lived in on the rock walls of their shelters. They were also master craftsmen, producing tools, musical instruments and material crafts from wood, leather and ostrich eggshells. This fundamental artistic aesthetic in the most utilitarian pots, fabrics, baskets and tools is one of Botswana's (and Africa's) greatest artistic legacies. But the contemporary art scene in Botswana is not confined to the material arts; there are also talented painters and sculptors producing some dynamic modern artwork.

Architecture

Traditional Batswana architecture is compact and beautiful, and blends well with the landscape. A typical village would have been a large, sprawling and densely populated affair, comprising hundreds of round mud-brick houses (*ntlo* or *rondavel*) topped with neat thatched roofs of *motshikiri* (thatching grass).

The mud bricks used for construction are ideally made from the concrete-like earth of the termite mound, and then plastered with a mixture of soil and cow dung. Often, the exterior is then decorated with a paint made from a mixture of cow dung and different coloured soils. The paint is spread by hand using the unique *lekgapho* designs, which are lovely and quite fanciful.

The thatch on the roofs is also an intricate business. Roof poles are taken from strong solid trees, lashed together with flexible branches and covered with tightly packed grass. When it's finished, the thatch is coated with oil and ash to discourage infestation by termites. Barring bad weather, a good thatching job can last five to 15 years and a *rondavel* can last 30 years or more.

These days, cement is the building material of choice, so the traditional home with its colourful designs may eventually die out. *Decorated Homes in Botswana*, by Sandy and Elinah Grant, is an attempt to capture just some of the wonderful examples of traditional architecture and promote the art of home decorating.

One interesting and accessible village where visitors can see traditional Botswanan architecture is Mochudi, near Gaborone.

Traditional Arts & Crafts

Handwoven baskets and the traditional crafts of the San are the best of a fairly modest collection of locally made traditional handicrafts. You will see some impressive woodcarvings and textiles in Botswana, but very few are produced here – most come from West Africa (Mali in particular) or the Democratic Republic of Congo. One exception is Oodi Weavers, close to Gaborone.

BASKET WEAVING

Botswana is most famous for the basketry produced in the northwestern regions of the Okavango Delta by Wayeyi and Mbukushu women. Like most material arts in Africa, they have a practical purpose, but their intricate construction and evocative designs – with names like Tears of the Giraffe or Flight of the Swallows – are anything but.

In the watery environs of the delta, the baskets serve as watertight containers for grains and seeds. The weaving is so tight on some that they were also used as beer kegs. All the baskets are made from the leaf fibre of the real fan palm (*mokolane*) and colours are derived from soaking the fibres in natural plant dyes. The work is incredibly skilful and provides one of the most important sources of income for rural families.

One of the best places to purchase the work is the Shorobe Baskets Cooperative in Shorobe, north of Maun. While it is always better to buy craftwork in the area in which it is produced (you tend to get better prices and the proceeds go directly to the community in question), another good place to browse for high-quality crafts is Botswanacraft Marketing (p54) in Gaborone.

SAN CRAFTS

Traditional San crafts include ostrich-eggshell jewellery, leather aprons and bags and strands of seeds and nuts (you may not be able to import these into some countries).

In recent years, traditional San painting has been experiencing something of a revival, with traditional themes wedded to contemporary techniques. The best places to see San art and handicrafts:

» Botswanacraft Marketing (p54), Gaborone
» Gantsi Craft (p119), Ghanzi
» Kuru Art Project (p119), D'kar

Dance

In traditional tribal societies, dance has an important symbolic role in expressing social values and marking the different stages of life. It is also a key component of traditional medicine and ancestor worship, where dance is a medium of communication with the spiritual realm. In a world without TV, it's also a great excuse for a community knees-up.

The best-documented dances in popular travel literature such as *The Healing Land* and films such as *The Great Dance* are those of the San, whose traditional dances have many different meanings. They were a way to thank the gods for a successful hunt and plentiful rains, to cure the sick and to celebrate a girl's transition into womanhood. Implements used in San dancing include decorated dancing sticks, fly whisks created from wildebeest tails, and dancing rattles, which are leather strings through cocoons full of tiny stones or broken ostrich eggshells.

One of the more interesting dances is the *ndazula* dance, a rain dance used to thank the gods for a plentiful harvest. Another is *borankana*, which originated in southern Botswana but is now enjoyed all over the country. It features in dance and music competitions and exhibitions, and is practised by school groups across Botswana. *Borankana*, which is Setswana for 'traditional entertainment', includes the unique *setlhako* and *sephumuso* rhythms, which feature in music by artists such as Nick Nkosanah Ndaba.

Most visitors will encounter traditional dancing in the rather staged displays at top-end safari camps. While they may lack the passion and spontaneity of traditional performances, such performances are important in preserving traditions that might otherwise be lost. A more genuine and less affected arena is the Maitisong Festival (p51), Botswana's biggest arts festival, held at the end of March in Gaborone.

Literature

The first work to be published in Setswana was the Holy Bible (completed by 1857), shortly followed by *The Pilgrim's Progress*. As you may gather from this, Botswana had

BEST BOTSWANA READS

Fiction

No.1 Ladies' Detective Agency (Alexander McCall Smith) The book that created a phenomenon.

Jamestown Blues (Caitlin Davies) Set in a poor salt-mining town, it explores the disparities between expatriate and local life through the eyes of a young Motswana girl.

Whites and **Mating** (Norman Rush) The first is a collection of short stories on expatriate life, the second a prize-winning comedy of manners featuring two Americans in 1980s Botswana.

Far and Beyon' (Unity Dow) Well-told chronicle of a family struggling with the often-contradictory pull of modern and traditional Botswana life.

Nonfiction

The Lost World of the Kalahari (Laurens van der Post) A classic and often eulogistic account of the disappearing culture of the San in the 1950s.

Cry of the Kalahari (Mark and Delia Owens) A wonderfully written tale of seven years spent living among the wildlife of the Kalahari.

Botswana Time (Will Randall) An endearing story of the author's time spent travelling with his school football team.

Twenty Chickens for a Saddle (Robyn Scott) Funny yet enlightening retelling of a childhood in the Botswana wilderness.

Place of Reeds (Caitlin Davies) Fascinating story of life as a Motswana wife and mother.

Serowe: Village of the Rain Wind (Bessie Head) An intriguing cultural study of life in Serowe in eastern Botswana.

little literary tradition to speak of until well into the 20th century.

Botswana's most famous modern literary figure was South African–born Bessie Head (1937–86), who fled apartheid in South Africa and settled in Sir Seretse Khama's village of Serowe. Her writings, many of which are set in Serowe, reflect the harshness and beauty of African village life and the physical attributes of Botswana itself. Her most widely read works include *Serowe – Village of the Rain Wind, When Rain Clouds Gather, Maru, A Question of Power, The Cardinals, A Bewitched Crossroad* and *The Collector of Treasures*, which is an anthology of short stories.

Since the 1980s Setswana novel writing has had something of a revival with the publication in English of novels like Andrew Sesinyi's *Love on the Rocks* (1983) and Gaele Sobott-Mogwe's haunting collection of short stories, *Colour Me Blue* (1995), which blends fantasy and reality with the everyday grit of African life.

Other novels that lend insight into contemporary Batswana life are *Jamestown Blues* (1997) and *Place of Reeds* (2005) by Caitlin Davies, who was married to a Motswana and lived in Botswana for 12 years.

Unity Dow, Botswana's first female High Court judge, has also authored four books to date, all of them dealing with contemporary social issues in the country; we recommend *Far and Beyon'* (2002).

POETRY

Like many African cultures, Botswana has a rich oral tradition of poetry, and much of Botswana's literary heritage, its ancient myths and poetry, is still unavailable in translation. One of the few books that is available is *Bayeyi & Hambukushu: Tales from the Okavango*, edited by Thomas J Larson, which is a primary source of oral poetry and stories from the Okavango Panhandle region.

Botswana's best-known poet is probably Barolong Seboni, who, in 1993, was poet in residence at the Scottish Poetry Library in Edinburgh. He has written several books of poems, including the short volume *Love Songs* (1994) and *Windsongs of the Kgalagadi* (1995), which details some of the Batswana traditions, myths and history that have been recited for centuries.

More modern poetry tends to highlight current issues. For example, *The Silent Bomb* aimed to promote awareness of HIV/AIDS. It was written by AIDS activist Billy Mosedame (1968–2004), who himself succumbed to the virus.

Music

Musical traditions run deeply through Botswana's culture and have done so ever since the earliest San societies where men gathered around their campfires playing their thumb pianos (*mbira*) accompanied by music bows. Compact discs and cassettes of traditional San music are available in D'kar and at Botswanacraft outlets in Gaborone.

Jazz, reggae, gospel and hip hop are the most popular forms of modern music – almost nothing else features on Batswana radio or is played live in nightclubs and bars.

One reliable measure of local talent is *My African Dream*, Botswana's version of *Pop Idol*. The show is faithfully watched across the country and, as these things are wont to do, has plucked at the musical dreams of many a Gaborone-bound Motswana youth.

JAZZ & REGGAE

Bojazz is the colloquial term for a form of music called Botswana jazz. It has been immortalised by Nick Nkosanah Ndaba, among others, who recently released *Dawn of Bojazz,* the first bojazz album to be produced in Botswana.

Another popular artist is Ras Baxton, a Rastafarian who plays what he calls 'tswana reggae', but he, like many other Batswana artists, has to go to South Africa to make a living. Banjo Mosele is huge all around the nation, while Bonjour Keipidile is perhaps the greatest living guitarist in Botswana.

Jazz performances are staged every few weeks in the winter (dry season) in and around Gaborone, including Bojanala Waterfront at the picturesque Gaborone Dam and at the huge National Stadium. These festivals are great fun, safe and cheap. Details are advertised in the English-language newspapers.

FUSION & HIP HOP

Other fusion sounds are *gumba-gumba,* a modern blend of Zulu and Tswana music mixed with a dose of traditional jazz – the word comes from the township slang for 'party'. Alfredo Mos is the father of *rumba kwasa,* that African bum-gyrating jive that foreigners have so such trouble emulating. Hot on his heels is *kwasa kwasa* king Franco, one of the most successful artists in Botswana at the moment, alongside the Wizards, Vee and Jeff Matheatau.

Wildly popular is Botswana's version of hip hop, championed by the Wizards, who fuse the style with ragga and R&B. It's nearly always been the case that talented Batswana musicians have had to move to South Africa to make a living, but at the time of writing there was still some decent talent here, including Kast, Scar, Vee and

THE NO.1 LADIES' DETECTIVE AGENCY & ITS AUTHOR

Gaborone may once have been one of the world's lesser-known capitals, but Alexander McCall Smith's runaway international success *No.1 Ladies' Detective Agency* has changed that forever. Based around the exploits of the Motswana Mma Precious Ramotswe, Botswana's first female detective, the book spawned a whole series of novels (13 at last count, plus two novellas for younger readers) with names like *Morality for Beautiful Girls, The Kalahari Typing School for Men* and *The Double Comfort Safari Club.* This is crime writing without a hard edge, a delightfully whimsical and almost gentle series of tales that seems to fit perfectly within Botswana's relatively peaceful society.

The author was born in Rhodesia (now Zimbabwe) in 1948 and went on to become a leading international expert in medical law. Before turning his hand to crime fiction, he wrote a number of children's books (among them *The White Hippo* and *Akimbo and the Lion*). He lectured at the University of Botswana from 1981 to 1984, but it was not until 1999 that his *No.1 Ladies' Detective Agency* was published, changing his life forever and putting Botswana on the literary map. Although he lives in Scotland, he has sponsored a number of projects in Botswana, including Gaborone's No.1 Ladies' Opera House (p54). And if you're a fan of the series, don't miss one of the themed tours of Gaborone (p51) and visit the author's website (www.alexandermccallsmith.co.uk).

Stagga-Don Dada. Kwaito music, the South African–township fusion of hip hop, house and all things that make booties shake, is also hugely popular.

Botswana Cuisine
Local Dishes

Local Batswana cooking is, for the most part, aimed more at sustenance than exciting tastes. Forming the centre of most Batswana meals nowadays is *mabele* (sorghum) or *bogobe* (porridge made from sorghum), but these staples are rapidly being replaced by imported maize mealies, sometimes known by the Afrikaans name mealie pap, or just plain pap. This provides the base for an array of meat and vegetable sauces like *seswaa* (shredded goat or lamb), *morogo* (wild spinach) or *leputshe* (wild pumpkin). For breakfast, you might be able to try *pathata* (sort of like an English muffin) or *megunya,* also known as fat cakes. These are little balls of fried dough that are kind of like doughnuts minus the hole and, depending on your taste, the flavour.

Oh, and don't forget mopane worms. These fat suckers are pulled off mopane trees and fried into little delicacies – they're tasty and a good source of protein. You might be able to buy some from ladies selling them by the bag in the Main Mall in Gaborone; otherwise, they're pretty common up in Francistown.

Kalahari Cooking

The more challenging environment of the Kalahari means that the San have an extraordinary pantry, including desert plants like *morama,* which produces leguminous pods that contain edible beans. There is also an immense tuber that contains large quantities of water. Other desert delectables include marula fruit, wild plums, berries, tsama melons, wild cucumbers and honey. There's also a type of edible fungus (grewia flava) related to the European truffle but now known to the marketing people as the 'Kalahari truffle'.

What You'll Actually Eat

Sadly, most travellers rarely encounter local dishes, not least because self-drivers are usually also self-caterers. Some top-end safari lodges do make variations on some of the more conventional Batswana meat and veg-etable recipes. In general, however, you'll be dining on international fare, some of which is quite sumptuous considering the logistical problems of getting food in and out of remote locations. One plate where local and international tastes converge is in the local obsession with steaks – Botswana's cattle industry is well regarded and its steaks are available in restaurants in most cities and larger towns.

Gaborone's Courtyard Restaurant (p52) is a rare and welcome exception to the separation of international clientele from local dishes – it serves impala or guinea-fowl stews among other local dishes.

Otherwise, many hotels offer buffets, and there's always a good range of fruit and vegetables. In larger towns you'll even find a selection of Indian and Chinese restaurants.

Drinks

Decent locally made beers include Castle Lager (made under licence from the South African brewery), St Louis Special Light and Lion Lager; also available are the excellent Windhoek Lager (from Namibia) and Zambezi Lager (from Zimbabwe).

Traditional drinks are plentiful. Legal home brews include the common *bojalwa,* an inexpensive sprouted-sorghum beer that is brewed commercially as Chibuku. Another serious drink is made from fermented marula fruit. Light and nonintoxicating *mageu* is made from mealies or sorghum mash. Another is *madila,* a thickened sour milk that is used as a relish or drunk ('eaten' would be a more appropriate term) plain.

Mosukujane tea and lengane tea are used to treat headaches/nausea and arthritis respectively. They're a bit strong in flavour, but locals faithfully tout their remedial properties.

Environment
The Land

Botswana is the geographic heart of sub-Saharan Africa, extending over 1100km from north to south and 960km from east to west, an area of 582,000 sq km that's equivalent in size to France. The country is entirely landlocked, and is bordered to the south and southeast by South Africa, across the Limpopo and Molopo Rivers; to the northeast by Zimbabwe; and to the north and west by Namibia.

THE KALAHARI

Around 100 million years ago the supercontinent Gondwanaland dramatically broke up. As the land mass ripped apart, the edges of the African continent rose up, forming the mountain ranges of Southern and Central Africa. Over the millennia, water and wind weathered these highlands, carrying the fine dust inland to the Kalahari Basin. At 2.5 million sq km, it's the earth's largest unbroken tract of sand, stretching from northern South Africa to eastern Namibia and Angola, and to Zambia and Zimbabwe in the west.

Depending on who you believe, between 68% and 85% of the country, including the entire central and southwestern regions, is taken up by the Kalahari. The shifting sand dunes that compose a traditional desert are found only in the far southwest, in the Kgalagadi Transfrontier Park. In the northeast are the great salty deserts of the Makgadikgadi Pans; in ancient times part of a vast superlake, they're now the largest (about 12,000 sq km) complex of salt pans in the world and considered to be part of the Kalahari.

In Botswana, large tracts of the Kalahari are protected, with at least five protected areas (listed from north to south):

Nxai Pans National Park (p74)

Makgadikgadi Pans National Park (p74)

Central Kalahari Game Reserve (p120)

Khutse Game Reserve (p124)

Kgalagadi Transfrontier Park (p126)

OKAVANGO DELTA

The Okavango Delta is one of Africa's most extraordinary landscapes, not to mention the antidote to the Kalahari's endless sea of sand. Covering between 13,000 and 18,000 sq km, it snakes into the country from Angola to form a watery paradise of convoluted channels and islands that appear and disappear depending on the water levels. The delta is home to more than 2000 plant species, 450 bird species and 65 fish species, not to mention an estimated 200,000 large mammals.

The delta owes its existence to a tectonic trough in the Kalahari basin, a topographical depression that ensures that the waters of the Okavango River evaporate or are drunk by plants without ever reaching the sea; the delta is extremely flat with no more than 2m variation in the land's altitude, which means that the waters simply come to a halt. The delta's waters surge and subside at the behest of the rains in far-off Angola, and every year around 11 cu km of water flood into the delta. The flooding is seasonal, beginning in the Angolan highlands in January and February, the waters travelling approximately 1200km in a month. Having reached the delta, the waters disperse across the delta from March to June, before peaking in July and August – during these months, the water surface area of the delta can be three times that of the nonflooding periods.

MOUNTAINS

Botswana could be one of the flattest countries on earth, but there are a few sites of topographical interest. The country's highest point above sea level is the rather modest Otse Hill (1489m) which lies around 45km south of Gaborone.

Of far greater interest are the Tsodilo Hills in the country's far northwest, with dramatic scenery and prehistoric rock art; the Tswapong Hills, a range of low, flat-topped hills cut through with vertiginous canyons, good for hiking and birdwatching; and the Tuli Block, shadowing the Limpopo River in Botswana's far east, with otherworldy *kopjes* rising up from the riverine plains.

Wildlife

Botswana is home to anywhere between 160 and 500 different mammal species, 593 species of birds, 150 different reptiles, over 8000 species of insects and spiders, and more than 3100 types of plants and trees.

LIONS

Lions may be the easiest of the big cats to spot – leopards are notoriously secretive and largely keep to the undergrowth, while cheetahs live in similarly low-density populations and can also prove elusive. But don't let appearances fool you: the lion is the most endangered of Africa's three big cats.

Fewer than 30,000 lions are thought to remain in Africa (there is a tiny, highly inbred population of Asian lions in the Gir Forest in Gujarat state in India), although most conservationists agree that the number is most likely considerably below that figure. Only six lion populations in Africa – the Okavango Delta is one of these – are sufficiently protected to hold at least 1000 lions, the conservation gold standard that the peak cat conservation body Panthera (www.panthera.org) applies for guaranteeing the long-term survival of the species. One of the

WHICH FIELD GUIDE?

Field guides can be invaluable tools for identifying animals while on safari, apart from being damned interesting to read. Our favourites:

A Field Guide to the Carnivores of the World (Luke Hunter, 2011) Wonderfully illustrated, up to date and filled with fascinating detail.

The Kingdon Field Guide to African Mammals (Jonathon Kingdon, 2003) The latest edition of the classic field guide covering over 1150 species.

Watching Wildlife: Southern Africa (Matthew Firestone and Nana Luckham, 2nd edn, 2003) Lonely Planet's very own field guide, complete with colour photographs.

Mammals of Botswana & Surrounding Areas (Veronica Roodt, 2011) Handy, well-written guide available in many lodges and bookstores around Botswana.

Birds of Southern Africa (Ian Sinclair et al, 4th edn, 2011) Easily the best field guide to the country's birds.

most comprehensive surveys of Africa-wide lion populations came up with an estimated population in Botswana of around 3000 lions (or roughly 10% of all lions left in Africa). Of these, the most important populations were in the Okavango Delta (1438 lions), the Central Kalahari Game Reserve (312), the Kgalagadi Transfrontier Park (458) and the Chobe River area (213). As such, Botswana is one of the lion's most important strongholds.

Like lions elsewhere, those in Botswana are facing threats from poisoning, in retaliation for either killing livestock or encroaching onto farming lands.

ELEPHANTS

Botswana has more elephants within its borders than any other country on earth. While elephants elsewhere are facing a renewed threat from poaching – an estimated 25,000 elephants were killed for their ivory in 2011 – Botswana's elephant populations remain in rude health. Latest estimates suggest that there are 130,000 elephants in Botswana, including as many as 71,000 in Chobe National Park alone – the Chobe population represents the densest concentration of elephants on the planet.

RHINOS

Rhinoceroses were once plentiful across Botswana, particularly in the north, with black rhinos concentrated around the Chobe River and white rhinos more widely spread across Chobe, Moremi and elsewhere in the Okavango Delta. But the poaching holocaust in the 1970s and 1980s that sent numbers of both black and white rhinos plummeting

across Africa saw the rhino all but disappear from Botswana. By 1992 the black rhino was considered extinct in Botswana, with just 19 white rhinos remaining in the country.

At around the same time, the 4300-hectare Khama Rhino Sanctuary was established, and all remaining rhinos were shut away there in a bid to save the species. The sanctuary has been something of a success story, protecting around 40 white rhinos and four blacks. Better still, in 2001 the Botswana Rhino Reintroduction Project, a collaboration between the government, conservation groups and tourism operators, began the process of sending rhinos once more out into the Botswana wild. At the time of writing, 32 white rhinos have been set free in Botswana's Moremi Game Reserve, particularly around Chief's Island and the exclusive Mombo Camp (the owners, Wilderness Safaris, were involved in the project from the beginning). Poachers killed two rhinos in 2003, but otherwise the population has continued to grow – with an estimated 11 calves having been born to released rhinos, the current population is believed to be 38 wild rhinos.

Two females refused to be confined to their new surroundings and were last seen in Makgadikgadi Pans National Park; in 2008 a male white rhino was sent to Makgadikgadi from the Khama Rhino Sanctuary in the hope of establishing a small population there.

Despite Botswana's relative distance from the epicentre of poaching, it cannot entirely escape the debate. In 2012 Botswana – along with Zimbabwe, Zambia, Angola and Namibia – took the controversial decision to sell rhino-horn powder to medical clinics and pharmacies in the region in a bid to undermine the illegal trade. A recent upsurge in rhino poaching – rhino horn had an estimated black-market value of €52,000 per kilo in 2012 – has seen the number of rhinos killed in neighbouring South Africa rise from 13 in 2007 to as many as 600 in 2012; with approximately 19,000 rhinos, South Africa is home to an estimated 90% of the world rhinoceros population.

AFRICAN WILD DOGS

One of Botswana's most charismatic creatures, the African wild dog (also known as the Cape hunting dog) is under serious threat. Where once half a million wild dogs roamed 39 African countries, only 3000 to 5300 remain in the wild in just 14 countries today.

African wild dogs live in packs of up to 28 animals, which may account for the fact that they have one of the highest hunting success rates (as high as 70%) of all carnivores. That and their maximum speed of 66km/h. Their preferred prey includes impala, red *lechwe*, wildebeest, steenbok and warthog.

Moremi Game Reserve is believed to be home to 30% of the world's population, with the Linyanti Marshes one of the best places to spot wild dog packs. Numbers are lower, but the species is believed to persist in the Central Kalahari Game Reserve. When we were in Botswana, an entire pack was wiped out when a cow carcass was laced with poison next to a wild dog den in the Tuli Block, an all-too-common scenario as this wideranging carnivore comes increasingly into contact with humans.

REPTILES

Botswana's dry lands are home to over 150 species of reptile. These include 72 species of snake, such as the poisonous Mozambique spitting cobra, Egyptian cobra and black mamba. Although about 80% of snakes in Botswana are not venomous, watch out for the deadly puff adder, much more frequently seen than the cobras and mamba. Tree snakes, known as boomslangs, are also common in the delta.

Lizards are everywhere; the largest are *leguaans* (water monitors), docile creatures that reach over 2m in length. Smaller versions, savannah *leguaans*, inhabit small hills and drier areas. Also present in large numbers are geckos, chameleons and rock-plated lizards.

Although Nile crocodiles are threatened elsewhere in Southern Africa, the Okavango Delta is full of them. You will hear rather than see them while gliding through the channels in a *mokoro* (traditional dugout canoe). Frogs of every imaginable shape, size and colour are more delightful; they jump from reeds to a *mokoro* and back again, and provide an echoing chorus throughout the delta (and elsewhere such as the Boteti River in Makgadikgadi Pans National Park) at night.

INSECTS & SPIDERS

Botswana boasts about 8000 species of insects and spiders. The most colourful butterflies can be found along the Okavango Panhandle (the northwestern extension of the delta), and include African monarchs and citrus swallowtails. Other insects of note include stick insects, expertly camouflaged among the reeds of the Okavango Delta; large, scary but harmless button spiders; and sac spiders, which look harmless but are poisonous (although rarely fatal) and live mainly in rural homes. The delta is also home to grasshoppers, mopane worms and locusts, as well as mosquitoes and tsetse flies in increasing and potentially dangerous numbers.

Scorpions are not uncommon in the Kalahari; although their sting is not fatal, it can be painful.

BIRDS

Botswana is not only a big wildlife country but also a birding paradise. Between September and March, when the delta is flush with water, you should be able to train the lenses of your binoculars on any number of Botswana's 593 recorded species, including the delta's famous African skimmers, the endangered wattled crane, slaty egrets, African

---

BOTSWANA'S ENDANGERED SPECIES

According to the International Union for the Conservation of Nature (IUCN), species which are listed as 'vulnerable' in Botswana include the cheetah, black-footed cat, lion and hippo. In greater trouble and listed as 'endangered' is the African wild dog, while the black rhino is considered 'critically endangered'.

USEFUL RESOURCES

Birding Botswana (☎7219 1472; www.birdingbotswana.com) Maun-based operator specialising in birdwatching safaris.

BirdLife Botswana (☎319 0540; www.birdlifebotswana.org.bw) BirdLife International's local chapter is actively involved in conservation projects, such as building observation posts, and organising birdwatching trips.

jacanas, bee-eaters, pygmy geese and the shy Pel's fishing owl. You can still see many bird species in the dry season, when it's often easier to spot them around the few remaining water sources.

BIRDWATCHING AREAS

Most of Botswana's best birding is concentrated in the north of the country around the Okavango Delta, including the Okavango Panhandle; the Chobe Riverfront; the Central Kalahari Game Reserve; Khama Rhino Sanctuary; and the Tuli Block, especially around the Limpopo River.

One especially good site is the Nata Bird Sanctuary which is home to over a quarter of Botswana's birds. The sanctuary is covered in a sea of pink flamingos, and other migratory birds, during the rainy season from November to March.

ENDANGERED BIRD SPECIES

Inevitably, the birdlife in Botswana is under threat from overgrazing, urban sprawl and insecticides that are used to tackle the scourge of tsetse flies that sometimes plague the delta.

Endangered among Botswana's birds are wattled cranes and African skimmers. Cape vultures, which are protected in the Mannyelanong Game Reserve in Otse, also have important breeding colonies in the Moremi Gorge in the Tswapong Hills in Botswana's east.

PLANTS

More than 2500 species of plants and 650 species of trees have been recorded in Botswana.

The Okavango Delta enjoys a riparian environment dominated by marsh grasses, water lilies, reeds and papyrus, and is dotted with well-vegetated islands thick with palms, acacias, leadwood and sausage trees. At the other extreme, the Kalahari is characterised by all sorts of savannah, including bush savannah with acacia thorn trees, grass savannah and arid shrub savannah in the southwest.

The country's only deciduous mopane forests are in the north, where six forest reserves harbour stands of commercial timber, as well as both mongonga and marula trees. Also common around Botswana are camel-thorn trees, which some animals find tasty and which the San use for firewood and medicinal purposes; and motlopi trees, also called shepherd's tree, which have edible roots.

For more on the plant life of the Okavango, pick up a copy of *Common Wildflowers of the Okavango Delta* and *Trees & Shrubs of the Okavango Delta* by Veronica Roodt. Both have informative descriptions with useful paintings and drawings.

Environmental Issues

As a relatively large country with a very low population density, Botswana is one of Africa's most unpolluted and pristine regions. It faces most of the ecological problems experienced elsewhere in Africa, such as land degradation and desertification, deforestation (around 21% of the country is covered by forests), water scarcity and urban sprawl. In addition to these, some major ecological and conservation issues continue to affect the country's deserts, wetlands and savannahs.

THE FENCE DILEMMA

If you've been stopped at a veterinary checkpoint, or visited the eastern Okavango Delta, you'll be familiar with the country's 3000km of 1.5m-high 'buffalo fence', officially called the Veterinary Cordon Fence. It's not a single fence but a series of high-tensile steel-wire barriers that run cross-country through some of Botswana's wildest terrain.

The fences were first erected in 1954 to segregate wild buffalo herds from domestic free-range cattle in order to thwart the spread of foot-and-mouth disease. Botswana's beef-farming industry is one of the most important in the country, both economically and in terms of the status conferred by cattle upon their owners in Batswana society. At the same time, wildlife tourism is a major money earner and the country's international reputation is often tied to its perceived willingness to protect the country's wildlife. Balancing these two significant yet sometimes-conflicting industries is one of the most complicated challenges facing Botswana's government.

DANGERS THREATENING THE DELTA

Despite its status as a biodiversity hot spot and the largest Ramsar Wetland Site on the planet, the Okavango Delta has no international protection (apart from the Moremi Game Reserve), even though many prominent conservationists consider it to be critically endangered and think that it should be awarded Unesco World Heritage status.

Wetland ecosystems are disappearing globally at an alarming rate, partly due to climate change and partly due to mismanagement and unsustainable development, and the Okavango Delta is no exception. Already a survey team from the DWNP and BirdLife Botswana has concluded that the delta is shrinking. The Kubango River – originating in the highlands of Angola – carries less water and floods the delta for a shorter period of the year.

Other key threats include overgrazing, which is already resulting in accelerated land and soil degradation; commercial gill netting and illegal fire lighting; unplanned developments in Angola as post-civil war resettlement occurs; and pressure for new and increased abstraction of water for mining, domestic use, agriculture and tourism. Most worrying of these is the proposed extraction of water from the Okavango River to supply the growing needs of Namibia. One such proposal is the construction of a 1250km-long pipeline from the Okavango River to Namibia's capital, Windhoek, which first reared its head in 1997 and has grown and faltered in fits and starts since.

In 1994 Botswana, Namibia and Angola signed the **Okavango River Basin Commission** (Okacom; www.okacom.org), aimed at coordinating the sustainable management of the delta's waters. Although the commission has high principles, the practicalities on

FENCES: A HISTORY OF CONFLICT

The main problem with Botswana's 'buffalo fence' is that many of the fences prevent wild animals from migrating to water sources along age-old seasonal routes. While Botswana has set aside large areas for wildlife protection, these areas rarely constitute independent or self-contained ecosystems. As a result, Botswana's wildebeest population has declined by 99% over the past 20 years and all remaining buffaloes and zebras are stranded north of the fences.

The worst disaster occurred in the drought of 1983, in which the Kuke Fence barred herds of wildebeest heading for the Okavango waters, resulting in the death of 65,000 animals. The final section of Mark and Delia Owens' *Cry of the Kalahari* chronicles another heartbreaking example, with wildebeest from the southern Kalahari suddenly barred from their grazing grounds around Lake Xau. The Owens' publicising of the issue ultimately led to their expulsion from the country.

The 80km-long Northern Buffalo Fence located north of the Okavango Delta has opened a vast expanse of wildlife-rich – but as yet unprotected – territory to cattle ranching. Safari operators wanted the fence set as far north as possible to protect the seasonally flooded Selinda Spillway; prospective cattle ranchers wanted it set as far south as possible, maximising new grazing lands. The government sided with the ranchers and the fence opened up to 20% of the Okavango Delta to commercial ranching.

In 2003 the controversy started up again with the proposal of a new cordon fence around the Makgadikgadi Pans. When completed, the fence will extend for 480km and is intended to limit predator–livestock conflict along the Boteti River. However, on the completion of the western section of the fence, the **Environmental Investigation Agency** (EIA; www.eia-international.org) found that the alignment failed to adhere to the suggestions of the Department of Wildlife and National Parks' (DWNP) Environmental Appraisal, and as a result the majority of the Boteti River now lies outside the park, cutting off the animals within. The net effect was immediately felt: in early 2005 some 300 zebras died trying to reach the river. In addition, the cattle fence around the Okavango Delta has already been damaged by roving elephant herds.

THE HUNTING DEBATE

Hunting in Africa has, in recent times, largely operated in the shadows of international attention, which may be why there was such a commotion when Spain's King Juan Carlos I injured himself while on a hunting trip to Botswana in early 2011. Pictures soon emerged of the king standing alongside an elephant he had shot on a previous hunting trip to Botswana. Leaving aside for a moment the fact that the king was at the time the honorary president of the Spanish chapter of the World Wildlife Fund (WWF), the episode both cast an uncomfortable spotlight on the industry and brought to the fore one of the most contentious issues in African conservation.

While it is abhorrent to many conservationists, some recognise that controlled hunting can play an important part in preserving species. If we can distil the argument in favour of hunting to its essence, it would be as follows. Tourism revenues (whether national park fees or lodge revenues) sometimes fail to reach local communities, reinforcing a perception that wildlife belongs to the government. Hunting on private concessions, however, generally attracts massive fees (lion licences sold for US$20,000 before the 2001 ban), of which, the theory goes, a significant proportion is fed back into local community projects, thereby giving wildlife a tangible economic value for local people. If controlled strictly – through the use of quotas and killing only a limited number of solitary male lions who are past their prime, for example – hunting can, according to its proponents (including many in the conservation community), play a part in saving species from extinction.

At the same time, opponents of hunting argue that the whole debate is premised on the failure of governments and private operators to fairly redistribute their revenues from nonlethal forms of tourism – why, they ask, should we expect that hunting be any different? They also argue that the solution lies in a fairer distribution of tourism revenues and greater community involvement in conservation rather than in killing the very animals upon which tourism depends. And finally, some critics point to the double standards of arresting and imprisoning locals who hunt wildlife (whether for commercial or subsistence reasons), while permitting rich (and usually white) hunters to shoot animals during short visits to the continent.

The debate continues.

the ground are far from simple and the process of moving towards a sustainable management plan and eventual treaty has been very slow. As Angola, the basin state where 95% of the water flow originates, settles into its first period of peace in some 30 years, it is hoped that the pace will accelerate.

HUNTING

In mid-2001 the government initiated a complete ban on all hunting of lions and cheetahs due to concerns over the increasing gender imbalances in the populations of these two big cats. At the time, local people were none too happy, saying that the ban would prevent them from protecting valuable livestock. Hunters, too, were metaphorically speaking up in arms. The ban was lifted in 2005, only to be reinstated two years later. Over the course of 2011 and 2012, Botswana's government, responding to what it called 'catastrophic' declines in some species, made a series of an-

nouncements that seemed to suggest a near-total ban on hunting was imminent. If these policy pronouncements are fulfilled, hunting will be almost completely phased out from 2013. Hunting will, for the time being, be restricted to plains wildlife on game ranches and auctions for a few licences to shoot elephants outside of wilderness areas and in areas with high human populations.

POACHING

Poaching is not common in Botswana due to its relatively stable economy, which makes such a risky and illegal undertaking unnecessary and unattractive. Also, transporting hides and tusks overland from remote areas of Botswana to ports hundreds of kilometres away in other countries is well nigh impossible, especially considering Botswana's well-patrolled borders, which are monitored by the Botswana Defence Force (BDF). What little poaching there is seems to be 'for the pot' – local people supplementing their diets by hunting wild animals – rather than large-scale commercial enterprises.

National Parks & Reserves

Around one-third of Botswana's land mass is officially protected, representing one of the highest proportions of protected areas on earth. According to the United Nations Environment Program (UNEP), the figure is 30.2%. Government sources put the figure at around 17% of the country protected in national parks or game reserves, with another 20% vaguely defined as 'wildlife management areas' (WMA). Either way, the figures reinforce the perception that Botswana is serious about preserving its wildlife and has long pursued a far-sighted policy of sustainable tourism that is aimed at preserving the country's pristine natural environment.

Budget travellers may feel excluded by some of the prohibitive costs, but the money you pay on entering the national parks goes a long way in both contributing to the development of local communities and bolstering conservation strategies.

Most of the national parks in Botswana are characterised by vast open spaces with a few private safari concessions, next to no infrastructure and limited amenities. Exceptions include the Chobe National Park and Moremi Game Reserve, which both have relatively larger volumes of travellers visiting each year.

Most national parks in Botswana boast four of the Big Five – buffaloes, elephants, leopards and lions. In Chobe National Park alone, the elephant population has swelled to an estimated 71,000 (at last count), and in Moremi Game Reserve (the only part of the Okavango Delta to be officially protected) there survives one of the few healthy wild dog populations in Africa. Because the

NATIONAL PARKS – BEST OF BOTSWANA

PARK	FEATURES	ACTIVITIES	BEST TIME
Central Kalahari Game Reserve	52,800 sq km; one of the largest protected areas in the world; semi-arid grassland	wildlife viewing; walking; visiting San villages	Jun-Oct
Chobe National Park	11,700 sq km; mosaic of grassland & woodland; high elephant population	wildlife viewing; birdwatching; fishing	year-round
Kgalagadi Transfrontier Park	38,000 sq km; straddles the South African border; semi-arid grassland	wildlife viewing; birdwatching	Dec-May
Khama Rhino Sanctuary	43 sq km; last refuge of Botswana's rhinos	wildlife viewing; birdwatching	May-Sep
Khutse Game Reserve	2590 sq km; adjoins Central Kalahari Game Reserve; same features	wildlife viewing; walking; visiting San villages	Jun-Oct
Makgadikgadi & Nxai Pans NPs	7300 sq km; largest saltpans in the world; migratory zebras & wildebeest; flamingos	wildlife viewing; trekking with San; quad biking	Mar-Jul
Moremi Game Reserve	3800 sq km; grassland, flood plains & swamps; huge wildlife density	wildlife viewing; walking; scenic flights; boating	Aug-Dec
Northern Tuli Game Reserve	collection of private reserves; unique rock formations	wildlife viewing; horse riding; walking; night drives	May-Sep

Okavango Delta and Chobe River provide an incongruous water supply in a semi-arid environment, nearly all Southern African mammal species are present in the Moremi Game Reserve, parts of the Chobe National Park and the Linyanti Marshes. In the Makgadikgadi & Nxai Pans National Park, herds of wildebeest, zebras and other hoofed mammals migrate between their winter range on the Makgadikgadi plains and the summer lushness of the Nxai Pan region, one of the largest such migrations on earth.

Visiting National Parks

All public national parks and reserves in Botswana are run by the **Department of Wildlife & National Parks** (DWNP; ☑397 1405; www.mewt.gov.bw/DWNP/). There are other park offices in Maun (p99) and Kasane (p81).

There are a few things worth remembering about visiting Botswana's national parks and reserves:

» Park fees were slated for a rise at the time of writing – don't be surprised if they're significantly above those listed here by the time you arrive.

» Although there are exceptions (such as the Chobe Riverfront section of Chobe National Park) and it may be possible on rare occasions to get park rangers to bend the rules, no one is allowed into a national park or reserve without an accommodation booking for that park.

» It is once again possible to pay park entrance fees at park entrance gates, after a spell in which places had to be reserved and fees paid in advance at DWNP offices in Gaborone, Maun or Kasane (you'll still see some signs around Botswana to that effect). Even so, you should always try to book in advance.

» The gates for each DWNP park are open from 6am to 6.30pm (1 April to 30 September) and from 5.30am to 7pm (1 October to 31 March). It is vital that all visitors be out of the park, or settled into their campsite, outside of these hours. Driving after dark is strictly forbidden (although it is permitted in private concessions).

CAMPING & BOOKING

The DWNP ran all of the campsites within national parks and reserves until a recent shift in policy saw most of these tendered out to private companies.

The DWNP still runs a small number of campsites (especially in the Central Kalahari Game Reserve and Kgalagadi Transfrontier Park), and reservations for any DWNP campsite can be made up to 12 months in advance at the DWNP offices in Maun or Gaborone; Chobe National Park bookings are also possible at the Kasane DWNP office. It's at these offices that you also pay the park entry fees (upon presenting proof of a confirmed campsite reservation).

We recommend that, wherever possible, you make the bookings in person or arrange for someone to do so on your behalf. In theory, the DWNP also allows you to make bookings over the phone or via email, but in practice getting anyone to answer the phone or reply to emails is far more challenging than it should be. If you do manage to make a phone or email booking, insist on receiving (by fax, email or letter) a receipt with a reference number on it that you must keep and quote if you need to change your reservation.

When making the reservation, you need to give the DWNP:

» the name of your preferred campsite(s) within the park, in order of preference

» the number of nights required, and the date of your arrival to and departure from the park and campsite

---

NATIONAL PARK FEES PER DAY IN BOTSWANA

Infants and children up to the age of seven are entitled to free entry into the national parks.

	FOREIGNERS
adult	P120
child (8-17)	P60
camping	P50
vehicles <3500kg	P50

» the number of adults and children camping

» the vehicle's number plates and also the country in which the vehicle is registered (this may be waived if you don't yet have a vehicle)

» proof of your status if you are not paying 'foreigner' rates

Once you have booked it is difficult to change anything, so be sure to plan your trip well and allow enough time to get there and look around. A refund (less a 10% administration charge) is only possible with more than 30 days' notice.

SURVIVAL GUIDE

Directory A–Z

Accommodation

The story of Botswana's accommodation is one of extremes. At one end, there are fabulously sited campsites for self-drivers (the closest the country comes to budget accommodation). At the other extreme, there are top-end lodges where prices can be eye-wateringly high. In between, you will find some midrange options in the major towns and places such as the Okavango Panhandle, but elsewhere there's very little for the midrange (and nothing for the noncamping budget) traveller.

PRICES

The order of accommodation listings is by author preference, and each place to stay is accompanied by one of the following symbols (the price relates to a high-season double room with private bathroom and, unless stated otherwise, includes breakfast). Upmarket places tend to price in US dollars as opposed to pula.

$	<US$50
$$	US$50-100
$$$	>US$100

BED LEVY & GOVERNMENT TAX

Please note that all hotels, lodges, campsites and other forms of accommodation are required by the government to charge a P10 bed levy per person per night. This levy is rarely if ever included in quoted accommodation rates.

> **BOOK YOUR STAY ONLINE**
>
> For more accommodation reviews by Lonely Planet authors, check out http://hotels.lonelyplanet.com.
>
> You'll find independent reviews, as well as recommendations on the best places to stay. Best of all, you can book online.

In addition to the levy, there is a 12% government tax on hotels and lodges (but not all campsites) and, unlike the levy, *is* usually included in prices.

SEASONS

While most budget and midrange options tend to have a standard room price, many top-end places change their prices according to season. High season is usually from June to November (and may also apply to Christmas, New Year and Easter, depending on the lodge), low season corresponds to the rains (December to March or April) and the shoulder is a short April and May window. The only exception is the Kalahari, where June to November is generally (but not always) considered to be low season.

ACCOMMODATION TYPES

CAMPING

Just about everywhere of interest, including all major national parks, has a campsite. Once the domain of the Department of Wildlife and National Parks (DWNP), most of the campsites are now privately run.

The jury remains out on whether the change has been a good thing. The change in ownership has seen prices rise considerably. In some cases, the companies in question have upgraded the ablutions blocks to have hot and cold showers and flush toilets, and generally make sure the sites are in good nick. Others do little to maintain their sites, offer cold-bucket showers and pit latrines, and run inefficient booking systems. All campsites have *braai* (barbecue) pits. While we were in Botswana, rumours were circulating that the DWNP's patience was running out and had plans to reclaim some (if not all) of the campsites. As a result, some of the following information may be subject to change.

All campsites *must* be booked in advance and they fill up fast in busy periods, such as during South African school holidays. And

PRACTICALITIES

Newspapers Government-owned *Daily News, Botswana Advertiser* (Gaborone & Eastern Botswana), *Ngami Times* (a regional Maun weekly).

Radio Yarona (106.6FM) and GABZFM (96.2FM) broadcast around Gaborone, while RB2 (103FM) is the commercial network of Radio Botswana. With a short-wave radio, you can easily pick up the BBC World Service and international services from Europe.

TV Botswana TV (BTV) broadcasts news (in Setswana) and sports (in English and Setswana), and an array of US sitcoms. Government-run South African stations are also available. Most top-end hotels also offer satellite TV.

Weights & Measures Metric system.

it is very important to remember that you will not be allowed into any park run by the DWNP without a reservation for a campsite.

Camping areas are usually small (often with only two or three places to pitch a tent and/or park a vehicle).

Outside of the parks and reserves, some hotels and lodges also provide camping areas. Most private and hotel/lodge campsites have sit-down toilets, showers (often hot), *braai* pits and washing areas. One definite attraction is that campers can use the hotel bars and restaurants and splash around the hotel swimming pool for free.

Other places where camping is possible include the Tsodilo Hills and Khama Rhino Sanctuary.

Elsewhere, camping in the wild is permitted outside national parks, reserves or private land and away from government freehold areas. If you want to camp near a village, obtain permission from the village leader or police station and inquire about a suitable site.

HOTELS

Every major town has at least one hotel, and the larger towns and tourist areas, such as Gaborone, Maun, Francistown and Kasane, offer several in different price ranges. In general, midrange and top-end travellers are well looked after, but budget travellers will struggle to find anything as cheap as the budget accommodation in Namibia; the really cheap places in Botswana often double as brothels. There's a relatively high demand for hotel rooms in Gaborone, in particular from business travellers, so it pays to book ahead here and also elsewhere in the high season.

The range of hotel accommodation available includes: *rondavels,* which are detached rooms or cottages with a private bathroom;

B&B-type places, often with a shared bathroom – mostly in Gaborone; motel-style units with a private bathroom, and sometimes, cooking facilities, usually along the highways of eastern Botswana; and luxury hotels in major towns.

LODGES

Botswana's claim to being Africa's most exclusive destination is built around its luxury lodges (sometimes called 'camps'). You'll find them where there are decent concentrations of wildlife, most notably in Chobe National Park, the Tuli Block, Moremi Game Reserve, all over the Okavango Delta and, to a lesser extent, the parks and reserves of the Kalahari. It's impossible to generalise about them, other than to say that most pride themselves on their isolation, exclusivity, luxury and impeccable service. Most feature permanent or semipermanent luxury tents, a communal dining area overlooking a waterhole or other important geographical feature, and a swimming pool.

For many visitors, they're once-in-a-lifetime places with accommodation rates to match – some start at around US$1000/1500 per person per night in the low/high season, but many cost considerably more than that. Usually included in these rates are all meals, some drinks and most wildlife drives and other activities. Most places are only accessible by 4WD transfer or air; the latter will cost an extra US$100 to US$200.

🏃 Activities

Such is the nature of travelling in Botswana that even the most tranquil holidays will involve some form of activities, from rugged 4WD excursions to poling gently along the Okavango Delta's waterways in a traditional *mokoro* (dugout canoe). Most activities that are possible are organised as part of a lodge package rather than designed for individual travellers.

HIKING

Botswana lags behind neighbours Namibia and Zambia as a hiking destination, although a number of hikes are possible.

Walking safaris in the company of an armed guard form part of the available activities at many lodges, and leaving the safety of your vehicle will sharpen your senses and your awareness of your surroundings. Places where such hiking excursions along nature trails are possible include the Okavango Delta, the Central Kalahari Game

CAMP SITES

PARK/RESERVE/ SECTOR	CAMPSITE	OPERATOR	PRICE PER ADULT/ CHILD
Central Kalahari Game Reserve	Kori, Deception Valley, Leopard Pan, Phokoje Pan, Xade, Bape and Xaka	**DWNP** (for bookings email dwnp@gov.bw or ☑318 0774 Gaberone office)	P200/100
	Passarge Valley, Piper Pan, Motopi, Lekhubu, Leatihau and Sunday Pan	**Big Foot Tours** (www. bigfoottours.co.bw)	P200/100
Chobe Riverfront	Ihaha	**Kwalate** (for bookings email kwalatesafari@ gmail.com)	P260/130 (US$40/20)
Kgalagadi Transfrontier Park	All sites	**DWNP** (for bookings email dwnp@gov.bw or ☑318 0774 Gaberone office)	P30/15
Khutse Game Reserve	All sites	**Big Foot Tours** (www. bigfoottours.co.bw)	P200/100
Kubu Island	Kubu Island	**Gaing-O-Community Trust** (www.kubu island.com)	P100/50
Linyanti	Linyanti Camp	**SKL** (sklcamps.com)	P240/120 (US$50/25)
Makgadikgadi Pans National Park	Khumaga	**SKL** (sklcamps.com)	P240/120 (US$50/25)
Moremi Game Reserve	Khwai	**SKL** (sklcamps.com)	P240/120 (US$50/25)
	South Camp	**Kwalate** (for bookings email kwalatesafari@ gmail.com)	P260/130 (US$40/20)
	Third Bridge	**Xomae** (www.xomae sites.com)	P226/113
	Xakanaxa	**Kwalate** (for bookings email kwalatesafari@ gmail.com)	P260/130 (US$40/20)
Nxai Pans National Park	Baines Baobab	**Xomae** (www.xomae sites.com)	P350/175
	South Camp	**Xomae** (www.xomae sites.com)	P226/113
Savuti	Savuti Camp	**SKL** (sklcamps.com)	P240/120 (US$50/25)

Reserve (CKGR) and the Makgadikgadi Pans. The treks run out of the luxury lodges of the Makgadikgadi Pans or the CKGR, for example, are a fascinating opportunity to explore the arid environs with San guides, who can point out the hidden details of the landscape and its specially adapted flora and fauna.

You don't need to be staying at a luxury lodge or tented camp to explore a small corner of the Delta on foot, as many of the *mokoro* expeditions organised from Maun include walking components. Also, a small but growing number of mobile safaris in the delta and Moremi Game Reserve, organised from Maun, involve multiday hikes.

Options are limited for more free-range hiking, but the Tsodilo Hills, where trails lead up to thousands of rock-art sites, is undoubtedly the premier spot. Guides are available from the main campsite in the region. Another possibility is the Tswapong Hills in the country's east, which sees very few tourists. For both, you'll need to be entirely self-sufficient.

HORSE RIDING

Cantering among herds of zebras and wildebeest is an unforgettable experience and the horse-riding safaris in Botswana are second to none. You'll need to be an experienced rider as most horseback safaris in Botswana don't take beginners – after all, you need to be able to get yourself out of trouble should you encounter it.

Try the following operators.

African Animal Adventures (p89) Expeditions from Maun.

Grassland Safari Lodge (p120) Safaris into the CKGR.

Mashatu Game Reserve (p67) In the Tuli Block.

Uncharted Africa (p73) Out onto the salt pans of Makgadikgadi.

MOKORO TRIPS

Travelling around the channels of the Okavango Delta in a *mokoro* is a wonderful experience that is not to be missed. The *mokoro* is poled along the waterways by a skilled poler, much like an African gondola. Although you won't be spotting much wildlife from such a low viewpoint, it's a great way to appreciate the delta's birdlife and gain an appreciation, hopefully from a distance, of the formidable bulk of hippos.

MOTORBOAT & FISHING TRIPS

The only two places where motorboats can operate for wildlife cruises and fishing trips are along the Okavango and Chobe Rivers.

For fishing, the only stretches of water to consider are the deep and fast-flowing waters of the Okavango Panhandle. The most popular form of freshwater fishing is fly fishing for tigerfish, although pike, barbel (catfish) and bream are also plentiful. Tigerfish season runs from September to June, while barbel are present from mid-September to December.

QUAD BIKES

Some lodges in the Makgadikgadi Pans area in northeastern Botswana offer trips across the expansive salt pans on four-wheeled quad bikes, also called ATVs (all-terrain vehicles). These are safe to drive, require no experience, do not need a car or motorbike licence and are great fun. Most are reputable operators, but sadly in recent years some travellers have begun to bring their own quad bikes to Botswana, where they crisscross the pans with little concern for the wildlife of the area.

SCENIC FLIGHTS

A scenic flight of fancy in a light aircraft or helicopter high above the Okavango Delta is a thrilling activity. These can be arranged either in Maun directly with the operator or through your accommodation.

Children

Botswana can be a challenging destination for families travelling with children. That's primarily because the distances here can be epic and long days in the vehicle along bumpy trails will test the patience of most kids. It's also worth remembering that many upmarket lodges and safari companies won't accept children under a certain age (sometimes seven, more often 12), and those that do will probably require you to book separate game drives.

On the other hand, if you can keep the kids entertained on the long drives (bring lots of activity books, CDs and games), camping out in the wilds can be a wonderful family experience. It may require eternal vigilance – almost no private or public campsite in the country has enough fencing to keep animals out and children in, and there are the additional hazards of campfires, mosquitoes, snakes and biting/stinging insects. But long distances and these basic rules of camping life aside, a self-driving camping safari is something your kids will remember forever.

The best piece of advice we can give to make the most out of Botswana's abundant attractions is to not be too ambitious. Instead of trying to cover the whole country, concentrate on really getting to know just one or two places over the course of a week or 10 days, thereby cutting travel times.

There are lodges and safari operators that do offer family packages that can be worth checking out. Some offer specialist children's guides and imaginative activity programs, which might include things such as making paper from elephant dung! Most lodges and tented camps also have swimming pools, which provide a fine reward for long hours spent in the car.

PRACTICALITIES

Unless you're planning to be in Botswana for the long haul, we advise you to bring everything with you that you think you'll need. For invaluable general advice on taking the family abroad, see Lonely Planet's *Travel with Children* by Brigitte Barta et al.

» **Babysitting** Many lodges make a point of saying they are not babysitting agencies (in other words, your kids are your responsibility), and such agencies are otherwise extremely rare.

» **Car seats** These may be available from car-hire firms, but you'd be better off bringing your own; no car seats in safari vehicles.

» **Changing facilities** Almost unheard-of.

» **Cots** Rarely available in hotels or lodges.

» **Health** A check-up with your doctor back home is a good idea before setting out for Botswana, but this is a comparatively safe country and medical facilities are good.

» **High chairs** Almost nonexistent in restaurants.

» **Mosquito repellent** Check with your doctor before setting out, as most mosquito repellents with high levels of DEET may be unsuitable for young children. Some lodges have mosquito nets; if you're camping, bring your own.

» **Nappies and baby food** These are available from supermarkets in larger towns, but they may not be the brands you're used to and you don't want to find

yourself in trouble if you're in town on a Sunday or public holiday.

» **National park entry fees** Free for children under eight and half-price for those aged from eight to 17 years old.

SIGHTS & ACTIVITIES

Wildlife densities are at their highest in the north, especially the Okavango Delta, Moremi Game Reserve and Chobe National Park. As a result, you shouldn't need to spend too long in the car before tracking down elephants or lions.

Although they're rarely aimed at a young audience, older kids will get a kick out of quad biking in the Makgadikgadi Pans, horse-riding safaris, *mokoro* trips in the reedy waters of the delta, or even scenic flights high above the delta. Fishing in the Okavango Panhandle might also appeal. There's an even greater range of activities just across the border at Victoria Falls.

Customs Regulations

Most items from elsewhere in the Southern African Customs Union (SACU) – Namibia, South Africa, Lesotho and Swaziland – may be imported duty free. You may be asked to declare new laptops and cameras, but this is rarely enforced.

Visitors may bring into Botswana the following amounts of duty-free items: up to 400 cigarettes, 50 cigars or 250g of tobacco; 2L of wine or 1L of beer or spirits; and 50mL of perfume or 250mL of eau de cologne.

The most rigorous searches at customs posts are for fresh meat products – don't buy succulent steaks in South Africa for your camping barbecue and expect them to be allowed in.

There is no restriction on currency; however, you might need to declare any pula or foreign currency you have on you when entering or leaving the country, but this depends on the border crossing and who is on duty.

Discount Cards

There is no uniformly accepted discount-card scheme in Botswana, but a residence permit entitles you to claim favourable residents' rates at hotels. Hostel cards are of little use, but student cards score a discount (usually around 15%) on some buses. Seniors over 60, with proof of age, also receive a discount on some buses and airfares.

Embassies & High Commissions

Most diplomatic missions are in Gaborone. Many more countries have embassies or consulates in South Africa.

France (Map p53; ☑397 3863; www.am bafrance-bw.org; 761 Robinson Rd, PO Box 1424; ☺8am-4pm Mon-Fri)

Germany (☑395 3143; www.gaborone.diplo. de; Segoditshane Way, 3rd fl, Professional House, Broadhurst Mall; ☺9am-noon Mon-Fri)

Namibia (Map p50; ☑390 2181; nhc.gabs@ info.bw; Plot 186, Morara Close; ☺7.30am-1pm & 2-4.30pm Mon-Fri)

South Africa (Map p53; ☑390 4800; sahc gabs@botsnet.bw; 29 Queens Rd, Plot 29, PO Box 00402; ☺8am-12.45pm & 1.30-4.30pm Mon-Fri)

UK (Map p53; ☑395 2841; ukinbotswana.fco.gov. uk/en/; Queens Rd, Plot 1079-1084 Main Mall, PO Box 0023; ☺8am-12.30pm & 1.30-4.30pm Mon-Thu, to 1pm Fri)

US (Map p50; ☑395 3982; botswana.usembassy. gov; Embassy Dr, Government Enclave; ☺7.30am-5pm Mon-Thu, to 1.30pm Fri)

Zambia (Map p53; ☑395 1951; Plot No 1118 Queens Rd, the Mall; ☺8.30am-12.30pm & 2-4.30pm Mon-Fri)

Zimbabwe (Map p50; ☑391 4495; www.zimga borone.gov.zw; Plot 8850, Orapa Close, Government Enclave; ☺8am-1pm & 2-4.30pm Mon-Fri)

Food

The order of restaurant listings follows the author's preference, and each place to eat is accompanied by one of the following symbols.

$	<US$10 per main course
$$	US$10-20 per main course
$$$	>US$20 per main course

Gay & Lesbian Travellers

Homosexuality, both gay and lesbian, is illegal in Botswana and carries a minimum sentence of seven years if you're caught. Intolerance has increased further over the last few years due to the homophobic statements of leaders in neighbouring Namibia and Zimbabwe.

To tackle this widespread homophobia, a group of lesbians, gays and bisexuals established the group **LeGaBiBo** (Lesbians, Gays and Bisexuals of Botswana; ☑393 2516; www.lega bibo.org.bw; 5062 Medical Mews, Fairgrounds, Ga-borone) in 1998. The first thing they did was to publish a human-rights charter under the auspices of Ditshwanelo, the Botswana Centre for Human Rights, and they have since run safe-sex workshops to highlight the risks of HIV/AIDS.

Arrests are rare, but the Botswana High Court has ruled on a case involving two gay men. In its judgment, passed in July 2003, it found that 'the time has not yet arrived to decriminalise homosexual practices even between consenting adult males in private'. Ditshwanelo continues to advocate and lobby for the decriminalisation of homosexuality. In 2011 LeGaBiBo launched a legal case against the government, arguing that current laws criminalising homosexuality were unconstitutional and that homophobia was 'un-African'.

Given the sensitivity of the subject and the strongly held views of many Batswana, it is advisable to refrain from any overt displays of affection in public.

USEFUL RESOURCES

Afriboyz (www.afriboyz.com/Homosexuality-in-Africa.html) Links to gay topics in an African context.

David Tours (www.davidtravel.com) Can arrange seven- and 12-day trips to northern Botswana, all with a gay focus.

Global Gayz (www.globalgayz.com) Links to country-by-country gay issues, including Botswana.

Purple Roofs (www.purpleroofs.com/africa/kenyata.html) Lists a number of gay or gay-friendly tour companies in South Africa and elsewhere that may be able to help you plan your trip.

Insurance

Two words: get some! A travel-insurance policy to cover theft, loss and medical problems is a very sensible precaution. Worldwide travel insurance is available at www.lonelyplanet.com/travel_services. You can buy, extend and claim online anytime – even if you're already on the road.

Medical cover is the most vital element of any policy, but make sure you check the small print.

Some policies specifically exclude 'dangerous activities', which can even include motorcycling and hiking. If such activities are on your agenda you'll need a fully comprehensive policy, which may be more ex-

CHANGING MONEY AT THE BORDER

A word of warning: if you're changing money at or near border posts and not doing so through the banks, be aware that local businesses (sometimes bureaux de change, sometimes just shops with a sideline in currencies so that arriving travellers can pay their customs duties) usually have *abysmal* rates. Change the minimum that you're likely to need and change the rest at a bank or bureau de change in the nearest large town.

pensive. Using a locally acquired motorcycle licence may not be valid under your policy.

You may prefer a policy that pays doctors or hospitals direct rather than you having to pay on the spot and claim later. If you have to claim later, make sure you keep all documentation.

Some policies ask you to call back (reverse charges) to a centre in your home country, where an immediate assessment of your problem is made.

Check that the policy covers ambulances or an emergency flight home.

Internet Access

Establishments with internet access are identified in this book with the @ icon, while those with wireless have the 🛜 icon.

Cyber cafes Common in large and medium-sized towns; connection speeds fluctuate wildly and prices range from P12 per hour in Gaborone to P40 elsewhere.

Post offices Some post offices, including in Kasane, have a few internet-enabled PCs.

Wireless Reasonably common in mid-range and top-end hotels in towns, but very rarely available in safari lodges.

Maps

The best paper map of Botswana is the *Botswana* (1:1,000,000) map published by Tracks4Africa (www.tracks4africa.co.za). Updated every couple of years using detailed traveller feedback, the map is printed on tear-free, waterproof paper and includes distances *and* estimated travel times. Used in conjunction with Tracks4Africa's unrivalled GPS maps, it's far and away the best mapping product on the market. Even so, be aware that, particularly in the Okavango Delta, last year's trails may this year be underwater depending on water levels, so these maps should never be a substitute for expert local knowledge.

If for some reason you are unable to get hold of the Tracks4Africa map, the only other maps that we recommend are those published by Shell Oil Botswana and Veronica Roodt. The *Shell Tourist Map of Botswana* (1:1,750,000) is available at major bookshops in Botswana and South Africa.

Probably of more interest are Shell's zoomed-in maps (with varying scales) of the various reserves and other popular areas. These include numerous GPS coordinates for important landmarks and the tracks are superimposed onto satellite images of the area in question. Some are a little out of date, but they're still excellent. Titles include *Okavango Delta*, *Chobe National Park*, *Moremi Game Reserve* and *Kgalagadi Transfrontier Park*.

Money

The unit of currency is the Botswanan pula (P). Pula means 'blessings' or 'rain', the latter of which is as precious as money in this largely desert country. Notes come in denominations of P10, P20, P50 and P100, and coins (thebe, or 'shield') are in denominations of 5t, 10t, 25t, 50t, P1, P2 and P5.

Prices can be quoted in US dollars and pula. At top-end hotels, lodges and camps, things are priced and you can pay in US dollars. Otherwise, you'll be making most transactions in Botswana pula.

Most banks and foreign exchange offices won't touch Zambian kwacha and (sometimes) Namibian dollars; in border areas you can sometimes pay at some businesses with the latter. To make sure you don't get caught out, buy/sell these currencies at or near the respective borders.

ATMS

Credit cards can be used in ATMs displaying the appropriate sign, or to obtain cash advances over the counter in many banks – Visa and MasterCard are among the most widely recognised. Transaction fees can be prohibitive and usually apply per transaction rather than by the amount you're withdrawing – take out as much as you can each time. Check also with your bank before leaving home to see if some banks have agreements with your home bank and work out cheaper than others.

You'll find ATMs at all the main bank branches throughout Botswana, including in Gaborone, Maun, Francistown and Kasane, and this is undoubtedly the simplest (and safest) way to handle your money while travelling.

CASH

Most common foreign currencies can be exchanged, but not every branch of every bank will do so. Therefore, it's best to stick to US dollars, euros, UK pounds and South African rand, which are all easy to change.

Foreign currency, typically US dollars, is also accepted by a number of midrange and top-end hotels, lodges and tour operators. South African rand can also be used on Botswanan combis (minibuses) and buses going to/from South Africa, and to pay for Botswanan vehicle taxes at South African/Botswanan borders.

There are five commercial banks in the country with branches in all the main towns and major villages. Although you will get less favourable rates at a bureau de change, they are a convenient option if the lines at the banks are particularly long.

There is no black market in Botswana. Anyone offering to exchange money on the street is doing so illegally and is probably setting you up for a scam, the exception being the guys who change pula for South African rand in front of South Africa-bound minibuses – locals use their services, so they can be trusted.

For current exchange rates, log on to www.xe.com.

CREDIT/DEBIT CARDS

All major credit cards, especially Visa and MasterCard, but also American Express and Diners Club, are widely accepted in most shops, restaurants and hotels (but only in *some* petrol stations).

Major branches of Barclays Bank and Standard Chartered Bank also deal with cash advances over the counter and don't charge commissions for Visa and MasterCard. Almost every town has at least one branch of Barclays and/or Standard Chartered that offers foreign-exchange facilities, but not all have the authority or technology for cash advances.

EXCHANGE RATES

Australia	A$1	P8.38
Canada	C$1	P8.08
Europe	€1	P10.59
Japan	¥100	P9.03
New Zealand	NZ$1	P6.69
South Africa	R1	P0.90
UK	UK£1	P12.75
US	US$1	P7.97

For current exchange rates see www.xe.com

TIPPING

While tipping isn't obligatory, the government's official policy of promoting upmarket tourism has raised expectations in many hotels and restaurants. A service charge may be added as a matter of course, in which case there's no need to leave a tip. If there is no service charge and the service has been good, leave around 10%.

It is also a good idea to tip the men who watch your car in public car parks and the attendants at service stations who wash your windscreens. A tip of around P5 to P10 is appropriate.

Guides and drivers of safari vehicles will also expect a tip, especially if you've spent a number of days under their care.

TRAVELLERS CHEQUES

Travellers cheques can be cashed at most banks and exchange offices. American Express (Amex), Thomas Cook and Visa are the most widely accepted brands. Banks charge anywhere between 2% and 3% commission to change the cheques; Barclays usually offers the most efficient service and charges 2.5% commission for most brands.

As a general rule, it is preferable to buy travellers cheques in US dollars, euros or UK pounds rather than any other currency. Get most of the cheques in largish denominations to save on per-cheque commissions.

You must take your passport with you when cashing cheques.

Opening Hours

Lonely Planet reviews don't list business hours unless they differ significantly from

GOVERNMENT TRAVEL ADVICE

The following government websites offer travel advisories and information for travellers.

Australian Department of Foreign Affairs & Trade (www.smartraveller.gov.au)

Canadian Department of Foreign Affairs & International Trade (www.voyage.gc.ca)

French Ministère des Affaires Étrangères et Européennes (www.diplomatie.gouv.fr/fr/fr/conseils-aux-voyageurs_909/index.html)

Italian Ministero degli Affari Esteri (www.viaggiaresicuri.mae.aci.it)

New Zealand Ministry of Foreign Affairs & Trade (www.mft.govt.nz/travel)

UK Foreign & Commonwealth Office (www.fco.gov.uk)

US Department of State (www.travel.state.gov)

the following standards. The whole country practically closes down on Sunday.

Banks Barclays Bank 8.30am to 3.30pm Monday to Friday, 8.15am to 10.45am Saturday; Standard Chartered Bank 8.30am to 3.30pm Monday to Friday, 8.15am to 11am Saturday

National Parks 6am to 6.30pm April to September, 5.30am to 7pm October to March

Post Offices 9am to 5pm Monday to Friday, 9am to noon Saturday or 7.30am to noon and 2pm to 4.30pm Monday to Friday, 7.30am to 12.30pm Saturday

Restaurants 11am to 11pm Monday to Saturday; some also open the same hours on Sundays

Photography

While many Batswana enjoy being photographed, others do not; always ask permission and respect the wishes of the person in question. Avoid taking pictures of bridges, dams, airports, military equipment, government buildings and anything that could be considered strategic.

Digital memory cards, CDs and the like can be purchased in Gaborone in large malls like Game City. They're a bit harder to find in Maun and Kasane, but it's possible.

Post

Botswana Post (www.botspost.co.bw) is generally reliable, although it can be slow, so allow at least two weeks for delivery to or from any overseas address.

To send parcels, go to the parcel office at the main post office, fill out the customs forms and pay the duties (if required). Parcels may be plastered with sticky tape but they must also be tied up with string and sealing wax, so bring matches to seal knots with the red wax provided.

Public Holidays

During official public holidays, all banks, government offices and major businesses are closed. However, hotels, restaurants, bars, smaller shops, petrol stations, museums, national parks, border crossings and public transport continue operating as normal. Government offices, banks and some businesses also take the day off after New Year's Day, President's Day, Botswana/Independence Day and Boxing Day.

New Year's Day 1 January

Easter March/April – Good Friday, Easter Saturday and Easter Monday

Labour Day 1 May

Ascension Day May/June, 40 days after Easter Sunday

Sir Seretse Khama Day 1 July

President's Day Third Friday in July

Botswana/Independence Day 30 September

Christmas Day 25 December

Boxing Day 26 December

Safe Travel

Botswana is modern and developed, and most things work. You can safely drink the tap water in the towns and cities, and you do not need protection against cholera or yellow fever.

HIV/AIDS is a serious issue but, unless you fail to take common-sense precautions, there should be no undue risk. In fact, the greatest danger to the traveller is posed by wildlife and the risks of driving in the bush.

CRIME

Crime is rarely a problem in Botswana, and doesn't usually extend beyond occasional pickpocketing and theft from parked cars.

Maun's recently acquired reputation for such petty theft resulted in a rigorous police crackdown, with a resulting drop in crime.

POLICE & MILITARY

Although police and veterinary roadblocks, bureaucracy and bored officials may be tiresome, they're mostly harmless. Careful scrutiny is rare, but drivers may have to unpack their luggage for closer inspection at a border or veterinary checkpoint.

The Botswana Defence Force (BDF), takes its duties seriously and is best not crossed. The most sensitive base, which is operated jointly with the US government, lies in a remote area off the Lobatse road, southwest of Gaborone. Don't stumble upon it accidentally! Also avoid State House, the official residence of the president in Gaborone, especially after dark. It's located near the government enclave, where there's not much else going on in the evening, so anyone caught 'hanging around' is viewed suspiciously.

ROAD SAFETY

Although vehicle traffic is light on most roads outside of the major towns and cities, the most significant concern for most travellers is road safety. Botswana has one of the highest accident rates in the world, and drunk and reckless driving are common, especially at month's end (wage day). Cattle, goats, sheep, donkeys and even elephants are deadly hazards on the road, especially at dusk and after dark when visibility is poor. Never drive at night unless you absolutely have to.

Telephone

The operator of Botswana's fixed-line telephone service is Botswana Telecom (BTC; www.btc.bw). Local and domestic calls at peak times start at P35 per minute and rise according to the distance. When deciding when to call, remember that prices drop by up to one-third for local and domestic calls and 20% for international calls from 8pm

IMPORTANT NUMBERS	
Country code	☑267
Area codes	Botswana does not use area codes
International access codes	☑00
Emergency	☑999

to 7am Monday to Friday, 1pm to midnight Saturday and all day Sunday. These discounts don't apply if you use the operator.

AC Braby (www.brabys.com) also has a reasonable online phone directory.

MOBILE PHONES

Botswana has two main mobile (cell) phone networks, Mascom Wireless (www.mascom. bw) and Orange Botswana (www.orange. co.bw), of which Mascom is by far the largest provider. Both providers have dealers where you can buy phones, SIM cards and top up your credit in most large and medium-sized towns.

The coverage map for these two providers is improving with each passing year, but when deciding whether or not to get a local SIM card, remember that there's simply no mobile coverage across large swaths of the country (including much of the Kalahari and Okavango Delta). That said, the main highway system is generally covered.

Most Botswana mobile numbers begin with ☑071 or ☑072.

PHONECARDS

Telephone booths can be used for local, domestic and international calls, and can be found in and outside all BTC offices, outside all post offices and around all shopping centres and malls. Blue booths (with the English and Setswana words 'coin' and *madi*) take coins, and the green booths (with the words 'card' and *karata*) use phonecards.

Phonecards can be bought at BTC offices, post offices and some small grocery shops. Local and long-distance telephone calls can also be made from private telephone agencies, often called 'phone shops'.

Time

Botswana is two hours ahead of GMT/UTC, so when it's noon in Botswana, it's 10am in London, 5am in New York, 2am in Los Angeles and 8pm in Sydney (not taking into account daylight-saving time in these countries). There is no daylight-saving time in Botswana.

Tourist Information

For many years the tourism industry in Botswana was controlled by a few exclusive operators who brought guests from abroad and ferried them hither and thither until their departure date. There was little need for a local network of tourist offices as people simply didn't require them.

More recently, independent travel to Botswana has been on the rise and the government is finally acknowledging the need for some sort of network of information offices both inside and outside the country.

The Department of Tourism, rebranded in the public sphere as Botswana Tourism (www.botswanatourism.co.bw) has an excellent website and a growing portfolio of tourist offices around the country. These tourist offices don't always have their finger on the pulse, but they can be an extremely useful source of brochures from local hotels, tour operators and other tourist services.

For information on national parks, you're better off contacting the Department of Wildlife and National Parks (p152).

Another useful resource is the Regional Tourism Organisation of Southern Africa (in South Africa 011-315 2420; www.retosa.co.za), which promotes tourism throughout Southern Africa, including Botswana.

Travellers with Disabilities

People with limited mobility will have a difficult time travelling around Botswana – although there are many people with disabilities living in the country, facilities here are very few and much of the country can be an obstacle course. Along streets and footpaths, kerbs and uneven surfaces will often present problems for wheelchair users, and only a very few upmarket hotels/lodges and restaurants have installed ramps and railings. Also, getting to and around any of the major lodges or camps in the national wildlife parks will be extremely difficult given their remote and wild locations.

If you are contemplating travelling to Botswana, be sure to choose the areas you visit carefully, and clearly explain your requirements to the lodge and/or safari operator when making your original enquiry. The swampy environs of the Okavango Delta will be particularly challenging for people who have special needs, although the lodges in both the Kalahari and the Makgadikgadi Pans are relatively accessible, providing you are travelling with an able-bodied companion. It is also worth bearing in mind that almost any destination in Botswana will require a long trip in a 4WD and/or a small plane.

Visas

Most visitors can obtain tourist visas at the international airports and borders (and the nearest police stations in lieu of an immigration official at remote border crossings). Visas on arrival are valid for 30 days – and possibly up to 90 days if requested at the time of entry – and are available for free to passport holders from most Commonwealth countries (but not Ghana, India, Nigeria, Pakistan and Sri Lanka), all EU countries, the USA and countries in the Southern African Customs Union (SACU), ie South Africa, Namibia, Lesotho and Swaziland.

If you hold a passport from any other country, apply for a 30-day tourist visa at an overseas Botswanan embassy or consulate. Where there is no Botswanan representation, try going to a British embassy or consulate.

Tourists are allowed to stay in Botswana for a maximum of 90 days every 12 months, so a 30-day visa may be extended twice. Visas can be extended for free at immigration offices in Gaborone, Francistown, Maun and Kasane. Whether you're required to show an onward ticket and/or sufficient funds at this time depends on the official(s).

Anyone travelling to Botswana from an area infected with yellow fever needs proof of vaccination before they can enter the country.

Volunteering

There are very few volunteering opportunities in Botswana. The community and conservation projects that exist are usually small, focused grassroots projects that simply aren't set up for drop-in volunteers. Another factor is that Botswana is a pretty well-organised, wealthy country and the need for volunteer projects simply doesn't exist, with the exception of nongovernmental organisations (NGOs) working with HIV/AIDS sufferers.

BOTSWANA PROJECTS

The following specific volunteering opportunities were available within Botswana at the time of writing.

Frontier Conservation Expeditions (www.frontier.ac.uk) Teaching and wildlife conservation.

Project Trust (www.projecttrust.org.uk) Schoolteaching near Maun.

Working Abroad (www.workingabroad.com) Cheetah conservation near Ghanzi and Gaborone in the Mokolodi Nature Reserve.

The following international organisations are good places to start gathering information on volunteering, although they won't necessarily always have projects on the go in Botswana.

Coordinating Committee for International Voluntary Service (ccivs.org)

Earthwatch (www.earthwatch.org)

Idealist.org (www.idealist.org)

International Volunteer Programs Association (www.volunteerinternational.org)

Peace Corps (www.peacecorps.gov)

Worldwide Experience (www.worldwideexperience.com)

Worldwide Volunteering (www.wwv.org.uk)

Women Travellers

In general, travelling around Botswana poses no particular difficulties for women travellers. For the most part, men are polite and respectful, and women can often meet and communicate with local men without their intentions necessarily being misconstrued. However, unaccompanied women should be cautious in nightclubs or bars, as generally most instances of hassle tend to be the advances of men who have had one too many drinks.

The threat of sexual assault isn't any greater in Botswana than in Europe, but women should still avoid walking alone in parks and backstreets, especially at night. Don't hitch alone or at night and, if you can, find a companion for trips through sparsely populated areas. Use common sense and things should go well.

Dress modestly. Short sleeves are fine, and baggy shorts and loose T-shirts are acceptable where foreigners are common, but in villages and rural areas try to cover up as much as possible.

Getting There & Away

Botswana is not the easiest or cheapest place in the world to get to. Surprisingly few international airlines fly to and from Botswana; the long-distance airlines prefer to fly into Johannesburg (Jo'burg) or Cape Town in South Africa, where connecting flights depart to Maun or Gaborone. Many people prefer to enter the country overland from South Africa or, more recently, Namibia as part of a longer safari.

Flights, tours and rail tickets can be booked online at www.lonelyplanet.com/travel_services.

Entering Botswana

Entering Botswana is usually straightforward provided you are carrying a valid passport. Visas are available on arrival for most nationalities and are issued in no time. If you're crossing into the country overland and in your own (or rented) vehicle, expect to endure (sometimes quite cursory) searches for fresh meat, fresh fruit and dairy products, most of which will be confiscated if found. For vehicles rented in South Africa, Namibia or other regional countries, you will need to show a letter from the owner that you have permission to drive the car into Botswana, in addition to all other registration documents.

At all border posts you must pay P120 (a combination of road levy and third-party insurance) if you're driving your own vehicle. Hassles from officialdom are rare.

For a moderately useful list of the government's entry requirements, see www.botswanatourism.co.bw/entryFormalities.php. The Tracks4Africa *Botswana* map has opening hours for all border posts, some of which we have covered in detail.

PASSPORT

All visitors entering Botswana must hold a passport that is valid for at least six months. Also, allow a few empty pages for stamp-happy immigration officials, especially if you plan on crossing over to Zimbabwe and/or Zambia to Victoria Falls.

Air

AIRLINES

The national carrier is Air Botswana (BP; ☎390 5500; www.airbotswana.co.bw), which flies routes within Southern Africa. Air Bot-

CLIMATE CHANGE & TRAVEL

Every form of transport that relies on carbon-based fuel generates CO_2, the main cause of human-induced climate change. Modern travel is dependent on aeroplanes, which might use less fuel per kilometre per person than most cars but travel much greater distances. The altitude at which aircraft emit gases (including CO_2) and particles also contributes to their climate change impact. Many websites offer 'carbon calculators' that allow people to estimate the carbon emissions generated by their journey and, for those who wish to do so, to off set the impact of the greenhouse gases emitted with contributions to portfolios of climate-friendly initiatives throughout the world. Lonely Planet off-sets the carbon footprint of all staff and author travel.

swana has offices in Gaborone, Francistown, Maun, Kasane and Victoria Falls (Zimbabwe). It's generally cheaper to book Air Botswana tickets online than it is through one of its offices.

The only scheduled flights to Botswana come from Jo'burg and Cape Town (South Africa), Victoria Falls and Harare (Zimbabwe), Lusaka (Zambia) and Windhoek (Namibia). No European or North American airline flies directly into Botswana, and most travellers fly into either Jo'burg or Cape Town in South Africa (both of which are served by an array of international and domestic carriers) and hop on a connecting flight.

In addition to the following two airlines which do fly into Botswana, the country is served by a number of special charter flights.

Air Namibia (☑in Maun 686 0391; www.airnamibia.com)

South African Airways (☑in Gaborone 397 2397; www.flysaa.com)

AIRPORTS

Kasane Airport (BBK; ☑625 0133)

Maun Airport (MUB; ☑686 1559)

Sir Seretse Khama International Airport (GBE; ☑391 4401) Botswana's main airport is located 11km north of Gaborone. Although it's well served with flights from Jo'burg and Harare, it's seldom used by tourists as an entry point into the country.

Land

Botswana has a well-developed road network with easy access from neighbouring countries. All borders are open daily. It is advisable to try to reach the crossings as early in the day as possible to allow time for any potential delays. Remember also that, despite the official opening hours listed

throughout this book, immigration posts at some smaller border crossings sometimes close for lunch between 12.30pm and 1.45pm. At remote borders on the Botswanan side, you may need to get your visa at the nearest police station in lieu of an immigration post.

TO/FROM NAMIBIA

BORDER CROSSINGS

There are five border crossings between Botswana and Namibia:

Gcangwa–Tsumkwe Little-used crossing along a 4WD-only track close to Botswana's Tsodilo Hills.

Kasane–Mpalila Island Crossing this border is only possible for guests who have prebooked accommodation at upmarket lodges on the island.

Mamuno Remote crossing on the road between Ghanzi and Windhoek.

Mohembo Connects Shakawe, Maun and the Okavango Panhandle with northeastern Namibia.

Ngoma Bridge East of Kasane and connects to Namibia's Caprivi Strip.

BUS

The public transport options between the two countries are few. One option is to catch the daily combi (minibus) from Ghanzi to Mamuno (three hours) and then to cross the borders on foot, bearing in mind that this crossing is about a kilometre long. You will then have to hitch a ride from the Namibian side at least to Gobabis, where you can catch a train or other transport to Windhoek. It's time-consuming and unreliable at best.

CAR & MOTORCYCLE

Drivers crossing the border at Mohembo must secure an entry permit for Mahango Game Reserve. This is free if you're transiting or N$80 per person per day plus N$40 per vehicle per day if you want to drive around the reserve (which is possible in a 2WD).

From Divundu, turn west towards Rundu and then southwest for Windhoek, or east towards Katima Mulilo (Namibia), Kasane (Botswana) and Victoria Falls (Zimbabwe), or take the ferry to Zambia.

TO/FROM SOUTH AFRICA

Gaborone is only 280km as the crow flies from Jo'burg along a good road link.

BORDER CROSSINGS

There are 14 border crossings between South Africa and Botswana. Five of these provide access of sorts from the South African side of the Kgalagadi Transfrontier Park, five are handy for Gaborone, and the remaining four are good for Eastern Botswana and the Tuli Block.

The major crossings:

Bokspits The best South African access to the Kgalagadi Transfontier Park.

Martin's Drift, Zanzibar, Platjan & Pont Drift Eastern Botswana and the Tuli Block from the Northern Transvaal.

Pioneer Gate Connects Gaborone (via Lobatse and Zeerust) with Jo'burg.

Ramatlabama Connects Gaborone with Mafikeng.

Tlokweng Connects Gaborone and Jo'burg via the Madikwe Game Reserve in South Africa.

BUS & COMBI

Intercape Mainliner (☎in Botswana 397 4294, in South Africa 021-380 4400; www.intercape.co.za) runs a service from Jo'burg to Gaborone (from SAR240, 6½ hours, one daily); while you need to get off the bus to sort out any necessary visa formalities, you'll rarely be held up for too long at the border. In Gaborone, the Intercape Mainliner leaves from the petrol station beside the Mall and tickets should be booked a week or so in advance; this can be done online.

You can also travel between South Africa and Botswana by combi. From the far (back) end of the bus station in Gaborone, combis leave when full to a number of South African destinations including Jo'burg (P210/ SAR220, six to seven hours). Be warned that you'll be dropped in Jo'burg's Park Station, which is *not* a safe place to linger in. Combis also travel from Selebi-Phikwe to the border at Martin's Drift (P34, two hours).

Public transport between the two countries bears South African number plates and/or signs on the door marked 'ZA Cross Border Transport'.

CAR & MOTORCYCLE

Most border crossings are clearly marked, but it is vital to note that some crossings over the Limpopo and Molopo Rivers (the latter is in Botswana's south) are drifts (river fords) that cannot be crossed by 2WD in wet weather. In times of very high water, these crossings may be closed to all traffic.

TO/FROM ZIMBABWE

BORDER CROSSINGS

There are three land border crossings between Botswana and Zimbabwe.

Kazungula The main crossing point from Kasane to Victoria Falls.

Pandamatenga A little-used backroads crossing off the road between Kasane and Nata.

Ramokgweban–Plumtree Connects Francistown with Bulawayo and Harare.

BUS

Incredibly, there is *no* public transport between Kasane, the gateway to one of Botswana's major attractions (ie Chobe National Park), and Victoria Falls. Other than hitching, the only cross-border options are the 'tourist shuttle' minibuses that take about one hour and can be arranged through most hotels, camps and tour operators in Kasane. There is little or no coordination between combi companies in either town, so combis often return from Victoria Falls to Kasane empty. Most combis won't leave Kasane unless they have at least two passengers.

Some hotels and lodges in Kasane also offer private transfers to Livingstone/Victoria Falls (from P1250, two hours). They usually pick up booked passengers at their hotels around 10am.

From the Zimbabwean side of the border, try Backpackers Bazaar in Victoria Falls. Some hotels and hostels in Zimbabwe will arrange for your transport from the border, but you need to contact them beforehand.

Elsewhere, buses leave early- to mid-afternoon from the bus station in Francistown bound for Bulawayo (P60, two hours) and Harare (P160, five hours). For anywhere else in western Zimbabwe, get a connection in Bulawayo.

River

Botswana and Zambia share one of the world's shortest international borders: about 750m across the Zambezi River. The only way across the river is by ferry from Kazungula, which normally operates from 6am to 6pm daily.

If you're driving, ferry costs depend on which ferry you catch. The Botswana-registered ferry costs P200 for foreign vehicles and P80 for Botswana-registered vehicles to make the crossing. The Zambian-run ferry charges ZMK134 per vehicle.

At the time of writing there was no cross-border public transport. A combi from Kasane to the border post at Kasungula should cost no more than P35. Once there, you'll need to complete the formalities and take the ferry on foot. There is no regular public transport from the Zambian side of the river, although there is one combi that goes to Dambwa, 3km west of Livingstone. If you don't have a vehicle, ask for a lift to Livingstone, Lusaka or points beyond at the ferry terminal or on the ferry itself.

Getting Around

Botswana's public-transport network is limited. Although domestic air services are fairly frequent and usually reliable, Air Botswana (and charter flights) is not cheap and only a handful of towns are regularly served. Public buses and combis (minibuses) are also cheap and reasonably frequent but confined to sealed roads between towns. All in all, hiring a vehicle is the best and most practical option.

Air

Air Botswana (p164) operates a limited number of domestic routes. It's usually much cheaper to purchase the tickets online through the Air Botswana website than in person at one of its offices. Sample one-way fares at the time of writing:

Gaborone–Francistown from P680

Gaborone–Kasane from P1050

Gaborone–Maun from P882

Kasane–Maun from P369

One-way fares are usually more expensive than return fares, so plan your itinerary accordingly; children aged under two sitting on the lap of an adult cost 10% of the fare and children aged between two and 12 cost

50% of the fare. Passengers are allowed 20kg of luggage (unofficially, a little more is often permitted if the flight is not full).

CHARTER FLIGHTS

Charter flights are often the best – and sometimes the only – way to reach remote lodges, but they are an expensive extra cost; fares are not usually included in the quoted rates for most lodges.

On average, a one-way fare between Maun and a remote lodge in the Okavango Delta will set you back around US$150 to US$250. These services are now highly regulated and flights must be booked as part of a safari package with a mandatory reservation at one of the lodges. This is essential as you can't simply turn up in these remote locations and expect to find a bed for the night, as many lodges are very small. Likewise, you are not permitted to book accommodation at a remote lodge in the delta without also booking a return airfare at the same time. Packages can be booked through agencies in Maun.

It is very important to note that passengers on charter flights are only allowed 10kg to 12kg (and rarely 20kg) of luggage each; check the exact amount when booking. However, if you have an extra 2kg to 3kg, the pilot will usually only mind if the plane is full of passengers.

If you can't stretch the budget to staying in a remote lodge you can still book a flight over the delta with one of the scenic flight companies in Maun.

Bicycle

Botswana is largely flat – and that's about the only concession it makes to cyclists. Unless you're an experienced cyclist and equipped for the extreme conditions, abandon any ideas you may have about a Botswanan bicycle adventure. Distances are great; the climate and landscapes are hot and dry; and, even along major routes, water is scarce and villages are widely spaced. Also bear in mind that bicycles are not permitted in Botswana's national parks and reserves, and cyclists may encounter potentially dangerous wildlife while travelling along any highway or road.

Bus & Combi

Buses and combis regularly travel to all major towns and villages throughout Botswana but are less frequent in sparsely populated areas such as western Botswana and the

Kalahari. Public transport to smaller villages is often nonexistent, unless the village is along a major route.

The extent and frequency of buses and combis also depends on the quantity and quality of roads; for example, there is no public transport along the direct route between Maun and Kasane (ie through Chobe National Park), and services elsewhere can be suspended if roads are flooded. Also, bear in mind that there are very few long-distance services, so most people travelling between Gaborone and Kasane or Maun, for example, will need a connection in Francistown.

Buses are usually comfortable, and normally leave at a set time regardless of whether they're full or not. Finding out the departure times for buses is a matter of asking around the bus station, because schedules are not posted anywhere. Combis leave when full, usually from the same station as the buses. Tickets for all public buses and combis cannot be bought in advance; they can only be purchased on board.

Car & Motorcycle

The best way to travel around Botswana is to hire a vehicle. With your own car you can avoid public transport and organised tours. Remember, however, that distances are long and we generally recommend that you rent a vehicle outside the country (preferably South Africa), where the range of choice is greater and prices are generally lower.

You cannot hire motorbikes in Botswana and, unlike Namibia, the terrain is not well suited to biking. It's also important to note that motorbikes are *not* permitted in national parks and reserves for safety reasons.

DRIVING LICENCE

Your home driving licence is valid for six months in Botswana, but if it isn't written in English you must provide a certified translation. In any case, it is advisable to obtain an International Driving Permit (IDP). Your national automobile association can issue this and it is valid for 12 months.

FUEL & SPARE PARTS

Fuel is relatively expensive in Botswana – at the time of writing it was P9.15 for petrol, P9.40 for diesel – but prices vary according to the remoteness of the petrol station. Petrol stations are open 24 hours in Gaborone, Francistown, Maun, Mahalapye and Pal-

apye; elsewhere, they open from about 7am to 7pm daily.

HIRE

If you're looking to hire a car for exploring Botswana, consider hiring a vehicle in South Africa. Otherwise, we recommend booking through companies who offer specialist rental of fully equipped 4WDs with all camping equipment.

Mainstream international car rental agencies have offices in Botswana. That said, most have only a handful of 4WDs and you should always read the fine print of any rental contracts – some such agencies are known for including a clause that forbids off-road driving! As such, renting through these companies is more likely to be of interest if you'll only be travelling between major population centres along sealed roads.

To hire a car you must be aged at least 21 (some companies require drivers to be over 25) and have been a licensed driver in your home country for at least two years (sometimes five).

Drive Botswana CAR HIRE
(☎in Palapye 492 3416; www.drivebotswana.com) Arranges 4WDs through Explorer Safaris in South Africa, but also organises a complete package itinerary including maps, trip notes and bookings for campsites, all at no extra cost. We found the owner, Andy Raggett, to be outstanding and unfailingly professional.

Self Drive Adventures CAR HIRE
(☎in Maun 686 3755; www.selfdriveadventures. com)

Travel Adventures Botswana CAR HIRE
(☎in Maun 686 1211; www.traveladventuresbotsw ana.com)

INSURANCE

Insurance is *strongly* recommended. No matter who you hire your car from, make sure you understand what is included in the price (such as unlimited kilometres, tax and so on) and what your liabilities are. Most local insurance policies do not include cover for damage to windshields and tyres.

Third-party motor insurance is a minimum requirement in Botswana. However, it is also advisable to take a Damage (Collision) Waiver, which costs around P150 extra per day for a 2WD and about P300 per day for a 4WD. Loss (Theft) Waiver is also an extra worth having. For both types of insurance, the excess liability is about P5000 for a 2WD and P9000 for a 4WD. If you're only going for a short period of time, it may be worth taking out the Super Collision Waiver, which covers absolutely everything, albeit at a price.

ROAD CONDITIONS

With the upgrading of the road between Kasane and Nata, good sealed roads link most major population centres. The most notable exception is the direct route between Kasane and Maun – a horribly corrugated gravel track. The road from Maun to Shakawe past the Okavango Panhandle is generally reasonable but beware of potholes.

Tracks with sand, mud, gravel and rocks (and sometimes all four) – but normally accessible by 2WD except during exceptional rains – connect most villages and cross a few national parks.

Most other 'roads' are poorly defined – and badly mapped – tracks that should only be attempted by 4WD. In the worst of the wet season (December to February), 4WDs should carry a winch on some tracks (eg through Chobe or Moremi National Parks). A compass or, better, Global Positioning System (GPS) equipment with the Tracks4-Africa maps loaded, is essential for driving by 4WD around the salt pans of the Kalahari or northern Botswana at any time.

ROAD RULES

To drive a car in Botswana, you must be at least 18 years old. Like most other Southern African countries, traffic keeps to the left side of the road. The national speed limit is 60km/h up to 120km/h on sealed roads; when passing through towns and villages, assume a speed limit of 60km/h, even in the absence of any signs. Mobile police units routinely set up speed cameras along major roads, particularly between Gaborone and Francistown – on-the-spot fines operate on a sliding scale, but can go as high as P500 if you're 30km/h over the limit and you'll be expected to pay on the spot. On gravel roads, limits are set at 60km/h to 80km/h, while it's 40km/h in all national parks and reserves.

Other road rules to be aware of:

» Sitting on the roof of a moving vehicle is illegal.

» Wearing seat belts (where installed) is compulsory in the front (but not back) seats.

» Drink-driving is also against the law, and your insurance policy will be invalid if you have an accident while drunk.

» Driving without a licence is a serious offence.

» If you have an accident causing injury, it must be reported to the authorities within 48 hours. If vehicles have sustained only minor damage and there are no injuries – and all parties agree – you can exchange names and addresses and sort it out later through your insurance companies.

» In theory, owners are responsible for keeping their livestock off the road, but in practice animals wander wherever they want. If you hit a domestic animal, your distress (and possible vehicle damage) will be compounded by trying to find the owner and the red tape involved when filing a claim.

» Wild animals, including elephants and the estimated three million wild donkeys in Botswana, are a hazard, even along the highways. The Maun–Nata and Nata–Kasane roads are frequently traversed by elephants. The chances of hitting a wild or domestic animal are far, far greater after dark, so driving at night is definitely not recommended.

» One common, but minor, annoyance are the so-called 'buffalo fences' (officially called Veterinary Cordon Fences). These are set up to stop the spread of disease from wild animals to livestock. In most cases your vehicle may be searched (they're looking for fresh meat or dairy products) and you may have to walk (and put additional pairs of shoes) through a soda solution and drive your car through soda-treated water.

Hitching

Hitching in Botswana is an accepted way to get around, given that public transport is sometimes erratic, or nonexistent, in remote areas. Travellers who decide to hitch, however, should understand that they are taking a small but potentially serious risk. People who do choose to hitch will be safer if they travel in pairs and let someone know where they are planning to go.

The equivalent of a bus fare will frequently be requested in exchange for a lift, but to prevent uncomfortable situations at the end of the ride, determine a price before climbing in.

It is totally inadvisable to hitch along the backroads, for example through the Tuli Block or from Maun to Kasane through Chobe National Park. This is because traffic along these roads is virtually nonexistent; in fact, vehicles may only come past a few times a day, leaving the hopeful hitchhiker at risk of exposure or, even worse, running out of water. One way to circumvent this problem is to arrange a lift in advance at a nearby lodge.

Local Transport

Public transport in Botswana is geared towards the needs of the local populace and is confined to main roads between major population centres. Although cheap and reliable, it is of little use to the traveller as most of Botswana's tourist attractions lie off the beaten track.

COMBI

Combis, recognisable by their blue number plates, circulate according to set routes around major towns; ie Gaborone, Kasane, Ghanzi, Molepolole, Mahalapye, Palapye, Francistown, Selebi-Phikwe, Lobatse and Kanye. They are very frequent, inexpensive and generally reliable. However, they aren't terribly safe (most drive too fast), especially on long journeys, and they only serve the major towns. They can also be crowded.

TAXI

Licensed taxis are also recognisable by their blue number plates. They rarely bother hanging around the airports at Gaborone, Francistown, Kasane and Maun, so the only reliable transport from the airport is usually a courtesy bus operated by a top-end hotel or lodge. These are free for guests, but anyone else can normally negotiate a fare with the bus driver. Taxis are always available *to* the airports, however.

It is not normal for taxis to cruise the streets for fares – even in Gaborone. If you need one, telephone a taxi company to arrange a pick-up or go to a taxi stand (usually near the bus or train stations). Some taxi companies include Speedy Cabs (p57) and Final Bravo Cabs (p57). Fares for taxis are negotiable, but fares for occasional shared taxis are fixed. Taxis can be chartered – about P300 to P400 per day, although this is negotiable depending on how far you want to go.

TRAIN

The Botswana Railways system no longer takes passengers. In case passenger services do resume, services are likely to be limited to one line running along eastern Botswana from Ramokgwebana on the Zimbabwean border to Ramatlabama on the South African border.

Victoria Falls

Best Places to Eat

» Cafe Zambezi (p180)

» In Da Belly (p184)

» Olga's Italian Corner (p180)

» Mama Africa (p185)

Best Places to Stay

» Victoria Falls Hotel (p183)

» Elephant Camp (p184)

» Jollyboys Backpackers (p177)

» Stanley Safari Lodge (p179)

Why Go?

Taking its place alongside the Pyramids and the Serengeti, Victoria Falls (*Mosi-oa-Tunya* – the 'smoke that thunders') is one of Africa's original blockbusters. And although Zimbabwe and Zambia share it, Victoria Falls is a place all of its own.

As a magnet for tourists of all descriptions – backpackers, tour groups, thrill seekers, families, honeymooners – Vic Falls is one of the earth's great spectacles. View it directly as a raging mile-long curtain of water, in all its glory, from a helicopter ride or peek precariously over its edge from Devil's Pools; the sheer power and force of the falls is something that simply does not disappoint.

Whether you're here purely to take in the sight of a natural wonder of the world, or for a serious hit of adrenaline via rafting or bungee jumping into the Zambezi, Victoria Falls is a place where you're sure to tick off numerous items from that bucket list.

When to Go

There are two main reasons to go to Victoria Falls – to view the falls and to experience the outdoor activities – and each has its season.

July to December is the season for white-water rafting, especially August for hardcore rapids.

From February to June don't forget your raincoat as you'll experience the falls at their full force.

From July to September You'll get the best views of the falls, combined with lovely weather and all activities to keep you busy.

Victoria Falls

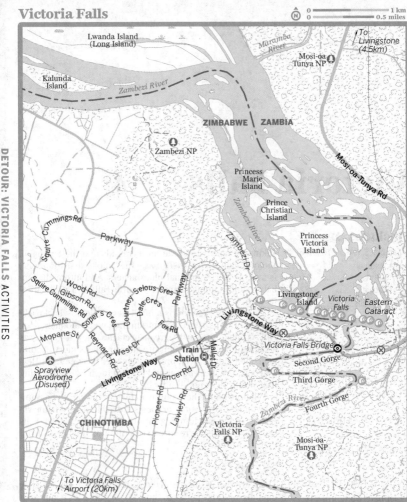

Seventh Natural Wonder of the World

Victoria Falls is the largest, most beautiful and most majestic waterfall on the planet, and is the Seventh Natural Wonder of the World as well as being a UNESCO World Heritage Site. A trip to Southern Africa would not be complete without visiting this unforgettable place.

One million litres of water fall – per second – down a 108m drop along a 1.7km wide strip in the Zambezi Gorge; an awesome sight. Victoria Falls can be seen, heard, tast-ed and touched: it is a treat that few other places in the world can offer, a 'must see before you die' spot.

Victoria Falls is spectacular at any time of year, yet varies in the experiences it offers.

🏃 Activities

While of course it's the spectacular sight of Vic Falls that lures travellers to the region, the astonishing amount of activities to do here is what makes them hang around. White-water rafting, bungee jumping, tak-ing a chopper ride over the falls, walking with rhinos: Vic Falls is well and truly established as one of the world's premier adventure destinations.

To get the best value out of your time here, look into packages which combine various adrenaline leaps, slides and swings for around US$125. Confirm any extra costs such as park or visa fees at the time of booking.

Costs are fairly standard across the board and activities can be organised through accommodation providers and tour operators.

Abseiling
Strap on a helmet, grab a rope and spend the day rappelling down the 54m sheer-drop cliff face for US$40.

Birdwatching
Twitchers will want to bring binoculars to check out 470 species of birds that inhabit the region, including Schalow's turaco, the African finfoot and half-collared kingfisher. Spot them on foot in the parks or on a canoe trip along the Zambezi.

Bungee Jumping & Swings
The third-highest bungee in the world (111m), this famous jump is from atop the iconic Victoria Falls bridge. It's a long way down, but man, it's a lot of fun. It costs US$125 per person.

Otherwise there's the bridge swing where you jump feet first, and free fall for four seconds; you'll end up swinging the right way up, not upside down. There are two main spots, one right off the Victoria Falls Bridge, and the other a bit further along the Batoka Gorge. Costs for single/tandem are US$125/195.

Combine bungee with a bridge swing and bridge slide, and it'll cost US$160.

Canoeing & Kayaking
On the Zambian side, take on the Zambezi's raging rapids in an inflatable kayak on a full-day trip (US$155), or learn to eskimo roll by signing up for half-/one-/three-day courses for US$82/145/412.

Otherwise there are peaceful canoe trips along the Upper Zambezi River on two-person inflatable canoes for US$125 or even more relaxed three-hour guided sunset trips for US$60 including wine and beer. Overnight jaunts cost US$200, with longer trips available.

Cultural Activities
Spend an evening by a campfire drumming under the Southern African sky, which includes a traditional meal, for US$25 for the hour. You can arrange to watch and participate in traditional dance for US$40.

Fishing
Grab a rod and cruise out to the Zambezi for the opportunity to reel in a mighty tiger fish, for around US$125 for a half day, and

THE FALLS VIEWING SEASON

Though spectacular at any time of year, the falls has a wet and dry season and each brings a distinct experience.

When the river is higher and the falls fuller it's the Wet, and when the river is lower and the falls aren't smothered in spray it's the Dry. Broadly speaking, you can expect the following conditions during the year:

January to April The beginning of the rainy season sees the falls begin their transitional period from low to high water, which should give you decent views, combined with experiencing its famous spray.

May to June Don't forget your raincoat, as you're gonna get drenched! While the falls will be hard to see through the mist, it'll give you a true sense of its power as 500 million litres of water plummets over the edge. The mist during this time can be seen from 50kms away. If you want views, don't despair, this is the best time for aerial views with a chopper flight taking you up and over this incredible sight.

July to October The most popular time to visit, as the mist dissipates to unveil the best views and photography options from directly across the falls, while the volume maintains its rage to give you an idea of its sheer force.

November to January The least popular time to visit, as temperatures rise and the falls are at their lowest flow. But they're still impressive nevertheless, as the curtain of water divides into sections. The advantage of this time of year is you're able to swim right up to the edge of Devil's Pool on the Zambian side.

ZIM OR ZAM?

Victoria Falls straddles the border between Zimbabwe and Zambia, and is easily accessible from both countries. However, the big question for most travellers is: do I visit the falls from the town of Victoria Falls, Zimbabwe, or from Livingstone, Zambia? The answer is simple: visit the falls from both sides and, if possible, stay in both towns.

From the Zimbabwean side you're further from the falls, though the overall views are better. From the Zambian side, for daring souls you can literally stand on top of the falls from Devil's Pool, though from here your perspective is narrowed.

The town of Victoria Falls was built for tourists, so it's easily walkable and located right next to the entrance to the Falls. It has a natural African bush beauty.

Livingstone is an attractive town with a relaxed ambience and a proud, historic air. Since the town of Victoria Falls was the main tourist centre for so many years, Livingstone feels more authentic, perhaps because locals earn their livelihood through means other than tourism. Livingstone is bustling with travellers year round, though the town is fairly spread out, and is located 11km from the falls.

US$255 for a full day, which includes beer, fuel and transfers. Get in touch with Angle Zambia (☑327489; www.zambezifishing.com) for more info.

Horse Riding

Indulge in a bit of wildlife spotting from horseback along the Zambezi. Rides for 2½ hours cost around $US90, and full-day trips for experienced riders are US$145.

Jet Boats

Power straight into whirlpools! This hair-raising trip costs US$97, and is combined with a cable-car ride down into the Batoka Gorge.

Quad biking

Discover the spectacular landscape around Livingstone, Zambia and the Batoka Gorge, spotting wildlife as you go on all-terrain quad bikes. Trips vary from ecotrail riding at Batoka Land to longer-range cultural trips in the African bush. Trips are 1 hour (US$80) or 2½ hours (US$150).

Rafting

This is one of the best white-water rafting destinations in the world, both for experienced rafters and newbies. Rafting can be done on either side of the Zambezi, in Zim or Zam, and fills up between mid-February and July, high-water season. In the river below Vic Falls you'll find Grade 5 rapids – very long with huge drops and big kicks, and not for the faint-hearted. In high-water season, day trips move downstream from rapids 11 to 24, covering a distance of around 18km.

Low-water (open) season is between July and mid-February and is considered the best time for rafting. Day trips run between rapids 1 and 19, covering a distance of around 25km. The river will usually close for its 'off season' around April/May, depending on the rain pattern for the year.

Half-/full-day trips cost about US$120/130. Overnight and multiday jaunts can also be arranged.

Other options include **riverboarding**, which is basically lying on a boogie board and careering down the rapids for US$135/150 for a half/full day. The best time of year for riverboarding is February to June. A rafting/riverboarding combo is available, US$165.

River Cruises

River cruises along the Zambezi range from civilised jaunts on the grand *African Queen* to all-you-can-drink sunset booze cruises. Prices range from US$30 to US$60. Great for spotting wildlife, though some tourists get just as much enjoyment out of the bottomless drinks. Highly recommended.

Scenic Flights

Just when you thought the falls couldn't get any more spectacular, discover the 'flight of angels' helicopter ride that flies you right by the drama for the undisputed best views available. Rides aren't cheap, but it's worth it. Zambezi Helicopter Company (www.shearwatervictoriafalls.com/helicopters; flights 13/25 mins US$130/250, plus US$10 park entry fee) in Zimbabwe and United Air Charter (☑213

323095; www.uaczam.com; Baobab Ridge, Livingstone) in Zambia both offer flights.

Another option is motorised hang-gliders, which also offer fabulous aerial views, and the pilot will take pictures for you with a camera fixed to the wing. It costs US$140 for 15 minutes over the falls.

Steam-train Journeys

To take in the romance of yesteryear, book yourself a ride on a historical steam train. On the Zimbabwe side there is the 1953 class 14A Garratt steam train through Victoria Falls Steam Train Co (☑13 42912; steamtraincompany.com; incl drinks US$40, incl dinner from US$75), that will take you over the iconic bridge at sunset or through the Zambezi National Park with either a full dinner or gourmet canapes and unlimited drinks. Even if you're not booked on a trip it's worth getting along to the station to watch the incredible drama of its departure. There are also daily vintage tram trips (one way/return US$15/30) that head over the bridge and which also have a drinks and canapes option (US$40).

In Zambia the Royal Livingstone Express (☑213 323232; www.royal-livingstone-express.com; Mosi-oa-Tunya Rd, Livingstone; incl dinner & drinks US$170; ☾Wed & Sat) takes you on a 3½-hour ride including five-course dinner and drinks on a 1922 10th-class steam engine that will chug you through Mosi-oa-Tunya National Park on plush leather couches.

Wildlife Safaris

There are plenty of options for wildlife watching in the area, both in the nearby national parks and private game reserves, or further afield. Both guided walks and jeep safaris are available in the parks on both sides of the border. At Mosi-oa-Tunya Game Park (wildlife sanctuary admission US$10; ☾wildlife sanctuary 6am-6pm) in Zambia, there's a chance to see white rhinos, while the Zambezi National Park in Zimbabwe has a small population of lions. Walks cost around US$70, and drives US$50 to US$90. There are also dusk, dawn or night wildlife drives (US$50 to US$90). River safaris (US$30) along the Zambezi River are another popular way to see various wildlife including elephants, hippos and plenty of birdlife.

Another convenient option, only 15km from Victoria Falls town, is the Victoria Falls Private Game Reserve (☑44471;

www.shearwatervictoriafalls.com/safaris), a 4000-hectare private reserve run by Shearwaters. Here you can track the Big Five on a game drive (US$90), where apparently you stand a 97% (to be precise) chance of encountering a black rhino.

You can travel further afield, with operators arranging day trips to Chobe National Park (see p75) in Botswana for US$170 (excluding visas). It's only a one-hour drive from Victoria Falls, and includes a breakfast boat cruise, a game drive in Chobe National Park, lunch and transfer back to Victoria Falls by 5pm. Wildlife viewing is excellent: lions, elephants, wild dogs, cheetahs, buffaloes and plenty of antelopes.

Hwange National Park (admission per day US$15; ☾about 6am-6pm) in Zimbabwe is the other option, with one of the largest number of elephants in the world. A day trip will cost around US$250.

Zipline & Slides

Glide at 106km/h along a zipline (single/tandem US$66/105), or soar like a superhero from one country to another (from Zim to Zam) on the 'bridge slide' as you whiz over Batoka Gorge (single/tandem US$35/50). Other similar options are flying-fox rides (US$40).

ℹ Information

Tourist Information

Hands down the best independent advice is from Backpackers Bazaar (p186) in the town of Victoria Falls, run by the passionate owner, Joy, who is a wealth of all info and advice for Vic Falls and beyond. In Livingstone, the folks at Jollyboys Backpackers (p177) are also extremely knowledgeable on all the latest happenings. Both are good places to book activities and onward travel.

Travel & Adventure Companies

With activities and prices standardised across the board, all bookings can conveniently be arranged through backpacker accommodation and big hotels.

You can also go directly to the tour operators. The main ones in Zimbabwe are **Wild Horizons** (☑0712-213721, 13 42013; www.wildhorizons.co.za; 310 Parkway Dr) and **Shearwater** (☑13 44471; www.shearwatervictoriafalls.com; Parkway Dr). In Zambia try **Safari Par Excellence** (☑213 320606; www.safpar.net) and **Livingstone's Adventure** (☑213 323587; www.livingstonesadventure.com) both in Livingstone. All cover activities on either side.

VISAS

You will need a visa to cross sides between Zim and Zam. These are available at the border crossings, open from around 7am to 10pm. Note that you can't get multi-entry visas at these crossing; in most cases you need to apply at the embassy in your home country before travelling.

Crossing into Zambia, a day visit costs US$20 for 24 hours, a single-entry visa costs US$50 and double entry is US$80.

Crossing into Zimbabwe, a single-entry visa costs US$30 for most nationalities (US$55 for British/Irish, US$75 for Canadian). Double entry is US$45 for most nationalities (US$75 for British/Irish, and unavailable for Canadians).

ZAMBIA

☑ 260

As Zambia continues to ride the wave of tourism generated by the falls, it manages to keep itself grounded, offering a wonderfully low-key destination that has been recognised as such; it's co-host of the 2013 United Nations World Tourism Assembly. The waterfront straddling the falls continues its rapid development and is fast becoming one of the most exclusive destinations in Southern Africa.

Livingstone & Around

☑ 0213

Set 11km away from Victoria Falls, the relaxed town of Livingstone has taken on the role of a backpacking mecca. It attracts travellers not only to experience the falls, but to tackle the thrilling adventure scene. The town is not much to look at, but it is a safe, lively place with some fantastic restaurants. Those looking for a more scenic and luxurious experience can treat themselves to the natural setting along the Zambezi River at any number of plush lodges with river and wildlife views.

The town centres itself around one main road, Mosi-oa-Tunya Rd, 11km from the entrance to the falls. Several establishments are set right on the Zambezi River, but most of the action is set a bit back from the waterfront.

◉ Sights & Activities

TOP CHOICE Victoria Falls World Heritage National Monument Site   WATERFALL
(admission ZMW103.5; ⊘6am-6pm) This is what you're here for, the mighty Victoria Falls. It's a part of the Mosi-oa-Tunya National Park, 11km outside town before the Zambia border crossing; a path here leads to the visi-

tor information centre, which has modest displays on local fauna, geology and culture.

From the centre, a network of paths leads through thick vegetation to various viewpoints. You can walk upstream along a path free of fences – and warning notices (so take care!) – to watch the Zambezi waters glide smoothly through rocks and little islands towards the lip of the falls.

For close-up views of the **Eastern Cataract**, nothing beats the hair-raising (and hair-wetting) walk across the footbridge, through swirling clouds of mist, to a sheer buttress called the **Knife Edge**. If the water is low, or the wind is favourable, you'll be treated to a magnificent view of the falls as well as the yawning abyss below. Otherwise, your vision (and your clothes) will be drenched by spray. Then you can walk down a steep track to the banks of the great Zambezi to see the huge whirlpool called the **Boiling Pot**. Watch out for cheeky baboons.

The park is open again in the evenings during (and just before and after) a full moon in order to see the amazing lunar rainbow. The tickets cost an extra ZMW51 – hours of operation vary, so inquire through your accommodation.

TOP CHOICE Livingstone Island   VIEWPOINT
One of the most thrilling experiences not only at the falls, but in Africa, is the hair-raising journey to Livingstone Island. Here you will bathe in **Devil's Pool** – nature's ultimate infinity pool, set directly on the edge of the raging drama of Victoria Falls. You can leap into the pool and then poke your head over the edge to get an extraordinary view of the 100m drop.

Livingstone Island is in the middle of the Zambezi River, located at the top of the falls, and here you'll see a plaque marking the spot where David Livingstone first sighted the falls. The island is accessed via boat, and prices include either breakfast (ZMW333), lunch (ZMW615) or high tea (ZMW486). When the water is low, you're able to access it via walking or swimming across, but a guide is compulsory. Note that access to the island is closed from around March to May when the water levels are too high.

Mosi-oa-Tunya Game Park   WILDLIFE RESERVE
(admission US$10; ☺6am-6pm) The other part of the Mosi-oa-Tunya National Park is up-river from the falls, and only 3km southwest of Livingstone. The tiny wildlife sanctuary has a surprising range of animals including rhinos, zebras, giraffes, buffaloes, elephants and antelopes. It's most famous for tracking white rhinos on foot. Walks cost ZMW435 per person, for groups of up to eight.

Livingstone Museum   MUSEUM
(Mosi-oa-Tunya Rd; admission ZMW25; ☺9am-4.30pm) The excellent Livingstone Museum is divided into five sections covering archaeology, history, ethnography, natural history and art, and is highlighted by Tonga ritual artefacts, a life-sized model African village, a collection of David Livingstone memorabilia and historic maps dating back to 1690.

🛏 Sleeping

TOWN CENTRE

TOP CHOICE **Jollyboys Backpackers**   BACKPACKERS $
(✆324229; www.backpackzambia.com; 34 Kanyanta Rd; campsite/dm/r ZMW40/50/205; @ 🛜 🛒) The British and Canadian owners of Jollyboys know exactly what backpackers want, and it is wildly popular for a good reason. They have kept the needs of independent travellers at the forefront, from the sunken lounge and excellent coffee to the sparkling pool, cheap restaurant-bar and clean bright rooms. Things can get a bit hectic in the evenings, so they've

DETOUR: VICTORIA FALLS LIVINGSTONE & AROUND

LIVINGSTONE – THE MAN, THE MYTH, THE LEGEND

David Livingstone is one of a few European explorers who is still revered by modern-day Africans. His legendary exploits on the continent border the realm of fiction, though his life's mission to end the slave trade was very real (and ultimately very successful).

Born into rural poverty in the south of Scotland on 19 March 1813, Livingstone worked in London for several years before being ordained as a missionary in 1840. The following year he arrived in Bechuanaland (now Botswana) and began travelling inland, looking for converts and seeking to end the slave trade.

As early as 1842 Livingstone had already become the first European to penetrate the northern reaches of the Kalahari. For the next several years he explored the African interior with the purpose of opening up trade routes and establishing missions. In 1854 Livingstone discovered a route to the Atlantic coast, and arrived in present-day Luanda. However, his most famous discovery occurred in 1855 when he first set eyes on Victoria Falls during his epic boat journey down the Zambezi River. Livingstone returned to Britain a national hero, and recounted his travels in the 1857 publication *Missionary Travels and Researches in South Africa*.

In 1858 Livingstone returned to Africa as the head of the 'Zambezi Expedition', a government-funded venture that aimed to identify natural resource reserves in the region. Unfortunately, the expedition ended when a previously unexplored section of the Zambezi turned out to be unnavigable.

In 1869 Livingstone reached Lake Tanganyika despite failing health, though several of his followers abandoned the expedition en route. These desertions were headline news in Britain, sparking rumours regarding Livingstone's health and sanity. In response to the growing mystery surrounding Livingstone's whereabouts, the *New York Herald* arranged a publicity stunt by sending journalist Henry Morton Stanley to find Livingstone.

After arriving in Zanzibar and setting out with nearly 200 porters, Stanley finally found Livingstone on 10 November 1871 in Ujiji near Lake Tanganyika and famously greeted him with the line 'Dr Livingstone, I presume?'.

Although Stanley urged him to leave the continent, Livingstone was determined to find the source of the Nile, and penetrated deeper into the continent than any European prior. On 1 May 1873 Livingstone died from malaria and dysentery near Lake Bangweula in present-day Zambia. His body was carried for thousands of kilometres by his attendants, and now lies in the ground at Westminster Abbey in London.

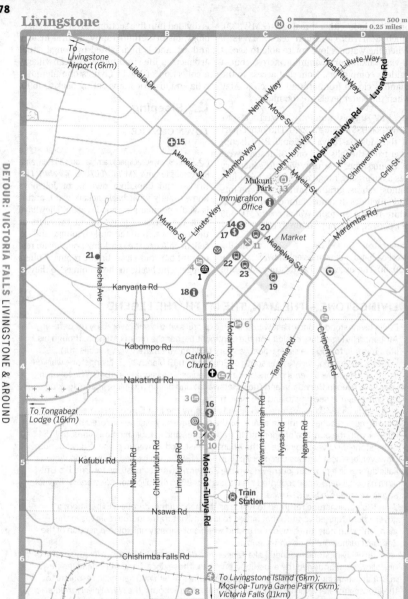

opened up the quieter **Jollyboys Camp** (Chipembi Rd) guesthouse nearby, in Chipembi Rd, to suit couples and families.

Fawlty Towers   BACKPACKERS, LODGE **$$**
(☏323432; www.adventure-africa.com; 216 Mosi-oa-Tunya Rd; campsite/dm/tr ZMW40/76/215, d

with/without bathroom ZMW307/205; ✳@🛜🏊) Once a backpacker institution, things have been spruced up here into a guesthouse full of upmarket touches: free internet and wi-fi, shady lawns, a great pool and some of the nicest and most spacious dorms we've seen. No Basil or Manuel in sight.

Livingstone

ZigZag   GUESTHOUSE $$
(☏322814; www.zigzagzambia.com; off Mosi-oa-Tunya Rd; s/d ZMW280/410; P❋@🛜❄) Don't be deceived by the motel-meets-caravan-park exterior; the rooms here are more boutique B&B with loving touches throughout. Run by a friendly Scottish and Namibian couple, the lovely swimming pool, great restaurant and playground for kids give it a classic holiday feel.

Olga's Guesthouse   GUESTHOUSE $$
(☏324160; www.olgasproject.com; cnr Mosi-oa-Tunya & Nakatindi Rds; s/d/f ZMW256/358/460; ❋🛜) If you need a lie down after gorging at Olga's Italian Corner restaurant, Olga's has it covered. Clean, spacious rooms with cool tiled floors, teak furniture and slick bathrooms are just a few feet away. Profits go towards helping an organisation supporting local youth.

Livingstone Backpackers   BACKPACKERS $
(☏324730; www.livingstonebackpackers.com; 559 Mokambo Rd; campsite/dm ZMW40/50; 🛜❄) Resembling the *Big Brother* household, this place can be a bit 'party central', particularly when the Gen Y volunteer brigade is on holiday. You'll find them lounging by the pool or in the sandy outdoor cabana, swinging in hammocks or tackling the rock-climbing wall! There is also a hot tub, open-air kitchen and living room.

ZAMBEZI RIVERFRONT

Most prices include meals and transfers from Livingstone and reservations are recommended.

Stanley Safari Lodge   LODGE $$$
TOP CHOICE
(☏in South Africa 27-72-170 8879; www.stanley safaris.com; per person with full board and activities from ZMW2,203; @🛜❄) Intimate and indulgent, Stanley is a 10km drive from the falls in a peaceful spot surrounded by mopane forest. Rooms are as plush as can be expected at these prices; the standouts are the open-air suites where you can soak up nature from your own private plunge pool. When you tire of that, curl up by the fire in the open-air lounge. Rates are all-inclusive.

David Livingstone   LODGE $$$
(☏324601; www.thedavidlivingstone.com; River Side Dr, Mosi-oa-Tunya National Park; s/d incl breakfast & activities ZMW1,745/2,675; 🛜❄) The newest addition to Livingstone's luxury hotels: all rooms have river views, Rhodesian teak furniture, concertina doors, four-poster beds and stand-alone bathtubs looking out to the water. It's set within the national park, hippos honk around at night, and the decking and bar around the riverfront infinity pool is a wonderful spot for a sundowner. It's located halfway between Livingstone and the falls.

Jungle Junction
Bovu Island LODGE, CAMPGROUND $
(☎0978-725282, 323708; www.junglejunction.
info; campsite per person ZMW50, hut per person
ZMW128–179; ☒) Hippos, hammocks and
harmony. On a lush island in the middle of
the Zambezi River, around 50km from Livingstone, Jungle Junction attracts travellers
who just want to lounge beneath palm trees,
or engage in some fishing (ZMW77 including equipment and guide). Meals are available (ZMW36 to ZMW60).

Zambezi Waterfront LODGE $$$
(☎320606; www.safpar.net/waterfront.html; camp-
site per person ZMW50, s/d tent ZMW155/200,
s/d incl breakfast from ZMW640/920; ❄️☎☒)
Another waterfront lodge, things feel more
rustic here with a wilderness charm, as crocs
inhabit a small creek on the property. Ac-
commodation ranges from luxury tents and
riverside chalets to executive rooms or family
suites. The riverside open-air beer garden is
unsurprisingly popular at sunset. It's located
4km south of Livingstone, and a handy free
shuttle service takes you to the falls and
town.

Zambezi Sun RESORT $
(☎321122; www.suninternational.com; s/d incl break-
fast from ZMW2,355/2,510, f ZMW2,550; ❄️@☎☒)
Only a 10-minute walk from the falls, this
sprawling resort provides a great base for ex-
ploring the area. The North African kasbah-
inspired rooms are vibrant while plenty of
pools and a playground are perfect for fami-
lies. It's within the perimeter of the national
park, so expect to see grazing zebras but keep
your distance. Rates include falls entry.

Tongabezi Lodge LODGE $$$
(☎323235; www.tongabezi.com; cottage/house per
person ZMW2,200/2,710; ❄️☒) Here you'll find
sumptuous spacious cottages and open-
faced 'treehouses' and private dining decks.
Guests are invited to spend an evening on
nearby Sindabezi Island (per person per
night US$350), selected by the *Sunday
Times* as the best remote place to stay in the
world.

✖ Eating & Drinking
Livingstone is home to a number of high-
quality restaurants, including a batch of
excellent newcomers. Enjoy a sundowner
at any of the the Zambezi riverfront resorts
that allow nonguests to pop in for a drink
and a stellar sunset.

TOP CHOICE ⟩ **Cafe Zambezi** AFRICAN $$
(☎0978-978578; 217 Mosi-oa-Tunya Rd; mains
ZMW30-48; ☺9am-midnight; ☎🍴) Bursting
with local flavour; vibrant decor flows from
the indoor dining room to the outdoor
courtyard, sunny by day and candlelit by
night. The broad menu covers local *braai*
(barbecue) favourites of goat meat and mo-
pane caterpillars or an international twist
of roasted veg with feta, served with *sadza*
(maize porridge). Authentic wood-fired
pizzas are a winner or sink your teeth into
crocodile or eggplant-and-haloumi burgers.

TOP CHOICE ⟩ **Olga's Italian Corner** ITALIAN $$
(www.olgasproject.con; cnr Mosi-oa-Tunya & Nakatindi
Rds; pizza & pasta from ZMW40; ☺7am-10pm; ☎🍴)
Olga's does authentic wood-fired thin-crust
pizzas, as well as delicious homemade pasta
classics all served under a large thatched roof.
Great options for vegetarians, include the la-
sagna with its crispy blackened edge served in
the dish. All profits go to a community centre
to help disadvantaged youth.

ZigZag CAFE $$
(off Mosi-oa-Tunya Rd; mains from ZMW25; ☺7am-
9pm; ☎) Another string to Livingstone's bow
of culinary choices, ZigZag has a drool-
inducing menu of homemade muffins (such
as cranberry and white chocolate), smooth-
ies using fresh fruit from the garden, and a
changing small menu of comfort food.

Spot CAFE $
(Mosi-oa-Tunya Rd; mains from ZMW40; ☺10am-
10pm) Promising 'forkin good food', this at-
tractive little outdoor eatery with picnic tables
delivers with its mix of local and international
dishes, including a mean chicken schnitzel.

Wonderbake CAFE, BAKERY $
(Mosi-oa-Tunga Rd; ☺8am-9pm; ☎) There's
nothing fancy about this bakery cafeteria,
but it has a good local flavour, sells cheap
pies and has free wi-fi.

Fez Bar BAR
(Mosi-oa-Tunya Rd) This open-air bar set under
a garage tin roof is a popular place to kick on
to with its drinking games, pool tables and
menu of soft-shell tacos.

🔒 Shopping
Mukuni Crafts CRAFTS
(Mosi-oa-Tunya Rd) The craft stalls in the south-
ern corner of Mukuni Park are a pleasant,
and hassle-free place to browse for souvenirs.

❶ Information

Dangers & Annoyances

Don't walk from town to the falls as there have been a number of muggings along this stretch of road – even tourists on bicycles have been attacked. It's a long and not terribly interesting walk anyway, and simply not worth the risk. Take a minivan for under ZMW5 or a blue taxi for ZMW40.

Emergency

Police (☏320116; Maramba Rd)

Internet Access

Computer Centre (216 Mosi-oa-Tunya Rd; internet per hr US$2; ☺8am-8pm) Also offers international phone calls and faxes. All the hostels now have wi-fi or at least internet access.

Medical Services

Livingstone General Hospital (☏321475; Akapelwa St)

Money

Barclays Bank (cnr Mosi-oa-Tunya Rd & Akapelwa St) and **Standard Charted Bank** (Mosi-oa-Tunya Rd) both accept Visa cards, while **Stanbic** (Mosi-oa-Tunya Rd) accepts MasterCard.

Post

Post Office (Mosi-oa-Tunya Rd) Has a *poste restante* and fax service.

Tourist Information

Tourist Centre (☏321404; www.zambia tourism.com; Mosi-oa-Tunya Rd; ☺8am-5pm Mon-Fri) Mildly useful and can help with booking tours and accommodation, but Jollyboys and Fawlty Towers have all the information you need.

❶ Getting There & Away

Air

South African Airways (☏0212-612207; www.flysaa.com) and **British Airways** (www.british airways.com) have daily flights to and from Johannesburg. **1Time** (☏322744; www.1time.aero) flies three times a week. The cheapest economy fare starts at around US$400 return. **Proflight Zambia** (☏0211-845944; www.proflight-zambia.com) flies daily from Livingstone to Lusaka.

Bus & Combi (Minibus)

The Zambian side of the falls is 11km south of Livingstone and along the main road to the border with Zimbabwe. Plenty of minibuses and shared taxis ply the route from the minibus terminal along Senanga Rd in Livingstone. As muggings have been reported, it is best to take a taxi.

TO LUSAKA

CR Holdings (☏0977-861063; cnr Mosi-oa-Tunya Rd & Akapelwa St) Runs four services a day to Lusaka (ZMW80, seven hours).

Mazhandu Family Bus (☏0975-805064) Seven daily buses to Lusaka (ZMW80 to ZMW115) from 6am till 10.30pm.

Shalom Bus (☏0977-747013; Mutelo St) Eight buses a day travelling to Lusaka (ZMW75, six hours), from 5.30am till 10pm, as well as to many other parts of Zambia

TO NAMIBIA

For travelling to Namibia, and crossing the Zambia–Namibia border at Katima Mulilo, see p252.

TO BOTSWANA

Buses to Shesheke (ZMW60, two hours) depart with Mazhandu Family Bus at 5am and 2pm. Otherwise there are buses to Sesheke (ZMW50) departing when full from Mingongo bus station next to the Catholic church at Dambwa village, 3km west of the town centre. To get to Mongu from Livingstone, it's best to head to Sesheke or Lusaka, and then transfer to a Mongu bus.

Combis (minibuses) to the Botswana border at Kazungula depart when they are full from Mingongo bus station and cost ZMW30. Shared taxis can be taken from the taxi rank by Shoprite and cost ZMW40.

For information about travelling to Botswana, and crossing the Zambia–Botswana border at Kazungula, see p83.

Car & Motorcycle

If you're driving a rented car or motorcycle, be sure to carefully check all info regarding insurance, and that you have all the necessary papers for checks and border crossings such as 'owners' and 'permission to drive' documents, insurance papers and a copy of carbon tax receipt. Expect to pay around $US55 in various fees when crossing the border into Zimbabwe.

Train

While the bus is a much quicker way to get around, the *Zambezi Express* is more for lovers of slow travel or trains. It leaves Livingstone for Lusaka (economy/1st class/sleeper ZMW30/45/45, 15 hours), via Choma, on Tuesday and Friday at 8pm. Reservations are available at the **train station** (☏320001), which is signed off Mosi-oa-Tunya Rd.

❶ Getting Around

To/From the Airport

Livingstone Airport is located 6km northwest of town, and is easily accessible by taxi (ZMW50 each way).

Combis & Taxis

Combis run regularly along Mosi-oa-Tunya Rd to Victoria Falls and the Zambian border, 11km south of Livingstone (ZMW5, 15 minutes). Blue taxis cost ZMW40 to ZMW50 from the border to Livingstone. Coming from the border, combis are parked just over from the waiting taxis, and depart when full.

Car Hire

Hemingways (☑320996; www.hemingways zambia.com; Mosi-oa-Tunya Rd) in Livingstone has new Toyota Hi-Lux 4WDs for around US$210 per day. Prices include cooking and camping equipment. Drivers must be over 25.

ZIMBABWE

☑ 263

There may still be a long way to go, but finally things seem to be looking up for Zimbabwe. All the bad news that has kept it in the glare of the spotlight – rampant land reform, hyper inflation and food shortages – fortunately now seem to be a thing of the past. In reality, safety has never been a concern for travellers here and, even during the worst of it, tourists were never targets for political violence. Word of this seems to have spread, as tourists stream back to the Zim side of the falls.

Victoria Falls

☑ 013

Having temporarily lost its mantle to Livingstone as the falls' premier tourist town, the town of Victoria Falls has reclaimed what's historically theirs as tourists return across the border in numbers.

Unlike Livingstone, the town was built for tourism. It is right upon the falls with neat, walkable streets (though not at dark, because of the wild animals) lined with hotels, bars and some of the best crafts you'll find in Southern Africa. While for a few years it felt like a resort in off-season, there's

Victoria Falls

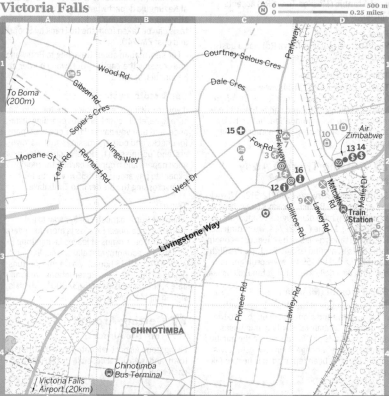

no mistake about it now – it's officially reopened for business.

◉ Sights & Activities

TOP CHOICE Victoria Falls National Park WATERFALL (admission US$30; ⊙6am-6pm) Located just before the border crossing and about 1km from the town centre, here on the Zim side of the falls you're in for a real treat. The walk is along the top of the gorge on a path, with various viewing points opening up to the extraordinary front-on panoramas of these world-famous falls. One of the most dramatic spots is the westernmost point known as **Cataract View**. Another track leads to the aptly named **Danger Point**, where a sheer, unfenced 100m drop-off will rattle your nerves. From there, you can follow a side track for a view of the **Victoria Falls Bridge**.

Hire a raincoat and umbrella just inside the gates if you go in April, or you may as well walk in your swimsuit – you will get soaked! The park is open again in the evenings during (and just before and after) a full moon, in order to see the amazing lunar rainbow (tickets cost an extra US$10).

Zambezi National Park WILDLIFE RESERVE (admission US$15; ⊙6am-6.30pm) Consisting of 40km of Zambezi River frontage and a spread of wildlife-rich mopane forest and savannah, this national park is best known for its herds of sable antelopes, but it is also home to giraffes, elephants and an occasional lion. The entrance to the park is only 5km northwest of the Victoria Falls town centre, and is easily accessible by private vehicle. Tour operators on both sides of the border offer wildlife drives, guided hikes and fishing expeditions.

FREE Jafuta Heritage Centre CULTURAL CENTRE (www.elephantswalk.com/heritage; Elephant's Walk Shopping Village, off Adam Stander Dr; ⊙8am-6pm) This worthwhile collection details the cultural heritage of local ethnic groups, from Shona, Ndebele, Tonga and Lozi people.

🛏 Sleeping

TOP CHOICE Victoria Falls Hotel LUXURY HOTEL $$$ (☎44751; www.victoria-falls-hotels.net; 2 Mallet Dr; s/d incl breakfast from US$312/336; ❄🛜🏊) Built in 1904, this historic hotel (the oldest in Zimbabwe) oozes elegance and sophistication, and occupies an impossibly scenic location. Looking across manicured lawns (with roaming warthogs) to the gorge and bridge, you can't see the falls as such but you do see the spray from some rooms. High tea here at Stanley's Terrace is an institution.

Shoestrings Backpackers BACKPACKERS $ (☎40167; 12 West Dr; campsite per person US$6, dm/d US$9/35; @🛜🏊) A perennial favourite

Victoria Falls & Mosi-oa-Tunya National Parks

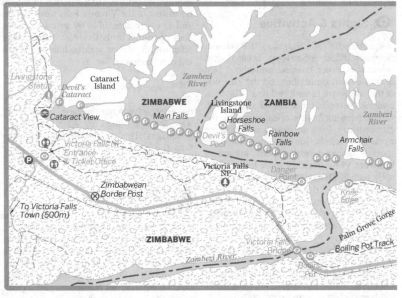

for backpackers, both the overland truck crowd and independent variety, who are here for its laid-back ambience, swimming pool and social bar (things gets very rowdy here on weekends). Rooms are a mix of dorms or privates, or pitch a tent. They also book all activities.

Elephant Camp LUXURY LODGE $$$
(www.theelephantcamp.com; s/d full board US$350/700; @🛜🏊) One of the best spots to splash out; the luxurious 'tents' have a classic lodge feel and are set on a private game reserve looking out to the mopane woodland savannah. Each room has its own outdoor private plunge pool and balcony decking to spot grazing animals or the spray of the falls. You might get to meet Sylvester, the resident cheetah.

Victoria Falls
Restcamp & Lodges CAMPSITE, LODGE $
(🖉40509; www.vicfallsrestcamp.com; cnr Parkway & West Dr; campsite/dm/fitted dome tents US$10/11/20, s/d chalets without bathroom US$25/34, cottages US$67; 🛜🏊) A great alternative for budget travellers wanting to avoid the party atmosphere of other backpackers. Rooms are basic no-frills lodge-style and tented camps. There's a lovely pool and fantastic

open-air restaurant, In Da Belly. Rooms are basic, but spotless.

Victoria Falls Backpackers BACKPACKERS $
(🖉42209; www.victoriafallsbackpackers.com; 357 Gibson Rd; campsite per person US$4, dm US$8, s/d without bathroom US$10/20; @🏊) Slightly rough around the edges, and a bit further away from the centre of town, it nevertheless remains a very good choice for budget travellers wanting a more laid-back environment.

Bengula Cottages GUESTHOUSE $$
(🖉45945, 0778-173286; www.bengulacottages.com/; 645 Mahogany Rd; s/d/f low season US$60/100/120, high season $US100/160/220; 🏊) In the leafy suburbs, these attractive units are a solid midrange choice set around a shady pool with paper lanterns strung up and a relaxed atmosphere. The communal kitchen comes well equipped.

✖ Eating

In Da Belly
Restaurant AFRICAN, INTERNATIONAL $
(🖉332077; Victoria Falls Restcamp & Lodges; meals US$5-15; ⏰7am-9.30pm) Under a large thatched hut, looking out to a sparkling pool, this relaxed open-air eatery has a menu of warthog schnitzel, crocodile curry and impala burgers, as well as one of the

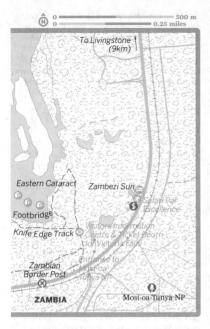

best breakfast menus in town. The name is a play on Ndebele, one of the two major population tribes in Zimbabwe.

Africa Cafe CAFE $
(www.elephantswalk.com/africa_cafe.htm; Elephant's Walk Shopping & Art Village; ⊘8am-5pm; ☑) This appealing outdoor cafe at the Elephant's Walk Shopping & Artist Village, with smiley staff, is a great place to refuel with quality coffee, delicious breakfast, burgers and vegetarian food.

Lola's Tapas & Bar SPANISH $$
(☑42994; 8B Landela Complex; tapas US$2-9; ⊘8am-10pm; ☎) Tapas such as *patatas bravas* and *calamares a la Romana* served by a welcoming couple from Barcelona. Dine outdoors or in the more intimate indoor area. Jugs of sangria available (US$15).

Mama Africa AFRICAN $$
(☑41725; www.mamaafricaeatinghouse.com; meals US$5-8; ⊘10am-10pm) This long-time tourist haunt behind the Landela Centre specialises in local dishes, steaks and game meats. Also has regular live music and traditional dance performances.

Boma AFRICAN $$
(off Map p182; ☑43211; www.thebomarestaurant. com; Squire Cummings Rd, Victoria Falls Safari Lodge; buffet US$40; ⊘dinner 7pm) While it may be a bit of a tourist trap, Boma manages to be more genuine than tacky. Enjoy a taste of Africa at this buffet restaurant set under a massive thatched roof. Dine on smoked guinea-fowl starter, impala-knuckle terrine or spit-roast warthog. There's also traditional dancing, interactive drumming and fortune telling by a witch doctor.

🍷 Drinking

[TOP CHOICE] **Stanley's Terrace** RESTAURANT
(Mallet Dr, Victoria Falls Hotel; high tea for 2 people US$30; ⊘high tea 3-6pm; ☎) The Terrace at the stately Victoria Falls Hotel just brims with English colonial ambience. High tea is served with a postcard-perfect backdrop of the gardens and Vic Falls Bridge, with polished silverware, decadent cakes and three-tiered trays of finger sandwiches (cucumber? why yes, of course). Jugs of Pimms are perfect on a summer day at US$22. The only thing missing is the croquet.

Shoestrings Backpackers BAR
(12 West Dr) It's fairly laid back during the week, while weekends often feel like a house party as the dance floor gets a lot of action.

🛍 Shopping

A good selection of craft shops are located along Adam Stander Dr, with a quality items such as Shona sculpture and pieces made from recycled materials.

[TOP CHOICE] **Elephant's Walk Shopping & Artist Village** SHOPPING CENTRE
(☑0772-254552; www.elephantswalk.com; Adam Stander Dr) A must for those in the market for quality Zimbabwean and African craft, this shopping village is home to boutique stores and galleries owned by a collective that aims to promote and set up local artists.

Prime Art Gallery ART
(☑342783; www.primeart-gallery.com; Elephant's Walk Shopping & Arts Village) Sells original pieces by Dominic Benhura, Zimbabwe's most prominent current-day Shona sculptor whose worked has been exhibited around the world.

Matsimela BEAUTY
(www.matsimela.co.za; Elephant's Walk Shopping & Arts Village; ⊘8am-5pm) South African bodycare brand Matsimela has set up store here with an enticing aroma of natural scented soaps and body scrubs such as rose and

lychee and baobab-seed oil. Also has a branch at Doon Estate in Harare.

Jairos Jiri Crafts
CRAFTS

(Victoria Falls Curio Village; ☺8am-5pm Mon-Fri, 8.30am-4.30pm Sat, 8.30am-1pm Sun) Good range of Shona arts and crafts, with proceeds assisting disadvantaged locals.

Ndau Collection
JEWELLERY

(✆386221; www.ndaujewelry.com) Watch local artisans hand-make individually pieced silver bracelets, rings and necklaces at this store-workshop. They also sell exquisite antique African trade beads to be incorporated into custom-made jewellery.

ⓘ Information

Dangers & Annoyances

Mugging is not such a problem anymore, but at dawn and dusk wild animals such as elephants and warthogs do roam the streets away from the town centre, so take taxis at these times. Although it's perfectly safe to walk to and from the falls, it's advisable to stick to the more touristed areas.

Emergency

Medical Air Rescue Service (MARS; ✆44764)
Police (✆44206; Livingstone Way)
Victoria Falls Surgery (✆43356; West Dr)

Internet Access

Econet (Park Way; per 30min/1hr US$1/2; ☺8am-5pm Mon-Fri, to 1pm Sat & Sun)
Telco (✆43441; Phumula Centre; per hr US$1; ☺8am-6pm)

Money

Barclays Bank (off Livingstone Way)
Standard Chartered Bank (off Livingstone Way)

Post

Post Office (off Livingstone Way)

Tourist Information

Backpackers Bazaar (✆013-45828; www.backpackersbazaarvicfalls.com; off Parkway; ☺8am-5pm Mon-Fri, 9am-4pm Sat & Sun) Definitive place for all tourist info and bookings.
Zimbabwe Tourism Authority (✆44202; zta@vicfalls.ztazim.co.zw; 258 Adam Stander Dr; ☺8am-5pm Mon-Fri, 8am-1pm Sat) A few brochures, but not very useful.

ⓘ Getting There & Away

Air

Check out www.flightsite.co.za or www.travelstart.co.za, where you can search all the airlines including low-cost carriers (and car-hire companies) for the cheapest flights and book yourself. **South African Airways** (✆011-808678; www.flysaa.com) and **British Airways** (www.britishairways.com) fly every day to Johannesburg from around US$320 return. **Air Namibia** (www.airnamibia.com) flies to Windhoek for around US$530 return.

Bus & Minibus

TO JOHANNESBURG

By road the easiest option is Pathfinder from VicFalls to Bulawayo (arrives 1pm) then connect with Intercaper Greyhound at 4pm to Johannesburg.

TO BULAWAYO/HWANGE

Pathfinder has a daily service to Bulawayo (US$30, six hours) en route to Harare (US$60, 12 hours), stopping outside Hwange National Park on the way. Bravo Tours also plies the route for similar prices. Otherwise combis (US$20) and local buses (US$15) head to Bulawayo.

Car & Motorcycle

If you're driving a rented vehicle into Zambia, you need to make sure you have insurance and carbon tax papers, as well original owner documents. When you enter Zambia you are issued with a Temporary Import Permit, valid for while you are in the country. This must be returned to immigration for them to acquit the vehicle.

Train

A popular way of getting to/from Vic Falls is by the overnight Mosi-oa-Tunya train that leaves Victoria Falls daily at 7pm for Bulawayo, Zimbabwe (economy/2nd/1st class US$8/10/12, 12 hours). First class is the only way to go. Make reservations at the **ticket office** (✆44392; ☺7am-10am & 2.30-6.45pm Mon-Fri, 9-10am & 4.30-6.45pm Sat & Sun) inside the train station.

ⓘ Getting Around

To/From the Airport

Victoria Falls Airport is located 20km southeast of town, and is easily accessible by taxi (US$30 each way). Another option is to book a transfer with one of the companies through your hostel or travel agent in Vic Falls. Transfers are US$15 per person one way.

Car & Motorcycle

At the time of research, petrol was readily available in petrol stations. Avis and Europcar both have offices at the Vic Falls airport.

Taxis

A taxi around town costs about US$10, slightly more after dark.

Wildlife

by David Lukas

Despite Botswana being mostly covered in sand, and Namibia being one of the driest places on earth, huge numbers of wildlife still wander their ancestral routes. In fact Botswana and Namibia both offer superb wildlife-viewing opportunities, particularly in the north where the Chobe and Okavango Rivers create one of the world's premier wetland ecosystems.

Running giraffes, Okavango Delta (p88)

DOUG McKINLAY / GETTY IMAGES ©

Cats

With their excellent vision and keen hearing, the cats found in Botswana and Namibia are superb hunters. Some of the most stunning scenes in Africa are the images of big cats making their kills.

Caracal

1 *Weight 8–19kg; length 80–120cm* The caracal is a tawny cat with long, pointy tufted ears and jacked up hind legs, enabling it to make vertical leaps of 3m to swat birds out of the air.

Leopard

2 *Weight 30–60kg (female), 40–90kg (male); length 170–300cm* Leopards rely on expert camouflage to stay hidden. During the day you might only spot one reclining in a tree after it twitches its tail, but at night there is no mistaking its bone-chilling groans.

Lion

3 *Weight 120–150kg (female), 150–225kg (male); length 210–275cm (female), 240–350cm (male)* Lions are Africa's most feared predators, with teeth that tear through bone and tendon. Each group of adults (a pride) is based around generations of females that do all the hunting.

Cheetah

4 *Weight 40–60kg; length 200–220cm* A world-class sprinter reaching speeds of 112km/h, the cheetah runs out of steam after 300m and must cool down for 30 minutes before hunting again.

Black-Footed Cat

5 *Weight 1–2kg; length 40–60cm* This pint-sized predator is one of the smallest cats in the world. Though only 25cm high, this nocturnal cat is a fearsome hunter that can leap six times its height.

Wildcat

6 *Weight 3–6.5kg; length 65–100cm* Found near villages, the wildcat looks like a common tabby and is the direct ancestor of our domesticated house cats. It's best identified by its unmarked rufous ears and longish legs.

Primates

Botswana and Namibia are home to a mere three species of primates. Of these, only the Chacma baboon is common and widespread, but they are so fascinating to watch that they make up for the absence of other primates.

Vervet Monkey

1 *Weight 4–8kg; length 90–140cm* Found in northern Botswana and Namibia, vervets spend a lot of time on the ground, but always near to trees where they can escape from predators. Each troop is composed of females, while males fight each other for bragging rights and access to females.

Lesser Galago

2 *Weight 100–250g; length 40cm* The nocturnal lesser galago (commonly called 'bushbaby') is phenomenally agile and acrobatic, making 5m-long leaps between trees and even leaping into the air to catch flying prey. In Botswana and Namibia they are only found in lush forested woodlands along the rivers of the north.

Chacma Baboon

3 *Weight 12–30kg (female), 25–45kg (male); length 100–200cm* Chacma baboons are worth watching because they have exceedingly complex social dynamics. See if you can spot signs of friendship, deception or deal-making within a troop.

Cud-Chewing Mammals

Many of Africa's ungulates (hoofed mammals) live in groups to protect themselves from the continent's formidable predators. The subgroup of ungulates that ruminate (chew their cud) and have horns are called bovines. Among this family, the antelopes are particularly numerous, with over a dozen species in Botswana and Namibia.

Hartebeest

1 *Weight 120–220kg; length 190–285cm* The long face allows this short-necked antelope to reach down and graze while still looking up for predators.

Gemsbok

2 *Weight 180–240kg; length 230cm* With straight 1m-long horns, this desert antelope can survive for months on the scant water it derives from the plants it eats. Other adaptations include being able to survive temperatures that would kill other animals.

African Buffalo

3 *Weight 250–850kg; length 220–420cm* Imagine a cow on steroids, then add a fearsome set of curling horns, and you get the African buffalo. Fortunately they're usually docile, because an angry or injured buffalo is an extremely dangerous animal.

Impala

4 *Weight 40–80kg; length 150–200cm* With a prodigious capacity to reproduce, impalas can reach great numbers quickly, outstripping predators' ability to eat them all. Visit Namibia's Etosha National Park to see the unique black-faced impala.

Wildebeest

5 *Weight 140–290kg; length 230–340cm* The wildebeest of northern Botswana are rather sedentary creatures, moving only when conditions fluctuate seasonally. Because they favour expansive views, wildebeest are in turn easily viewed themselves.

Hoofed Mammals

Apart from giraffes, these ungulates are not ruminants and can be seen over a much broader range of habitats than bovines. They have been at home in Africa for millions of years and are among the most successful mammals to have ever wandered the continent.

Black Rhinoceros

1 *Weight 700–1400kg; length 350–450cm* Once widespread and abundant, the rhino has been poached to the brink of extinction for having a horn worth more than gold. The best viewing location might be at Etosha National Park's Okaukuejo waterhole.

Mountain Zebra

2 *Weight 230–380kg; length 260–300cm* The unique mountain zebras of central Namibia differ from their savannah relatives in having unstriped bellies and rusty muzzles.

African Elephant

3 *Weight 2200–3500kg (female), 4000–6300kg (male); height 2.4–3.4m (female), 3–4m (male)* Elephants are abundant at Chobe National Park, where up to 55,000 congregate in the lush wetlands. Even more interesting are the unique desert-loving elephants of Namibia.

Hippopotamus

4 *Weight 510–3200kg; length 320–400cm* Designed like a big grey floating beanbag with tiny legs, the 3000kg hippo spends all its time in or very near water. Hippos display a tremendous ferocity and strength when provoked.

Giraffe

5 *Weight 450–1200kg (female), 1800–2000kg (male); height 3.5–5.2m* The 5m-tall giraffe does such a good job reaching up to high branches that stretching down to get a simple drink of water is difficult. Though they stroll along casually, they can outrun any predator.

Carnivores

As well as the cats, Botswana and Namibia are home to a couple of dozen carnivores, ranging from slinky mongooses to highly social hunting dogs. All are linked in having 'carnassial' (slicing) teeth, but visitors may be more interested in witnessing their hunting prowess.

Bat-Eared Fox

1 *Weight 3–5kg; length 70–100cm* This animal has huge ears that it swivels in all directions to pick up the sounds of subterranean food like termites. Monogamous pairs of these social foxes will often mingle with other pairs and families when hunting for food.

Meerkat

2 *Weight 0.5–1kg; length 50cm* The area's several species of mongoose may be best represented by the meerkat (also known as a suricate). Spending much of their time standing up, if threatened they all spit and jump up and down together.

Hunting Dog

3 *Weight 20–35kg; length 100–150cm* Uniquely patterned, hunting dogs run in packs of 20 to 60. These highly social but endangered canids are incredibly efficient hunters. Look for them at Botswana's Moremi Game Reserve.

Cape Fur Seal

4 *Weight 80kg (females), 350kg (males); length 120–200cm* Several giant breeding colonies of seals are located on Namibia's Skeleton Coast. Forced to gather in dense numbers as protection against marauding hyenas, these colonies are turbulent, noisy and exciting to watch.

Spotted Hyena

5 *Weight 40–90kg; length 125–215cm* The spotted hyena is one of Southern Africa's most unusual animals. Living in packs ruled by females, these savage fighters use their bone-crushing jaws to disembowel prey or to do battle with lions.

Birds of Prey

Botswana and Namibia are home to about 70 species of hawk, eagle, vulture and owl, meaning that you are likely to see an incredible variety of birds of prey here. Look for them perching on trees, soaring high overhead or gathered around a carcass.

Lappet-Faced Vulture

1 *Length 115cm* Vultures mingle with predators around carcasses in Botswana and Namibia. Here, through sheer numbers, they compete for scraps of flesh and bone. The monstrous lappet-faced vulture gets its fill before other vultures move in.

Pale Chanting Goshawk

2 *Length 55cm* Small clusters of these slim grey raptors with red beaks and legs are often seen perched low on bushes. Look closely because they are probably following some other small hunter like a honey badger.

Bateleur

3 *Length 60cm* French for 'tightrope-walker', the name refers to its distinctive low-flying aerial acrobatics. In flight, look for its white wings and tailless appearance; at close range look for the bold colour pattern and scarlet face.

African Fish Eagle

4 *Length 75cm* With a wingspan over 2m, this replica of the American bald eagle hunts for fish around water, but it is most familiar for its loud ringing vocalisations that have become known as 'the voice of Africa'.

Secretary Bird

5 *Length 100cm* With the body of an eagle and the legs of a crane, the secretary bird towers 1.3m tall and walks up to 20km a day across the savannah in search of vipers, cobras and other snakes that it kills with lightning speed and agility.

2

Birds

Come to Botswana and Namibia prepared to see an astounding number of birds in every shape and colour. You may find them a pleasant diversion after a couple of days of staring at sleeping lions.

Lilac-Breasted Roller

1 *Length 40cm* Related to kingfishers, the gorgeously coloured lilac-breasted roller gets its name from the tendency to 'roll' from side to side in flight as a way of showing off its iridescent blues, purples and greens.

Cape Gannet

2 *Length 85cm* These crisply marked seabirds congregate by the thousands to catch fish with high-speed dives into the waves.

Lesser Flamingo

3 *Length 100cm* Coloured deep rose pink and gathering by the hundreds of thousands on shimmering salt lakes, the lesser flamingo creates one of Africa's most dramatic wildlife spectacles.

Ostrich

4 *Length 200–270cm* Standing 2.7m and weighing upwards of 130kg, these flight-less birds escape predators by running away at 70km/h or lying flat on the ground to re-semble a pile of dirt. Genuinely wild ostriches are still found in the Kalahari Desert.

Jackass Penguin

5 *Length 60cm* Jackass penguins are actu-ally named for their donkeylike calls, part of the courtship displays given by the males. Found along the Namibian coast and on offshore islands, some penguin colonies are ridiculously tame.

Hamerkop

6 *Length 60cm* The hamerkop is a stork rela-tive with an oddly crested, woodpecker-like head. Nicknamed the 'hammerhead', it is frequently observed hunting frogs and fish at the water's edge. Look for its massive 2m-wide nests in nearby trees.

Namibia

Namibia

264 / POP 2.1 MILLION

Best for Wildlife Watching

» Etosha National Park (p237)

» Waterberg Plateau (p231)

» Bwabwata National Park (p248)

» Khaudum National Park (p247)

» Mamili National Park (p253)

Best of the Outdoors

» Swakopmund (p274)

» Fish River Canyon (p316)

» Damaraland (p260)

» The Kaokoveld (p265)

» The Skeleton Coast (p269)

Why Go?

Namibia posesses some of the most stunning landscapes in Africa, and a trip through the country is one of the great road adventures. Natural wonders such as that mighty gash in the earth at Fish River Canyon and the wildlife utopia of Etosha National Park enthrall, but it's the lonely desert roads, where mighty slabs of granite rise out of swirling desert sands, that will sear themselves in your mind. It's like a coffee-table book come to life as sand dunes in the world's oldest desert meet the crashing rollers along the wild Atlantic coast. Among all this is a German legacy, evident in the cuisine and art nouveau architecture and in festivals such as Windhoek's legendary Oktoberfest.

Namibia is also the headquarters of adventure activities in the region, so whether you're a dreamer or love hearing the crunch of earth under your boots, travel in Namibia will stay with you long after the desert vistas fade.

When to Go

Windhoek

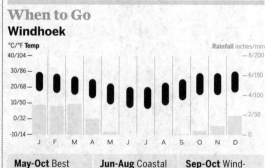

May-Oct Best time of the year for wildlife viewing.

Jun-Aug Coastal towns of Swakopmund and Walvis Bay are subject to miserable sandstorm conditions.

Sep-Oct Windhoek comes alive with festivals that include arts events and Oktoberfest.

WINDHOEK

📞061 / POP 340,000 / ELEV 1660M

Central Windhoek is a surprisingly modern, well-groomed city where office workers lounge around Zoo Park at lunchtime, tourists funnel through Post Street Mall admiring African curios and taxis whizz around honking at potential customers. In fact, first impressions confirm that the city wouldn't look out of place in the West.

It's not a big city and is eminently walkable; add to this a mixed population, a pedestrian-friendly city centre, a relaxed, relatively hassle-free pace and an utterly cosmopolitan outlook and Windhoek makes for a very pleasant exploration indeed. Neobaroque cathedral spires, as well as a few seemingly misplaced German castles, punctuate the skyline and complement the steel-and-glass high-rises.

Of course that's only part of the story; a trip into Katutura, the once-ramshackle township on the outskirts of the city, now just another outer suburb, gives insight into the reality of most people's lives within the boundaries of the capital.

Windhoek makes a great place to begin or break a journey through Namibia. The accommodation choices, food variety, cultural sights, shopping and African urban buzz give it an edge not found anywhere else in Namibia.

History

The city of Windhoek has existed for just over a century, but its history is as diverse as its population. During the German colonial occupation it became the headquarters for the German Schutztruppe (Imperial Army), which was ostensibly charged with brokering peace between the warring Herero and Nama in exchange for whatever lands their efforts would gain for German occupation. For over 10 years at the turn of the 20th century, Windhoek served as the administrative capital of German South West Africa.

In 1902 a narrow-gauge railway was built to connect Windhoek to the coast at Swakopmund, and the city experienced a sudden spurt of growth. During this period Windhoek began to evolve into the business, commercial and administrative centre of the country, although the modern city wasn't officially founded until 1965.

◉ Sights

Windhoek is not really known for its tourist attractions, but if you're here for a few days and have time to kill it's an easy and interesting city for a stroll.

Zoo Park PARK
(Map p210; ☉dawn-dusk) Although this leafy park served as a public zoo until 1962, today it functions primarily as a picnic spot and shady retreat for lunching office workers. Five thousand years ago the park was the site of a Stone Age elephant hunt, as evidenced by the remains of two elephants and several quartz tools found here in the early 1960s. This prehistoric event is honoured by the park's prominent elephant column, designed by Namibian sculptor Dörthe Berner.

A rather anachronous mate to the elephant column is the Kriegerdenkmal (War Memorial), topped by a rather frightening golden imperial eagle, which was dedicated in 1987 to the memory of German Schutztruppe soldiers who died in the Nama wars of 1893–94.

Christuskirche CHURCH
(Map p210; Fidel Castro St) Windhoek's best-recognised landmark, and something of an unofficial symbol of the city, this German Lutheran church stands on a traffic island and lords it over the city centre. This unusual building, which was constructed from local sandstone in 1907, was designed by architect Gottlieb Redecker in conflicting neo-Gothic and art nouveau styles. The resulting design looks strangely edible, and is somewhat reminiscent of a whimsical gingerbread house. The altarpiece, the *Resurrection of Lazarus,* is a copy of the renowned work by Rubens. To view the interior, pick up the key during business hours from the nearby church office on Peter Müller St.

FREE **Tintenpalast** NOTABLE BUILDING
(Map p210; 📞288 9111; www.parliament.gov.na; ☉tours 9am-12pm & 2-4pm Mon-Fri) The former administrative headquarters of German South West Africa have been given a new

IMPORTANT NUMBERS

Country code	📞264
Area codes	Namibia uses three-digit area codes
International access code	📞00
Emergency	📞10111

Namibia Highlights

1 Admire the ancient petroglyphs of the San people in **Brandberg** (p260) and **Twyfelfontein** (p262)

2 Get off the beaten track (and the sealed road) in the true African wilderness of the **Skeleton Coast** (p269) and **Kaokoveld** (p265)

3 Explore the wildlife reserves while they're still undiscovered and pop into Botswana's delta region in the **Caprivi Strip** (p248)

4 Hike through **Fish River Canyon** (p316), one of Africa's greatest natural wonders

5 Crouch by a waterhole in one of the world's premier wildlife venues, **Etosha National Park** (p237)

6 Hike to the top of the **Waterberg Plateau** (p231) for breathtaking views, keeping an eye out for rare sable and roan

7 Watch the sun rise from the top of fiery-coloured dunes of **Sossusvlei** (p297)

8 Get your adrenaline fix at **Swakopmund** (p274), the extreme-sports capital of Namibia

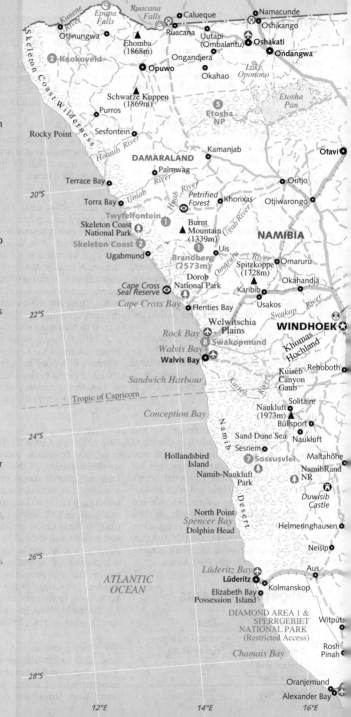

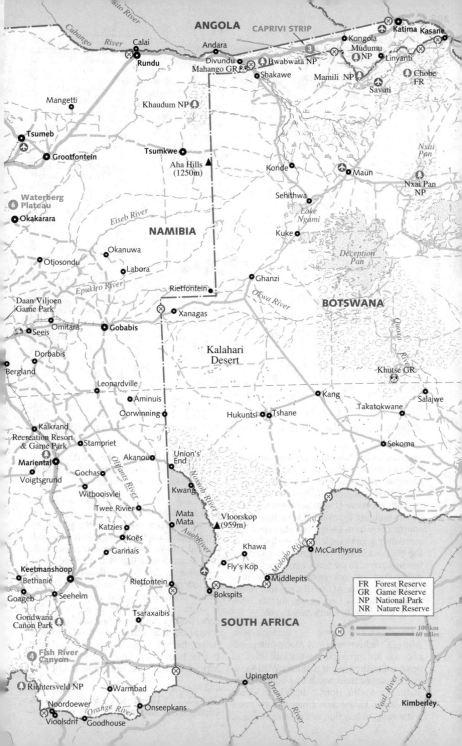

Windhoek

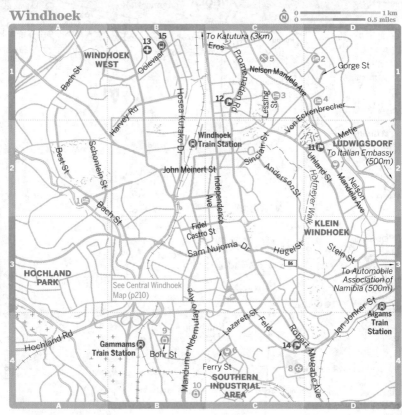

mandate as the Namibian parliament building. As a fitting homage to the bureaucracy of government, the name of the building means 'Ink Palace', in honour of all the ink spent on typically excessive official paperwork.

The building is remarkable mainly for its construction from indigenous materials. The surrounding gardens, which were laid out in the 1930s, include an olive grove and a proper bowling green. In the front, have a look at Namibia's first post-independence monument, a bronze-cast statue of the Herero chief Hosea Kutako, who was best known for his vehement opposition to South African rule.

Gathemann's Complex   HISTORIC BUILDING
(Map p210; Independence Ave) Along Independence Ave are three colonial-era buildings, all designed by the famous architect Willi Sander. The one furthest south was built in 1902 as the Kronprinz Hotel, which later joined Gathemann House (now home to a gourmet restaurant) to function as a private business.

The most notable of the three is the Erkrath Building, which was constructed in 1910 as a private home and business.

Turnhalle   HISTORIC BUILDING
(Map p210; Bahnoff St) The Turnhalle was built in 1909 as a practise hall for the Windhoek Gymnastic Club, though in 1975 it was modernised and turned into a conference hall. On 1 September of that year it served as the venue for the first Constitutional Conference on Independence for South West Africa, which subsequently – and more conveniently – came to be called the Turnhalle Conference. During the 1980s the building hosted several political summits and debates that paved the way to Namibian independence. It now houses a tribunal for the Southern Africa Development Community (SADC).

Old Magistrates' Court   HISTORIC BUILDING
(Map p210; cnr Lüderitz & Park Sts; ⊙8am-1pm & 2-5pm Mon-Fri, 8am-1pm Sat) This old court-

Windhoek

NAMIBIA WINDHOEK

house was built in 1898 for Carl Ludwig, the state architect, but it was never used and was eventually drafted into service as the magistrates' court. Take a look at the verandah on the south side, which provided a shady sitting area for people waiting for their cases to be called. The building has been given new life as the Namibia Conservatorium.

Kaiserliche Realschule HISTORIC BUILDING
(Map p210; Robert Mugabe Ave) Windhoek's first German primary school was built in 1908, and opened the following year with a class size of 74 students. Notice the curious turret with wooden slats, which was designed to provide ventilation for European children unaccustomed to the African heat. The building later housed Windhoek's first German high school and an English middle school, and today it's the administrative headquarters of the National Museum of Namibia.

FREE **National Museum of Namibia** MUSEUM
(Map p210; Robert Mugabe Ave; ☉9am-6pm Mon-Fri, 3-6pm Sat & Sun) There is an excellent display on Namibia's independence at the country's historical museum, which provides some enlightening context to the struggles of this young country. But probably the most interesting part of the museum is the rock-art display, with some great reproductions, and it would definitely be worth a nose around before heading to the Brandberg or Twyfelfontein.

It's housed in Windhoek's oldest surviving building, dating from the early 1890s,

and originally served as the headquarters of the German Schutztruppe. The rest of the museum contains memorabilia and photos from the colonial period as well as indigenous artefacts.

Outside the museum, don't miss the somewhat incongruous collection of railway engines and coaches, which together formed one of the country's first narrow-gauge trains. This open-air exhibit is lorded over by a bronze statue known as the **Reiterdenkmal (Rider's Memorial)**, which commemorates Schutztruppe soldiers killed during the Herero-Nama wars of 1904–08. For history buffs, note that the statue was unveiled on 27 January 1912, which coincided with Kaiser Wilhelm II's birthday.

FREE **Owela Museum** MUSEUM
(State Museum; Map p210; 4 Robert Mugabe Ave; ☉9am-6pm Mon-Fri, 3-6pm Sat & Sun) The other half of the National Museum of Namibia, about 600m from the main building, is known as the Owela Museum. Exhibits focus on Namibia's natural and cultural history and it has been popular with readers; note it may sometimes close early.

Trans-Namib Transport Museum MUSEUM
(Map p210; ☎298 2186; admission N$5; ☉8am-1pm & 2-5pm Mon-Fri) Windhoek's beautiful old Cape Dutch–style train station on Bahnhof St was constructed by the Germans in 1912, and was expanded in 1929 by the South African administration. Across the driveway from the entrance is the German steam locomotive *'Poor Old Joe'*, which was shipped

to Swakopmund in 1899 and reassembled for the treacherous journey across the desert to Windhoek. Upstairs in the train station is the small but worthwhile Trans-Namib Transport Museum outlining Namibian transport history, particularly that of the railway.

Owambo Campaign Memorial MONUMENT
(Map p210; Bahnhof St) At the entry to the train station parking area, you'll see the Owambo Campaign Memorial, which was erected in 1919 to commemorate the 1917 British and South African campaign against Chief Mandume of the Kwanyama Owambo. Heavily

Central Windhoek

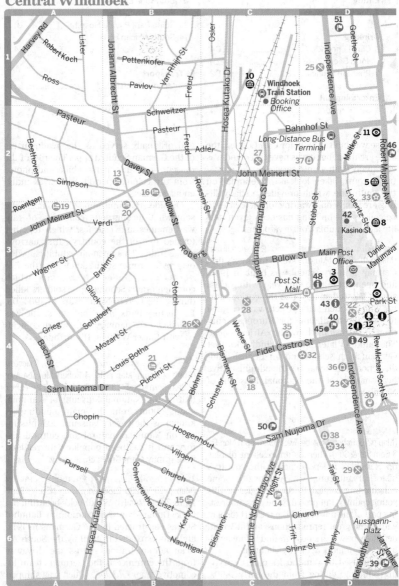

NAMIBIA WINDHOEK

outmatched by the colonial armies, the chief depleted all of his firepower and committed suicide rather than surrendering.

National Art Gallery   GALLERY
(Map p210; cnr Robert Mugabe Ave & John Meinert St; admission Mon-Fri/Sat free/N\$20; ☺8am-5pm

Tue-Fri, 9am-2pm Sat) This art gallery contains a permanent collection of works reflecting Namibia's historical and natural heritage. The collection displays works by Muafangejo – Namibia's first black artist to gain international acclaim. His linocuts depict the liberation struggle from a religious and narrative perspective.

Daan Viljoen Game Park   WILDLIFE RESERVE
(per person/vehicle N\$40/10; ☺visitors sunrise-6pm) This beautiful wildlife park sits in the Khomas Hochland about 18km west of Windhoek.

You can walk to your heart's content through lovely wildlife-rich desert hills, and spot gemsboks, kudu, mountain zebras, springboks, hartebeest, warthogs and eland. Daan Viljoen is also known for its birdlife, and over 200 species have been recorded, including the rare green-backed heron and pin-tailed whydah.

Daan Viljoen's hills are covered with open thorn-scrub vegetation that allows excellent wildlife viewing, and three walking tracks have been laid out. The 3km Wag-'n-Bietjie Trail follows a dry riverbed from near the park office to Stengel Dam. A 9km circuit, the Rooibos Trail crosses hills and ridges and affords great views back to Windhoek in the distance. The 34km Sweet-Thorn Trail circuits the empty eastern reaches of the reserve.

If you can't be bothered getting back to Windhoek, Daan Viljoen Lodge provides luxury accommodation within the park.

To get to Daan Viljoen, take the C28 west from Windhoek; Daan Viljoen is clearly signposted off the Bosua Pass Hwy, about 18km from the city.

✯✯ Festivals & Events

Bank Windhoek Arts Festival   ARTS
(www.bankwindhoekarts.com.na) This is the largest arts festival in the country, with events running from February to September.

Mbapira/Enjando Street Festival   ARTS
Windhoek's big annual bash is held in March around the city centre. It features colourful gatherings of dancers, musicians and people in ethnic dress.

Independence Day   NATIONAL
On 21 March, this national day is celebrated in grand style, with a parade and sports events.

Windhoek Karneval (WIKA) CARNIVAL
(www.windhoek-karneval.com) The German-style carnival takes place in late April and features music performances, a masked ball and a parade down Independence Ave.

Wild Cinema Festival CINEMA
An annual international film festival that takes place in late spring and early summer.

Windhoek Show AGRICULTURE
(www.windhoekshow.na) In late September or early October the city holds the Windhoek show, with its roots in agriculture, on the showgrounds near the corner of Jan Jonker and Centaurus Sts.

/AE//Gams Arts Festival ARTS
Highlighting Namibian artwork, it's held in venues around Windhoek in October.

Oktoberfest BEER
True to its partially Teutonic background, Windhoek stages this festival towards the end of October – beer lovers should not miss it.

GET YOUR BEARINGS

Set among low hills, Windhoek enjoys dry, clean air and a healthy highland climate, which means in winter the nights are *cold*.

Central Windhoek is bisected by Independence Ave, where most shopping and administrative functions are concentrated. The shopping district is focused on the Post Street pedestrian mall and the nearby Gustav Voigts Centre, Wernhill Park Centre and Levinson Arcade. Zoo Park, beside the main post office, provides a green lawn and shady lunch spots.

North along Independence Ave are the industrial expanses of Windhoek's Northern Industrial Area. To the west and northwest are the high-density townships of Khomasdal and Katutura, which are slowly developing into amenable neighbourhoods, but still have several pockets of serious poverty. In other directions, middle- and upper-class suburbs such as Klein Windhoek and Eros Park sprawl across the hills that encircle the city, affording impressive views.

Immediately beyond the city limits, the wild country begins. Approximately 40km to the east lies Hosea Kutako International Airport, completely surrounded by the encroaching bush. Just to the west is Daan Viljoen Game Park, where wild animals roam in the shadow of the capital.

Sleeping

Whether you bed down in a bunkhouse or slumber the night away in a historic castle, Windhoek has no shortage of appealing accommodation options. Compared to the rest of the country, prices in the capital are relatively high, though you can usually be assured of a corresponding level of quality. Note that in a city this small, space is limited, so consider booking your bed well in advance, especially if you're travelling during the high season, holidays or even on busy weekends.

TOP CHOICE Guesthouse Tamboti   GUESTHOUSE $$
(Map p210; ☎235515; www.guesthouse-tamboti. com; 9 Kerby St; s/d from N$415/620; ❈@🛜🏊) Hands-down our favourite place in Windhoek to stay, Tamboti is very well priced, and has a great vibe and terrific hosts who will go out of their way to ensure you are comfortable (such as driving you to the airport if you have a flight to catch). The rooms here are spacious and well set up – it's situated on a small hill just above the city centre. Book ahead as it's popular.

Hotel-Pension Steiner   HOTEL $$
(Map p210; ☎222898; www.natron.net/tour/stein er/main.html; 11 Wecke St; s/d from N$540/850; 🛜🏊) Although it has an excellent city-centre location just a few minutes' walk from Independence Ave, this small hotel-pension is sheltered from the hustle and bustle of the street scene. Simple but comfortable rooms open to a thatched bar and swimming pool, where you can quickly unwind.

Vondelhof Guesthouse   GUESTHOUSE $$
(Map p210; ☎248320; www.vondelhof.com; 2 Puccini St; s/d N$625/900; ❈@🏊) This rather grand-looking affair has great-sized rooms, the very friendly staff have a good attitude towards hospitality and serve a decent breakfast. Ask to have a look at a few rooms but we try to snare room 8, which is a beauty. Don't let the horrible green colour on the outside of the building put you off; the interior is far more palatable.

Rivendell Guest House   GUESTHOUSE $$
(Map p210; ☎250006; www.rivendellnamibia. com; 40 Beethoven St; s/d N$450/600, without bathroom from N$345/450; @🏊) This homey setup gets good reviews from travellers. It's a very relaxed guesthouse located in a shady suburb within easy walking distance of the city centre. Bright and airy rooms open to a lush garden and a sparkling pool. It's a good place to try if everywhere is full as the owner will try and help with alternative accommodation. Rates do not include breakfast.

Daan Viljoen Lodge   LODGE $$$
(☎232 393; info@sunkarros.com.na; campsites per person N$200, s/d chalet from N$1090/1960; @) Daan Viljoen Lodge provides luxury accommodation within Daan Viljoen Game Park. Chalets have captivating views and private barbecues or you can take advantage of the well-stocked restaurant. Wildlife drives are also available.

Chameleon Backpackers Lodge & Guesthouse   BACKPACKERS $
(Map p210; ☎244347; www.chameleonbackpack ers.com; 5-7 Voight St; campsite N$80, dm/r inc

KATUTURA – A PERMANENT PLACE?

In 1912, during the days of the South African mandate – and apartheid – the Windhoek town council set aside two 'locations', which were open to settlement by black Africans working in the city: the Main Location, which was west of the city centre, and Klein Windhoek, to the east. The following year, people were forcibly relocated to these areas, which effectively became haphazard settlements. In the early 1930s streets were laid out in the Main Location and the area was divided into regions. Each subdivision within these regions was assigned to an ethnic group and referred to by that name (eg Herero, Nama, Owambo, Damara), followed by a soulless numerical reference.

In the 1950s the Windhoek municipal council, with encouragement from the South African government (which regarded Namibia as a province of South Africa), decided to 'take back' Klein Windhoek and consolidate all 'location' residents into a single settlement northwest of the main city. There was strong opposition to the move, and in early December 1959 a group of Herero women launched a protest march and boycott against the city government. On 10 December unrest escalated into a confrontation with the police, resulting in 11 deaths and 44 serious injuries. Frightened, the roughly 4000 residents of the Main Location submitted and moved to the new settlement, which was ultimately named Katutura. In Herero the name means 'we have no permanent place', though it can also be translated as 'the place we do not want to settle'.

Today in independent Namibia, Katutura is a vibrant Windhoek suburb – Namibia's Soweto – where poverty and affluence brush elbows. The town council has extended municipal water, power and telephone services to most areas of Katutura, and has also established the colourful and perpetually busy Soweto Market, where traders sell just about anything imaginable. Unlike its South African counterparts, Katutura is relatively safe by day, assuming you can find a trustworthy local who can act as a guide.

The tourist office can book township tours but even better is **Katu Tours** (☎081 3032856; www.katuturatours.com; tours per person N$350), which offers guided tours by bike. You get a good taste of township life and the chance to meet plenty of locals; it also includes dropping into Penduka, where local women produce a range of handicrafts and textiles. Tours depart at 8am from Katutura and take 3½ hours.

breakfast from N$120/300; @🛜🏊) With a chilled vibe emanating from its considerable range of accommodation options, this well-matched rival to the Cardboard Box caters to a slightly more subdued crowd. It offers decent-sized, luxurious African-chic rooms and spick-and-span dorms at shoestring prices. There are also three self-catering flats if you're in town for an extended period. The on-site safari centre offers some of the most affordable trips in Namibia.

Cardboard Box Backpackers BACKPACKERS $
(Map p210; ☎228994; www.cardboardbox. na; 15 Johann Albrecht St; campsite/dm N$70/95, r from N$300; @🛜🏊) Hostels are hard to come by in this country but 'the Box' has been doing it for years, with a rep as one of Windhoek's wildest backpackers. It has a fully stocked bar and swimming pool to cool off in, and travellers have a tough time leaving this oasis of affordable luxury. If you do decide to motivate yourself, the city centre is just a short walk away, and the excel-

lent on-site Travel Shop gives useful information and can help sort out your future travel plans. Rates include free coffee and pancakes in the morning and there are free pickups from the Intercape bus stop.

Olive Grove BOUTIQUE HOTEL $$$
(Map p208; ☎239199; www.olivegrove-namibia. com; 20 Promenaden St; s/d standard N$735/1260, luxury N$1130/2030, ste from N$2000; ❄@🏊) Refined elegance is the order of the day at this boutique hotel in Klein Windhoek, which features 10 individually decorated rooms and two suites awash with fine linens, hand-crafted furniture and all-around good taste. Guests in need of some pampering can indulge in a massage, or warm their toes on a cold Windhoek night in front of the crackling fire. If the package here isn't high-end enough for you, check out their exclusive lodging next door.

Villa Verdi BOUTIQUE HOTEL $$$
(Map p210; ☎221994; www.leadinglodges.com/villa verdi.htm; 4 Verdi St; s/d budget N$735/1260,

standard N$1075/1930; ❄@❄) This utterly unique Mediterranean-African hybrid features whimsically decorated rooms complete with original paintings and arty touches. Straddling the divide between midrange and top-end properties, Villa Verdi competes in opulence and class with the bigger hitters on the block, yet offers more affordably priced rooms by targeting the boutique market rather than the tour-group crowd.

Hotel Thule HOTEL $$$
(Map p208; ☑371950; www.hotelthule.com; 1 Gorge St; s/d from N$1410/1960; ❄@❄) Perched on a towering hilltop in Eros Park, which is something along the lines of the Beverly Hills of Windhoek, Hotel Thule commands some of the most impressive views of any hotel in the capital. Cavernous rooms with a touch of European elegance are complemented by a classy restaurant and wraparound sundowner bar where you can sip a cocktail while watching the twinkling lights of the city switch on for the night. Email the hotel for better rates than listed here.

Roof of Africa HOTEL $$
(Map p208; ☑254708; www.roofofafrica.com; 124-126 Nelson Mandela Ave; s N$660-1070, d N$860-1420; ❄@❄) A pleasant haven located about 30 minutes by foot from the city centre, Roof of Africa has a rustic barnyard feel, offering well-designed rooms of varying price and luxury that attract laid-back travellers looking for a quiet retreat from the city. It's worth shelling out a few more Namib dollars for the luxury rooms, which come with far more space, sink-in-and-smile beds and modern bathrooms; ask to see a few though, as they do vary.

Hotel Heinitzburg HOTEL $$$
(Map p210; ☑249597; www.heinitzburg.com; 22 Heinitzburg St; s/d from N$1530/2200; ❄@) This is Windhoek's most royal B&B option – quite literally, as it's located inside Heinitzburg Castle, which was commissioned in 1914 by Count von Schwerin for his fiancée, Margarethe von Heinitz. A member of the prestigious Relais & Chateaux hotel group, the Heinitzburg is far and beyond the most personable upmarket accommodation in Windhoek. Rooms have been updated for the 21st century with satellite TV and aircon, though the highlight of the hotel is the palatial dining room, which offers excellent gourmet cuisine and an extensive wine cellar.

Hotel Cela HOTEL $$
(Map p210; ☑226295; info@hotelcela.com; Bulow St; s N$480-650, d N$660-850) This varied and well-located set-up has a range of rooms to suit most tastes. The more expensive, renovated rooms are the best. It's a good place to try when everywhere else in the city is full.

Haus Ol-Ga B&B $$
(Map p208; ☑235853; 91 Bach St; s/d N$350/500) The name of this German-oriented place is derived from the owners' names: Gesa Oldach and Erno Gauerke, who go out of their way to provide a good measure of Deutsch hospitality here in Namibia. Haus Ol-Ga enjoys a nice, quiet garden atmosphere in Windhoek West, and is a good choice if you're looking for accommodation that is more reminiscent of a homestay (it's like staying at your grandma's). Rooms are simple, neat and unfussy.

✖ Eating

Namibia's multicultural capital provides a range of restaurants. It's worth stretching your budget and indulging the in gourmand lifestyle while you're in town. Be advised that reservations are a very good idea on Friday and Saturday nights.

Windhoek is a grocery paradise for self-caterers. The big names are **Pick & Pay** (Map p210; Wernhill Park Centre) and **Checkers** (Map p210; Gustav Voigts Centre).

Paul's INTERNATIONAL $
(Map p210; ☑307176; Old Breweries Complex, Craft Market Inner Courtyard, cnr Garten & Tal Sts; mains N$30-60; ☺8am-5pm Mon-Fri, to 2pm Sat) Mixing brasserie, coffeeshop, and patisserie is this impressive eatery at the heart of Windhoek's craft market. Dining takes place in an industrial space made much more interesting with modern African prints and decor. It's a quirky mix – as are the menu options, which include tapas in the evenings, salads, freshly baked rolls and more substantial meals. Linking it all is a policy of low fat, no MSG and the use of fresh ingredients. The owner is a champion of disabled rights and has a great attitude towards the preparation of food. Call ahead as it can close at odd times.

Sardinia's Restaurant ITALIAN $$
(Map p210; 39 Independence Ave; dishes N$60-100; ☺lunch, dinner) An energetic restaurant that is

NAMIBIA WINDHOEK

a focal point for dining along the main drag. There's always a crowd, and understandably so, as it churns out first-class pizzas and an impressive array of pasta dishes. And it doesn't stop there: chicken and beef dishes and salads are also offered (the baby chicken with herb and lemon is excellent).

Namibia Crafts Cafe   CAFE $

(Map p210; Old Breweries Complex, cnr Garten & Tal Sts; mains N$40-80; ⊙9am-6pm Mon-Fri, to 3.30pm Sat & Sun) This cafe-restaurant-bar is a great spot to perch yourself above Tal St, checking out the local action and taking in the breeze from the outside deck. It's one of the capital's more pleasant places to consume food or have a cold drink – the extensive drinks menu includes health shakes and freshly squeezed juices. Meals in the way of salads, large pitas, cold meat platters, open sandwiches and healthy (or just filling) breakfasts hit the spot.

Gourmet   INTERNATIONAL $$

(Map p210; ☑232360; Kaiserkrone Centre, Post St Mall; mains N$70-180; ⊙breakfast, lunch & dinner Mon-Sat) Tucked away in a lovely, peaceful courtyard just off Post Street Mall, this alfresco bistro has one of the most comprehensive menus you've ever seen. The unifying trend is its adherence to using gourmet ingredients to create a blend of Namibian, German, French and Italian dishes that are as innovative as they are delicious. The carpaccio of ostrich is recommended but ask them to go easy on the oil.

O Pensador   ANGOLAN, SEAFOOD $$

(Map p210; ☑221223; cnr Mandume Ndemufayo Ave & John Meinert St; mains N$130-200; ⊙dinner) A quality seafood restaurant with a twist of Angolan here and a hint of Portuguese there; the food may not be squirming on your plate but our overall impression was one of freshness, tasty morsels and attentive service.

Café Balalaika   CAFE $$

(Map p210; ☑233479; Independence Ave, Zoo Park; sushi N$80, mains N$80-100; ⊙11am-2am; ⊛) This sheltered spot beneath a giant rubber tree with outdoor terrace on the edge of Zoo Park is just lovely for a cappuccino accompanied by a sushi plate. With some decent beer on tap and a large menu covering pizza, salads and meat dishes, it's a great spot to while away an afternoon. It also morphs into

a bar-club in the evening but keeps serving food until the wee hours.

Nice   INTERNATIONAL $$

(Map p210; ☑300710; cnr Mozart St & Hosea Kutako Dr; mains N$70-130; ⊙lunch Mon-Fri, dinner daily) The Namibian Institute of Culinary Education – or 'nice' for short – operates this wonderfully conceived 'living classroom' where apprentice chefs can field test their cooking skills. Spanning several indoor rooms and a beautiful outdoor courtyard, the restaurant itself is more akin to a stylish gallery (think white tablecloths and clinking wine glasses too), and also here is a sushi and wine bar. Lunch dishes include tiger prawn and avocado salad, slow-cooked lamb shank and game meat such as oryx. The menu is short and targeted and service is very good.

La Marmite   WEST AFRICAN $$

(Map p210; Independence Ave; mains N$100; ⊙lunch & dinner) Commanding a veritable legion of devoted followers, this humble West African eatery deserves its long-garnered popularity. Here you can sample wonderful North and West African cuisine, including Algerian, Senegalese, Ivorian, Cameroonian (try the curry) and Nigerian dishes, all of which are prepared with the finesse of the finest French haute cuisine.

Restaurant Gathemann   NAMIBIAN $$$

(Map p210; ☑223853; 179 Independence Ave; mains N$120-240; ⊙dinner) Located in a prominent colonial building overlooking Independence Ave, this splash-out spot serves gourmet Namibian cuisine that fully utilises this country's unique list of ingredients. From Kalahari truffles and Owamboland legumes to tender cuts of game meat and Walvis Bay oysters, Restaurant Gathemann satisfies the pickiest of appetites.

Crafter's Kitchen   CAFE $

(Map p210; 109 Independence Ave; mains N$30-45; ⊙breakfast & lunch Mon-Sat) You can shop for handicrafts here and get a bite at the same time from the busy little kitchen which churns out decent fuel, such as toasties, burgers and soups, for locals and tourists alike. Takeaway is available, and consider dropping in for the cake and coffee too.

Leo's   INTERNATIONAL $$$

(Map p210; ☑249597; www.heinitzburg.com; 22 Heinitzburg St; mains N$250) Leo's takes its regal setting in Heinitzburg Castle to heart by welcoming diners into a banquet hall that previously served the likes of royalty. The formal settings of bone china and polished crystal glassware are almost as extravagant as the food itself, which spans cuisines and continents and land and sea.

Joe's Beer House   PUB **$**
(Map p208; 160 Nelson Mandela Ave; mains N$60-120; ☺dinner) A legendary Windhoek institution, this is where you can indulge (albeit with a little guilt...) in flame-broiled fillets of all those amazing animals you've seen on safari! Seriously. We're talking huge cuts of zebra tenderloin, ostrich skewers, peppered springbok steak, oryx sirloin, crocodile on a hotplate, and marinated kudu steak.

🍷 Drinking

There are some perennially popular spots where you can enjoy a few drinks and maybe even a bit of dancing. Many restaurants also double as late-night watering holes, particularly tourist-friendly establishments such as Nice which is also a great spot for a drink. While the nightlife scene in Windhoek is relaxed and generally trouble-free, you should always travel by taxi when heading to and from establishments.

El Cubano   NIGHTCLUB
(Map p210; cnr Sam Nujoma Dr & Independence St; ☺Fri & Sat) Offering up a little bit of Havana, Namibian-style, El Cubano reopened in 2012 in the basement of the Hilton Hotel. It's the capital's most popular club with a suave, modern interior, a mixed crowd and of course a Facebook page.

Joe's Beer House   PUB
(Map p208; 160 Nelson Mandela Ave) True to its moniker, Joe's stocks a wide assortment of Namibian and German beers, and you can count on prolonged drinking here until early in the morning. It's the favoured drinking hole of Afrikaners.

Café Balalaika   BAR
(Map p210; Independence Ave, Zoo Park) This spot, cafe by day, bar by night, features a terrace with the capital's largest rubber tree. Live music and karaoke features, as does a cool bar scene with some great beer on tap.

Pharaoh Lounge   BAR
(Map p208; 22 Nelson Mandela Ave) Good for a cocktail and a dance or just a chill out in lounge chairs, this bar is located on the corner of Nelson Mandela and Sam Nujoma Aves.

Club London   NIGHTCLUB
(Map p208; 4 Nasmith St, Southern Industrial Area; ☺Wed-Sat) Formerly La Dee Da's, this is another relocated club that has undergone a makeover. Check out the Facebook page to see whether it's a foam party, glowstick event or some other inventive idea enticing patrons to show their moves. At other times you can dance to Angolan *kizomba* (fast-paced Portuguese-African music), hip-hop, rave, traditional African, rock and commercial pop accompanied by special effects.

Wine Bar   WINE BAR
(Map p210; ☎226514; 3 Garten St; ☺4-11.30pm Mon-Thu, 3pm-midnight Fri, 5-10.30pm Sat) In a lovely historic mansion that actually used to store the town's water supply, but now houses the city's premium wine selection, staff here have an excellent knowledge of their products. Playing off this ambience, your hosts will satiate your palate with an admirable South African wine selection, paired with Mediterranean-style tapas and small snacks. It's a beautiful spot for a glass of wine and a fiery African sunset. There's a wine shop here too.

☆ Entertainment

Whether you're in the mood for a night out at the theatre or a Hollywood screening, Windhoek can provide.

National Theatre of Namibia   THEATRE
(Map p210; ☎234 633; Robert Mugabe St) Located south of the National Art Gallery, the national theatre stages infrequent theatrical performances; for information see the *Namibian* newspaper.

Playhouse Theatre   THEATRE
(Map p210; ☎402253; 48 Tal St, Old South-West Brewery Bldg) This place used to be a warehouse for the breweries but has been converted into a full-scale, state-of-the-art theatre. The industrial interior and versatility of its design makes the Playhouse ideal for staging live African and European music and theatre productions. There's also a permanent exhibition space and an internet cafe here.

Ster Kinekor   CINEMA
(Map p208; ☎215912; Maerua Park Centre) Off Robert Mugabe Ave, this place shows recent films and has half-price admission on Tuesday.

DAVID WALL PHOTO / GETTY IMAGES ©

1. Kolmanskop (p313)
Once a thriving diamond-mining town, Kolmanskop now lies deserted and at the mercy of encroaching desert sands.

2. Etosha National Park (p237)
Attracting enormous congregations of animals, Etosha is one of the best places on earth for watching wildlife.

3. Kokerbooms
A unique floral oddity, the *kokerboom* (quiver tree) is a species of aloe that grows only in southern Namibia.

4. Moremi Game Reserve (p103)
Named after the Batawana chief Moremi III, Moremi Game Reserve has habitats ranging from woodland and grassland to flood plains, marshes, lagoons and islands.

GEM CONSCIOUSNESS

The former owner of House of Gems, Sid Pieters, who passed away in 2003, was once Namibia's foremost gem expert. In 1974, along the Namib coast, Pieters uncovered 45 crystals of jeremejevite, a sea-blue tourmaline containing boron – the rarest gem on earth. His discovery was only the second ever; the first was in Siberia in the mid-19th century. Another of his finds was the marvellously streaky 'crocidolite pietersite' (named for Pieters himself), from near Outjo in North-Central Namibia. Pietersite, a beautiful form of jasper shot through with asbestos fibres, is certainly one of the world's most beautiful and unusual minerals, and some believe that it has special energy and consciousness-promoting qualities. Other New Age practitioners maintain that it holds the 'keys to the kingdom of heaven'; stare at it long enough and perhaps you'll agree.

College of the Arts (COTA)   CLASSICAL MUSIC
(Map p210; ☑225 841; 41 Fidel Castro St) The conservatorium in this college occasionally holds classical concerts.

🛍 Shopping

The handicrafts sold in Post Street Mall are largely imported from neighbouring countries, though there is still an excellent selection of woodcarvings, baskets and other African curios on offer. You're going to have to bargain hard if you want to secure a good price, though maintain your cool and always flash a smile – you'll win out with politeness in the end! Another spot with a good range of curios is along Fidel Castro St, near the corner of Independence, snaking up the hill towards Christuskirche

Mall culture is alive and well in Windhoek, and you'll find them scattered throughout the city centre and out in the 'burbs. Most of the stores are South African standards, which generally offer high-quality goods at a fraction of the price back home. Katutura's Soweto Market is more reminiscent of a traditional African market, though it's best to visit either with a local or as part of an organised tour.

You can find gear for 4WD expeditions at Safari Den (Map p208; ☑290 9294; www.safariden.com; 20 Bessemer St) and also try Gräber's (Map p208; ☑222732; Bohr St) in the Southern Industrial Area.

Namibia Crafts Centre   CRAFT
(Map p210; ☑242222; 40 Tal St, Old Breweries Craft Market; ☺9am-5.30pm Mon-Fri, to 3.30pm Sat & Sun) This place is an outlet for heaps of wonderful Namibian inspiration – leatherwork, basketry, pottery, jewellery, needlework, hand-painted textiles and other material

arts – and the artist and origin of each piece is documented. We like the root carvings.

Old Breweries Craft Market   CRAFT
(Map p210; cnr Garten & Tal Sts) This hive of tourist shopping euphoria contains a heap of small and large shops with a range of African arts and crafts on offer. A couple of our favourite shops are Woven Arts of Africa, with some wonderfully fine weavings in the form of wall-hangings and rugs; and Arti-San, a small pokey little shop with genuine Bushman crafts.

House of Gems   GEMS
(Map p210; ☑225202; www.namrocks.com; 131 Werner List St) This is the most reputable shop in Windhoek for buying both raw and polished minerals and gemstones.

Penduka   CRAFT
(☑257210; www.penduka.com) Penduka, which means 'wake up', operates a nonprofit women's needlework project at Goreangab Dam, 8km northwest of the city centre. You can purchase needlework, baskets, carvings and fabric creations for fair prices and be assured that all proceeds go to the producers. To get there, take the Western Bypass north and turn left on Monte Cristo Rd, left on Otjomuise Rd, right on Eveline St and right again on Green Mountain Dam Rd. Then follow the signs to Goreangab Dam/Penduka.

Cymot Greensport   OUTDOOR EQUIPMENT
(Map p210; ☑234131; 60 Mandume Ndemufayo St) This is the place to head for supplies before you head off into the Namibian wilds – it's good for air compressors, a vital accessory. It is also a supplier of quality camping, hiking, cycling and vehicle outfitting equipment, as is Cape Union Mart (Map p208; Maerua Park Centre).

ℹ Information

Dangers & Annoyances

Central Windhoek is actually quite relaxed and hassle free. As long as you stay alert, walk with confidence, keep a hand on your wallet and avoid wearing anything too flashy, you should encounter nothing worse than a few persistent touts and the odd con artist.

However, you do need to be especially wary when walking with any kind of bag, especially on backstreets. Most importantly, don't use bumbags or carry swanky camera or video totes – they're all prime targets.

During the research for this book, a popular con was for would-be-thieves to play on the conscience of tourists and get their attention by posing the question, 'why won't you talk to a black man?' Ignore this and keep walking. As an extra precaution, always travel by taxi at night, even in the wealthy suburbs. The streets in Windhoek are ominously quiet once the sun goes down, which sadly means that foreign tourists quickly become easy targets.

The most likely annoyance for travellers is petty theft, which more often than not occurs at budget hotels and hostels around the city. As a general rule, you should take advantage of the hotel safe, and never leave your valuables out in the open.

If you're driving, avoid parking on the street, and never leave anything of value visible in your vehicle. Also, never leave your car doors unlocked, even if you're still in the car: a common ploy is for one guy to distract you while another opens one of the other doors, grabs a bag and does a runner.

During the day, the safest and most convenient parking is the underground lot beneath the Wernhill Park Centre. At night, you should stay at accommodation that provides off-street secure parking.

The township of Katutura and the northwestern industrial suburbs of Goreangab, Wanaheda and Hakahana are not as dangerous as their counterparts in South Africa, and are reasonably safe during the daytime. However, if you do visit these neighbourhoods, it's best to either go with a local contact or as part of an organised tour.

Emergency

Ambulance (☏211 111)
National Police (☏10111)
City Police (☏290 2239; ⊗24hr)

Internet Access

Virtually all hotels and hostels offer cheap and reliable internet access, with wi-fi increasingly the norm. If you're out and about, internet cafes can be found in every mall in the city.

Medical Services

Rhino Park Private Hospital (Map p208; ☏225434; Sauer St) Provides excellent care and service, but patients must pay up front.

Mediclinic Windhoek (☏222687; Heliodoor St, Eros; ⊗24hr) Emergency centre and a range of medical services.

Money

Major banks and bureaux de change are concentrated around Independence Ave, and all will change foreign currency and travellers cheques, and give credit-card advances. As a general rule, ATMs in Namibia handle Visa and MasterCard.

Post & Telephone

The modern **main post office** (Independence Ave) can readily handle overseas post. It also has telephone boxes in the lobby, and next door is the **Telecommunications Office** (Independence Ave), where you can make international calls and send or receive faxes.

Tourist Information

Namibia Wildlife Resorts (NWR; Map p210; ☏285 7200; www.nwr.com.na; Independence Ave) Books national park accommodation and hikes.

Windhoek Information & Publicity Office (Main Office) (Map p210; ☏290 2092, 290 2596; www.cityofwindhoek.org.na; Independence Ave; ⊗7.30am-4.30pm) The friendly staff at this office answer questions and distribute local publications and leaflets, including *What's On in Windhoek* and useful city maps. There's another branch (Map p210; Post Street Mall; ⊗7.30am-noon and 1-4.30pm) in the Post Street Mall that is open the same hours but closes from noon to 1pm.

Travel Agencies

Cardboard Box Travel Shop (Map p210; ☏256580; www.namibian.org) Attached to the backpacker hostel of the same name, this recommended travel agency can arrange both budget and upmarket bookings all over the country.

Chameleon Safaris (Map p210; ☏247668; www.chameleonsafaris.com) Attached to the backpacker hostel of the same name, this travel agency is recommended for all types of safaris around the country.

ℹ Getting There & Away

Air

Chief Hosea Kutako International Airport, which is located about 40km east of the city centre, serves most international flights into and out of Windhoek. **Air Namibia** (☏299 6333; www.air namibia.com.na) operates flights daily between Windhoek and Cape Town and Johannesburg,

CYCLING THE ELEPHANT HIGHWAY *MARA VORHEES*

When I was contemplating the possibility of a bike ride across Botswana and Namibia, I turned to my trusty Lonely Planet: 'Unless you're an experienced cyclist and equipped for the extreme conditions, abandon any ideas you may have about a...bicycle adventure'. The book went on to emphasise the scorching sun, the paucity of water and the vast distances. 'If you try to ride your bike here,' I inferred, 'you will die.' What had I got myself into?

I was reassured by the fact that I would be riding as a part of an organised tour. The **Tour d'Afrique** (TDA; www.tourdafrique.com) is an 11,800km expedition from Cairo to Cape Town that is divided into eight legs. As a member of a Lonely Planet relay team, I would ride the penultimate leg – the Elephant Hwy – from Victoria Falls to Windhoek.

So, thankfully, I did not have to worry about pesky details like drinking water. Namibia and especially Botswana are sparsely populated countries. Even on the country's major highways, we rode for hours at a time without passing any sign of civilisation. In fact, we spent every second night at a bush camp, sleeping in the wilderness with no facilities except those provided by the TDA truck. Remember that this is the desert. Without a support vehicle, cyclists should be prepared to carry or pull at least two days' worth of food and water.

The other aspect of the climate – the heat – was also not a major concern, since my trip took place in April. As it turns out, autumn in Southern Africa offers conditions that are close to perfect for cycling. We would set out at sunrise to take advantage of the cool morning air. I always needed a jacket to start, but that never lasted long; by midday it would be hot. Of course, by midday the speedier riders had already reached our destination. As one of the slower riders, I endured some hot afternoons, but the temperature rarely went above 30°C.

The sun is brutal, no doubt, and the application of sunscreen was a ritual that took place every morning and every few hours on the road. Some cyclists wore a long-sleeved, lightweight base layer under their jersey to protect their arms from the sun. In any case, there was no escaping the 'biker's tan' showing off the line from the chamois shorts.

So I could handle the heat and the limited water supply, but what about the distances? At 1576km, the Elephant Hwy is one of the longest sections of the tour and it was certainly further than I had ever ridden my bike. The good news is that the landscape is mostly flat and the roads are paved. The bad news is that it can be monotonous when you are riding for six to eight hours a day. So how to prepare? Take care of your body: make sure you have trained properly by logging many, many kilometres. Take care of your mind: bring an iPod.

Desolate landscapes aside, there's plenty to see along the Elephant Hwy. Yes, *elephants*. They are frequently sighted along the main road north and west of Nata. I was thrilled when I cycled past a group of ellies congregating around a watering hole, and later when a big one created a roadblock ahead of me. I was not so thrilled when I saw – or rather smelled – a carcass at the side of the road.

In case you're wondering, an elephant's top speed is 40km/h when alarmed or upset. Fortunately, they can't sustain this speed for more than a few seconds. So, as long as you get a head start on your bike, you can probably outride them.

There is other wildlife in the vicinity, although it can be difficult to spot from the road: keep your eyes peeled for giraffes, warthogs, various antelopes, iguanas and plenty of birds.

That said, if wildlife watching is your game, you'll want to schedule some time out of the saddle. Park your bike in Maun and take an excursion into the Okavango Delta. Spend a few nights at a lodge between Nata and Maun so you can explore the Makgadikgadi Pans. Trade your bike for a boat in Kasane and cruise along the Zambezi River. Cyclists are not permitted in the national parks, for good reason: nobody wants to be meals on wheels.

Author Mara Vorhees was one of 16 Lonely Planet riders to participate in the 2009 Tour d'Afrique. She rode 1546km of the Elephant Hwy.

as well as daily flights to and from Frankfurt. Several airlines including Air Namibia also offer international services to and from Maun (Botswana) and Victoria Falls (Zimbabwe).

Eros Airport, immediately south of the city centre, serves most domestic flights into and out of Windhoek. Air Namibia offers around three weekly flights to and from Katima Mulilo, Ondangwa, Rundu and Swakopmund/Walvis Bay.

Coming from Windhoek, make sure the taxi driver knows which airport you are going to.

Other airlines with flights into and out of Windhoek:

Lufthansa Airlines (☑415 3747; www.lufthansa.com)

South African Airways (p354)

TAAG Angola (☑226625; www.taag.com.br) All of these airlines have offices at Chief Hosea Kutako International Airport or in Windhoek at the **Sanlaam Centre** (Map p210; Fidel Castro St), though you can easily make travel arrangements in advance by going online.

Bus

From the main long-distance **bus station** (cnr Independence Ave & Banhof St), the Intercape Mainliner (p357) runs to and from Cape Town, Johannesburg, Victoria Falls and Swakopmund, serving a variety of local destinations along the way. Tickets can be purchased through your accommodation, from the Intercape Mainliner office or online – given the popularity of these routes, advance reservations are highly recommended.

There are some useful shuttle services out to Swakopmund and Walvis Bay (the tourist office has details) such as the **Town Hoppers** (☑081 210 3062), departing daily at 2.30pm (N$250, four hours), and returning in the morning to Windhoek.

Local combis (minibuses) leave when full from the Rhino Park petrol station, Katutura (get there very early in the morning) and can get you to most urban centres in central and southern Namibia. For northern destinations such as Tsumeb, Grootfontein and Rundu you need to go to the local minibus station opposite the hospital on Independence Ave, Katutura.

Generally, combi routes do not serve the vast majority of Namibia's tourist destinations, which are located well beyond major population centres. Still, they're a fine way to travel if you want to visit some of the country's smaller towns and cities, and it's great fun to roll up your sleeves and jump into the bus with the locals.

Car & Motorcycle

Windhoek is literally the crossroads of Namibia – the point where the main north–south route (the B1) and east–west routes (B2 and B6) cross –

and all approaches to the city are extremely scenic, passing through beautiful desert hills. Roads are clearly signposted; those travelling between northern and southern Namibia can avoid the city centre by taking the Western Bypass.

Hitching

Due to its location and traffic, hitching to or from Windhoek is easier than anywhere else in Namibia.

Train

Windhoek train station has a **booking office** (☑298 2175; ☾7.30am-4pm Mon-Fri) where you are able to reserve seats on any of the country's public rail lines. Routes are varied, and include overnight trains to Keetmanshoop, Tsumeb and Swakopmund, though irregular schedules, lengthy travel times and far better bus connections make train travel of little interest for the majority of overseas travellers.

❶ Getting Around

Collective taxis from the main ranks at Wernhill Park Centre follow set routes to Khomasdal and Katutura, and if your destination is along the way, you'll pay around N$5 to N$15. With taxis from the main bus stations or by radio dispatch, fares are either metered or are calculated on a per-kilometre basis, but you may be able to negotiate a set fare per journey. Plan on N$50 to anywhere around the city.

If you're arriving at Hosea Kutako International Airport, taxis typically wait outside the arrivals area. It's a long drive into the city, so you can expect to pay anywhere from N$270 to N$300 depending on your destination. For Eros Airport, fares are much more modest at around N$50. In the city there are always reliable taxis that hang around the tourist office on Independence Ave. If you flag one down off the streets just be aware there are plenty of cowboys around and often not much English is spoken.

NORTH-CENTRAL NAMIBIA

When you have little more than a car window separating you from the surrounding white plains, and with a thermos of early-morning coffee and cameras ready, there are few places that can match the wildlife prospects of dawn in Etosha National Park. Home to a network of artificial waterholes and naturally up-welling springs, the southern boundary of the Etosha Pan harbours enormous congregations of African animals. Just one day of wildlife watching at a single waterhole can produce literally thousands of sightings, which has justifiably earned Etosha the reputation as one of the best reserves in the world.

Unlike the vast majority of safari parks in Africa, all roads inside Etosha are 2WD accessible and open to private vehicles. This, of course, means that if you've been fortunate enough to rent your own vehicle, you're in for one of the most memorable safaris of your life. Anyone can tell their friends and family back home how quickly their guide spotted a pride of lions, but how many people can say that they drove on the edges of a salt pan while tracking herds of zebra in the distance?

The crown jewel in Namibia's rich treasure trove of protected areas, Etosha dominates the tourism circuit in North-Central Namibia. However, there are plenty of worthwhile opportunities here for hiking and exploring, and there's a good chance that the tourist crowds will be elsewhere. If you have the time to spare, don't overlook the region's other highlights, which run the gamut from lofty plateaus and art-laden caves to hulking meteorites and dino footprints.

Geography

Although the Etosha Pan is the most prominent feature in the region, the area is primarily known as a mining and cattle-ranching centre. Large-scale mining, particularly in the Tsumeb area, dates back to the early 1900s, while pastoralism, especially among the Herero, pre-dates the German colonial era. North-Central Namibia is also known for its unique natural landscapes, particularly the Waterberg Plateau Park, a lovely island in the sky, and the Erongo Mountains (Erongoberg), which form a dramatic backdrop along the route from Windhoek to Swakopmund.

❶ Getting Around

Since the majority of sites in North-Central Namibia are outside population centres, you will need a private vehicle to access most of the region. Etosha itself is easy enough to visit as part of an organised tour, but most visitors prefer the thrill and excitement of a self-drive safari. Even in the rainy season, the paved approach to the park, in addition to all internal roads, is easily accessible to 2WD vehicles.

Outside of Etosha, North-Central Namibia benefits from an excellent network of sealed roads. This is one region where a 4WD vehicle

is largely unnecessary, aside from a few minor access roads in the Erongo Mountains.

East to Botswana

The seemingly never-ending B6 runs east from Windhoek to the Botswana border, passing through the heart of one of Namibia's most important ranching centres. Together, the 970 farms of the Omaheke region cover nearly 5 million hectares, and provide over one-third of Namibia's beef. While passionate carnivores can certainly rejoice at these numbers, the road east to the Botswana border is a long and monotonous slog – fortunately it is sealed, flat and in excellent condition.

GOBABIS

📝 062

Gobabis is situated on the Wit-Nossob River, 120km from the Botswana border at Buitepos. The name is Khoikhoi for 'place of strife', but a slight misspelling (Goabbis) renders it 'place of elephants', which locals seem to prefer despite its obvious shortage of elephants.

Although Gobabis is the main service centre of the Namibian Kalahari, there isn't a lot to look at. The town's only historic building is the old military hospital, the Lazarett, which once served as a town museum. It's not officially open, but you can pick up a key at the library in the centre of town.

The Harnas Wildlife Foundation & Guest Farm (📝568828; www.harnas.org; campsite per person N$180, igloos/cottages per person N$750/950, igloos/cottages per person with full board N$935/1135) is a rural development project that likens itself to Noah's Ark. Here you can see wildlife close up, including cheetahs, leopards and lions. Many of the animals are caged, but since they were either orphaned or injured, they would be unable to survive were it not for the foundation. A wide range of accommodation is available, including options for full board, and there are plenty of activities to keep you amused for a couple of days. To get here, turn north on the C22 past Gobabis and continue for 45km, then drive east on the D1668 for another 45km (following the signs).

Public transport is unreliable along this route, and it's recommended that you head east from Windhoek in a private vehicle. If you're planning on crossing into Botswana in a hire car, be sure in advance that all of your paperwork is in order.

BUITEPOS

Buitepos, a wide spot in the desert at the Namibia-Botswana border crossing, is little more than a petrol station and customs and immigration post. The border itself is open from 7am to midnight, though you should try to cross with plenty of daylight since it's a long drive to Ghanzi, the next settlement of major size along the Trans-Kalahari Hwy.

The **East Gate Service Station & Rest Camp** (062-560405; www.eastgate-namibia.com; Trans-Kalahari Hwy; campsite per person N$70, cabins without bathroom per person N$130, 2-person bungalows N$450; ❋) rises from the desert like a mirage, and is a decent enough place to crash if you're not particularly fussy.

On the other side of the border, the paved road continues to Ghanzi.

North to Etosha

The immaculate B1 heads north from Windhoek, and provides access to Outjo as well as Tsumeb and Grootfontein. Prominent towns in their own right, together they serve as the launching point for excursions into nearby Etosha National Park. While it's very tempting to strike north with safari fever, it's definitely worth slowing down and taking a bit of time to explore the quirky sights of this comparatively untouristed section of North-Central Namibia.

OKAHANDJA & AROUND

062

Okahandja is a busy little place, but not as busy as Windhoek – it's far more manageable than the capital and it makes a great alternative base, especially for forays further north to Etosha and west to Swakopmund.

From the mid-19th century to the early 20th century the town served as a German-run mission and a colonial administrative centre, remnants of which still dot the town centre.

Sights

Friedenskirche   CHURCH
(Church of Peace; Kerk St; ⊙dawn-dusk) In the churchyard and across the road from the 1876 Friedenskirche are the graves of several historical figures, including Herero leader Willem Maherero, Nama leader Jan Jonker Afrikaner and Hosea Kutako, the 'father of

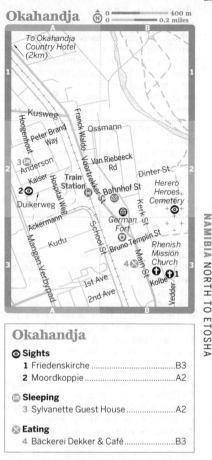

Okahandja

Okahandja

◎ **Sights**
  1 Friedenskirche B3
  2 Moordkoppie A2

◎ **Sleeping**
  3 Sylvanette Guest House A2

◎ **Eating**
  4 Bäckerei Dekker & Café......................B3

Namibian independence', who was the first politician to petition the UN against the South African occupation of Namibia.

Moordkoppie   HISTORIC SITE
The historical animosity between the Nama and the Herero had its most emphatic expression at the Battle of Moordkoppie (Afrikaans for 'Murder Hill') on 23 August 1850. During the battle, 700 Herero under the command of chief Katjihene were massacred by Nama forces. Half of the victims were women or children, whose bodies were dismembered for the copper bangles on their arms and legs. The scene of this tragedy was a small rocky hill near the centre of town between the B2 and the railway line, 500m north of the Gross Barmen turn-off.

NAMIBIA NORTH TO ETOSHA

✲ Festivals & Events

Maherero Day
REMEMBERANCE

On the weekend nearest 26 August is Maherero Day, which is when the Red Flag Herero people meet in traditional dress in memory of their fallen chiefs, killed in battles with the Nama and the Germans. A similar event is held by the Mbanderu (Green Flag Herero), on the weekend nearest 11 June.

🛏 Sleeping & Eating

Sylvanette Guest House
GUESTHOUSE

(📞505550; www.sylvanette.com; Anderson St; s/d from N$390/600; ✳@🛜🌊) This cosy little guesthouse is located in a quiet and garden-like suburban setting and centred on a refreshing swimming pool surrounded by all manner of potted plants. Well-priced rooms pay tribute to the wilds of Namibia with ample animal prints.

Okahandja Country Hotel
HOTEL $$

(off Map p225; 📞504 299; www.okahandjahotel.com; campsite N$125, d N$880) This big old stalwart is a great bastion of hospitality. The stone buildings with sweeping thatched roofs stay cool in summer and have plenty of room. The rooms are old-fashioned and a little frumpy but very comfortable. A little green oasis in an otherwise dusty setting, it's 2km north of town, opposite the D2110 turn-off.

Von Bach Dam Resort
RESORT

(📞500162; campsite per person N$100, s/d chalets from N$580/900; 🌊) Located just south of Okahandja on the B1 and also known as Tungeni, this place was transformed several years ago from a relatively low-key resort into a much larger (and busier) enterprise. It has dozens of chalets, as well as campsites with their own *braais* (barbecues). There's also a swimming pool and spa, and cruises can be organised. A fee of N$10 per car plus N$10 per person must be paid to enter the park surrounding the dam.

Bäckerei Dekker & Café
BAKERY $

(Martin Neib St; meals & snacks N$25-50; ⏱6.30am-3.30pm Mon-Fri, to noon Sat) This German cafe and bakery serves, along with hot and cold drinks, tasty breakfasts and lunches including toasties, bread rolls, sandwiches, salads, freshly made pies, a cold platter and game steaks.

❶ Getting There & Away

BUS

Intercape Mainliner (p355) buses make the trip between Windhoek and Okahandja (from N$190,

one hour, four weekly). Book your tickets in advance online as this service continues on to Victoria Falls and fills up quickly.

Combis (minibuses) also run up and down the B1 with fairly regular frequency, and a ride between Windhoek and Okahandja shouldn't cost more than N$80. Okahandja is a minor public-transport hub, serving various regional destinations by combi with fares averaging between N$40 and N$60.

CAR

Okahandja is 70km north of Windhoek on the B1, the country's main north–south highway.

TRAIN

Trans-Namib (📞061-298 2175) operates trains between Windhoek and Okahandja (fares from N$70, two hours, daily except Saturday), though very limited early-morning and late-night departures are inconvenient for most.

ERONGO MOUNTAINS (ERONGOBERG)
📞 064

The volcanic Erongo Mountains, often referred to as the Erongoberg, rise as a 2216m massif north of Karibib and Usakos. The Erongo range is best known for its caves and rock paintings, particularly the 50m-deep Phillips Cave.

After the original period of volcanism, some 150 million years ago, the volcano collapsed on its magma chamber, allowing the basin to fill with slow-cooling igneous material. The result is this hard granite-like core, which withstood the erosion that washed away the surrounding rock. Much later in prehistory, the site was occupied by the San, who left behind a rich legacy of cave paintings and rock art that has weathered remarkably well throughout the ages.

◎ Sights

Phillips Cave
CAVE

(day permit N$50) This cave, 3km off the road, contains the famous humpbacked white elephant painting. Superimposed on the elephant is a large humpbacked antelope (perhaps an eland), and around it frolic ostriches and giraffes. These paintings were brought to attention in the book *Phillips Cave* by prehistorian Abbè Breuil, but his speculations about their Mediterranean origins have now been discounted. The site is open to day hikers via Ameib Ranch.

The Ameib picnic site is backed up by outcrops of stacked boulders, one of which, the notable Bull's Party, resembles a circle of gossiping bovines. Other formations that are often photographed include one resembling an elephant's head and another that recalls a Herero woman in traditional dress, standing with two children.

🛏 Sleeping

Ameib Ranch GUESTHOUSE $$$
(☑684151; campsite per person N$130, s/d from N$600/1200; ☀) Located at the base of the Erongo foothills, the 'Green Hill' Ranch was established in 1864 as a Rhenish mission station, though it operates today as a guest farm and campsite. Accommodation is in the historic farmhouse, which is adjacent to a landscaped pool, a *lapa* (a circular area with a fire pit, used for socialising) and the well-maintained campsite. Ameib Ranch owns the concessions on Phillips Cave, and issues permits for the site in addition to guided hikes and day tours.

Erongo Wilderness Lodge LODGE $$$
(☑570537; www.erongowilderness-namibia.com; per person tented bungalows with full board from N$1515; ✱@☀) This highly acclaimed wilderness retreat combines spectacular mountain scenery, wildlife viewing, birdwatching and environmentally sensitive architecture to create one of Namibia's most memorable lodges. Accommodation is in one of 10 tented bungalows, which are built on wooden stilts and situated among towering granite pillars. When you're not lounging in front of the fireplace in the main lodge, you can take a guided walk (cost included in the full-board price) or a nature drive (N$440). To get to the lodge, go to Omaruru, turn west on the D2315 (off the Karibib road 2km south of town) and continue for 10km.

ℹ Getting There & Away

North of Ameib, the D1935 skirts the Erongo Mountains before heading north into Damaraland. Alternatively, you can head east towards Omaruru on the D1937. This route virtually encircles the Erongo massif and provides access to minor 4WD roads into the heart of the mountains.

OMARURU
☑ 064
Omaruru's dry and dusty setting beside the shady Omaruru riverbed lends it a real outback feel. The town has a growing reputation as an arts and crafts centre and in recent years has become home to the Artist's Trail, an annual arts event in September; you can pick up a free copy of the program of events around town.

The town itself is a welcoming little oasis with some great accommodation options, good food and one of the very few wineries in the country – there's little as surreal as enjoying a platter of meats and cheeses under trees while wine tasting in the Namibian outback.

◉ Sights

Franke Tower HISTORIC SITE
In January 1904 Omaruru was attacked by Herero forces under chief Manassa. German captain Victor Franke, who had been engaged in suppressing an uprising in southern Namibia, petitioned Governor Leutwein for permission to march north and relieve the besieged town. After a 20-day, 900km march, Franke arrived in Omaruru and led the cavalry charge, which defeated the Herero attack.

For his efforts Franke received the highest German military honours, and in 1908 the grateful German residents of Omaruru erected the Franke Tower in his honour. The tower, which was declared a national monument in 1963, holds a historical plaque and affords a view over the town. It's normally locked, though if you want to climb it you can pick up a key at the Central Hotel.

Kristall Kellerei Winery WINERY
(☑570083; ◷8am-4.30pm Mon-Fri, to 12.30pm Sat) One of only three wineries in Namibia, this is a lovely spot to come for lunch. In the afternoon you can enjoy light meals – cheese and cold-meat platters (N$70) – while tasting their wines and other products. Sit out in the garden full of works of art and enjoy a platter over a glass of Namibian wine. Apart from schnapps the winery produces Colombard, a white wine, and Paradise Flycatcher, a red blend of Ruby Cabernet, Cabernet Sauvignon and Tinta Barocca. The winery is 4km east of town on the D2328.

✲ Festivals & Events

Omaruru has been home to the Artists Trail since 2007, marking it as Namibia's artist town. Music and dance events feature over three days in September, along with food and wine, jewellery, photography and painting.

Each year on the weekend nearest to 10 October the White Flag Herero people hold a procession from the Ozonde suburb to the graveyard, opposite the mission station, where their chief Wilhelm Zeraua was buried after his defeat in the German-Herero wars.

🛏 Sleeping & Eating

Central Hotel Omaruru HOTEL $$
(☑570030; Wilhelm Zeraua St; s/d from
N$300/400; ✻🐾) This place is the town's
focal point for eating and drinking and has
rondavels (round, traditional-style huts)in
the huge garden – they are simple concrete
set-ups with small beds, clean linen and
good bathrooms. The dining room may well
be the only show in town in the evening for
dinner. Fortunately, the standard of food is
pretty good for a remote pub with German
faves plus a nod to the local game (mains
N$75).

Kashana Hotel HOTEL $$$
(☑571434; www.kashana-namibia.com; Dr I Scheep-
ers St; r per person from N$400; ✻🛜🐾) Offering a
swag of accommodation, upmarket Kashana
has luxury bungalows and rooms set around
a large shady courtyard. In the main building
is a bar and restaurant. Also based here is a
goldsmith and a shop selling herbal products.

River Guesthouse GUESTHOUSE $$
(☑570274; Dr I Scheepers St; campsite N$90, s/d
N$390/610; 🐾) The camping here is the best
in town with some great shady trees to pitch
a tent under and excellent facilities, which
include fireplaces and power outlets. You
may just have four dogs keeping you com-
pany as well – they make a good blanket in
winter. The rooms are fine and surround a
shady courtyard well set up for relaxing.

Omaruru Souvenirs & Kaffestube CAFE
(Wilhelm Zeraua St; meals N$20-55) The build-
ing housing this intimate cafe dates from
1907. This place is a good choice for a
strong cup of coffee and traditional Ger-
man baked goods, as well as for a cold pint
of Hansa and some pub grub in the outdoor
beer garden.

🛍 Shopping

CmArte Gallery ARTS & CRAFTS
(☑570017; Wilhelm Zeraua St; ⊙9am-5pm) This
arts and crafts outlet has some really good
crafts including some from local artists,
alongside imported antiques from both An-
gola and the DRC. It's worth sticking your
nose in here and having a good rummage
around, as you just may find a gem. We like
the black-and-white wildlife sketches, both
framed (N$1600) and unframed (N$1300).

Omaruru Souvenirs & Kaffestube SOUVENIRS
(Wilhelm Zeraua St;) The extensive souvenir
range at this place is worth a browse. And
you can always grab a hot/cold drink in be-
tween foraging.

ℹ Getting There & Away

With your own vehicle, the sealed C33 which-
passes through Omaruru provides the quickest
route between Swakopmund and Etosha.

UIS
☑064
Just over an hour's drive from Omaruru, Uis
is a small, dusty settlement that's at a handy
crossroads for those heading north through
Damaraland, or southwest to the Skeleton
Coast or Swakopmund. It has an array of
affordable accommodation including the
very welcoming **White Lady B&B** (☑504102;
whitelady@iway.na; campsite N$80, s/d incl break-
fast N$380/680; 🛜🐾), where simple rooms
are a good size and well kept; and the small
orderly campsite has some shady trees. Din-
ner is also available.

KALKFELD
☑067
Around 200 million years ago, Namibia was
covered in a shallow sea, which gradually
filled with wind-blown sand and eroded silt.
Near the tiny town of Kalkfeld, these sand-

THE LIVING MUSEUM OF THE SAN PEOPLE

The **Living Museum** (☑064-571086; www.omandumba.de; Farm Omandumba) is a unique
opportunity in Namibia to interact with, and learn about, the San people, one of the
oldest traditional hunter-and-gatherer cultures in the world. Experiencing traditional
San culture includes learning how to make arrows, jewellery and traditional medicine.
Tourists can also go on bushwalks and hunting trips, and enjoy tribal song and dance.
The museum features a typical San village and proceeds go towards a school, also here.
Tours to rock paintings in the area run from the museum and there's accommodation in
the way of campsites and simple rooms. The open-air museum is located 50km south-
west of Omaruru on D2315.

stone layers bear the evidence of a 25m-long dinosaur stroll, which took place an estimated 170 million years ago. The tracks were made in what was then soft clay by a three-toed dinosaur that walked on its hind legs – probably a forerunner of modern birds.

The **dinosaur footprints** (admission N$20), which were declared a national monument in 1951, are located on a farm 29km from Kalkfeld, just off route D2414. Aside from hosting the dino tracks, **Otjihaenamparero Farm** (290153; www.dinosaurstracks. com/home.html; campsite per person N$80, s/d N$350/600) has a three-room guesthouse offering B&B; dinner can be organised for an additional cost (N$160). There's also a small campground.

The nearby **Mt Etjo Safari Lodge** (290173; www.mount-etjo.com; 4-person campsite N$400, s/d N$1590/3180; ✿@✿), in the heart of a private nature reserve, provides access to a smaller set of dinosaur tracks, which are located on the edge of the appropriately named Dinosaur Campsite. 'Mt Etjo' means place of refuge, and refers to the nearby table mountain. Its place in history was sealed in April 1989 when the Mt Etjo Peace Agreement was signed, ending the South-West African People's Organisation's (Swapo) liberation struggle and setting the stage for Namibian independence the following March. Accommodation is either in the main safari lodge, an upmarket affair that benefits from the beauty of the surrounding nature, or in the expensive but entirely private campsite, located a few kilometres down the road. The lodge is situated 35km from Kalkfeld via the D2414 and the D2483 – just follow the brightly painted signs.

Kalkfeld is located just off the C33 approximately halfway between Omaruru and Otjiwarongo.

OTJIWARONGO
067

Handy as a jumping-off point for Etosha, and particularly the Waterberg Plateau, Otjiwarongo is especially pleasant in September and October when the town explodes with the vivid colours of blooming jacaranda and bougainvillea.

The town was officially founded in 1906 with the arrival of the narrow-gauge railway from Swakopmund to the mines at Otavi and Tsumeb. An old locomotive still rests in town, proudly marking this historical legacy.

Sights

Locomotive No 41 TRAIN
At the train station stands Locomotive No 41, which was manufactured in 1912 by the Henschel company of Kassel (Germany), and then brought all the way to Namibia to haul ore between the Tsumeb mines and the port at Swakopmund. It was retired from service in 1960 when the 0.6m narrow gauge was replaced with the wider 1.067m gauge.

Crocodile Ranch CROCODILE FARM
(cnr Zingel & Hospital Sts; admission N$25; 9am-5pm Mon-Fri, to 3pm Sat & Sun) Otjiwarongo is home to Namibia's first crocodile ranch. This ranch produces crocodile skins for export, and you can do a worthwhile tour of the crocs. There's a shop which has mainly wooden carvings with some jewellery and metalwork, though not much in the way of croc-skin products. The restaurant has a fullblown menu for breakfast and lunch; try any number of croc delicacies such as a croc wrap or kebabs.

Sleeping

Okonjima Lodge LODGE $$$
(687032; www.okonjima.com; s/d with half board from N$1500/2300) Okonjima Lodge, 'the Place of Baboons', is home to the AfriCat Foundation, which sponsors a cheetah and leopard rehabilitation centre as well as a sanctuary for orphaned or problem lions, cheetahs and other cats. Guests are able to participate in cheetah- and leopard-tracking (including on foot) expeditions, in addition to more relaxing activities, including hiking, bird-watching and wildlife drives. Accommodation is in a variety of chalets, luxury tents and rooms with private bathrooms, scattered throughout the reserve. To reach Okonjima, turn west onto the D2515, 49km south of Otjiwarongo; follow this road for 15km and then turn left onto the farm road for the last 10km.

Bush Pillow GUESTHOUSE $$
(303885; http://bushpillow.com; 47 Son Rd; s/d incl breakfast N$490/620; ✿✿) This great little guesthouse styles itself as 'executive accommodation' by targeting the business market, but with comfortable modern rooms and wi-fi connectivity throughout it also makes an ideal pit stop for travellers. The seven rooms include a couple set up for families and the kids will love the pool.

C'est Si Bon Hotel
HOTEL **$$**
(☑301240; www.cestsibonhotel.com; Swembad Rd; s/d from N$570/670; ❄❄) Named after a common French expression that translates to 'it is so good', this charmer of a hotel takes its moniker to heart, blending Namibian design with European flourishes. After a few laps in the pool, a cappuccino on the sundeck and a glass of wine in the bar, you'll probably agree that indeed, *c'est si bon.*

Out of Africa Town Lodge
LODGE **$$**
(☑302230; Long St; s/d from N$570/670; ❄❄) This attractive whitewashed, colonial-style lodge is a nice place to break up the drive to Etosha if you accidentally get a late start. Lofty rooms retain their historical accents, though frequent renovations have kept them in sync with the times.

❶ Getting There & Away
The Intercape Mainliner (p355) service that departs Windhoek for Victoria Falls passes through Otjiwarongo (from N$300, 3½ hours, twice weekly), and minibuses travelling between Windhoek and the north stop at the Engen petrol station. All train services between Tsumeb and Windhoek or Walvis Bay (via Swakopmund) also pass through.

OUTJO
☑ 067

Given the tourist traffic through this small town it has retained a surprisingly country, low-key feel. Although it's primarily a stopover with few attractions, the eating and accommodation options available make it a good place to chill out for a day or two on the way to or from Etosha National Park. Outjo is the last major rest stop before reaching Okaukuejo, the administrative headquarters of and western gateway to Etosha.

◎ Sights
Naulila Monument
HISTORIC SITE
This monument commemorates the 19 October 1914 massacre of German soldiers and officials by the Portuguese near Fort Naulila on the Kunene River in Angola. It also commemorates soldiers killed on 18 December 1914, under Major Franke, who was sent to avenge earlier losses.

Outjo Museum
MUSEUM
(admission N$5; ⊙8am-1pm & 2-5pm Mon-Fri) Originally called the Kliphuis (stone house), Franke House is one of Outjo's earliest buildings and now houses the town's museum. It was constructed in 1899 by order of Major von Estorff as a residence for himself and subsequent German commanders. It was later occupied by Major Franke, who posthumously gave it his name, though the current focus of the museum within it is political and natural history.

🛏 Sleeping & Eating
Etotongwe Lodge
LODGE **$$**
(☑313333; www.etotongwelodge.com; campsite per person N$90, s/d N$410/680) This refreshing place on the way to Etosha, just outside of town, feels like a little outpost. Its neat appearance and trim lawns break up the concrete, stone and thatched roofs which are spun around an attractive area. Rooms are fairly bare inside, but have some nice African touches and are neat as a pin and very roomy. Probably the best feature is the small front porch with chairs and table. Etotongwe is friendly and professionally run and there's a bar and restaurant on site.

Etosha Garden Hotel
HOTEL **$$**
(☑313130; www.etosha-garden-hotel.com; s/d incl breakfast N$360/580; ❄❄) Just a short walk from the town centre, this old place features curio-filled rooms surrounding plush greenery and a swimming pool. It's looking a bit run down these days and is pretty disorganised, but it's worth dropping into to see if they will give you a decent walk-in rate.

Farmhouse
CAFE, GUESTHOUSE **$$**
(☑313444; www.thefarmhouse-outjo.com; mains N$50-80; ⊙breakfast, lunch & dinner) This all-rounder is the centre of food and drink in town, serving meals all day, every day. Its pleasant beer garden is a great spot to check your emails (N$30 per 30 minutes for wireless or terminals). Burgers, grills (including game such as kudu, eland and oryx), wraps, pizza, salads and ever-changing daily specials are on offer, as is a tempting array of cakes. It might not pull off the farmhouse feel, but it does have rustic overtones inside and serves the best coffee in town. The Farmhouse also has a single and three double rooms on offer, all of a very comfortable standard.

❶ Getting There & Away
Combis run between the OK Supermarket in Outjo to towns and cities around North-Central Namibia, though there is no public transport leading up to Okaukuejo and the Andersson Gate of Etosha National Park. If you're driving, however, the sealed road continues north as far as the park gate.

WATERBERG PLATEAU PARK

The wild Waterberg is highly recommended – there is nothing quite like it in Namibia. It takes in a 50km-long, 16km-wide sandstone plateau, looming 150m above the desert plains. It doesn't have the traditional big wildlife attractions (such as lions or elephants). What it does have is animals that are rarely seen, and even here you have to be lucky because they are skittish and the bush is very thick. The park protects these rare and threatened species, which include sable and roan antelope, and white and black rhino. Most animals here have been introduced and, after breeding successfully, some are moved to other parks.

History

While Waterberg is known among tourists as a unique safari park, the plateau has played a prominent role in Namibian history.

In 1873 a Rhenish mission station was established at Waterberg, but it was destroyed in 1880 during the Herero-Nama wars. In 1904 it was the site of the decisive Battle of the Waterberg between German colonial forces and the Herero resistance. Due to superior weaponry and communications, the Germans prevailed and the remaining Herero were forced to flee east into the Kalahari. The final death blow was dealt by German soldiers, who were sent ahead to refuse the retreating Herero access to the region's few waterholes.

🏃 Activities

Wildlife Drive   WILDLIFE DRIVE
(incl breakfast pack N$450; ☺6am or 3pm) If you're not doing a hike, wildlife drives are the only way to get onto the plateau to spot the animals (self-drives are not allowed). The four-hour drive takes you to hides cleverly hidden around waterholes. Antelope, including eland, sable, roan and red hartebeest are the ones you're most likely to spot. Leopards, cheetahs and brown hyeanas are around but rarely seen.

Waterberg Unguided Hiking Trail   HIKING
A four-day, 42km unguided hike around a figure-eight track begins at 9am every Wednesday from April to November. It costs N$100 per person, and groups are limited to between three and 10 people. Book through Namibia Wildlife Resorts (p221) in Windhoek.

Hikers stay in basic shelters along the course and don't need to carry a tent but must otherwise be self-sufficient, ie carry food, sleeping bag, torch (flashlight) etc. Shelters have drinking water, but you'll need to carry enough to last you between

NAMIBIA WATERBERG PLATEAU PARK

Waterberg Plateau Park

NAMIBIA WATERBERG PLATEAU PARK

times – plan on drinking 3L to 4L per day, especially in the hot summer months.

The first day begins at the visitor centre (which is the Waterberg Camp), and follows the escarpment for 13km to Otjozongombe shelter. The second day's walk to Otjomapenda shelter is just a three-hour, 7km walk. The third day consists of an 8km route that loops back to Otjomapenda for the third night. The fourth and final day is a six-hour, 14km return to the visitor centre.

Waterberg Wilderness Trail   HIKING
From April to November the four-day, guided Waterberg Wilderness Trail operates every Thursday. The walks, which are led by armed guides, need a minimum of two people. They begin at 2pm on Thursday from the visitor centre and end early on Sunday afternoon. They cost N$220 per person and also must be prebooked through NWR in Windhoek. There's no set route,

and the itinerary is left to the whims of the guide. Accommodation is in simple huts, but participants must carry their own food and sleeping bags.

Resort Walking Trails   HIKING
Around the pink-sandstone-enclosed rest camp are nine short walking tracks, including one up to the plateau rim at Mountain View. They're great for a pleasant day of easy walking, but watch for snakes, which sun themselves on rocks and even on the actual tracks. No reservations are required for these trails.

🛏 Sleeping
The Waterberg Camp should be booked in advance through NWR in Windhoek, although walk-ins are accepted, subject to availability. The Waterberg Wilderness Lodge is privately owned and accepts walk-ins, though advance reservations are recommended, given its popularity.

Waterberg Camp CAMPGROUND, LODGE **$$**
(⌖067-305001; 2-person campsite N$300, bush chalet N$1200) Together with its sibling properties in Etosha, the Waterberg Camp is part of NWR's Classic Collection. At Waterberg, campers can pitch a tent in any number of scattered sites around *braai* pits and picnic tables. Campsites benefit from space, views of the plateau and the plains beyond, and well-kept amenities. Self-caterers can pick up firewood, alcohol, basic groceries and other supplies from the shop, while others can sink their teeth into a fine oryx steak at the restaurant (a rather grand stone building up the hill from the campsite – it's a bit of a slog on foot – complete with old pics and chandeliers) and wash it down with a glass of South African Pinotage from the bar. One word of warning, though: Waterberg is overrun with crafty baboons, so keep your tents zipped and your doors closed, and watch where you leave your food.

Waterberg Wilderness Lodge LODGE **$$$**
(⌖067-687018; www.waterberg-wilderness.com; camp site N$150, s/d with half board from N$1050/1800; ✴@⌖❄) While it's considerably more expensive than the Waterberg Camp, Waterberg Wilderness occupies a vast private concession within the park and is a wonderful upmarket alternative if you've got a bit of extra cash to burn. The Rust family has painstakingly transformed the property (formerly a cattle farm) by repopulating wildlife and allowing nature to return to

its pre-grazed state. The main lodge rests in a sun-drenched meadow at the end of a valley, where you'll find red-sandstone chalets adorned with rich hardwood furniture. Alternatively, you can choose from a handful of more secluded chalets perched high on a rock terrace deeper in the concession, or save a bit of money and pitch your own tent in the high-lying plateau campsite. To reach Waterberg Wilderness Lodge, take the D2512 gravel road 8km northeast of the park entrance.

Wabi Lodge LODGE **$$$**
(⌖067-306500; www.wabi.ch; per person sharing from N$650) Wabi is a private luxury setup almost 30km from Waterberg Plateau on the D2512. The Swiss owners have imparted their heritage on the design and furnishing of the eight bungalows and in the well-prepared food. It runs its own wildlife drives including night drives where you've a chance to see honey badgers, caracals, genets, brown hyenas, and even cheetahs and leopards.

❶ Information

Waterberg Plateau Park is accessible by private vehicle, though visitors must explore the plateau either on foot or as part of an official wildlife drive conducted by NWR.

With the exception of walking trails around the Waterberg Resort, both unguided and guided hiking routes in Waterberg must be booked well in advance through Namibia Wildlife Resorts (p221) in Windhoek.

THE RED LINE

Between Grootfontein and Rundu, and Tsumeb and Ondangwa, the B8 and B1 cross the 'Red Line', the Animal Disease Control Checkpoint veterinary control fence separating the commercial cattle ranches of the south from the communal subsistence lands to the north. Since the 1960s this fence has barred the north–south movement of animals as a precaution against foot-and-mouth disease and rinderpest. Animals bred north of this line have not been allowed to be sold to the south or exported to overseas markets.

As a result, the Red Line has effectively marked the boundary between the developed and developing world. The landscape south of the line is characterised by a dry, scrubby bushveld (open grassland) of vast ranches, which are home only to cattle and a few scattered ranchers. North of the Animal Disease Control Checkpoint, travellers enter a landscape of dense bush, baobab trees, mopane scrub and small *kraals* (hut villages), where the majority of individuals struggle to maintain subsistence lifestyles.

This impasse may soon be resolved, however. In late 2012, the Namibian government stepped up its efforts to have much of the existing 'protected' area internationally recognised as being free of livestock disease. This could see the Red Line shifted up as far as the western boundary of Bwabwata National Park (the Caprivi Strip is still regarded as a high-risk zone for foot-and-mouth disease). And perhaps, one day, the line will be erased.

❶ Getting There & Away

Waterberg Plateau Park is only accessible by private car – motorcycles are not permitted anywhere within the park boundaries. From Otjiwarongo it's about 90km to the park gate via the B1, C22 and the gravel D512. While this route is passable for 2WD vehicles, go slow in the final stretches as the road can be in bad shape after the rainy season. An alternative route is the D2512, which runs between Waterberg and Grootfontein – this route is OK during winter but can be terrible during summer, the rainy season, when it requires a high-clearance 4WD.

GROOTFONTEIN

☑ 067

With a pronounced colonial feel, Grootfontein (Afrikaans for Big Spring) has an air of uprightness and respectability, with local limestone constructions and avenues of jacaranda trees that bloom in the autumn. The springboard for excursions out to Khaudum National Park and the San villages in Otjozondjupa, Grootfontein is the last town of any real significance that you see before heading out into the deep, deep bush.

History

It was the town's eponymous spring that managed to attract Grootfontein's earliest travellers, and in 1885 the Dorsland (Afrikaans for Thirst Land) trekkers set up the short-lived Republic of Upingtonia. By 1887 the settlement was gone, but six years later Grootfontein became the headquarters for the German South-West Africa Company, thanks to the area's abundant mineral wealth. In 1896 the German Schutztruppe constructed a fort using local labour, and Grootfontein became a heavily fortified garrison town. The fort and nearby colonial cemetery are still local landmarks.

◉ Sights

German Fort & Museum
FORT, MUSEUM

(adult/child N$25/15; ☺8.30am-4.30pm Mon-Fri) Historical settler history is depicted here through some fascinating black-and-white photos. The Himba, Kavango and Mbanderu collections of artefacts and photographs are also interesting, as is the history of research into the area's rock paintings. It's a huge museum; put a couple of hours aside at least.

The 1896 fort that the museum is housed in was enlarged several times in the early 20th century and in 1922 a large limestone extension was added. Later the building served as a boarding school, but in 1968 it fell into disuse.

Cemetery
CEMETERY

In the town cemetery, off Okavango Rd, you can wander the graves of several Schutztruppe soldiers who died in combat with local forces around the turn of the century.

Grootfontein

◉ Sights

🛏 Sleeping

❶ Transport

Grootfontein

Hoba Meteorite
NATURAL SITE

(admission adult/child N$20/10; ⊙dawn-dusk)
Near the Hoba Farm, the world's largest
meteorite was discovered in 1920 by hunter
Jacobus Brits. This cuboid bit of space debris is composed of 82% iron, 16% nickel and
0.8% cobalt, along with traces of other metals. No one knows when it fell to earth (it's
thought to have been around 80,000 years
ago), but since it weighs around 54,000kg, it
must have made a hell of a thump.

In 1955, after souvenir hunters began
hacking off bits to take home, the site was
declared a national monument. There's
now a visitors information board, a short
nature trail and a shady picnic area. Unless
you have a specialised interest, however, it's
worth a quick stop only, and its size is not all
that impressive.

From Grootfontein, follow the C42 towards Tsumeb. After 500m, turn west on
the D2859 and continue 22km; then follow
the clearly marked signs until you reach the
complex.

🛏 Sleeping & Eating

Roy's Rest Camp
CAMPGROUND, BUNGALOWS **$$**

(☏240302; www.roysrestcamp.com; campsite per
person N$90, s/d N$700/1190; ☒) Accommo-
dation in this recommended place looks
like a fairy-tale illustration – the handmade
wooden furnishings are all fabulously rustic,
while the thatched bungalows sit tranquilly
beneath towering trees. Possible activities
include a 2.5km hiking trail, drives around
the large farm on which the camp is set, and
a day trip to a traditional San village. Roy's is
located 55km from Grootfontein on the road
towards Rundu, and it's a convenient stop if
you're heading to Tsumkwe.

Courtyard Guesthouse
GUESTHOUSE **$$**

(☏240027; 2 Gauss St; s/d N$430/660; ❄@🛜☒)
The top spot in Grootfontein is modest by
any standard, but its truly enormous rooms
(not all – ask to see a few) leave you plenty

of space to unpack your bag and take stock
of your gear. If you're about to embark on a
bush outing, spend the afternoon poolside
and bask in comfort while you can. Probably
the best place in town for food too. The restaurant (mains N$60 to N$80, open 7am to
10pm) serves fish, salads, pastas and grills
dabbling in a bit of everything.

❶ Getting There & Away

Minibuses run frequently between Grootfontein
and Tsumeb, Rundu, Katima Mulilo and Windhoek, departing when full from informal bus
stops along Okavango Rd at the appropriate
ends of town. The Intercape Mainliner (p355)
bus that departs Windhoek for Victoria Falls also
passes through Grootfontein (from N$350, six
hours, twice weekly).

If you're heading out to Tsumkwe, you will need
a private vehicle. The gravel road into town is
accessible by 2WD if you take it slow, but you will
need a high-clearance vehicle to reach the various villages in Otjozondjupa, and a 4WD might
be necessary in the rainy season. If you're heading to Khaudum, a sturdy 4WD is a requirement,
as is travelling as part of a well-equipped convoy.

TSUMEB
☑ 067

Tsumeb is one Namibian town worth a poke
around, especially if you are trying to get a
feel for the country's urban side. The streets
are very pleasant to wander, made more so
by the plentiful shady trees, it's reasonably
compact, and there's usually a smile or two
drifting your way on the busy streets.

◉ Sights & Activities

Tsumeb Mining Museum
MUSEUM

(cnr Main St & 8th Rd; adult/child N$30/5; ⊙9am-
5pm Mon-Fri, to noon Sat) Tsumeb's history is
told in this museum, which is housed in a
1915 colonial building that once served as
both a school and a hospital for German
troops. In addition to outstanding mineral
displays (you've never seen anything like
psitticinite!), the museum also houses mining machinery, stuffed birds, Himba and

---

MIGHTY MINERALS, WORLDLY WONDERS

The prosperity of Tsumeb is based on the presence of 184 known minerals, including 10
that are unique to this area. Its deposits of copper ore and a phenomenal range of other
metals and minerals (lead, silver, germanium, cadmium and many others), brought to
the surface in a volcanic pipe – as well as Africa's most productive lead mine – give it
the distinction of being a metallurgical and mineralogical wonder of the world. Tsumeb
specimens have found their way into museum collections around the globe, but you'll
also see a respectable assembly of the region's mineralogical largesse and historical
data in the town museum.

Tsumeb

Tsumeb

Sights

1 St Barbara's Church...........................C1
2 Tsumeb Arts & Crafts Centre............B1
3 Tsumeb Mining Museum....................C2

Sleeping

4 Makalani Hotel.................................C1
5 Mousebird Backpackers &
   Safaris..C2
6 Travel North Namibia
   Guesthouse..................................C2

Information

Travel North Namibia Tourist
Office...(see 6)

Transport

7 Bahnhof St Minibus Terminus............A1

Herero artefacts, and weapons recovered from Lake Otjikoto. There is also a large collection of militaria, which was dumped here by German troops prior to their surrender to the South Africans in 1915.

Tsumeb Arts & Crafts Centre   CRAFT
(☎220257; 18 Main St; ⊗9am-5pm Mon-Fri, to 1pm Sat) This craft centre markets Caprivian woodwork, San arts, Owambo basketry (also some great basketry from the San), European-Namibian leatherwork, karakul weavings, and other traditional northern Namibian arts and crafts. There's a very helpful, jolly lady overseeing what is a small but interesting selection.

St Barbara's Church   CHURCH
(cnr Main St & Sam Nujoma Dr) Tsumeb's distinctive Roman Catholic church was consecrated in 1914 and dedicated to St Barbara, the patron saint of mineworkers. It contains some fine colonial murals and an odd tower, which makes it look less like a church than a municipal building in some small German town.

Tsumeb Cultural Village   CULTURAL VILLAGE
(☎220787; admission N$22; ⊗8am-4pm Mon-Fri, to 1pm Sat) This complex, located 3km outside the town on the road to Grootfontein, showcases examples of housing styles, cultural demonstrations and artefacts from all major Namibian traditions.

🛏 Sleeping & Eating

**Travel North Namibia
Guesthouse**   GUESTHOUSE $$
(☎220728; http://natron.net/tnn/index.htm; Sam Nujoma Dr; s/d N$365/480; ❇@🛜) This budget guesthouse is a wonderful spot if you're

counting your Nam dollars. It's a fantastically friendly place delivering decent, good value accommodation. Rooms are a bit old-fashioned and some of the decor wouldn't look out of place at grandma's, but it's well kept and well run. The smallish beds still have enough life left to ensure a good night's snooze.

**Mousebird Backpackers
& Safaris**   BACKPACKERS $
(☎221777; 533 4th St; campsite per person N$90, dm/tw N$120/380; @) Tsumeb's long-standing backpacker spot continues to stay true to its roots, offering economical accommodation without sacrificing personality or character – there's a really good feel to this place. It's a small house-style set-up with decent com-

LAKE OTJIKOTO

In May 1851 explorers Charles John Andersson and Francis Galton stumbled across the unusual **Lake Otjikoto** (admission N$25; ⊙8am-6pm summer, to 5pm winter). The name of the lake is Herero for 'deep hole' and its waters fill a limestone sinkhole measuring 100m by 150m, reaching depths of 55m. Interestingly, Lake Otjikoto and nearby Lake Guinas are the only natural lakes in Namibia, and they're also the only known habitats of the unusual mouth-brooding cichlid fish. These fish are psychedelic in appearance – ranging from dark green to bright red, yellow and blue – and are believed by biologists to eschew camouflage due to the absence of predators in this isolated environment. It's thought that these fish evolved from tilapia (bream) washed into the lake by ancient floods.

In 1915 the retreating German army dumped weaponry and ammunition into the lake to prevent it from falling into South African hands. It's rumoured that they jettisoned five cannons, 10 cannon bases, three Gatling guns and between 300 and 400 wagonloads of ammunition. Some of this stuff was salvaged in 1916 at great cost and effort by the South African army, the Tsumeb Corporation and the National Museum of Namibia. In 1970 divers discovered a Krupp ammunition wagon 41m below the surface; it's on display at the Owela Museum in Windhoek. In 1977 and 1983 two more ammunition carriers were salvaged as well as a large cannon, and are now on display at the Tsumeb Mining Museum.

Lake Otjikoto is located 25km north of Tsumeb along the B1, and there are signs marking the turn-off. Note that the entry to the lake is just past the sign for it (about 100m) coming from Etosha. Although the site is undeveloped, there is a ticket booth, an adjacent car park and several small kiosks selling cold drinks and small snacks, as well as quite a bit of shade. While treasure seekers have been known to don scuba gear and search the lake under cover of night, diving (and swimming for that matter) is presently forbidden.

munal areas including a kitchen. The best twin rooms share a bathroom inside the house, although the twin outside does have its own bathroom. The four-bed dorm is also very good.

Makalani Hotel HOTEL **$$**
(☎221051; www.makalanihotel.com; Ndilimani Cultural Troupe St; s/d from N$460/680; ❄🤶🏊) Situated in the town centre, the upmarket Makalani Hotel is a rather garish-looking place that markets itself as both a small hotel and almost a miniresort complete with casino. But it can't have it both ways and it sits uncomfortably between the two. What it does have is excellent rooms – if you prefer slightly more comfy hotel-like options then this place is for you.

ⓘ Information
Travel North Namibia Tourist Office
(☎220728; 1551 Sam Nujoma Dr; 🤶) Inside the guesthouse of the same name. Provides nationwide information, arranges accommodation, transport, car hire and Etosha bookings, and has internet access. No maps available.

ⓘ Getting There & Away

BUS

Intercape Mainliner (p355) buses make the trip between Windhoek and Tsumeb (from N$310,

5½ hours, twice weekly). Book your tickets in advance online as this service continues on to Victoria Falls and fills up quickly.

Combis also run up and down the B1 with fairly regular frequency, and a ride between Windhoek and Tsumeb shouldn't cost more than N$220. If you're continuing on to Etosha National Park, be advised that there is no public transport serving this route.

CAR

Tsumeb is an easy day's drive from Windhoek along paved roads and serves as the jumping-off point for Namutoni and the Von Lindequist Gate of Etosha National Park. The paved route continues north as far as the park gate, though keep your speed under control as wildlife is frequently seen along the sides of the highway.

Etosha National Park
☑ 067

Etosha National Park ranks as one of the world's great wildlife-viewing venues. Its unique nature is encapsulated by the vast Etosha pan – an immense, flat, saline desert that, for a few days each year, is converted by the rains into a shallow lagoon teeming with flamingos and pelicans. In contrast, the surrounding bush and grasslands provide habitat for Etosha's diverse wildlife. And

Etosha National Park

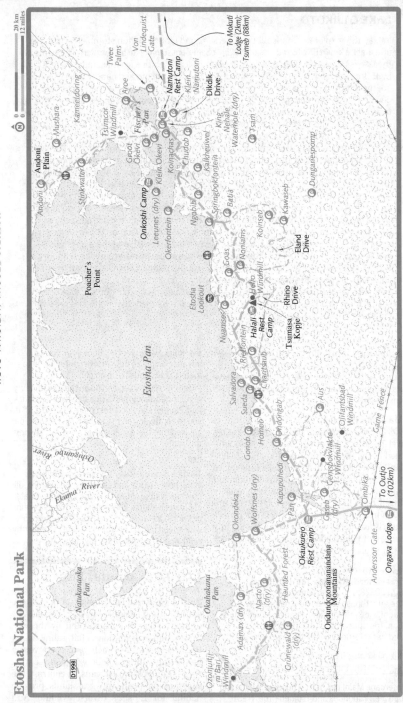

20 km
12 miles

To Mokuti
Lodge (2km);
Tsumeb (88km)

Von
Lindequist
Gate

Twee
Palms

Namutoni
Rest Camp

Klein
Namutoni

Dikdik
Drive

Aroe

Fischer's
Pan

King
Nehale
Waterhole (dry)

Tsam

Kameeldoring

Mushara

Tsumcor
Windmill

Groot
Okevi

Klein Okevi

Koinachas

Chudob

Kalkheuwel

Andoni
Plain

Stinkwater

Andoni

Onkoshi Camp

Leeunes (dry)

Okerfontein

Ngobib

Springbokfontein

Batia

Dungariespomp

Goas

Nonams

Koinseb

Kawaseb

Poacher's
Point

Etosha Pan

Etosha
Lookout

Njamses

Helio
Windmill

Rhino
Drive

Eland
Drive

Rietfontein

Halali
Rest
Camp

Tsumasa
Kopje

Salvadora

Sueda

Gonob

Homeb

Ondongab

Aus

Olifantsbad
Windmill

Game Fence

Chaursaub

Oshigambo River

Ekuma
River

Okondeka

Wolfsnes (dry)

Kapupuhedi

Gaseb (dry)

Gemsbokvlakte
Windmill

Ombika

To Outjo
(102km)

Okaukuejo
Rest Camp

Andersson Gate

Ongava Lodge

Natukanaoka
Pan

Okahakana
Pan

Nacto
(dry)

Haunted Forest

Ondundozonanandana
Mountains

Adamax (dry)

Grünewald
(dry)

Ozonjuitji
m'Bari
Windmill

D1998

ETOSHA NATIONAL PARK AT A GLANCE

Why Go?
Etosha is completely unique in Namibia and indeed in Southern Africa: the desolate nature of the pan, the low-cut landscapes, and, of course, the waterholes mean that wildlife viewing is some of the easiest and most productive on the continent. It's also one of the best places to spot the highly endangered black rhino in southern Africa, and you can do it from the relative ease of the waterholes right next to the camps.

Gateway Town
Most people call in at Outjo, if approaching from the south – it's about 100km to Andersson Gate in Etosha from here on a smooth sealed road. Outjo is a fine place to stock up on supplies at the supermarket, use the internet and indulge in some good food. If you're heading straight to the eastern side of the park (if you were coming from the Caprivi Strip or Rundu, for example) you'll go via Tsumeb, another handy launching point for the park; it's about 110km from Von Lindequist Gate.

Wildlife
The opportunity to see black rhinos is a big draw here; they are usually very difficult to spot but as they come to some of the waterholes around the camps, it couldn't be easier! We found jackals and giraffes to be quite prolific as well, and if you don't see antelopes such as springbok and gemsbok you must be wearing a blindfold.

When to Go
Etosha is really a year-round destination but May through to October (the dry season) is really the ideal time to go as the grass is short and water supplies have dwindled to a few waterholes making wildlife easier to spot.

Moving Around
You need your own transport to get to the park and using your own car, preferably one with high-clearance, giving you a better view, is an ideal way to explore Etosha.

Author Tips
If you're self-catering – and you really should be, as the food at the camp restaurants inside the park is generally pretty ordinary – bring your own supplies into the park, as the food selection in the shops is abysmal.

At the camps, try hanging around the floodlit waterholes late, after most folk have gone to bed. We did just that at Halali and had one of the best wildlife encounters – watching black rhinos – we have had in Africa.

what wildlife there is – if you've had a taste of African wildlife watching previously, you are likely to be mesmerised by it here.

Unlike many other parks in Africa, where you can spend days looking for animals across the plains, one of Etosha's charms is its ability to bring the animals to you. Just park your car next to one of the many waterholes, wait with bated breath and watch while a host of animals – lions, elephants, springboks, gemsbok etc – come by, not two by two but in the hundreds.

Although it may look barren, the landscape (covering an area of more than 20,000 sq km) fringing the pan is home to 114 mammal species as well as 340 bird species, 16 reptile and amphibian species, one fish species and countless insects.

History
The first Europeans in Etosha were traders and explorers Charles John Andersson and Francis Galton, who arrived by wagon at Namutoni in 1851. They were later followed in 1876 by an American trader, G McKeirnan, who observed: 'All the menageries in the world turned loose would not compare to the sight I saw that day'.

However, Etosha didn't attract the interest of tourists or conservationists until after the turn of the 20th century, when the governor of German South West Africa, Dr von Lindequist, became concerned about diminishing animal numbers and founded a 99,526-sq-km reserve, which included Etosha Pan.

At the time the land was still unfenced and animals could follow their normal migration routes. In subsequent years, however, the park boundaries were altered a few times, and by 1970 Etosha had been reduced to its present size.

🏃 Activities

Wildlife Watching

Etosha's most widespread vegetation type is mopane woodland, which fringes the pan and constitutes about 80% of the vegetation. The park also has umbrella-thorn acacias and other trees that are favoured by browsing animals, and from December to March this sparse bush country has a pleasant green hue.

Depending on the season, you may observe elephants, giraffes, Burchell's zebras, springboks, red hartebeest, blue wildebeests, gemsboks, eland, kudu, roans, ostriches, jackals, hyenas, lions, and even cheetahs and leopards. Among the endangered animal species are the black-faced impala and the black rhinoceros.

The park's wildlife density varies with the local ecology. As its Afrikaans name would suggest, Oliphantsbad (near Okaukuejo) is attractive to elephants, but for rhinos you couldn't do better than the floodlit waterhole at Okaukuejo. In general, the further east you go in the park, the more wildebeest, kudu and impalas join the springboks and gemsboks. The area around Namutoni, which averages 443mm of rain annually (compared with 412mm at Okaukuejo), is the best place to see the black-faced impala and the Damara dik-dik, Africa's smallest antelope. Etosha is also home to numerous smaller species, including both yellow and slender mongooses, honey badgers and *leguaans* (water-monitor lizards).

In the dry winter season wildlife clusters around waterholes, while in the hot, wet summer months animals disperse and spend the days sheltering in the bush. In the afternoon, even in the dry season, look carefully for animals resting beneath the trees, especially prides of lions lazing about. Summer temperatures can reach 44°C, which isn't fun when you're confined to a vehicle, but this is the calving season and you may catch a glimpse of tiny zebra foals and fragile newborn springboks.

Birdlife is also profuse. Yellow-billed hornbills are common, and on the ground you should look for the huge kori bustard, which weighs 15kg and seldom flies. You might also observe ostriches, korhaans (a type of bustard), marabous, white-backed vultures and many smaller species.

The best times for wildlife drives are at first light and late in the evening, though visitors aren't permitted outside the camps after dark. Guided night drives (N$600 per person) can be booked through any of the main camps and are your best chance to see lions hunting as well as the various nocturnal species. Each of the camps also has a visitor register, which describes any recent sightings in the vicinity.

🛏 Sleeping & Eating

The main camps inside the park are open year-round, and have restaurants, bars, shops, swimming pools, picnic sites, petrol stations, kiosks and floodlit watering holes that attract game throughout the night. Although fees are normally prepaid through NWR in Windhoek, it is sometimes possible to reserve accommodation at either gate. However, be advised that the park can get very busy on weekends, especially during the dry season – if you can manage it, pre-booking is recommended.

IN THE PARK

All accommodation listed here is generally much cheaper in the off season (ie November to June). Most visitors spend a couple of nights at one of the three rest camps, Namutoni, Halali and Okaukuejo, which are spaced at 70km intervals.

Okaukuejo Rest Camp   LODGE, CAMPGROUND **$$** (campsite per site N$200 plus per person N$110, s/d from N$1020/1840, chalets from N$1100/2000; ❈ ▨) Pronounced 'o-ka-kui-yo', this is the site of the Etosha Research Station, and it functions as the official park headquarters and main visitor centre. The Okaukuejo waterhole is probably Etosha's best rhino-viewing venue, particularly between 8pm and 10pm, though you're almost guaranteed to spot zebras, wildebeest, jackals and even elephants virtually any time of the day. Okaukuejo's campsite can get very crowded, but the shared facilities are excellent, and include washing stations, *braai* pits, and bathroom and toilet facilities with hot water. The self-catering accommodation includes older but refurbished rooms alongside stand-alone chalets. If you want to splurge, the luxury chalet is a stunning two-storey affair complete with a furnished centre-stage balcony boasting unmatched views of animals lining up to drink.

Halali Rest Camp   LODGE, CAMPGROUND **$$**
(campsite per site N$200 plus per person N$100, s/d from N$800/1400, chalets from N$1000/1700; ❄️❄️) Etosha's middle camp, Halali, nestles between several incongruous dolomite outcrops. The short Tsumasa hiking track leads up Tsumasa Kopje, the hill nearest the rest camp, from where you can snap wonderful panoramic shots of the park. The best feature of Halali is its floodlit waterhole, which is a 10-minute walk from the rest camp and is sheltered by a glen of trees with huge boulders strewn about. While it's not as dramatic in scope as Okakuejo, it's a wonderfully intimate setting where you can savour a glass of wine in peace, all the while scanning the bush for rhinos and lions, which frequently stop by to drink in the late-evening hours. Like Okakuejo, there is a very well-serviced campsite here, in addition to a fine collection of luxury chalets that make for a wonderfully relaxed night of sleep despite being deep in the African bush.

Namutoni Rest Camp   LODGE, CAMPGROUND **$$**
(campsite per site N$200 plus per person N$110, s/d from N$850/1500, chalets from N$1000/1800; ❄️❄️) Etosha's easternmost camp is defined by its landmark whitewashed German fort, a colonial relic that casts a surreal shadow over the rest of the camp. Beside the fort is a lovely freshwater limestone spring and the floodlit King Nehale waterhole, which is filled with reed beds and some extremely vociferous frogs. The viewing benches are nice for lunch or watching the pleasant riverbank scene, but the spot attracts surprisingly few thirsty animals. Again, like Okakuejo and Halali, Namutoni offers an immaculate campsite (the only campsite in the park with grass) in addition to a few luxury chalets on the edge of the bush.

Onkoshi Camp   LODGE **$$$**
(per person with half board incl transfers from Namutoni N$2000; ❄️❄️) If you feel like a splashout, book yourself into Onkoshi Camp. Upon arrival in Namutoni, you will be chauffeured to a secluded peninsula on the rim of the pan, and then given the keys to one of only 15 thatch-and-canvas chalets that rest on el-evated wooden decks and occupy exclusive locations well beyond the standard tourist route. The interiors, which blend rich hardwoods, delicate bamboo, elaborate metal flourishing, finely crafted furniture, hand-painted artwork and fine porcelain fixtures, create an overwhelmingly opulent atmosphere. While the temptation certainly exists to spend your days lounging about in such regal settings, guests are treated to personalised wildlife drives (from N$500 per person) conducted by Etosha's finest guides, and dinners are multicourse affairs that are illuminated by candlelight.

Dolomite Camp   LODGE **$$$**
(s/d with half board from N$1250/2300; ❄️❄️) Recently opened in a previously restricted area of the park in western Etosha, Dolomite Camp is beautifully carved into its rocky surrounds. Accommodation is in thatched chalets (actually luxury tents) including a couple with their own plunge pool. The views of surrounding plains are wonderful and there's even a waterhole at the camp so spotting the wildlife doesn't mean moving far from your bed. When you do get out and about, the wildlife viewing around here is superb as the area has been free from human activity for half a century.

OUTSIDE THE PARK
There plenty of top-end lodges located on the periphery of Etosha. At all of these properties, prebooking is essential to ensure a room, and access is via private vehicle or charter flight. All published rates are for the high season and include full board and wildlife drives; transfers from Windhoek are also possible with advance notice.

⬛TOP CHOICE **Sachsenheim**   CAMPING, CHALETS **$$**
(📞081 215 0100, 067-230011; campsite without/with bathroom N$110/150, s/d chalets N$500/900) This guest farm has some great options and is 3km north of the C38/B1 junction (off the B1). You can camp on grass under shady trees with *braai*, running water and communal or private facilities. Large-roomed stone chalets are simply but beautifully decorated. The linen is particularly good. The location gives this place a rather remote, harsh feel which is softened by the grassed areas and plenty of shady trees. It's a very affordable spot close to Etosha – the best camping in the area. Meals available (breakfast/lunch N$80/160).

Etosha Aoba Lodge LODGE $$$

(☑229100; www.etosha-aoba-lodge.com; s/d with half board from N$1240/1980; ✳@☎) Situated on a 70-sq-km private concession about 10km east of the Von Lindequist Gate, this tranquil lodge is located in tamboti forest next to a dry river bed. The property comprises 10 cottages that blend effortlessly into their riverine environment. The atmosphere is peaceful and relaxing, though the main lodge is conducive to unwinding with other guests after a long day on safari.

Taleni Etosha Village TENTED CAMP $$

(☑067-687190; s/d self-catering N$900/1100; ✳☎) This little hideaway just a couple of kilometres outside Etosha has self-catering safari tents (half- and full-board options available) that are very well equipped and come with outdoor seating area, *braai*, wooden floors, power points and many little luxuries. The tents are nestled into bushland among mopane trees and the friendly staff can also organise food if you are self-catering. The internet is available for N$60 per hour and there's a restaurant and great bar area. Walk-in rates are about half those listed here. Etosha Village is situated 2km before the Andersson Gate.

Mokuti Lodge LODGE $$$

(☑229084; www.kempinski.com/mokuti; tw incl breakfast N$1300, chalet N$2300; ✳✳☎) This sprawling lodge, located just 2km from the Von Lindequist Gate, has rooms, chalets and luxurious suites, as well as several swimming pools, spa and tennis courts, though the low-profile buildings create an illusion of intimacy. The accommodation mixes contemporary fittings with African style, creating a funky blend. Chalets have sink-in-and-smile sofas and welcome platters. The lodge seeks to create an informal, relaxed atmosphere (there's a *boma* with firepit and nightly storytelling), which makes this a good choice if you're travelling with the little ones. Don't miss the attached reptile park and its resident snake collection, which features locals captured around the lodge property.

Ongava Lodge LODGE $$$

(☑061-225178; www.wilderness-safaris.com; per person from N$2280; ✳@☎) The most exclusive luxury lodge in the Etosha area is located on a private reserve near Andersson Gate that protects several prides of lions, a few black and white rhinos, and your standard assortment of herd animals. Ongava is actually divided into two properties; the main Ongava Lodge is a collection of safari-chic chalets surrounding a small waterhole, while the Ongava Tented Camp consists of eight East African–style canvas tents situated a bit deeper in the bush.

Toshari LODGE $$

(☑067-333440; campsite per person N$105, d chalet N$1100) This convenient alternative to staying in the park is 25km from Etosha, right on the C38. It has cubicle-type chalets that are rather ugly but forgiven due to their comfort and bushy setting. The campsites (only three) are excellent, and all have that unusual feature in Namibia – grass. Each also has its own bathroom, *braai*, stone bench and shade. When camping, you can use the lodge facilities including free tea and coffee, a well-stocked bar and relaxing communal area complete with pet mongoose.

Etosha Safari Camp CAMP $$$

(☑061-230066; www.gondwana-collection.com; campsite per person N$120, s/d chalet N$1300/2000; ✳☎) Excellent grassed campsites spill over a large area here, so there's a good chance you'll get a pitch even if you haven't booked. This whole place is set up like a small village complete with *shebeen* bar; be warned there is plenty of kitsch, including a shop in a railway carriage. Safari drives into Etosha are available. It's 9km from the park on the C38, just off the road and well signed. Etosha Safari Lodge next door is also owned by the Gondwana group.

❶ Information

Only the eastern two-thirds of Etosha are open to the general public; the western third is reserved exclusively for tour operators. Etosha's three main entry gates are Von Lindequist (Namutoni), west of Tsumeb; King Nehale, southeast of Ondangwa; and Andersson (Okaukuejo), north of Outjo.

Visitors are encouraged to check in at either Von Lindequist Gate or Andersson Gate (King Nehale Gate is frequently closed), where you then must purchase a permit costing N$80 per person plus N$10 per vehicle per day. The permits are to be presented at your reserved rest camp, where you pay any outstanding camping or accommodation fees.

Those booked into the rest camps must show up before sunset, and can only leave after sunrise; specific times are posted on the gates.

Pedestrians, bicycles, motorcycles and hitching are prohibited in Etosha, and open trucks must be screened off. Outside the rest camps, visitors must stay in their vehicles (except at toilet stops).

❶ Getting There & Around

There's no public transport into and around the park, which means that you must visit either in a private vehicle or as part of an organised tour.

All roads in the eastern section of Etosha are passable to 2WD vehicles. The park speed limit is set at 60km/h both to protect wildlife and keep down the dust.

The park road between Namutoni and Okaukuejo skirts Etosha Pan, providing great views of its vast spaces. Driving isn't permitted on the pan, but a network of gravel roads threads through the surrounding savannahs and mopane woodland and even extends out to a viewing site, the Etosha Lookout, in the middle of the salt desert.

NORTHERN NAMIBIA

The country's most densely populated region, and undeniably its cultural heartland, northern Namibia is a place for some serious African adventure. It is where endless skies meet distant horizons in an expanse that will make you truly wonder if this could be your greatest road trip of all time. There is space out here to think, and you may just find yourself belting down a dirt road hunched over the steering wheel, pondering in detail whatever's on your mind...for many hours. Northern Namibia is the place for serious problem solving, all induced by that unforgettable landscape.

Northern Namibia takes form and identity from the Caprivi Strip, where, alongside traditional villages, a collection of national parks are being repopulated with wildlife after many decades of war and conflict. At the time of independence, these parks had been virtually depleted by poachers, though years of progressive wildlife management have firmly placed the region back on the safari circuit.

Geography
Known as the Land of Rivers, Northern Namibia is bounded by the Kunene and Okavango Rivers along the Angolan border, and in the east by the Zambezi and the Kwando/Mashe/Linyanti/Chobe river systems. In the northeast, the gently rolling Kavango region is dominated by the Okavango River. East of Kavango is the spindly Caprivi Strip, a flat, unexceptional landscape that is character-

ised by expanses of acacia forest. Along the border with Botswana is the Otjozondjupa region, a wild and thinly populated strip of scrub forest that is home to several scattered San villages.

❶ Getting Around

As a major population centre, Owamboland is comparatively well served by combis (minibuses), and hitching here is fairly easy due to the higher density of people. The C46 and B1 are both sealed and in good condition, but off these routes road maintenance is poor, and a 4WD is required in places, especially after the rain. Petrol is available at Oshakati, Ondangwa, Oshikango and Uutapi (Ombalantu).

If you're transiting the Caprivi Strip en route to Victoria Falls, Intercape Mainliner connects Livingstone (Zambia) to Windhoek. This route is sealed in its entirety and suitable for all 2WD vehicles. However, a high-clearance vehicle, preferably with 4WD, is necessary for visiting any of the national parks.

Finally, the town of Tsumkwe in Otjozondjupa can be reached by 2WD, though you will need a sturdier vehicle if you plan to visit outlying San villages. If you're continuing on to Khaudum National Park, a fully equipped 4WD vehicle is a necessity, and ideally you'll be travelling as part of a convoy.

The North

The regions of Omusati, Oshana, Ohangwena and Otjikoto comprise the homeland of the Owambo people, Namibia's largest population group. Although there's little in terms of tourist attractions in this region, Owambo country is home to a healthy and prosperous rural society that buzzes with activity. It's also a good place to stock up on the region's high-quality basketry and sugarcane work, which is often sold at roadside stalls. Designs are simple and graceful, usually incorporating a brown geometric pattern woven into the pale-yellow reed.

ONDANGWA
☑ 065
The second-largest Owambo town is known as a minor transport hub, with combis fanning out from here to other cities and towns in the north. Its large number of warehouses provide stock to the 6000 tiny cuca shops (small bush shops named after the brand of Angolan beer they once sold) that serve the area's rural residents.

◉ Sights

Lake Oponono   LAKE

The main attraction in the area is Lake Oponono, a large wetland fed by the Culevai *oshanas* (underground river channels). After a heavy rainy season, the lake shores attract a variety of birdlife, including saddlebill storks, crowned cranes, flamingos and pelicans. The edge of the lake is located 27km south of Ondangwa.

Nakambale Museum   MUSEUM

(admission N$10; ☺8am-1pm & 2-5pm Mon-Fri, 8am-1pm Sat, noon-5pm Sun) Nakambale, which was built in the late 1870s by Finnish missionary Martti Rauttanen, is believed to be the oldest building in northern Namibia. It now houses a small museum on Owambo history and culture. Nakambale is part of Olukonda village, which is located 20km south of Ondangwa on the D3629.

⮞ Sleeping & Eating

Nakambale Campsite   CAMPGROUND $

(☎245668; campsites N$50, huts per person N$100) Here's your opportunity to sleep in a basic hut that would have been used historically by an Owambo chief or one of his wives. Nakambale is located on the outskirts of Olukonda village, 20km south of Ondangwa on the D3629.

Protea Hotel Ondangwa   HOTEL $$$

(☎241900; www.proteahotels.com/protea-hotel-ond angwa.html; s/d from N$765/1050; ✳✿) This plush business hotel features bright rooms decorated with tasteful artwork as well as modern furnishings. The attached Chatters restaurant serves decent European-inspired cuisine, and there's also a small espresso shop and takeaway in the lobby.

❶ Getting There & Away

AIR

Air Namibia flies to and from Windhoek's Eros Airport daily. Note that the airstrip in Oshakati is for private charters only, which means that Ondangwa serves as the main access point in the north for airborne travellers.

BUS

Combis run up and down the B1 with fairly regular frequency, and a ride between Windhoek to Ondangwa shouldn't cost more than N$160. From Ondangwa, a complex network of combi routes serves population centres throughout the north, with fares typically costing less than N$30 a ride.

CAR

The B1 is sealed all the way from Windhoek to Ondangwa and out to Oshakati.

The Oshikango border crossing to Santa Clara in Angola is 60km north of Ondangwa; to travel further north, you'll need an Angolan visa that allows overland travel.

OSHAKATI
☑ 065

The Owambo capital is an uninspiring commercial centre that is little more than a strip of characterless development along the highway. But it's worth spending an hour or so at the large covered market, which proffers everything from clothing and baskets to mopane *tambo* (beer).

If you're looking to apply for an Angolan visa, the **Angola Consulate** (☎221799; Dr Agostinho Neto Rd) is currently the best place to submit an application.

If you get stuck here for the night, **Oshandira Lodge** (☎220443; oshandira@iway.na; s/d N$490/690; ✿), next to the airstrip, offers simple but spacious rooms that surround a landscaped pool and thatched open-air restaurant. A slightly more upmarket option is the **Oshakati Country Lodge** (☎222380; Robert Mugabe Rd; s/d from N$550/800; ✳@✿), a favourite of visiting government dignitaries and business people, though it's your best bet if you're a slave to modern comforts.

From the bus station at the market, combis leave frequently for destinations in the north.

UUTAPI (OMBALANTU) & AROUND
☑ 065

The area around Uutapi (also known as Ombalantu), which lies on the C46 between Oshakati and Ruacana, is home to a number of widely revered national heritage sites, and warrants a quick visit if you've got your own wheels and are passing through the area.

The most famous attraction in Uutapi is the former South African Defence Force (SADF) base, which is dominated by an enormous baobab tree. This tree, known locally as *omukwa,* was once used to shelter cattle from invaders, and later was used as a turret from which to ambush invading tribes. It didn't work with the South African forces, however, who invaded and used the tree for everything from a chapel to a coffeehouse.

To reach the fort, turn left at the police station 350m south of the petrol station and look for an obscure grassy track winding between desultory buildings towards the conspicuous baobab.

ONGULUMBASHE

The town of Ongulumbashe is regarded as the birthplace of modern Namibia. On 26 August 1966 the first shots of the war for Namibian independence were fired from this patch of scrubland. The site is also where the People's Liberation Army of Namibia enjoyed its first victory over the South African troops, who had been charged with rooting out and quelling potential guerrilla activities. At the site, you can still see some reconstructed bunkers and the 'needle' monument marking the battle. An etching on the reverse side honours the Pistolet-Pulemyot Shpagina (PPSh), the Russian-made automatic rifle that played a major role in the conflict.

From Uutapi, turn south on the D3612 to the village of Otsandi (Tsandi). At the eastern edge of the village, turn west down an unnumbered track and continue 20km to Ongulumbashe. Be advised that this area is considered to be politically sensitive – you will need permission to visit the site from the Swapo office in Uutapi.

ONGANDJERA

If you're feeling especially patriotic, you can visit the town of Ongandjera, which is the birthplace of former president Sam Nujoma. The rose-coloured *kraal* that was his boyhood home is now a national shrine, and is distinguished from its neighbours by a prominent Swapo flag hung in a tree. It's fine to look from a distance, but the *kraal* remains a private home and isn't open to the public.

Ongandjera lies on the D3612, 52km southeast of Uutapi near Okahao. It's also accessible via the C41 from Oshakati.

RUACANA
☑ 065

The tiny Kunene River town of Ruacana (from the Herero words *orua hakahana* – the rapids) is the jumping-off point for visiting the Ruacana Falls. Here, the Kunene River splits into several channels before plunging 85m over a dramatic escarpment and through a 2km-long gorge of its own making. The town was built as a company town to serve the 320-megawatt underground Ruacana hydroelectric project, which now supplies over half of Namibia's power requirements.

◉ Sights

Ruacana Falls   WATERFALL

At one time, Ruacana Falls was a natural wonder, though all that changed thanks to Angola's Calueque Dam, 20km upstream, and NamPower's Ruacana power plant. The little water that makes it past the first barrage is collected by an intake weir, 1km above the falls, which ushers it into the hydroelectric plant to turn the turbines. On the rare occasions when there's a surfeit of water, Ruacana returns to its former glory. In wetter years, it's no exaggeration to say it rivals Victoria Falls – if you hear that it's flowing, you certainly won't regret a side trip to see it (and it may be the closest you ever get to Angola).

To reach the falls, turn north 15km west of Ruacana and follow the signs towards the border crossing. To visit the gorge, visitors must temporarily exit Namibia by signing the immigration register. From the Namibian border crossing, bear left (to the right lies the decrepit Angolan border crossing) to the end of the road. There you can look around the ruins of the old power station, which was destroyed by Namibian liberation forces. The buildings are pockmarked with scars from mortar rounds and gunfire, providing a stark contrast to the otherwise peaceful scene.

⌂ Sleeping

Hippo Pools Camp Site   CAMPGROUND $

(☑270120; campsite per person N$50) Also known as Otjipahuriro, this community-run campsite sits alongside the river and has a good measure of shade and privacy. There are also *braai* pits, hot showers and environmentally friendly pit toilets. Local community members can organise trips to Ruacana Falls or to nearby Himba villages for a small fee.

Ruacana Eha Lodge   LODGE $$$

(☑271500; www.ruacanaehalodge.com.na; Springbom Ave; campsite per person N$70, huts per person N$220, s/d N$775/1080; ❄@♨) This upmarket lodge appeals to travellers of all budgets by offering manicured campsites and rustic A-frame huts alongside its polished rooms. An attractive oasis in the middle of Ruacana, the Eha Lodge is highlighted by its lush gardens and refreshing plunge pool.

① Getting There & Away

Ruacana is near the junction of roads between Opuwo, Owambo country and the rough 4WD route along the Kunene River to Swartbooi's

Drift. Note that mileage signs along the C46 confuse Ruacana town and the power plant, which are 15km apart. Both are signposted 'Ruacana' – don't let them throw you too badly.

For westbound travellers, the 24-hour petrol station is the last before the Atlantic; it's also the terminal for afternoon minibuses to and from Oshakati and Ondangwa, costing around N$30.

Kavango Region

The heavily wooded and gently rolling Kavango region is dominated by the Okavango River and its broad flood plains. The rich soil and fishing grounds support large communities of Mbukushu, Sambiyu and Caprivi peoples, who are renowned for their high-quality woodcarvings – animal figures, masks, wooden beer mugs, walking sticks and boxes are carved in the light *dolfhout* (wild teak) hardwood and make excellent souvenirs. Although there's little wildlife nowadays outside Khaudum, the national park itself arguably rivals Etosha as Namibia's top safari experience.

At Sambiu, east of Rundu and 30km along the Okavango River road, is a Roman Catholic mission museum (☑251111; admission free; ◷by appointment), which exhibits crafts and woodcarvings from Angola and Kavango. Phone to arrange a visit, or take your chances and simply stop by during daylight hours.

RUNDU
☑ 066

Rundu, a sultry tropical outpost on the bluffs above the Okavango River, is a major centre of activity for Namibia's growing Angolan community. Although the town has little of specific interest for tourists, the area is home to a number of wonderful lodges where you can laze along the riverside, and spot crocs and hippos doing pretty much the same.

Take a stroll around the large covered market, which is one of Africa's most sophisticated informal sales outlets. From July to September, don't miss the fresh papayas, sold straight from the trees. Alternatively, head for the Khemo Open Market (◷daily) where you can shop for both African staples and Kavango handicrafts.

Very reasonably priced woodcarvings from a sustainable source are on offer at Ncumcara Community Forestry Craft Centre (B8; ◷Mon-Sat, after church Sun), a neighbourhood craft shop. The carvings are high quality with proceeds going back to the local community. It's 35km south of Rundu; if the shop is unattended, just wait for someone to show up and open the gate.

🛏 Sleeping & Eating

Lodges in Rundu and the surrounding region offer a variety of excursions, including sunset cruises, canoeing and fishing.

Self-caterers will find supplies at the well-stocked Shoprite Supermarket in the town centre.

BORDER CROSSING: RUNDU–ANGOLA

The border crossing here is almost one-way traffic, with plenty of Angolans coming into Namibia to purchase goods from the shops, seek medical help and visit relatives; however, we heard reports of Namibians getting a lot of hassle when they try to enter Angola. As for tourists, they are seen as easy pickings for the Angolan authorities, and you may be asked for a bribe or even arrested. Basic Portuguese-language skills would be a huge bonus, as English is not widely spoken. Getting an Angolan visa (US$100) in Windhoek is very difficult, and you need time and patience (one traveller we heard about waited for months with no success). It may just depend on who you deal with at the Angolan embassy and, of course, your nationality. For one thing, you need a letter of invitation from somebody in Angola as part of your visa application, as well as a copy of their ID. At the time of writing, Oshakati in Namibia was the best place to try to lodge an Angolan visa application in Namibia.

There are a few travel agents running basic organised trips into Angola, which consists of you and your guide, your vehicle and all your own camping equipment; Walvis Bay is a good place to make inquiries. The bonus here is that they will organise your visa including letter of invitation.

Some lodges, such as N'Kwazi Lodge in Rundu, run boat trips along the Okavango River and will dock on the Angolan side to give you a chance to get some Angolan soil on the soles of your shoes.

Rundu

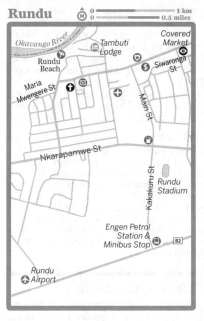

gotten resort, which gives it an allure all of its own. Rooms are large, and come with big freestanding bathtub, mosquito nets and small porches. It's good value for two people sharing, but not so good for singles. The lodge also arranges boat trips on the Okavango River separating Nambia from Angola.

Sarasungu River Lodge · LODGE $$

(☑255161; www.sarasunguriverlodge.com; campsite per person N$70, s/d/tr N$530/750/1000; ❄🛜🏊) Sarasunga River Lodge is a very laid-back place, situated in a secluded riverine clearing 4km from the town centre. It has attractive thatched chalets that surround a landscaped pool, and a decent-sized grassed camping area with basic amenities and beautiful sunsets. There is also a bar-restaurant onsite with ordinary food but cold beer and good chat. It's a bit out of town but the value for money and quiet setting make it well worthwhile. Room rates are often reduced.

Hakusembe Lodge · LODGE $$

(☑257010; campsite per person N$100, chalets per person with half board from N$1100; ❄🏊) This secluded hideaway sits amid lush riverside gardens, and comprises luxury chalets (one of which is floating) decked out in safari prints and locally crafted furniture. It lies 17km down the Nkurenkuru Rd, then 2km north to the riverbank.

ⓘ Getting There & Away

BUS

Several weekly Intercape Mainliner (p355) buses make the seven-hour trip between Windhoek and Rundu (fares from N$380). Book your tickets in advance online, as this service continues on to Victoria Falls and fills up quickly.

Combis connect Windhoek and Rundu with fairly regular frequency, and a ride shouldn't cost more than N$250. From Rundu, routes fan out to various towns and cities in the north, with fares costing less than N$40 a ride. Both buses and combis depart and drop off at the Engen petrol station.

CAR & MOTORCYCLE

Drivers will need to be patient on the road (B8) to Rundu from Grootfontein. It's in good condition but passes by many schools where the speed limit drops suddenly – fertile ground for speed cameras.

KHAUDUM NATIONAL PARK

☑066
Exploring the undeveloped 384,000-hectare Khaudum National Park is an intense

---

⭐**TOP** **N'Kwazi Lodge** · LODGE $
CHOICE

(☑081 242 4897; www.nkwazilodge.com; campsite/r per person N$120/420) Situated on the banks of the Okavango, about 20km from Rundu's town centre, this is a tranquil and good-value riverside retreat where relaxation is a by-product of the owners' laid-back approach. The entire property blends naturally into the surrounding riverine forest, while the rooms are beautifully laid out, with personal touches; there's a great campsite, although it's sometimes overrun by safari trucks. The lodge represents incredibly good value with no surcharge for singles and a justifiably famous buffet dinner for N$175 at night.

The lodge's owners, Valerie and Weynand Peyper, are active in promoting responsible travel and have rebuilt a preschool that was previously washed away in the 2009 floods. They also have many other ongoing projects, including supporting orphans in the area. Guests can visit the preschool and also local villages (N$50 for a village walk).

Tambuti Lodge · LODGE $$

(☑255711; www.tambuti.com.na; campsites N$60, s/d incl breakfast N$510/610; 🛜) An old place that has been around for a while, Tambuti leaks faded grandeur from its stone walls. Less than 1km from town, it feels like a for-

wilderness challenge that is guaranteed not to disappoint. Meandering sand tracks lure you through pristine bush and across *omiramba* (fossil river valleys), which run parallel to the east–west-oriented Kalahari dunes.

As there is virtually no signage, and navigation is largely based on GPS coordinates and topographic maps, few tourists make the effort to extend their safari experience beyond the secure confines of Etosha. But that is precisely why Khaudum is worth exploring – as one of Namibia's most important game reserves, Khaudum is home to one of only two protected populations of lions, and it's the only place in the country where African wild dogs can be spotted.

In order to explore the reserve by private 4WD vehicle, you will have to be completely self-sufficient, as petrol and supplies are only available in towns along the Caprivi Strip. Water is available inside the reserve, though it must be boiled or treated prior to drinking.

Tracks in the reserve are mostly sand, though they deteriorate into mud slicks after the rains. As a result, NWR requires that parties travel in a convoy of at least two self-sufficient 4WDs, and are equipped with enough food, water and petrol to survive for at least three days. Caravans, trailers and motorcycles are prohibited.

🏃 Activities
WILDLIFE WATCHING

The park protects large populations of elephants, zebras, giraffes, wildebeest, kudu, oryxes and tsessebes, and there's a good chance you'll be able to spot large herds of roan antelopes here. If you're an avid birder, Khaudum supports 320 different species, including summer migratory birds such as storks, crakes, bitterns, orioles, eagles and falcons.

Wildlife viewing is best from June to October, when herds congregate around the waterholes and along the *omiramba*. November to April is the richest time to visit for birdwatchers, though you will have to be prepared for a difficult slog through muddy tracks.

🛏 Sleeping

Namibia Wildlife Resorts (NWR) used to administer two official campsites in the park, but after one too many episodes of elephants gone wild, it decided to close up shop. These two sites have been neglected for a long time: if you are planning to stay at either one, keep your expectations low. Rumours of impending development in Khaudum persist, but to date that's all they are.

Sikereti Camp ('Cigarette' camp) is located in a shady grove of terminalia trees, though full appreciation of this place requires sensitivity to its subtle charms, namely isolation and silence. **Khaudum Camp** is somewhat akin to the Kalahari in miniature.

ℹ️ Getting There & Away

From the north, take the sandy track from Katere on the B8 (signposted 'Khaudum'), 120km east of Rundu. After 45km you'll reach the Cwibadom Omuramba, where you should turn east into the park.

From the south, you can reach Sikereti Camp via Tsumkwe. From Tsumkwe, it's 20km to Groote Döbe and another 15km from there to the Dorslandboom turning. It's then 25km north to Sikereti Camp.

The Caprivi Strip

Namibia's spindly northeastern appendage, the Caprivi Strip is typified by expanses of mopane and terminalia broadleaf forest, and punctuated by *shonas*, fossilised parallel dunes that are the remnants of a drier climate. For most travellers, the Caprivi serves as the easiest access route connecting the main body of Namibia with Victoria Falls and Botswana's Chobe National Park. However, visitors with time and patience can get off the beaten path here, exploring such hidden gems as Mudumu, Mamili and Bwabwata national parks.

BWABWATA NATIONAL PARK
🌀 066

Only recently recognised as a national park, Bwabwata was established to rehabilitate local wildlife populations. Prior to the 2002 Angolan ceasefire, this area saw almost no visitors, and wildlife had been virtually wiped out by rampant poaching instigated by ongoing conflict. Now that a decade of peace has returned, the animals are miraculously back again, and tourism is starting to pick up once more.

If you come here expecting Etosha, you'll be severely disappointed, though if you're looking to get off the beaten path, this is a great area to explore while it's still relatively undiscovered.

Bwabwata includes five main zones: the Divundu area, the West Caprivi Triangle, the

Mahango Game Reserve, Popa Falls and the now-defunct West Caprivi Game Reserve. The Mahango Game Reserve presently has the largest concentrations of wildlife, and is therefore the focus of most safaris in the area.

Divundu, with two (nominally) 24-hour petrol stations and a relatively well-stocked supermarket, is merely a product of the road junction. The real population centres are the neighbouring villages of Mukwe, Andara and Bagani. Divundu is marked as Bagani on some maps and road signs, though technically they're separate places about 2km apart.

The West Caprivi Triangle, the wedge bounded by Angola to the north, Botswana to the south and the Kwando River to the east, was formerly the richest wildlife area in the Caprivi. Poaching, bush clearing, burning and human settlement have greatly reduced wildlife, though you can still access the area via the road along the western bank of the Kwando River near Kongola.

Finally, the Golden Hwy between Rundu and Katima Mulilo traverses the former West Caprivi Game Reserve. Although this was once a haven for large herds of elephants, it served as a pantry for local hunters and poachers for decades, and is now largely devoid of wildlife.

◉ Sights

Mahango Game Reserve   WILDLIFE RESERVE
(per person/vehicle N$40/10; ☺sunrise-sunset)
This small but diverse 25,000-hectare park occupies a broad flood plain north of the Botswana border and west of the Okavango River. It attracts large concentrations of thirsty elephants and herd animals, particularly in the dry season.

With a 2WD vehicle, you can either zip through on the Mahango transit route or follow the Scenic Loop Drive past Kwetche picnic site, east of the main road. With a 4WD you can also explore the 20km Circular Drive Loop, which follows the *omiramba* and offers the best wildlife viewing. It's particularly nice to stop beside the river in the afternoon and watch the elephants swimming and drinking among hippos and crocodiles.

Popa Falls   WATERFALL
(per person/vehicle N$40/10; ☺sunrise-sunset)
Near Bagani, the Okavango River plunges down a broad series of cascades known as Popa Falls. The falls are nothing to get steamed up about, especially if Victoria Falls lies in your sights. In fact, the falls are actually little more than large rapids, though periods of low water do expose a drop of 4m. Aside from the 'falls', there are good

NAMIBIA THE CAPRIVI STRIP

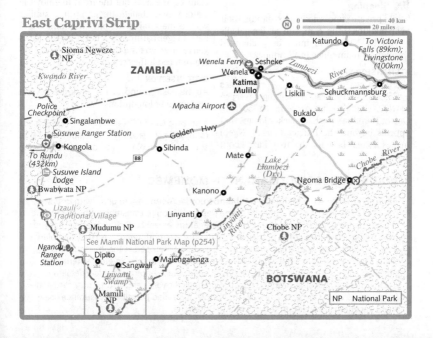

East Caprivi Strip

Bwabwata NP (Western Section)

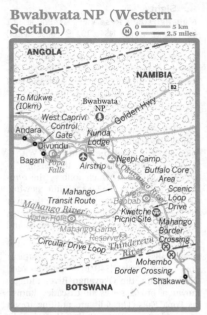

in lovely green, shady common areas during the day and find a chat partner at the happening bar in the evening. Crash for the night in a bush hut or tree hut, or pitch a tent on grass right by the river's edge and let the sounds of hippos splashing about ease you into a restful sleep. There's also a wide range of inexpensive excursions, including Mahango wildlife drives (N$420, three hours), canoe trips, booze cruises (N$190, 1½ hours) and *mokoro* (traditional dugout canoe) trips (N$190, 2½ hours) in the Okavango Panhandle. Or try a local village walk for N$100. The camp is located 4km off the main road, though the sandy access can prove difficult without a high-clearance vehicle. Phone the lodge if you need a lift from Divundu.

Nunda Lodge　　　　　　　　　　LODGE **$$$**
(☑686070; www.nundalodge.com; campsites/safari tents per person N$110/665, chalets N$760) This very welcoming lodge has an appealing aesthetic comprising stone buildings with thatched roofs and wooden decks on the river's edge. It's really well set up, with relaxing common areas overlooking the water where you can catch the breeze. The campsites are excellent, with sites 6 and 7 the best; all have power, *braai* plates and bins. Safari tents are also on the riverbank, with a small table and chair on the deck out the front to enjoy the water views. Chalets are set up in a similar way to the safari tents but are roomier and have bigger bathrooms – but if it's the views you're after, go for a safari tent. Rates are often reduced if they're not busy.

opportunities here for hiking and bird-watching, though swimming is definitely not safe as there are hungry crocs about.

🛏 Sleeping

While private concessions here handle their own bookings, the campsite at Popa Falls is run by NWR and must be prebooked through its main office in Windhoek.

WESTERN SECTION

Ngepi Camp　　　　　　　　　　LODGE **$**
(☑259903; www.ngepicamp.com; campsite per person N$100, bush/tree huts per person N$350/500) One of Namibia's top backpacker lodges that appeals beyond the budget market, Ngepi makes a great base for the area. Laze about

EASTERN SECTION

At the eastern end of the park are several accommodation options.

Nambwa Camp Site　　　　　CAMPGROUND **$**
(campsite per person N$60) Nambwa, 14km south of Kongola, is the only official camp

---

BORDER CROSSING: MAHANGO–MOHEMBO

About 12km before the **Mahango–Mohembo** border (open 6am to 6pm) with Botswana is the entry point to the Mahango Game Reserve. If you're transiting to the border there is no fee payable – just fill out the register at the entrance gate, indicating that you have entered the area. At the border, formalities are straightforward – on the Namibian side, just fill in a departure card and get your passport stamped at the Immigration desk. On your way to the Botswana side, you need to stop at the exit gate, enter a small office and fill out the registration book (you'll need your licence and vehicle details).

On the Botswana side, fill in the registration book for your vehicle, the entry card and get your passport stamped. Pay P110 (or N$160) for a road permit and insurance (payment accepted in either currency). Exit into Botswana.

THE SHAPE OF THINGS PAST

The Caprivi Strip's notably odd shape is a story in itself. When Germany laid claim to British-administered Zanzibar in 1890, Britain naturally objected, and soon after the Berlin Conference was called to settle the dispute. In the end, Britain kept Zanzibar, but Germany was offered a vast strip of land from the British-administered Bechuanaland protectorate (now Botswana). Named the Caprivi Strip after German chancellor General Count Georg Leo von Caprivi di Caprara di Montecuccoli, this vital tract of land provided Germany with access to the Zambezi River.

For the Germans, the motivation for this swap was to ultimately create a colonial empire that spanned from the south Atlantic Coast to Tanganyika (now Tanzania) and the Indian Ocean. Unfortunately for them, the British colonisation of Rhodesia stopped the Germans well upstream of Victoria Falls, which proved a considerable barrier to navigation on the Zambezi.

Interestingly enough, the absorption of the Caprivi Strip into German South West Africa didn't make world news, and it was nearly 20 years before some of its population discovered that they were under German control. In 1908 the German government finally dispatched one Hauptmann Streitwolf to oversee local administration, a move that prompted the Lozi tribe to round up all the cattle – including those belonging to rival tribes – and drive them out of the area. The cattle were eventually returned to their rightful owners, but most of the Lozi people chose to remain in Zambia and Angola rather than submit to German rule.

On 4 August 1914 Britain declared war on Germany and, just over a month later, the German administrative seat at Schuckmannsburg was attacked by the British from their base at Sesheke and then seized by the police. An apocryphal tale recounts that German governor Von Frankenberg was entertaining the English resident administrator of Northern Rhodesia (now Zambia) when a servant presented a message from British authorities in Livingstone. After reading it, the British official declared his host a prisoner of war, and thus, Schuckmannsburg fell into British hands. Whether the story is true or not, the seizure of Schuckmannsburg was the first Allied occupation of enemy territory in WWI.

in the park, and it provides easy access to the wildlife-rich oxbow lagoon, about 5km south. Book and pick up a permit at the Susuwe ranger station, about 4km north of Kongola (4WD access only) on the west bank of the river. To reach the camp, follow the 4WD track south along the western bank of the Kwando River.

Susuwe Island Lodge LODGE $$$
(☎061-401047; www.islandsinafrica.com/susuwe-island-lodge; per person Jan-Apr from N$3220, Jun-Dec from N$5480; ✳@☎) This posh safari lodge is located on a remote island in the Kwando River, and surrounded by a diverse habitat of savannah, woodland and wetland. Accommodation is in six stylish brick-and-thatch chalets adorned in soft earth tones. Amenities include an open-fire lounge, a gourmet bar-restaurant, private plunge pools and an outdoor viewing deck for taking in the beauty of the area. Susuwe is accessible only by charter flight or 4WD. Prebooking is mandatory.

❶ Getting There & Away

The paved road between Rundu and Katima Mulilo is perfectly suited to 2WD vehicles, as is the gravel road between Divundu and Mohembo (on the Botswana border). Drivers may transit the park without charge, but you will incur national park entry fees if you use the loop drive through the park.

KATIMA MULILO
☑ 066

Out on a limb at the eastern end of the Caprivi Strip lies remote Katima Mulilo, which is as far from Windhoek (1200km) as you can get in Namibia. Once known for the elephants that marched through the village streets, Katima is devoid of wildlife these days – apart from the hippos and crocodiles in the Zambezi – though it continues to thrive as a border town and minor commercial centre.

🛏 Sleeping & Eating

Mukusi Cabins CABINS $$
(☎253255; Engen petrol station; campsites N$80, s/d from N$460/640; ✳) Although it lacks the

BORDER CROSSINGS: EASTERN CAPRIVI STRIP

Botswana–Kasane & Chobe

With a private vehicle, the **Ngoma Bridge** (8am to 6pm) border crossing enables you to access Chobe National Park (Botswana) and Kasane (Botswana) in just a couple of hours. If you stick to the Chobe National Park Transit Route, you're excused from paying Botswana park fees.

Zambia–Victoria Falls

The 1km-long **Wenela Bridge** (7am to 6pm) spans the Zambezi between Katima Mulilo and Wenela, providing easy access to Livingstone and other destinations in Zambia. If you're heading to the falls, the road is sealed all the way to Livingstone, and is accessible by 2WD vehicle, even in the rainy season. If you're heading west to Mongu in Zambia, check the state of the road first as it can get washed away during the rainy season.

riverside location of other properties in the area, this oasis behind the Engen petrol station has a good range of accommodation, from simple rooms with fans to small but comfortable air-con cabins. The lovely bar-restaurant dishes up a range of unexpected options – including calamari, snails and king-klip – as well as steak and chicken standbys.

Caprivi River Lodge　　　　LODGE $$
(☑252288; www.capririverlodge.com; s N$415-1075, d N$620-1375; ❋@❋) This diverse lodge offers options to suit travellers of all budgets, from rustic cabins with shared bathrooms to luxurious chalets facing the Zambezi River. It also offers a decent variety of activities, including boating, fishing and wildlife drives in the various Caprivi parks. The lodge is 5km from town along Ngoma Rd.

Protea Hotel Zambezi Lodge　　LODGE $$$
(☑251500; www.proteahotels.com/katima-mulilo .html; campsite per person N$70, s/d from N$700/1050; ❋@❋) This stunning riverside lodge is perched on the banks of the Zambezi and features a floating bar where you can watch the crocs and hippos below. The campsite is amid a flowery garden, while accommodation is in well-equipped modern rooms that open up to small verandahs and ample views.

🛍 Shopping

Caprivi Arts Centre　　　　CRAFT
(◷8am-5.30pm) Run by the Caprivi Art & Cultural Association, the centre is a good place to look for local curios and crafts, including elephant and hippo woodcarvings, baskets, bowls, kitchen implements, and traditional knives and spears.

ℹ Getting There & Away

AIR
Air Namibia has several weekly departures between Windhoek's Eros Airport and Katima's Mpacha Airport, located 18km southwest of town.

BUS & MINIBUS
Several weekly Intercape Mainliner (p355) buses make the 16-hour run between Windhoek and Katima Mulilo. Book your tickets (fares from N$460) in advance online, as this service continues on to Victoria Falls and fills up quickly.

Combis connect Windhoek and Katima with fairly regular frequency, and a ride shouldn't cost more than N$230. From Katima, routes fan out to various towns and cities in the north, with fares costing less than N$40 a ride.

CAR
The sealed Golden Hwy runs between Katima Mulilo and Rundu, and is accessible to all 2WD vehicles.

HITCHING
The best places to wait for lifts between Katima Mulilo and Rundu are at the petrol stations in Divundu and Kongola. Chances are that any eastbound/westbound vehicle from Rundu/Katima Mulilo will be doing the entire route.

MPALILA ISLAND
☑ 066
Mpalila (Impalilia) Island, a wedge driven between the Chobe and Zambezi Rivers, represents Namibia's outer limits at the 'four-corners meeting' of Zimbabwe, Botswana, Namibia and Zambia. The island itself, which is within easy reach by boat from Chobe National Park, is home to a handful of exclusive lodges catering to upmarket tourists in search of luxurious isolation.

Prebooking is essential for all accommodation on the island. All lodges offer a variety of activities for guests, including cruises on the Chobe River, guided wildlife drives, fishing expeditions, island walks and *mokoro* trips. Rates include full board and transfers.

Access to Mpalila Island is either by charter flight or by boat from Kasane (Botswana), though lodges will organise all transport for their booked guests.

🛏 Sleeping

Impalila Island Lodge   LODGE $$$
(☏061-401047; www.islandsinafrica.com/impalila-island-lodge/; per person Jan-Apr N$2860, Jun-Dec N$4840; ✳✳) Overlooking the impressive Mombova rapids, Impalila Island Lodge is a stylish retreat of eight luxury chalets built on elevated decks at the water's edge. The centrepiece of the lodge is a pair of ancient baobab trees, which tower majestically over the grounds.

Chobe Savannah Lodge   LODGE $$
(☏in South Africa 021-4241037; www.desertdelta.co.za; per person Jan-Apr US$410, Jun-Dec US$650; ✳✳) The most famous spot on the island is Chobe Savannah Lodge, which is renowned for its panoramic views of the wildlife-rich Puku Flats. Each stylishly decorated room has a private verandah where you can spot animals without ever having to change out of your pyjamas.

MUDUMU NATIONAL PARK
✔ 066

Mudumu National Park has a tragic history of environmental abuse and neglect. Although it was once one of Namibia's most stunning wildlife habitats, by the late 1980s the park had become an unofficial hunting concession gone mad. In under a decade the wildlife was decimated by trophy hunters, which prompted the Ministry of Environment and Tourism (MET) to gazette Mudumu National Park in a last-ditch effort to rescue the area from total devastation. Mudumu's wildlife has begun to return, but it will take years of wise policy-making and community awareness before the area approaches its former glory.

◉ Sights

The culmination of a joint partnership between the owners of a one-time local lodge (Lianshulu, now closed), MET, private benefactors and the Lizauli community, the **Lizauli Traditional Village** (admission N$20; ☺9am-5pm Mon-Sat) was established to educate visitors about traditional Caprivian lifestyles, and to provide insight into the local diet, fishing and farming methods, village politics, music, games, traditional medicine, basketry and tool making. After the guided tour, visitors can shop for good-value local handicrafts without the sales pressure.

The aforementioned partnership has also enabled the recruitment of Mudumu game scouts from Lizauli and other villages, and was given responsibility for community conservation and antipoaching education. Most importantly, the project provides a forum in which locals can interact with tourists, and benefit both economically and culturally from the adoption of a strict policy of environmental protection.

MAMILI NATIONAL PARK

In years of good rains, this wild and seldom-visited national park becomes Namibia's equivalent of Botswana's Okavango Delta. Forested islands fringed by reed and papyrus marshes foster some of the country's richest birdwatching, with more than 430 recorded species to count. Poaching has taken a toll, though Mamili's wildlife, mainly semiaquatic species such as hippos, crocodiles, pukus, red lechwes, sitatungas and otters, will still impress.

Birding is best from December to March, though the vast majority of the park is inaccessible during this time. Wildlife viewing is best from June to August, and is especially good on Nkasa and Lupala islands.

You must bring everything with you, including your own water, and be prepared for extremely rough road conditions. Although there is generally a ranger to collect park fees at the entrance gate, you're all alone once inside, and it's highly recommended that you travel as part of a convoy. Needless to say, a 4WD vehicle with high clearance is mandatory, and you can expect lots and lots of deep mud.

Access to the park is by 4WD track from Malengalenga, northeast of the park, or from Sangwali village, which is due north.

🛏 Sleeping

There are two officially designated camping areas in the park: Liadura, beside the Kwando River, and Mparamura.

🏷**Nkasa Lupala Lodge**   LODGE $$$
(☏081 147 7798; www.nkasalupalalodge.com; d per person N$1400) Located 30km from Mudumu, and just outside the entrance to Mamili National Park, this remote luxury lodge

NAMIBIA THE CAPRIVI STRIP

Mamili National Park

sits on the banks of the Kwando–Linyanti River system. The lodge gets rave reviews from travellers and offers activities such as game drives in both national parks. Accommodation is in tents on stilts, from where you might just spot elephants trooping past your deck.

🛈 Getting There & Away

Nkasa Lupala lodge is about 75km from Kongola and 130km from Katima Mulilo. Take the C49 (a maintained gravel road from Kongola and sealed from Katima Mulilo) to Sangwali. From Sangwali, head to the Mamili National Park – you'll need a 4WD, or call for a pick-up. From the Shisintze ranger station at the park boundary, drive east for 1km to reach the lodge.

Otjozondjupa

Otjozondjupa is commonly referred to as Bushmanland, a pejorative term that unfortunately seems to resist dying away. A large-

ly flat landscape of scrub desert lying at the edge of the Kalahari, Otjozondjupa is part of the traditional homeland of the Ju/'hoansi San, who were among the original inhabitants of Southern Africa. Following a spurt in worldwide interest in Kalahari cultures, tourist traffic has increased throughout the region, though any expectations you might have of witnessing an entirely self-sufficient hunter-gatherer society will, sadly, not be met here.

For some people, witnessing the stark reality of the modern Ju/'hoansi San lifestyle is a sobering experience fraught with disappointments. Hunting is forbidden throughout the region, and most communities have largely abandoned foraging in favour of cheap, high-calorie foods such as *pap* (corn meal) and rice, which are purchased in bulk from shops. Try to look beyond the dire realities of the San's economic situation, and attempt to use the experience as a rare chance to interact with the modern-day descendants of perhaps all of our ancestors.

If you're visiting the region as a tourist, you are required to stop by the office of the **Nyae Nyae Conservancy** (☎244011; ⏱8am-5pm Mon-Fri) in central Tsumkwe. It's recommended that you book/get recommendations for activities through here rather than striking off on your own. This practice ensures that the money you spend ends up in the community fund rather than in the pockets of one or two individuals.

There are no officially posted prices for activities, though you can expect to be charged a reasonably modest amount for every person that accompanies you. English-speaking guides command the largest fee, generally in the realm of N$250 per day plus food, while hunters and foragers should be organised in the villages – ask in the office where to do this. It is also possible to arrange overnight stays in villages.

While you are out travelling in the bush, you will inevitably come across San communities, and the temptation to snap photos without permission inevitably exists. However photogenic a situation might be, it is important to always ask permission before taking a photo, especially since your subject will generally ask for either money or a small gift. Before leaving Tsumkwe, it's a good idea to stock up on small bills or, better yet, do some grocery shopping in town

and be prepared to trade healthy food items for snapshots. The San have a long history of gift giving, and an appreciation of this tradition will quickly win you respect.

When visiting San villages, visitors are expected to either purchase or trade for beadwork, walking sticks, ostrich-shell necklaces, bow-and-arrow sets, and so on. Trading is a wonderful practice worth encouraging, and prized items include T-shirts, shoes, trousers, baseball caps and other useful items. People will also ask for sugar and tobacco – you'll have to decide whether to trade these products, given their attendant health risks. In any case, please trade fairly, avoid excessive payment and help keep local dignity intact by resisting the urge to hand out gifts for nothing.

History

Of the six sub-Saharan countries where the San reside, Namibia is home to the second-largest population, numbering nearly 33,000 individuals. Although they once controlled expansive n!oresi (lands where one's heart is), these homelands were commandeered by the South African Defence Force (SADF) as military bases during the Namibian War of Independence. After being reduced to refugees, many San migrated to towns like Tsumkwe in search of work.

Some San succeeded in finding work as unskilled farm labourers, while others worked as army trackers for the SADF,

NAMIBIA OTJOZONDJUPA

THE JU/'HOANSI SAN TODAY

The enforcement of conservation laws, most notably the establishment of Khaudum National Park, has negatively affected the ability of the San to continue hunting and gathering. While some communities have successfully shifted to agriculture and herding, the majority scrape by on a subsistence lifestyle.

On the other hand, the Ju/'hoansi San are permitted to hunt with traditional bows and arrows within their concession, and the reintroduction of game has enabled some successful hunters to earn a respectable living.

The Nyae Nyae Conservancy was also successful in facilitating the passage of the Traditional Authorities Act by the Namibian government, which officially recognised the political power of local chiefs. Today, these individuals work alongside the Nyae Nyae Conservancy at the local, regional and national levels to find sustainable land-use solutions. Furthermore, tourism has firmly taken hold in Otjozondjupa, and the Nyae Nyae Conservancy now envisions Tsumkwe emerging as a prominent ecotourism hot spot.

While visiting Otjozondjupa, please be extremely sensitive to the plight of the San, though do take comfort in the fact that your visit can indeed help. Revenue from tourism plays a vital role in the development of the region, particularly if you are buying locally produced crafts or paying for the services of a guide. Perhaps more importantly, indigenous tourism helps to reassure communities like the San that their traditional culture is worth preserving, ensuring that future generations can continue to learn about our common human heritage.

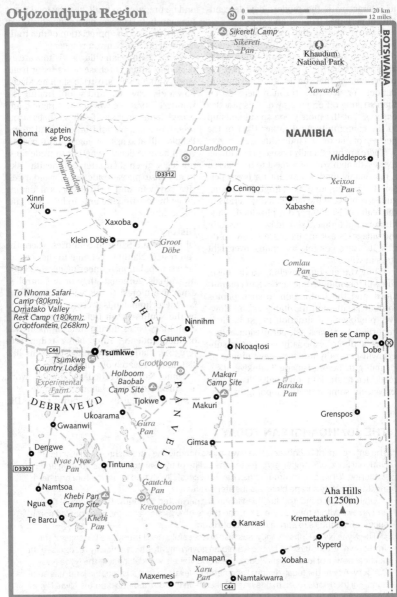

who were waging a war against Swapo in northern Namibia and Angola. Still, the majority met with grinding unemployment, a demographic shift that resulted in disease, prostitution, alcoholism, domestic violence, malnutrition and other social ills.

Following Namibian independence, the San territory shrank from 70,000 sq km to less than 10,000 sq km, and a large portion of their boreholes were expropriated by other interests, possibly in retaliation for their partnership with SADF. As a result, the San were left without sufficient land to maintain their traditional lifestyle, which further aggravated pre-existing poverty and dispossession.

Fortunately, a number of influential Westerners, ranging from academics and journalists to development workers and cultural survivalists, have long been interested in the advocacy of indigenous rights throughout Southern Africa. In northern Namibia, US filmmaker John Marshall and his British colleague Claire Marshall established the Nyae Nyae Conservancy in the late 1980s to encourage the Ju/'hoansi San to return to their traditional lands. Unfortunately, the foundation has suffered from a number of ideological conflicts, including to what extent tourism should be fostered in the region.

TSUMKWE
🗎 067

Tsumkwe is the only real permanent settlement in the whole of Otjozondjupa, though it's merely a wide spot in the sand with a few rust-covered buildings. Originally constructed as the regional headquarters of the SADF, Tsumkwe was then given a mandate as the administrative centre of the Ju/'hoansi San community, and is home to the Nyae Nyae Conservancy. While organised tourism in the region is still something of a work in progress, Tsumkwe is where you can arrange everything from bushwalks to hunting safaris, and inject some much-needed cash into the local community.

◉ Sights

Hunting and foraging trips are the highlight of any visit to Otjozondjupa. Much as they have for generations, the San still use traditional gear, namely a bow with poisoned arrows for men, and a digging stick and sling for women. In the past, men would be gone for several days at a time in pursuit of herds, so you shouldn't expect to take down any big game on an afternoon excursion. But it's fascinating to see trackers in pursuit of their quarry, and you're likely to come across spoor and maybe even an antelope or two.

Foraging is very likely to turn up edible roots and tubers, wild fruits and nuts, and even medicinal plants. At the end of your excursion, the women will be more than happy to slice up a bush potato for you, which tastes particularly wonderful when roasted over a bed of hot coals. Baobab fruit is also surprisingly sweet and tangy, while protein-

SAN INTERACTIONS

About 25km out of Tsumkwe, heading towards Khaudum National Park, is the **Living Hunter's Museum of the Ju/'hoansi** (D3315; ⊘sunrise-sunset), which has been established for about 2½ years and is run and managed independently by the San. A lot of effort has gone into representing the old San hunter-gather culture as authentically as possible. Cultural interactions on offer include hunting trips (N$200 per person) with San hunters using traditional methods and equipment. There are also bushwalks (N$100) and singing/dancing shows.

rich nuts are an exotic yet nutritious desert treat.

While stereotypes of the San abound, from misleading Hollywood cinematic representations to misconstrued notions of a primitive people living in the bush, San society is extremely complex. Before visiting a San village, take some time to read up on their wonderfully rich cultural heritage – doing so will not only provide some context to your visit but also help you better engage your hosts.

AROUND TSUMKWE

In addition to village visits, the area around Tsumkwe is home to a number of natural attractions that are accessible by private 4WD vehicle.

Panveld   NATURAL SITE

Forming an arc east of Tsumkwe is a remote landscape of phosphate-rich pans. After the rains, the largest of these, Nyae Nyae, Khebi and Gautcha (all at the southern end of the arc), are transformed into superb wetlands. These ephemeral water sources attract itinerant water birds – including throngs of flamingos – but they are also breeding sites for waterfowl: ducks, spurwing geese, cranes, crakes, egrets and herons. Other commonly observed birds include teals, sandpipers and reeves, as well as the rare black-tailed godwit and the great snipe.

Baobabs   NATURAL SITE

The dry, crusty landscape around Tsumkwe supports several large baobab trees, some of which have grown quite huge. The imaginatively named **Grootboom** (Big Tree) is one of the largest, with a circumference of over 30m. One tree with historical significance is the **Dorslandboom**, which was visited by the Dorsland (Thirst Land) trekkers who camped here on their trek to Angola in 1891 and carved their names into the tree. Another notable tree, the immense **Holboom** (Hollow Tree), dominates the bush near the village of Tjokwe.

Aha Hills   HILLS

Up against the Botswana border, the flat landscape is broken only by the Aha Hills. Given the nearly featureless landscape that surrounds them, you may imagine that these low limestone outcrops were named when the first traveller uttered, 'Aha, some hills.' In fact, it's a rendition of the sound made by the endemic barking gecko.

The region is pockmarked with unexplored caves and sinkholes, but don't attempt to enter them unless you have extensive caving experience. The hills are also accessible from the Botswana side. A border crossing is open between Tsumkwe (though this is 30km to the west of the border) and Dobe.

🛏 Sleeping & Eating

There's a restaurant at the Tsumkwe Country Lodge, and the **Tsumkwe Winkel** in town sells limited groceries, but self-caterers would be wise to stock up on supplies before driving out here.

Nyae Nyae Conservancy
Camp Sites   CAMPGROUND **$**
(campsite per person from N$60) The Nyae Nyae Conservancy has several campsites, the most popular being: the Holboom Baobab at Tjokwe, southeast of Tsumkwe; Makuri, a few kilometres east of that; and Khebi Pan, well out in the bush south of Tsumkwe. Water is sometimes available in adjacent villages, but generally it's best to carry in all of your supplies and be entirely self-sufficient. Avoid building fires near the baobabs – it damages the trees' roots.

Omatako Valley Rest Camp   CAMPGROUND **$**
(☎255977; campsite per person N$60) Outside the conservancy at the junction of the C44 and D3306, this community-run camp has solar power, a water pump, hot showers and a staff of local San. It offers both hunting and gathering trips as well as traditional music presentations.

Tsumkwe Country Lodge   LODGE **$$**
(☎061-374750; www.namibialodges.com/tsumkwe_en.htm; campsite per person N$80, s/d from N$580/800; ❄@≋) The only tourist lodge in Tsumkwe proper is an upmarket affair with a bar, restaurant, small shop and pool. Guests can base themselves here and visit surrounding villages as part of an organised tour.

Nhoma Safari Camp   TENTED CAMP **$$$**
(☎081-273 4606; www.tsumkwel.iway.na; campsite per person N$150, full board per person from N$2200; ❄) The former owners of the Tsumkwe Country Lodge, Arno and Estelle, have lived in the area for much of their lives and are well respected by the local San communities. Their luxury tented camp is perched between a fossilised river valley and a verdant teak grove, though the main attraction continues to be their wonderful excursions into local San villages. The camp is located 280km east of Grootfontein and 80km west of Tsumkwe along the C44. You must book in advance to stay here – as mobile phone reception at the camp is unreliable (there's no landline), it's best to email them.

❶ Getting There & Away

Note that you will need your own transport; a 4WD with good clearance is recommended. There are no sealed roads in the region, and only the C44 is passable for 2WD vehicles. Petrol is sometimes available at the Tsumkwe Country Lodge, though it's best to carry a few jerry cans with you. If you're planning to explore the bush around Tsumkwe, it is recommended that you hire a local guide and travel as part of a convoy.

The Dobe border crossing to Botswana requires a 4WD and extra fuel to reach the petrol stations at Maun or Etsha 6, which are accessed by a difficult sand track through northwestern Botswana.

NORTHWESTERN NAMIBIA

For those who like to take a walk (or even a drive) on the wild side, northwestern Namibia is a stark, desolate environment where some of the most incredible landscapes imaginable lie astride 4WD tracks. Along the Skeleton Coast, seemingly endless expanses of foggy beach are punctuated by rusting shipwrecks and flanked by wandering dunes. Here, travellers are left entirely alone to bask in this riveting isolation, both-

SAVE THE RHINO TRUST

The Save the Rhino Trust (SRT) is dedicated to stopping illegal poaching. Since the trust was formed, it has collaborated with both the Namibian government and local communities in order to provide security and monitor population size of the only free-ranging black-rhino population in the world. To date SRT has successfully protected these rhinos and allowed the rhino group to expand in number. Census results have revealed that the population of 1130 rhinos has been preserved, with an annual growth rate of 5%. In fact, the International Union for Conservation of Nature (IUCN) has identified the population as the fastest growing in Africa.

SRT operates in Damaraland, a sparsely populated region that is lacking in resources and deficient in employment opportunities. As a result, it has worked to include locals in conservation efforts in the hope that they will benefit from the preservation of the species. This is especially important as Damaraland does not have a formal conservation status and thus does not receive government funding.

Although the organisation has been successful in stabilising rhino populations, SRT still faces challenges, such as the increasing demand in Namibia for arable farmland. According to SRT, the future of the rhino is dependent on the effective resolution of this issue, and it argues that government policy must include the establishment of stable rhino populations in parks, reserves and private lands throughout the country.

For visitors interested in tracking black rhinos through the bush, SRT operates the exclusive **Desert Rhino Camp** (✆061-225178; www.wilderness-safaris.com; per person from US$650), a joint venture with Wilderness Safaris. Accommodation is in eight East Africa–style linen tents with private bathroom and hot-water bucket showers. Rates include all meals, wildlife drives and rhino-tracking excursions. Prebooking is essential; 4WD transfers and air charters are available.

ered only by the concern of whether their vehicles can survive the journey unscathed.

Not to be outdone by the barren coastline, the Kaokoveld is a photographer's dreamscape of wide-open vistas, lonely desert roads and hardly another person around to ruin your shot. A vast repository of desert mountains, this is one of the least developed regions of the country, and arguably Namibia at its most primeval. The Kaokoveld is also the ancestral home of the Himba people, a culturally rich tribal group that has retained its striking appearance and dress.

And then there's Damaraland, home to the Brandberg Massif, Namibia's highest peak, and Twyfelfontein, which together contain some of Southern Africa's finest prehistoric rock paintings and engravings. A veritable window into the past, these two sites help to illuminate the hidden inner workings of our collective forebears, who roamed the African savannah so many eons ago.

Geography

Northwestern Namibia is synonymous with the Skeleton Coast, a formidable desert coastline engulfed by icy breakers. As one moves inland, the sinister fogs give way to the wondrous desert wilderness of Dama-

raland and the Kaokoveld. The former is known for its unique geological features, including volcanic mounds, petrified forests, red-rock mesas and petroglyph-engraved sandstone slabs. The latter is known as one of the last great wildernesses in Southern Africa. Despite their unimaginably harsh conditions, both regions are also rich in wildlife, which have adapted to the arid environment and subsequently thrived.

❶ Getting Around

Since there is virtually no public transport anywhere in the region, and hitching is practically impossible, the best way to explore northwestern Namibia is with a private vehicle. A 2WD vehicle is suitable for the sealed highway to Opuwo, as well as the graded dirt C-roads and most D-roads in Damaraland. However, be advised that the roads in the Kaokoveld require a high-clearance vehicle, and some may require a 4WD, especially if driving during the rainy season.

Routes through the western Kaokoveld are all rugged 4WD tracks that were laid down by the South African Defence Force (SADF) during the Namibian War of Independence, and they've been maintained only by the wheels of passing vehicles. Off the main tourist route from Sesfontein to Opuwo, Okongwati and Epupa Falls, there's little traffic, and the scattered villages lack hotels, shops, showers, hospitals and vehicle spares or repairs. If that makes you uncomfortable, you may want to consider visiting the region with an established tour operator or as part of a larger convoy.

Damaraland

Moving inland from the dunes and plains of the bleak Skeleton Coast, the terrain gradually rises through wild desert mountains towards the scrubby plateaus of central Namibia. Damaraland, which occupies much of this transition zone, is laced with springs and ephemeral rivers that provide streaks of greenery and moisture for wildlife, people and livestock. Its broad spaces are one of Southern Africa's last 'unofficial' wildlife areas, and you can still see zebras, giraffes, antelopes, elephants and even black rhinos ranging outside national parks or protected reserves.

THE SPITZKOPPE

📝] 064

One of Namibia's most recognisable landmarks, the 1728m-high Spitzkoppe rises like a mirage above the dusty pro-Namib plains of southern Damaraland. Its dramatic shape has inspired its nickname, the Matterhorn of Africa, but similarities between this ancient volcanic remnant and the glaciated Swiss alp begin and end with its sharp peak. First summited in 1946, the Spitzkoppe continues to attract hard-core rock climbers bent on tackling Namibia's most challenging peak.

The Spitzkoppe is administered by the Ministry of Environment & Tourism (MET), and attended to by the local community. Local guides are also available for a negotiable price, and they provide some illuminating context to this rich cultural site.

◉ Sights & Activities

Beside the Spitzkoppe rise the equally impressive Pondoks, which are composed of enormous granite domes. At the eastern end of this rocky jumble, a wire cable climbs the granite slopes to a vegetated hollow known as Bushman's Paradise, where an overhang shelters a vandalised panel of ancient rhino paintings.

Although you do not need technical equipment and expertise to go scrambling, climbing to the top of the Spitzkoppe is a serious and potentially dangerous endeavour. For starters, you must be fully self-sufficient in terms of climbing gear, food and water,

and preferably be part of a large expedition. Before climbing the Spitzkoppe, seek local advice and be sure to inform others of your intentions. Also be advised that it can get extremely hot during the day and surprisingly cold at night and at higher elevations – bring proper protection.

🛏 Sleeping & Eating

Spitzkoppe Rest Camp LODGE $
(Groot Spitzkoppe village; campsite per person N$45, bungalows from N$120) The sites at this excellent camp are dotted around the base of the Spitzkoppe and surrounding outcrops. Most are set in magical rock hollows and provide a sense of real isolation. Facilities at the entrance include a reception office, eco-friendly ablutions blocks and *braai* stands, plus a bar and restaurant. The site was taken over by a private investor in mid-2012, who has pledged to upgrade the facilities while ensuring the local community continues to benefit from the enterprise.

ⓘ Getting There & Away

Under normal dry conditions, a 2WD is sufficient to reach the mountain. Turn northwest off the B2 onto the D1918 towards Henties Bay. After 18km, turn north onto the D3716.

THE BRANDBERG

Driving around this massive pink granite bulge, and marvelling at the ethereal light during sunset which appears to bounce off it, is a highlight of the region. But inside lies the real treasure – one of the finest remnants of prehistoric art on the African continent.

The Brandberg (Fire Mountain) is named for the effect created by the setting sun on its western face, which causes this granite massif to resemble a burning slag heap. Its summit, Königstein, is Namibia's highest peak at 2573m.

The Brandberg is a reserve and the entry fee for admission is N$50 per person and N$20 per car. Note that this includes being allocated a compulsory guide – you cannot just walk around these fragile treasures by yourself. It's good to tip the guide afterwards if you're happy with their service.

◉ Sights

Tsisab Ravine ARCHAEOLOGICAL SITE
The most famous figure in the ravine is the White Lady of the Brandberg, which is located in Maack's Shelter. The figure, which isn't necessarily a lady (it's still open to interpretation), stands about 40cm high, and is part of a larger painting that depicts

The Spitzkoppe & Pondoks

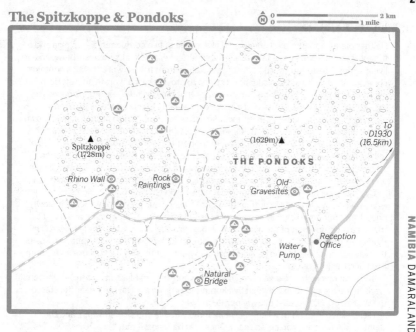

a bizarre hunting procession. In one hand, the figure is carrying what appears to be a flower or possibly a feather. In the other, the figure is carrying a bow and arrows. However, the painting is distinct because 'her' hair is straight and light-coloured – distinctly un-African – and the body is painted white from the chest down.

The first assessment of the painting was in 1948, when Abbé Henri Breuil speculated that the work had Egyptian or Cretan origins, based on similar ancient art he'd seen around the Mediterranean. However, this claim was eventually dismissed, and recent scholars now believe the white lady may in fact be a San boy, who is covered in white clay as part of an initiation ceremony.

Numas Ravine   ARCHAEOLOGICAL SITE

Numas Ravine, slicing through the western face of the Brandberg, is another treasure house of ancient paintings. Most people ask their guide to take them to the rock facing the southern bank of the riverbed, which bears paintings of a snake, a giraffe and an antelope. It lies about 30 minutes' walk up the ravine. After another half-hour you'll reach an oasis-like freshwater spring and several more paintings in the immediate surroundings.

🛏 Sleeping

There are unofficial campsites near the mouths of both the Numas and Tsisab Ravines, but neither has water or facilities.

Brandberg White Lady Lodge   LODGE $$

(☑684004; www.brandbergwllodge.com; campsite per person N$80, tw luxury tent N$545, s/tw with halfboard N$775/1330) The Brandberg White Lady has something for just about every kind of traveller. Campers can pitch a tent along the riverine valley, all the while taking advantage of the lodge's upmarket facilities, while lovers of their creature comforts can choose from rustic bungalows and chalets that are highlighted by their stone interiors and wraparound patios. The lodge does wildlife drives (N$200) where oryx, springboks, zebras and mountain cheetahs can be seen, along with desert elephants (from August to December).

Ugab Wilderness Camp   CAMPSITE $

(campsite per person N$70) Facilities are basic here, though the camp is well run and a good base for organising guided Brandberg hikes or climbs. The turn-off is signposted from the D2359 and the camp is 10km from here.

LICHEN FIELDS

Neither plants nor animals, lichens actually consist of two components – an alga and a fungus – and perhaps provide nature's most perfect example of symbiosis between two living things. The fungus portion absorbs moisture from the air, while the alga contains chlorophyll, which produces sugar and starch to provide carbohydrate energy. Both algae and fungi are cryptogams, which means that they lack the sex organs necessary to produce flowers and seeds, and are therefore unable to reproduce as plants do.

Lichens come in many varieties, including crustose, which form orange, black, brown or pale-green ring patterns on rocks, and foliose, which are actually free-standing. In fact, the gravel plains of the Namib Desert support the world's most extensive fields of foliose lichen, which provide stability for the loose soil in this land of little vegetation. These fields are composed mostly of stationary grey lichen, free-standing black lichen and the rarer orange lichen, which is surprisingly bushy and can grow up to 10cm high.

By day, the lichen fields very much resemble thickets of dead, shrivelled shrubs. However, when heavy fogs roll in during the night-time, the dull grey and black fields slowly uncurl, and burst into blue, green and orange blooms. Water droplets are absorbed by the fungus component of the lichen, which also provides the root system and physical rigidity. At the first light of dawn, however, the alga kicks in with its contribution by using the water droplets, light and carbon dioxide to photosynthesise carbohydrates for both itself and the fungus.

The best places to observe lichen fields are southwest of Messum Crater, in scattered areas along the salt road between Swakopmund and Terrace Bay, and near the start of the Welwitschia Drive, east of Swakopmund.

Please keep in mind that lichens are incredibly fragile and slow growing, and the slightest disturbance can crush them. Once that happens, it may take 40 or 50 years before any regeneration is apparent. In particular, you should never thoughtlessly drive off-road, and always follow pre-existing tracks when you're bush driving.

ⓘ Getting There & Away

To reach Tsisab Ravine from Uis, head 15km north and turn west on the D2359, which leads 26km to the Tsisab car park. To reach Numas Ravine, head 14km south of Uis and follow the D2342 for 55km, where you'll see a rough track turning eastwards. After about 10km, you'll reach a fork; the 4WD track on the right leads to the Numas Ravine car park.

MESSUM CRATER

One of Damaraland's most remote natural attractions is the highly mysterious-looking Messum Crater, which comprises two concentric circles of hills created by a collapsed volcano in the Goboboseb Mountains. The crater measures more than 20km in diameter, creating a vast lost world that you're likely to have all to yourself.

Camping is prohibited inside the crater.

Of its three main entrances, Messum is best accessed along the Messum River from the D2342 west of the Brandberg. Note that you must stick to the tracks at all times, especially if you choose either route involving the fragile lichen plains of the Dorob National Park. If you are driving in this area,

you will require the relevant topographic sheets, which are available from the Office of the Surveyor General in Windhoek.

TWYFELFONTEIN & AROUND
🔊 067

Twyfelfontein (Doubtful Spring), at the head of the grassy Aba Huab Valley, is one of the most extensive rock-art galleries on the continent.

In the ancient past, this perennial spring most likely attracted wildlife, creating a paradise for the hunters who eventually left their marks on the surrounding rocks. Animals, animal tracks and geometric designs are well represented here, though there are surprisingly few human figures. Many of the engravings depict animals that are no longer found in the area – elephants, rhinos, giraffes and lions – and an engraving of a sea lion indicates contact with the coast more than 100km away.

To date over 2500 engravings have been discovered, and Twyfelfontein became a national monument in 1952. Unfortunately, the site did not receive formal protection until 1986, when it was designated a natural reserve. In the interim, many petroglyphs were damaged by vandals, and some were even removed altogether.

A significant amount of restoration work has taken place here in recent years, a welcome development that hasn't gone unnoticed by the international community. In 2007 Twyfelfontein was declared a Unesco World Heritage Site, the first such distinction in the whole of Namibia.

◉ Sights

Rock Engravings   ROCK ART
(per person/car N$50/20; ☉sunrise-sunset) Most dating back at least 6000 years to the early Stone Age, Twyfelfontein's rock engravings were probably the work of ancient San hunters, and were made by cutting through the hard patina covering the local sandstone. In time, this skin reformed over the engravings, protecting them from erosion. From colour differentiation and weathering, researchers have identified at least six distinct phases, but some are clearly the work of copycat artists and are thought to date from the 19th century. Guides are compulsory; note that tips are their only source of income.

AROUND TWYFELFONTEIN

Burnt Mountain   HILL
Southeast of Twyfelfontein rises a barren 12km-long volcanic ridge, at the foot of which lies the hill known as Burnt Mountain, an expanse of volcanic clinker that appears to have been literally exposed to fire. Virtually nothing grows in this eerie panorama of desolation. Burnt Mountain lies beside the D3254, 3km south of the Twyfelfontein turn-off.

Organ Pipes   NATURAL SITE
Over the road from Burnt Mountain, you can follow an obvious path into a small gorge that contains a 100m stretch of unusual 4m-high dolerite (coarse-grained basalt) columns known as the Organ Pipes.

Petrified Forest   NATURAL SITE
(per person/car N$40/20; ☉sunrise-sunset) The petrified forest is an area of open veld scattered with petrified tree trunks up to 34m long and 6m in circumference, which are estimated to be around 260 million years old. The original trees belonged to an ancient group of cone-bearing plants that are known as *Gymnospermae,* which includes such modern plants as conifers, cycads and welwitschias. Because of the lack of root or branch remnants, it's thought that the

trunks were transported to the site in a flood.

About 50 individual trees are visible, some half buried in sandstone and many perfectly petrified in silica – complete with bark and tree rings. In 1950, after souvenir hunters had begun to take their toll, the site was declared a national monument, and it's now strictly forbidden to carry off even a small scrap of petrified wood. Guides are compulsory.

The Petrified Forest, signposted 'Versteende Woud', lies 40km west of Khorixas on the C39.

Wondergat   NATURAL SITE
Wondergat is an enormous sinkhole with daunting views into the subterranean world. Turn west off the D3254, 4km north of the D2612 junction. It's about 500m further on to Wondergat.

🍴 Sleeping & Eating

Campsites such as Aba Huab Camp beside a riverbed (immediately north of the Twyfelfontein turn-off) are worth trying if you're on a budget, although we've heard very mixed reports regarding this place, including that it's in a pretty bad state of disrepair. Otherwise, there are mainly luxury, upmarket options near the rock-art site.

Camp Kipwe   LODGE $$$
(☏232009, 687211; www.kipwe.com; r with half board per person N$1800; ☒) Brilliantly located among the boulders and rocks littered throughout its premises, Kipwe is languidly draped over the stunning landscape in very unobtrusive large *rondavels* with thatched roofs that blend in beautifully with their surrounds. There are nine standard rooms and one honeymoon suite (rooms 3 and 4 are family rooms with kids' tents); all come with outdoor bathrooms so you can stargaze while you wash. Great views from the dining/lounge area – catch the breeze with your cocktail. The lodge also runs nature drives (N$540) and excursions to the rock art. The entrance to Kipwe is just across the road (D2612) from the entrance to Mowani Mountain Camp.

Twyfelfontein Country Lodge   LODGE $$$
(☏374750; www.namibialodges.com; s/d from N$1324/1860; ☀@☒) Over the hill from Twyfelfontein, this architectural wonder is embedded in the red rock. On your way in, be sure not to miss the ancient rock engravings, as well as the swimming pool with

NAMIBIA DAMARALAND

its incongruous desert waterfall. The lodge boasts stylish rooms, an immense and airy elevated dining room, and a good variety of excursions throughout Damaraland. It's very close to Twyfelfontein and the rock art, fairly well signposted and easy to find.

Mowani Mountain Camp LODGE $$$
(☑232009; www.mowani.com; r per person with full board from N$2700; @☎) There's little to prepare you for this beautiful lodge – its domed buildings seem to disappear into the landscape and you don't see it until you're there. The main buildings all enjoy an ingenious natural air-conditioning system, and the accommodation nestles out of sight amid the boulders. The mountain camp is located 5km north of the Twyfelfontein turn-off from the D2612.

ⓘ Getting There & Away

There's no public transport in the area and little traffic. Turn off the C39, 73km west of Khorixas, turn south on the D3254 and continue 15km to a right turning signposted Twyfelfontein. It's 5km to the petroglyph site.

KAMANJAB
☑ 067

Flanked by lovely low rock formations, tiny Kamanjab functions as a minor service centre for northern Damaraland, and serves as an appealing stopover en route between Damaraland and Kaokoveld. Kamanjab's scenic hinterland also supports a pair of wonderful lodges that are in the business of protecting Namibia's population of feline predators.

🛏 Sleeping & Eating

Otjitotongwe Cheetah Lodge LODGE $$$
(☑687056; s/d with full board N$990/1830; ☎) Otjitotongwe is run by cheetah aficionados Tollie and Roeleen Nel, who keep tame cheetahs around their home and have set up a 40-hectare enclosure for wilder specimens, which they feed every afternoon. The project started when the Nels trapped several wild cheetahs that were poaching their livestock, in the hopes of releasing them in Etosha National Park. After learning that the government was opposed to the idea, they released the animals into the wild, though they kept a litter of cubs born in captivity. Since then, the Nels have taken in a number of recovered cheetahs and operate the wildlife farm in the hope of increasing awareness of the plight of these endangered predators. Otjito-

tongwe is located 24km south of Kamanjab on the C40.

Kavita Lion Lodge LODGE $$$
(☑687107; www.kavitalion.com; s/d incl breakfast from N$900/1400; ☎) This lodge is situated on the borders of Etosha National Park, and is the home of the Afri-Cat Foundation. This nonprofit organisation works to ensure the long-term survival of lions in Namibia. In addition to advocacy, the owners also take care of injured and unruly lions. Apart from guided walks and drives through their private reserve, the favoured activity here is the Africat Project (N$220) which involves an early-morning introduction to the works of the foundation, and lion viewing from a hide. Accommodation at Kavita is in attractive thatched chalets that surround the main lodge. The standard of hospitality is very high, rooms have lots of personal touches to make you feel welcome and the food is excellent, especially local game meats such as oryx. Be warned though, it's a favourite with German groups, which can make it a little cliquey, and meals are at a communal table with the owners. Kavita is located 36km north of Kamanjab on the C35.

Oase Guest House GUESTHOUSE $$
(☑330286; s/d N$420/600; ☎) This delightful guesthouse is located in the heart of Kamanjab, and features warm and cosy rooms. The bar-restaurant is the centre of nightlife in town. Even if you're not staying here, it's worth stopping by for a cold beer and a fresh cut of kudu or gemsboks. The owners also arrange tours to a nearby Himba village as well as local rock-art galleries.

ⓘ Getting There & Away

The good road north to Ruacana is open to 2WD vehicles, though you need to exercise caution once you cross the Red Line. Just north of Etosha, this veterinary cordon fence marks the boundary between commercial ranching and subsistence herding.

PALMWAG

Palmwag is a rich wildlife area amid stark red hills and plains, surrounded by a bizarre landscape of uniformly sized stones. The area is home to a handful of luxury lodges, and also serves as a study centre for the Save the Rhino Trust (SRT).

🛏 Sleeping

The majority of lodges must be prebooked. Rates usually include all meals and activities. Transfers by 4WD and air charters are available through the operator.

Grootberg Lodge   LODGE $$$

(067-333 212; www.grootberg.com; s/d with half board N$1450/2150) An extraordinary location with the best views we witnessed on this research trip of Namibia, this is one of the best places in the area to do black rhino tracking (N$1200) – yes, you get to drive down into that valley! It is a genuinely wild, open space – there are no fences. The rhino are elusive, however, and much of the tracking is spent in the vehicle, or on foot either following the trackers or waiting around for them to get a new lead. But the prize is a chance to see one of Africa's most endangered animals in the wild. Other animals you may see are desert elephants, mountain cheetahs, lions, antelopes such as steenboks, klipspringers, springboks and gemsboks, as well as zebras. It's located 25km east of Palmwag and 90km west of Kamanjab – take the C40.

Palmwag Lodge   LODGE $$$

(061-225178; www.wilderness-safaris.com; s/d with full board from N$1720/2540; ⛱) The oldest accommodation in the Palmwag area, nowadays run by Wilderness Safaris, is situated on a private concession adjacent to the Uniab River. The property contains several excellent hiking routes, and the human watering hole (swimming pool) has a front-row view of its palm-fringed elephantine counterpart – even black rhinos drop by occasionally.

Etendeka Mountain Camp   TENTED CAMP $$$

(061-239199; www.etendeka-namibia.com; r per person from N$2000; ⛱) The focus of Etendeka, an ecofriendly tented camp set beneath the foothills of the Grootberg Mountains, is on conservation, not luxury. Guests usually check out with an in-depth understanding of the Damaraland environment.

Damaraland Camp   TENTED CAMP $$$

(061-225178; www.wilderness-safaris.com; s/d with full board from N$3680/4540; ⛱) This solar-powered desert outpost has distant views of stark, truncated hills and is an oasis of luxury amid a truly feral and outlandish setting. When you're not living out your end-of-the-world fantasies in your luxury tent, you can do a few laps in the novel pool that occupies a rocky gorge formed by past lava flows.

ℹ Getting There & Away

Palmwag is situated on the D3706, 157km from Khorixas and 105km from Sesfontein. Coming from the south, you'll cross the Red Line, 1km south of Palmwag Lodge.

SESFONTEIN

Damaraland's most northerly outpost is almost entirely encircled by the Kaokoveld, and is somewhat reminiscent of a remote oasis in the middle of the Sahara. Fed by six springs (hence its name), the town was established as a military outpost in 1896 following a rinderpest outbreak. A barracks was added in 1901, and four years later a fort was constructed to control cattle disease, arms smuggling and poaching. This arrangement lasted until 1909, when the fort appeared to be redundant and was requisitioned by the police, who used it until the outbreak of WWI. In 1987 the fort was restored by the Damara Administration (regional government) and converted into a comfortable lodge, which is now one of the most unusual accommodation options in the whole of Namibia.

For adventurers who dream of uncharted territory, the spectacular and little-known **Otjitaimo Canyon** lurks about 10km north of the main road, along the western flanks of the north–south mountain range east of Sesfontein. To get here would involve a major expedition on foot, but if you're up for it, pick up the topographic sheets from the Office of the Surveyor General in Windhoek, pack lots of water (at least 4L per person per day), and expect unimaginable scenery and solitude.

Ever fancy spending the night in a colonial fort out in the middle of the desert? At **Fort Sesfontein** (065-685034; www.fort-sesfontein.com; r per person N$950; ⛱) you and 43 other guests can live out all your Lawrence of Arabia fantasies. Accommodation is basic but incredibly atmospheric, and there's a good restaurant that serves German-inspired (what a surprise!) dishes.

The road between Palmwag and Sesfontein is good gravel, and you'll only have problems if the Hoanib River is flowing. Unless it has been raining, the gravel road from Sesfontein to Opuwo is accessible to all vehicles.

The Kaokoveld

Often described as one of the last true wildernesses in Southern Africa, the Kaokoveld is largely devoid of roads and is crossed only by sandy tracks laid down by the SADF decades ago. In this harsh wilderness of arid conditions, wildlife has been forced to adapt in miraculous ways – consider the critically endangered desert elephant, which has especially spindly legs suited for long walks in search of precious water. Beyond wildlife, the Kaokoveld is also home to the Himba, a group of nomadic pastoralists who are famous for covering their skin with a traditional mixture of ochre butter and herbs to protect themselves from the sun.

OPUWO
☑ 065

In the Herero language, Opuwo means 'the end', which is certainly a fitting name for this dusty collection of concrete commercial buildings ringed by traditional *rondavels* and huts. While first impressions are unlikely to be very positive, a visit to Opuwo is one of the cultural highlights of Namibia, particularly for anyone interested in interacting with the Himba people. As the unofficial capital of Himbaland, Opuwo serves as a convenient jumping-off point for excursions into the nearby villages, and there is a good assortment of lodges and campsites in the area to choose from.

◉ Sights & Activities
Tourism is booming in Himbaland, as evidenced by the sealing of the road all the way up to Opuwo (but not to the border with Angola!), and the inauguration of the Opuwo Country Hotel by the Namibian president himself. Ever-so-photogenic shots of Himba women appear on just about every Namibian tourism brochure, and busloads of tourists can be seen whizzing through Opuwo's dusty streets virtually every day.

Throughout Opuwo you will see Himba wherever you go – they will be walking the streets, shopping in the stores and even waiting in line behind you at the supermarket. However tempting it might be, please do not sneak a quick picture of them, as no one appreciates having a camera waved in front of their face.

🛏 Sleeping & Eating
For self-caterers, there's an **OK Grocer** in town.

Ohakane Lodge   LODGE $$
(☑273031; s/d N$520/900; ❀☀) This well-established and centrally located lodge sits along the main drag in Opuwo and does good business with tour groups. Fairly standard but fully modern rooms are comfortable enough, but if it's in your budget, it's worth shelling out a bit more for a bungalow at the Opuwo Country Hotel.

Opuwo Country Hotel   HOTEL $$$
(☑061-374750; www.namibialodges.com/opuwo_en .htm; campsite per person N$100, s/d from N$920/1320; ❀@☀) Far and away the area's swankiest accommodation option, the hilltop Opuwo Country Hotel is an enormous thatched building (reportedly the largest in Namibia) that elegantly lords it over the town below. The hotel faces across a valley towards the Angolan foothills, and most of your time here will be spent soaking your cares away in the infinity-edge pool. If the standard rooms are taken and you can't afford a luxury version, consider pitching a tent in the secluded campsite, which grants you complete access to the hotel's amenities, including a fully stocked wine bar and a regal dining hall. The turn-off leading up to the

---

EXPLORING THE KAOKOVELD

Even if you're undaunted by extreme 4WD exploration, you still must make careful preparations for any trip off the Sesfontein–Opuwo and the Ruacana–Opuwo–Epupa Falls routes. To summarise, you will need a robust 4WD vehicle, plenty of time and enough supplies to see you through the journey. It's also useful to take a guide who knows the region, and to travel in a convoy of at least two vehicles.

Poor conditions on some tracks may limit your progress to 5km/h but, after rains, streams and mud can stop a vehicle in its tracks. Allow a full day to travel between Opuwo and Epupa Falls, and several days each way from Opuwo to Hartmann's Valley and Otjinjange (Marienflüss) Valley. Note that Van Zyl's Pass may be crossed only from east to west. Alternative access is through the Rooidrum road junction north of Orupembe (via Otjihaa Pass).

Camping in the Kaokoveld requires awareness of the environment and people.

THE HIMBA, ETIQUETTE & TAKING PICS

In the past, rural Himba people were willing models for photography. These days, however, you are likely to encounter traditionally dressed Himba people who will wave you down and ask for tips in exchange for having their photograph taken. Naturally, whether you accept is up to you, but bear in mind that encouraging this trade works to draw people away from their traditional lifestyle, and propels them towards a cash economy that undermines longstanding values and community cooperation.

It's recommended that instead you trade basic commodities for photographs. In times of plenty, Himba grow maize to supplement their largely meat- and milk-based diet, though rain is highly unpredictable in Namibia. *Pap* (corn meal) is a very desirable gift for the Himba, as are rice, bread, potatoes and other starches. Try to resist giving sugar, soft drinks and other sweets, as the majority of Himba may never meet a dentist in their lifetime.

If you would like to have free rein with the camera, visiting a traditional village – if done in the proper fashion – can yield some truly amazing shots. Needless to say, a guide who speaks both English and the Himba language is essential to the experience. You can either join an organised tour through your accommodation, or stop by the Kaoko Information Centre in Opuwo.

Before arriving in the village, please do spend some time shopping for gifts – entering a village with food items will garner a warm welcome from the villagers, who will subsequently be more willing to tolerate photography. At the end of your time in the village, buying small bracelets and trinkets directly from the artisan is also a greatly appreciated gesture.

NAMIBIA THE KAOKOVELD

hotel is a bit tricky to find, but there are signs posted throughout the town.

🛍 Shopping

Kunene Craft Centre   CRAFT
(⊘8am-5pm Mon-Fri, 9am-1pm Sat) Opuwo's brightly painted self-help curio shop sells local arts and crafts on consignment. You'll find all sorts of Himba adornments smeared with ochre: conch-shell pendants, wrist bands, chest pieces and even the headdresses worn by Himba brides. There's also a range of original jewellery, appliquéd pillowslips, Himba and Herero dolls, drums and wooden carvings.

ℹ Information

Kaoko Information Centre (✆273420; ⊘8am-6pm) KK and Kemuu, the friendly guys at this information centre (look for the tiny, tiny yellow shack), can arrange visits to local Himba villages in addition to providing useful information for your trip through the Kaokoveld region.

ℹ Getting There & Away

The paved C41 runs from Outjo to Opuwo, which makes Himbaland accessible even to 2WD vehicles. Although there is a temptation to speed along this long and lonely highway, keep your lead foot off the pedal north of the veterinary control fence, as herds of cattle commonly stray across the road. If you're heading deeper into

the Kaokoveld, be advised that Opuwo is the last opportunity to buy petrol before Kamanjab, Ruacana or Sesfontein.

SWARTBOOI'S DRIFT
⊿ 065

From Ruacana, a rough track heads west along the Kunene to Swartbooi's Drift, where a monument commemorates the Dorsland trekkers who passed en route to their future homesteads in Angola. The town is a good place to break up the drive to Epupa Falls, and it's also a good base to go white-water rafting on the Kunene River.

The very friendly **Kunene River Lodge** (✆274300; www.kuneneriverlodge.com; campsite per person N$105, s/d chalets N$720/1440, r N$790/1420; ⊛), approximately 5km east of Swartbooi's Drift, makes an idyllic riverside stop. Campsites are sheltered beneath towering trees, and the rooms and thatched chalets enjoy a pleasant garden setting. Guests can hire canoes, mountain bikes and fishing rods, as well as go on birdwatching excursions and booze cruises. With a minimum of two participants, the lodge also operates half-day, full-day and multiday white-water rafting trips, starting at N$420 per person, from the class IV Ondarusu rapids (upstream from Swartbooi's Drift) to Epupa Falls.

At Otjikeze/Epembe, 73km northwest of Opuwo, an eastward turning onto the D3701 leads 60km to Swartbooi's Drift. This is the easiest access route, and it's open to 2WD vehicles. The river road from Ruacana is extremely rough, but in dry conditions it can be negotiated by high-clearance 2WD vehicles. On the other hand, the 93km river road to Epupa Falls – along the lovely 'Namibian riviera' – is extremely challenging even with a 4WD and can take several days.

EPUPA FALLS

At Epupa, which means 'falling waters' in Herero, the Kunene River fans out into a vast flood plain and is ushered through a 500m-wide series of parallel channels, dropping a total of 60m over 1.5km. The greatest single drop, an estimated 37m, is commonly identified as the Epupa Falls. Here the river tumbles into a dark, narrow, rainbow-wrapped cleft, which is a spectacular sight to behold, particularly when the Kunene is in peak flow from April to May.

Although you'd think this remote corner of the Kaokoveld would be off the tourist trail, Epupa Falls is a popular stopover for overland trucks and organised safaris, and unfortunately can get swamped with tourists. But if you're passing through the area, a dip in the falls is certainly worth the detour, and the sight of so much water in the middle of the dry Kaokoveld is miraculous to say the least.

◉ Sights & Activities

During periods of low water, the **pools** above the Epupa Falls make fabulous natural jacuzzis. You're safe from crocodiles in the eddies and rapids, but hang onto the rocks and keep away from the lip of the falls; once you're caught by the current, there's no way to prevent being swept over. Every couple of years some unfortunate locals and foreign tourists drown in the river, and it's difficult at best to retrieve their bodies. Swimming here is most definitely not suitable for children.

There's also excellent **hiking** along the river west of the falls, and plenty of mountains to climb, affording panoramic views along the river and far into Angola. Keen hikers can manage the route along the 'Namibian riviera' from Swartbooi's Drift to Epupa Falls (93km, five days) or from Ruacana to Epupa Falls (150km, eight days). You're never far from water, but there are lots of crocodiles and, even in winter, the heat can be oppressive and draining. It's wise to plan your trip

around a full moon, when you can beat the heat by walking at night.

As with most adventure activities in Kaokoveld, you need to be self-sufficient, as there is no support network here to help you in the event of trouble. Carry extra supplies, especially since you may have to wait for lifts back. And, whenever possible, always advise someone of your intended route and itinerary before striking out into the deep bush.

⌷ Sleeping

Omarunga Lodge LODGE $$$
(☐064-403096;www.natron.net/omarunga-camp/main.html; campsite per person N$100, s/d chalets with full board N$1600/2200) This German-run camp operates through a concession granted by a local chief, and has a well-groomed campsite with modern facilities as well as a dozen luxury chalets. It's a very attractive spot, but it can't hold a candle to the slightly more upmarket Epupa Camp.

Epupa Camp LODGE $$$
(☐061-232740; www.epupa.com.na; per person with full board NS$1260; ▨) Located 800m upstream from the falls, this former engineering camp for a now-shelved hydroelectric project has been converted into beautifully situated accommodation among a grove of towering baobab trees. There are nine luxury tents filled to the brim with curios, and a slew of activities is on offer, including Himba visits, sundowner hikes, birdwatching walks and trips to rock-art sites. Five campsites are also available.

⊙ Getting There & Away

The road from Okongwati is accessible to high-clearance 2WD vehicles, but it's still quite rough. As the rugged 93km 4WD river route from Swartbooi's Drift may take several days, it's far quicker to make the trip via Otjiveze/Epembe.

THE NORTHWEST CORNER

West of Epupa Falls is the Kaokoveld of travellers' dreams: stark, rugged desert peaks, vast landscapes, sparse, scrubby vegetation, drought-resistant wildlife, and nomadic bands of Himba people and their tiny settlements of beehive huts. This region, which is contiguous with the Skeleton Coast Wilderness, has been designated the Kaokoveld Conservation Area.

◉ Sights

Van Zyl's Pass NATURAL SITE
The beautiful but frightfully steep and challenging Van Zyl's Pass forms a dramatic

transition between the Kaokoveld plateaus and the vast, grassy expanses of Otjinjange Valley (Marienflüss). This winding 13km stretch isn't suitable for trailers and may only be passed from east to west, which means you'll have to return via Otjihaa Pass or through Purros.

Otjinjange & Hartmann's Valleys
NATURAL SITE

Allow plenty of time to explore the wild and magical Otjinjange (better known as Marienflüss) and Hartmann's Valleys – broad sandy and grassy expanses descending gently to the Kunene River. Note that camping outside campsites is prohibited in both valleys.

🛏 Sleeping

Except for in Otjinjange (Marienflüss) and Hartmann's Valleys, unofficial bush camping is possible throughout the northwest corner.

Okarohombo Camp Site   CAMPGROUND $

(campsite per person N$60) This community-run campsite is located at the mouth of the Otjinjange Valley. Facilities include flushable toilets, showers and a communal kitchen.

Purros Camp Site   CAMPGROUND $

(campsite per person N$50; 🐾) A community-run campsite, Purros, also known as Ngatutunge Pamwe, is located beside the Hoarusib River, 2km from Purros village. It has hot showers, flush toilets and a bar, and is a good spot for hiring guides to visit nearby Himba villages or observing desert-adapted wildlife.

Elephant Song Camp   CAMPGROUND $

(☑064-403829; campsite per person N$80) Community-run Elephant Song is located in the Palmwag Concession, a very rough 25km down the Hoanib River from Sesfontein. This camp caters to outdoorsy types, with great views, hiking, birdwatching and the chance to see rare desert elephants.

❶ Getting There & Away

From Okongwati, the westward route through Etengwa leads to either Van Zyl's Pass or Otjihaa Pass. From Okauwa (with a landmark broken windmill) to the road fork at Otjitanda (which is a Himba chief's *kraal*), the journey is extremely rough and slow going – along the way, stop for a swim at beautiful Ovivero Dam. From Otjitanda, you must decide whether you're heading west over Van Zyl's Pass (which may only be traversed from east to west!) into Otjinjange (Marienflüss) and Hartmann's Valleys, or south over the equally beautiful but much easier Otjihaa Pass towards Orupembe.

You can also access Otjinjange (Marienflüss) and Hartmann's Valleys without crossing Van Zyl's Pass by turning north at the three-way junction in the middle of the Onjuva Plains, 12km north of Orupembe. At the T-junction in Rooidrum (Red Drum), you can decide which valley you want. Turn right for Otjinjange (Marienflüss) and left for Hartmann's. West of this junction, 17km from Rooidrum, you can also turn south along the fairly good route to Orupembe, Purros (provided that the Hoarusib River isn't flowing) and on to Sesfontein.

Alternatively, you can head west from Opuwo on the D3703, which leads 105km to Etanga; 19km beyond Etanga, you'll reach a road junction marked by a stone sign painted with white birds. At this point, you can turn north toward Otjitanda (27km away) or south towards Otjihaa Pass and Orupembe.

The Skeleton Coast

This treacherous coast – a foggy region with rocky and sandy coastal shallows – has long been a graveyard for unwary ships and their crews, hence its forbidding name. Early Portuguese sailors called it *As Areias do Inferno* (The Sands of Hell), as once a ship washed ashore, the fate of the crew was sealed. This protected area stretches from Sandwich Harbour, south of Swakopmund, to the Kunene River, taking in around 2 million hectares of dunes and gravel plains to form one of the world's most inhospitable waterless areas.

DOROB NATIONAL PARK

The recently (December 2010) declared Dorob National Park consumes the old 'National West Coast Tourist Recreation Area', and broadens out, especially to the south, beyond the borders of the old recreation area. Dorob extends beyond the Swakop River and down to Sandwich Harbour in the south, while its northern border is the Ugab River.

The area focused on in this section is a 200km-long and 25km-wide strip that extends from Swakopmund to the Ugab River. The area is extremely popular with South African fishermen, who flock here to tackle such saltwater species as galjoen, steenbra, kabeljou and blacktail. In fact, between Swakopmund and the Ugab River are hundreds of concrete buildings, spaced at intervals of about 200m. Although these appear to be coastal bunkers guarding against

NAMIBIA THE SKELETON COAST

an offshore attack, they are actually toilet blocks for fishermen and campers.

Entry fees and a whole stack of regulations are supposed to apply to Dorob National Park, but information on this is confusing. At the time of research no fees were payable for ducking in and out of the park. Don't assume that this is still the case though; check with the nearest tourist office or NWR before you head into the park.

HENTIES BAY
☑ 064

At Henties Bay, 80km north of Swakopmund, the relatively reliable Omaruru River issues into the Atlantic (don't miss the novel golf course in the riverbed!). It was named for Hentie van der Merwe, who visited its spring in 1929. Today it consists mainly of holiday homes and refuelling and provisioning businesses for anglers headed up the coast.

The **tourist information office** (☑501143; www.hentiesbaytourism.com; Nickey Iyambo Rd; ☺8am-1pm & 2-5pm Mon-Fri) is an excellent resource. This recently established office is very helpful for info on the area and also sells artwork and crafts. The coffeehouse here is recommended as well.

Buck's Camping Lodge (☑501039; Nickey Iyambo Rd; campsites N$230), near the police station in town, is expensive but for the extra dollars you get a campsite with your own private bathroom. Look for the caravan sign just off the road

The **De Duine Country Hotel** (☑081 124 1181; www.deduinehotel.com; s/d N$400/600; ❊❃), the most established hotel in Henties Bay, sits on the coast, though not a single room has a sea view – go figure! The German colonial-style property does feature rooms with swimming-pool and garden views, though.

The C34 salt road, which begins in Swakopmund and ends 70km north of Terrace Bay, provides access to Dorob National Park and the southern half of the Skeleton Coast Park. The park is also accessible via the C39 gravel road that links Khorixas with Torra Bay. Henties Bay lies at the junction of the coastal salt road and the C35, which turns inland towards Damaraland.

Note that motorcycles are not permitted in Skeleton Coast Park. No permits are required to transit the area, and the salt road from Swakopmund is passable year-round with a 2WD.

CAPE CROSS SEAL RESERVE

The best-known breeding colony of Cape fur seals along the Namib coast is this **reserve** (per person/car N$40/10; ☺10am-5pm), where the population has grown large and fat by taking advantage of the rich concentrations of fish in the cold Benguela current. The sight of more than 100,000 seals basking on the beach and frolicking in the surf is impressive to behold, though you're going to have to contend with the overwhelming odoriferousness of piles and piles of stinky seal poo. Bring a handkerchief or bandana to cover your nose – seriously, you'll thank us for the recommendation.

No pets or motorcycles are permitted, and visitors may not cross the low barrier between the seal-viewing area and the rocks where the colony lounges.

Although it's primarily known for the seals, Cape Cross has a long and illustrious history. In 1485 Portuguese explorer Diego Cão, the first European to set foot in Namibia, planted a 2m-high, 360kg *padrão* (a stone cross in tribute to Portuguese king João II) at Cape Cross.

In 1893 however, a German sailor, Captain Becker of the *Falke,* removed the cross and hauled it off to Germany. The following year, Kaiser Wilhelm II ordered that a replica be made with the original inscriptions in Latin and Portuguese, as well as a commemorative inscription in German. This cross remains at the site, in addition to a second cross, made of dolerite, which was erected in 1980 on the site of Cão's original cross.

There are **campsites** (per person N$100) here on the water's edge, which appear well set up a bit away from the stink, but were closed when we called through and it was unclear when they would reopen.

Cape Cross Lodge (☑064-694012; www.capecross.org; campsites N$380, s/d N$1300/1950; ❊@) has an odd but strangely appealing architecture, which is self-described as a cross between Cape Dutch and fishing-village style. The nicer rooms have spacious outdoor patios that overlook the coastline, though you really can't choose a bad room at this all-around stunner of a lodge, conveniently located just before the official reserve entrance. It's a superb, isolated spot right on a sweeping bend of the bay overlooking blue seas and rollers lolling in and crashing over white sand beaches. The restaurant (mains N$70 to N$100) dishes out plenty of seafood

CAPE FUR SEALS

There are seven seal species in Southern African waters but, except for very occasional vagrants from the Antarctic and sub-Antarctic islands, the only mainland species is the Cape fur seal. Communal to the extreme, this massive population is divided between only about 25 colonies; a few of them, such as Cape Cross on Namibia's western coast, number more than 100,000.

Despite their gregariousness, Cape fur seals are not especially sociable; colony living makes sense for breeding opportunities, and to reduce the chance of predators sneaking up, but individual seals are essentially loners on land, and they constantly quarrel over their own little patch. Except for pups playing with each other in crèche-like 'playgrounds', virtually every interaction in the colony is hostile, creating extraordinary opportunities for watching behaviour.

Cape fur seals have a thick layer of short fur beneath the coarser guard hairs, which remain dry and trap air for insulation. This enables the animals to maintain an internal body temperature of 37°C and spend long periods in cold waters.

Male Cape fur seals weigh less than 200kg on average, but during the breeding season they take on a particularly thick accumulation of blubber and balloon out to more than 360kg. Females are much smaller, averaging 75kg, and give birth to a single, blue-eyed pup during late November or early December. About 90% of the colony's pups are born within just over a month.

Pups begin to suckle less than an hour after birth but are soon left in communal nurseries while their mothers leave to forage for food. When the mothers return to the colony, they identify their own pup by a combination of scent and call.

The pups moult at the age of four to five months, turning from a dark grey to olive brown. Mortality rates in the colony are high, and up to a quarter of the pups fail to survive their first year, with the bulk of deaths occurring during the first week after birth. The main predators are the brown hyena and the black-backed jackal, which account for 25% of pup deaths. Those pups that do survive may remain with their mothers for up to a year.

Cape fur seals eat about 8% of their body weight each day, and the colonies along the western coast of Southern Africa annually consume more than 1 million tonnes of fish and other marine life (mainly shoaling fish and squid). That's about 300,000 tonnes more than is taken by the fishing industries of Namibia and South Africa put together!

NAMIBIA THE SKELETON COAST

including a fish sandwich (with admittedly weird mayo) and a seafood platter for N$195.

Cape Cross is located 46km north of Henties Bay along the coastal salt road.

SKELETON COAST PARK

At Ugabmund, 110km north of Cape Cross, the salt road passes through the entry gate to the Skeleton Coast Park, where rolling fogs and dusty sandstorms encapsulate its eerie, remote and wild feel. Despite the enduring fame of this coastline, surprisingly few travellers ever reach points north of Cape Cross. In order to preserve this incredibly fragile environment, Namibian Wildlife Resorts (NWR) imposes very strict regulations on individual travellers seeking to enter the park.

Although this can be a deterrent for some, permits are easily obtainable if you do some planning. And, while you may have to sacrifice a bit of spontaneity to gain admittance to the park, the enigmatic Skeleton Coast really does live up to all the hype.

The zone south of the Hoanib River is open to individual travellers, but you need a permit, which costs N$80 per person and N$10 per vehicle per day. These are available through the NWR office in Windhoek. Accommodation is available only at Terrace Bay and Torra Bay (the latter is open only in December and January), either of which must be booked at NWR concurrently with your permit. To stay in either camp, you must pass the Ugabmund entrance before 3pm and/or Springbokwater before 5pm.

No day visits to the park are allowed, but you can obtain a transit permit to pass between Ugabmund and Springbokwater, which can be purchased at the gates. To transit the park, you must pass the entry

SKELETONS ON THE COAST

Despite prominent images of rusting ships embedded in the hostile sands of the Skeleton Coast, the most famous shipwrecks have long since disappeared. The harsh winds and dense fog that roll off the South Atlantic are strong forces of erosion, and today there are little more than traces of the countless ships that were swept ashore during the height of the mercantile era. In addition, the few remaining vessels are often in remote and inaccessible locations.

One such example is the *Dunedin Star*, which was deliberately run aground in 1942 just south of the Angolan border after hitting some offshore rocks. The ship was en route from Britain around the Cape of Good Hope to the Middle East war zone, and was carrying more than 100 passengers, a military crew and cargo.

When a rescue ship arrived two days later, getting the castaways off the beach proved an impossible task. At first, the rescuers attempted to haul the castaways onto their vessel by using a line through the surf. However, as the surge grew stronger, the rescue vessel was swept onto the rocks and wrecked alongside the *Dunedin Star*. Meanwhile, a rescue aircraft, which managed to land on the beach alongside the castaways, became bogged in the sand. Eventually all the passengers were rescued, though they were evacuated with the help of an overland truck convoy. The journey back to civilisation was two weeks of hard slog across 1000km of desert.

Further south on the Skeleton Coast – and nearly as difficult to reach – are several more intact wrecks. The *Eduard Bohlen* ran aground south of Walvis Bay in 1909 while carrying equipment to the diamond fields in the far south. Over the past century the shoreline has changed so much that the ship now lies beached in a dune nearly 1km from the shore.

On picturesque Spencer Bay, 200km further south and just north of the abandoned mining town of Saddle Hill, is the dramatic wreck of the *Otavi*. This cargo ship beached in 1945 following a strong storm, and is now dramatically perched on Dolphin's Head, the highest point on the coast between Cape Town's Table Mountain and the Angolan border. Spencer Bay also claimed the Korean cargo ship *Tong Taw* in 1972, which is currently one of the most intact vessels along the entirety of the Skeleton Coast.

gate before 1pm and exit through the other gate before 3pm the same day. Note that transit permits aren't valid for Torra Bay or Terrace Bay.

🏃 Activities

Ugab River Guided Hiking Route HIKING
The 50km-long route is open to groups of between six and eight people on the second and fourth Thursday of each month from April to October. Hikes start at 9am from Ugabmund and finish on Saturday afternoon. Most hikers stay Wednesday night at the Mile 108 Camp Site, 40km south of Ugabmund, which allows you to arrive at Ugabmund in time for the hike. The hike must be booked through NWR; hikers must provide and carry their own food and camping equipment. The route begins by crossing the coastal plain, then climbs into the hills and follows a double loop through lichen fields and past caves, natural springs and unusual geological formations.

🛏 Sleeping

All accommodation (with the exception of the Ugab River Camp Site) must be pre-booked through NWR.

Ugab River Camp Site CAMPGROUND $
(www.rhino-trust.org.na; campsite per person N$60) Outside the Skeleton Coast Park, this campsite is administered by the Save the Rhino Trust. This remote landscape is truly enigmatic, and those who've visited have only glowing comments. To get there, turn east onto the D2303, 40km north of Cape Cross; it's then 70km to the camp.

Torra Bay Camping Ground CAMPGROUND $
(campsite per person N$125; ☉Dec & Jan) This campsite, which is open to coincide with the Namibian school holidays, is flanked by a textbook field of barchan dunes. These dunes are actually the southernmost extension of a vast sand sea that stretches all the way to the Curoca River in Angola. Petrol, water, firewood and basic supplies are avail-

able, and campers may use the restaurant at Terrace Bay Resort. Torra Bay is located 215km north of Cape Cross.

Terrace Bay Resort   CHALETS $$$
(campsite per person N$125, s/d N$800/1600, 4–10-person beach chalets per person N$700) Open year-round, this resort is a luxurious alternative to camping at Torra Bay. Around the camp you may spot black-backed jackals or brown hyenas, and the scenery of sparse coastal vegetation and lonely dunes is the Skeleton Coast at its finest. The site has a restaurant, a shop and a petrol station. Terrace Bay is located 49km north of Torra Bay.

❶ Getting There & Away
The Skeleton Coast Park is accessed via the salt road from Swakopmund, which ends 70km north of Terrace Bay. The park is also accessible via the C39 gravel road which runs between Khorixas and Torra Bay. Note that motorcycles are not permitted in the Skeleton Coast Park. Hitchhikers may be discouraged by the bleak landscape, cold sea winds, fog, sandstorms and sparse traffic.

SKELETON COAST WILDERNESS AREA
The Skeleton Coast Wilderness Area, stretching between the Hoanib and Kunene Rivers, makes up the northern third of the Skeleton Coast and is a part of the Skeleton Coast Park. This section of coastline is among the most remote and inaccessible areas in Namibia, though it's here in the wilderness that you can truly live out your Skeleton Coast fantasies. Since the entire area is a private concession, you're going to have to part with some serious cash to visit. Up until late 2012, the sole accommodation here was at the Skeleton Coast Wilderness Camp, which was accessible only by charter flight. That camp was closed after being gutted by a fire, but it's rumoured that a new luxury operation, the Hoanib Skeleton Coast Camp, will open for business in the region in early to mid-2013.

History
In the early 1960s, Windhoek lawyer Louw Schoemann began bringing business clients to the region, and became involved in a consortium to construct a harbour at Möwe Bay, at the southern end of the present-day Skeleton Coast Wilderness Area. In 1969, however, the South African government dropped the project, and in 1971 it declared the region a protected reserve. Five years later, when the

government decided to permit limited tourism, the concession was put up for bid, and Schoemann's was the only tender.

For the next 18 years, his company led small group tours and practised ecotourism long before it became a buzz word. Louw Schoemann passed away in 1993, but his sons have since carried on the business.

◉ Sights & Activities
The wonders of this region defy description. For instance, the barchan dunes of the northern Skeleton Coast hold a unique distinction: they roar. If you don't believe it, sit down on a lee face, dig in your feet and slide slowly down. If you feel a jarring vibration and hear a roar akin to a four-engine cargo plane flying low, don't bother looking up – it's just the sand producing its marvellous acoustic effect. It's thought that the roar is created when air pockets between electrically charged particles are forced to the surface. The effect is especially pronounced in the warmth of the late afternoon, when spaces between the sand particles are at their greatest.

❶ Getting There & Away
The Skeleton Coast Wilderness Area is closed to private vehicles. Access is restricted to fly-in trips.

CENTRAL NAMIBIA

Central Namibia zeroes in on the tourist trade but it does so Namibian-style offering epic road journeys, big skies and mesmerising landscapes. In that sense its not unlike other parts of the country – except here it is home to two large cities and a spectacular desert.

Walvis Bay and Swakopmund were originally established as port towns during the colonial era. The drive into them defines their surreal nature as desert wildernesses, which is magically replaced by (in the case of Swakopmund) a Germanic urban landscape that would be a colonial relic if it weren't for the life and energy brought to bear by a thriving tourist industry.

Adventure sports and Swakopmund go hand in hand. From quad biking up the crest of a soaring seaside dune to jumping out of a plane at 3000m, Swakop is where you can test your limits and go wild amid a stunningly beautiful natural setting unlike any other on the planet.

The region is defined by the Namib Desert though, a barren and desolate landscape of undulating apricot-coloured dunes interspersed with dry pans. Indeed, the Nama word 'Namib', which inspired the name of the entire country, rather prosaically means 'vast dry plain'. Nowhere is this truer than at Sossusvlei, Namibia's most famous strip of sand, where gargantuan dunes tower more than 300m above the underlying strata.

Geography

The Namib Desert is one of the oldest and driest deserts in the world. As with the Atacama in northern Chile, it is the result of a cold current – in this case, the Benguela current – sweeping north from Antarctica, which captures and condenses humid air that would otherwise be blown ashore. Although travellers to Namibia and Botswana are surprised (and even a bit disappointed) by the lushness of the Kalahari, the soaring sand dunes of the Namib rarely cease to amaze. Much of the surface between Walvis Bay and Lüderitz is covered by enormous linear dunes, which roll back from the sea towards the inland gravel plains that are occasionally interrupted by isolated mountain ranges.

ⓘ Getting Around

If you don't have a private vehicle, Swakopmund is serviced by a variety of transport options, and Sossusvlei is visited on virtually every organised tour of Namibia. Like the rest of the country though, you really need your own wheels to fully appreciate the full expanse of the desert.

Sealed roads connect Windhoek to Swakopmund and continue south to Sesriem, the base town for Sossusvlei. If you have a 2WD vehicle, you can get within a couple of kilometres of Sossusvlei, though the final stretch is only accessible by 4WD (taxis are available). Otherwise, most of the region is 2WD accessible, aside from a few minor 4WD roads in and around Namib-Naukluft Park.

Swakopmund

🗘 064 / POP 45,000

From Windhoek, the Khomas Hochland mountain range stretches west to form a scenic transition zone between the high central plateau and the Namib plains. En route to Swakopmund and Walvis Bay, this scenic landform facilitates some truly pleasurable driving, though the real highlight awaits

you on the coast. Just as the road begins to flatten out, falling in line with surrounding gravel plains, deep orange dunes appear on your left, while your nose first catches the salty breeze of the ocean just ahead – welcome to Swakopmund!

It can be an eerie feeling entering Swakop, especially out of tourist season when the city, sandwiched between Atlantic rollers and the Namib Desert, feels like a surreal colonial remnant. Some find it soothing, others weird – personally we have a leg in either camp. The people of Swakopmund are a quirky mix of German-Namibian residents and overseas German tourists, who feel right at home with the town's pervasive *Gemütlichkeit,* a distinctively German appreciation of comfort and hospitality. With its seaside promenades, half-timbered homes and colonial-era buildings, it seems that only the wind-blown sand and the palm trees distinguish Swakop from holiday towns along Germany's North Sea and Baltic coasts.

One thing Swakopmund isn't is boring. It's Namibia's most popular holiday destination, and there are myriad attractions for enjoying the great climate, including surfing, fishing, lolling around on the beach and finding ways to terrify yourself – it's the adventure sports capital of Namibia.

History

Small bands of Nama people have occupied the Swakop River mouth from time immemorial, but the first permanent settlers were Germans who didn't arrive until early 1892. Because nearby Walvis Bay had been annexed by the British-controlled Cape Colony in 1878, Swakopmund remained German South West Africa's only harbour, and consequently rose to greater prominence than its poor harbour conditions would have otherwise warranted. Early passengers were landed in small dories, but after the pier was constructed they were winched over from the ships in basketlike cages.

Construction began on the first building, the Alte Kaserne (Old Barracks), in September 1892. By 1893 it housed 120 Schutztruppe soldiers, and ordinary settlers arrived soon after to put down roots. The first civilian homes were prefabricated in Germany, and then transported by ship. By 1909 Swakopmund had officially become a municipality.

The port emerged as the leading trade funnel for all of German South West Africa and attracted government agencies and transport companies. During WWI however, South West Africa was taken over by South Africa, and the harbour was allowed to silt up as maritime operations moved to nearby Walvis Bay. Strangely enough, this ultimately turned Swakopmund into a holiday resort, which is why the city is generally more pleasant on the eye than the industrial-looking Walvis Bay.

◉ Sights

Swakopmund brims with numerous historic examples of traditional German architecture. For further information on the town's colonial sites, pick up *Swakopmund – A Chronicle of the Town's People, Places and Progress,* which is sold at Swakopmund Museum and in local bookshops.

Woermannhaus   HISTORIC BUILDING
(Bismarck St) From the shore, the delightful German-style Woermannhaus stands out above surrounding buildings. Built in 1905 as the main offices of the Damara & Namaqua Trading Company, it was taken over four years later by the Woermann & Brock Trading Company, which supplied the current name. In the 1920s it was used as a school dormitory and later served as a merchant sailors' hostel. It eventually fell into disrepair, but was declared a national monument and restored in 1976.

Kaiserliches Bezirksgericht
(State House)   HISTORIC BUILDING
(Daniel Tjongarero St) This rather stately building was constructed in 1902 to serve as the district magistrates' court. It was extended in 1905, and again in 1945 when a tower was added. After WWI it was converted into the official holiday home of the territorial administrator. In keeping with that tradition, it's now the official Swakopmund residence of the president.

Marine Memorial   MONUMENT
(Daniel Tjongarero St) Often known by its German name, Marine Denkmal, this memorial was commissioned in 1907 by the Marine Infantry in Kiel (Germany) and designed by sculptor AM Wolff. It commemorates the German First Marine Expedition Corps, which helped beat back the Herero uprisings of 1904. As a national historical monument, it will continue to stand, but one has to wonder how long it will be before the Herero erect a memorial of their own.

Hohenzollern Building   HISTORIC BUILDING
(Libertine St) This imposing baroque-style building was constructed in 1906 to serve as a hotel. Its rather outlandish decor is crowned by a fibreglass cast of Atlas supporting the world, which replaced the precarious cement version that graced the roof prior to renovations in 1988.

German Evangelical
Lutheran Church   CHURCH
(Daniel Tjongarero Av) This neo-baroque church was built in 1906 to accommodate the growing Lutheran congregation of Dr Heinrich Vedde – it still holds regular services.

Swakopmund Museum   MUSEUM
(☎402046; Strand St; adult/student N$20/10; ☺10am-5pm) When ill winds blow, head for this museum at the foot of the lighthouse, where you can hole up and learn about the town's history. The museum occupies the site of the old harbour warehouse, which was destroyed in 1914 by a 'lucky' shot from a British warship.

Displays include exhibits on Namibia's history and ethnology including information on local flora and fauna. Especially good is the display on the !nara melon, a fruit that was vital to the early Khoikhoi people of the Namib region.

It also harbours a reconstructed colonial home interior, Emil Kiewittand's apothecary shop and an informative display on the Rössing Mine. Military buffs will appreciate the stifling uniforms of the Camel Corps and the Shell furniture, so called because it was homemade from 1930s depression-era petrol and paraffin tins.

National Marine Aquarium   AQUARIUM
(Strand St) This waterfront aquarium provides an excellent introduction to the cold offshore world in the South Atlantic Ocean. Most impressive is the tunnel through the largest aquarium, which allows close-up views of graceful rays, toothy sharks (you can literally count all the teeth!) and other little marine beasties found on Namibia's seafood platters. The place was getting a revamp when we called through in mid-2012, so drop in to check out the admission price and opening hours.

Kristall Galerie   GALLERY
(☎406080; cnr Garnison St & Theo-Ben Gurirab Ave; admission N$20; ☺9am-5pm Mon-Sat) This architecturally astute gallery features some of the planet's most incredible crystal

Swakopmund

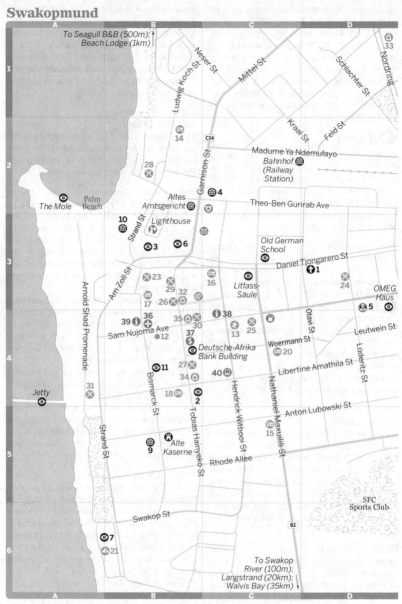

To Seagull B&B (500m);
Beach Lodge (1km)

Neser St
Mittel St
Ludwig Koch St
Schlachter St
Nordring

C34
Garrison St
Kraal St
Feld St

Madume Ya Ndemufayo
Bahnhof
(Railway
Station)

The Mole
Palm
Beach

Altes
Amtsgericht
Theo-Ben Gurirab Ave

Strand St
Lighthouse

Old German
School

Daniel Tjongarero St

Am Zoll St

Litfass-
Säule

OMEG
Haus

Arnold Shad Promenade

Sam Nujoma Ave

Deutsche-Afrika
Bank Building

Woermann St
Olavi St
Leutwein St
Libertine Amathila St
Lüderitz St

Bismarck St

Jetty

Tobias Hanyeko St

Alte
Kaserne

Hendrick Witbooi St
Anton Lubowski St
Nathaniel Maxuilili St

Rhode Allee

Strand St

Swakop St

B2

SFC
Sports Club

To Swakop
River (100m);
Langstrand (20km);
Walvis Bay (35km)

formations, including the largest quartz crystal that has ever been found. The adjacent shop sells lovely mineral samples, crystal jewellery, and intriguing plates, cups and wine glasses that are carved from the local stone.

Living Desert Snake Park ZOO
(405100; Sam Nujoma Ave; admission N$20; 8am-5pm Mon-Fri, 9am-1pm Sat) This park houses an array of serpentine sorts. The owner knows everything you'd ever want to know – or not know – about snakes, scor-

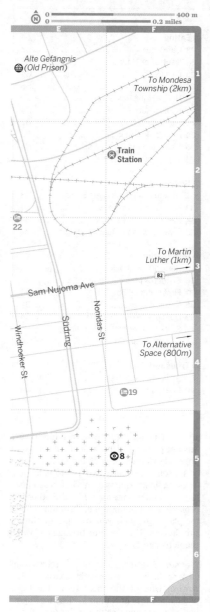

warmer than around 15°C (remember, the Benguela current sweeps upwards from Antarctica). **Swimming** in the sea is best in the lee of the Mole sea wall.

At the **lagoon** at the Swakop River mouth you can watch ducks, flamingos, pelicans, cormorants, gulls, waders and other birds. North of town you can stroll along kilometres and kilometres of deserted beaches stretching towards the Skeleton Coast. The best **surfing** is at Nordstrand (Thick Lip) near Vineta Point.

A fascinating short **hike** will take you across the Swakop River to the large dune fields south of town. The dune formations and unique vegetation are great for solo exploring.

Swakopmund is one of the top destinations in southern Africa for extreme sports enthusiasts. Although filling your days with adrenaline-soaked activities is certainly not cheap, there are few places in the world where you can climb up, race down and soar over towering sand dunes.

Most activity operators don't have offices in town, which means that you need to arrange all of your activities through either your accommodation or the Namib-i (p285) tourist information centre.

Alter Action   ADVENTURE SPORTS

(☎ 402737; www.alter-action.info; lie-down/stand-up US$40/55) Sandboarding with Alter Action is certain to increase your heart rate. If you have any experience snowboarding or surfing, it's highly recommended that you have a go at the stand-up option. You will be given a snowboard, gloves, goggles and enough polish to ensure a smooth ride. While you can't expect the same speeds as you would on the mountain, you can't beat the experience of carving a dune face, and falling on sands hurts a lot less than ice!

The lie-down option (which makes use of a greased-up sheet of masonite) requires much less finesse but is equally fun. The highlight is an 80km/h 'schuss' down a 120m mountain of sand, which finishes with a big jump at the end. Slogging up the dunes can be rather taxing work, so you need to be physically fit and healthy. Trips depart in the morning and last for approximately four hours. The price includes the equipment rental, pick-up, transport to and from the dunes, instruction, lunch and either a beer or soft drink upon completion.

pions, spiders and other widely misunderstood creatures.

🏃 **Activities**

Swakopmund is Namibia's main beach resort, but even in summer the water is never

Swakopmund

◉ Sights
1 German Evangelical Lutheran
  Church...D3
2 Hohenzollern Building...........................B4
3 Kaiserliches Bezirksgericht
  (State House)....................................B3
4 Kristall Galerie.....................................C2
5 Living Desert Snake Park......................D3
6 Marine Memorial..................................B3
7 National Marine Aquarium B6
8 Old German Cemetery..........................F5
9 Prinzessin Rupprecht Heim B5
10 Swakopmund Museum..........................B3
11 Woermannhaus......................................B4

◉ Activities, Courses & Tours
12 Charly's Desert Tours B4
13 Pleasure Flights....................................C4

◉ Sleeping
14 Brigadoon Bed & Breakfast..................B2
15 Desert Sky Backpackers........................C5
16 Hansa Hotel C3
17 Hotel Pension Rapmund.......................B3
18 Hotel-Pension d'Avignon B4
  Prinzessin Rupprecht Residenz.....(see 9)
19 Sam's Giardino Hotel F4
  Schweizerhaus Hotel ....(see 23)
20 Swakop Lodge.......................................C4
21 Tiger Reef Campsite..............................B6
22 Villa Wiese..E3

◉ Eating
23 Cafe Anton B3
24 Deutsches Haus D3
25 Fish Deli C4
26 Garden Cafe..B3
  Hansa Hotel Restaurant...............(see 16)
27 Kücki's Pub..B4
28 Lighthouse Pub & Cafe.........................B2
29 Raith's Gourmet B3
30 Swakopmund Brauhaus.........................B4
31 Tug..A4

◉ Shopping
32 Die Muschel Book & Art Shop B3
33 Karakulia Weavers D1
34 Peter's Antiques...................................B4
35 Swakopmunder Büchhandlung............B4

◉ Information
  Bank of Windhoek ....(see 37)
36 Bismarck Medical Centre......................B4
37 First National Bank...............................B4
38 Namib-i...C4
39 Namibia Wildlife Resorts Office.............B4
  Swakopmunder Buchhandlung
  Commercial Bank.........................(see 35)

◉ Transport
  Air Namibia Office ....(see 12)
40 Intercape Mainliner Bus Stop...............C4

Ground Rush Adventures   ADVENTURE SPORTS
(402841; www.skydiveswakop.com.na; tandem jump N$1950, handycam/professional video N$450/850) Ground Rush Adventures provides the ultimate rush, and skydiving in Swakopmund is sweetened by the outstanding dune and ocean backdrop. The crew at Ground Rush has an impeccable safety record to date, and they make even the most nervous participant feel comfortable about jumping out of a plane at 3000m and freefalling for 30 seconds at 220km/h. If you're having any second thoughts taking the plunge, know that your tandem master has been pulling the cord several times a day for years and years on end!

The price also includes a 25-minute scenic flight in a tiny Cessna aircraft, which provides striking views of the coastline between Swakop and Walvis Bay to the south. It is worth pointing out that the ascent can often be the scariest part, especially if you're afraid of flying (though it certainly makes the jump that much easier!). If you want physical evidence of your momentary lapse of reason, there are two photo/video options available: one is a handycam strapped to your tandem master, while the other is a professional photographer jumping out of the plane alongside you and filming the entire descent. Have a light breakfast – you'll thank us later!

Pleasure Flights   SCENIC FLIGHTS
(404500; www.pleasureflights.com.na; prices variable) One of the most reputable light-plane operators in Namibia, Pleasure Flights has been offering scenic aerial cruises for almost 20 years. Considering that so much of the South Atlantic coastline is inaccessible on the ground, taking to the skies is a wonderful way to appreciate the wild nature that typifies most of the region. Several uniquely designed routes are available for your choos-

THE MARTIN LUTHER

In the desert 4km east of Swakopmund, a lonely and forlorn steam locomotive languished for several years. The 14,000kg machine was imported to Walvis Bay, from Halberstadt in Germany, in 1896 to replace the ox wagons used to transport freight between Swakopmund and the interior. However, its inauguration into service was delayed by the outbreak of the Nama-Herero wars, and in the interim its locomotive engineer returned to Germany without having revealed the secret of its operation.

A US prospector eventually got it running, but it consumed enormous quantities of locally precious water. It took three months to complete its initial trip from Walvis Bay to Swakopmund, and subsequently survived just a couple of short trips before grinding to a halt just east of town. Clearly this particular technology wasn't making life easier for anyone, and it was abandoned and dubbed the *Martin Luther*, in reference to the great reformer's famous words to the Diet of Reichstag in 1521: 'Here I stand. May God help me, I cannot do otherwise.'

Although the *Martin Luther* was partially restored in 1975, and concurrently declared a national monument, it continued to suffer from the ravages of nature. Fortunately, in 2005 students from the Namibian Institute of Mining and Technology restored the locomotive to its former grandeur. They also built a protective encasement that should keep the *Martin Luther* around at least for another century.

NAMIBIA SWAKOPMUND

ing, which take in a range of destinations, including the Salt Works, Sandwich Harbour, Welwitschia Drive, the Brandberg Mountains, Sossusvlei, the Skeleton Coast and beyond.

Prices start at around N$850 per person for a one-hour circuit, though prices are dependent on the length of the flight and the number of passengers on board as well as the fluctuating price of aviation fuel. Generally speaking, if you can put together a large group, and you spring for the longer flight, you will get much better value for your dollars. Regardless, chartering a private plane is a privileged experience that is well worth the splurge, and there are few places in the world that can rival the beauty and grandeur of Central Namibia.

Okakambe Trails HORSE RIDING
(✆402799; www.okakambe.iway.na; prices variable) Meaning 'horse' in the local Herero and Oshivambo languages, Okakambe specialises in horse riding and trekking through the desert. The German owner cares immensely for her horses, so you can be assured that they're well fed and looked after. Prices for a one-hour solo ride along the Swakop River to the Moon Landscape start at N$460, but discounts are available for larger groups and longer outings. More experienced riders can organise multiday treks with full board, as well as moonlight outings and jaunts along the beach and through the dunes. You'll find it 12km east of Swakopmund on the D1901.

Camel Farm ADVENTURE SPORTS
(✆400363; 20min ride N$120) If you want to live out all your *Lawrence of Arabia*–inspired desert fantasies, visit the Camel Farm (on the D1901, 12km east of Swakopmund, adjacent to Okakambe Trails). After donning the necessary amount of Bedouin kitsch, you can mount your dromedary and make haste for the horizon. While camels run the gamut from uncouth to downright mean-tempered, don't underestimate their speed and grace! A camel galloping in full stride can cover an enormous distance, and their unique physiology justifiably earns them the nickname 'ships of the desert'.

☞ Tours

If you've arrived in Swakopmund by public transport, and don't have access to a private vehicle, then consider booking a tour through a recommended operator. Central Swakop is compact and easily walkable, but you need to escape the city confines if you really want to explore the area.

Prices are variable depending on the size of your party and the length of tour. As with activities in Swakop, money stretches further if you get together with a few friends and combine a few destinations to make a longer outing.

Possible tours include: the Cape Cross seal colony; Rössing Mine gem tours; Welwitschia Drive; Walvis Bay Lagoon; and various destinations in the Namib Desert and Naukluft Mountains.

TREKKOPJE MILITARY CEMETERY

In January 1915, after Swakopmund was occupied by South African forces, the Germans retreated and cut off supplies to the city by damaging the Otavi and State railway lines. However, the South Africans had already begun to replace the narrow-gauge track with a standard-gauge one, and at Trekkopje, their crew met German forces. When the Germans attacked their camp on 26 April 1915, the South Africans defended themselves with guns mounted on armoured vehicles and won easily. All fatalities of this battle are buried in the Trekkopje cemetery – 112km northeast of Swakopmund along the B2 – which is immediately north of the railway line, near the old train station.

The most popular operators are **Charly's Desert Tours** (404341; www.charlysdesert tours.com; Sam Nujoma Ave), **Namib Tours and Safaris** (406038; www.namibia-tours-safaris. com) and **Turnstone Tours** (403123; www. turnstone-tours.com). With the exception of Charly's, most operators do not have central offices, so it's best to make arrangements through your accommodation.

If you're interested in arranging a visit to the Mondesa township, **Hafeni Cultural Tours** (400731; hafenictours@gmail.com; 4hr tour N\$420) runs a variety of different excursions that provide insight into how the other half of Swakopmunders live.

Rössing Mine   GUIDED TOUR
(402046; mine tours per person N\$50) This mine, 55km east of Swakopmund, is the world's largest open-cast uranium mine. Uranium was first discovered here in the 1920s by Peter Louw, though his attempts at developing the mine quickly failed. In 1965 the concession was transferred to Rio Tinto-Zinc, and comprehensive surveys determined that the formation measured 3km long and 1km wide. Ore extraction came on line in 1970, but didn't reach capacity for another eight years.

Rössing, with 2500 employees, is currently a major player in Swakopmund's economy. The affiliated Rössing Foundation provides an educational and training centre in Arandis, northeast of the mine, as well as medical facilities and housing for its Swakopmund-based workers. It has promised that the eventual decommissioning of the site will entail a massive clean-up, but you may want to temper your enthusiasm about its environmental commitments until something is actually forthcoming.

Three-hour **mine tours** leave at 10am on the first and third Friday of each month; book at least one day in advance at the Swakopmund Museum (tours depart from here).

You can also arrange a visit through most tour companies.

🛌 Sleeping

Swakopmund has a number of budget hotels and hostels that are of a high standard, as well as family-run guesthouses and B&Bs. There are also a handful of attractive midrange and top-end hotels that are definitely worth the splurge.

Given Swakopmund's chilly climate, air-conditioning is absent at most hotels, though you won't miss it once the sea air starts blowing through your room. On the contrary, a heater is something of a requirement in the winter months when the mercury drops along the coast.

During the school holidays in December and January, accommodation books up well in advance – make reservations as early as possible.

TOP CHOICE   **Sea Breeze Guesthouse**   GUESTHOUSE \$\$
(463348; www.seabreeze.com.na; Turmalin St; s/d incl breakfast N\$700/1000; @) This upmarket guesthouse is right on the beach about 4.5km north of town, and is an excellent option if you're looking for a secluded retreat. Ask to see a few of the rooms as several of them have spectacular sea views; and there's a great family room for N\$1050. There's plenty of advice available on what to see and do around town. Follow the Strand north and keep an eye out for signs.

Hotel-Pension d'Avignon   GUESTHOUSE \$\$
(405821; www.natron.net/tour/davignon/main. html; 25 Libertine Amathila St; s/d incl breakfast N\$320/520;) A great option close to town that won't break the budget, d'Avignon is a smart, well-run guesthouse that has been recommended by travellers. Triple rooms are also available and there's a TV lounge to collapse into in the evenings.

Hotel Pension Rapmund GUESTHOUSE $$
(☎402035; www.hotelpensionrapmund.com; 6-8
Bismarck St; s/d N$585/770, luxury r N$1240)
Overlooking the park promenade, this long-
standing hotel pension has light and airy
rooms that are adorned with rich woods
and plenty of African and German-inspired
flourishing to create an attractive accommo-
dation spot. The location is on the money
and some rooms have terrific views.

Sophiadale
Base Camp CAMPGROUND, CHALETS $$
(☎403264; www.sophiadale.org; campsite per
person N$90, 2-person rondavel N$500; d incl
breakfast N$660) Campsites here have large,
shady trees and there are even sunroofs
around the camping ground. Fireplaces and
electrical powerpoints are big ticks, and the
amenities block is scrubbed clean on a regular basis. Or if you feel like a roof over your
head, upgrade to a large, solid *rondavel*
which is basic, good value and comes with a
braai area. The camp is 12km east of town,
take the turn-off from the road to Windhoek.

Tiger Reef Campsite CAMPGROUND $
(☎081 380 6014; campsite N$200, plus per person
N$75) This campsite sits right on the sand at
the beach front, sheltered from the wind by
lovely tamarisk trees. It's convenient to the
city centre.

Prinzessin Rupprecht Residenz HOTEL $$
(☎412540; www.prinzrupp.com.na; 15 Anton
Lubowski Ave; s/d from N$440/750) With 24
rooms, you have a good chance of snagging
accommodation here if you haven't booked
ahead. Housed in the former colonial mili-
tary hospital, the hotel appeals to history
buffs looking to catch a glimpse of the Swa-
kopmund of old. The interior has been large-
ly retained, and you can still stroll along the
hospital corridors and try to picture the
building's former life.

Sam's Giardino Hotel HOTEL $$$
(☎403210; www.giardinonamibia.com; 89 Anton
Lubowski Ave; s/d from N$650/1200; 🛜🏊) Sam's
Giardino Hotel is a touch of luxury in the
backstreets emphasising superb wines, fine
cigars and relaxing in the rose garden with
a Saint Bernard dog named Ornelia. There's
a lovely front garden and a lot of common
areas including a grotto with stacks of wine
bottles. The rooms are tasteful and refined
and cheaper at the walk-in rate if the hotel
isn't busy.

NAMIBIA SWAKOPMUND

A TERN FOR THE WORSE

Around 90% of the world population of the tiny Damara tern, of which less than 2000
breeding pairs remain, are endemic to the open shores and sandy bays of the Namib
coast from South Africa to Angola. Adult Damara terns, which have a grey back and
wings, a black head and white breast, measure just 22cm long, and are more similar in
appearance to swallows than to other terns.

Damara terns nest on the Namib gravel flats well away from jackals, hyenas and other
predators, though their small size renders them incapable of carrying food for long distances. As a result, they must always remain near a food source, which usually consists
of prawns and larval fishes.

When alarmed, Damara terns try to divert the threat by flying off screaming. Since the
nest is usually sufficiently well camouflaged to escape detection, this is effective behaviour. However, if the breeding place is in any way disturbed, the parent tern abandons
the nest and sacrifices the egg or chick to the elements. The following year, it seeks out
a new nesting site, but more often than not, it discovers that potential alternatives are
already overpopulated by other species, which it instinctively spurns.

Over the past few seasons, this has been a serious problem along the Namib coast,
mainly due to the proliferation of unregulated off-road driving along the shoreline between Swakopmund and Terrace Bay. This problem is further compounded by the fact
that Damara terns usually hatch only a single chick each year. In recent years the terns
have failed to breed successfully and, if the current situation continues, they may well be
extinct within just a few years.

Although the biggest risk to the Damara tern continues to be off-road drivers, the
increase in tourist activities on the dunes is also taking its toll. One way of reducing the
environmental impact of activities is for a company to operate in a confined area. When
you're booking through a company, inquire about its conservation policies.

THE PATH TO BOTANICAL DISCOVERY

Among Namibia's many botanical curiosities, the extraordinary *Welwitschia mirabilis*, which exists only on the gravel plains of the northern Namib Desert from the Kuiseb River to southern Angola, is probably the strangest of all. It was first noted in 1859, when Austrian botanist and medical doctor Friedrich Welwitsch stumbled upon a large specimen east of Swakopmund.

Welwitschias

Despite their dishevelled appearance, welwitschias actually have only two long and leathery leaves, which grow from opposite sides of the corklike stem. Over the years, these leaves are darkened in the sun and torn by the wind into tattered strips, causing the plant to resemble a giant wilted lettuce. Pores in the leaves trap moisture, and longer leaves actually water the plant's own roots by channelling droplets onto the surrounding sand.

Welwitschias have a slow growth rate, and it's believed that the largest ones, whose tangled masses of leaf strips can measure up to 2m across, may have been growing for up to 2000 years! However, most midsized plants are less than 1000 years old. The plants don't even flower until they've been growing for at least 20 years. This longevity is probably only possible because they contain some compounds that are unpalatable to grazing animals, although black rhinos have been known to enjoy the odd plant.

The plants' most prominent inhabitant is the yellow and black pyrrhocorid bug, which lives by sucking sap from the plant. It's commonly called the push-me-pull-you bug, due to its almost continuous back-to-back mating.

Welwitschia Drive

This worthwhile excursion by vehicle or organised tour is recommended if you want to see one of Namibia's most unusual desert plants, the Welwitschia. Welwitschias reach their greatest concentrations on the Welwitschia Plains east of Swakopmund, near the confluence of the Khan and Swakop Rivers, where they're the dominant plant species.

In addition to this wilted wonder itself, Welwitschia Drive also takes in grey and black **lichen fields**, which were featured in the BBC production *The Private Life of Plants*. It was here that David Attenborough pointed out these delightful examples of plant-animal symbiosis, which burst into 'bloom' with the addition of fog droplets. If you're not visiting during a fog, sprinkle a few drops of water on them and watch the magic.

Further east is the **Moon Landscape**, a vista across eroded hills and valleys carved by the Swakop River. Here you may want to take a quick 12km return side-trip north to the farm and oasis of **Goanikontes**, which dates from 1848. It lies beside the Swakop River amid fabulous desert mountains, and serves as an excellent picnic site.

The Welwitschia Drive, which turns off the Bosua Pass route east of Swakopmund, lies inside the Dorob National Park. Most often visited as a day trip from Swakopmund, the drive can be completed in two hours, but allow more time to experience this otherworldly landscape.

Alternative Space GUESTHOUSE $$
(off Map p276; ☎402713; 46 Dr Alfons Weber St; s/d from N$450/750; @) Located on the desert fringe, 800m east of town, this delightfully alternative place is run by Frenus and Sybille Rorich. The main attractions are the castlelike architecture, saturation artwork and an industrial scrap-recycling theme. Dune carts (free to guests) are guaranteed to provide a thrilling experience, especially with the dunes lying just off in the distance. Be advised that this is most definitely not a party place.

Beach Lodge HOTEL $$$
(off Map p276; ☎414500; www.beachlodge.com. na; Stint St; s/d from N$860/1260; @) This boat-shaped place, which sits right on the sand about 1km north of town, allows you to watch the sea through your very own personal porthole. Rooms vary in size and amenities and some come complete with window-side bathtubs.

Seagull B&B B&B $
(off Map p276; ☎405287; www.seagullbandb.com. na; 60 Strand St North; s/d from N$240/300) Right on the waterfront, this budget B&B

features a variety of rooms to suit travellers with wallets of varying sizes. Just a short walk north of town along Neser St, it's one of the most affordable B&Bs in Swakopmund, and is a much more personal place than some of the larger backpacker joints.

Desert Sky Backpackers BACKPACKERS $
(☑402339; Anton Lubowski Ave St; campsite per person N$70, dm/r N$80/200; @) This centrally located backpackers haunt is an excellent place to drop anchor in Swakopmund. The indoor lounge is simple and homey, while the outdoor picnic tables are a nice spot for a cold beer and warm conversation. Free coffee is available all day, and you're within stumbling distance of the pubs if you want something stronger.

Villa Wiese B&B $$
(☑407105; www.villawiese.com; cnr Theo-Ben Gurirab Ave and Windhoeker St; dm N$120, s/d N$450/550; @) Villa Wiese is a friendly and funky guest lodge occupying a historic colonial mansion complete with vaulted ceilings, rock gardens and period furniture. It draws a very eclectic mix of overlanders, backpackers and independent travellers, and serves as a slightly more sophisticated alternative to other budget-oriented options in town. The nearby Dunedin Star is its overflow property, and has similar costs and atmosphere.

Schweizerhaus Hotel HOTEL $$$
(☑400331; www.schweizerhaus.net; 1 Bismarck St; s/d from N$625/1020; @) Although it's best known for the landmark institution that is Cafe Anton, the Schweizerhaus Hotel itself is also a class act. Standard but comfortable rooms benefit from spectacular views of the beach and the adjacent lighthouse, which lights up the sky when the heavy fog rolls in from sea.

Brigadoon Bed & Breakfast B&B $$$
(☑406064; www.brigadoonswakopmund.com; 16 Ludwig Koch St; s/d N$925/1400; @) This Scottish-run B&B occupies a pleasant garden setting opposite Palm Beach, and recently underwent a major refurbishment giving it stylish, contemporary rooms boasting flat screen TVs, minibars and brand spanking new bathrooms. Each room also has its own private patio area.

Hansa Hotel HOTEL $$$
(☑414200; www.hansahotel.com.na; 3 Hendrick Witbooi St; s/d from N$1380/2000; @) Swakopmund's most established upmarket hotel

bills itself as 'luxury in the desert'. Individually decorated rooms with lofty ceilings and picture windows are tasteful and elegant, though the highlight of the property is its classic dining hall with white-glove service, bone china, sterling silver and fine crystal stemware.

Swakop Lodge BACKPACKERS $
(☑402030; 42 Nathaniel Maxuilili St; dm/s/d N$150/450/650; @) This backpacker-orientated hotel is the epicentre of the action in Swakopmund, especially since this is where many of the adrenaline activities depart from and return to, and where many of the videos are screened each night. The hotel is extremely popular with overland trucks, so it's a safe bet that the attached bar is probably bumping and grinding most nights of the week.

Eating
True to its Teutonic roots, Swakopmund's restaurants have a heavy German influence, though there's certainly no shortage of local seafood and traditional Namibian favourites, as well as a surprising offering of cosmopolitan fare. While Windhoekers might disagree, Swakopmund can easily contend for the title of Namibia's culinary capital.

Self-caterers can head for the well-stocked supermarket on Sam Nujoma Ave near the corner with Hendrick Witbooi St. Most backpacker spots have kitchens on the premises.

Garden Cafe CAFE $$
(Tobias Hainyeko St; mains N$40-80; ⊙8am-6pm Mon-Fri, 8am-3pm Sat & Sun) Set in a nice little garden away from the main street, Garden Cafe has open-air tables and chairs, changing specials and freshly prepared cafe food including salads, wraps and burgers (desserts are yummy too). It's pleasantly topped off by friendly and efficient service. In winter, the cafe is still in full swing with patrons huddled around tables basking in skinny shafts of sunlight.

Deutsches Haus GERMAN $$$
(☑404896; 13 Luderitz St; lunch N$70-120, dinner N$100-150) The fine dining at Deutsches Haus takes place in the well-organised upmarket, country dining room or the bench seating out the front of the building. It's one of the best-run restaurants in town as evidenced by the attentive and professional

NAMIBIA SWAKOPMUND

service. German dishes are freshly prepared and quickly served.

Swakopmund Brauhaus   GERMAN $$
(22 Sam Nujoma Ave; mains N$75-100; ⊘closed Sun) This excellent restaurant and boutique brewery offers one of Swakopmund's most sought-after commodities, namely authentic German-style beer. And, so as not to break with tradition, feel free to accompany your frothy brew with a plate of mixed sausages, piled sauerkraut and a healthy dollop of spicy mustard.

Kücki's Pub   PUB $$
(☑402407; Tobias Hainyeko St; mains N$100-120) A Swakopmund institution, Kücki's has been in the bar and restaurant biz for a couple of decades. The menu is full of seafood and meat dishes alongside comfort food, and everything is masterfully prepared. The warm and congenial atmosphere is a welcome complement to the food.

Tug   SEAFOOD $$$
(☑402356; mains US$80-140; ⊘lunch Sat-Sun, dinner daily) Housed in the beached tugboat *Danie Hugo* near the jetty, the Tug is something of an obligatory destination for any dinner-goer in Swakopmund. Regarded by many as the best restaurant in town, the Tug is an atmospheric, upmarket choice for meat and seafood, though a sundowner cocktail will do just fine. Due its extreme popularity and small size, advance bookings are recommended.

Lighthouse Pub & Cafe   PUB $$
(☑400894; The Mole, Main Beach; mains US$80-120) With a postcard-perfect view of the beach and crashing surf, the Lighthouse Pub & Cafe is an atmospheric choice for lovers of fine seafood. Depending on what the fishing boats are catching in their nets, lines and pots, you'll find everything from kingklip and lobster to kabeljou and calamari. It also does some delicious pizza meals (half-price on Monday).

Fish Deli   SEAFOOD $$
(Sam Nujoma St; N$70-90; ⊘8.30am-5pm Mon, Tue, Thu, Fri, 8.30am-2pm Wed, 9am-1pm Sat) Recommended by locals as the best place for a seafood meal in town. It's a simple but clean set-up inside and importantly the fish comes straight from the water to your plate – no frozen stuff.

Hansa Hotel Restaurant   INTERNATIONAL $$$
(☑400311; www.hansahotel.com.na; 3 Hendrick Witbooi St; mains N$120-240) It's hard to top history, and the Hansa Hotel is steeped in it. In the main dining hall at this classic colonial spot, you can indulge in culinary excesses and wash them down with a bottle from the extensive wine list.

Cafe Anton   CAFE $$
(1 Bismarck St; light meals N$40-70) This much-loved local institution, located in the Schweizerhaus Hotel, serves superb coffee, *Apfelstrudel, Kugelhopf* (cake with nuts and raisins), *Mohnkuchen* (poppy-seed cake), *Linzertorte* (cake flavoured with almond meal, lemon and spices, and spread with jam) and other European delights. The outdoor seating is inviting for afternoon snacks in the sun.

Raith's Gourmet   CAFE-BAKERY $
(Tobias Hainyeko St; snacks & mains N$20-40; ⊘from 7am daily) Very central and convenient and open all weekend, this proclaims itself to be a bakery-deli-gelateria-bistro (that might be stretching it). It's mainly a bakery with freshly made rolls and sandwiches for lunch, pies and pasties. Indulge in a croissant and scrambled eggs for breakfast. There's a good selection of meats and cheeses too if you're self-catering.

KALAHARI TRUFFLES

There is certainly no shortage of gourmet foods on the menu in Swakop, though one of the more heavenly items for foodies is the much-celebrated Kalahari truffle. A somewhat distant cousin of the more widely known European truffle, the Kalahari truffle is a *terfeziaceae* (desert truffle), which is endemic to arid and semi-arid areas of Africa and the Middle East. In the Kalahari, they can grow to several centimetres across, and reach weights of up to 300g. Although their flavour is not nearly as rich as the white and black truffles from Italy and France, Kalahari truffles are much more common, and thus much, much more affordable. When thinly sliced, braised in olive oil and served over a fine cut of ostrich steak, Kalahari truffles are simply divine.

🍷 Drinking & Entertainment

Swakopmund likes to party, and there are a few bars to find your favourite drink. **Tug** and the **Lighthouse** are popular happy-hour spots to coincide with Swakop sunsets. And both **Kücki's Pub** and **Swakopmund Brauhaus** are also good places to prop up the bar. But if you really want to feel like you're in Africa, the beach bar at **Tiger Reef (p281)** is all the rage and what better way to send off the day than feel the sand between your toes over a cold beer.

🔒 Shopping

Street stalls sell Zimbabwean crafts on the waterfront by the steps below Cafe Anton on Bismarck St.

Karakulia Weavers   CARPETS
(☑461415; www.karakulia.com.na; 2 Rakotoka St) This local carpet factory produces original and beautiful African rugs, carpets and wall hangings in karakul wool and offers tours of the spinning, dyeing and weaving processes.

Die Muschel Book & Art Shop   BOOKS
(☑402874; Hendrick Witbooi St; ⊙8.30am-6pm Mon-Fri, 8.30am-1pm & 4-6pm Sat, 10am-6pm Sun) German- and English-language books. Great for guides and maps. Esoteric works on art and local history are also available here.

Peter's Antiques   ANTIQUES
(☑405624; www.peters-antiques.com; 24 Tobias Hainyeko St) This place is an Ali Baba's cave of treasures, specialising in colonial relics, historic literature, West African art, politically incorrect German paraphernalia and genuine West African fetishes and other artefacts from around the continent.

Swakopmunder Buchhandlung   BOOKS
(☑402613; Sam Nujoma Ave) A wide selection of literature from various genres.

ℹ️ Information

Thanks to the mild temperatures and negligible rainfall, Swakopmund enjoys a statistically superb climate (25°C in the summer and 15°C in the winter), but there's a bit of grit in the oyster. When an easterly wind blows, the town gets a good sandblasting, and the cold winter sea fogs often create an incessant drizzle and an unimaginably dreary atmosphere. However, take comfort in the fact that this fog rolls up to 50km inland, and provides life-sustaining moisture for desert plants and animals.

Note that there is a continuing programme of street name changes (eg Lazarett St to Anton Lubowski Ave) around town which can be confusing – where possible we've used new names (as signed in the town) or both in the text.

Dangers & Annoyances

Although the palm-fringed streets and cool sea breezes in Swakopmund are unlikely to make you tense, you should always keep your guard up in town. Regardless of how relaxed the ambience might be, petty crime unfortunately occurs.

If you have a private vehicle, be sure that you leave it all locked up with no possessions inside visible during the day. At night, you need to make sure you're parked in a gated parking lot and not on the street. Also, when you're choosing a hotel or hostel, be sure that the security precautions (ie an electric fence and/or a guard) are up to your standards. Finally, although Swakopmund is generally safe at night, it's best to stay in a group, and when possible, take a taxi to and from your accommodation.

Emergency
Ambulance (☑081 124 0019)
Police (☑402431, 10111)

Internet Access
Swakopmund Internet Cafe (Shop 1, Atlanta Cinema Building, Nedbank Arcade; 30min N$20; ⊙closed Sun morning) Down the mall that is opposite the Garden Cafe.

Medical Services
Bismarck Medical Centre (☑405000; cnr Bismarck St & Sam Nujoma Ave) For doctors' visits, go to this recommended centre.

Money
There are plenty of banks in the centre of town with ATMs – try around the corner of Tobias Hainyeko St and Sam Nujoma Ave.

Post
Main Post Office (Garnison St) Also sells telephone cards and offers fax services.

Tourist Information
Namib-i (☑404827; www.natron.net/tour/swakop/infoe.htm; Sam Nujoma Ave; ⊙8am-5pm Mon-Fri, 9am-5pm Sat, 9am-1pm Sun) This tourist information centre is a very helpful resource. In addition to helping you get your bearings, it can also act as a booking agent for any activities and tours that happen to take your fancy.

Namibia Wildlife Resorts Office (NWR; ☑402172; www.nwr.com.na; Woermannhaus, Bismarck St; ⊙8am-1pm & 2-5pm Mon-Fri) Like its big brother in Windhoek, this office sells Namib-Naukluft Park and Skeleton Coast permits, and can also make reservations for other NWR-administered properties around the country.

❶ Getting There & Away

Air

Air Namibia (p354) has several flights a week between Windhoek's Eros Airport and Walvis Bay, from where you can easily catch a bus or taxi to Swakopmund.

Bus

There are several weekly buses between Windhoek and Swakopmund (around N$230, five hours) on the Intercape Mainliner (p355). Also consider **Town Hopper** (☑407223; www. namibiashuttle.com), which runs private shuttle buses between Windhoek and Swakopmund (N$270), and also offers a door-to-door pick-up and drop-off service.

Finally, **combis** (minibuses) run this route fairly regularly, and a ride between Windhoek and Swakopmund shouldn't cost more than N$120. Swakopmund is also a minor public transport hub, serving various regional destinations including Walvis Bay by combi, with fares averaging between N$20 and N$40.

Car

Swakopmund is about 400km west of Windhoek on the B2, the main east–west highway.

Hitching

Hitching isn't difficult between Swakopmund and Windhoek or Walvis Bay, but conditions can be rough if heading for Namib-Naukluft Park or the Skeleton Coast; hitchers risk heatstroke, sandblasting and hypothermia – sometimes all in the same day.

Train

Trans-Namib (☑061-2981111) trains operate throughout the day and night (from N$100), though they're not very convenient or popular, especially given the ease of bus travel.

The plush *Desert Express* 'rail cruise' runs to and from Windhoek.

Walvis Bay

☑ 064 / POP 65,000

Walvis Bay (vahl-fis bay) is pleasant enough, particularly around the new waterfront development and along the esplanade. The town is not so compact and having your own wheels makes life easier. It's a good alternative to staying in Swakopmund if that city is all a bit glitzy and urban for you – Walvis Bay has a far more relaxed feel to it and the accommodation options and food choices are excellent.

Unlike Swakopmund, Walvis Bay was snatched by the British years before the Germans colonists could get their hands on it. As a result, the town is architecturally uninspiring, and lacks the Old World ambience of its northerly neighbour. In marked contrast, the area around Walvis Bay is home to a number of unique natural attractions, including one of the largest flocks of flamingos in the whole of Southern Africa.

Walvis Bay is situated 30km south of Swakopmund, and is the only real port between Lüderitz and Luanda (Angola). The natural harbour at Walvis Bay is the result of the sand spit Pelican Point, which forms a natural breakwater and shelters the city from the strong ocean surge.

History

Although Walvis Bay was claimed by the British Cape Colony in 1795, it was not formally annexed by Britain until 1878 when it was realised that the Germans were eyeing the harbour. In 1910 Britain relinquished its hold on Walvis Bay, and it became part of the newly formed Union of South Africa.

When the Germans were defeated after WWI, South Africa was given the UN mandate to administer all of German South West Africa as well as the Walvis Bay enclave. This stood until 1977, when South Africa unilaterally decided to return it to the Cape Province. The UN was not impressed by this unauthorised act, and insisted that the enclave be returned to the mandate immediately. In response, South Africa steadfastly refused to bow.

When Namibia achieved its independence in 1990, Namibians laid claim to Walvis Bay. Given the strategic value of the natural harbour, plus the salt works (which produced 40,000 tonnes annually – some 90% of South Africa's salt), the offshore guano platforms and the rich fishery, gaining control over Walvis Bay became a matter of great importance for Namibia.

In 1992, after it had become apparent that white rule in South Africa was ending, the two countries agreed that South Africa would remove its border posts, and that both countries would jointly administer the enclave. Finally, facing growing domestic troubles and its first democratic elections, South Africa gave in, and at midnight on 28 February 1994, the Namibian flag was raised over Walvis Bay for the first time.

⊙ Sights

Dune 7   NATURAL SITE
In the bleak expanse just off the C14, 6km by road from town, Dune 7 is popular with

locals as a slope for sandboarding and skiing. The picnic site, which is now engulfed
by sand, has several shady palm trees tucked
away in the lee of the dune.

Rhenish Mission Church CHURCH
(5th Rd) Walvis Bay's oldest remaining building, the Rhenish Mission Church was prefabricated in Hamburg (Germany) reconstructed beside the harbour in 1880 and
consecrated the following year. Because of
machinery sprawl in the harbour area, it
was relocated to its present site in the mid-
20th century, and functioned as a church
until 1966.

The Railway TRAIN
During the winter, rail services between
Swakopmund and Walvis Bay are often
lagued by windblown sand, which covers
the tracks and undermines the track bed
and sleepers. This isn't a new problem –
5km east of town on the C14, notice the em-
bankment, which has buried a section of
narrow-gauge track from the last century. In
front of the train station are the remains of
the *Hope*, an old locomotive that once ran
on the original narrow-gauge railway. Both
were abandoned after the line was repeated-
ly buried beneath 10m sand drifts. The *Hope*
is now a national monument and stands on
6th St in front of the train station.

FREE Walvis Bay Museum MUSEUM
(Nangolo Mbumba Dr; ⊙9am-5pm Mon-Thu, closes
4.30pm Fri) The town museum is located in
the library. It concentrates on the history
and maritime background of Walvis Bay, but

NAMIBIA WALVIS BAY

FLAMINGOS AT WALVIS

Lesser and greater flamingos flock in large numbers to pools along the Namib Desert
coast, particularly around Walvis Bay and Lüderitz. They're excellent fliers, and have
been known to migrate up to 500km overnight in search of proliferations of algae and
crustaceans.

The lesser flamingo filters algae and diatoms (microscopic organisms) from the water
by sucking in, and vigorously expelling water from its bill. The minute particles are caught
on fine hairlike protrusions, which line the inside of the mandibles. The suction is created
by the thick fleshy tongue, which rests in a groove in the lower mandible and pumps back
and forth like a piston. It has been estimated that a million lesser flamingos can consume
over 180 tonnes of algae and diatoms daily.

While lesser flamingos obtain food by filtration, the greater flamingo supplements its
algae diet with small molluscs, crustaceans and other organic particles from the mud.
When feeding, it will rotate in a circle while stamping its feet in an effort to scare up a
tasty potential meal.

The greater and lesser flamingos are best distinguished by their colouration. Greater
flamingos are white to light pink, and their beaks are whitish with a black tip. Lesser flamingos are a deeper pink – often reddish – colour, with dark-red beaks.

Located near Walvis Bay are three diverse wetland areas; the lagoon, the salt works
and the Bird Paradise at the sewage works. Together they form Southern Africa's single
most important coastal wetland for migratory birds, with up to 150,000 transient avian
visitors stopping by annually, including massive flocks of both lesser and greater flamingos. The three wetland areas are as follows:

» **The Lagoon** This shallow and sheltered 45,000-hectare lagoon, southwest of
Walvis Bay and west of the Kuiseb River mouth, attracts a range of coastal water birds
in addition to enormous flocks of lesser and greater flamingos. It also supports chest-
nut banded plovers and curlew sandpipers, as well as the rare Damara tern.

» **The Salt Works** Southwest of the lagoon is this 3500-hectare saltpan complex,
which currently supplies over 90% of South Africa's salt. As with the one in Swakopmund, these pans concentrate salt from seawater with the aid of evaporation. They
also act as a rich feeding ground for prawns and larval fish.

» **Bird Paradise** Immediately east of town along the C14 at the municipal sewage
purification works is this nature sanctuary, which consists of a series of shallow artificial pools, fringed by reeds. An observation tower and a short nature walk afford
excellent birdwatching.

Walvis Bay

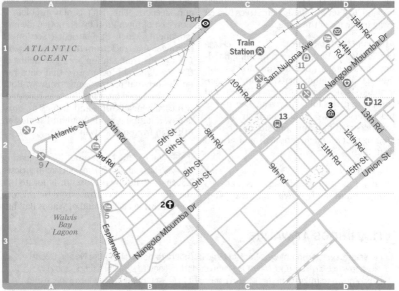

also has archaeological exhibits, a mineral collection and natural history displays on the Namib Desert and the Atlantic Coast.

AROUND WALVIS BAY

Sandwich Harbour   HARBOUR
(N$850) Sandwich Harbour, located 56km south of Walvis Bay in Dorob National Park, historically served as a commercial fishing and trading port. Some historians suggest that the name may be derived from an English whaler, the *Sandwich,* whose captain produced the first map of this coastline. Others contend that the name may also be a corruption of the German word *sandfische,* a type of shark often found here. History aside, at present the harbour is a total wilderness devoid of any human settlement.

Dunes up to 100m high slope into the Atlantic which washes into the picturesque lagoon. Birdwatchers will have a field day and **Sandwich Harbour 4x4** (☑207663; www.sandwich-harbour.com; Waterfront) facilitate shalf- and full-day (N$1050) trips down here.

Activities

Eco Marine Kayak Tours   KAYAKING
(☑203144; www.emkayak.iway.na) Sea-kayaking trips around the beautiful Walvis Bay wetlands are conducted by this outfit. Note that there is no central office, though bookings can be made over the phone or through your accommodation.

Mola Mola Safaris   BOAT TOUR
(☑205511; www.mola-namibia.com; Waterfront) This marine safari company offers fully customisable boating trips around the Walvis Bay and Swakopmund coastal areas, where you can expect to see dolphins, seals and countless birds. Prices are dependent on your group size and length of voyage.

Sleeping

Accommodation options are located in the city centre, on the waterfront, or at Langstrand (Long Beach), which is 10km north of Walvis Bay on the road to Swakopmund.

Self-catering is a good option in Walvis Bay with houses and apartments available both on the coast and in the city. A two-bedroom place can be found for around N$650; contact **Remax** (☑212451; www.remax.co.za; Sam Nujoma St).

Oyster Box Guesthouse   GUESTHOUSE **$$$**
(☑202247; www.oysterboxguesthouse.com; cnr Esplanade & 2nd St West; s/d N$750/1200; ❈ 🐾) More like a classy boutique hotel, this guest-

NAMIBIA WALVIS BAY

house is a stylish affair right on the waterfront, a short walk from the Raft restaurant. Rooms are very contemporary and bedding includes crispy sheets and fluffy pillows. Helpful staff can book activities for you around town and arrange transport.

Lagoon Lodge   HOTEL $$$
(✆200850; www.lagoonlodge.com.na; 2 Nangolo Mbumba Dr; s/d N$600/1200; ⌛) A garish yellow facade greets visitors to this French-run lodge which commands a magnificent location next to the lagoon, and features individually decorated rooms with private terraces facing out towards the sand and sea. As well as the heartfelt welcome, the free wireless and unbroken views over the water are highlights. The location on the promenade is handy for an evening/early morning walk along the waterfront.

Courtyard Hotel Garni   HOTEL $$
(✆206252; 16 3rd Rd; r per person incl breakfast N$580; @⌛⌛) This low-rise place in a quiet neighbourhood near the water has generous rooms that are a bit beaten around the edges – it's comfortable enough and there are nice common areas but it's probably a tad overpriced and the beds are quite small. Kitchenette useful for self-caterers. Guests can access the indoor heated pool and sauna.

Burning Shore   RESORT $$$
(✆064-207568; www.proteahotels.com/protea-hotel-burning-shore.html; s/d from N$1600/2250; ⌛⌛) At the Burning Shore, a secluded retreat (managed by the Protea Hotel chain) with only a dozen rooms, you can soak up the beauty and serenity of the adjacent dunes and the ocean. Rooms are luxurious without being pretentious, which lends a relaxed elegance and cool sophistication to the entire property. It's 15km from Walvis Bay at Longbeach.

✖ Eating & Drinking

The Waterfront area is a development claiming a cluster of bars and restaurants right on the water overlooking the harbour and the big machinery of the port not far away. It has a very genuine feel, unlike some of its counterparts in South Africa that have suffered from overdevelopment. There's a small but classy selection of places to sit outside on the water's edge and enjoy a cold drink and a meal.

Anchor   INTERNATIONAL $$
(Waterfront; breakfast/mains N$45/70; ⊙breakfast, lunch & dinner) The food is OK at the Anchor but the real attraction is the location

NEWEST NATIONAL PARK

The area between Swakopmund and Walvis Bay is slated to become the country's newest conservation area – the **Walvis Bay National Park**. There was no word on when this would occur during research of this book, but it could well be up and running by the time you read this.

overlooking the water. It makes a particularly lovely spot for breakfast, and if you're tired of eating stodgy food it does a pretty mean fruit salad. Sit at a table right on the water and watch the morning cruise boats slink out of the bay. The Anchor is a hotspot throughout most of the day receiving much passing trade – its distinctive building and nautical theme attracts both locals and tourists.

Raft   SEAFOOD $$
(☎204877; Esplanade; mains N$75-125; ☺dinner) This Walvis Bay landmark sits on stilts offshore, and has a great front-row view of the ducks, pelicans and flamingos. From this partner restaurant to the Tug in Swakopmund, you can expect a similar offering of high-quality meats and seafood in addition to spectacular sunsets and ocean views. The seafood extravaganza is well worth the extravagant N$340 price tag.

Bon Aroma   INTERNATIONAL $$
(☎220226; Sam Nujoma Ave; starters N$50, mains N$70-120; ☺lunch, dinner, closed Sun) A stylish restaurant with a sunny courtyard, Bon Aroma serves up a variety of dishes with a healthy bent toward seafood. Beef 'Gordon' Bleu also features and you can sniff out pizzas, pastas, salads and grills on the menu. The sound system belts out good 'ole boy country tunes in the background and there's a decent wine list.

Willi Probst Bakery & Cafe   CAFE $
(cnr 12th Rd & 9th St; light meals N$20-40; ☺closed Sun) If you're feeling nostalgic for Swakopmund (or Deutschland for that matter), take comfort in knowing that Probst specialises in stodgy German fare: pork, meatballs, schnitzel and the like. A range of sweet treats ensures that it is everyone's friend.

❶ Information

Police (☎10111; cnr 11th St & 13th Rd)

Post office (Sam Nujoma Ave) Provides public telephones and fax services.

Welwitschia Medical Centre (13th Rd; ☺24hr) For medical services.

❶ Getting There & Away

Air Namibia (p354) has around seven flights a week between Windhoek's Eros Airport and Walvis Bay's Rooikop Airport, located 10km southeast of town on the C14.

All buses and combis to Walvis Bay run via Swakopmund. The Intercape Mainliner stop is the Spur Restaurant – Ben Gurirab St. There are also other private bus services running between Windhoek and Walvis Bay.

Hitching isn't difficult between Walvis Bay and Swakopmund, but weather conditions can be rough if heading for Namib-Naukluft Park or the Skeleton Coast.

Namib-Naukluft Park & Sossusvlei

This is desert country and the swirling sand dunes here are one of the highlights of a visit to Namibia. Nowhere else in the country defines Namibia so much as the much-photographed dunes: silent, constantly shifting and ageless.

The present boundaries of Namib-Naukluft Park, one of the world's largest national parks, were mostly established in 1978 by merging the Namib Desert Park and the Naukluft Mountain Zebra Park with parts of Diamond Area 1 and bits of surrounding government land. However, the park's northern border was adjusted in December 2010 with the establishment of Dorob National Park (formerly the National West Coast Tourist Recreation Area), which stretches south as far as Sandwich Harbour.

The Namib-Naukluft Park takes in around 23,000 sq km of arid and semi-arid land, and protects various areas of vast ecological importance in the Namib and the Naukluft. The park also abuts the NamibRand Nature Reserve, the largest privately owned property in Southern Africa, forming a massive wildlife corridor that promotes migratory movement.

NAMIB SECTION

While most people associate the Namib solely with Sossusvlei, the desert sweeps across most of Central Namibia, and is character-

ised by a large array of geological formations. Given the extremes of temperature
and environment, you will need a 4WD vehicle in addition to good navigation skills in
order to properly explore the Namib. Truly
this is one place where the journey itself is
worth much more than the destination.

◎ Sights

Kuiseb Canyon   CANYON
Located on the Gamsberg Pass route west
of the Khomas Hochland, Kuiseb Canyon
contains the ephemeral Kuiseb River, which
is no more than a broad sandy riverbed for
most of the year. Although it may flow for
two or three weeks during the rainy season,
it only gets as far as Gobabeb before seeping
into the sand. At Rooibank, drinking water
for Walvis Bay is pumped from this subterranean supply.

It was in Kuiseb Canyon that the famous
geologists Henno Martin and Hermann
Korn went into hiding for three years during WWII, as recounted in Martin's book
The Sheltering Desert. Today, the canyon's
upper reaches remain uninhabited, though
there are scattered Topnaar Khoikhoi villages where the valley broadens out near the
north riverbank.

Hamilton Hills   HILLS
The range of limestone hills known as the
Hamilton Hills, south of Vogelfederberg
campsite, rises 600m above the surrounding desert plains. It provides lovely desert
hikes, and the fog-borne moisture supports
an amazing range of succulents and other
botanical wonders.

🛏 Sleeping

The Namib-Naukluft Park has eight exclusive camps, some of which have multiple but
widely spaced campsites. Sites have tables,
toilets and *braai* pits, but no washing facilities. Brackish water is available for cooking
and washing but not drinking – be sure that
you bring enough water. All sites must be
prebooked through Namibia Wildlife Resorts (NWR) in Windhoek or Swakopmund.
Camping costs N$110 per person (maximum
of eight people) plus N$80/10 per person/
car per day in park fees; fees are payable
when the park permit is issued.

Bloedkoppie   CAMPGROUND $
(Blood Hill) These camping spots are among
the most beautiful and popular sites in the
park. If you're coming from Swakopmund,
they lie 55km northeast of the C28, along
a signposted track. The northern sites may
be accessed with 2WD, but they tend to be
more crowded. The southern sites are quieter and more secluded, but can be reached
only by 4WD. The surrounding area offers
some pleasant walking, and at Klein Tinkas,
5km east of Bloedkoppie, you'll see the ruins of a colonial police station (basically a
ruined hut) and the graves of two German
police officers dating back to 1895.

Groot Tinkas   CAMPGROUND $
Groot Tinkas must be accessed with 4WD
and rarely sees much traffic. It enjoys a
lovely setting beneath shady rocks and the
surroundings are super for nature walks.
During rainy periods, the brackish water in
the nearby dam attracts a variety of birdlife.

Vogelfederberg   CAMPGROUND $
Vogelfederberg is a small facility, 2km south
of the C14, and makes a convenient overnight camp. Located just 51km from Walvis
Bay, it's more popular for picnics or short
walks. It's worth looking at the intermittent
pools on the summit that shelter a species
of brine prawn whose eggs hatch only when
the pools are filled with rainwater. The only
shade is provided by a small overhang where
there are two picnic tables and *braai* pits.

Ganab   CAMPGROUND $
Ganab is a dusty, exposed facility, translat-
ing to 'Camelthorn Acacia', that sits beside a
shallow stream bed on the gravel plains. It's
shaded by hardy acacia trees, and a nearby
bore hole provides water for antelopes.

Kriess-se-Rus   CAMPGROUND $
Kriess-se-Rus is a rather ordinary site in a
dry stream bank on the gravel plains, 107km
east of Walvis Bay on the Gamsberg Pass
Route. It is shaded, but isn't terribly pre-
possessing, and is best used simply as a convenient stop en route between Windhoek
and Walvis Bay.

Kuiseb Canyon   CAMPGROUND $
Kuiseb Canyon is a shady site at the Kuiseb
River crossing along the C14 and is also a
convenient place to break up a trip between
Windhoek and Walvis Bay. The location is
scenic enough, but the dust and noise from
passing vehicles makes it less appealing
than other campsites. There are pleasant
short canyon walks, but during heavy rains
in the mountains the site can be flooded;
during summer months, keep tabs on the
weather.

Namib-Naukluft Park

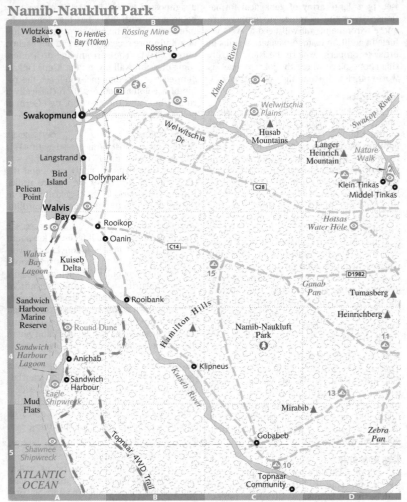

Mirabib
CAMPGROUND $

Mirabib is a pleasant facility that accommodates two parties at separate sites, and is comfortably placed beneath rock overhangs along a large granite escarpment. There's evidence that these shelters were used by nomadic peoples as early as 9000 years ago, and also by nomadic shepherds in the 4th or 5th century.

Homeb
CAMPGROUND $

Homeb is located in a scenic spot upstream from the most accessible set of dunes in the Namib-Naukluft Park, and can accommodate several groups. Residents of the nearby Topnaar Khoikhoi village dig wells in the Kuiseb riverbed to access water beneath the surface, and one of their dietary staples is the !nara melon, which obtains moisture from the water table through a long taproot. This hidden water also supports a good stand of trees, including camelthorn acacia and ebony.

ℹ Getting There & Away

The main park transit routes, the C28, C14, D1982 and D1998, are all open to 2WD traffic. However, the use of minor roads requires a park permit (N$80 per day plus N$10 per vehicle), which can either be picked up at any of the park

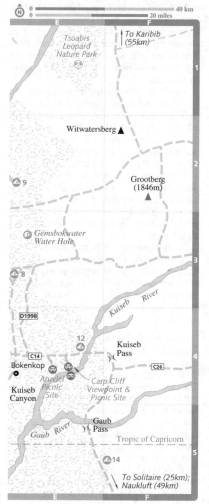

NAMIBIA NAMIB-NAUKLUFT PARK & SOSSUSVLEI

leopards, springboks and klipspringers. In addition to wildlife watching, the Naukluft is home to a couple of challenging hikes that open up this largely inaccessible terrain.

History
In the early 1890s the Naukluft was the site of heated battle between the German colonial forces and the Nama. In January 1893 a contingent of Schutztruppe soldiers estimated that they could force the Nama to flee their settlement at Hoornkrans in three days. However, due to their unfamiliarity with the terrain and their lack of experience in guerrilla warfare, the battle waged for months, resulting in heavy losses on both sides. Eventually, the Nama offered to accept German sovereignty if they could retain their lands and weapons. The Germans accepted, thus ending the Battle of the Naukluft.

◎ Sights & Activities
Waterkloof Trail   HIKING
This lovely 17km anticlockwise loop takes about seven hours to complete, and begins at the Naukluft (Koedoesrus) campsite, located 2km west of the park headquarters. It climbs the Naukluft River and past a frog-infested weir (don't miss the amazing reed tunnel!) and a series of pools, which offer cool and refreshing drinking and swimming. About 1km beyond the last pool, the trail then turns west, away from the Naukluft River and up a *kloof* (ravine). From there to

gates or arranged in advance through NWR. While some minor roads in the park are accessible to high-clearance 2WD vehicles, a 4WD is highly recommended.

NAUKLUFT MOUNTAINS
063 / ELEV 1973M
The Naukluft Mountains, which rise steeply from the gravel plains of the central Namib, are characterised by a high plateau bounded by gorges, caves and springs cut deeply from dolomite formations. The Tsondab, Tsams and Tsauchab Rivers all rise in the massif, and the relative abundance of water creates ideal habitats for mountain zebras, kudu,

the halfway point, the route traverses an increasingly open plateau.

Shortly after the halfway mark, the trail climbs steeply to a broad 1910m ridge, which is the highest point on the route. Here you'll have fabulous desert views before you begin a long, steep descent into the Gororosib Valley. Along the way, you'll pass several inviting pools full of reeds and tadpoles, and climb down an especially impressive waterfall before meeting up with the Naukluft River. Here, the route turns left and follows the 4WD track back to the park headquarters.

Olive Trail   HIKING

The 11km Olive Trail, named for the wild olives that grow alongside it, begins at the car park 4km northeast of the park headquarters. The walk runs clockwise around the triangular loop and takes four to five hours.

The route begins with a steep climb onto the plateau, affording good views of the Naukluft Valley. It then turns sharply east and descends a constricted river valley, which becomes deeper and steeper and makes a couple of perfect U-turns before it reaches a point where hikers must traverse a canyon wall – past a pool – using anchored chains. In several places along this stretch, the dramatic geology presents an astonishing gallery of natural artwork. Near the end of the route, the trail strikes the Naukluft 4WD route and swings sharply south, where it makes a beeline back to the car park.

Four-Day & Eight-Day Loops   HIKING

The two big loops through the massif can be hiked in four and eight days. For many people the Naukluft is a magical place, but its charm is more subtle than that of Fish River Canyon in southern Namibia. For example, some parts are undeniably spectacular, such as the Zebra Highway, Ubusis Canyon and Die Valle (look for the fantastic stallion profile on the rock beside the falls). However, a couple of days involve walking in relatively open country or along some maddeningly rocky riverbeds.

The four-day 60km loop is actually just the first third of the eight-day 120km loop, combined with a 22km cross-country jaunt across the plateau back to park headquarters. It joins up with the Waterkloof Trail at its halfway point, and follows it the rest of the way back to park headquarters. Alternatively, you can finish the four-day route at Tsams Ost Shelter, midway through the

eight-day loop, where a road leads out to the Sesriem-Solitaire Rd. However, you must prearrange to leave a vehicle there before setting off from park headquarters. Note that hikers may not begin from Tsams Ost without special permission from the rangers at Naukluft.

These straightforward hikes are marked by white footprints (except those sections that coincide with the Waterkloof Trail, which is marked with yellow footprints). Conditions are typically hot and dry, and water is only reliably available at overnight stops (at Putte, it's 400m from the shelter).

To shorten the eight-day hike to seven days, it's possible to skip Ubusis Canyon by turning north at Bergpos and staying the second night at Adlerhorst. Alternatively, very fit hikers combine the seventh and eighth days.

In four places – Ubusis Canyon, above Tsams Ost, Die Valle and just beyond Tufa Shelter – hikers must negotiate dry waterfalls, boulder-blocked kloofs and steep tufa formations with the aid of chains. Some people find this off-putting, so be sure you're up to it.

Naukluft 4WD Trail Off-road   DRIVING

Off-road enthusiasts can exercise their machines on the 73km, two-day Naukluft 4WD Trail. It begins near the start of the Olive Trail and follows a loop near the northeastern corner of the Naukluft area. Accommodation is provided in one of the stone-walled A-frames at the 28km point. Facilities include shared toilets, showers and braai pits. Up to four vehicles/16 people are permitted here at a time. Book through the NWR office in Windhoek; the route (including accommodation) costs N$220 per vehicle plus an additional N$80 per person per day.

🛏 Sleeping

In addition to the unofficial campsites along the trails, there are several accommodation options outside the park.

Tsauchab River Camping   CAMPSITE $

(📞293416; www.tsauchab.com; campsite N$150, plus per person N$100, s/d chalet N$760/1300) If you're an avid hiker (or just love excellent settings!), you're in for a treat. The scattered campsites here sit beside the Tsauchab riverbed – one occupies a huge hollow tree – and each has a private shower block, a sink and braai area. The 6km Kudu Hiking Trail climbs to the summit of Rooikop. Beside a spring 11km away from the main site is the 4WD exclusive site, which is the starting point for the wonderful 21km Mountain Zebra Hiking Trail.

Büllsport Guest Farm FARMSTAY **$$**
(☏693371; www.buellsport.com/main.html; s/d with half board from N$840/1460) This scenic farm, owned by Ernst and Johanna Sauber, occupies a lovely, austere setting below the Naukluft Massif, and features a ruined colonial police station, the Bogenfels arch and several resident mountain zebras. A highlight is the 4WD excursion up to the plateau and the hike back down the gorge, past several idyllic natural swimming pools.

Zebra River Lodge LODGE **$$**
(☏061-301934; www.zebrariver.com; s/d with full board from N$1160/1630) Occupying a magical setting in the Tsaris Mountains, this is Rob and Marianne Field's private Grand Canyon. The surrounding wonderland of desert mountains, plateaus, valleys and natural springs is accessible on a network of hiking trails and 4WD tracks. If you take it very slowly, the lodge road is accessible by 2WD vehicles.

ℹ Information

Most Naukluft visitors come to hike either the Waterkloof or Olive Trails. These hikes are open

Naukluft Mountains

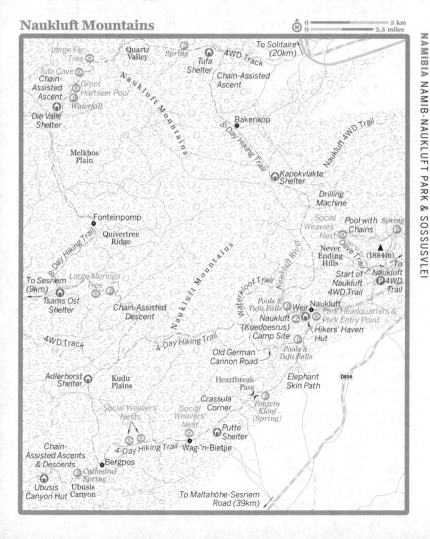

THE NAMIB DUNES

The Namib dunes stretch from the Orange to the Kuiseb Rivers in the south, and from Torra Bay in Skeleton Coast Park to Angola's Curoca River in the north. They're composed of colourful quartz sand and come in varying hues – from cream to orange and red to violet.

Unlike the ancient Kalahari dunes, those of the Namib are dynamic, which means that they shift with wind, and are continuously sculpted into a variety of distinctive shapes. The top portion of the dune, which faces the direction of migrations, is known as the slipface, and is formed as the sand spills from the crest and slips down. Various bits of plant and animal detritus also collect here and provide a meagre food source for dune-dwelling creatures, and it's here that most dune life is concentrated.

The following is a list of the major types of dunes found in the Namib:

» **Parabolic dunes** Along the eastern area of the dune sea (including those around Sossusvlei), the dunes are classified as parabolic or multicyclic, and are the result of variable wind patterns. These are the most stable dunes in the Namib, and therefore the most vegetated.

» **Transverse dunes** The long, linear dunes along the coast south of Walvis Bay are transverse dunes, which lie perpendicular to the prevailing southwesterly winds. As a result, their slipfaces are oriented towards the north and northeast.

» **Seif dunes** Around the Homeb campsite in the Namib-Naukluft Park are the prominent linear or seif dunes, which are enormous all-direction-oriented sand ripples. With heights of up to 100m, they're spaced about 1km apart and show up plainly on satellite photographs. They're formed by seasonal winds; during the prevailing southerly winds of summer, the slipfaces lie on the northeastern face. In the winter, the wind blows in the opposite direction, which causes slipfaces to build up on the southern-western faces.

» **Star dunes** In areas where individual dunes are exposed to winds from all directions, a formation known as a star dune appears. These dunes have multiple ridges, and when seen from above may appear to have a star shape.

» **Barchan dunes** These dunes prevail around the northern end of the Skeleton Coast and south of Lüderitz, and are the most mobile as they are created by unidirectional winds. When shifting, barchan dunes take on a crescent shape, with the horns of the crescent aimed in the direction of migration. In fact, it is barchan dunes that are slowly devouring the ghost town of Kolmanskop near Lüderitz.

» **Hump dunes** Typically forming in clusters near water sources, hump dunes are considerably smaller than other dune types. They are formed when sand builds up around vegetation (such as a tuft of grass), and held in place by the roots of the plant, forming a sandy tussock. Generally, hump dunes rise less than 3m from the surface.

to day visitors, but most hikers want to camp at Naukluft (Koedoesrus), which must be pre-booked.

The four-day and eight-day loops have more restrictions attached. Thanks to stifling summer temperatures and potentially heavy rains, these two are only open from 1 March to the third Friday in October. Officially, you can only begin these hikes on the Tuesday, Thursday and Saturday of the first three weeks of each month. The price of N$100 per person includes accommodation at the Hikers' Haven hut on the night before and after the hike, as well as camping at trailside shelters and the Ubusis Canyon Hut. In addition, you'll have to pay

N$80 per person per day and another N$10 per day for each vehicle you leave parked. Groups must comprise three to 12 people.

Due to the typically hot, dry conditions and lack of reliable natural water sources, you must carry at least 3L to 4L of water per person per day, as well as food and emergency supplies.

ℹ Getting There & Away

The Naukluft is best reached via the C24 from Rehoboth and the D1206 from Rietoog; petrol is available at Büllsport and Rietoog. From Sesriem, 103km away, the nearest access is via the dip-ridden D854.

SESRIEM & SOSSUSVLEI

☑ 063

Appropriate for this vast country with its epic landscapes – its number-one tourist attraction – Sossusvlei still manages to feel isolated. The dunes, appearing otherworldly at times, especially when the light hits them just so, are part of the 32,000 sq km sand sea that covers much of the region. The dunes reach as high as 325m, and are part of one of the oldest and driest ecosystems on earth. However, the landscape here is constantly changing – wind forever alters the shape of the dunes, while colours shift with the changing light, reaching the peak of their brilliance just after sunrise.

The gateway to Sossusvlei is Sesriem (Six Thongs), which was the number of joined leather ox-wagon thongs necessary to draw water from the bottom of the nearby gorge. Sesriem remains a lonely and far-flung outpost, home to little more than a petrol station and a handful of tourist hotels and lodges.

◉ Sights & Activities

Sossusvlei   NATURAL SITE

Sossusvlei, a large ephemeral pan, is set amid red sand dunes that tower up to 200m above the valley floor and more than 300m over the underlying strata. It rarely contains any water, but when the Tsauchab River has gathered enough volume and momentum to push beyond the thirsty plains to the sand sea, it's completely transformed. The normally cracked dry mud gives way to

an ethereal blue-green lake, surrounded by greenery and attended by aquatic birdlife, as well as the usual sand-loving gemsboks and ostriches.

This sand probably originated in the Kalahari between three and five million years ago. It was washed down the Orange River and out to sea, where it was swept northwards with the Benguela current to be deposited along the coast. The best way to get the measure of this sandy sprawl is to climb a dune, as most people do. And of course, if you experience a sense of déjà vu here, don't be surprised – Sossusvlei has appeared in many films and advertisements worldwide, and every story ever written about Namibia features a photo of it.

At the end of the 65km 2WD road from Sesriem is the 2WD car park, and only 4WDs can drive the last 4km into the Sossusvlei Pan itself. Visitors with lesser vehicles park at the 2WD car park and walk, hitch or catch the shuttle to cover the remaining distance. If you choose to walk, which really is the best way to take in all the desert scenery, allot about 90 minutes, carry enough water and be prepared for a hot, sandy slog in the blazing sun.

Sesriem Canyon   CANYON

The 1km-long, 30m-deep Sesriem Canyon, 4km south of the Sesriem headquarters, was carved by the Tsauchab River through the 15-million-year-old deposits of sand and gravel conglomerate. There are two pleasant walks: you can hike upstream to the

---

!NARA MELONS

Historically, human existence in the Namib Desert has been made possible by an unusual spiny plant, the !nara melon. It was first described taxonomically by the same Friedrich Welwitsch who gave his name to the welwitschia plant.

Although the !nara bush lives and grows in the desert, it is not a desert plant since it lacks the ability to prevent water loss through transpiration. So it must take in moisture from the groundwater table via a long taproot. As a result, !nara melons are an effective way of monitoring underground water tables: when the plants are healthy, so is the water supply. Its lack of leaves also protects it from grazing animals, although ostriches do nip off its tender growing shoots.

As with the welwitschia, the male and female sex organs in the !nara melon exist in separate plants. Male plants flower throughout the year, but it's the female plant that produces the 15cm melon each summer, providing a favourite meal for jackals, insects and humans. In fact, it remains a primary food of the Topnaar Khoi-Khoi people, and has also become a local commercial enterprise. Each year at harvest time the Topnaar erect camps around the Kuiseb Delta to collect the fruits. Although melons can be eaten raw, most people prefer to dry them for later use, or prepare, package and ship them to urban markets.

Sesriem & Sossusvlei

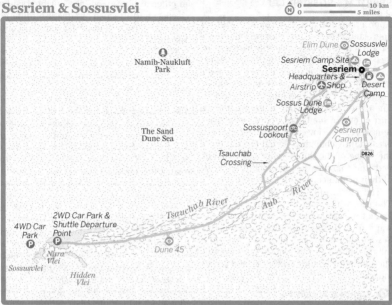

brackish pool at its head or 2.5km downstream to its lower end. Check out the natural sphinxlike formation on the northern flank near the canyon mouth.

Dune 45   NATURAL SITE
The most accessible of the large red dunes along the Sossusvlei road is Dune 45, so-called because it's 45km from Sesriem. It rises over 150m above the surrounding plains, and is flanked by several scraggly and often photographed trees.

Elim Dune   NATURAL SITE
This often visited red dune, 5km north from the Sesriem Camp Site, can be reached with 2WD vehicles, but also makes a pleasant morning or afternoon walk.

Hidden Vlei   HIKING
The rewarding 4km return hike from the 2WD Car Park to Hidden Vlei, an unearthly dry *vlei* (low, open landscape) amid lonely dunes, makes a rewarding excursion. The route is marked by white-painted posts. It's most intriguing in the afternoon, when you're unlikely to see another person.

Dead Vlei   HIKING
The rugged 6km return walk from Sossusvlei to Dead Vlei is popular with those who think the former is becoming overly touristy.

Despite the name, it's a lovely spot and is just as impressive as its more popular neighbour.

Namib Sky
Balloon Safaris   ADVENTURE SPORTS
(☎683188; www.namibsky.com) Floating over the dunes in a hot air balloon (N$3950 per person including champagne breakfast) is a breathtaking way to appreciate the stunning landscape. Pick-ups a half-hour before sunrise are arranged at many accommodation places in the area.

🛏 Sleeping
Advanced reservations are essential, especially during the high season, school holidays and busy weekends.

Sesriem Camp Site   CAMPGROUND $$
(campsite per person N$130) With the exception of the upmarket Sossus Dune Lodge, this is the only accommodation inside the park gates – staying here guarantees that you will be able to arrive at Sossusvlei in time for sunrise. The campsite is rudimentary – sandy sites with bins, taps, and trees for shade – and expensive for what you get, but you pay for the location inside the park. Given its popularity, you must book in advance at the NWR office in Windhoek, and arrive by sunset or the camp staff will reassign

your site on a standby basis. A small shop at the office here sells snacks and cold drinks, and the campsite bar provides music and alcohol nightly.

Sossusvlei Lodge   LODGE **$$$**

(✆293636; www.sossusvleilodge.com; campsite for 2 persons N$300, s/d from N$2330/3150; ❄) People either love this curious place or hate it, but it does make a statement. Accommodation is in self-contained chalets with private verandahs, and guests can mingle with one another in the swimming pool, bar-restaurant and observatory. Walk-in rates are often cheaper. There's an adventure centre here that organises scenic flights, hot-air ballooning, quad biking and many other activities. The lodge also runs **Sossus Oasis campsite**, near the petrol station – an exposed site with good facilities.

Sossus Dune Lodge   LODGE **$$$**

(✆061-2857200; www.nwr.com.na/sossus_dune_ lodge.html; s/d dune chalet with half board N$2400/4600; ❄) Splash out at this ultra-exclusive lodge, which is administered by NWR, and is one of only two properties located inside the park gates. Constructed entirely of local materials, the lodge consists of elevated bungalows that run alongside a curving promenade, and face out towards the silent desert plains. In the morning, you can roll out of your plush queen-sized bed, take a hot shower, sit down to a light breakfast of filter coffee and fresh fruits, and then be one of the first people to watch the morning light wash over Sossusvlei.

La Mirage Desert Lodge   HOTEL **$$$**

(✆063-693019; www.leadinglodges.com/lodges/lod ges-in-namibia/le-mirage-lodge-spa; r per person N$2300; ❄) This extravagant stone mock-castle rises like a mirage out of the desert. The whole affair is over the top, but it's a very comfortable place to stay with pool, grass and sunbeds set around a bar area, a restaurant and large rooms sumptuously furnished – rooms come in different sizes so ask to see a few: Room 26 is a good one. Sundowner spot out the back for a cocktail at day's end. It's on the C27, 21km from Sesriem

Desert Camp   TENTED CAMP **$$**

(✆683205; www.desertcamp.com; per person N$1000; ❄) The sister property of the Sossusvlei Lodge, located 3km outside the park gate, targets midrange travellers who want the comforts of a lodge without having to part with too much cash. Desert Camp consists of 20 East African–style canvas tents, complete with private bathrooms, kitchenettes and *braai* pits, which fan out from the central communal area.

❶ Information

Sesriem Canyon and Sossusvlei are open year-round between sunrise and sunset. If you want to see the sunrise over Sossusvlei, you must stay inside the park, either at the Sesriem Camp Site or the Sossus Dune Lodge. From both places, you are allowed to start driving to Sossusvlei before the general public is admitted through the main gates. If you're content with simply enjoying the morning light, however, you can stay in Sesriem or Solitaire and simply pass through the park gate once the sun rises above the horizon.

All visitors headed for Sossusvlei must check in at the park office and secure a park entry permit.

Namib-Naukluft **park entry** at Sossusvlei is N$80 per person, N$10 per car. There's an **internet cafe** at the petrol station near Sossus Oasis campsite (N$30 for half an hour).

❶ Getting There & Away

Sesriem is reached via a signposted turn-off from the C14, and petrol is available in town. There is no public transport leading into the park, though hotels can arrange tours if you don't have your own vehicle.

The road leading from the park gate to the 2WD car park is paved, though the speed limit remains 60km/h. Although the road is conducive to higher speeds, there are oryx and springboks dashing about, so drive with extreme care.

SOLITAIRE & AROUND

Solitaire is a lonely and aptly named settlement of just a few buildings about 80km north of Sesriem along the A46. Although the town is nothing more than an open spot in the desert, the surrounding area is home to several guest farms and lodges, which can serve as an alternative base for exploring Sossusvlei.

🛏 Sleeping & Eating

TOP CHOICE **Agama River Camp**   LODGE, CAMPGROUND **$$**

(✆683245; www.agamarivercamp.com; campsite/ bungalow per person N$120/400) This relatively new lodge is in a handy spot between Sousslevi and Sesriem (34km from Sesriem). The bungalows here have rooftop decks and staff will set up a sleeping kit on the deck for you, so you can sleep under the stars. If you're tenting it in the excellent campsite, and the weather is foul, the friendly owners may let you sleep in the sitting room next to the fire. In the main lodge there is a sundowner deck (best enjoyed by admiring the surrounding hills in pink and red hues over a cold beer) and lounge; meals are only available if booked well in advance.

Solitaire Guest Farm FARMSTAY $$
(☑062-682033;www.solitaireguestfarm.com;campsite per site N$120, s/d with half board from N$800/1440; ☎) This inviting guest farm, located 6km east of Solitaire on the C14, is a peaceful oasis situated between the Namib plains and the Naukluft Massif. Bright rooms, home-cooked meals and relaxing surroundings make it a good choice.

Solitaire Country Lodge LODGE $$
(☑063-293621; www.namibialodges.com; campsite per person N$100, s/d N$495/805; @☎) Despite its relative youth, the property was designed to evoke images of a colonial-era farmhouse, albeit one with a large swimming pool in the backyard! Serviceable rooms are fairly sparse, a decent size and set around a large, grassed square.

Rostock Ritz LODGE $$$
(☑064-694000; www.rostock-ritz-desert-lodge.com; campsite per person from N$130, s/d chalets from N$1200/1900; ☎) This unique accommodation is known for its bizarre water gardens and cool and cave-like cement-domed chalets. The Rostock Campsite is a peaceful 7km from the lodge itself. The staff can arrange a number of activities, including hiking, a visit to the nearby hot springs and the obligatory trip to Sossusvlei. The Ritz lies east of the C14, just south of the C26 junction.

❶ Getting There & Away

Solitaire is connected to Sesriem by the unsealed C19, and petrol is available in town.

There was a shuttle service just beginning to run from Solitaire petrol station to Sousslevi for N$100 return, in mid-2012; check with the station to see if it's still going and for the times the service runs.

NAMIBRAND NATURE RESERVE

Bordering the Namib-Naukluft Park, this reserve (www.namibrand.org) is essentially a collection of private farms that together protect over 200,000 hectares of dunes, desert grasslands and wild, isolated mountain ranges. Currently, several concessionaires operate on the reserve, offering a range of experiences amid one of Namibia's most stunning and colourful landscapes. A surprising amount of wildlife can be seen here, including large herds of gemsboks, springboks and zebras, as well as kudu, klipspringers, spotted hyenas, jackals, and Cape bat-eared foxes.

Access by private vehicle is restricted in order to maintain the delicate balance of the reserve. Accommodation prices are also extremely high, which seeks to limit the tourist footprint. As a result, you must book in advance through a lodge, and then arrange either a 4WD transfer or a chartered fly-in.

🛏 Sleeping

Wolwedans Dune Lodge LODGE $$$
(☑061-230616; www.wolwedans.com; chalet per person with full board incl activities from N$4280; ✳☎) One of the more affordable lodges in the NamibRand (in this price bracket, affordable is a relative term), Wolwedans features an architecturally arresting collection of raised wooden chalets that are scattered amid towering red sand dunes. Service is impeccable, and the atmosphere is overwhelmingly elegant, yet you can indulge in your wild side at anytime with chauffeured 4WD dune drives and guided safaris.

Sossusvlei Desert Lodge LODGE $$$
(☑in Johannesburg 27-11-809 4300; www.andbeyondafrica.com; chalet per person with full board incl activities from N$3690; ✳☎) This fashionable accommodation frequently appears in *Condé Nast* as one of the top lodges in the world. The property contains 10 chalets, which are constructed from locally quarried stone, and appear to blend effortlessly into the surrounding landscape. The interiors are nothing short of regal and feature personal fireplaces, marble baths and linen-covered patios. Of special interest is the on-site observatory, which boasts a high-powered telescope and local star charts.

SOUTHERN NAMIBIA

If you're beginning a regional odyssey in South Africa, one of the best ways to approach Namibia is from South Africa's vast Northern Cape, crossing the border into the infinite, desert-rich south of the country. Once in Namibia, the landscape, noticeably starker than its southern neighbour, is tinged with a lunar feel from the scattered rocky debris, and is marked from the irrepressible movement of the oldest sand dunes on the planet.

Although the tourist trail in Namibia firmly swings north towards Etosha National Park, the deserts of Southern Namibia sparkle beneath the sun – quite literally – as they're filled with millions of carats of diamonds.

The port of Lüderitz has long been a traveller's favourite. A surreal colonial relic that has largely disregarded the 21st century, Lüderitz clings fiercely to its European roots, with traditional German architecture set against a backdrop of fiery sand dunes and deep blue seas.

Your first sight of Fish River Canyon will, more than any place in Namibia, leave you with feelings of awe and grandeur – it is Mother Earth at its very finest. One of the largest canyons in the world, it's also one of the most spectacular sights in the whole of Africa.

Geography

Southern Namibia takes in everything from Rehoboth in the north to the Orange River along the South African border, and westward from the Botswana border to the Forbidden Coast. The central plateau is characterised by wide open country, and the area's widely spaced rural towns function mainly as commercial and market centres. Further south, the landscape opens up into seemingly endless plains, ranges and far horizons. In the far south of the region, the Fish River Canyon forms a spectacular gash across the otherwise flat landscape.

🛈 Getting Around

While sparse public transport connects Windhoek to the border, and Keetmahshoop out to Lüderitz, a private vehicle is necessary if you want to access any of the stunning nature that defines this region. A 2WD vehicle can tackle the vast majority of the roads down south, and you'll have no problems accessing the trailheads for Fish River Canyon or the long and lonely road out to Lüderitz.

Outside of the rainy season, a 2WD with reasonable clearance will survive most of the coastal roads around the Lüderitz peninsula, but you'd be wise to avoid the off-road sand tracks. For any excursion into the Sperrgebiet, a sturdy 4WD with full support equipment is absolutely essential.

The Central Plateau

The central plateau is bisected by the B1, which is the country's main north–south route, stretching from the South African border to Otjiwarongo. For most drivers, this excellent road is little more than a mesmerising broken white line stretching towards a receding horizon – a paradise for lead-foot drivers and cruise-control potatoes. Most of the central plateau's towns are situated off the main B1 route, and serve either as good bases for exploring the region's natural attractions, or, at the very least, obligatory fuel stops en route to destinations further south.

DORDABIS
📱 062

The lonely ranching area around Dordabis is the heart of Namibia's karakul country, and supports several sheep farms and weaveries. At the **Farm Ibenstein Weavery** (📱573524; ⊘by appointment), located 4km down the C15 from Dordabis, you can learn about spinning, dyeing and weaving, as well as purchase handwoven rugs and carpets.

Yes, the name **Eningu Clayhouse Lodge** (📱581880; www.eningulodge.com; Peperkorrel Farm; s/d with half board N$1050/1840) sounds a lot like the title of a children's book but, appropriately enough, this place is a bit of a fantasy. It was painstakingly designed and constructed by Volker and Stephanie Hümmer, whose efforts with sun-dried adobe have resulted in an appealing African-Amerindian architectural cross. It really is visually arresting, and activities here include wonderful hiking trails (with a mountain hut en route), wildlife viewing, archery, and star-gazing through their telescope. To get there, follow the D1458 for 63km southeast of Chief Hosea Kutako International Airport and then turn west on the D1471; travel for 1km to the Eningu gate.

To reach Dordabis, head east from Windhoek on the B6 and turn right onto the C23, 20km east of town; the town centre is 66km down this road.

ARNHEM CAVE

With a subterranean length of 4.5km, Arnhem Cave is the longest cave system in Namibia. Formed in a layer of limestone and dolomite, Arnhem was sandwiched between folds of stratified quartzite and shale, and discovered in 1930 by farmer DN Bekker. Shortly thereafter, mining operations began extracting the deposits of lucrative bat guano, which were commonly used at the time as fertiliser.

Guided tours (1/2hr tours N$80/100) dive into darkness, beyond the reach of sunlight. Because it's dry, there are few stalagmites or

REHOBOTH

If you're looking to rehabilitate your travel-worn body and mind, a surprisingly relaxing retreat is the **Lake Oanob Resort** (☎062-522370; www.oanob.com.na; campsites N$70-130, s/d N$780/1030, 6-bed chalets N$2420; ⌧), located alongside the Oanob Dam, just west of Rehoboth. The resort is centred on a stunningly calm and tranquil blue lake. Amenities include a shaded camping area, a thatched bar and restaurant, and beautiful stone self-catering bungalows on the lake's shores. Rehoboth lies 85km south of Windhoek and just a stone's throw north of the Tropic of Capricorn.

The **town museum** (☎062-522954; www.rehobothmuseum.com; admission N$25; ◷by appointment), housed in the 1903 residence of the settlement's first colonial postmaster, recounts the historical roots of Rehoboth from 1844.

Intercape Mainliner (p355) buses running from Windhoek to Keetmanshoop pass through Rehoboth (from N$230, one hour, four weekly).

stalactites, but it's possible you could see up to six bat species: the giant leaf-nosed bat, the leaf-nosed bat, the long-fingered bat, Geoffroy's horseshoe bat, Denti's horseshoe bat and the Egyptian slit-faced bat. It's also inhabited by a variety of insects, worms, shrews and prawns. The grand finale is the indescribable first view of the blue-cast natural light as you emerge from the depths.

Arnhem Cave & Lodge (☎581885; www.arnhemcave.com; campsite per person N$90, chalets per person from N$470) lies within an hour's walk of Arnhem Cave, and is located on the same farm. Day visitors can arrange guided tours here, while overnight visitors are treated to a bucolic retreat lying just beyond the lights of the capital.

To get to the guesthouse, turn south 3km east of Chief Hosea Kutako International Airport on the D1458. After 66km, turn northeast on the D1506 and continue for 11km to the T-junction, where you turn south on the D180. The guesthouse is 6km down this road.

MARIENTAL
☑ 063

The small administrative and commercial centre of Mariental is home to the large-scale Hardap irrigation scheme, which allows citrus-growing and ostrich farming. For most travellers, however, Mariental is little more than a petrol stop before heading out west to Sesriem and Sossusvlei.

If you get stuck for the night, the well-established **Mariental Hotel** (☎242466; Marie Brandt St; s/d N$350/480; ⌧) has plush rooms with modern amenities as well as an attractive dining room serving Namibian standards.

Intercape Mainliner (p355) buses travelling from Windhoek to Keetmanshoop

pass through Mariental (from N$250, three hours, four weekly).

HARDAP DAM GAME RESERVE
☑ 063

This **reserve** (per person N$20, plus per vehicle N$10; ◷sunrise-6pm), 15km northwest of Mariental, is a 25,000-hectare wildlife park with 80km of gravel roads and a 15km hiking loop. Hardap is Nama for 'nipple'; it was named after the conical hills topped by dolerite knobs that dot the area.

There are several picnic sites east of the lake, and between sunrise and sunset you can walk anywhere in the reserve. Note that swimming isn't permitted in the dam.

Most travellers come for the **blue lake**, which breaks up the arid plateau landscape and provides anglers with carp, barbel, mudfish and blue karpers. The lake also supports countless species of water bird, including flamingos, fish eagles, pelicans, spoonbills and Goliath herons.

To get to the reserve, you will need your own vehicle – take the signposted turning off the B1, 15km north of Mariental, and continue 6km to the entrance gate.

BRUKKAROS

With a 2km-wide crater, this extinct volcano (1586m) dominates the skyline between Mariental and Keetmanshoop. It was formed some 80 million years ago when a magma pipe encountered groundwater about 1km below the earth's surface and caused a series of violent volcanic explosions.

From the car park, it's a 3.5km hike to the crater's southern entrance; along the way, watch for the remarkable **quartz formations** embedded in the rock. From here, you can head for the otherworldly **crater floor**, or turn left and follow the southern rim up to the abandoned sunspot research centre, which was established by the US Smithsonian Institute in the 1930s.

The basic **Brukkaros Campsite** (campsite per person N$50) has sites with toilets and a bush shower, but you must supply your own drinking water. Half of the campsites are literally carved out of the volcano and offer some truly stunning views across the valley.

Brukkaros rises 35km west of Tses on the B1. Follow the C98 west for 40km and then turn north on to the D3904 about 1km east of Berseba. It's then 8km to the car park. Note that a 4WD is required to access some of the higher campsites at Brukkaros Campsite.

KEETMANSHOOP
☑ 063

Keetmanshoop (*kayt*-mahns-*hoo*-up) sits at the main crossroads of Southern Namibia, and this is why you may end up here. More of a place to overnight than spend any time, it's a friendly enough little town.

There are a few examples of German colonial architecture, including the 1910 **Kaiserliches Postampt** (Imperial Post Office; cnr 5th Ave & Fenschel St), and the **town museum** (cnr Kaiser St & 7th Ave; admission free; ⏰7.30am-4.30pm Mon-Fri), which is housed in the 1895 Rhenish Mission Church, which itself is arguably more interesting than the contents of the museum inside. The ramshackle bits and pieces on display are good for killing an hour or so.

About 14km east of town, the **Quivertree Forest Rest Camp** (☑683421; www.quivertreeforest.com; campsite per person N$100, s/d/tr/q bungalows from N$420/580/700/1000, day admission per person N$55) proudly boasts Namibia's largest stand of *kokerboom* (quiver trees). Rates include use of picnic facilities and entry to the Giant's Playground, a bizarre natural rock garden 5km away.

In the quiet Westdene neighbourhood of the town itself, **Pension Gessert** (☑081 4347379, 223892; gesserts@iafrica.com.na; 138 13th St; s/d incl breakfast N$320/560; ☒) offers quaint and homey rooms with modern touches, a beautiful cooling green garden to relax in and a swimming pool. There's a cheaper option without breakfast available too.

Although down a dirt road and without a street address, **Bernice B&B** (☑224851; bernicebeds@iway.na; s/d N$240/360) is extremely well signed from any direction that you approach town – just follow the signs! Book ahead as it does get busy. There are family options, DSTV and good-sized rooms with a contemporary touch.

❶ Getting There & Away
Intercape Mainliner (p355) runs buses between Windhoek and Keetmanshoop (from N$280, 5½ hours, four weekly). Book your tickets in advance online as this service continues on to Cape Town (South Africa) and fills up quickly.

Combis (minibuses) also run up and down the B1 with fairly regular frequency, and a ride between Windhoek to Keetmanshoop shouldn't cost more than N$100. Less regular combis connect Keetmanshoop to the township in Lüderitz, with fares averaging around N$175.

Trans-Namib (p226) operates a night train between Windhoek and Keetmanshoop (from N$90, 12 hours, daily except Saturday).

NAUTE DAM
Naute Dam is an attractive spot that is surrounded by low truncated hills, and attracts

BEWARE OF FALLING ROCKS

A meteorite is an extraterrestrial body that survives its impact with the earth's surface without being destroyed. Although it's estimated that about 500 meteorites land each year, only a handful are typically recovered. However, in a single meteor shower sometime in the dim and distant past, more than 21 tonnes of 90% ferrous extraterrestrial boulders crashed to earth in southern Namibia. It's rare for so many meteorites to fall at once, and these are thought to have been remnants of an explosion in space, which were held together as they were drawn in by the earth's gravitational field.

Thus far, at least 77 meteorite chunks have been found within a 2500-sq-km area around the former Rhenish mission station of Gibeon, 60km south of Mariental. The largest chunk, which weighs 650kg, is housed in Cape Town Museum (South Africa) while other bits have wound up as far away as Anchorage (Alaska). Between 1911 and 1913, soon after their discovery, 33 chunks were brought to Windhoek for safekeeping. Over the years, they've been displayed in Zoo Park and at Alte Feste in Windhoek, but have now found a home on Post Street Mall.

large numbers of water birds. Camping is permitted, though there are no official facilities, and you must be self-sufficient. To get to the dam, drive 30km west of Keetmanshoop on the B4 and turn south on the D545.

SEEHEIM

It's a long and lonely drive southwest to Lüderitz, which is why you might want to consider stopping for the night at the Seeheim rail halt, 48km southwest of Keetmanshoop. Although the tiny town is home to little more than petrol stations and small shops, about 13km west on the B4 is the Naiams farm, where a signpost indicates a 15-minute walk to the remains of a 1906 German fort. The fort was raised to prevent Nama attacks on German travellers and Lüderitz-bound freight.

Accommodation of all varieties is available at the historic Seeheim Hotel (☎250503; campsite per person N$75, s/d N$420/760), which features an atmospheric old bar as well as period furniture. Campsites on terraced grass at the front of hotel and a clean amenities block are available, while rooms are simple, clean affairs with mosquito nets (upstairs rooms are better).

The sealed B4 highway connects Keetmanshoop with Lüderitz, though you're going to need your own vehicle if you want to access this stretch of highway.

DUWISIB CASTLE
☎ 063

A curious neo-baroque structure located about 70km south of Maltahöhe smack dab in the middle of the barren desert, this European castle (admission N$60; ☉8am-1pm & 2-5pm) is smaller than some grandiose descriptions suggest and only really worth a stop if you're passing by. The portraits and scant furniture certainly give it a European feel, though, and the pleasant courtyard is a good place to relax in the shade of some majestic trees.

It was built in 1909 by Baron Captain Hans Heinrich von Wolf. After the German-Nama wars, the loyal Baron commissioned architect Willie Sander to design a castle that would reflect his commitment to the German military cause. He also married the stepdaughter of the US consul to Dresden, Miss Jayta Humphreys, and planned on ruling over his personal corner of German South West Africa.

Although the stone for the castle was quarried nearby, much of the raw material was imported from Germany, and required 20 ox wagons to transport it across the 330km of desert from Lüderitz. Artisans and masons were hired from as far away as Ireland, Denmark, Sweden and Italy. The result was a U-shaped castle with 22 rooms, all suitably fortified and decorated with family portraits and military paraphernalia. Rather than windows, most rooms have embrasures, which emphasise Von Wolf's apparent obsession with security.

As history would have it, WWI broke out, and the Baron re-enlisted in the Schutzruppe, only to be killed two weeks later

BETHANIE

One of Namibia's oldest settlements, Bethanie was founded in 1814 by the London Missionary Society. After seven years the mission was abandoned due to tribal squabbling and although a German missionary Heinrich Schmelen attempted to revive it several times, he was thwarted by drought.

Schmelen's original 1814 mission station, Schmelenhaus, occupied a one-storey cottage. It was burnt to the ground when he left Bethanie in 1828, and later rebuilt in 1842 by the first Rhenish missionary, Reverend Hans Knudsen. The building now sits on the grounds of the Evangelical Lutheran Church and houses a museum full of old photos of the mission. If it's locked, a notice on the door will tell you where to pick up a key.

Also worth a look is the 1883 home of Captain Joseph Fredericks, the Nama chief who signed a treaty with the representatives of Adolf Lüderitz on 1 May 1883 for the transfer of Angra Pequena (present-day Lüderitz). It was here in October 1884 that Captain Fredericks and the German Consul General, Dr Friedrich Nachtigal, signed a treaty of German protection over the entire territory.

The sole accommodation in town is the Bethanie Hotel, a personality-steeped building that's more like an expansive guesthouse, with good facilities including camping and modern rooms. This place was being sold at the time of writing so call by to see if it has reopened.

The Bethanie turn-off is signposted on the B4, 140km west of Keetmanshoop.

ALL-IN ONE

A welcoming stop on the road in these parts is **Betta Camp Site** (☎081 128 4419; www.
bettacamp.net; cnr C27 & D826; campsite/chalets per person N$80/200), roughly 20kms
past Duwisib. Apart from petrol and campsites if you want to crash the night, make a
beeline for the kiosk where you can stock up on supplies and indulge in the most delicious homemade goodies. Snaffle down freshly baked farm bread, apple pie, pancakes
and mouth-watering sweet treats (breakfast N$50, dinner N$100). There is even firewood
and barbecue packs.

---

at the Battle of the Somme. The Baroness
never returned to Namibia, though some
people claim that the descendants of her
thoroughbred horses still roam the desert.
In the late 1970s, ownership of the Duwisib
Castle and its surrounding 50 hectares was
transferred to the state, and is now administered by NWR.

🛏 Sleeping

Duwisib Castle Rest Camp   CAMPGROUND **$**
(campsites per person N$90) This very amena-
ble camp (with sparkling amenities block)
occupies one corner of the castle grounds
and is well set up with campsites containing bin, *braai* and bench seating. The
adjoining kiosk sells snacks, coffee and cool
drinks. Book through the NWR office in
Windhoek.

Duwisib Guest Farm   GUESTHOUSE **$$**
(☎293344; www.farmduwisib.com; campsite per
person N$90, s/d with half board N$760/1300)
Located 300m from the castle, this pleas-
ant guest farm has rooms with views of the
main attraction, and self-catering family
units that sleep up to eight people. While
you're there, be sure to check out the historic
blacksmith shop up the hill.

❶ Getting There & Away

There isn't any public transport to Duwisib
Castle. If you're coming from Helmeringhausen,
head north on the C14 for 62km and turn north-
west on to the D831. Continue for 27km, then
turn west onto the D826 and travel a further
15km to the castle.

MALTAHÖHE
☎ 063

Maltahöhe, lying at the heart of a commer-
cial ranching area, is a convenient stopover
along the back route between Namib-
Naukluft Park and Lüderitz. The area sup-
ports a growing number of guest farms and
private rest camps.

In town, you can bed down for the night
at the **Hotel Maltahöhe** (☎293013; s/d

N$475/750), which has won several national
awards for its amenable, spic-and-span ac-
commodation. It also has a restaurant and
bar offering continental cuisine.

HELMERINGHAUSEN
☎ 063

Helmeringhausen is little more than a
homestead, hotel and petrol station, and has
been the property of the Hester family since
1919. The highlight is the idiosyncratic **Ag-
ricultural Museum** (Main St; admission free;
☺on request from hotel), established in 1984
by the Helmeringhausen Farming Associa-
tion. It displays all sorts of interesting old
furniture and farming implements collected
from local properties, as well as an antique
fire engine.

Helmeringhausen Hotel (☎233083; s/d
N$520/960; ☒) is a surprisingly swish hotel
with basic, elegant rooms in addition to a
very popular restaurant (lunch mains N$60)
and bar. The menu is limited, but the beer
is cold and it has a well-stocked wine cel-
lar. Those who like eating game meat may
feel uncomfortable being watched by all
those accusing trophies. There's also a great
courtyard area for soaking up the sun and
enjoying a cold drink; it gets busy with tour
groups – book ahead in high season.

Helmeringhausen is 130km south of Mal-
tahöhe on the C14.

The South Coast

The south coast of Namibia is dominated
by Sperrgebiet (Forbidden Area), which
plays host to the country's highly lucrative
and highly secure diamond mining efforts.
Although much of the park has yet to open
up, the town of Lüderitz, which is rich in
German colonial architecture and occupies
an otherworldly setting between the dunes
and sea, is a pleasant place to spend a few
days.

NAMIBIA THE CENTRAL PLATEAU

AUS
☑ 063

A stop on the long drive west to Lüderitz, Aus is the home to a former prison camp and, aside from the prison camp, also boasts two highly recommendable guest farms where you can slow down and spend some time soaking up the desolate beauty of the shifting sands.

Aus Information Centre (☑258151; ⊘8am-5pm Mon-Fri, 8am-2pm Sat & Sun) just off the B4 has a cafe, internet and lots of information on nature, war and wild horses of the area. Ask here about the Aus Walking Trail which begins at the info centre.

🛏 Sleeping

Klein-Aus Vista　　　　LODGE $$
(☑258021; www.namibhorses.com; campsite per person N$90, cabin N$175, r/chalet per person from N$780/1250; ✴ ☒) This 10,000-hectare ranch, 3km west of Aus, is a hiker's paradise with six different trails you can do, from 4km to 20km in length. Accommodation is provided in the main lodge; in the dormitory hut Geister Schlucht, in a Shangri-la-like valley; or in the opulent Eagle's Nest complex, where several chalets are built right into the boulders. Meals are available at the main lodge. Apart from the wonderful hiking, activities include horse riding and 4WD tours of the ranch's vast desert concession.

Namtib Biosphere Reserve　　LODGE $$$
(☑683055; www.namtib.net; campsite per person N$90, s/d N$800/1270) In the beautiful Tirasberge, this private reserve is run by ecologically conscious owners who've created a self-sustaining farm in a narrow valley, with distant views of the Namib plains and dune sea. There is an incredible wealth of nature on display here, and it's certainly worth spending a night or two out here getting acquainted with all the empty space. To reach the reserve, take the C13 north of Aus for 55km, then turn west on the D707; after 48km turn east onto the 12km farm road to the lodge.

❶ Getting There & Away

Aus is 125km east of Lüderitz on the B4. Travel in this region typically requires a private vehicle.

THE AUS-LÜDERITZ ROAD

If you've come to Aus, chances are you're heading for Lüderitz. Between Aus and the coast, the road crosses the desolate southern Namib, which is distinct from the gravel plains to the north. The area is distinguished by the pastel-coloured Awasib and Uri-Hauchab ranges, which rise from the plains through a mist of windblown sand and dust – the effect is mesmerising and ethereal.

About 10km from Aus, start watching out for feral desert horses. About 20km west of Aus, turn north at the sign 'Feral Horses' and follow the track for 1.5km to Garub Pan, which is home to an artificial waterhole.

When the wind blows – which is most of the time – the final 10km into Lüderitz may be blocked by a barchan dune field that seems bent upon crossing the road. Conditions do get hazardous, especially if it's foggy, and the drifts pile quite high before road crews clean them off. Obey local speed limits, and avoid driving at night if possible.

LÜDERITZ
☑ 063

Before travelling to Lüderitz, pause for a moment to study the map, and you'll realise the fact that the town is sandwiched between the barren Namib Desert and the windswept

---

WARTIME AUS

After the Germans surrendered to the South African forces in 1915, Aus became one of two internment camps for German military personnel – military police and officers were sent to Okahandja in the north while non-commissioned officers went to Aus. Since the camp quickly grew to 1500 prisoners and 600 South African guards, residents were forced to seek shelter in flimsy tents. However, the resourceful inmates turned to brick-making and constructed houses for themselves – they even sold the excess bricks to the guards for 10 shillings per 1000. The houses weren't opulent – roofs were tiled with unrolled food tins – but they did provide protection from the elements. The prisoners also built several wood stoves and even sank boreholes.

After the Treaty of Versailles the camp was dismantled, and by May 1919 it was closed. Virtually nothing remains, though several of the brick houses have been reconstructed. The former camp is 4km east of the village of Aus, down a gravel road, then to the right; there's now a national plaque commemorating it.

WILD HORSES

On the desert plains west of Aus live some of the world's only wild desert-dwelling horses. The origin of these eccentric equines is unclear, though several theories abound. One theory suggests that the horses are descended from Schutztruppe (German Imperial Army) cavalry horses abandoned during the South African invasion in 1915, while others claim they were brought in by Nama raiders moving north from beyond the Orange River. Yet another theory asserts that they descended from a load of ship-wrecked horses en route from Europe to Australia. Still others maintain that the horses descended from the stud stock of Baron Captain Hans-Heinrich von Wolf, the original owner of the Duwisib Castle.

These horses, whose bony and scruffy appearance belies their probable high-bred ancestry and apparent adaptation to the harsh conditions, are protected inside the Diamond Area 1. In years of good rain, they grow fat and their numbers increase to several hundred. Their only source of water is Garub Pan, which is fed by an artificial borehole.

If not for the efforts of a few concerned individuals, the horses would probably have been wiped out long ago. These individuals, led by security officer Jan Coetzer of Consolidated Diamond Mines (CDM), recognised that the horses were unique, and managed to secure funding to install the borehole at Garub Pan. At one stage, the Ministry of Environment & Tourism (MET) considered taming the horses for use on patrols in Etosha National Park, though the proposal fell through. There have also been calls to exterminate the horses by individuals citing possible damage to the desert environment and gemsbok herds. So far, however, the tourism value of the horses has swept aside all counter-arguments.

The horses may also be valuable for scientific purposes. For instance, they urinate less than domestic horses, and are smaller than their supposed ancestors. The horses are also able to go without water for up to five days at a time. These adaptations may be valuable in helping scientists understand how animals cope with changing climatic conditions.

NAMIBIA LÜDERITZ

South Atlantic coast. As if Lüderitz's wholly unique geographical setting wasn't impressive enough, its surreal German art nouveau architecture will seal the deal. Something of a colonial relic scarcely touched by the 21st century, Lüderitz might recall a Bavarian village, with churches, bakeries and cafes.

Unlike its more well-heeled Teutonic rival Swakopmund on the central coast, relative isolation, poor transport links and a struggling economy have worn heavy on Lüderitz over the decades. The town itself feels a bit like it's stuck in a time warp – a perception that delivers both gloom and a certain charm (at least for visitors).

In the natural environment surrounding the town Southern Namibia really comes to life. The rocky coastline of the Lüderitz peninsula harbours flamingo flocks and penguin colonies, while the adjacent Sperrgebiet National Park is arguably the country's wildest and most pristine landscape.

History

In April 1883 Heinrich Vogelsang, under orders from Bremen merchant Adolf Lüderitz, entered into a treaty with Nama chief Joseph Fredericks and secured lands within an 8km radius of Angra Pequeña (Little Bay). Later that year Lüderitz made an appearance in Little Bay and, following his recommendation, the German chancellor Otto von Bismarck designated southwestern Africa a protectorate of the German empire. Following the discovery of diamonds in the Sperrgebiet in 1908, the town of Lüderitz was officially founded, and quickly prospered from the gem trade.

Indeed, the history of diamond mining in Namibia parallels the history of Lüderitz. Although diamonds were discovered along the Orange River in South Africa, and among the guano workings on the offshore islands as early as 1866, it apparently didn't occur to anyone that the desert sands might also harbour a bit of crystal carbon. In 1908, however, railway worker Zacharias Lewala found a shiny stone along the railway line near Grasplatz and gave it to his employer, August Stauch. Stauch took immediate interest and, to his elation, the state geologist confirmed that it was indeed a diamond. Stauch applied for a prospecting licence from the Deutsche Koloniale Gesellschaft (German Colonial Society) and set up his own mining company, the Deutsche Diamanten Gesellschaft (German Diamond Company), to begin exploiting the presumed windfall.

In the years that followed, hordes of prospectors descended upon the town of Lüderitz with dreams of finding wealth buried in the sands. Lüderitz became a boom town as service facilities sprang up to accommodate the growing population. By September 1908, however, diamond dementia was threatening to escalate out of control, so the German government intervened by establishing the Sperrgebiet. This 'Forbidden Zone' extended from latitude 26°S southward to the Orange River mouth, and stretched inland for 100km. Independent prospecting was henceforth *verboten,* and those who'd already staked their claims were forced to form mining companies.

In February 1909 a diamond board was created to broker all diamond sales and thereby control prices. However, after WWI ended, the world diamond market was so depressed that in 1920, Ernst Oppenheimer of the Anglo-American Corporation was able to purchase Stauch's company, along with eight other diamond-producing companies. This ambitious move led to the formation of Consolidated Diamond Mines (CDM), which was administered by De Beers South Africa and headquartered in Kolmanskop.

In 1928 rich diamond fields were discovered around the mouth of the Orange River, and in 1944 CDM decided to relocate to the purpose-built company town of Oranjemund. Kolmanskop's last inhabitants left in 1956, and the sand dunes have been encroaching on the town ever since.

In 1994 CDM gave way to Namdeb Diamond Corporation Limited (Namdeb), which is owned in equal shares by the government of Namibia and the De Beers Group. De Beers is a Johannesburg- and London-based diamond mining and trading corporation that has held a virtual monopoly over the diamond trade for much of its corporate history. Today, diamonds are still Lüderitz's best friend, though it's also home to several maritime industries, including the harvesting of crayfish, seaweed and seagrass, as well as experimental oyster, mussel and prawn farms.

LÜDERITZ TOWN

Lüderitz is chock-a-block with colonial buildings, and every view reveals something interesting. The curiously intriguing architecture, which mixes German imperial and art nouveau styles, makes this bizarre little town appear even more other-worldly.

◉ Sights

Goerke Haus   HISTORIC HOUSE
(Diamantberg St; admission N$25; ⊘guided tour 2-4pm Mon-Fri, 4-5pm Sat-Sun) The sheer scale of Goerke Haus and the way it blends into the rockface is very impressive. Originally the home of Lieutenant Hans Goerke, designed by architect Otto Ertl and constructed in 1910 on Diamond Hill, it was one of the town's most extravagant properties. The house has undergone an admirable renovation job and is certainly worth a look.

FREE **Felsenkirche**   CHURCH
(Kirche St; ⊘4-5pm Mon-Sat) The prominent Evangelical Lutheran church dominates Lüderitz from high on Diamond Hill. It was designed by Albert Bause, who implemented the Victorian influences he'd seen in the Cape. With assistance from private donors in Germany, construction of the church began in late 1911 and was completed the following year. The brilliant stained-glass panel situated over the altar was donated by Kaiser Wilhelm II, while the Bible was a gift from his wife. Come for the views over the water and the town.

Lüderitz Museum   MUSEUM
(🖉202582; Diaz St; admission N$15; ⊘3.30-5pm Mon-Fri) This museum contains information on the town's history, including displays on natural history, local indigenous groups and the diamond-mining industry. Phone to arrange a visit outside standard opening hours.

LÜDERITZ PENINSULA

The Lüderitz Peninsula, much of which lies outside the Sperrgebiet, makes an interesting half-day excursion from town.

Agate Bay, just north of Lüderitz, is made up of tailings from the diamond workings. There aren't many agates these days, but you'll find fine sand partially consisting of tiny grey mica chips.

The picturesque and relatively calm bay, **Sturmvogelbucht**, is a pleasant place for a *braai,* though the water temperature would be amenable only to a penguin or polar bear. The rusty ruin in the bay is the remains of a 1914 Norwegian whaling station; the salty pan just inland attracts flamingos and merits a quick stop.

At **Diaz Point**, 22km by road from Lüderitz, is a classic lighthouse and a replica of the cross erected in July 1488 by Portuguese navigator Bartolomeu Dias on his return from the Cape of Good Hope. Portions of the original have been dispersed as far as Lisbon, Berlin and Cape Town. From the point, there's a view of a nearby seal colony and you can also see cormorants, flamingos, wading birds and even the occasional pod of dolphins.

Also at the point is a **cafe** serving hot/cold drinks, toasties (N$20), oysters, beer and great chocolate cake. It's possible to **camp** (campsite N$75, per person N$45) on rocky, flat ground roped off between the lighthouse and water. There are decent amenities although the site is more exposed to the wind than Shark Island.

Halifax Island, a short distance offshore south of Diaz Point, is home to Namibia's best-known jackass penguin colony. Jackass or Cape penguins live in colonies on rocky offshore islets off the Atlantic Coast. With binoculars, you can often see them gathering on the sandy beach opposite the car park.

Grosse Bucht (Big Bay), at the southern end of Lüderitz peninsula, is a wild and scenic beach favoured by flocks of flamingos, which feed in the tidal pools. It's also the site of a small but picturesque shipwreck on the beach.

Just a few kilometres up the coast is **Klein Bogenfels,** a small rock arch beside the sea. When the wind isn't blowing a gale, it makes a pleasant picnic spot.

☞ Tours

With the exception of the Kolmanskop ghost town, allow at least five days to plan any excursion into the Sperrgebiet as tour companies need time to fill out all of the paperwork and acquire all of the necessary permits.

Coastway Tours Lüderitz   ADVENTURE TOUR
(☏202002; www.coastways.com.na) This highly reputable company runs multiday self-catering 4WD trips deep into the Sperrgebiet. Note that the cost of the permit (N$250) is included in the price of the relevant tour.

Lüderitz Safaris & Tours   ADVENTURE TOUR
(☏202719; ludsaf@africaonline.com.na; Bismarck St; ☉daily) Provides useful tourist information, organises visitor permits for the Kolmanskop ghost town and books seats on the schooner *Sedina* (N$330 per person), which sails past the Cape fur seal sanctuary at Diaz Point and the penguin colony on Halifax Island. It conducts guided oyster tours (N$50 for tour, N$30 for tastings) as well. Also a great information service with very knowledgeable staff and sells curios, books, stamps and phonecards.

🛏 Sleeping

Kairos B&B   B&B $$
(☏081 650 5598; Shark Island; s/d N$400/520) This brand spanking new, cheerful, white-washed building houses a promising new guesthouse and overlooks the water just before Shark Island. It's in a lovely location and is just a few minutes drive from the town centre. Also here is a cafe serving breakfast and lunch.

Krabbenhoft une Lampe   APARTMENT $$
(☏081 447 1151, 202674; 25 Bismarck St; tw flat N$500) One of the more unusual sleeping options in town, the Krabbenhoft is a converted carpet factory that now offers a number of self-catering flats upstairs from a furniture shop and Avis car rental office. Accommodation has loads of character, floor-to-ceiling bookshelves, high ceilings, lots of natural light, good kitchen facilities and the novelty factor can't be beat.

Kratzplatz   B&B $$
(☏202458; www.kratzplatz.com; 5 Nachtigal St; s/d incl breakfast from N$400/750) Housed in a converted church complete with vaulted ceilings, this centrally located B&B offers a variety of different rooms to choose from set amidst a patch of greenery. Rooms are in varying condition – some are a little worn but comfortable and the upstairs ones come with outside chair and table on the balcony. The attached Barrels restaurant has a lively beer garden and a wonderful German kitchen that draws both guests and outside diners.

Haus Sandrose   SELF-CATERING $$
(☏202630; www.haussandrose.com; 15 Bismarck St; s/d from N$410/750) Haus Sandrose comprises uniquely decorated self-catering rooms surrounding a sheltered garden. The bright rooms are good value and exude a cheerful and spacious feel. It's a great

Lüderitz

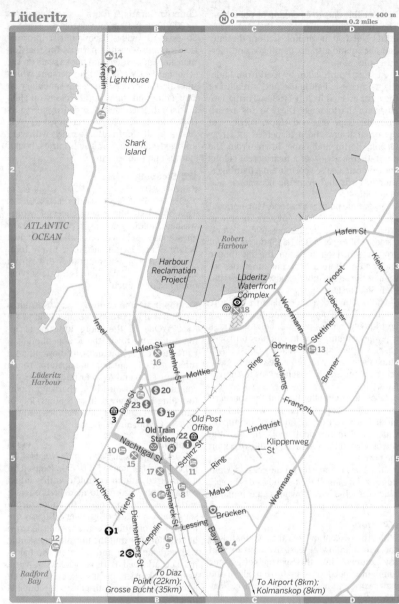

location and very friendly – note some rooms are bigger than others.

Shark Island Camp Site   CAMPGROUND **$**
(campsite per person N$100, 6-person bungalow per person N$220, lighthouse per person N$220) This

is a beautifully situated but aggravatingly windy locale. Shark Island is connected to the town by a causeway but is no longer an island, thanks to the harbour reclamation project that attached it to the mainland. The centrepiece of the island is a historic

Lüderitz

NAMIBIA LÜDERITZ

lighthouse that caps the central rock, and features two bedrooms, a living room and a kitchen – perfect for self-caterers! Book accommodation through the NWR office in Windhoek; bookings can also be made at the entrance.

Kapps Hotel　　　　　　　HOTEL **$$**
(☏202345; www.kappshotel.com; Bay Rd; s/d N$400/650) This is the town's oldest hotel, dating back to 1907, which has managed to retain some historical ambience while adding a touch of modernity. Darkish downstairs rooms have huge bathrooms. The attached **Rumour's Grill** is a great place to drop into for either a cold beer at the end of a long drive or a strong nightcap on the way up to bed.

Bay View Hotel　　　　　　HOTEL **$$**
(☏202288; www.luderitzhotels.com; Diaz St; s/d incl breakfast N$500/900; 🛜🐾) This historic complex, owned by the Lüderitz family, is one of the most established hotels in town. Airy rooms surround a courtyard and a swimming pool, and there's also an on-site bar and restaurant. The sun-blasted, blockhouse rooms are better value without breakfast (N$100 less).

Lüderitz Nest Hotel　　　　HOTEL **$$$**
(☏204000; www.nesthotel.com; 820 Diaz St; s/d N$930/1500; ❄🐾) Lüderitz's oldest upmarket hotel occupies a jutting peninsula in the southwest corner of town complete with

its own private beach. Each room is stylishly appointed with modern furnishings and faces out towards the sea. Amenities include a pool, sauna, kids' playground, car hire, terraced bar and a collection of gourmet restaurants. This hotel is what you would expect – decent service, clean and good facilities. It's overpriced but its drawcard is the magnificent water views from the rooms.

Lüderitz Backpackers　　　BACKPACKERS **$**
(☏174513, 202000; www.namibweb.com/backpackers.htm; 7 Schinz St; campsite N$70, dm/d/f N$100/250/380) Housed in a historic colonial mansion, this is the only true backpackers spot in town, with rudimentary accommodation. The vibe is congenial and low-key and the friendly management is helpful in sorting out your onward travels. And of course, the usual backpacker amenities are on offer here, including a communal kitchen, braai pit, TV lounge and laundry facilities. Prices may increase when it's busy.

**Protea Sea-View Hotel
Zum Sperrgebiet**　　　　　　HOTEL **$$$**
(☏203411; www.seaview-luederitz.com; cnr Woermann & Göring Sts; s/d from N$670/1060; ❄🛜🐾) In a town defined by its colonial heritage, the Protea bucks the trend with a modern offering of polished steel and sparkling glass. There are only 22 sun-blessed rooms here, each accented by a sweeping terrace facing out towards the sea.

✗ Eating & Drinking

If the sea has been bountiful, various hotels serve the catch of the day, though you
can always count on a long list of German
specialities. If you're self-catering, there are
a number of supermarkets as well as small
seafood merchants in town. And finally, if
you're a drinker, most restaurants double as
watering holes, though Lüderitz tends to be
fairly subdued once the sun drops.

Bistro D'Cafe BISTRO $$
(Hafen St; mains N$60-90; ⊘breakfast & lunch, din-
ner, closed Sun; 🖥) This cosy little restaurant
has a simple set-up with the emphasis on
the lovingly prepared food not the aesthet-
ics. The cute menus (remember the Rubik's
cube?) reveal seafood dishes (such as the plat-
ter, N$180) and a smattering of other options
including coronation chicken. The presenta-
tion of the food is delightful and everything is
cooked fresh – love and time are the two most
important ingredients in the food.

Barrels GERMAN $$
(📞202458; 5 Natchtigal St; mains N$45-100;
⊘dinner Mon-Fri) A wonderfully festive bar-
restaurant accented by occasional live
music, Barrels offers rotating daily specials
highlighting fresh seafood and German
staples. Portions are hefty and the buffet
(N$120) is great value. Bar opens at 6pm.

Ritzi's Seafood Restaurant SEAFOOD $$
(📞202818; Waterfront; mains N$80; ⊘breakfast,
lunch & dinner, closed Mon breakfast & Sun) Oc-
cupying a choice location in the waterfront
complex, Ritzi's is the town's top spot for
amazing seafood matched with equally
amazing sunset views. Try the assorted sea-
food curry (N$75), or seafood platter (one/
two persons N$200/300); there's a decent
wine selection, and outside dining catches
the breeze and the views.

Diaz Coffee Shop CAFE $
(cnr Bismarck & Nachtigal Sts; snacks & meals
N$25-45; ⊘breakfast, lunch) The cappuccinos
are strong and the pastries are sweet, and
the ambience wouldn't at all look out of
place in Munich. Patrons sit in a large room
with some comfy seating and receive quick
service; the food, such as hot wraps or chick-
en schwarma, is delicious. Try the speciality
coffee – if you dare.

Seabreeze Coffee Shop CAFE $
(Waterfront Complex; snacks & meals N$10-40;
⊘7.15am-4.30pm Mon-Fri, 8am-1pm Sat) This
waterfront cafe offers attractive sea views, so
make it a double espresso and linger a bit
longer than you normally would. Bratwurst
sausage, boerewors (farmer's sausage) in a
hotdog, burgers and toasties feature on the
menu, along with breakfasts. It's a well-run
place with outdoor seating that does indeed
catch the breeze.

❶ Information

Several banks on Bismarck St change cash and
travellers cheques. There is a new **tourist infor-
mation office** at the waterfront but it has very
erratic opening hours.

Stay well clear of the Sperrgebiet, unless
you're part of an organised tour, as much of
the area remains strictly off limits despite its
national park status. The northern boundary is
formed by the B4 and extends almost as far east
as Aus. The boundary is patrolled by some fairly
ruthless characters, and trespassers will be
prosecuted (or worse).

❶ Getting There & Away

Air Namibia (p354) travels about three times a
week between Windhoek and Lüderitz. The air-
port is 8km southeast of town.

Somewhat irregular combis connect Lüderitz
to Keetmanshoop, with fares averaging around
N$200. Buses depart from the southern edge of
town at informal bus stops along Bismarck St.

Lüderitz and the scenery en route are worth
the 334km trip from Keetmanshoop via the
sealed B4.

SPERRGEBIET NATIONAL PARK

Although the area has been off limits to the
public for most of the last century, in 2008
the Namibian government inaugurated
the Sperrgebiet as a national park. Known
worldwide as the source of Namibia's exclu-
sive diamonds, the Sperrgebiet (Forbidden
area) could become the gem of Namibia's
protected spaces. Geographically speak-
ing, the park encompasses the northern tip
of the Succulent Karoo Biorne, an area of
26,000 sq km of dunes and mountains that
appear dramatically stark but represent one
of 25 outstanding global 'hotspots' of unique
biodiversity.

The Sperggebiet originally consisted of
two private concessions: Diamond Area 1
and Diamond Area 2. The latter, home to
the Kolmanskop ghost town and Elizabeth
Bay, has been open to the public for some
time now. Since 2004 parts of the former
have also been opened up to specialist con-
servation groups, though given the diamond
industry's security concerns, access has been
carefully controlled.

At the time of research, it appeared that disagreement between internal government departments was holding back further development and access for tourists in the park. Hopefully, once this has been resolved, more of this unique area will be open to visitors.

History

The 'Forbidden Zone' was established in 1908 following the discovery of diamonds near Lüderitz. Although mining operations were localised along the coast, a huge swath of Southern Namibia was sectioned off in the interest of security.

As a diamond mining concession, the Sperrgebiet has been off limits to the public and scientists for most of the last century, and the tight restrictions on access have helped to keep much of the area pristine. De Beers Centenary, a partner in De Beers Consolidated Diamond Mines, continues to control the entire area until the MET establishes a management plan for the park.

Wildlife & Conservation

Forty per cent of the park is desert, and 30% is grassland; the rest is rocks, granite mountains and moonscape. Though the area has yet to be fully explored, initial scientific assessments have discovered 776 plant species, 230 of which are thought to be unique to the park. There are also populations of gemsbok, brown hyenas and rare, threatened reptile species, including the desert rain frog. Bird species are extremely varied, and include the dune lark, black-headed canary and the African oystercatcher.

The **Namibian Nature Foundation** (NNF; www.nnf.org.na) will eventually take over the planning for the park and will focus on community-based initiatives to ensure that locals benefit. The eventual development of tourism in the Sperrgebiet is expected to stimulate the economy of Lüderitz, which will serve as the main gateway to the park.

◉ Sights

Kolmanskop Ghost Town   HISTORIC TOWN
(tour adult/child incl permit fee N$55/35) Given that permits can be arranged from Namdeb with relative ease, the most popular excursion from Lüderitz is the ghost town of Kolmanskop. Named after an early Afrikaner trekker, Jani Kolman, whose ox wagon became bogged in the sand here, Kolmanskop was originally constructed as the CDM headquarters. Although Kolmanskop once boasted a casino, bowling alley and a theatre with fine acoustics, the slump in diamond sales after WWI and the discovery of richer pickings at Oranjemund ended its heyday. By 1956 the town was totally deserted, and left to the mercy of the shifting desert sands. Today, Kolmanskop has been partially restored as a tourist attraction, and the sight of decrepit buildings being invaded by dunes is simply too surreal to describe.

You can turn up at any time, and you're not required to arrive as part of an organised tour, though you do need to purchase a permit in advance through either the NWR office in Lüderitz or a local tour operator. Guided tours (in English and German; at 9.30am and 11am Monday to Friday, and 10am Sunday), which are included in the price of the permit, depart from the museum in Kolmanskop. After the tour you can return to the museum, which contains relics and information on the history of Namibian diamond mining.

☞ Tours

Until the park loosens its tight restrictions on public access, it's in your own best interest to have a healthy respect for the boundaries. Armed guards in the Sperrgebiet have a lot of time on their hands – don't make their day. Selected sights in the national park are open to visitors on private tours.

GHOSTLY GOINGS-ON

Kolmanskop Ghost Tours (tour adult/child incl permit fee N$55/35) can be organised in Lüderitz. Unfortunately the cafe and gift shop and often large tourist numbers dampen the potential eerie effect of this old town. If there are a lot of tourists around (likely) then you're better off skipping the organised tour part of the trip here and focusing instead on wandering around the decrepit buildings and piles of sand, getting a bit of a taste for this old deserted town. Kolmanskop is only a 15-minute drive from Lüderitz, just off the main B4 highway. Tour agencies sell tours to Kolmanskop, or you can drive yourself, as long as you have arranged the permit beforehand .

DIAMOND DEMENTIA

Geology & the 4 Cs

Diamonds are the best known allotrope (form) of carbon, and are characterised by their extreme hardness (they are the hardest naturally occurring mineral) and high dispersion of light (diamonds are prismatic when exposed to white light). As a result, they are valued for industrial purposes as abrasives since they can only be scratched by other diamonds, and for ornamental purposes since they retain lustre when polished. It's estimated that 130 million carats (or 26,000kg) of diamonds is mined annually, yielding a market value of over US$9 billion.

Diamonds are formed when carbon-bearing materials are exposed to high pressures and temperatures for prolonged periods of time. With the exception of synthetically produced diamonds, favourable conditions only occur beneath the continental crust, starting at depths of about 150km. Once carbon crystallises, a diamond will then continue to grow in size so long as it is exposed to both sufficiently high temperatures and pressures. However, size is limited by the fact that diamond-bearing rock is eventually expelled towards the surface through deep-origin volcanic eruptions. Eventually they are forced to the surface by magma, and are expelled from a volcanic pipe.

Since the early 20th century the quality of a diamond has been determined by four properties, now commonly used as basic descriptors of a stone: carat, clarity, colour and cut. The **carat** weight measures the mass of a diamond, with one carat equal to 200mg. Assuming all other properties are equal, the value of a diamond increases exponentially in relation to carat weight since larger diamonds are rarer.

Clarity is a measure of internal defects known as inclusions, which are foreign materials or structural imperfections present in the stone. Higher clarity is associated with value, and it's estimated that only about 20% of all diamonds mined have a high enough clarity rating to be sold as gemstones.

Although a perfect diamond is transparent with a total absence of hue, virtually all diamonds have a discernable **colour** due to chemical impurities and structural defects. Depending on the hue and intensity, a diamond's colour can either detract from or enhance its value (yellow diamonds are discounted, while pink and blue diamonds are more valuable).

Elizabeth Bay
SCENIC TOUR

In 1986 CDM again began prospecting in the northern Sperrgebiet, and found bountiful diamond deposits around Elizabeth Bay, 30km south of Kolmanskop. The estimated 2.5 million carats weren't expected to last more than 10 years, but CDM installed a full-scale operation and rather than duplicate its Lüderitz facilities here, the company provided its workers with daily transport from the town. Half-day tours to Elizabeth Bay, which must be booked through tour operators in Lüderitz, also take in Kolmanskop and the Atlas Bay Cape fur seal colony.

Bogenfels Sea Arch
SCENIC TOUR

One-third of the way down the Forbidden Coast between Lüderitz and Oranjemund is the 55m natural sea arch known as Bogenfels (Bow Rock). Bogenfels has only been opened to private tours for a few years, which also take in the mining ghost town of Pomona, the Maerchental Valley, the Bogenfels ghost town and a large cave near the arch itself. You must book this trip in Lüderitz.

Coastway Tours Lüderitz (p309) conducts daily sightseeing tours from Lüderitz out to Bogenfels (from N$1250 per person depending on numbers on tour), via Pomona.

🛏 Sleeping

There are no tourist lodges within the national park, and bush camping is strictly forbidden. While it is likely that some form of accommodation will be constructed in the years to come, in the meantime your best option is to base yourself in Lüderitz.

❶ Getting There & Away

Do not attempt to access the Sperrgebiet in a private vehicle as you will be inviting a whole mess of trouble. The only exception to this state-

Finally, the **cut** of a diamond describes the quality of workmanship and the angles to which a diamond is cut.

International Trade

The international trade in diamonds as gemstones is unique in comparison to precious metals such as gold and platinum since diamonds are not traded as a commodity. As a result, the price of diamonds is artificially inflated by a few key players, and there exists virtually no secondary market. For example, wholesale trade and diamond cutting was historically limited to a few locations, including New York, Antwerp, London, Tel Aviv and Amsterdam, though recently centres have been established in China, India and Thailand.

Since its establishment in 1888, De Beers has maintained a virtual monopoly on the world's diamond mines and distribution channels for gem-quality stones. At one time it was estimated that over 80% of the world's uncut diamonds were controlled by the subsidiaries of De Beers, though this percentage has dropped below 50% in more recent years. However, De Beers continues to take advantage of its market position by establishing strict price controls, and marketing diamonds directly to preferential consumers (known as sight holders) in world markets.

Once purchased by sight holders, diamonds are then cut and polished to sell as gemstones, though these activities are limited to the select locations mentioned earlier. Once they have been prepared, diamonds are then sold on one of 24 diamond exchanges known as bourses. This is the final tightly controlled step in the diamond supply chain, as retailers are only permitted to buy relatively small amounts of diamonds before preparing them for final sale to the consumer.

In recent years the diamond industry has come under increasing criticism regarding the buying and selling of conflict or 'blood' diamonds, those diamonds mined in war zones and sold to finance the ongoing conflict. In response to increasing public concern, the Kimberley Process was instituted in 2002, which was aimed at preventing the trade of conflict diamonds on the international market. The main mechanism by which the Kimberley Process operates is by documenting and certifying diamond exports from producing countries in order to ensure that proceeds are not being used to fund criminal or revolutionary activities.

NAMIBIA THE FAR SOUTH & FISH RIVER CANYON

ment is Kolmanskop, which can be accessed if you have the necessary permits.

The Far South & Fish River Canyon

Situated within the angle between Southern Africa's two most remote quarters, Namaqualand and the Kalahari, Namibia's bleak southern tip exudes a sense of isolation from whichever direction you approach it. As you travel along the highway, the seemingly endless desert plains stretch to all horizons, only to suddenly tear asunder at the mighty Fish River Canyon. This gash across the desert landscape is one of Namibia's most stunning geological formations, luring in determined bands of trekkers each winter, bent on traipsing across its vast expanse.

GRÜNAU
☑ 063

For most travellers, Grünau is either the first petrol station north of the South African border or a logical overnight stop for weary drivers between Cape Town and Windhoek.

An excellent spot to lie down for the night is the White House Guest Farm (☑262061; r N$400). Dolf and Kinna de Wet's wonderful and popular B&B – yes, it is a white house – has well-priced, self-catering accommodation. This renovated farmhouse, which dates from 1912, is architecturally stunning. Kitchen facilities are available, though the hosts will also provide set meals and *braai* packs on request. To get there, head 11km towards Keetmanshoop on the B1 and turn west at the White House signpost; it's 4km off the road.

Grünau is 144km northwest of the Velloorsdrift border crossing along the C10, and 142km north of the Noordoewer border crossing along the B1.

FISH RIVER CANYON
☑ 063

Nowhere else in Africa will you find anything quite like Fish River Canyon. Despite the seeming enormity of this statement, the numbers don't lie: the canyon measures 160km in length and up to 27km in width, and the dramatic inner canyon reaches a depth of 550m. Although these figures by themselves are impressive, it's difficult to get a sense of perspective without actually witnessing the enormous scope of the canyon. In order to do this, you will need to embark on a monumental five-day hike that traverses half the length of the canyon, and ultimately tests the limits of your physical and mental endurance. Your reward, however, will be the chance to tackle one of Namibia's and, indeed, one of Africa's greatest natural wonders.

Fish River Canyon is part of the |Ai- |Ais Richtersveld Transfrontier Park, one of an increasing number of 'peace' or cross-border parks in southern Africa. Straddling southern Namibia and South Africa (and measuring 6045 sq km) it boasts one of the most species-rich arid zones in the world. It also encompasses Richtersveld National Park (in South Africa) and the Orange River valley.

History

The San have a legend that the wildly twisting Fish River Canyon was gouged out by a frantically scrambling snake, *Koutein Kooru*, as he was pursued into the desert by hunters. However, the geological story is a bit different...

Fish River, which joins the Orange River 110km south of the canyon, has been gouging out this gorge for aeons. Surprisingly, Fish River Canyon is actually two canyons, one inside the other, which were formed in entirely different ways. It's thought that the original sedimentary layers of shale, sandstone and loose igneous material around Fish River Canyon were laid down nearly two billion years ago, and were later metamorphosed by heat and pressure into more solid materials, such as gneiss. Just under a billion years ago, cracks in the formation admitted intrusions of igneous material, which cooled to form the dolerite dykes (which are now exposed in the inner canyon).

Fish River Canyon

FIRST IMPRESSIONS: FISH RIVER CANYON

The canyon, seen most clearly in the morning, is stark, very beautiful and seemingly carved into the earth by a master builder – it flaunts an otherworldliness. The exposed rock and lack of plant life is quite startling. Its rounded edges and sharp corners create a symphony in stone of gigantic and imposing proportions. If you have a viewpoint to yourself it's a perfect place to reflect on this country's unique landscape, harsh environment and immense horizons.

The surface was then eroded into a basin and covered by a shallow sea, which eventually filled with sediment – sandstone, conglomerate, quartzite, limestone and shale – washed down from the surrounding exposed lands. Around 500 million years ago a period of tectonic activity along crustal faults caused these layers to rift and to tilt at a 45° angle. These forces opened a wide gap in the earth's crust and formed a large canyon.

This was what we now regard as the outer canyon, the bottom of which was the first level of terraces that are visible approximately 170m below the eastern rim and 380m below the western rim. This newly created valley naturally became a watercourse (the Fish River, oddly enough), which began eroding a meandering path along the valley floor and eventually gouged out what is now the 270m-deep inner canyon.

◉ Sights

HOBAS

From Hobas, it's 10km on a gravel road to the Main Viewpoint with probably the best – and most photographed – overall canyon view. Hikers' Viewpoint a few kilometres north (at the start of the hiking route) is even more stunning. You can walk along the canyon rim between these two viewpoints and both vistas take in the sharp river bend known as Hell's Corner. Tracking the other way from the main viewpoint (ie turn left as you approach it) is a road to the Sunset Viewpoint, another well-located vantage point. A few kilometres before you reach the main viewpoint a 4WD-only track winds 13km out to other viewpoints including Sulphur Springs and Eagle Rock.

AI-AIS

The hot springs (adult/child N\$80/free; ☉sunrise-sunset) at Ai-Ais (Nama for 'scalding hot') are beneath the towering peaks at the southern end of the Fish River Canyon. Although the 60°C springs have probably been known to the San for thousands of years, the legend goes that they were 'discovered' by a nomadic Nama shepherd rounding up stray sheep. They're rich in chloride, fluoride and sulphur, and are reputedly therapeutic for sufferers of rheumatism or nervous disorders. The hot water is piped to a series of baths and jacuzzis as well as an outdoor swimming pool.

A pleasant diversion is the short scramble to the peak, which rises above the opposite bank (note that the trail is not marked). It affords a superb view of Ai-Ais, and you will even see the four pinnacles of Four Finger Rock rising far to the north. The return trip takes approximately two hours.

Amenities include a shop, restaurant, petrol station, tennis courts, post office and, of course, a swimming pool, spa and mineral bath facilities.

Be advised that during the summertime, there's a serious risk of flooding – Ai-Ais was destroyed by floods in both 1972 and 2000.

🏃 Activities

Fish River Hiking Trail   HIKING
(per person N\$250) The five-day hike from Hobas to Ai-Ais is Namibia's most popular long-distance walk – and with good reason. The magical 85km route, which follows the sandy riverbed past a series of ephemeral pools, begins at Hikers' Viewpoint and ends at the hot spring resort of Ai-Ais.

Due to flash flooding and heat in summer months, the route is open only from 15 April to 15 September. Groups of three to 30 people may begin the hike every day of the season, though you will have to book in advance as the trail is extremely popular. Reservations can be made at the NWR office in Windhoek.

Officials may need a doctor's certificate of fitness, issued less than 40 days before your hike, though if you look young and fit they may not ask. Hikers must arrange their own transport to and from the start and finish as well as accommodation in Hobas and Ai-Ais.

NAMIBIA THE FAR SOUTH & FISH RIVER CANYON

FISH RIVER CANYON HIKING ROUTE

From Hobas, it's 10km to **Hikers' Viewpoint**, which is the start of the trail – hikers must find their own transport to this point. The steep and scenic section at the beginning takes you from the canyon rim to the river, where you'll have a choice of fabulous sandy campsites beside cool, green river pools.

Although some maps show the route following the river quite closely, it's important to note that the best route changes from year to year. This is largely due to sand and vegetation deposited by the previous year's floods. In general, the easiest hiking will be along the inside of the river bends, where you're likely to find wildlife trails and dry, non-sandy terrain that's free of vegetation tangles, slippery stones or large boulders.

After an exhausting 13km hike through the rough sand and boulders along the east bank, the **Sulphur Springs Viewpoint** track joins the main route. If you're completely exhausted at this stage and can't handle the conditions, this route can be used as an emergency exit from the canyon. If it's any encouragement, however, the going gets easier as you move downstream, so why not head a further 2km to **Sulphur Springs**, set up camp and see how you feel in the morning?

Sulphur Springs – more commonly called **Palm Springs** – is an excellent campsite with thermal sulphur pools (a touch of paradise) to soothe your aching muscles. The springs, which have a stable temperature of 57°C, gush up from the underworld at an amazing 30L per second and contain not only sulphur but also chloride and fluoride.

Legend has it that during WWI two German prisoners of war hid out at Sulphur Springs to escape internment. One was apparently suffering from asthma and the other from skin cancer but thanks to the spring's healing powers, both were cured. It's also said that the palm trees growing here sprang up from date pips discarded by these two Germans.

The next section of the hike consists mostly of deep sand, pebbles and gravel. The most direct route through the inside river bends requires hikers to cross the river several times. The Table Mountain formation lies 15km beyond Sulphur Springs, and a further 15km on is the first short cut, which avoids an area of dense thorn scrub known as Bushy Corner. Around the next river bend, just upstream from the Three Sisters rock formation, is a longer short cut past Kanebis Bend up to Kooigoedhoogte Pass. At the top, you'll have a superb view of Four Finger Rock, an impressive rock tower consisting of four thick pinnacles (though they more closely resemble a cow's udder than fingers).

After descending to the river, you'll cross to the west bank and start climbing over yet another short cut (although you can also follow the river bend). At the southern end of this pass, on the west bank of the river, lies the grave of Lieutenant Thilo von Trotha, who was killed here after a 1905 confrontation between the Germans and the Nama.

The final 25km into Ai-Ais, which can be completed in one long day, follows an easy but sandy and rocky route. South of von Trotha's grave, the canyon widens out and becomes drier. Be advised that, during the end of winter, the final 15km are normally completely dry, so you will need to carry sufficient water.

Thanks to the typically warm, clear weather, you probably won't need a tent, but you must carry a sleeping bag and food. In Hobas, check on water availability in the canyon. In August and September the last 15km of the walk can be completely dry and hikers will need several 2L water bottles to manage this hot, sandy stretch. Large, plastic soft-drink bottles normally work just fine.

🛏 Sleeping

Accommodation inside the park must be prebooked through the NWR office in Windhoek.

Hobas Camp Site CAMPGROUND $
(campsite N$125; 🌊) Administered by NWR, this pleasant and well-shaded camping ground near the park's northern end is about 10km from the main viewpoints. Facilities

are clean, and there's a kiosk and swimming pool, but no restaurant or petrol station.

Ai-Ais Hot Springs Spa   RESORT $$
(campsite N$125, mountain/river view d N$900/1100; 🌊) Also administered by NWR, amenities include washing blocks, *braai* pits and use of the resort facilities, including the hot springs. There are also family chalets available and an on-site restaurant and small grocery store.

Fish River Lodge   LODGE $$$
(☑683005; www.fishriverlodge-namibia.com; s/d N$1500/2250) Twenty chalets located on the western rim of the canyon, this is a magical spot to enjoy the landscape. Activities include a five-night canyon hike (75km, April to September) or a day hike for the less ambitious; both are in a private concession so there is no need to book through NWR. Access to the lodge is from the D463, which links the B4 in the north and the C13 to the west.

❶ Information
The main access points for Fish River Canyon are at Hobas, near the northern end of the park, and Ai-Ais, near the southern end. Both are administered by the NWR. Accommodation must be booked in advance through the Windhoek office. Daily park permits, N$80 per person and N$10 per vehicle, are valid for both Hobas and Ai-Ais.

The **Hobas Information Centre** (⊘7.30am–noon & 2–5pm) at the northern end of the park is also the check-in point for the five-day canyon hike. Packaged snacks and cool drinks are available here, but little else. If you're on your way to view the canyon, use the toilets here if you need them – there are none further on.

The Fish River typically flows between March and April. Early in the tourist season, from April to June, it may diminish to a trickle and by midwinter, to just a chain of remnant pools along the canyon floor.

Following the death of an ill-prepared hiker in 2001, the NWR decided to prohibit day hikes into Fish River Canyon – day hikes and leisure walks are strictly prohibited.

❶ Getting There & Away
There's no public transport to Hobas or Ai-Ais, and you'll really need a private vehicle to get around. The drive in from Grünau to Hobas is on a decent gravel road.

GONDWANA CAÑON PARK
Founded in 1996, the 100,000-hectare Gondwana Cañon Park was created by merging several former sheep farms and removing the fences to restore the wilderness country immediately northeast of |Ai- |Ais Richtersveld Transfrontier Park. Waterholes have been established and wildlife is returning to this wonderful, remote corner of Namibia. In the process, the park absorbed the former Augurabies-Steenbok Nature Reserve, which had been created earlier to protect not only steenboks, but also Hartmann's mountain zebras, gemsboks and klipspringers.

🛏 Sleeping
A wide range of activities, from 4WD excursions and guided hikes to horseback riding and scenic flights, are available at the places below.

🔝CHOICE Cañon Lodge   LODGE $$$
(☑061-230066; www.gondwana-collection.com; s/d from N$1400/2240; ❋🌊) This mountain retreat is one of Namibia's most stunning accommodation options. The whole place, but especially the luxury stone bungalows, is sympathetically integrated into its boulder-strewn backdrop. The outlook is dramatic and the bungalows have great privacy. The restaurant, housed in a 1908 farmhouse, is tastefully decorated with historic farming implements and has rambling gardens. It's a very friendly place, the food is first class and we've never met a nicer barman.

Cañon Roadhouse   GUESTHOUSE $$
(☑061-230066; www.gondwana-collection.com; campsite per person N$100, s/d from N$815/1300; 🌊) This wonderfully unique (and terribly kitsch) place attempts to recreate a roadhouse out on the wildest stretches of Route 66 – at least as it exists in the collective imagination. Buffets are served on an antique motorcycle, the stunning window shades are made from used air filters and the bar stools are air filters from heavy-duty vehicles. Rooms (which are all the same) are brightly coloured with low-slung roofs and modern touches. The walk-in shower is a luxury and the cheapish furniture is offest by a Mediterranean feel. There are also 12 campsites with toilets and *braai* facilities. It's a handy place to stop for lunch during the day (toasties N$30) too – try the Amarula cheesecake.

Cañon Mountain Camp   LODGE $
(☑061-230066; www.gondwana-collection.com; r per person from N$310; 🌊) One of the more budget orientated properties in the Cañon collection, this remote mountain camp occupies a high altitude setting amid dolerite

NAMIBIA THE FAR SOUTH & FISH RIVER CANYON

BORDER CROSSING: SOUTH AFRICA

Formalities crossing from or to South Africa via the **Vioolsdrif–Noordoewer border crossing** (open 24 hours) are straightforward. If coming from South Africa, first go to office 1: Immigration, then make sure you also pop into office 3: Police. If you have nothing to declare then you are not required to go through the Customs office. On the Namibia side of the border you'll need to complete the Entry/Departure card in the Immigration office (and fill in every category possible or they'll pull you up). Then, if you are driving, look for the 'Road Fund Administration' sign, go into that small office and pay a Cross Border Charge for bringing your vehicle into Namibia (N$220 for campers, 4WDs and cars). You will be issued with a CBC permit – keep this handy as you may need to present it at police roadblocks around the country. And through into Namibia! As soon as you're through the border crossing there are a couple of cheap lodges if you get stuck and two 24-hour petrol stations.

hills. Self-caterers can take advantage of the fully equipped kitchen, *braai* pits and communal lounges.

Cañon Village
COTTAGES $$$

(☏061-230066; www.gondwana-collection.com; s/d from N$1075/1750; ❄❄) Drawing inspiration from the Cape-Dutch villages of yesteryear, this wonderfully bucolic spot hugs a rock face on the outskirts of Fish River Canyon. Cottages are spacious and comfortable, and afford great views of the area. The centrepiece is a thatched restaurant serving traditional Afrikaner specialities.

❶ Getting There & Away
Gondwana Cañon Park can be accessed via private vehicle along the C37.

NOORDOEWER
☏ 063

Noordoewer sits astride the Orange River, which has its headwaters in the Drakensberg Mountains of Natal (South Africa) and forms much of the boundary between Namibia and South Africa. Although the town primarily serves as a border post and a centre for viticulture, it serves as a good base for organising a canoeing or rafting adventure on the Orange River.

🏃 Activities
Canoe and rafting trips are normally done in stages and last three to six days. The popular trips from Noordoewer north to Aussenkehr aren't treacherous by any stretch – the white-water never exceeds Class II – but they do provide access to some wonderfully wild canyon country. Other possible stages include: Aussenkehr to the Fish River mouth; Fish River mouth to Nama Canyon

(which has a few more serious rapids); and Nama Canyon to Selingsdrif.

Amanzi Trails
CANOEING

(☏in South Africa 27-21-559 1573; www.amanzi trails.co.za) This well-established South African company is based in Abiqua Camp, and specialises in four-/five-day guided canoe trips down the Orange River costing N$2020/2360 per person. It also arranges shorter self-guided trips and longer excursions up Fish River for more experienced clients.

Felix Unite
CANOEING

(☏in South Africa 27-21-702-9400; www.felixunite. com) Another highly reputable South African operator, Felix Unite is based in Provenance Camp, and specialises in four-/six-day guided canoe and rafting trips down the Orange River costing N$3175/3650 per person. It can also combine these excursions with lengthier trips around the Western Cape of South Africa.

🛏 Sleeping

Abiqua Camp
CAMPGROUND $$

(☏297255; www.amanzitrails.co.za/abiqua_river_ camp/abiqua_camp.html; campsite per person N$70, plus per vehicle N$30, s/d/tr chalet N$350/ 420/490) This well-situated camp, 15km down Orange River Rd, sits on the riverbank. It's the launch point for Amanzi Trails, so you can stock up on supplies, indulge in a hot meal and get a good night's rest before embarking on your canoe trip.

Camp Provenance
CAMPGROUND $$

(☏in South Africa 27-21-702-9400; www.felixunite. com; campsite per person N$100, permanent tw tent N$600, tw cabana N$800) Approximately 10km west of Noordoewer is this safari-chic river camp and launch point for Felix Unite. Purists can pitch their own tent on the grassy field, while lovers of creature comforts can bed down in a permanent tent or chalet, and stockpile their reserves for the paddling ahead.

❶ Getting There & Away

Noordoewer is located just off the B1 near the South African border, and is only accessible by private transport.

UNDERSTAND NAMIBIA

Namibia Today

Namibia is presently one of the better-performing democracies in Africa, and it scores comparatively well in world development indicators assessed by the World Bank. Although it was affected by the global recession in 2008–09, its mineral deposits have ensured its economy rebounded as uranium and diamond prices recovered in 2010. In 2011 the government announced it had discovered an estimated 11 billion barrels of offshore oil reserves.

Following a visit by the Chinese president Hu Jintao in 2007, China has provided loans, grants and credits to Namibia as their relationship has continued to strengthen. Trade has increased enormously between the two countries in recent years. China has also shown a firm interest in Namibia's mineral deposits, with Chinese state interests applying for many exclusive prospecting licences; Chinese mineral exploration and development companies are also jointly developing mineral deposits, especially around Grootfontein. The China Guangdong Nuclear Power Corp (CGNPC) plans to open one of the world's biggest uranium mines in Namibia by the end of 2015.

With inflation topping 7% in late 2012, living costs are on the rise for most Namibians. Worryingly, food prices are part of the core reason for the increase. The rise in inflation was attributed to a weaker exchange rate, in part due to the recent labour unrest in South Africa, which resulted in the country's credit rating being downgraded.

Although Namibia is in relatively good shape compared to the rest of the region, and for that matter the continent, poverty and disease are still enormous challenges for the government. Namibia has one of the

most unequal income distributions in the world. According to the United Nations Development Programme, the recent Namibia Household Income and Expenditure Survey found more than one in four households lived in poverty, and the poorest 10% of households commanded just 1% of the country's total income while the wealthiest 10% controlled more than half. These are shocking statistics in a country with so much apparent wealth and resource potential, and clearly put into context the challenge for the Namibian government.

In an example that more politicians across the region could follow, a local Windhoek councillor is using his entertainment allowance to buy gardening tools, seeds and manure to help needy residents in his constituency. Most of the people he supports are tuberculosis patients and people living with HIV, as well as orphans and vulnerable children. It's a small contribution but a good example of how grassroots initiatives begin.

With around 180,000 people living with AIDS (according to UNAIDS), half of them women over the age of 15, it's still a massive problem for the country. In 2008 the problem of coerced or forced sterilisations for women living with HIV came to light, and only after four years of proceedings did the High Court of Namibia rule in July 2012 that medical practitioners have a 'legal duty to obtain informed consent from a patient'. Although the findings did not include a link between the sterilisations and the HIV status of the women, the court's ruling has been acknowledged as an important step in recognising the reproductive health rights of women regardless of whether they are HIV-positive. The case has brought widespread global attention as more HIV-positive women who claim they were forcibly sterilized continue to come forward in Namibia, although the government denies that forced sterilisations for HIV-positive women is government policy.

On the environmental front, Dorob National Park is Namibia's newest national park, opened in 2011. Dorob basically replaces the old National West Coast Tourist Recreation Area on Namibia's Atlantic Coast, although the new boundaries are bigger. Although entry fees and applicable regulations are still murky, what is clear is that the creation of this park means that Namibia's entire coastline is now protected, beginning with Skeleton Coast Park in the

NAMIBIA NAMIBIA TODAY

north, then Dorob, Namib-Naukluft, and finally Sperrgebiet in the south. In fact, the Namibian Government eventually hopes to consolidate all four parks into a proposed Namib Skeleton Coast National Park, which would cover nearly 11 million hectares.

History

In the Beginning

Namibia's history extends back into the mists of time, a piece in the jigsaw that saw the evolution of the earliest human beings. The camps and stone tools of *Homo erectus* (literally 'man who stands upright') have been found scattered throughout the region. One archaeological site in the Namib Desert provides evidence that these early people were hunting the ancestors of present-day elephants, and butchering their remains with stone hand axes, as early as 750,000 years ago.

By the middle Stone Age, which lasted until 20,000 years ago, the Boskop, the presumed ancestors of the San, had developed into an organised hunting and gathering society. Use of fire was universal, tools (made from wood and animal products as well as stone) had become more sophisticated and natural pigments were being used for personal adornment. From around 8000 BC (the late Stone Age) they began producing pottery, and started to occupy rock shelters and caves such as those at Twyfelfontein, Brandberg and the Tsodilo Hills in Botswana.

The Settlement of Namibia

The archaeological connection between the late Stone Age people and the first Khoisan arrivals isn't clear, but it is generally accepted that the earliest documented inhabitants of Southern Africa were the San, a nomadic people organised into extended family groups who were able to adapt to the severe terrain.

During the early Iron Age, between 2300 and 2400 years ago, rudimentary farming techniques appeared on the plateaus of south-central Africa. However, whether or not the earliest farmers were Khoisan, who had adapted to a settled existence, or migrants from East and Central Africa, remains in question. Regardless, as the centuries came and went, Bantu-speaking groups began to arrive in sporadic southward waves.

The first agriculturists and iron workers of definite Bantu origin belonged to the Gokomere culture. They settled the temperate savannah and cooler uplands of southeastern Zimbabwe, and were the first occupants of the Great Zimbabwe site. Cattle ranching became the mainstay of the community, and earlier hunting and gathering San groups retreated to the west, or were enslaved and/or absorbed.

At the same time, the San communities were also coming under pressure from the Khoikhoi (the ancestors of the Nama), who probably entered the region from the south. The Khoikhoi were organised loosely into tribal groups, and were distinguished by their reliance on raising livestock. They gradually displaced the San, becoming the dominant group in the region until around 1500 AD.

During the 16th century, the Herero arrived in Namibia from the Zambezi Valley, and proceeded to occupy the north and west of the country. As ambitious pastoralists, they inevitably came into conflict with the Khoikhoi over the best grazing lands and water sources. Eventually, given their superior strength and numbers, the Herero came to dominate nearly all of the indigenous Namibian groups. By the late 19th century a new Bantu group, the Owambo, settled in the north along the Okavango and Kunene Rivers.

European Exploration & Incursion

In 1486 the Portuguese captain Diego Cão sailed as far south as Cape Cross, where he erected a stone cross in tribute to his royal patron, João II. The following year, another cross was erected by Bartolomeu Dias at Lüderitz, but it wasn't really until the early 17th century that Dutch sailors from the Cape colonies began to explore the desert coastline, although they refrained from setting up any permanent stations.

Soon after, however, growing European commercial and territorial interests were to send ambitious men deeper into Namibia's interior, and in 1750 the Dutch elephant hunter Jacobus Coetsee became the first European to cross the Orange River. In his wake came a series of traders, hunters and missionaries, and by the early 19th century there were mission stations at Bethanie, Windhoek, Rehoboth, Keetmanshoop and various other sites. In 1844 the German Rhenish Missionary Society, under Dr Hugo Hahn, began working among the Herero. More successful were the Finnish Lutherans, who arrived in the north in 1870 and established missions among the Owambo.

By 1843 the rich coastal guano deposits of the southern Namib Desert were attracting commercial attention. In 1867, the guano islands were annexed by the British, who then proceeded to take over Walvis Bay in 1878. The British also mediated the largely inconclusive Khoisan-Herero wars during this period.

The Scramble for Africa

The Germans, under Chancellor Otto von Bismarck, were late entering the European scramble for Africa. Bismarck had always been against colonies; he considered them an expensive illusion, famously stating, 'My map of Africa is here in Europe'. But he was to be pushed into an ill-starred colonial venture by the actions of a Bremen merchant called Adolf Lüderitz.

Having already set up a trading station in Lagos, Nigeria in 1881, Lüderitz convinced the Nama chief, Joseph Fredericks, to sell Angra Pequena, where he established his second station trading in guano (made from excrement, this manure was an effective fertiliser and gunpowder ingredient). He then petitioned the German chancellor for protection. Bismarck, still trying to stay out of Africa, politely requested the British at Walvis Bay to say whether they had any interest in the matter, but they never bothered to reply. Subsequently, in 1884, Lüderitz was officially declared part of the German Empire.

Initially, German interests were minimal, and between 1885 and 1890 the colonial administration amounted to three public administrators. Their interests were served largely through a colonial company (along the lines of the British East India Company in India prior to the Raj), but the organisation couldn't maintain law and order.

So in the 1880s, due to renewed fighting between the Nama and Herero, the German government dispatched Curt von François and 23 soldiers to restrict the supply of arms from British-administered Walvis Bay. This seemingly innocuous peacekeeping regiment slowly evolved into the more powerful Schutztruppe (German Imperial Army),

which constructed forts around the country to combat growing opposition.

At this stage, Namibia became a fully fledged protectorate known as German South West Africa. The first German farmers arrived in 1892 to take up expropriated land on the central plateau, and were soon followed by merchants and other settlers. In the late 1890s the Germans, the Portuguese in Angola and the British in Bechuanaland (present-day Botswana) agreed on Namibia's boundaries.

Reaping the Whirlwind

Meanwhile, in the south, diamonds had been discovered at Grasplatz, east of Lüderitz, by South African labourer Zacharias Lewala. Despite the assessment of diamond-mining giant De Beers that the find probably wouldn't amount to much, prospectors flooded in to stake their claims. By 1910, the German authorities had branded the entire area between Lüderitz and the Orange River a *Sperrgebiet* (closed area), chucked out the prospectors and granted exclusive rights to Deutsche Diamanten Gesellschaft (German Diamond Company).

But for all the devastation visited upon the local populace, Germany was never to benefit from the diamond riches they found. The outbreak of WWI in 1914 was to mark the end of German colonial rule in South West Africa. By this time, however, the Germans had all but succeeded in devastating the Herero tribal structures, and taken over all Khoikhoi and Herero lands. The more fortunate Owambo, in the north, managed to avoid German conquest, and they were only subsequently overrun during WWI by Portuguese forces fighting on the side of the Allies.

In 1914, at the beginning of WWI, Britain pressured South Africa into invading Namibia. The South Africans, under the command of Prime Minister Louis Botha and General Jan Smuts, pushed northwards, forcing the outnumbered Schutztruppe to retreat. In May 1915 the Germans faced their final defeat at Khorab near Tsumeb, and a week later, a South African administration was set up in Windhoek.

By 1920, many German farms had been sold to Afrikaans-speaking settlers, and the German diamond-mining interests in the south were handed over to the South Africa–based Consolidated Diamond Mines

DARK TIMES

Once the Germans had completed their inventory of Namibia's natural resources, it is difficult to see how they could have avoided the stark picture that presented itself. Their new colony was a drought-afflicted land enveloped by desert, with a nonexistent transport network, highly restricted agricultural opportunities, unknown mineral resources and a sparse, well-armed indigenous population. In fact, the only option that presented itself was to follow the example of the Herero, and pursue a system of seminomadic pastoralism. But the problem with this was that all the best land fell within the territories of either the Herero or the Nama.

In 1904 the paramount chief of the Herero invited his Nama, Baster and Owambo counterparts to join forces with him to resist the growing German presence. This was an unlikely alliance between traditional enemies. Driven almost all the way back to Windhoek, the Schutztruppe (GermanImoerial Army) brought in reinforcements, and under the ruthless hand of General von Trotha went out to meet the Herero forces at their Waterberg camp.

On 11 August 1904 the Battle of Waterberg commenced. Although casualties on the day were fairly light, the Herero fled from the scene of battle east into the forbidding Omaheke Desert. Seizing the opportunity, von Trotha ordered his troops to pursue them to their death. In the four weeks that followed, some 65,000 Herero were killed or died of heat, thirst and exhaustion. In fact, the horror only concluded when German troops themselves began to succumb to exhaustion and typhoid, but by then, some 80% of the entire Herero population had been wiped out.

Since the early 1990s, traditional Herero leaders have been lobbying for an official apology as well as monetary compensation from the German government. Finally in 2004, on the 100th anniversary of the Battle of Waterberg, Heidemarie Wieczorek-Zeul, Germany's development aid minister, apologised for the genocide, and in 2005 Germany pledged US$28 million to Namibia over a 10-year period as a reconciliation initiative.

Still many problems remain. The Namibian government, almost exclusively made up of Owambo members, believes that any compensation should be channelled through it rather than go directly to the Herero, citing its policy of nontribalism as a key concern. But as the chairman of the Namibian National Society for Human Rights points out, 'Not all the country suffered from the genocide, so it is ridiculous to say that the Hereros should not be specifically compensated'.

What may have been a minor episode in German colonial history was a cataclysm for the Herero nation. Demographic analysts suggest there would be 1.8 million Herero in Namibia today if it were not for the killings, making it rather than the Owambo the dominant ethnic group. In reality there are only about 120,000 Herero. For many this is a bitter pill to swallow, as the comments of Chief Kuaima Riruako illustrate. 'We ought to be in control of this country,' he said, 'and yet we are not.' Old rivalries still run deep.

(CDM), which later gave way to the Namdeb Diamond Corporation Limited (Namdeb).

South African Occupation

Under the Treaty of Versailles in 1919, Germany was required to renounce all of its colonial claims, and in 1920 the League of Nations granted South Africa a formal mandate to administer Namibia as part of the Union of South Africa.

While the mandate was renewed by the UN following WWII, South Africa was more interested in annexing South West Africa as a full province in the Union, and decided to scrap the terms of the mandate and rewrite the constitution. In response, the International Court of Justice determined that South Africa had overstepped its boundaries, and the UN established the Committee on South West Africa to enforce the original terms of the mandate. In 1956 the UN further decided that South African control should be terminated.

Undeterred, the South African government tightened its grip on the territory, and in 1949 granted the white population parliamentary representation in Pretoria. The bulk of Namibia's viable farmland was parcelled into some 6000 farms for white settlers, while other ethnic groups were relegated to newly demarcated 'tribal homelands'. The official intent was ostensibly to 'channel economic development into predominantly poor rural areas', but it was all too obvious that it was simply a convenient way of retaining the majority of the country for white settlement and ranching.

As a result, a prominent line of demarcation appeared between the predominantly white ranching lands in the central and southern parts of the country, and the poorer but better-watered tribal areas to the north. This arrangement was retained until Namibian independence in 1990, and to some extent continues to the present day.

Swapo

Throughout the 1950s, despite mounting pressure from the UN, South Africa refused to release its grip on Namibia. This intransigence was based on its fears of having yet another antagonistic government on its doorstep, and of losing the income that it derived from the mining operations there.

Forced labour had been the lot of most Namibians since the German annexation, and was one of the main factors that led to mass demonstrations and the increasingly nationalist sentiments in the late 1950s. Among the parties was the Owamboland People's Congress, founded in Cape Town under the leadership of Samuel Daniel Shafiishuna Nujoma and Herman Andimba Toivo ya Toivo.

In 1959 the party's name was changed to the Owamboland People's Organisation, and Nujoma took the issue of South African occupation to the UN in New York. By 1960 his party had gathered increased support, and they eventually coalesced into the South-West African People's Organisation (Swapo), with its headquarters in Dar es Salaam, Tanzania.

In 1966 Swapo took the issue of South African occupation to the International Court of Justice. The court upheld South Africa's right to govern South West Africa, but the UN General Assembly voted to terminate South Africa's mandate and replace it with a Council for South West Africa (renamed the Commission for Namibia in 1973) to administer the territory.

In response, on 26 August 1966 (now called Heroes' Day), Swapo launched its campaign of guerrilla warfare at Ongulumbashe in northern Namibia. The next year,

one of Swapo's founders, Toivo ya Toivo, was convicted of terrorism and imprisoned in South Africa, where he would remain until 1984. Nujoma, however, stayed in Tanzania, and avoided criminal prosecution. In 1972 the UN finally declared the South African occupation of South West Africa officially illegal and called for a withdrawal, proclaiming Swapo the legitimate representative of the Namibian people.

In 1975 Angola gained independence under the Cuban-backed Popular Movement for the Liberation of Angola (MPLA). Sympathetic to Swapo's struggle for independence in neighbouring Namibia, the fledgling government allowed it a safe base in the south of the country from where it could step up its guerrilla campaign against South Africa.

South Africa responded by invading Angola in support of the opposition party National Union for the Total Independence of Angola (Unita), an act that prompted the Cuban government to send hundreds of troops to the country to bolster up the MPLA. Although the South African invasion failed, and troops had to be withdrawn in March 1976, furious and bloody incursions into Angola continued well into the 1980s.

In the end, it was neither solely the activities of Swapo nor international sanctions that forced the South Africans to the negotiating table. On the contrary, all players were growing tired of the war, and the South African economy was suffering badly. By 1985, the war was costing some R480 million (around US$250 million) per year, and conscription was widespread. Mineral exports, which once provided around 88% of the country's gross domestic product (GDP), had plummeted to just 27% by 1984.

Independence

In December 1988, a deal was finally struck between Cuba, Angola, South Africa and Swapo that provided for the withdrawal of Cuban troops from Angola and South African troops from Namibia. It also stipulated that the transition to Namibian independence would formally begin on 1 April 1989, and would be followed by UN-monitored elections held in November 1989 on the basis of universal suffrage. Although minor score settling and unrest among some Swapo troops threatened to derail the whole process, the plan went ahead, and in September, Sam Nujoma returned from his

30-year exile. In the elections, Swapo garnered two-thirds of the votes, but the numbers were insufficient to give the party the sole mandate to write the new constitution, an outcome that went some way to allaying fears that Namibia's minority groups would be excluded from the democratic process.

Following negotiations between the Constituent Assembly (soon to become the National Assembly) and international advisers, including the USA, France, Germany and the former USSR, a constitution was drafted. The new constitution established a multiparty system alongside an impressive bill of rights. It also limited the presidential executive to two five-year terms. The new constitution was adopted in February 1990, and independence was granted a month later, with Sam Nujoma being sworn in as Namibia's first president.

Post-independence

In those first optimistic years of his presidency, Sam Nujoma and his Swapo party based their policies on a national reconciliation program aimed at healing the wounds left by 25 years of armed struggle. They also embarked on a reconstruction program based on the retention of a mixed economy and partnership with the private sector.

These moderate policies and the stability they afforded were well received, and in 1994 President Nujoma and his party were re-elected with a 68% landslide victory over the main opposition party, the Democratic Turnhalle Alliance (DTA). Similarly, in 1999 Swapo won 76.8% of the vote, although concerns arose when President Nujoma amended the constitution to allow himself a rather unconstitutional third term.

Other political problems included growing unrest in the Caprivi Strip. On 2 August 1999, rebels – mainly members of Namibia's Lozi minority led by Mishake Muyongo, a former vice president of Swapo and a longtime proponent of Caprivian independence – attempted to seize Katima Mulilo. However, the poorly trained perpetrators failed to capture any of their intended targets, and after only a few hours, they were summarily put down by the Namibian Defence Force (NDF).

Later that year, Nujoma also committed troops from the NDF to support the Angolan government in its civil war against Unita rebels – an act that triggered years of strife for the inhabitants of the Caprivi Strip,

where fighting and lawlessness spilled over the border. When a family of French tourists was robbed and murdered while driving between Kongola and Divundu, the issue exploded in the international press, causing tourist numbers to plummet. Continuing reports of fighting, attacks on civilians and land-mine detonations caused a huge exodus of people from the region, and kept tourists firmly away until the cessation of the conflict in 2002.

In 2004 the world watched warily to see if Nujoma would cling to power for a fourth term, and an almost audible sigh of relief could be heard in Namibia when he announced that he would finally be stepping down in favour of his chosen successor, Hifikepunye Pohamba.

Like Sam Nujoma, Pohamba is a Swapo veteran, and he swept to power with nearly 77% of the vote. In 2009 he was re-elected for a second term. He left behind the land ministry, where he presided over one of Namibia's most controversial schemes – the expropriation of land from white farmers. This policy formed part of the 'poverty agenda' which, along with Namibia's HIV/AIDS crisis, the unequal distribution of incomes, fair management of the country's resource wealth and the challenge of raising living standards for Namibia's poor, are the defining domestic issues of his presidency.

The Namibian People

Namibia's population in 2012 was estimated at 2,165,828 people, with an annual population growth rate of 0.82%. This figure takes into account the effects of excess mortality due to AIDS, which became the leading cause of death in Namibia in 1996. At approximately two people per square kilometre, Namibia has one of Africa's lowest population densities.

The population of Namibia comprises 12 major ethnic groups. Half the people come from the Owambo tribe (50%), with other ethnic groups making up a relatively small percentage of the population: Kavango (9%), Herero/Himba (7%), Damara (7%), Caprivian (4%), Nama (5%), Afrikaner and German (6%), Baster (6.5%), San (1%) and Tswana (0.5%).

Like nearly all other sub-Saharan nations, Namibia is struggling to contain its HIV/AIDS epidemic, which is impacting heavily on average life expectancy and population

THE POVERTY AGENDA

Land reform has been a contentious issue in Southern Africa (including in Namibia, where most of the arable land is owned by white farmers), with the government seeking to redistribute land to landless black Namibians. The Namibian government has been pursuing a policy of 'willing seller, willing buyer', whereby they have compensated those who have voluntarily chosen to sell their farms.

The Legal Assistance Centre (LAC), a nongovernmental human rights organisation based in Windhoek, says that the government's resettlement scheme has 'placed 800 farms in black hands in the 17 years since independence'. It is the equivalent of about 12% of all farms. The Namibian Agricultural Union (NAU) puts the figure at over 1000 farms or the equivalent of 16%. However, there are concerns that the pace of the reform is too slow. The LAC report also states that no resettlement farms are doing well, and that black farmers get subdivided portions of previous farms to support the same numbers of livestock, giving them no chance to be profitable. In fact, the scheme amounts to swapping one form of poverty for another.

Despite calls for the speed of the process to be increased, the NAU says disadvantaged Namibians currently own more than 9 million hectares of commercial farm land in the country, nearly two-thirds of the government's resettlement target for 2020. It argues that land reform is a process on track and needs time.

The past few years have seen politicians call for compulsory land acquisitions to increase the pace of land reform, but sceptics say there are few economic benefits to be had from such a policy. Although in principle many people support land reform, Namibia's arid environment is badly suited to a system of smallholdings farmed by poor Namibians who have neither the economic nor technical resources to develop the land. The real social issue, some say, is not so much land reform, but the government's failure to provide work opportunities for ordinary Namibians.

Whatever the problems, it is clear that most Namibians don't relish the economic and social chaos in neighbouring Zimbabwe. As an article in the *Namibian* so succinctly says, 'We emulate them at our peril.'

NAMIBIA THE NAMIBIAN PEOPLE

growth rates. Life expectancy in Namibia has dropped to 52 years, although some other estimates place it as low as 43. In 2009 13% of the population were HIV-positive, and by 2021, it is estimated that up to a third of Namibia's children under the age of 15 could be orphaned.

Although Namibia is one of the world's least densely populated countries, its rich mix of ethnic groupings provides a wealth of social and cultural diversity. The indigenous people of Namibia, the Khoisan (comprised of San hunter-gatherers and Nama pastoralists), have inhabited the region from time immemorial. They were followed by Bantu-speaking herders, with the first Europeans trickling in during the 17th century.

San

The word San is a collective term referring to the traditional groups of hunter-gatherers that occupy sub-Saharan Africa, and whose languages belong to the Khoisan family of languages. According to archaeological evidence, San communities were present in Namibia as early as 20,000 years ago, and left behind written records in the form of rock paintings. By AD 1000, however, the southward Bantu migration pushed the San into inhospitable areas, including the Kalahari. Regardless, anthropologists have dubbed the San our 'genetic Adam', stating that all living humans can ultimately trace back their lineage to this population group.

One of the most striking findings based on anthropological research is that traditional San communities were nonhierarchical and egalitarian, and grouped together based on kinship and tribal membership. Since groups were never able to build up a surplus of food, full-time leaders and bureaucrats never emerged.

Although village elders did wield a measure of influence over the mobile group, the sharpest division in status was between the sexes. Men provided for their families by hunting game, while women supplemented this diet by foraging for wild fruits, vegetables and nuts. While Thomas Hobbes famously noted in the 17th century that this lifestyle was 'solitary, poor, nasty, brutish and short', more recent ethnographic data has shown that hunter-gatherers worked fewer hours and enjoyed more leisure time than members of industrial societies.

Owambo

As a sort of loose confederation, the Owambo have always been strong enough to deter outsiders, including the slavers of yore and the German invaders of the last century. They were historically an aggressive culture, which made them the obvious candidates to fight the war of independence. They also make up Namibia's largest ethnic group (about 50% of the population) and, not surprisingly, most of the ruling South West Africa People's Organisation (Swapo) party.

The Owambo traditionally inhabited the north of the country, and are subdivided into 12 distinct groups. Four of these occupy the Kunene region of southern Angola, while the other eight comprise the Owambo groups in Namibia. The most numerous group is the Kwanyama, which makes up 35% of Namibia's Owambo population and dominates the government.

Recently large numbers of Owambo have migrated southwards to Windhoek, or to the larger towns in the north, to work as professionals, craftspeople and labourers. They have enjoyed considerable favour from the government over the years, and with the exception of white Namibians of European descent, are among the most successful of the tribal groups.

Kavango

The Kavango originated from the Wambo tribe of East Africa, who first settled on the Kwando River in Angola before moving south in the late 18th century to the northern edges of the Okavango. Since the outbreak of civil war in Angola in the 1970s, however, many Kavango have emigrated further south, swelling the local Namibian population, and making them Namibia's second-largest ethnic group. They are divided into five distinct subgroups: the Mbukushu, the Sambiyu, the Kwangari, the Mbunza and the Geiriku.

The Kavango are famous for their highly skilled woodcarvers. However, as with other groups in northern Namibia, large numbers of Kavango are now migrating southwards

in search of employment on farms, in mines and around urban areas.

Herero/Himba

Namibia's 120,000 Herero occupy several regions of the country, and are divided into several subgroups. The largest groups include the Tjimba and Ndamuranda groups in Kaokoveld, the Maherero around Okahandja, and the Zeraua, who are centred on Omaruru. The Himba of the Kaokoveld are also a Herero subgroup, as are the Mbandero, who occupy the colonially demarcated territory formerly known as Hereroland, around Gobabis in eastern Namibia.

The Herero were originally part of the early Bantu migrations south from central Africa. They arrived in present-day Namibia in the mid-16th century, and after a 200-year sojourn in the Kaokoveld, they moved southwards to occupy the Swakop Valley and the central lateau. Until the colonial period, they remained as seminomadic pastoralists in this relatively rich grassland, herding and grazing cattle and sheep.

However, bloody clashes with the northwards migrating Nama, as well as with German colonial troops and settlers, led to a violent uprising in the late 19th century, which culminated in the devastating Battle of Waterberg in August 1904. In the aftermath, 80% of the country's Herero population was wiped out, and the remainder were dispersed around the country, terrified and demoralised. Large numbers fled into neighbouring Botswana, where they settled down to a life of subsistence agriculture (although they have since prospered to become the country's richest herders).

The characteristic Herero women's dress is derived from Victorian-era German missionaries. It consists of an enormous crinoline worn over a series of petticoats, with a horn-shaped hat or headdress. If you happen to be in Okahandja on the nearest weekend to 23 August, you can witness the gathering of thousands of Hereros immaculately turned out in their traditional dress who come to honour their fallen chiefs on Maherero Day.

The Himba, a tribal group numbering not more than 50,000 people, are a seminomadic pastoral people that are closely related to the Herero, yet continue to live much as they have for generations on end. The women in particular are famous for smearing themselves with a fragrant mixture

BEYOND THE CLICHÉS: A TRAVELLER'S PERSPECTIVE
IAN KETCHESON

It's hard to write about the Himba in a way that doesn't sound like a cliché or a *National Geographic* article. They are the widely photographed subject of many travel brochures and glossy coffee-table books. They are often portrayed as an 'early people' who have lived untouched by outside influence for thousands of years. Their practice of smearing red ochre over their bodies, and their not-so-modest attire of leather miniskirts and loin-cloths, has also made them quite popular on the tourist circuit for those wishing to travel to a remote corner of the continent for a glimpse of 'traditional' Africa.

While these stereotypes might seem accurate at first glance, the reality is much more complex. In fact, the Himba have only lived in this part of Namibia for about 200 years. After being on the losing end of many ethnic battles during the 18th and 19th centuries, this group of people managed some success on the battlefield in the late 19th century, stole a bunch of cattle and goats, and headed off to the remote northwestern corner of the country where they could finally get some peace and quiet – at least until the tourists started turning up in the 1990s.

As for their attire, it's just a sign of the lack of success that 19th-century Christian missionaries had in colonising the Himba. One of the top priorities of missionaries across Namibia (and beyond) was to convince people that the first thing a 'civilised' person could do was to put on hot, uncomfortable and expensive clothes. After they had proper clothes, all they had to do was get a 'real' (read Christian) name, renounce polygamy and sit through long church services. Next stop, heaven.

Although the Himba are also widely portrayed as victims of the steady march of modernisation, their leaders have shown themselves to be quite adept at dealing with the outside world. In the late 1990s the Namibian government was moving ahead with plans to dam Epupa Falls in order to reduce the country's dependence on imported electricity. The plan would have flooded large areas of Himba land, and posed a major threat to their way of life.

Chief Kapika, the Himba leader for the area bordering the falls, with the assistance of some of the top lawyers in the country, mounted a campaign of opposition to the scheme that included a high-profile trip to Europe, where he spoke to foreign investors, NGOs and activists. Chief Kapika quite successfully managed to shine a bit of the international spotlight on his cause, attracting attention and generating support to help in the fight against the government. In recent years, the dam proposal has fallen through, although the Namibian government has been making noises about the prospect of a dam on the Cunene River, which has its source in Angola and demarcates the border between the two countries before spilling into the Atlantic. The Himba are also fiercely opposed to this dam project.

NAMIBIA THE NAMIBIAN PEOPLE

of ochre, butter and bush herbs, which dyes their skin a burnt orange hue, and serves as a natural sunblock and insect repellent. As if this wasn't striking enough, they also use the mixture to cover their braided hair, which has an effect similar to dreadlocking. Instead of wearing Western clothes, they prefer to dress traditionally, bare-breasted, with little more than a pleated animal-skin skirt in the way of clothing.

Similar to the Masai of Kenya and Tanzania, the Himba breed and care for herds of cattle in addition to goats and sheep. Unlike the East African savannah, Himba homelands are among the most extreme environments in the world, and their survival is ultimately dependent on maintaining strong community alliances. It was this very climactic harshness and resulting seclusion from outside influences that enabled the Himba to maintain their cultural heritage over the centuries.

During the 1980s and early 1990s, the Himba were severely threatened by war and drought, though they have experienced a tremendous resurgence in past years. At present, the population as a whole has succeeded in gaining control of their homelands, and in exerting real political power on the national stage.

Damara

The Damara resemblance to some Bantu of West Africa has led some anthropologists to believe they were among the first people to migrate into Namibia from the north, and that perhaps early trade with the Nama and San caused them to adopt Khoisan as a lingua franca.

What is known is that prior to the 1870s, the Damara occupied much of central Namibia from around the site of Rehoboth, westwards to the Swakop and Kuiseb Rivers, and north to present-day Outjo and Khorixas. When the Herero and Nama began expanding their domains into traditional Damara lands, large numbers of Damara were displaced, killed or captured and enslaved. The enmity between them resulted in Damara support for the Germans against the Herero during the colonial period. As a reward, the Damara were granted an enlarged homeland, now the southern half of Kunene province.

When Europeans first arrived in the region, the Damara were described as semi-nomadic pastoralists, who also maintained small-scale mining, smelting and trading operations. However, during the colonial period, they settled down to relatively sedentary subsistence herding and agriculture. In the 1960s the South African administration purchased for the Damara over 4.5 million hectares of marginal European-owned ranch land in the desolate expanses of present-day Damaraland.

It has not done them much good – the soil in this region is generally poor, most of the land is communally owned, and it lacks the good grazing that prevails in central and southern Namibia. Nowadays, most of Namibia's 80,000 Damara work in urban areas and on European farms, and only about a quarter of them actually occupy Damaraland.

Namibians of European Descent

There were no European settlers in Namibia until 1884, when the Germans set up a trading depot at Lüderitz Bay. By the late 1890s, Namibia was a German colony, and settlers began to arrive in ever-greater numbers. At the same time, Boers (white South Africans of Dutch origins) were migrating north from the Cape. Their numbers continued to increase after Namibia came under South African control following WWI.

Nowadays, there are around 85,000 white Namibians, most of whom are of Afrikaans descent. They are concentrated in the urban, central and southern parts of the country, and are involved mainly in ranching, commerce, manufacturing and administration. Furthermore, white Namibians almost exclusively manage and control the tourism industry.

Caprivians

In the extreme northeast, along the fertile Zambezi and Kwando riverbanks, live the 80,000 Caprivians, comprising five main tribal groups: the Lozi, Mafwe, Subia, Yei and Mbukushu. Most Caprivians derive their livelihood from fishing, subsistence farming and herding cattle.

Until the late 19th century, the Caprivi Strip was under the control of the Lozi kings. Today, the lingua franca of the various Caprivian tribes is known as Rotse, which is a derivative of the Lozi language still spoken in parts of Zambia and Angola.

Nama

Sharing a similar language to the San of Botswana and South Africa, the Nama are another Khoisan group, and are one of Namibia's oldest indigenous peoples.

The Nama's origins are in the southern Cape. However, during the early days of European settlement, they were either exterminated or pushed northwards by colonial farmers. They eventually came to rest in Namaqualand, around the Orange River, where they lived as seminomadic pastoralists until the mid-19th century, when their leader, Jan Jonker Afrikaner, led them to the area of present-day Windhoek.

On Namibia's central plateau, they came into conflict with the Herero, who had already occupied that area, and the two groups fought a series of bloody wars. Eventually, the German government enforced the peace by confining both groups to separate reserves.

Today, there are around 60,000 Nama in Namibia, and they occupy the region colonially designated as Namaqualand, which stretches from Mariental southwards to Keetmanshoop. They're known especially for their traditional music, folk tales, proverbs and praise poetry, which have been handed down through the generations to form a basis for their culture today.

Topnaar

The Topnaar (or Aonin), who are technically a branch of the Nama, mainly occupy the western central Namib Desert, in and around Walvis Bay. However, unlike the Nama, who historically had a tradition of communal land ownership, the Topnaar passed their lands down through family lines.

Today the Topnaar are arguably the most marginalised group in Namibia. Historically, they were dependent upon the !nara melon, which was supplemented by hunting. Now their hunting grounds are tied up in Namib-Naukluft Park. Those that remain in the desert eke out a living growing !nara melons and raising stock (mainly goats).

Most Topnaar have migrated to Walvis Bay and settled in the township of Nar-

raville, from where they commute to fish-canning factories. Others live around the perimeter in shanty towns. In the Topnaar community, southeast of Walvis Bay, a primary school and hostel have been provided, although only a minority of students come from the Topnaar community.

Coloureds

After the transfer of German South West Africa (as Namibia used to be known) to South African control after WWI, the South African administration began to introduce the racial laws of apartheid. Thus, at the beginning of the 1950s, cohabitation of mixed-race couples became illegal, although marriage was still allowed. On Afrikaans and German farms all over the territory, farmers married

NAMIBIA THE NAMIBIAN PEOPLE

LEARNING TO SURVIVE *IAN KETCHESON*

Before my wife, daughter and I moved to the small northern Namibia community of Odibo, we thought we were well aware of the impact of HIV/AIDS on Namibia.

What we weren't prepared for, though, were the funerals. We lived next door to a large Anglican church, a massive white building that on any given Sunday will hold more than 1000 people for the marathon four-hour church services. During the rest of the week, the steady flow of funeral processions past our front door was a daily reminder of the deeply personal impact of the HIV/AIDS pandemic on the community. According to a former nurse and local historian, the number of funerals held at the church has risen almost five-fold in the last decade, from 37 in 1992 to 177 in 2003.

At the same time, the tremendous stigma that surrounds the disease has made it very difficult for Namibians to be open about their status. As is the case across much of Africa, HIV/AIDS is shrouded in denial and silence, and reinforced by fear, shame and a lack of understanding of the disease. Despite the prevalence of HIV/AIDS in Namibia, a study carried out by the Namibian government in 2000 found that two-thirds of women in the Ohangwena region said they would not buy food from a person they knew to be HIV positive.

In the midst of these seemingly insurmountable challenges, there are thousands of community workers and volunteers struggling to overcome the stigma and help those affected. In the small community in which we lived, projects include the Anglican Home-Based Care Project, which provides training and distributes home-based care kits to volunteers who visit patients too ill to leave their homesteads; and Omwene Tu Talulula (OTTA; the name means 'Learn to Survive'), a group of HIV-positive activists who travel to schools, churches and other community gatherings encouraging people to come out about their status, and calling for an end to discrimination.

While some progress has been made to improve conditions for people living with HIV/AIDS, with improved access to antiretrovirals over the last few years, the challenges remain daunting. For many residents of Ohangwena region in northern Namibia, it is difficult or impossible to make the long trip to a hospital or clinic, and people often don't have enough food to help them digest their medicine. Visiting homesteads served by the Anglican Home-Based Care Project, I was amazed to discover that volunteers dropped off a loaf of bread in most of the homesteads they visited. For many it would be their only substantial food of the day, and would mean that they would be able to tolerate that day's medication.

Damara and Herero women; but a few years later marriage, too, was forbidden.

This left the children of these unions in an unenviable position, shunned by black and white communities alike. There are now around 52,000 coloureds in Namibia, living mainly in Windhoek, Keetmanshoop and Lüderitz.

Basters

Although distinct from coloureds, Basters are also the result of mixed unions, specifically between the Nama and Dutch farmers in the Cape Colony. In the late 1860s, after coming under pressure from the Boer settlers in the Cape, they moved north of the Orange River and established the settlement of Rehoboth in 1871. There they established their own system of government with a *Kaptein* (headman) and *Volksraad* (legislative council). They also benefited from supporting the Germans during the colonial period with increased privileges and recognition of their land rights.

Most of Namibia's 35,000 Basters still live around Rehoboth, and either follow an urban lifestyle or raise livestock.

Tswana

Namibia's 8000 Tswana make up the country's smallest ethnic group. They are related to the Tswana of South Africa and Botswana, the Batswana, and live mainly in the eastern areas of the country, around Aminuis and Epukiro.

The Namibian Way of Life

On the whole, Namibians are a conservative and God-fearing people – an estimated 80% to 90% of the country is Christian – so modesty in dress is important. Keeping up appearances extends to behaving modestly and respectfully to one's elders and social superiors, performing religious and social duties, and fulfilling all essential family obligations.

Education, too, is very important and the motivation to get a good education is high. But getting an education is by no means easy for everyone, and for families living in remote rural areas, it often means that very young children must be sent to schools far away where they board in hostels. The literacy rate for Namibia is 85%.

Most Namibians still live in homesteads in rural areas, and lead typical village lives.

NAMIBIAN SOCIAL STRUCTURES

On a national level, Namibia is still struggling to attain a cohesive identity, and history weighs heavy on the generations who grew up during the struggle for independence. As a direct and unfortunate result, some formidable tensions still endure between various social and racial groups.

Although the vast majority of travellers will be greeted with great warmth and curiosity, some people may experience unpleasant racism or unwarranted hostility – this is not confined to black/white relations, and can affect travellers of all ethnicities as Namibia's ethnic groups are extremely varied. Acquainting yourself with Namibia's complex and often turbulent past will hopefully alert you to potentially difficult or awkward situations. Taking care of basic etiquette like dressing appropriately, greeting people warmly and learning a few words of the local languages will also stand you in good stead.

Socially, Namibians enjoy a rock-solid sense of community thanks to the clan-based system. Members of your clan are people you can turn to in times of need. Conversely, if someone from your clan is in trouble, you are obligated to help, whether that means providing food for someone who is hungry, caring for someone who is sick, or even adopting an orphaned child in some cases. This inclusiveness also extends to others, and it is not uncommon for travellers to be asked to participate in a spontaneous game of football or a family meal.

Such an all-embracing social structure also means that the traditional family nucleus is greatly extended. Many Namibian families will include innumerable aunts and uncles, some of whom might even be referred to as mother or father. Likewise, cousins and siblings are interchangeable, and in some rural areas, men may have dozens of children, some of whom they might not even recognise. In fact, it is this fluid system that has enabled families to deal in some way with the devastation wreaked by the HIV/AIDS crisis.

Villages tend to be family- and clan-based, and are presided over by an elected *elenga* (headman). The *elenga* is responsible for local affairs, everything from settling disputes to determining how communal lands are managed.

The sad reality is that life is a struggle for the vast majority of Namibians. Unemployment is high, and the economy remains dependent on the mining industry, and to a lesser extent fishing and canning. In recent years, tourism has grown considerably throughout the country, though white Namibians still largely control the industry.

Women in Namibia

In a culture where male power is mythologised, it's unsurprising that women's rights lag behind. Even today, it's not uncommon for men to have multiple sexual partners, and until recently, in cases where husbands abandoned their wives and their children, there was very little course for redress. Since independence, the Namibian government has been committed to improving women's rights with bills like the Married Persons Equality Act (1996), which equalised property rights and gave women rights of custody over their children.

Even the government acknowledges that achieving gender equality is more about changing grassroots attitudes than passing laws, as a survey into domestic violence in 2000 revealed. Of the women interviewed in Lüderitz, Karasburg and Keetmanshoop, 25% said they had been abused or raped by their husbands. Endemic social problems, such as poverty, alcoholism and the feeling of powerlessness engendered by long-term unemployment, only increase feelings of disaffection and fuel the flames of abuse. Although the government passed one of the most comprehensive legislative acts against rape in the world, it remains to be seen how effectively it is enforced.

Namibian women do feature prominently in local and civic life, and many a Namibian woman took a heroic stance in the struggle for independence, as the impressive stories in *Histories of Namibia* reveal.

According to a US Department of State Human Rights Report in 2010, women held 24 seats in the 78-seat National Assembly. There were five female ministers and four female deputy ministers among the 41 ministerial and deputy ministerial incumbents, and three female judges among the 11 permanent judges of the High Court.

Women are also undoubtedly the linchpin of the Namibian home. They shoulder a double responsibility in raising children and caring for family members as well as contributing to the family income. This load has only increased with the horrendous effects of HIV/AIDS on the family structure.

Religion

About 80% to 90% of Namibians profess Christianity, and German Lutheranism is the dominant sect in most of the country. As a result of early missionary activity and Portuguese influence from Angola, there is also a substantial Roman Catholic population, mainly in the central and northern areas.

Most non-Christian Namibians – mainly Himba, San and some Herero – live in the north, and continue to follow animist traditions. In general, their beliefs are characterised by ancestor veneration, and most practitioners believe that deceased ancestors continue to interact with the living, and serve as messengers between their descendants and the gods.

Economy

The Namibian people's way of life is in large part dictated by the country's economy, which is dominated by the extraction and processing of minerals for export. Although mining only accounts for 8% of the GDP, it provides more than half of foreign exchange earnings. Most famously, Namibia's large alluvial diamond deposits have earned it the enviable reputation as one of the world's primary sources for gem-quality stones. However, the country is also regarded as a prominent producer of uranium, lead, zinc, tin, silver and tungsten.

According to the African Development Bank, the Namibian economy slowed down in 2011 with a GDP growth rate of 3.8% and unemployment at over 50%, with a staggering 84% of 15- to 19-year-olds unemployed.

The mining sector employs only about 3% of the population, while about half of the population depends on subsistence agriculture for its livelihood. Namibia normally imports about 50% of its cereal requirements, and in drought years, food shortages are a major problem in rural areas. Although the fishing industry is also a large economic force, catches are typically canned and marked for export.

NAMIBIA THE NAMIBIAN WAY OF LIFE

AN ARGUMENT FOR MINIMUM WAGE *IAN KETCHESON*

A teller at an import/export shop in Oshikango can expect to earn around US$75 per month. These are the same shops that sell, in US dollars, everything from fridges to kitchen cupboards and motorcycles. The US$75 per month wage is not unusual, and would compare to salaries paid to most service-sector workers. Manual labourers and farm workers generally receive less.

To begin her day, the teller would need to walk several kilometres to her job in Oshikango. Transport into town costs one dollar each way, so it would eat up half of her salary. She would have to bring her own food and drink, as a Coke costs about US$0.75 and even the simplest lunch would cost at least US$2.

One night at the motel in Oshikango would cost her the equivalent of three weeks' salary; a tank of petrol would eat up six weeks' wages; and she would have to save all her salary for 15 years to buy a used truck. All this while she sells US$5000 motorcycles and US$500 fridges to wealthy Angolans, and converts their US hundred-dollar bills into Namibian dollars.

Like South Africa, Namibia's economy has been built on the apartheid system's legacy of cheap labour, and as a result, has produced an incredible gap between rich and poor in the country. While many things have changed in the years since independence, this gap remains.

At the time of writing, Namibia still lacked a statutory minimum-wage law. As a result, the mining, construction and agricultural sectors continue to set basic levels of pay through collective bargaining practices, which some economists have criticised for being extremely cumbersome and even exploitative.

The Namibian economy is closely linked to the regional powerhouse of South Africa, and the Namibian dollar is pegged one-to-one to the South African rand. In 2007 payments from the Southern African Customs Union (SACU) put Namibia's budget into surplus for the first time since independence.

The global recession greatly impacted Namibia's economic sector. Rising costs for mineral extraction and fish canning dented the profit margins on lucrative exports, and the global decline in the price of precious metals and diamonds hit the economy. But as prices recovered, Namibia's mineral riches, including some 11 billion barrels of oil reported to have been discovered off the coast in 2011, look set to boost the economy for decades to come, depending of course on global economic fortunes.

Arts

With its harsh environment and historically disparate and poor population, Namibia does not have a formal legacy of art and architecture. What it does have in abundance is a wealth of material arts: carvings, basketry, tapestry, beadwork and textile weaving.

There are some excellent festivals dedicated to the arts – for one of Namibia's newest, most exciting arts events head to Omaruru in September for the Artist's Trail.

Literature

Dogged by centuries of oppression, isolation, lack of education and poverty, it is hardly surprising that prior to independence there was a complete absence of written literature in Namibia, though there was a rich tradition of oral literature. What there was boils down to a few German colonial novels – most importantly Gustav Frenssen's *Peter Moor's Journey to Southwest Africa* (original 1905, English translation 1908) – and some Afrikaans writing. The best-known work from the colonial period is undoubtedly Henno Martin's *The Sheltering Desert* (1956, English edition 1957), which records two years spent by the geologist author and his friend Hermann Korn avoiding internment as prisoners of war during WWII.

Only with the independence struggle did an indigenous literature begin to take root. One of contemporary Namibia's most significant writers is Joseph Diescho (b 1955), whose first novel, *Born of the Sun,* was published in 1988, when he was living in the USA. To date, this refreshingly unpretentious work remains the most renowned Namibian effort. As with most African literature, it's largely autobiographical, describing the protagonist's early life in a tribal village, his coming of age and his first contact with Christianity. It then follows his path through the South African mines and his ultimate political awakening. Diescho's second novel, *Troubled Waters* (1993), focuses on a white South African protagonist, who is sent to Namibia on military duty and develops a political conscience.

Namibia also has a strong culture of women writers. Literature written by Namibian women after independence deals primarily with their experiences as women during the liberation struggle and in exile, as well as with the social conditions in the country after independence. Thus, the writing of Ellen Namhila (*The Price of Freedom;* 1998), Kaleni Hiyalwa (*Meekulu's Children;* 2000) and Neshani Andreas (*The Purple Violet of Oshaantu;* 2001) gives us a great insight into the sociopolitical world of post-colonial Namibia.

A New Initiation Song (1994) is a collection of poetry and short fiction published by the Sister Namibia collective. This volume's seven sections cover memories of girlhood, body image, and heterosexual and lesbian relationships. Among the best works are those of Liz Frank and Elizabeth !Khaxas. The most outstanding short stories include 'Uerieta' by Jane Katjavivi, which describes a white woman's coming to terms with African life, and 'When the Rains Came' by Marialena van Tonder, in which a farm couple narrowly survives a drought. One contributor, Nepeti Nicanor, along with Mar-jorie Orford, also edited another volume, *Coming on Strong* (1996).

Those who read German will appreciate the works of Giselher Hoffmann (b 1958), which address historical and current Namibian issues. His first novel, *Im Bunde der Dritte* (Three's Company; 1984), is about poaching. *Die Erstgeboren* (The Firstborn; 1991) is told from the perspective of a San group that finds itself pitted against German settlers. Similarly, the Nama-Herero conflict of the late 19th century is described from the Nama perspective in *Die Schweigenden Feuer* (The Silent Fires; 1994). It's also concerned with the impact of modernisation on indigenous cultures.

Cinema

Since 2002, the Namibian Film Commission has been encouraging local film production and promoting the country as a film location. In the same year, a little-known film called *Beyond Borders,* about the Ethiopian famine in 1984, was shot in the country – and the film's star, Angelina Jolie, returned in 2006 to give birth to her daughter. On a more serious note, the annual Wild Cinema Festival is gaining impressive ground, attracting thousands of theatregoers every autumn.

After a few hiccups, the story of Namibia's first president, Sam Nujoma, was turned into a film in the form of *Namibia: The Struggle for Liberation,* which received mixed critical acclaim. In July 2011 the filming of the on-again-off-again fourth *Mad Max* movie was moved to Namibia, after unexpected

---

GREETINGS

The Namibia greeting is practically an art form and goes something like this: *Did you get up well? Yes. Are you fine? Yes. Did you get up well? Yes. Are you fine? Yes.*

This is an example of just the most minimal greeting; in some cases greetings can continue at great length with repeated inquiries about your health, your crops and your family, which will demand great patience if you are in a hurry.

However, it is absolutely essential that you greet everyone you meet, from the most casual encounter in the corner store, to an important first meeting with a business associate. Failure to greet people is considered extremely rude, and it is without a doubt the most common mistake made by outsiders.

Learn the local words for 'hello' and 'goodbye', and use them unsparingly. If you have the time and inclination, consider broadening your lexicon to include longer and more complex phrases.

Even if you find yourself tongue-tied, handshakes are also a crucial ice-breaker. The African handshake consists of three parts: the normal Western handshake, followed by the linking of bent fingers while touching the ends of upward-pointing thumbs, and then a repeat of the conventional handshake.

rain turned the Australian desert into a very un-*Mad Max* carpet of flowers.

Music

Namibia's earliest musicians were the San, whose music probably emulated the sounds of animals, and was sung to accompany dances and storytelling. The early Nama, who had a more developed musical technique, used drums, flutes and basic stringed instruments, also to accompany dances. Some of these were adopted and adapted by the later-arriving Bantu, who added marimbas, gourd rattles and animal-horn trumpets to the range. Nowadays, drums, marimbas and rattles are still popular, and it isn't unusual to see dancers wearing belts of soft-drink (soda) cans filled with pebbles to provide rhythmic accompaniment to their steps.

A prominent European contribution to Namibian music is the choir. Early in the colonial period, missionaries established religious choral groups among local people, and both school and church choirs still perform regularly. Namibia's most renowned ensembles are the Cantare Audire Choir and the **Mascato Coastal Youth Choir** (www. mascatoyouthchoir.com), the country's national youth choir. The German colonists also introduced their traditional 'oompah' bands, which feature mainly at Oktoberfest and at other German-oriented festivals.

If you need some music to keep you company on those long, lonely Namibian roads, check out the soulful tunes of Hishishi Papa, a storyteller musician whose *Aantu Aantu* album is perfect driving music.

Architecture

While most visitors to Namibia have already set their sights on the country's natural wonders, there are a surprising number of architectural wonders to discover as well. Striking German colonial structures continue to stand as testament to the former European occupation of Namibia.

While most of Windhoek has modernised with the chock-a-block concrete structures that typify most African cities, there are a few remaining colonial gems. Towering over the city is the German Lutheran Christuskirche, which masterfully uses local sandstone in its European-leaning neo-Gothic construction. Another notable structure is the Alte Fest (Old Fort), which was constructed in 1890 by Curt von François and his men to serve as the barracks for the German army. It remains the oldest surviving building in the city, and now serves a much more peaceful function as the National Museum.

Of course, if you truly want to experience the shining jewels in Namibia's architectural crown, you're going to need to head out to the coast. Here, improbably squeezed between the frozen waters of the South Atlantic and the overbearing heat of the Namib Desert, are the surreal colonial relics of Swakopmund and Lüderitz. Walking the streets of either city, you'd be easily forgiven for thinking that you were in a Bavarian dorfchen (small village), albeit one on the African continent. Somewhat forgotten by time and history, both cities are characterised by a handsome blend of German imperial and art nouveau styles, which become all the more bizarre when viewed against the backdrop of soaring dunes and raging seas.

Dance

Each group in Namibia has its own dances, but common threads run through most of them. First, all dances are intended to express social values, to some extent, and many dances reflect the environment in which they're performed.

Dances of the Ju/'hoansi (!Kung) men (a San group in northeastern Namibia) tend to mimic the animals they hunt, or involve other elements that are important to them. For example, the 'melon dance' involves tossing and catching a *tsama* melon according to a fixed rhythm. The Himba dance *ondjongo* must be performed by a cattle owner, and involves representing care and ownership.

Specific dances are also used for various rituals, including rites of passage, political events, social gatherings and spiritual ceremonies. The Ju/'hoansi male initiation dance, the *tcòcmà*, for example, may not even be viewed by women. In the Kavango and Caprivi region, dances performed by traditional healers require the dancer to constantly shake rattles held in both hands. Most festive dances, such as the animated Kavango *epera* and *dipera,* have roles for both men and women, but are performed in lines with the genders separated.

Visual Arts

The majority of Namibia's established modern painters and photographers are of European origin, and concentrate largely on the country's colourful landscapes, bewitching light, native wildlife and, more recently, its diverse peoples. Well-known names include François de Necker, Axel Eriksson, Fritz Krampe and Adolph Jentsch. The well-known colonial landscape artists Carl Ossman and Ernst Vollbehr are exhibited in Germany. The work of many of these artists is exhibited in the permanent collection of the National Art Gallery in Windhoek, which also hosts changing exhibitions of local and international artists.

Non-European Namibians who have concentrated on three-dimensional and material arts have been developing their own traditions. Township art – largely sculpture made out of reclaimed materials like drink cans and galvanised wire – develops sober themes in an expressive and colourful manner. It first appeared in the townships of South Africa during the apartheid years. Over the past decade or two, it has taken hold in Namibia, and is developing into a popular art form.

In an effort to raise the standard and awareness of the visual arts in Namibia, a working group of artists – including Joseph Madesia and François Necker – established the Tulipamwe International Artists' Workshop in 1994. Since then they have held a long list of workshops in farms and in wildlife lodges around Namibia where Namibian, African and international artists can come together and share ideas and develop their skills base.

Namibian Cuisine

Staples & Specialities

Traditional Namibian food consists of a few staples, the most common of which is *oshifima*, a doughlike paste made from millet, and usually served with a stew of vegetables or meat. Other common dishes include *oshiwambo*, a rather tasty combination of spinach and beef, and *mealie pap*, an extremely basic porridge.

As a foreigner you'll rarely find such dishes on the menu. Most Namibian restaurants in big towns like Windhoek, Swakopmund and Lüderitz serve a variation on European-style foods, like Italian or French, alongside an abundance of seafood dishes. Outside these towns you'll rapidly become familiar with fried-food joints and pizza parlours.

Whatever the sign above the door, you'll find that most menus are meat-orientated, although you might be lucky to find a few vegetarian side dishes. The reason for this is pretty obvious – Namibia is a vast desert, and the country imports much of its fresh fruit and vegetables from South Africa. What is available locally is the delicious gem squash and varieties of pumpkin such as butternut squash. In season, Namibian oranges are delicious; in the Kavango region, papayas are served with a squeeze of lemon or lime.

More than anything else, German influences can be found in Namibia's *konditoreien* (cake shops), where you can pig out on *Apfelstrudel* (apple strudel), *Sachertorte* (a rich chocolate cake layered with apricot jam), *Schwartzwälder Kirschtorte* (Black Forest cake), and other delicious pastries and cakes. Several places in Windhoek and Swakopmund are national institutions. You may also want to try Afrikaners' sticky-sweet *koeksesters* (small doughnuts dripping with honey) and *melktart* (milk tart).

Cooked breakfasts include bacon and boerewors (farmer's sausage), and don't be surprised to find something bizarre – curried kidneys, for example – alongside your eggs. Beef in varying forms also makes an occasional appearance at breakfast time.

Evening meals feature meat, normally beef or game. A huge beef fillet steak or a kudu cutlet will set you back no more than N$100. Fish and seafood are best represented by kingklip, kabeljou and several types of shellfish. These are available all over Namibia, but are best at finer restaurants in Windhoek, Swakopmund and Lüderitz, where they'll normally be fresh from the sea.

Drinks

In the rural Owambo areas, people socialise in tiny makeshift bars, enjoying local brews like *oshikundu* (beer made from *mahango* – millet), *mataku* (watermelon wine), *tambo* (fermented millet and sugar) or *mushokolo* (a beer made from a small local seed) and *walende*, which is distilled from the *makalani* palm and tastes similar to vodka. All of these concoctions, except *walende*, are brewed in the morning and drunk the same day, and they're all dirt cheap.

For more conventional palates, Namibia is awash with locally brewed lagers. The most popular drop is the light and refreshing Windhoek Lager, but the brewery also produces Tafel Lager, the stronger and more bitter Windhoek Export, and the slightly

NAMIBIA NAMIBIAN CUISINE

rough Windhoek Special. Windhoek Light and DAS Pilsener are both drunk as soft drinks (DAS is often called 'breakfast beer'!), and in winter Namibia Breweries also brews a 7% stout known as Urbock. South African beers like Lion, Castle and Black Label are also widely available.

Although beer is the drink of choice for most Namibians, Namibia also has a few wineries, including the Kristall Kellerei, 3km east of Omaruru. Here it produces Paradise Flycatcher – a red blend of ruby cabernet, cabernet sauvignon and tinta barocca; co-lombard; and prickly-pear-cactus schnapps (a good blast). South African wines are also widely available. Among the best are the cabernet and pinot varieties grown in the Stellenbosch region of Western Cape Province. A good bottle of wine will set you back between N$80 and N$180.

Environment

The Landscape

It's the oldest desert in the world, a garden of burned and blackened-red basalt that spilled out of the earth 130 million years ago in southwest Africa, hardening to form the arid landscape of Namibia, the driest country south of the Sahara. Precious little can grow or thrive in this merciless environment, with the exception of a few uniquely adapted animals and plants, which illustrate the sheer ingenuity of life on earth.

Arid Namibia enjoys a wide variety of geographical and geological features. Broadly speaking, its topography can be divided into five main sections: the Namib Desert and the coastal plains of the south and central interior; the eastward-sloping central plateau, with its flat-topped *inselbergs* (isolated mountains); the Kalahari sands along the Botswana and South Africa borders; and the densely wooded bushveld of the Kavango and Caprivi regions. Most famous of all are the scorched dunes of the impossibly eerie but always captivating Skeleton Coast.

The Namib Desert extends along the country's entire Atlantic coast, and is scored by a number of rivers, which rise in the central plateau, but often run dry. Some, like the ephemeral Tsauchab, once reached the sea, but now end in calcrete pans. Others flow only during the summer rainy season, but at some former stage carried huge volumes of water, and carved out dramatic canyons

like the Fish River and Kuiseb, where Henno Martin and Hermann Korn struggled to survive WWII.

In wild contrast to the bleached-blue skies and vast, open expanses of most of the country, the Kavango and Caprivi regions are a well-watered paradise. Bordering Angola to the north, they are bounded by four great rivers – the Kunene, Okavango, Kwando/Mashi/Linyanti/Chobe and Zambezi – that flow year-round.

Wildlife

For wildlife watchers, there are really only three significant areas in Namibia: Kaokoland, where elusive desert elephants and black rhinos follow the river courses running to the Skeleton Coast; the isolated and rarely visited Khaudum, where Namibia's last African wild dogs find refuge; and Etosha National Park, one of the world's finest wildlife reserves.

Further south is the largest wildlife reserve in Africa, the Namib-Naukluft Park, which covers an astonishing 6% of Namibia's area. Much of it is true desert, and large mammals occur in extremely low densities, though local species include Hartmann's mountain zebra as well as more widespread Southern African endemics like springbok and gemsbok. For aficionados of smaller life, the Namib is an endemism hot spot: on the dunes, Gray's larks, dune larks, slip-face lizards and fog-basking beetles are found, while the scattered rocky plateaus host long-billed larks, rockrunners and Herero chats.

The severe Namibian coast is no place to expect abundant big wildlife, though it's the only spot in the world where massive fur-seal colonies are patrolled by hunting brown hyenas and black-backed jackals. The coast also hosts massive flocks of summer waders, including sanderlings, turnstones and grey plovers, while Heaviside's and dusky dolphins can often be seen in the shallow offshore waters.

In 2009 the Namibian government opened Sperrgebiet National Park, a vast 16,000-sq-km expanse of land home to the threatened desert rain frog, dramatic rock formations and disused diamond mines. The area's haunting beauty, which is highlighted by shimmering salt pans and saffron -coloured sand dunes, provides one of the world's most dramatic backdrops for adventurous wildlife watchers.

MAMMALS
Nowhere else on earth does such diverse mammal life exist in such harsh conditions. On the gravel plains live ostriches, zebras, gemsboks, springboks, mongooses, ground squirrels and small numbers of other animals, such as black-backed jackals, bat-eared foxes, caracals, aardwolfs and brown hyenas. Along the coast, penguins and seals thrive in the chilly Atlantic currents, and in the barren Erongo mountains and Waterberg plateau the last wild black rhinoceros populations are slowly recovering.

Namibia's largest and best-known wildlife park is Etosha. Its name means 'place of mirages', for the dusty saltpan that sits at its centre. During the dry season, huge herds of elephants, zebras, antelopes and giraffes, as well as rare black rhinos, congregate here against an eerie bleached-white backdrop.

To see the elusive wild dog, Khaudum National Park is your best bet. Namibia's other major parks for good wildlife viewing are Bwabwata National Park, Mudumu National Park and Mamili National Park.

Not all of Namibia's wildlife is confined to national parks. Unprotected Damaraland, in Namibia's northwest, is home to numerous antelope species and other ungulates, and is also a haven for desert rhinos, elephants and other specially adapted subspecies. Hikers in the Naukluft and other desert ranges may catch sight of the elusive Hartmann's mountain zebra, and along the desert coasts you can see jackass penguins, flamingos, Cape fur seals and perhaps even the legendary *strandwolf* (brown hyena).

For more in-depth information about the array of mammalian wildlife found in Namibia, pick up Lonely Planet's *Watching Wildlife Southern Africa*.

REPTILES
The dry lands of Namibia boast more than 70 species of snake, including three species of spitting cobra. It is actually the African puff adder that causes the most problems for humans, since it inhabits dry, sandy riverbeds. Horned adders and sand snakes inhabit the gravel plains of the Namib, and the sidewinder adder lives in the Namib dune sea. Other venomous snakes include the slender green vine snake; both the green and black mamba; the dangerous zebra snake; and the boomslang (Afrikaans for 'tree snake'), a slender 2m aquamarine affair with black-tipped scales.

Lizards, too, are ubiquitous. The largest of these is the *leguaan* (water monitor), a docile creature that reaches over 2m in length, swims and spends a lot of time laying around waterholes, probably dreaming of becoming a crocodile. A smaller version, the savannah leguaan, inhabits *kopjes* (small hills) and drier areas. Also present in large numbers are geckos, chameleons, legless lizards, rock-plated lizards and a host of others.

The Namib Desert supports a wide range of lizards, including a large vegetarian species, *Angolosaurus skoogi,* and the sand-diving lizard, *Aprosaura achietae,* known for its 'thermal dance'. The unusual bug-eyed palmato gecko inhabits the high dunes and there's a species of chameleon.

In the watery marshes and rivers of the north of the country, you'll find Namibia's reptile extraordinaire, the Nile crocodile. It is one of the largest species of crocodile on the planet, and can reach 5m to 6m in length. It has a reputation as a 'man-eater', but this is probably because it lives in close proximity to human populations. In the past, there have been concerns over excessive hunting of the crocodile, but these days numbers are well up, and it's more at risk from pollution and accidental entanglement in fishing nets.

INSECTS & SPIDERS
Although Namibia doesn't enjoy the profusion of bug life found in countries further north, a few interesting specimens buzz, creep and crawl around the place. Over 500 species of colourful butterflies – including the African monarch, the commodore and the citrus swallowtail – are resident, as well as many fly-by-night moths.

Interesting buggy types include the large and rarely noticed stick insects, the similarly large (and frighteningly hairy) baboon spider, and the ubiquitous and leggy shongololo (millipede), which can be up to 30cm long.

The Namib Desert has several wonderful species of spider. The tarantula-like 'white lady of the dunes' is a white hairy affair that is attracted to light. There's also a rare false spider known as a *solifluge* (sun spider). You can see its circulatory system through its light-coloured translucent outer skeleton. The dunes are also known for their extraordinary variety of *tenebrionid* (known as *tok-tokkie*) beetles.

Common insects such as ants, stink bugs, grasshoppers, mopane worms and locusts sometimes find their way into frying pans for snacks. For travellers, it takes something of a culinary daredevil to dive into a newspaper-wrapped ball of fried bugs, though for locals, the practice provides essential protein supplements.

BIRDS

Namibia's desert landscape is too harsh and inhospitable to support a great variety of birdlife. The exception to this is the lush green Caprivi Strip, which borders the Okavango Delta. Here, in the Mahango Game Reserve, you'll find the same exotic range of species as in Botswana, including the gorgeous lilac-breasted roller, pygmy goose (actually a duck) and white-fronted, carmine and little bee-eater. Other wetland species include the African jacana, snakebird, ibis, stork, egret, shrike, kingfisher, great white heron, and purple and green-backed heron. Birds of prey include Pel's fishing owl, goshawk, several species of vulture, and both bateleur and African fish eagle.

The coastal wildfowl reserves support an especially wide range of birdlife: white pelicans, flamingos, cormorants and hundreds of other wetland birds. Further south, around Walvis Bay and Lüderitz, flamingos and jackass penguins share the same desert shoreline.

Situated on a key migration route, Namibia also hosts a range of migratory birds, especially raptors, who arrive around September and October, and remain until April. The canyons and riverbeds slicing across the central Namib Desert are home to nine species of raptor, as well as the hoopoe, the unusual red-eyed bulbul and a small bird known as the familiar chat. Throughout the desert regions, you'll also see the intriguing social weaver, which builds an enormous nest that's the avian equivalent of a 10-storey block of flats. Central Namibia also boasts bird species found nowhere else, such as the Namaqua sand-grouse and Grey's lark.

FISH

The Namibian coastal waters are considered some of the world's richest, mainly thanks to the cold Benguela current, which flows northwards from the Antarctic. It's exceptionally rich in plankton, which accounts for the abundance of anchovies, pilchards, mackerel and other whitefish. But the limited offshore fishing rights have caused problems, and there is resentment that such countries as Spain and Russia have legal access to offshore fish stocks. Namibia has now declared a 200-nautical-mile exclusive economic zone to make Namibian fisheries competitive.

Endangered Species

Overfishing and the 1993–94 outbreak of 'red tide' along the Skeleton Coast have decimated the sea lion population, both through starvation and commercially inspired culling. Also, the poaching of desert rhinos, elephants and other Damaraland species has caused their numbers to decrease, and the desert lion, which once roamed the Skeleton Coast, is now considered extinct.

For the rest of Namibia's lions, survival is also precarious. From a high of 700 animals in 1980, the number has now decreased to no more than 400. Of these, nearly 85% are confined to Etosha National Park and Khaudum National Park. One problem is that reserve fences are penetrable, and once the lions have left protected areas, it's only a matter of time before they're shot by ranchers to protect cattle.

The stability of other bird and plant species, such as the lichen fields, the welwitschia plant, the Damara tern, the Cape vulture and numerous lesser-known species, has been undoubtedly compromised by human activities (including tourism and recreation) in formerly remote areas. However, awareness of the perils faced by these species is increasing among operators and tourists alike, which adds a glimmer of hope to the prospects of their future survival.

Hunting

As in Botswana, hunting is legal in Namibia, although it is strictly regulated and licensed. The Ministry of the Environment and Tourism along with the Namibia Professional Hunting Association (NAPHA) regulate hunting, which accounts for 5% of the country's revenue from wildlife.

The Namibian government views its hunting laws as a practical form of wildlife management and conservation. Many foreign hunters are willing to pay handsomely for big wildlife trophies (a leopard, for example, will fetch at least US$2500, while an elephant provides many times that amount) and farmers and ranchers frequently complain about the ravages of wildlife on their stock. The idea is to provide farmers with financial incentives to protect free-ranging

CONSERVATION ORGANISATIONS

Anyone with a genuine interest in a specific ecological issue should contact one or more of the following organisations. These organisations do not, however, provide tourist information or offer organised tours (unless stated otherwise).

Afri-Cat Foundation (www.africat.org) A nonprofit organisation focusing on research and the reintroduction of large cats into the wild. There's also an on-site education centre and a specialist veterinary clinic.

BirdLife International (www.birdlife.org) BirdLife International is actively involved in conservation projects, such as building observation posts, and organising bird-watching trips. Despite Namibia's variety of birdlife, the organisation has no in-country affiliations.

Cheetah Conservation Fund (CCF; www.cheetah.org) A centre of research and education on cheetah populations and how they are conserved. It's possible to volunteer with this organisation.

Integrated Rural Development and Nature Conservation (IRDNC; www.irdnc.org.na) IRDNC aims to improve the lives of rural people by diversifying their economic opportunities to include wildlife management and other valuable natural resources. Its two main projects are in the Kunene region and the Caprivi Strip.

Save the Rhino Trust (SRT; www.savetherhino.org) SRT has worked to implement community-based conservation since the early 1980s. By 2030, it hopes that its efforts will have succeeded in re-establishing the black rhino in Namibia in healthy breeding populations.

wildlife. Management strategies include encouraging hunting of older animals, evaluating the condition of trophies and setting bag limits in accordance with population fluctuations.

In addition, quite a few private farms are set aside for hunting. The owners stock these farms with wildlife bred by suppliers – mainly in South Africa – and turn it loose into the farm environment. Although community-based hunting concessions have appeared in the Bushmanland area, these still aren't widespread.

Plants

Because Namibia is mostly arid, much of the flora is typical African dry-land vegetation: scrub brush and succulents, such as euphorbia. Along the coastal plain around Swakopmund are the world's most extensive and diverse fields of lichen; they remain dormant during dry periods, but with the addition of water they burst into colourful bloom.

Most of the country is covered by tree-dotted, scrub savannah grasses of the genera *Stipagrostis, Eragrostis* and *Aristida.* In the south, the grass is interrupted by ephemeral watercourses lined with tamarisks, buffalo thorn and camelthorn. Unique floral oddities here include the *kokerboom*

(quiver tree), a species of aloe that grows only in southern Namibia.

In the sandy plains of southeastern Namibia, raisin bushes *(Grewia)* and candlethorn grow among the scrubby trees, while hillsides are blanketed with green-flowered *Aloe viridiflora* and camphor bush.

The eastern fringes of Namib-Naukluft Park are dominated by semidesert scrub savannah vegetation, including some rare aloe species *(Aloe karasbergensis* and *Aloe sladeniana).* On the gravel plains east of the Skeleton Coast grows the bizarre *Welwitschia mirabilis,* a slow-growing, ground-hugging conifer that lives for more than 1000 years.

In areas with higher rainfall, the characteristic grass savannah gives way to acacia woodlands, and Etosha National Park enjoys two distinct environments: the wooded savannah in the east and thorn-scrub savannah in the west. The higher rainfall of Caprivi and Kavango sustains extensive mopane woodland, and the riverine areas support scattered wetland vegetation, grasslands and stands of acacias. The area around Katima Mulilo is dominated by mixed subtropical woodland containing copalwood, Zambezi teak and leadwood, among other hardwood species.

National Parks & Reserves

Visiting National Parks in Namibia

Despite its harsh climate, Namibia has some of the world's grandest national parks, ranging from the world-famous, wildlife-rich Etosha National Park to the immense Namib-Naukluft Park, which protects vast dunefields, desert plains, wild mountains and unique flora. There are also the smaller reserves of the Caprivi region, the renowned Skeleton Coast and the awe-inspiring Fish River Canyon in |Ai- |Ais Richtersveld Transfrontier Park, which ranks among Africa's most spectacular natural wonders.

Around 15% of Namibia is designated as national park or conservancy. Access to most wildlife parks is limited to closed vehicles only. A 2WD is sufficient for most parks, but for Mamili National Park, Khaudum National Park and parts of Bwabwata National Park, you need a sturdy 4WD with high clearance.

Entry permits are available on arrival at park entrances, but campsites and resorts should be booked in advance, although it is possible to make a booking on arrival, subject to availability.

Namibia Wildlife Resorts (NWR)

The semiprivate Namibia Wildlife Resorts (p221) in Windhoek manages a large number of rest camps, campsites and resorts within the national parks. If you haven't prebooked (eg if you're pulling into a national park area on a whim), there's a good chance you'll find something available on the spot, but have a contingency plan in case things don't work out. This is not advised for Etosha or Sossusvlei, which are perennially busy.

BOOKING

When booking a campsite or resort with NWR, fees must be paid by credit card before the booking will be confirmed. Note that camping fees are good for up to four people; each additional person up to eight people will be charged extra.

To reserve a campsite, you need to provide the NWR the following:
» Your passport number.
» The name of the preferred campsite/resort within the park, in order of preference.
» The date of your arrival to and departure from the park.
» The number of adults and children (including ages) camping.
» The vehicle's number plates and also the country in which the vehicle is registered.
» Proof of your status if you are not paying 'foreigner' rates.

Prebooking is always advised. Bookings may be made up to 12 months in advance. Note that pets aren't permitted in any wildlife-oriented park or rest camp.

CAMPING & RESORTS

On average, campsites cost from N$50 for an undeveloped wilderness site to up to N$200 for the rest camps in Etosha, which feature pools, shops, restaurants, kiosks and well-maintained ablutions blocks with hot water. These rates are for one person, and you generally need to pay a bit more for your vehicle and any additional campers.

NWR also offers a range of other possibilities targeted at upmarket travellers. For example, Etosha National Park hosts luxury chalets that range from N$900 to N$2000 per person, and are stacked with modern amenities including air-con and satellite TV. These properties are also attractively perched around watering holes, which offer world-class game viewing from the comfort of your own private balcony.

National park accommodation may be occupied from noon on the day of arrival to 10am on the day of departure. During school

NATIONAL PARK FEES PER DAY IN NAMIBIA

	FOREIGNERS
adult	N$80
child (under 16)	free
camping	cost varies
vehicles	N$10

NATIONAL PARKS & RESERVES

Park	Features	Activities	Best time
Dorob National Park	Stretches from the Ugab River in the north down to Sandwich Harbour in the south (it consumes the old 'National West Coast Tourist Recreation Area'); coastal dune belt; vast gravel plains; prolific birdlife; major river systems	wildlife viewing; fishing; desert plants; sand dunes; birdwatching	Jun-Nov
Etosha National Park	22,275 sq km; semi-arid savannah surrounding saltpan; 114 mammal species	wildlife viewing; birdwatching; night drives	May-Sep
Fish River Canyon (part of |Ai- |Ais Richtersveld Transfrontier Park)	161km long; Africa's longest canyon; hot springs; rock strata of multiple colours	hiking; bathing	May-Nov
Khaudum National Park	3840 sq km; bushveld landscape crossed by fossilised river valleys	wildlife viewing; hiking; 4WD exploration	Jun-Oct
Mamili National Park	320 sq km; mini-Okavango; 430 bird species; canoe trails through park	wildlife viewing; birdwatching; canoe trips	Sep-Apr
Mudumu National Park	850 sq km; lush riverine environment; 400 bird species	wildlife watching; birdwatching; guided trails	May-Sep
Namib-Naukluft Park	50,000 sq km; Namibia's largest protected area; rare Hartmann's zebras	wildlife watching; walking	year-round
Skeleton Coast National Park	20,000 sq km; wild, foggy wilderness; desert-adapted animals	wildlife viewing; walking; fly-in safaris	year-round
Waterberg Plateau Park	400 sq km; table mountain; refuge for black and white rhinos and rare antelopes	wildlife viewing; rhino tracking; hiking	May-Sep

NAMIBIA NATIONAL PARKS & RESERVES

holidays, visitors are limited to three nights at each camp in Etosha National Park and Namib-Naukluft Park, and 10 nights at all other camps.

Conservancies & Private Game Reserves

In Namibia a conservancy is an amalgamation of private farms or an area of communal land where farmers and/or local residents agree to combine resources for the benefit of wildlife, the local community and tourism.

Conservancies can create important income for community development, and account for over 17% of Namibia. They are immense sanctuaries free from fencing, allowing wildlife to roam at will, and are often located in some of the country's most stunning landscapes. Lodges and community campsites offer great opportunities to experience these wild places.

Another sort of protected area is the private game reserve, of which there are now more than 180 in Namibia. The largest of these, by far, are the 200,000-hectare Namib-Rand Nature Reserve, adjoining the Namib-Naukluft Park, and the 102,000-hectare Gondwana Cañon Park, bordering Fish River Canyon. In both, concessionaires provide accommodation and activities for visitors. Most of the smaller game reserves are either private game farms or hunting farms, which sustain endemic animal species rather than livestock.

SURVIVAL GUIDE

Directory A–Z

Accommodation

Accommodation in Namibia is some of the most well priced and well kept in Southern Africa, and covers a huge range of options from hotels to rest camps, campsites, caravan parks, guest farms, backpacker hostels, B&Bs, guesthouses and luxury safari lodges. Most establishments are graded using a star system based on regular inspections carried out by the **Hospitality Association of Namibia** (HAN; hannamibia.com).

Hotels with restaurants also get a Y rating: YY means it only has a restaurant licence, while YYY indicates full alcohol licensing. For a full list of accommodation, pick up the comprehensive booklets *Namibia: Where to Stay, Welcome to Namibia – Official Visitor's Guide* and the *Namibia B&B Guide,* free from any tourist office. HAN also publishes a map showing the locations of most lodges and guest farms.

Many lower-budget and backpacker places do not include breakfast in the price. In B&Bs, guesthouses, farmstays and safari lodges, breakfast is usually included in the cost of the room along with either half-board or full-board options. The former would include breakfast and a set dinner, while the latter also provides lunch (either a set lunch or a buffet-style spread).

Price ranges in this book are as follows:

$	<US$50
$$	US$50-100
$$$	>US$100

While most budget and midrange options tend to have a standard room price, many top-end places change their prices according to the season. High season is from June

to December, while low season corresponds with the rains (January to April).

If you are booking one of the high-end lodges you will usually have to confirm your booking with a credit card; this is not necessary, however, for the bulk of accommodation.

In this book, sleeping listings are presented in order of author preference.

B&BS

Bed-and-breakfast (B&B) establishments are mushrooming all around the country. As private homes, the standard, atmosphere and welcome tends to vary a great deal. Generally speaking, B&Bs are a pleasure to frequent, and can be one of the highlights of any trip to Namibia. However, in some places in Swakopmund and Windhoek, readers have complained of unpleasant racism. Some places don't actually provide breakfast (!), so it pays to ask when booking.

For listings, pick up the *Namibia B&B Guide* or contact the **Accommodation Association of Namibia** (www.accommodation-association.com), which also lists a number of self-catering flats and guest farms.

CAMPING

Namibia is campers' heaven, and wherever you go in the country you'll find a campsite nearby. These can vary from a patch of scrubland with basic facilities to well-kitted-out sites with concrete ablution blocks with hot and cold running water.

In many of the national parks, campsites are administered by Namibia Wildlife Resorts (p221), and need to be booked beforehand online or through its offices in Windhoek, Swakopmund and Cape Town. These sites are all well maintained, and many of them also offer accommodation in bungalows.

To camp on private land, you'll need to secure permission from the landowner. On communal land – unless you're well away from human habitation – it's a courtesy to make your presence known to the leaders in the nearest community.

Most towns also have caravan parks with bungalows or *rondavels* (round huts), as well as a pool, restaurant and shop. Prices are normally per site, with a maximum of eight people and two vehicles per site; there's normally an additional charge per vehicle. In addition a growing number of private rest camps, with rooms and campsites and well-appointed facilities, are springing up in rural areas and along major tourist routes.

PRACTICALITIES

Newspapers There are a decent number of commercial newspapers, of which the *Namibian* and the *Windhoek Advertiser* are probably the best. The *Windhoek Observer*, published on Saturday, is also good. The two main German-language newspapers are *Allgemeine Zeitung* and *Namibia Nachrichten*.

Radio The Namibian Broadcasting Corporation (NBC) operates a dozen or so radio stations in nine languages. The two main stations in Windhoek are Radio Energy (100FM) and Radio Kudu (103.5FM); the best pop station is Radio Wave, at 96.7FM in Windhoek.

TV The NBC broadcasts government-vetted TV programs in English and Afrikaans. News is broadcast at 10pm nightly. Most top-end hotels and lodges with televisions provide access to satellite-supported DSTV, which broadcasts NBC and a cocktail of cable channels.

Weights & Measures Metric system.

Electricity Electrical plugs are three round pins (like South Africa).

GUEST FARMS

Farmstays are a peculiarly Namibian phenomenon, where tourists can spend the night on one of the country's huge private farms. They give an intriguing insight into the rural white lifestyle although, as with B&Bs, the level of hospitality and the standard of rooms and facilities can vary enormously. The emphasis is on personal service and quaint rural luxury, and bedding down on a huge rural estate in the middle of the bush can be a uniquely Namibian experience.

As an added bonus, many of these farms have designated blocks of land as wildlife reserves, and offer excellent wildlife viewing and photographic opportunities. With that said, many also serve as hunting reserves, so bear this in mind when booking if you don't relish the thought of trading trophy stories over dinner.

For all farmstays, advance bookings are essential.

HOSTELS

In Windhoek, Swakopmund, Lüderitz and other places, you'll find private backpacker hostels, which provide inexpensive dorm accommodation, shared ablutions and cooking facilities. Most offer a very agreeable atmosphere, and they are extremely popular with budget travellers. On average, you can expect to pay around N$90 per person per night. Some also offer private doubles, which cost around N$220 to N$350.

HOTELS

Hotels in Namibia are much like hotels anywhere else, ranging from tired old has-beens to palaces of luxury and indulgence. Rarely,

though, will you find a dirty or unsafe hotel in Namibia given the relatively strict classification system, which rates everything from small guesthouses to four-star hotels.

One-star hotels must have a specific ratio of rooms with private and shared facilities. They tend to be quite simple, but most are locally owned and managed, and provide clean, comfortable accommodation with adequate beds and towels. Rates range from around N$320 to N$400 for a double room, including breakfast. They always have a small dining room and bar, but few offer frills such as air-conditioning.

Hotels with two- and three-star ratings are generally more comfortable, and are often used by local businesspeople. Rates start at around N$450 for a double, and climb to N$600 for the more elegant places.

There aren't really many four-star hotels in the usual sense, though most high-end lodges could qualify for a four-star rating. To qualify for such a rating, a hotel needs to be an air-conditioned palace with a salon, valet service and a range of ancillary services for business and diplomatic travellers.

SAFARI LODGES

Over the last decade the Namibian luxury safari lodge has come along in leaps and bounds, offering the kind of colonial luxury that has been associated with Botswana. The Gondwana Desert Collection (www.gondwana-desert-collection.com) is a prime example.

Most of the lodges are set on large private ranches or in concession areas. Some are quite affordable family-run places with standard meals or self-catering options. In general they are still more affordable than comparable places in Botswana or the Victoria Falls area, yet more expensive than those in South Africa.

Activities

Given its stunning landscapes, Namibia provides a photogenic arena for the multitude of outdoor activities that are on offer. These range from the more conventional hiking and 4WD trails to sandboarding down mountainous dunes, quad biking, paragliding, ballooning and camel riding. Most of these activities can be arranged very easily locally, and are relatively well priced.

4WD TRAILS

Traditionally, 4WD trips were limited to rugged wilderness tracks through the Kaokoveld, Damaraland and Bushmanland, but an increasing number of 4WD trails have been established for 4WD enthusiasts. Participants must pay a daily fee, and are obligated to travel a certain distance each day and stay at pre-specified campsites. You'll need to book at least a few weeks in advance through Namibian Wildlife Resorts (p221). Contact them to see which trails are currently available. You could also try www.namibian.org/travel/adventure/4x4_action.htm, which includes a booking service; and www.drivesouthafrica.co.za/blog/best-4x4-trails-in-namibia for more information.

CANOEING & RAFTING

Along the Orange River, in the south of the country, canoeing and rafting trips are growing in popularity. Several operators in Noordoewer offer good-value descents through the spectacular canyons of the Orange River, along the South African border. White-water rafting on the Kunene River is available through the inexpensive Kunene River Lodge at Swartbooi's Drift, and also through several more upmarket operators.

FISHING

Namibia draws anglers from all over Southern Africa. The Benguela Current along the Skeleton Coast brings kabeljou, steenbras, galjoen, blacktails and copper sharks close to shore. Favoured spots include the various beaches north of Swakopmund, as well as more isolated spots further north.

In the dams, especially Hardap and Von Bach, you can expect to catch tilapia, carp, yellowfish, mullet and barbel. Fly-fishing is possible in the Chobe and Zambezi Rivers in the Caprivi region; here you'll find barbel, bream, pike and Africa's famed fighting tiger fish, which can grow up to 9kg.

HIKING

Hiking is a highlight in Namibia, and a growing number of private ranches have established wonderful hiking routes for their guests.

You'll also find superb routes in several national parks. Multiday walks are available at Waterberg Plateau, the four- or eight-day Naukluft loops, the Ugab River, Daan Viljoen Game Park and Fish River Canyon, but departures are limited, so book as far in advance as possible. See the destination sections for more detail on each of these hikes.

Hiking groups on most national park routes must consist of at least three but no more than 10 people, and each hiker needs a doctor's certificate of fitness (forms are available from the Windhoek Namibia Wildlife Resorts office) issued no more than 40 days before the start of the hike. If you're young and you look fit, this requirement might be waived on most trails, with the exception of the demanding 85km hike in Fish River Canyon. The NWR can recommend doctors, but again, in most cases this requirement is waived.

While this might seem restrictive to some folk who are accustomed to strapping on a pack and taking off, it does protect the environment from unrestrained tourism, and it ensures that you'll have the trail to yourself – you'll certainly never see another group.

If you prefer guided tramping, get in touch with **Trail Hopper** (☑061-264521; www.trailhopper.com), which offers hikes all over the country, including Fish River Canyon, a five-day Brandberg Ascent and a Naukluft Mountain Trek. Prices depend on the size of the group.

ROCK CLIMBING

Rock climbing is popular on the red rocks of Damaraland, particularly the Spitzkoppe and the Brandberg, but participants need their own gear and transport. For less-experienced climbers it's a dangerous endeavour in the desert heat, so seek local advice beforehand, and never attempt a climb on your own.

SANDBOARDING

A popular activity is sandboarding, which is commercially available in Swakopmund and Walvis Bay. You can choose between sled-style sandboarding, in which you lay on a masonite board and slide down the dunes at very high speeds, or the stand-up version, in which you schuss down on a snowboard. See those destinations for more information.

Business Hours

Banks 8am or 9am to 3pm Monday to Friday, 8am to 12.30pm Saturday

Information 8am or 9am to 5pm or 6pm Monday to Friday

Post offices 8am to 4.30pm Monday to Friday, 8.30 to 11am Saturday

Shopping 8am or 9am to 5pm or 6pm Monday to Friday, 9am to 1pm or 5pm Saturday; late-night shopping to 9pm Thursday or Friday

Eating Breakfast 8 to 10am, lunch 11am to 3pm, dinner 6 to 10pm; some places open 8am to 10pm Monday to Saturday

Drinking & entertainment 5pm to close (midnight to 3am) Monday to Saturday

Petrol Stations Only a few open 24 hours; in outlying areas fuel hard to find after hours or Sunday.

In this book reviews don't list hours unless they vary from the standard.

Children

Many parents regard Africa as just too dangerous for travel with children, but in reality, Namibia presents few problems to families travelling with children. As a destination it's relatively safe healthwise, largely due to its dry climate and good medical services; there's a good network of affordable accommodation, and an excellent infrastructure of well-maintained roads. In addition, foreigners who visit Namibia with children are usually treated with great kindness, and a widespread local affection for the younger set opens up all sorts of social interaction.

Still, it has to be said that travelling around Namibia with very small children (under-fives) will present some problems, not least because it's hot and distances can be vast. It's also difficult to see what very small children will take away from the experience, and parents will probably spend most of their time fretting over safety.

For invaluable general advice on taking the family abroad, see Lonely Planet's *Travel with Children.*

PRACTICALITIES

While there are few attractions or facilities designed specifically for children, Namibian food and lodgings are mostly quite familiar and manageable. Family rooms and chalets are normally available for only slightly more than double rooms; these normally consist of one double bed and two single beds. Other wise, it's usually easy to arrange more beds in a standard adult double room for a minimal extra charge.

Camping can be exciting, but you'll need to be extra vigilant so your kids don't just wander off unsupervised, and you'll also need to be alert to potential hazards such as mosquitoes and campfires. Most mosquito repellents with high levels of DEET may be unsuitable for young children. They should also wear sturdy enclosed shoes to protect them from thorns, bees and scorpion stings.

If you're travelling with kids, you should always invest in a hire car, unless you want to be stuck for hours on public transport. Functional seatbelts are rare even in taxis, and accidents are common – a child seat brought from home is a good idea if you're hiring a car or going on safari. Even with your own car, distances between towns and parks can be long, so parents will need to provide essential supplemental entertainment (toys, books, games, a Nintendo DS etc).

Canned baby foods, powdered milk, disposable nappies and the like are available in most large supermarkets.

SIGHTS & ACTIVITIES

Travelling by campervan and camping, or faking it in luxury tented lodges, are thrilling experiences for young and old alike, while attractions such as the wildlife of Etosha National Park or the world's biggest sandbox at Sossusvlei provide ample family entertainment.

Full-scale safaris are generally suited to older children. Be aware that some upmarket lodges and safari companies won't accept children under a certain age and those that do may require you to book separate game drives. Endless hours of driving and animal viewing can be an eternity for small children, so you'll need to break up your trip with lots of pit stops and picnics, and plenty of time spent poolside where possible.

Older children are well catered for with a whole host of exciting activities. Swakopmund is an excellent base for these. They include everything from horse riding and sandboarding to ballooning and paragliding. Less-demanding activities might include looking for interesting rocks (and Namibia has some truly incredible rocks!); beachcombing along the Skeleton Coast; or running and rolling in the dunes at Lüderitz, Sossusvlei, Swakopmund and elsewhere along the coast.

Customs Regulations

Most items from elsewhere in the Southern African Customs Union – Botswana, South Africa, Lesotho and Swaziland – may be imported duty-free. From elsewhere, visitors can import duty-free 400 cigarettes or 250g of tobacco, 2L of wine, 1L of spirits and 250ml of eau de cologne. Those aged under 18 do not qualify for the tobacco or drinks allowances. There are no limits on currency import, but entry and departure forms ask how much you intend to spend or have spent in the country.

Automobiles may not be sold in Namibia without payment of duty. For pets, you need a health certificate and full veterinary documentation; note that pets aren't permitted in national parks or reserves.

Discount Cards

Those with student cards score a 15% discount on Intercape Mainliner buses, and occasionally receive discounts on museum admissions. Seniors over 60, with proof of age, also receive a 15% discount on Intercape Mainliner buses, and good discounts on domestic Air Namibia fares.

Embassies & Consulates

It's important to realise what your own embassy – the embassy of the country of which you are a citizen – can and can't do to help you if you get into trouble. Generally speaking, it won't be much help in emergencies if the trouble you're in is remotely your own fault. Remember that you are bound by the laws of the country you are in. Your embassy will not be sympathetic if you end up in jail after committing a crime locally, even if such actions are legal in your own country. The embassies listed here are all in Windhoek.

Angola (Map p210; ☑227535; 3 Dr Agostino Neto St; ⊙9am-3pm)

Botswana (Map p208; ☑221941; 101 Nelson Mandela Ave; ⊙8am-1pm & 2-5pm)

Finland (Map p210; ☑221355; 2 Crohn St, cnr Bahnhof St; ⊙9am-noon Mon, Wed & Thu)

France (Map p208; ☑276700; 1 Goethe St; ⊙9am-noon, afternoons by appointment Mon-Thu, 9am-noon Fri)

Germany (Map p210; ☑273100; 154 Independence Ave, 6th fl, Sanlam Centre; ⊙9am-noon Mon-Fri, plus 2-4pm Wed)

Kenya (Map p210; ☑226836; 134 Robert Mugabe Ave, 5th fl, Kenya House; ⊙8.30am-1pm & 2-4.30pm Mon-Thu, to 3pm Fri)

South Africa (Map p208; ☑205 7111; cnr Jan Jonker St & Nelson Mandela Dr, Klein Windhoek; ⊙8.15am-12.15pm)

UK (Map p210; ☑274800; 116 Robert Mugabe Ave; ⊙8am-1pm & 2-5pm Mon-Thu, 8am-noon Fri)

US (Map p210; ☑295 8500; 14 Lossen St; ⊙8.30am-noon Mon-Thu)

Zambia (Map p210; ☑237610; 22 Sam Nujoma Dr, cnr Mandume Ndemufeyo Ave; ⊙9am-1pm & 2-4pm)

Zimbabwe (Map p210; ☑228134; Gamsberg Bldg, cnr Independence Ave & Grimm St; ⊙8.30am-1pm & 2-4.45pm Mon-Thu, 8.30am-2pm Fri)

Food

The order of restaurant listings follows the author's preference, and each place to eat is accompanied by one of the following symbols.

$	<US$10 per main course
$$	US$10-20 per main course
$$$	>US$20 per main course

Gay & Lesbian Travellers

As in many African countries, homosexuality is illegal in Namibia, based on the common-law offence of committing 'an unnatural sex crime'. Namibia is also very conservative in its attitudes, given the strongly held Christian beliefs of the majority. In view of this, discretion is certainly the better part of valour as treatment of gay men and women can range from simple social ostracism to physical attack. In 1996 Namibia's president Sam Nujoma initiated a very public campaign against homosexuals, recommending that all foreign gays and lesbians be deported or excluded from the country. One minister called homosexuality a 'behavioural disorder which is alien to African culture'.

Out-Right Namibia (http://outrightnamibia. org) is a human rights organisation based in Windhoek that was formed by gay and lesbian activists to challenge homophobia and advocate for equal rights. Its website contains information on its bimonthly events as well as links to other information sources. Namibian lesbians (and other women's interests) are also represented by Sister Namibia (www.sisternamibia.org).

Insurance

Travel insurance to cover theft, loss and medical treatment is strongly recommended. Some policies specifically exclude 'dangerous activities', which can include scuba diving, motorcycling and even trekking. If 'risky' activities are on your agendayou'll need the most comprehensive policy.

You may prefer to have an insurance policy that pays doctors or hospitals directly rather than you having to pay on the spot and claim later. If you have to claim later, make sure you keep all documentation. Some policies ask you to call back (reverse charges) to a centre in your home country, where an immediate assessment of your problem is made. Check that the policy covers ambulances or an emergency flight home. See also p358 for car insurance.

Worldwide travel insurance is available at www.lonelyplanet.com/travel_services. You can buy, extend and claim online anytime – even if you're already on the road.

Internet Access

Internet access is firmly established and widespread in Namibia, and connection speeds are fairly stable. Most larger or tourist-oriented towns have at least one internet cafe. Plan on spending around N$60 per hour online. An increasing number of backpacker hostels, hotels in larger towns and some top-end lodges also offer internet access. Still, the relatively high cost of accessing the internet is still a major constraint in rural areas.

If you're travelling with a notebook or hand-held computer, more and more hotels, guesthouses and lodges are offering wi-fi connectability to their guests.

Establishments with internet access are identified in this book with the @ icon, while those with wireless have the ⎙ icon.

Legal Matters

All drugs are illegal in Namibia, penalties are stiff and prisons are deeply unpleasant. So don't think about bringing anything over the borders or buying it while you're here. The police are also allowed to use entrapment techniques, such as posing as dealers, to catch criminals, so don't be tempted.

Police, military and veterinary officials are generally polite, and on their best behaviour. In your dealings with officialdom, you should always make every effort to be patient and polite in return.

Maps

A good all-round map of the region is the Michelin map *Central and South Africa* (series number 746) at a scale of 1:4,000,000, although it's not sufficiently detailed for Namibia. For more detail you might pick up the Namibia map produced by Reise-Know-How-Verlag (1:250,000) or the Freytag & Berndt map (1:200,000).

Shell Roadmap – Namibia or *InfoMap Namibia* are the best reference for remote routes. InfoMap contains GPS coordinates and both companies produce maps of remote areas such as Namibia's far northwest and the Caprivi Strip.

For the average tourist (ie if you're not planning your own remote self-drive safari), these are too detailed. Much better is the *Namibia Map* endorsed by the Roads Authority which shows major routes and lists accommodation. Even the Globetrotter *Namibia* map is easy to read and quite detailed.

Also consider *Namibia*, Nelles Vertag (1:1,500,000), and Map Studio, which also publish a Namibia map (1:1,550,000) and a road atlas (1:500,000).

The best place to purchase maps in Namibia is at petrol stations, although you can get your hands on more general maps at local bookshops.

In the USA, Trek Tools (www.trektools.com) is an excellent and exhaustive source for maps of Namibia. A similarly extensive selection of maps is available in the UK from Stanfords (www.stanfords.co.uk).

Money

The currency of Namibia is the Namibian dollar (N$). It's divided into 100 cents, and is linked to the South African rand. The rand is also legal tender in Namibia at a rate of 1:1. This can be confusing, given that there are three sets of coins and notes in use: old South African, new South African and Namibian. We quote prices in Namibian and occasionally US dollars.

Namibian dollar notes come in denominations of N$10, N$20, N$50, N$100 and N$200, and coins in values of 5, 10, 20 and 50 cents, and N$1 and N$5.

Money can be exchanged in banks and exchange offices. Banks generally offer the best rates, and travellers cheques normally fetch a better rate than cash. When changing money, you may be given either South African rand or Namibian dollars; if you'll need to change any leftover currency outside Namibia, the rand is a better choice.

There is no currency black market, so beware of street changers offering unrealistic rates.

ATMS

Credit cards can be used in ATMs displaying the appropriate sign or to obtain cash advances over the counter in many banks – Visa and MasterCard are among the most widely recognised. You'll find ATMs at all the main bank branches throughout Namibia, and this is undoubtedly the simplest (and safest) way to handle your money while travelling.

CASH

While most major currencies are accepted in Windhoek and Swakopmund, once away from these two centres you'll run into problems with currencies other than US dollars, euros, UK pounds and South African rand (you may even struggle with pounds). Play it safe and carry US dollars – it makes life much simpler.

CREDIT/DEBIT CARDS

Credit cards are accepted in most shops, restaurants and hotels, and credit-card cash advances are available from ATMs. Check charges with your bank.

Credit-card cash advances are available at foreign-exchange desks in most major banks, but set aside at least an hour or two to complete the rather tedious transaction.

Keep the card supplier's emergency number handy in case your card is lost or stolen.

EXCHANGE RATES

Australia	A$1	N$9.20
Canada	C$1	N$8.85
Europe	€1	N$11.65
Japan	¥100	N$9.76
New Zealand	NZ$1	N$7.31
South Africa	R10	N$10
UK	UK£	N$14.07
US	US$	N$8.71

For current exchange rates see www.xe.com

TIPPING

Tipping is welcomed everywhere, but is expected only in upmarket tourist restaurants where it's normal to leave a tip of 10% to 15% of the bill. Some restaurants add a service charge as a matter of course. As a rule, taxi drivers aren't tipped, but it is customary to give N$2 to N$5 to petrol-station attendants who clean your windows and/or check the oil and water. Note that tipping is officially prohibited in national parks and reserves.

At safari lodges, it's customary to tip any personal guides directly (assuming they merit a tip), and also to leave a tip with the proprietor, to be divided among all the staff.

TRAVELLERS CHEQUES

Travellers cheques can be cashed at most banks and exchange offices. American Express (Amex), Thomas Cook and Visa are the most widely accepted brands.

It's preferable to buy travellers cheques in US dollars, UK pounds or euros rather than another currency, as these are most widely accepted. Get most of the cheques in largish denominations to save on per-cheque rates. Travellers cheques may also be exchanged for US dollars cash – if the cash is available – but banks charge a hefty commission.

You must take your passport with you when cashing cheques.

Photography

While many Namibians enjoy being photographed, others do not; the main point is that you should always respect the wishes of the person in question, and don't snap a picture if permission is denied.

Officials in Namibia aren't as sensitive about photography as in some other African countries, but it still isn't a good idea to photograph borders, airports, communications equipment or military installations without first asking permission from any uniformed personnel that might be present.

If you're still shooting print and slide film, it's best to bring extra rolls from home. Memory cards for digital cameras are widely available in Windhoek and Swakopmund, and most internet cafes can burn your photos onto CD. Prices are generally very cheap for these services, and shouldn't cost more than a few US dollars.

For pointers on taking pictures in Africa, look out for Lonely Planet's *Travel Photography* book.

Post

Domestic post generally moves slowly; it can take weeks for a letter to travel from Lüderitz to Katima Mulilo, for example. Overseas airmail post is normally more efficient.

Public Holidays

Banks, government offices and most shops are closed on public holidays; when a public holiday falls on a Sunday, the following day also becomes a holiday.

New Year's Day 1 January
Good Friday March or April
Easter Sunday March or April
Easter Monday March or April
Independence Day 21 March
Ascension Day April or May
Workers' Day 1 May
Cassinga Day 4 May
Africa Day 25 May
Heroes' Day 26 August
Human Rights Day 10 December
Christmas 25 December
Family/Boxing Day 26 December

Safe Travel

Namibia is one of the safest countries in Africa. It's also a huge country with a very sparse population, and even the capital, Windhoek, is more like a provincial town than an urban jungle. Unfortunately however, crime is on the rise in the larger cities, in particular Windhoek, but a little street sense will go a long way here.

SCAMS

A common scam you might encounter in Namibia is the pretty innocuous palm-ivory nut scam practiced at various petrol stations. It starts with a friendly approach from a couple of young men, who ask your name. Without you seeing it they then carve your name onto a palm-ivory nut and then offer it to you for sale for anything up to N$70, hoping that you'll feel obligated to buy the personalised item. You can obtain the same sort of thing at any curio shop for around N$20. It's hardly the crime of the century but it pays to be aware.

A more serious trick, particularly prevalent in Walvis Bay in 2012, is for one guy to distract a parked motorist while their accomplice opens a door and grabs your bags from the back seat or from the front passenger seat. Aways keep the doors of your vehicle locked, and be aware of distractions.

THE SPERRGEBIET

En route to Lüderitz from the east, keep well clear of the Sperrgebiet (Forbidden Zone), the prohibited diamond area. Well-armed patrols can be overly zealous. The area begins immediately south of the A4 Lüderitz–Keetmanshoop road and continues to just west of Aus, where the off-limits boundary turns south towards the Orange River. It's best to have a healthy respect for the boundaries.

THEFT

Theft isn't rife in Namibia, but Windhoek, Swakopmund, Walvis Bay, Tsumeb and Grootfontein have problems with petty theft and muggings, so it's sensible to conceal your valuables, not leave anything in your car, and avoid walking alone at night. It's also prudent – and sensitive – to avoid walking around cities and towns bedecked in expensive jewellery, watches and cameras. Most hotels provide a safe or secure place for valuables, although you should be cautious of the security at some budget places.

Never leave a safari-packed vehicle anywhere in Windhoek or Swakopmund, other than in a guarded car park or private parking lot.

Theft from campsites can also be a problem, particularly near urban areas. Locking up your tent may help, but anything left unattended is still at risk.

VEGETATION

An unusual natural hazard is the euphorbia plant. Its dried branches should never be used in fires as they release a deadly toxin when burnt. It can be fatal to inhale the smoke or eat food cooked on a fire containing it. If you're in doubt about any wood you've collected, leave it out of the fire. Caretakers at campsites do a good job of removing these plants from around pitches and fire pits, so you needn't worry excessively. As a precaution, try to only use bundles of wood that

IMPORTANT NUMBERS

Country code	☑264
Area codes	Namibia uses 3-digit area codes
International access code	☑00
Emergency	☑10111

you've purchased in a store to start fires. If you're bush camping, best to familiarise yourself with the plant's appearance. There are several members of the family, and you can check out their pictures either online or at the tourist information centres in Windhoek.

Shopping

Namibia's range of inexpensive souvenirs includes all sorts of things, from kitsch African curios and batik paintings to superb Owambo basketry and Kavango woodcarvings. Most of the items sold along Post Street Mall in Windhoek are cheap curios imported from Zimbabwe. Along the highways around the country, roadside stalls sometimes appear, selling locally produced items, from baskets and simple pottery jars to the appealing woven mats and wooden aeroplanes that are a Kavango speciality. In Rundu, and other areas of the northeast, you'll find distinctive San material arts – bows and arrows, ostrich-egg beads and leather pouches. An excellent place to browse a whole range of craft work is the Namibia Crafts Centre in Windhoek.

The pastel colours of the Namib provide inspiration for a number of local artists, and lots of galleries in Windhoek and Swakopmund feature local paintings and sculpture. Also, some lovely items are produced in conjunction with the karakul wool industry, such as rugs, wall hangings and textiles. The better weaving outlets are found in Dordabis, Swakopmund and Windhoek.

Windhoek is the centre of the upmarket leather industry, and there you'll find high-quality products, from belts and handbags to made-to-measure leather jackets. Beware, however, of items made from crocodile or other protected species, and note that those comfortable shoes known as *Swakopmunders* are made from kudu leather. Several shops have now stopped selling them.

Minerals and gemstones are popular purchases. Malachite, amethyst, chalcedony, aquamarine, tourmaline, jasper and rose quartz are among the most beautiful. You'll find the best jewellery shops in Windhoek and Swakopmund and the most reputable of these is House of Gems (p220) in Windhoek.

If you're interested in something that appears to be exotic or resembles an artefact, ask about its provenance. Any antiquity must have an export/import permit and the dealer must have a licence to sell antiquities.

Buying souvenirs derived from protected wild species – cheetahs, leopards, elephants or (heaven forbid) rhinos – is prohibited. In Windhoek and other places, you'll see lots of ivory pieces and jewellery for sale. The only legitimate stuff is clearly marked as culled ivory from Namibian national parks.

BARGAINING

Bargaining is only acceptable when purchasing handicrafts and arts directly from the producer or artist, but in remote areas the prices asked normally represent close to market value. The exception is crafts imported from Zimbabwe, which are generally sold at large craft markets for inflated prices that are always negotiable.

Telephone

The Namibian fixed-line phone system run by **Telecom Namibia** (www.telecom.na) is very efficient, and getting through to fixed-line numbers is extremely easy. However, as in the rest of Africa, the fixed-line system is rapidly being overtaken by the massive popularity of prepaid mobile phones.

Fixed-line calls to the UK/US and Europe cost around N$3.50 to N$4.50 per minute at peak times; and around N$2 to N$3 per minute to neighbouring countries. See www.telecom.na/index.php/tariffs/international-services for exact charges.

Given the increasing number of wi-fi hot spots in the country, using Skype is also becoming a more common (and much cheaper) alternative.

MOBILE PHONES

MTC (www.mtc.com.na) is the largest mobile service provider in Namibia (others are Leo and Telecom Switch), operating on the GSM 900/1800 frequency, which is compatible with Europe and Australia but not with North America (GSM 1900) or Japan. There is supposedly comprehensive coverage across the country, although in reality Namibia is *huge* and it's hard to get a signal outside the major towns – the more remote you are the less likely you'll get coverage, which is why a satellite phone is an attractive proposition if you're travelling extensively away from population areas.

MTC offers a prepaid service, which since its introduction has become the package of choice in Namibia. After paying a one-off SIM-card fee, subscribers can buy prepaid vouchers at most stores across Namibia.

You can easily buy a handset in any major town in Namibia, which will set you back from N$600.

Most Namibian mobile phone numbers begin with 081, which is followed by a seven-digit number.

PHONE CODES

When phoning Namibia from abroad, dial the international access code (usually 00, but 011 from the USA), followed by the country code 264, the area code without the leading zero, and finally, the required number. To phone out of Namibia, dial 00 followed by the desired country code, area code (if applicable) and the number.

When phoning long-distance within Namibia, dial the three-digit regional area code, including the leading zero, followed by the six- or seven-digit number.

To phone some rural areas, you must dial the code and ask the exchange operator for the desired number.

PHONECARDS

Telecom Namibia phonecards are sold at post offices to the value of N$20, N$50 and N$100. They are also available at most shops and a number of hotels. Public telephone boxes are available at most post offices and can also be found scattered around towns.

Time

In the summer months (October to April), Namibia is two hours ahead of GMT/UTC. If it's noon in Southern Africa, it's 10am in London, 5am in New York, 2am in Los Angeles and 8pm in Sydney. In the winter (April to October), Namibia turns its clocks back one hour, making it only one hour ahead of GMT/UTC and one hour behind South African time.

Tourist Information

The level of service in Namibia's tourist offices is generally high, and everyone speaks impeccable English, German and Afrikaans.

In Windhoek, there are two branches of the local Windhoek Information & Publicity Office (p221). Also in Windhoek is the office of Namibia Wildlife Resorts (p221), where you can pick up information on the national parks and make reservations at any NWR campsite.

Other useful tourist offices include Lüderitz Safaris & Tours (p309) in Lüderitz and Namib-i (p285) in Swakopmund.

Travellers with Disabilities

There are very few special facilities, and people with limited mobility will not have an easy time in Namibia. All is not lost, however, and with an able-bodied travelling companion, wheelchair travellers will manage here. This is mainly because Namibia has some advantages over other parts of the developing world: footpaths and public areas are often surfaced with tar or concrete; many buildings (including safari lodges and national park cabins) are single-storey; car hire is easy and hire cars can be taken into neighbouring countries; and assistance is usually available on internal and regional flights. In addition, most safari companies in Namibia – including budget operators – are happy to 'make a plan' to accommodate travellers with special needs.

Visas

All visitors require a passport from their home country that is valid for at least six months after their intended departure date from Namibia. You may also be asked for an onward plane, bus or rail ticket, although checks are rarely made. Nationals of many countries, including Australia, the EU, USA and most Commonwealth countries do not need a visa to visit Namibia. Citizens of most Eastern European countries do require visas.

Tourists are granted an initial 90 days, which may be extended at the **Ministry of Home Affairs** (Map p210; ☑061-292 2111; www.mha.gov.na; cnr Kasino St & Independence Ave; ☺8am-1pm Mon-Fri) in Windhoek. For the best results, be there when the office opens at 8am, and submit your application at the 3rd-floor offices (as opposed to the desk on the ground floor).

Volunteering

Namibia has a good track record for grassroots projects and community-based tourism. However, it's seldom possible to find any volunteering work in-country due to visa restrictions and restricted budgets. Any organisations that do offer volunteer positions will need to be approached well in advance of your departure date. Many conservation outfits look for volunteers with specific skills that might be useful in the field.

The most well-known organisations offering volunteer positions (p137) are Save the Rhino Trust, the Afri-Cat Foundation and the Cheetah Conservation Fund. Projects like the Integrated Rural Development and Nature Conservation may also offer the occasional post.

Other international organisations which offer volunteering in Namibia include **Project Trust** (www.projecttrust.org.uk) in the UK and **World Teach** (www.worldteach.org) in the US.

Women Travellers

On the whole Namibia is a safe destination for women travellers, and we receive few complaints from women travellers about any sort of harassment. Having said that, Namibia is still a conservative society. Many bars are men only (by either policy or convention), but even in places that welcome women, you may be more comfortable in a group or with a male companion. Note that accepting a drink from a local man is usually construed as a come-on.

The threat of sexual assault isn't any greater in Namibia than in Europe, but it's best to avoid walking alone in parks and back streets, especially at night. Hitching alone is not recommended. Never hitch at night and, if possible, find a companion for trips through sparsely populated areas.

In Windhoek and other urban areas, wearing shorts and sleeveless dresses or shirts is fine. However, if you're visiting rural areas, wear knee-length skirts or loose trousers and shirts with sleeves. If you're poolside in a resort or lodge where the clientele is largely foreign, then somewhat revealing swimwear is acceptable, otherwise err on the side of caution and see what other women are wearing.

Getting There & Away

Unless you are travelling overland, most likely from Botswana or South Africa, flying is by far the most convenient way to get to Namibia. But, Namibia isn't exactly a hub of international travel, nor is it an obvious transit point along the major international routes. You're most likely to fly via South Africa or, for western European travellers, via Frankfurt.

A few adventurous and resourceful souls with their own vehicles still travel overland to Namibia from Europe, but most routes pass through several war zones and should only be considered after some serious planning and preparation.

Entering the Country

Entering Namibia is straightforward and hassle-free. Most nationalities (including nationals from the UK, USA, Australia, Japan and all the western European countries) don't even require a visa. If you are entering Namibia across one of its land borders, the process is painless. You will, however, need to have all the necessary documentation and insurance for your vehicle.

PASSPORTS

All visitors entering Namibia must hold a passport that is valid for at least six months after their intended departure date from Namibia. Also, allow a few empty pages for stamp-happy immigration officials, especially if you're crossing over to Zimbabwe and/ or Zambia to see Victoria Falls. In theory, although seldom in practice, you should also hold proof of departure either in the form of a return or onward ticket.

Air

Most international flights into Namibia arrive at Windhoek's **Hosea Kutako International Airport** (WDH; ☎061-299 6602; www.airports.com.na), 42km east of the capital. The main domestic carrier is **Air Namibia** (www.airnamibia.com.na), which flies routes to other parts of Southern Africa as well as long-haul flights to Frankfurt. Most international airlines stop at Johannesburg or Cape Town in South Africa, where you'll typically switch to a **South Africa Airlines** (☎273340; www.flysaa.com) flight for your final leg to Windhoek. It may also be cheaper to buy a cheap flight to South Africa and add on a flight to Windhoek (or elsewhere in Namibia) from there. South African Airways has daily flights connecting Cape Town and Johannesburg to Windhoek. Johannesburg is also the main hub for connecting flights to other African cities.

Return flights from Jo'burg to Windhoek are generally a few hundred dollars, although if you book your internal flight at the same time as your main flight, you'll always get a better deal. Note that the airport departure tax for international flights is included in the cost of your plane ticket.

For North American travellers, it's worth checking the price of a flight via Frankfurt, as this may be cheaper than a direct flight to South Africa.

Round-the-world tickets can work out cheaper than return tickets for travellers from Australia and New Zealand. The most common African stop is Jo'burg.

Book well in advance for flights from the following neighbouring countries:

Botswana Air Namibia runs several flights a week between Windhoek and Maun.

Zambia You will need to transit through Jo'burg for flights to Lusaka or Livingstone.

Zimbabwe Air Namibia flies to Victoria Falls (Zimbabwe) a few times a week.

Windhoek's in-town **Eros Airport** (ERS; ☑061-299 6500) is mainly for small charter flights, although Air Namibia also runs flights to Katima Mulilo, Ondangwa and Walvis Bay; see p357 for more details.

Land

Thanks to the Southern African Customs Union, you can drive through Namibia, Botswana, South Africa and Swaziland with a minimum of ado. To travel further north requires a *carnet de passage,* which can amount to heavy expenditure.

If you're driving a hire car into Namibia you will need to present a letter of permission from the hire company saying the car is allowed to cross the border.

BORDER CROSSINGS

Namibia has a well-developed road network with easy access from neighbouring countries. The main border crossings into Namibia are as follows:

Angola Oshikango, Ruacana, Rundu

Botswana Buitepos, Mahango and Mpalila Island

South Africa Noordoewer, Ariamsvlei

Zambia Katima Mulilo

All borders are open daily, and the main crossings from South Africa (Noordoewer and Ariamsvlei) are open 24 hours. Otherwise, border posts are generally open at least between 8am and 5pm. Immigration posts at some smaller border crossings close for lunch between 12.30pm and 1.45pm. It is always advisable to reach the crossings as early in the day as possible to allow time for any potential delays. There's no public access between Alexander Bay and Oranjemund (6am to 10pm) without permission from the diamond company Namdeb. For more information on opening hours check out the website www.namibweb.com/border.htm.

From Angola

To enter Namibia overland, you'll need an Angolan visa permitting overland entry. At Ruacana Falls, you can enter the border area temporarily without a visa to visit the falls by signing the immigration register.

From Botswana

The most commonly used crossing is at Buitepos/Mamuno, between Windhoek and Ghanzi, although the border post at Mohembo/Mahango is also popular. The only other real option is the crossing at Ngoma Bridge across the Chobe River. The Mpalila Island/Kasane border is only available to guests who have prebooked accommodation at upmarket lodges on the island.

Drivers crossing the border at Mahango must secure an entry permit for Mahango Game Reserve at Popa Falls. This is free if you're transiting, or US$3 per person per day plus US$3 per vehicle per day if you want to drive around the reserve (which is possible in a 2WD). No motorbikes are permitted in the national park.

From Zambia

A kilometre-long bridge spans the Zambezi between Katima Mulilo and Wenela, providing easy access to Livingstone and other destinations in Zambia. If you're heading to the Victoria Falls, the road is now sealed all the way to Livingstone, and is accessible by 2WD vehicle, even in the rainy season.

From Zimbabwe

There's no direct border crossing between Namibia and Zimbabwe. To get there you must take the Chobe National Park transit route from Ngoma Bridge through northern Botswana to Kasane/Kazungula, and from there to Victoria Falls.

BUS

There's only really one main inter-regional bus service connecting cities in Namibia with Botswana and South Africa. **Intercape Mainliner** (www.intercape.co.za) has services between Windhoek and Johannesburg and Cape Town (South Africa). They also travel northeast to Victoria Falls, and between larger towns within Namibia.

The public transport options between Botswana and Namibia are few and far between. **Monnakgotla Transport** (☑067-350 0419; www.monnakgotla.co.bw) is your best bet; it runs a twice-weekly service between Windhoek and Gaborone on Friday and Sunday. The cost is N$440 one way. If you're

PURCHASING A CAR IN SOUTH AFRICA

If you are planning an extended trip (three months or more) in Namibia, it may be worth considering purchasing a second-hand car in South Africa.

It's worth noting that cars bought in Cape Town will be viewed less favourably at sale time than those purchased in Johannesburg. This is because Cape Town cars are considered to be at risk of rust given the city's seaside location. On the flipside, cars with a Jo'burg registration tend to fetch a higher premium when resold in Cape Town.

If you're buying, newspapers in Jo'burg are obviously one place to start looking. Used-car dealers won't advertise the fact, but they may be willing to buy back a car bought from them after about three months for about 60% of the purchase price – if the car is returned in good condition.

Naturally, check the vehicle documents from the previous owner. A roadworthy certificate (usually included when a car is bought from a used-car dealer) is required; as is a certificate from the police (also provided by most car dealers) to prove that the car isn't stolen. Once bought, re-register the vehicle at a Motor Vehicle Registration Division in a major city. Also recommended is a roadworthiness test by the **Automobile Association** (www.dekraauto.co.za) before you buy anything; membership is not required.

For a *very* rough idea of prices, don't expect a vehicle for less than the rand equivalent of US$4000 to US$6000. A 4WD Land Rover or equivalent model will cost around US$8000 to US$10,000.

travelling on to Ghanzi or Maun, the bus connects with another service.

There are Intercape Mainliner services running between Windhoek and Cape Town, and between Windhoek and Livingstone.

CAR & MOTORCYCLE

Crossing land borders with your own vehicle or a hire car is generally straightforward as long as you have the necessary paperwork – the vehicle registration documents if you own the car, or a letter from the hire company stating that you have permission to take the car over the border, and proof of insurance.

Note that Namibia implements a road tax, known as the Cross-Border Charge (CBC) for foreign-registered vehicles entering the country. Passenger vehicles carrying fewer than 25 passengers are charged N$140 per entry; motorbikes are N$90. It is very important that you keep this receipt as you may be asked to produce it at police roadblocks, and fines will ensue if you can't produce it.

Before departure you should always contact your local automobile association to double-check that you have all the necessary documents for driving around Namibia.

Driving to/from South Africa

You can drive to Namibia along good, sealed roads from South Africa, either from Cape Town (1490km) in the south, crossing the border at Noordoewer, or from Jo'burg (1970km) in the east, in which case the border crossing is at Nakop.

Hiring a car in South Africa will probably work out cheaper than hiring one in Namibia. All major international car-hirel companies have offices all over South Africa. It's also worth trying **Around About Cars** (☎0860 422 4022; www.aroundaboutcars.com), **Britz** (☎in Jo'burg 27 11 230 5200, in Namibia 264-61-219590; www.britz.co.za) and **Buffalo Campers** (☎27-82 412 3099; www.buffalo.co.za), which offers fully equipped 4WD campers.

The cheapest 2WD will end up costing the rand equivalent of about US$50 per day, and a 4WD will cost in the region of US$100 per day.

Getting Around

Namibia is a sparsely populated country, and distances between towns can be vast. However, there is an excellent infrastructure of sealed roads, and to more remote locations there are well-maintained gravel and even salt roads. With such a low population density, it's hardly surprising that the public transport network is limited. Public buses do serve the main towns, but they won't take you to the country's major sights. By far the best way to experience Namibia is in the comfort of your own hire car.

Air

Air Namibia (p354) has an extensive network of local flights operating out of Eros Airport. There are six flights per week to Rundu, Katima Mulilo and Ondangwa.

From Windhoek, domestic destinations include Lüderitz and Oranjemund (three times per week) and Walvis Bay (daily).

Bicycle

Namibia is a desert country, and makes for a tough biking holiday. Distances are great and horizons are vast; the climate and landscapes are hot and very dry and the sun is intense; and, even along major routes, water is scarce and villages are widely spaced. As if all of this wasn't enough of a deterrent, also bear in mind that bicycles are not permitted in any national parks.

Of course, loads of Namibians do get around by bicycle, and cycling around small cities and large towns is much easier than a cross-country excursion. With that said, be wary of cycling on dirt roads as punctures from thorn trees are a major problem. Fortunately, many local people operate small repair shops, which are fairly common along populated roadsides.

Bus

Namibia's bus services aren't extensive. Luxury services are limited to the **Intercape Mainliner** (☑061-227847; www.intercape. co.za), which has scheduled services from Windhoek to Swakopmund, Walvis Bay, Grootfontein, Rundu, Katima Mulilo, Keetmanshoop and Oshikango. Fares include meals on the bus.

There are also local combis (minibuses), which depart when full and follow main routes around the country. From Windhoek's Rhino Park petrol station they depart for dozens of destinations.

Car

The easiest way to get around Namibia is in your own car, and an excellent system of sealed roads runs the length of the country from the South African border at Noordoewer to Ngoma Bridge on the Botswana border and Ruacana in the northwest. Similarly, sealed spur roads connect the main north–south routes to Buitepos, Lüderitz, Swakopmund and Walvis Bay. Elsewhere, towns and most sites of interest are accessible on good gravel roads. Most C-numbered highways are well maintained and passable to all

vehicles, and D-numbered roads, although a bit rougher, are mostly (but not always) passable to 2WD vehicles. In the Kaokoveld, however, most D-numbered roads can only be negotiated with a 4WD.

Nearly all the main car-hire agencies have offices at Hosea Kutako Airport. Ideally, you'll want to hire a car for the duration of your holiday, but if cost is an issue, you might consider a shorter hire from either Windhoek or Swakopmund. If you can muster a group of four, hiring a car will undoubtedly work out cheaper than an organised tour.

AUTOMOBILE ASSOCIATIONS

The **Automobile Association of Namibia** (AAN; ☑061-224201; www.aanamibia.com) is part of the international AA. It provides highway information and you can also acquire maps from them if you produce your membership card from your home country.

DRIVING LICENCE

Foreigners can drive in Namibia on their home driving licence for up to 90 days, and most (if not all) car-hire companies will accept foreign driving licences for car hire. If your home licence isn't written in English then you'd be better off getting yourself an International Driving Permit (IDP) before you arrive in Namibia.

FUEL & SPARE PARTS

The network of petrol stations in Namibia is good, and most small towns have a station. Mostly diesel, unleaded and super (leaded) are available, and prices vary according to the remoteness of the petrol station. Although the odd petrol station is open 24 hours, most are open 7am to 7pm.

All stations are fully serviced (there is no self-service), and a small tip of a couple of Namibian dollars is appropriate, especially if the attendant has washed your windscreen.

As a general road safety rule, you should never pass a service station without filling up, and it is advisable to carry an additional 100 litres of fuel (either in long-range tanks or jerry cans) if you're planning on driving in more remote areas. Petrol stations do run out of petrol in Namibia, so you can't always drain the tank and expect a fill-up at the next station.

Spare parts are readily available in most major towns, but not elsewhere. If you are planning on some 4WD touring, it is advisable to carry the following: two spare tyres, jump leads, fan belt, tow rope and cable, a few litres of oil, wheel spanner and a complete tool kit. A sturdy roll of duct tape will also do in a pinch.

If you're renting a hire car make sure you check you have a working jack (and know how to use it!) and a spare tyre. As an extra precaution, double-check that your spare tyre is fully pressurised as you don't want to get stuck out in the desert with only three good wheels.

HIRE

For a compact car, the least expensive companies charge around US$45 to US$65 per day (the longer the hire period, the lower the daily rate) with unlimited kilometres. Hiring a 4WD vehicle opens up remote parts of the country, but it can get expensive at US$85 to US$120 per day.

It's generally cheaper to hire a car in South Africa and drive it into Namibia, but you need permission from the rental agency, as well as the appropriate paperwork to cross the borders.

Most companies include insurance and unlimited kilometres in their standard rates, but some require a minimum hire period before they allow unlimited kilometres. Most companies also require a deposit, and won't hire to anyone under the age of 23 (although some go as low as 21).

Naturally, you should always check the paperwork carefully, and thoroughly examine the vehicle before accepting it. Car-hire agencies in Namibia have some very high excesses due to the general risks involved in driving on the country's gravel roads. You should also carefully check the condition of your car and never *ever* compromise if you don't feel totally happy with its state of repair.

Additional charges will be levied for dropping off or picking up the car at your hotel (rather than the car-hire office) and for each additional driver. A 'cleaning fee' (which can amount to US$50!) may be incurred – at the discretion of the hire company – and a 'service fee' may be added.

Always give yourself plenty of time when dropping off your hire car to ensure that the vehicle can be checked over properly for damage etc. The car-hire firm should then issue you with your final invoice before you leave the office.

Avis (www.avis.com) Offices in Windhoek, Swakopmund, Tsumeb and Walvis Bay as well as at Hosea Kutako Airport.

Budget (www.budget.co.za) Another big agency with offices in Windhoek and Walvis Bay as well as at Hosea Kutako Airport.

Europcar (www.europcar.co.za) Offices in Windhoek, Swakopmund, Tsumeb, Walvis Bay and at both Hosea Kutako and Eros airports.

INSURANCE

No matter who you hire your car from, make sure you understand what is included in the price (unlimited kilometres, tax, insurance, collision waiver and so on), and what your liabilities are. Most local insurance policies do not include cover damage to windshields and tyres.

Third-party motor insurance is a minimum requirement in Namibia. However, it is also advisable to take damage (collision) waiver, which costs around US$20 extra per day for a 2WD; and about US$40 per day for a 4WD. Loss (theft) waiver is also an extra worth having.

For both types of insurance, the excess liability is about US$1500 for a 2WD and US$3000 for a 4WD. If you're only going for a short period of time, it may be worth taking out the super collision waiver, which covers absolutely everything, albeit at a price.

PURCHASE

Unless you're going to be staying in Namibia for several years, it's not worth purchasing a vehicle in Namibia. The best place to buy a vehicle is across the border in South Africa (see p356).

ROAD HAZARDS

In addition to its fantastic system of sealed roads, Namibia has everything from high-speed gravel roads to badly maintained main routes, farm roads, bush tracks, sand tracks, salt roads and challenging 4WD routes. Driving under these conditions requires special techniques, appropriate vehicle preparation, a bit of practice and a heavy dose of caution.

Around Swakopmund and Lüderitz, watch out for sand on the road. It's very slippery, and can easily cause a car to flip over if you're driving too fast. Early-morning fog along the Skeleton Coast roads is also a hazard so keep within the prescribed speed limits.

ROAD RULES

To drive a car in Namibia, you must be at least 21 years old. Like most other Southern

African countries, traffic keeps to the left side of the road. The national speed limit is 120km/h on sealed roads out of habitation, 80km/h on gravel roads and 40km/h in all national parks and reserves. When passing through towns and villages, assume a speed limit of 60km/h, even in the absence of any signs.

Highway police use radar, and love to fine motorists (about N$70, plus an additional N$10 for every 10km you exceed the limit) for speeding. Sitting on the roof of a moving vehicle is illegal, and wearing seat belts (where installed) is compulsory in the front (but not back) seats. Drunk driving is also against the law, and your insurance policy will be invalid if you have an accident while drunk. Driving without a licence is also a serious offence. The legal blood-alcohol limit in Namibia is 0.05%.

If you have an accident causing injury, it must be reported to the authorities within 48 hours. If vehicles have sustained only minor damage, and there are no injuries – and all parties agree – you can exchange names and addresses and sort it out later through your insurance companies.

In theory, owners are responsible for keeping their livestock off the road, but in practice animals wander wherever they want. If you hit a domestic animal, your distress (and possible vehicle damage) will be compounded by the effort involved in finding the owner and the red tape involved when filing a claim. Wild animals can also be a hazard, even along the highways. The chances of hitting a wild or domestic animal is far, far greater after dark, so driving at night is definitely not recommended.

Hitching

Although hitching is possible in Namibia, it's illegal in national parks, and even main highways receive relatively little traffic. On a positive note, it isn't unusual to get a lift of 1000km in the same car. Truck drivers generally expect to be paid, so agree on a price beforehand; the standard charge is N$15 per 100km.

Lifts wanted and offered are advertised daily at Cardboard Box Backpackers and Chameleon Backpackers Lodge in Windhoek. At the Namibia Wildlife Resorts office, also in Windhoek, there's a notice board with shared car hire and lifts offered and wanted.

Hitching is never entirely safe in any country; if you decide to hitch, understand that you are taking a small but potentially serious risk. Travel in pairs and let someone know where you're planning to go if possible.

Local Transport

Public transport in Namibia is geared towards the needs of the local populace, and is confined to main roads between major population centres. Although cheap and reliable, it is of little use to the traveller as most of Namibia's tourist attractions lie off the beaten track.

Motorcycle

Biking holidays in Namibia are popular due to the exciting off-road riding on offer. Unfortunately, however, it's difficult to hire a bike in Namibia, though the bigger car companies generally have a couple in their fleet. Note that motorcycles aren't permitted in the national parks, with the exception of the main highway routes through Namib-Naukluft Park.

Train

Trans-Namib Railways ([☏]061-298 2032; www.transnamib.com.na) connects some major towns, but trains are extremely slow – as one reader remarked, they move 'at the pace of an energetic donkey cart'. In addition, passenger and freight cars are mixed on the same train, and trains tend to stop at every post, which means that rail travel isn't popular and services are rarely fully booked.

Windhoek is Namibia's rail hub, with services south to Keetmanshoop, west to Swakopmund and east to Gobabis. Trains carry economy and business-class seats but, although most services operate overnight, sleepers are not available. Book at train stations or through the Windhoek booking office; tickets must be collected before 4pm on the day of departure.

TOURIST TRAINS

There are also two tourist trains, which are upmarket private charters that aim to recreate the wondrous yesteryear of rail travel. The relatively plush 'rail cruise' aboard the **Desert Express** ([☏]061-298 2600; www.transnamib.com.na/desert-express.html) offers a popular overnight trip between Windhoek and Swakopmund (single/double from N$6000/9400) weekly in either direction. Ensuite cabins with proper beds and furniture are fully heated and air-conditioned, and have large picture windows for gazing out at the passing terrain. It also offers a special seven-day package combining Swakopmund and Etosha National Park, complete with wildlife drives, picnic bush lunches and plenty of long and glorious rail journeys to savour.

The **Shongololo Dune Express** (☑in South Africa 27-861-777 014; www.shongololo.com), which journeys between Johannesburg and Tsumeb via Mariental, Windhoek, Swakopmund and Otjiwarongo, does 12-day trips taking in Namibia's main sites. All-inclusive fares range from R25,800 for a single to R24,800 to R39,995 double per person depending on the type of cabin. Regardless of which level you choose, the Shongololo is one of the world's most luxurious trains, and is something akin to a 5-star hotel on wheels. Guests are wined and dined to their stomach's content, and you can expect fine linens, hot showers, ample lounge space and a permeating sense of railway nostalgia.

Survival
Guide

Health

As long as you stay up to date with your vaccinations and take basic preventive measures, you're unlikely to succumb to most serious health hazards. While Botswana and Namibia have an impressive selection of tropical diseases on offer, it's more likely you'll get a bout of diarrhoea or a cold than an exotic malady. The main exception to this is malaria, which is a real risk in lower-lying areas.

BEFORE YOU GO

A little predeparture planning will save you trouble later. Get a check-up from your dentist and from your doctor if you have any regular medication or chronic illness, eg high blood pressure or asthma. You should also organise spare contact lenses and glasses (and take your optical prescription with you); get a first-aid and medical kit together; and arrange necessary vaccinations.

Travellers can register with the International Association for Medical Advice to Travellers (IAMAT; www.iamat.org), which provides directories of certified doctors. If you'll be spending much time in more remote areas, consider doing a first-aid course (contact the Red Cross or St John's Ambulance), or attending a remote medicine first-aid course, such as that offered by Wilderness Medical Training (WMT; www.wildernessmedicaltraining.co.uk).

If you are bringing medications with you, carry them in their original containers, clearly labelled. A signed and dated letter from your physician describing all medical conditions and medications, including generic names, is also a good idea. If carrying syringes or needles, be sure to have a physician's letter documenting their medical necessity.

Insurance

Find out in advance whether your insurance plan will make payments directly to providers, or will reimburse you later for overseas health expenditures. In Botswana and Namibia, most doctors expect payment in cash. It's vital to ensure that your travel insurance will cover any emergency transport required to get you to a hospital in a major city, or all the way home, by air and with a medical attendant if necessary. Not all insurance covers this, so check the contract carefully. If you need medical assistance, your insurance company might be able to help locate the nearest hospital or clinic, or you can ask at your hotel. In an emergency, contact your embassy or consulate.

Recommended Vaccinations

The World Health Organization (www.who.int/en/) recommends that all travellers be covered for diphtheria, tetanus, measles, mumps, rubella and polio, as well as for hepatitis B, regardless of their destination. The consequences of these diseases can be severe, and outbreaks do occur.

According to the Centers for Disease Control & Prevention (www.cdc.gov), the following vaccinations are recommended for Botswana and Namibia: hepatitis A, hepatitis B, rabies and typhoid, and boosters for tetanus, diphtheria and measles. Yellow fever is not a risk in the region, but the certificate is an entry requirement if you're travelling from an infected region.

Medical Checklist

It's a very good idea to carry a medical and first-aid kit with you, to help yourself in the case of minor illness or injury. Following is a list of items to consider packing.

» antibiotics (prescription only), eg ciprofloxacin (Ciproxin) or norfloxacin (Utinor)
» antidiarrhoeal drugs (eg loperamide)
» acetaminophen (paracetamol) or aspirin
» anti-inflammatory drugs (eg ibuprofen)
» antihistamines (for hay fever and allergic reactions)

- » antibacterial ointment (eg Bactroban) for cuts and abrasions (prescription only)
- » antimalaria pills, if you'll be in malarial areas
- » bandages, gauze
- » scissors, safety pins, tweezers, pocket knife
- » DEET-containing insect repellent
- » permethrin-containing insect spray for clothing, tents and bed nets
- » prickly-heat powder for heat rashes
- » sunblock
- » oral rehydration salts
- » iodine tablets (for water purification)
- » sterile needles, syringes and fluids if travelling to remote areas

Websites

There is a wealth of travel health advice on the internet. The Lonely Planet website at www.lonelyplanet.com is a good place to start. The World Health Organization publishes the helpful *International Travel and Health*, available free at www.who.int/ith/. Other useful websites include **MD Travel Health** (www.mdtravelhealth.com) and **Fit for Travel** (www.fitfortravel.scot.nhs.uk).

Official government travel health websites:

Australia (www.smarttraveller.gov.au/tips/travelwell.html)

Canada (www.hc-sc.gc.ca/index_e.html)

UK (http://www.dh.gov.uk/en/Publicationsandstatistics/Publications/PublicationsPolicyAndGuidance/DH_4005547)

USA (www.cdc.gov/travel/)

Further Reading

- » *A Comprehensive Guide to Wilderness and Travel Medicine* (1998) Eric A Weiss
- » *Healthy Travel* (1999) Jane Wilson-Howarth

- » *Healthy Travel Africa* (2000) Isabelle Young
- » *How to Stay Healthy Abroad* (2002) Richard Dawood
- » *Travel in Health* (1994) Graham Fry
- » *Travel with Children* (2009) Brigitte Barta et al

IN BOTSWANA & NAMIBIA

Availability & Cost of Health Care

Good-quality health care is available in all major urban areas in Botswana and Namibia, and private hospitals are generally of excellent standard. Public hospitals by contrast are often underfunded and overcrowded, and in off-the-beaten-track areas, reliable medical facilities are rare.

Prescriptions are generally required in Botswana and Namibia. Drugs for chronic diseases should be brought from home. There is a high risk of contracting HIV from infected blood transfusions if you need to receive a blood transfusion. To minimise this, seek out treatment in reputable clinics. The **BloodCare Foundation** (www.bloodcare.org.uk) is a useful source of safe, screened blood, which can be transported to any part of the world within 24 hours.

Infectious Diseases

Following are some of the diseases that are found in Botswana and Namibia, though with a few basic preventative measures, it's unlikely that you'll succumb to any of these.

Cholera

Cholera is caused by a bacteria and spread via contaminated drinking water. The

main symptom is profuse watery diarrhoea, which causes debilitation if fluids are not replaced quickly. An oral cholera vaccine is available in the USA, but it is not particularly effective. Most cases of cholera can be prevented by not drinking tap water and avoiding unpeeled or uncooked fruits and vegetables. Treatment is by fluid replacement (orally or via a drip), but sometimes antibiotics are needed. Self-treatment is not advised.

Dengue Fever (Break-one Fever)

Dengue fever, spread through the bite of the mosquito, causes a feverish illness with headaches and muscle pains similar to those experienced with a bad, prolonged attack of influenza. There might be a rash. Mosquito bites should be avoided whenever possible. Self-treatment: paracetamol and rest.

Filariasis

Filariasis is caused by tiny worms migrating in the lymphatic system and is spread by the bite from an infected mosquito. Symptoms include localised itching and swelling of the legs and/or genitalia. Treatment is available. Self-treatment: none.

Hepatitis A

Hepatitis A, which occurs in both Botswana and Namibia, is spread through contaminated food (particularly shellfish) and water. It causes jaundice and, although it is rarely fatal, it can cause prolonged lethargy and delayed recovery. If you've had hepatitis A, you shouldn't drink alcohol for up to six months afterwards, but once you've recovered, there won't be any long-term problems. The first symptoms include dark urine and a yellow colour to the whites of the eyes. Sometimes a fever and abdominal pain might be present. Hepatitis A vaccine (Avaxim, VAQTA, Havrix) is given as an injection: a single dose will give protection for up to a year, and a booster after a year gives 10-year protection. Hepatitis A and typhoid vaccines can also be given as a single dose vaccine, hepatyrix or viatim. Self-treatment: none.

Hepatitis B

Hepatitis B, found in both countries, is spread through infected blood, contaminated needles and sexual intercourse. It can also be spread from an infected mother to the baby during childbirth. It affects the liver, causing jaundice and occasionally liver failure. Most people recover completely, but some people might be chronic carriers of the virus, which can lead eventually to cirrhosis or liver cancer. Those visiting high-risk areas for long periods or those with increased social or occupational risk should be immunised. Many countries now routinely give hepatitis B as part of the childhood vaccination program. It is given singly or can be given at the same time as hepatitis A (hepatyrix). A course will give protection for at least five years. It can be given over four weeks or six months. Self-treatment: none.

HIV

HIV, the virus that causes AIDS, is an enormous problem in Botswana and Namibia, with a devastating impact on local health systems and community structures. Botswana in particular has one of the highest rates of infection on the continent, with an HIV-positive incidence of 24.8%, second only to nearby Swaziland. The rate is more than 13% in Namibia. The virus is spread through infected blood and blood products, by sexual intercourse with an infected partner, and from an infected mother to her baby during childbirth and breastfeeding. It can be spread through 'blood to blood' contacts, such as with contaminated instruments during medical,

dental, acupuncture and other body-piercing procedures, and through sharing used intravenous needles.

At present there is no cure; but medication that might keep the disease under control is available. In 2002 the Botswana government elected to make antiretroviral drugs available to all citizens free of charge, becoming the first country in the world to offer this treatment for free. Still, for people living in remote areas of the country access to such treatment is a problem, as is the continuing stigma attached to 'owning up' to having the infection. In Namibia, antiretroviral drugs are still largely unavailable, or too expensive for the majority of Namibians.

If you think you might have been infected with HIV, a blood test is necessary; a three-month gap after exposure and before testing is required to allow antibodies to appear in the blood. Self-treatment: none.

Malaria

Apart from road accidents, malaria is probably the only major health risk that you face while travelling in this area, and precautions should be taken. The disease is caused by a parasite in the bloodstream spread via the bite of the female *Anopheles* mosquito. There are several types of malaria; falciparum malaria is the most dangerous type and the predominant form in Botswana and Namibia. Infection rates vary with season and climate, so check out the situation before departure. Several different drugs are used to prevent malaria and new ones are in the pipeline. Up-to-date advice from a travel health clinic is essential as some medication is more suitable for some travellers than others (eg people with epilepsy should avoid mefloquine, and doxycycline should not be taken by pregnant women or children aged under 12).

The early stages of malaria include headaches, fevers, generalised aches and pains, and malaise, which could be mistaken for flu. Other symptoms can include abdominal pain, diarrhoea and a cough. Anyone who

ANTIMALARIAL A TO D

A – Awareness of the Risk No medication is totally effective, but protection of up to 95% is achievable with most drugs, as long as other measures have been taken.

B – Bites To be avoided at all costs. Sleep in a screened room, use a mosquito spray or coils, sleep under a permethrin-impregnated net at night. Cover up at night with long trousers and long sleeves, preferably with permethrin-treated clothing. Apply appropriate repellent to all areas of exposed skin in the evenings.

C – Chemical prevention (ie antimalarial drugs) Usually needed in malarial areas. Expert advice is needed as resistance patterns can change, and new drugs are in development. Not all antimalarial drugs are suitable for everyone. Most antimalarial drugs need to be started at least a week before and continued for four weeks after the last possible exposure to malaria.

D – Diagnosis If you have a fever or an illness similar to flu within a year of travel to a malarial area, malaria is a possibility, and immediate medical attention is necessary.

develops a fever in a malarial area should assume malarial infection until a blood test proves negative, even if you have been taking antimalarial medication. If not treated, the next stage could develop within 24 hours, particularly if falciparum malaria is the parasite: jaundice, then reduced consciousness and coma (also known as cerebral malaria) followed by death. Treatment in hospital is essential, and the death rate might still be as high as 10% even in the best intensive-care facilities.

Many travellers think that malaria is a mild illness, and that taking antimalarial drugs causes more illness through side effects than actually getting malaria. This is unfortunately not true. If you decide against antimalarial drugs, you must understand the risks, and be obsessive about avoiding mosquito bites. Use nets and insect repellent, and report any fever or flu-like symptoms to a doctor as soon as possible. Some people advocate homeo-pathic preparations against malaria, such as Demal200, but there is no evidence that this is effective, and many homeopaths do not recommend their use.

Malaria in pregnancy frequently results in miscarriage or premature labour, and the risks to both mother and foetus during pregnancy are considerable. Travel throughout the region when pregnant should be carefully considered. Adults who have survived childhood malaria have developed immunity and usually only develop mild cases of malaria; most Western travellers have no immunity at all. Immunity wanes after 18 months of nonexposure, so even if you have had malaria in the past and used to live in a malaria-prone area, you may no longer be immune.

Rabies

Rabies is spread by receiving bites or licks from an infected animal on broken skin. Few human cases are reported in Botswana and Namibia, with the risks highest in rural areas. It is always fatal once the clinical symptoms start (which might be up to several months after an infected bite), so postbite vaccination should be given as soon as possible. Postbite vaccination (whether or not you've been vaccinated before the bite) prevents the virus from spreading to the central nervous system. Animal handlers should be vaccinated, as should those travelling to remote areas where a reliable source of postbite vaccine is not available within 24 hours. Three preventive injections are needed over a month. If you have not been vaccinated, you'll need a course of five injections starting 24 hours or as soon as possible after the injury. If you have been vaccinated, you'll need fewer postbite injections, and have more time to seek medical help. Self-treatment: none.

Schistosomiasis (Bilharzia)

This disease is a risk in parts of Botswana and Namibia. It's spread by flukes (minute worms) that are carried by a species of freshwater snail, which then sheds them into slow-moving or still water. The parasites penetrate human skin during swimming and then migrate to the bladder or bowel. They are excreted via stool or urine and could contaminate fresh water, where the cycle starts again. Swimming in suspect freshwater lakes or slow-running rivers should be avoided. Symptoms range from none, to transient fever and rash, and advanced cases might have blood in the stool or in the urine. A blood test can detect antibodies if you might have been exposed, and treatment is readily available. If not treated the infection can cause kidney failure or permanent bowel damage. It's not pos-

sible for you to infect others. Self-treatment: none.

Tuberculosis (TB)

Tuberculosis is spread through close respiratory contact and occasionally through infected milk or milk products. BCG vaccination is recommended if you'll be mixing closely with the local population, especially on long-term stays, although it gives only moderate protection against the disease. TB can be asymptomatic, only being picked up on a routine chest X-ray. Alternatively, it can cause a cough, weight loss or fever, sometimes months or even years after exposure. Self-treatment: none.

Typhoid

This is spread through food or water contaminated by infected human faeces. The first symptom is usually a fever or a pink rash on the abdomen. Sometimes septicaemia (blood poisoning) can occur. A typhoid vaccine (typhim Vi, typherix) will give protection for three years. In some countries, the oral vaccine Vivotif is also available. Antibiotics are usually given as treatment, and death is rare unless septicaemia occurs. Self-treatment: none.

Yellow Fever

Although not a problem within Botswana and Namibia, you'll need to carry a certificate of vaccination if you'll be arriving from an infected country. For a list of countries with a high rate of infection, see the websites of the **World Health Organization** (www.who.int/en/) or the **Centers for Disease Control & Prevention** (www.cdc.gov/travel/blusheet.htm).

Travellers' Diarrhoea

This is a common travel-related illness, sometimes simply due to dietary changes. It's possible that you'll succumb, especially if you're spending a lot of time in rural areas or eating at inexpensive local food stalls. Sometimes dietary changes, such as increased spices or oils, are the cause. To help prevent diarrhoea, avoid tap water unless you're sure it's safe to drink, only eat fresh fruits or vegetables that have been cooked or peeled, and be wary of dairy products that might contain unpasteurised milk. Although freshly cooked food can often be a safe option, plates or serving utensils might be dirty, so be selective when eating food from street vendors (make sure that cooked food is piping hot all the way through). If you develop diarrhoea, be sure to drink plenty of fluids, preferably an oral rehydration solution containing lots of water and some salt and sugar. A few loose stools don't require treatment but if you start having more than four or five stools a day you should start taking an antibiotic (usually a quinoline drug, such as cip-rofloxacin or norfloxacin) and an antidiarrhoeal agent (such as loperamide) if you're not within easy reach of a toilet. If diarrhoea is bloody, persists for more than 72 hours or is accompanied by fever, shaking chills or severe abdominal pain, you should seek medical attention.

Amoebic Dysentery

Contracted by eating contaminated food and water, amoebic dysentery causes blood and mucus in the faeces. It can be relatively mild and tends to come on gradually, but seek medical advice if you think you have the illness as it won't clear up without treatment (which is with specific antibiotics).

Giardiasis

This, like amoebic dysentery, is also caused by ingesting contaminated food or water. The illness usually appears a week or more after you have been exposed to the offend-ing parasite. Giardiasis might cause only a short-lived bout of typical travellers' diar-rhoea, but it can also cause persistent diarrhoea. Ideally, seek medical advice if you suspect you have giardiasis, but if you are in a remote area you could start a course of antibiotics.

Environmental Hazards

Heat Exhaustion

This condition occurs fol-lowing heavy sweating and excessive fluid loss with inad-equate replacement of fluids and salt, and is primarily a risk in hot climates when tak-ing unaccustomed exercise before full acclimatisation. Symptoms include head-aches, dizziness and tired-ness. Dehydration is already happening by the time you feel thirsty – aim to drink suf-ficient water to produce pale, diluted urine. Self-treatment: fluid replacement with water and/or fruit juice, and cool-ing by cold water and fans. The treatment of the salt-loss component consists of consuming salty fluids as in soup, and adding a little more table salt to foods than usual.

Heatstroke

Heat exhaustion is a precur-sor to the much more serious condition of heatstroke. In this case there is damage to the sweating mechanism, with an excessive rise in body temperature, irrational and hyperactive behaviour, and eventually loss of conscious-ness and death. Rapid cool-ing by spraying the body with water and fanning is ideal. Emergency fluid and electro-lyte replacement is usually also required by intravenous drip.

Insect Bites & Stings

Most hazardous insects are confined to the far northwest of the country in the watery environs of the Kunene, Okavango and Kwando river systems. Most nasty of all is the prevalence of tsetse flies in eastern Caprivi, which are especially active at dusk.

Mosquitoes might not always carry malaria or dengue fever, but they (and other insects) can cause irritation and infected bites. To avoid these, take the same precautions as you would for avoiding malaria. Use DEET-based insect repellents. Excellent clothing treatments are also available; mosquitos that land on treated clothing will die. Bee and wasp stings cause real problems only to those who have a severe allergy to the stings (anaphy-laxis). If you are one of these people, carry an EpiPen – an adrenalin (epinephrine) injection, which you can give yourself. This could save your life.

Scorpions are found in arid areas. They can cause a painful bite that is some-times life-threatening. If bitten by a scorpion, seek im-mediate medical assistance. Medical treatment should be sought if collapse occurs.

Ticks are always a risk away from urban areas. If you do get bitten, press down around the tick's head with tweezers, grab the head and gently pull upwards. Avoid pulling the rear of the body as this may squeeze the tick's gut contents through the attached mouth parts into the skin, increasing the risk of both infection and disease. Smearing chemicals on the tick will not make it let go and is not recommended.

Bed bugs are found in hostels and cheap hotels and lead to itchy, lumpy bites. Spraying the mattress with crawling-insect killer after changing bedding will get rid of them. Scabies are also found in cheap accommoda-tion. These tiny mites live in the skin, often between the fingers, and they cause an in-tensely itchy rash. The itch is easily treated with malathion and permethrin lotion from a pharmacy; other members of the household also need treating to avoid spreading scabies, even if they do not show any symptoms.

Snake Bites

Basically, avoid getting bitten! Don't walk barefoot, or stick your hand into holes or cracks. Boomslangs tend to hang out in trees, especially on overhanging limbs, so also exercise caution when walking in forests. If you're camping or trekking through any canyons or rocky areas, always pack away your sleeping bag when it's not in use, and tap out your boots to ensure that nothing has crept inside them during the night. Another sensible precaution is to shake out your clothes before you put them on. Remember, snakes don't bite unless threatened or stepped on.

However, about half of those bitten by venomous snakes are not actually injected with poison (envenomed). If bitten by a snake, do not panic. Immobilise the bitten limb with a splint (such as a stick) and apply a bandage over the site with firm pressure, similar to bandaging a sprain. Do not apply a tourniquet, or cut or suck the bite. Get medical help as soon as possible. It will help get you the correct antivenene if you can identify the snake, so try to take note of its appearance.

Water

Stick to bottled water while travelling in Botswana and Namibia, and purify stream water before drinking it.

Traditional Medicine

According to estimates, as many as 85% of residents of Botswana and Namibia rely in part, or wholly, on traditional medicine. Given the high costs and unavailability of Western medicine in many rural areas, traditional healers are the first contact for many when falling ill. The *sangoma* (traditional healer) and *inyanga* (herbalist) hold revered positions in many communities, and traditional medicinal products are widely available in local markets. Unfortunately, some traditional medicines are made from endangered or threatened species like aardvarks, cheetahs and leopards.

Language

WANT MORE?

For in-depth language information and handy phrases, check out Lonely Planet's *Africa Phrasebook*. You'll find it at **shop.lonely planet.com**, or you can buy Lonely Planet's iPhone phrasebooks at the Apple App Store.

English is the official language of Botswana, but the most common language is Setswana (Tswana). The second most common Bantu language is Sekalanga, a derivative of the Shona language spoken by the Bakalanga people who are centred around Francistown.

Namibia also has English as the official language, but the lingua franca is Afrikaans. Only in the Caprivi is English preferred over Afrikaans as a lingua franca. As their first language, most Namibians speak one of the many Bantu or Khoisan languages. The Bantu group includes Owambo, Kavango, Herero and Caprivian. Khoisan dialects include Khoikhoi (Nama), Damara and San dialects such as !Kung San. Many native Khoisan speakers also speak at least one Bantu and one European language, normally Afrikaans. Thanks to Namibia's colonial past, German is also widely spoken, while in the far north you'll also hear a lot of Portuguese.

AFRIKAANS

Afrikaans developed from the dialect spoken by the Dutch settlers in South Africa from the 17th century. Until the late 19th century it was considered a Dutch dialect, and in 1925 it became one of the official languages of South Africa. Today, it's the first language of around six million people. Afrikaans is the first language of over 150,000 Namibians.

If you read our coloured pronunciation guides as if they were English, you'll be understood. The stressed syllables are in italics. Note that aw is pronounced as in 'law', eu as the 'u' in 'nurse', ew as the 'ee' in 'see' with rounded lips, oh as the 'o' in 'cold', uh as the 'a' in 'ago', kh as the 'ch' in the the Scottish *loch*, zh as the 's' in 'pleasure', and r is trilled.

Basics

Hello.	*Hallo.*	ha·*loh*
Goodbye.	*Totsiens.*	tot·*seens*
Yes.	*Ja.*	yaa
No.	*Nee.*	ney
Please.	*Asseblief.*	a·si·*bleef*
Thank you.	*Dankie.*	*dang*·kee
Sorry.	*Jammer.*	*ya*·min

How are you?
Hoe gaan dit?   hu khaan dit

Fine, and you?
Goed dankie, en jy?   khut *dang*·kee en yay

What's your name?
Wat's jou naam?   vats yoh naam

My name is ...
My naam is ...   may naam is ...

Do you speak English?
Praat jy Engels?   praat yay *eng*·ils

I don't understand.
Ek verstaan nie.   ek vir·*staan* nee

Accommodation

Where's a ...?	*Waar's 'n ...?*	vaars i ...
campsite	*kampeerplek*	kam·*peyr*·plek
guesthouse	*gastehuis*	*khas*·ti·hays
hotel	*hotel*	hu·*tel*

Do you have a single/double room?
Het jy 'n enkel/   het yay i *eng*·kil/
dubbel kamer?   di·bil *kaa*·mir

How much is it per night/person?
Hoeveel kos dit per nag/   *hu*·fil kos dit pir nakh/
persoon?   pir·*soon*

Eating & Drinking

Can you recommend a ...?	*Kan jy 'n ... aanbeveel?*	kan yay i ... *aan*·bi·feyl
bar	*kroeg*	krukh
dish	*gereg*	khi·*rekh*
place to eat	*eetplek*	*eyt*·plek
I'd like ..., please.	*Ek wil asseblief ... hê.*	ek vil a·si·*bleef* ... he
a table for two	*'n tafel vir twee*	i *taa*·fil fir twey
the bill	*die rekening*	dee *rey*·ki·ning
the menu	*die spyskaart*	dee *spays*·kaart

Do you have vegetarian food?
Het julle vegetariese   het *yi*·li fe·gee·*taa*·ree·si
kos?   kos

beer	*bier*	beer
breakfast	*ontbyt*	awnt·*bayt*
coffee	*koffie*	*ko*·fee
dairy products	*suiwelprodukte*	*soy*·vil·pru·dik·ti
dinner	*aandete*	*aant*·ey·ti
drink	*drankie*	*drang*·kee
eggs	*eiers*	*ay*·irs
fish	*vis*	fis
fruit	*vrugte*	*frikh*·ti
lunch	*middagete*	*mi*·dakh·ey·ti
market	*mark*	mark
meat	*vleis*	vlays
milk	*melk*	melk
nuts	*neute*	*ney*·ti
restaurant	*restaurant*	*res*·toh·rant
seafood	*seekos*	*sey*·kaws
sugar	*suiker*	*say*·kir
tea	*tee*	tey
vegetable	*groente*	*khrun*·ti
water	*water*	*vaa*·tir
wine	*wyn*	vayn

Emergencies

Help!	*Help!*	help
Call a doctor!	*Kry 'n dokter!*	kray i *dok*·tir

Call the police!
Kry die polisie!   kray dee pu·*lee*·see

I'm lost.
Ek is verdwaal.   ek is fir·*dwaal*

Where are the toilets?
Waar is die toilette?   vaar is dee toy·*le*·ti

I need a doctor.
Ek het 'n dokter nodig.   ek het i *dok*·tir *noo*·dikh

It hurts here.
Dis hier seer.   dis heer seyr

I'm allergic to (penicillin).
Ek's allergies vir   eks a·*ler*·khees fir
(penisillien).   (pi·ni·si·*leen*)

Shopping & Services

I'm looking for ...
Ek soek na ...   ek suk naa ...

How much is it?
Hoeveel kos dit?   *hu*·fil kos dit

What's your lowest price?
Wat is jou laagste prys?   vat is yoh *laakh*·sti prays

There's a mistake in the bill.
Daar's 'n fout op   daars i foht op
die rekening.   dee *rey*·ki·ning

I want to buy a phonecard.
Ek wil asseblief   ek vil a·si·*bleef*
'n foonkaart koop.   i *foon*·kaart koop

I'd like to change money.
Ek wil asseblief   ek vil a·si·*bleef*
geld ruil.   khelt rayl

I want to use the internet.
Ek wil asseblief die   ek vil a·si·*bleef* dee
Internet gebruik.   *in*·tir·net khi·*brayk*

Time, Dates & Numbers

What time is it?
Hoe laat is dit?   hu laat is dit

It's (two) o'clock.
Dis (twee-)uur.   dis (*twey*·)ewr

Half past (one).
Half (twee).   half (twey)

yesterday	*gister*	*khis*·tir
today	*vandag*	fin·*dakh*
tomorrow	*môre*	*mo*·ri

Monday	Maandag	maan·dakh
Tuesday	Dinsdag	dins·dakh
Wednesday	Woensdag	wuns·dakh
Thursday	Donderdag	don·ir·dakh
Friday	Vrydag	vray·dakh
Saturday	Saterdag	sa·tir·dakh
Sunday	Sondag	son·dakh

1	een	eyn
2	twee	twey
3	drie	dree
4	vier	feer
5	vyf	fayf
6	ses	ses
7	sewe	see·vi
8	agt	akht
9	nege	ney·khi
10	tien	teen
20	twintig	twin·tikh
30	dertig	der·tikh
40	veertig	feyr·tikh
50	vyftig	fayf·tikh
60	sestig	ses·tikh
70	sewentig	sey·vin·tikh
80	tagtig	takh·tikh
90	negentig	ney·khin·tikh
100	honderd	hon·dirt
1000	duisend	day·sint

Transport & Directions

boat	boot	boot
bus	bus	bis
plane	vliegtuig	flikh·tayg
train	trein	trayn

A ... ticket, please.	Een ... kaartjie, asseblief.	eyn ... kaar·kee a·si·bleef
one-way	eenrigting	eyn·rikh·ting
return	retoer	ri·tur

How much is it to ...?
Hoeveel kos dit na ...?   hu·fil kos dit naa ...

Please take me to (this address).
Neem my asseblief na   neym may a·si·bleef naa
(hierdie adres).   (heer·dee a·dres)

Is this the road to ...?
Is dit die pad na ...?   is dit dee pat naa ...

Where's the (nearest) ...?
Waar's die (naaste) ...?   vaars dee (naas·ti) ...

Can you show me (on the map)?
Kan jy my   kan yay may
(op die kaart) wys?   (op dee kaart) vays

What's the address?
Wat is die adres?   vat is dee a·dres

How far is it?
Hoe ver is dit?   hu fer is dit

How do I get there?
Hoe kom ek daar?   hu kom ek daar

DAMARA/NAMA

The very similar dialects of the Damara and Nama peoples, whose traditional lands take in most of Namibia's wildest desert regions, belong to the Khoisan group of languages.

As with the San dialects, they feature several 'click' sounds, created by slapping the tongue against the teeth, palate or side of the mouth. These are normally represented by exclamation points (!), single or double slashes (/, //) and a vertical line crossed by two horizontal lines (‡).

Hello.	!Gâi tses.
Good morning.	!Gâi-//oas.
Good evening.	!Gâi-!oes.
Goodbye. (said by person leaving)	!Gâise hâre.
Goodbye. (said by person staying)	!Gâise !gûre.
Yes.	Î.
No.	Hâ-â.
Please.	Toxoba.
Thank you.	Aio.
Excuse me.	‡Anba tere.
Sorry.	Mati.
How are you?	Matisa?
I'm well.	!Gâi a.
Do you speak English?	Engels !khoa idu ra?
What is your name?	Mati du/onhâ?
My name is ...	Ti/ons ge a ...

Emergencies – Damara/Nama

Help!	Huitere!
Call a doctor!	Laedi aoba ‡gaire!
Call the police!	Lapa !nama ‡gaire!
Leave me alone.	//Naxu te.
I'm lost.	Ka tage hâi.

Where is the ...?	*Mapa ... hâ?*
Go straight.	*‡Khanuse ire.*
Turn left.	*//Are /khab ai ire.*
Turn right.	*//Am /khab ai ire.*
far	*!nu a*
near	*/gu a*
I'd like ...	*Tage ra ‡khaba ...*
How much?	*Mati ko?*
market	*‡kharugu*
shop	*!khaib*
small	*‡khariro*
large	*kai*
baboon	*//arub*
dog	*arib*
elephant	*‡khoab*
giraffe	*!naib*
goat	*piri*
horse	*hab*
hyena	*‡khira*
leopard	*/garub*
lion	*xami*
monkey	*/norab*
rabbit	*!oâs*
rhino	*!nabas*
warthog	*gairib*
zebra	*!goreb*
What time is it?	*Mati ko /laexa i?*
today	*nets*
tomorrow	*//ari*
1	*/gui*
2	*/gam*
3	*!nona*
4	*haka*
5	*kore*
6	*!nani*
7	*hû*
8	*//khaisa*
9	*khoese*
10	*disi*
50	*koro disi*
100	*/oa disi*
1000	*/gui /oa disi*

GERMAN

German (spoken in Namibia) is easy for English speakers to pronounce because almost all of its sounds are also found in English. If you read our coloured pronunciation guides as if they were English, you'll have no problems being understood. The stressed syllables are indicated with italics. Note that kh is like the 'ch' in 'Bach' or the Scottish 'loch' (pronounced at the back of the throat), r is also pronounced at the back of the throat (almost like a g, but with some friction), zh is pronounced as the 's' in 'measure', and ü as the 'ee' in 'see' but with rounded lips.

Basics

Hello.	*Guten Tag.*	goo·ten tahk
Goodbye.	*Auf Wiedersehen.*	owf vee·der·zay·en
Yes.	*Ja.*	yah
No.	*Nein.*	nain
Please.	*Bitte.*	bi·te
Thank you.	*Danke.*	dang·ke
You're welcome.	*Bitte.*	bi·te
Excuse me./ Sorry.	*Entschuldigung.*	ent·shul·di·gung

How are you?
Wie geht es Ihnen/dir? (pol/inf) — vee gayt es ee·nen/deer

Fine. And you?
Danke, gut. — dang·ke goot
Und Ihnen/dir? (pol/inf) — unt ee·nen/deer

What's your name?
Wie ist Ihr Name? (pol) — vee ist eer *nah*·me
Wie heißt du? (inf) — vee haist doo

My name is ...
Mein Name ist ... (pol) — main *nah*·me ist ...
Ich heiße ... (inf) — ikh *hai*·se ...

Do you speak English?
Sprechen Sie Englisch? (pol) — *shpre*·khen zee *eng*·lish
Sprichst du Englisch? (inf) — shprikhst doo *eng*·lish

I don't understand.
Ich verstehe nicht. — ikh fer·*shtay*·e nikht

Accommodation

campsite	*Campingplatz*	*kem*·ping·plats
guesthouse	*Pension*	pahng·*zyawn*
hotel	*Hotel*	ho·*tel*
room in a private home	*Privatzimmer*	pri·*vaht*·tsi·mer

Do you have a ... room?	*Haben Sie ein ...?*	hah·ben zee ain ...
double	*Doppelzimmer*	do·pel·tsi·mer
single	*Einzelzimmer*	ain·tsel·tsi·mer

How much is it per ...?	*Wie viel kostet es pro ...?*	vee feel kos·tet es praw ...
night	*Nacht*	nakht
person	*Person*	per·zawn

Is breakfast included?
Ist das Frühstück inklusive? — ist das frü·shtük in·kloo·zee·ve

Eating & Drinking

I'd like the menu, please.
Ich hätte gern die Speisekarte, bitte. — ikh he·te gern dee shpai·ze·kar·te bi·te

What would you recommend?
Was empfehlen Sie? — vas emp·fay·len zee

I'm a vegetarian.
Ich bin Vegetarier/ Vegetarierin. (m/f) — ikh bin ve·ge·tah·ri·er/ ve·ge·tah·ri·e·rin

Please bring the bill.
Bitte bringen Sie die Rechnung. — bi·te bring·en zee dee rekh·nung

beer	*Bier*	beer
bread	*Brot*	brawt
breakfast	*Frühstück*	frü·shtük
cheese	*Käse*	kay·ze
coffee	*Kaffee*	ka·fay
dinner	*Abendessen*	ah·bent·e·sen
egg/eggs	*Ei/Eier*	ai/ai·er
fruit	*Frucht/Obst*	frukht/awpst
grocery store	*Lebensmittel- laden*	lay·bens·mi·tel· lah·den
juice	*Saft*	zaft
lunch	*Mittagessen*	mi·tahk·e·sen
market	*Markt*	markt
meat	*Fleisch*	flaish
milk	*Milch*	milkh
restaurant	*Restaurant*	res·to·rahng
salt	*Salz*	zalts
seafood	*Meeresfrüchte*	mair·res·frükh·te
sugar	*Zucker*	tsu·ker
tea	*Tee*	tay
vegetable	*Gemüse*	ge·mü·ze
water	*Wasser*	va·ser
wine	*Wein*	vain

Emergencies

Help!
Hilfe! — hil·fe

Go away!
Gehen Sie weg! — gay·en zee vek

Call the police!
Rufen Sie die Polizei! — roo·fen zee dee po·li·tsai

Call a doctor!
Rufen Sie einen Arzt! — roo·fen zee ai·nen artst

Where are the toilets?
Wo ist die Toilette? — vo ist dee to·a·le·te

I'm lost.
Ich habe mich verirrt. — ikh hah·be mikh fer·irt

I'm sick.
Ich bin krank. — ikh bin krangk

Shopping & Services

I'd like to buy ...
Ich möchte ... kaufen. — ikh merkh·te ... kow·fen

Can I look at it?
Können Sie es mir zeigen? — ker·nen zee es meer tsai·gen

How much is this?
Wie viel kostet das? — vee feel kos·tet das

That's too expensive.
Das ist zu teuer. — das ist tsoo toy·er

Can you lower the price?
Können Sie mit dem Preis heruntergehen? — ker·nen zee mit dem prais he·run·ter·gay·en

ATM	*Geldautomat*	gelt·ow·to·maht
post office	*Postamt*	post·amt
tourist office	*Fremden- verkehrsbüro*	frem·den· fer·kairs·bü·raw

Time, Dates & Numbers

What time is it?
Wie spät ist es? — vee shpayt ist es

It's (10) o'clock.
Es ist (zehn) Uhr. — es ist (tsayn) oor

At what time?
Um wie viel Uhr? — um vee feel oor

At ...
Um ... — um ...

morning	*Morgen*	mor·gen
afternoon	*Nachmittag*	nahkh·mi·tahk
evening	*Abend*	ah·bent

yesterday	gestern	ges·tern
today	heute	hoy·te
tomorrow	morgen	mor·gen
Monday	Montag	mawn·tahk
Tuesday	Dienstag	deens·tahk
Wednesday	Mittwoch	mit·vokh
Thursday	Donnerstag	do·ners·tahk
Friday	Freitag	frai·tahk
Saturday	Samstag	zams·tahk
Sunday	Sonntag	zon·tahk
1	eins	ains
2	zwei	tsvai
3	drei	drai
4	vier	feer
5	fünf	fünf
6	sechs	zeks
7	sieben	zee·ben
8	acht	akht
9	neun	noyn
10	zehn	tsayn
20	zwanzig	tsvan·tsikh
30	dreißig	drai·tsikh
40	vierzig	feer·tsikh
50	fünfzig	fünf·tsikh
60	sechzig	zekh·tsikh
70	siebzig	zeep·tsikh
80	achtzig	akht·tsikh
90	neunzig	noyn·tsikh
100	hundert	hun·dert
1000	tausend	tow·sent

Transport & Directions

boat	Boot	bawt
bus	Bus	bus
plane	Flugzeug	flook·tsoyk
train	Zug	tsook

At what time's the ... bus?	Wann fährt der ... Bus?	van fairt dair... bus
first	erste	ers·te
last	letzte	lets·te

1st-class ticket	Fahrkarte erster Klasse	fahr·kar·te ers·ter kla·se
2nd-class ticket	Fahrkarte zweiter Klasse	fahr·kar·te tsvai·ter kla·se
one-way ticket	einfache Fahrkarte	ain·fa·khe fahr·kar·te
return ticket	Rückfahrkarte	rük·fahr·kar·te

At what time does it arrive?
Wann kommt es an? — van komt es an

Does it stop at ...?
Hält es in ...? — helt es in ...

What station is this?
Welcher Bahnhof ist das? — vel·kher bahn·hawf ist das

What's the next stop?
Welches ist der nächste Halt? — vel·khes ist dair naykh·ste halt

I want to get off here.
Ich möchte hier aussteigen. — ikh merkh·te heer ows·shtai·gen

Where's ...?
Wo ist ...? — vaw ist ...

What's the address?
Wie ist die Adresse? — vee ist dee a·dre·se

How far is it?
Wie weit ist es? — vee vait ist es

Can you show me (on the map)?
Können Sie es mir (auf der Karte) zeigen? — ker·nen zee es meer (owf dair kar·te) tsai·gen

HERERO/HIMBA

The Herero and Himba languages are quite similar, and are especially useful if travelling around remote areas of North-Central Namibia and particularly the Kaokoveld, where Afrikaans remains a lingua franca and few people speak English.

Herero is a rolling, melodious language, rich in colourful words. Most Namibian place names that begin with 'O' (eg Okahandja, Omaruru and Otjiwarongo) are derived from the Herero language.

Hello.	Tjike.
Good morning.	Wa penduka.
Good afternoon.	Wa uhara.
Good evening.	Wa tokerua.

Emergencies – Herero/Himba	
Help!	Vatera!
Call a doctor!	Isana onganga!
Call the police!	Isana oporise!
I'm lost.	Ami mba pandjara.

Good night.	Ongurova ombua.
Yes./No.	Ii./Kako.
Please.	Arikana.
Thank you.	Okuhepa.
How are you?	Kora?
Well, thank you.	Mbiri naua, okuhepa.
Pardon.	Makuvi.
Do you speak Afrikaans/English?	U hungira Otjimburu/Otjingirisa?
How many?	Vi ngapi?
When?	Rune?
Where?	Pi?
arrival	omeero
departure	omairo
from	okuza
one way (single)	ourike
return	omakotokero
ticket	okatekete
to	ko
travel	ouyenda
caravan park	omasuviro uo zo karavana
game reserve	orumbo ro vipuka
(short/long) hiking trail	okaira komakaendro uo pehi (okasupi/okare)
marsh	eheke
mountain	ondundu
point	onde
river (channel)	omuramba
today	ndinondi
tomorrow	muhuka
yesterday	erero
Monday	Omandaha
Tuesday	Oritjaveri
Wednesday	Oritjatatu
Thursday	Oritjaine
Friday	Oritjatano
Saturday	Oroviungura
Sunday	Osondaha
1	iimue
2	imbari
3	indatu
4	iine

5	indano
6	hamboumue
7	hambomabari
8	hambondatu
9	imuvyu
10	omurongo

!KUNG SAN

The languages of Namibia's several San groups are characterised by 'click' elements. Perhaps the most useful dialect for the traveller is that of the !Kung people, who are concentrated in Northern Namibia.

Clicks are made by compressing the tongue against different parts of the mouth to produce sounds. Names that include an exclamation mark are of Khoisan origin and should be rendered as a sideways click sound, similar to the sound one would make when encouraging a horse, but with a hollow tone (like the sound made when pulling a cork from a bottle).

In normal speech, the language features four different clicks (lateral, palatal, dental and labial), which are usually represented in Namibia by the symbols '//', '‡', '/' and '!', respectively. However, other orthographies are used around the region, and clicks may be represented as 'nx', 'ny', 'c', 'q', 'x', '!x', '!q', 'k', 'zh', and so on. To simplify matters, in the following list of basic phrases all clicks are represented by '!k' (locals will usually forgive you for pronouncing the clicks as a 'k' sound or for simplifying the four clicks to one).

Hello.	!Kao.
Good morning.	Tuwa.
Goodbye, go well.	!King se !kau.
How are you?	!Ka tseya? (to a man) !Ka tsiya? (to a woman)
Thank you (very much).	(!Kin)!Ka.
What is your name?	!Kang ya tsedia? (to a man) !Kang ya tsidia? (to a woman)
My name is ...	!Kang ya tse/tsi ... (m/f)

LOZI

Lozi (also known as Rotsi) is the most common Caprivian dialect, spoken throughout the Caprivi region, especially around Katima Mulilo. It originates from Barotseland in Zambia. As you can see from the list of options in the following phrases, social status is strongly reflected in spoken Lozi.

Hello.	*Eeni, sha.* (to anybody) *Lumela.* (to a peer) *Mu lumeleng' sha.* (to one or more persons of higher social standing)	1	*il'ingw'i*
		2	*z'e peli or bubeli*
Goodbye.	*Siala foo/hande/sinde.* (to a peer) *Musiale foo/hande/sinde.* (to more than one peer or one or more persons of higher social standing)	3	*z'e t'alu or bulalu*
		4	*z'e ne or bune*
		5	*z'e keta-lizoho*
		6	*z'e keta-lizoho ka ka li kang'wi*
Good morning.	*U zuhile.* (to a peer) *Mu zuhile.* (to more than one peer or one or more persons of higher social standing)	7	*supile*
		10	*lishumi*
		20	*mashumi a mabeli*
		1000	*likiti*

OWAMBO

There are eight dialects of Owambo; Kwanyama and Ndonga are the official Owambo languages. Owambo (or Oshiwambo) – specifically the Kwanyama dialect – is the first language of more Namibians than any other, and it's a second language for many non-Owambo Namibians of both Bantu and Khoisan origin.

Good evening/ afternoon.	*Ki manzibuana.* (to anybody) *U tozi.* (to a peer) *Mu tozi.* (to one or more persons of higher social standing)
Good night.	*Ki busihu.* (to anybody)
Please.	*Sha.* (only to people of higher social standing)
Thank you (very much).	*N'i tumezi (hahulu).*
Excuse me.	*Ni swalele.* (inf) *Mu ni swalele.* (pol)
Yes.	*Ee.* (to a peer) *Eeni.* (to more than one peer or one or more persons of higher social standing)
No.	*Awa.* (to a peer or peers) *Batili.* (to one or more persons of higher social standing)
Do you speak English?	*Wa bulela sikuwa?* (to peers) *W'a utwa sikuwa?* (to more than one peer or one or more persons of higher standing) *Mw'a bulela sikuwa?* *Mw'a utwa sikuwa?*
I don't understand.	*Ha ni utwi.*
What is your name?	*Libizo la hao ki wena mang'?* (to a peer) *Libizo la mina ki mina bo mang'?* (to a person of higher social standing)
What is that?	*S'ale king'?* (near) *Ki sika mang' s'ale?* (far)
Where?	*Kai?*
Here.	*Fa./Kafa./Kwanu.*
(Over) There.	*F'ale./Kw'ale.*
How much?	*Ki bukai?*
Enough.	*Ku felile.*
What time is it?	*Ki nako mang'?*
today	*kachenu*
tomorrow	*kamuso*
yesterday	*mabani*

Good morning.	*Wa lalapo.*
Good evening.	*Wa tokelwapo.*
How are you?	*Owu li po ngiini?*
I'm fine.	*Ondi li nawa.*
Yes.	*Eeno.*
No.	*Aawe.*
Please.	*Ombili.*
Thank you.	*Tangi.*
Excuse me.	*Ombili manga.*
I'm sorry.	*Onde shi panda.*
Do you speak English?	*Oho popi Oshiingilisa?*
Can you please help me?	*Eto vuluwu pukulule ndje?*
How much is this?	*Ingapi tashi kotha?*
I'm lost.	*Ombili, onda puka.*
Where is the ...?	*Openi pu na ...?*
here/there	*mpaka/hwii*
near/far	*popepi/kokule*
that way	*ondjila*
this way	*no onkondo*
Turn right.	*Uka kohulyo.*
Turn left.	*Uka kolumoho.*
today	*nena*
tomorrow	*ungula*
yesterday	*ohela*

Monday	*Omaandaha*
Tuesday	*Etiyali*
Wednesday	*Etitatu*
Thursday	*Etine*
Friday	*Etitano*
Saturday	*Olyomakaya*
Sunday	*Osoondaha*

1	*yimwe*
2	*mbali*
3	*ndatu*
4	*ne*
5	*ntano*
6	*hamano*
7	*heyali*
8	*hetatu*
9	*omugoyi*
10	*omulongo*

SETSWANA

Setswana (also commonly known as Tswana) is a Bantu language in the Sotho-Tswana language group that is understood by around 90% of Botswana's population. It is the language of the dominant ethnic group, the Batswana.

Setswana is pronounced more or less as it is written, except for *g*, which is pronounced as an English 'h' (or, more accurately, a strongly aspirated 'g') and *th*, which is pronounced as a slightly aspirated 't'.

Basics

Hello.	*Dumêla rra/mma.* (to a man/woman) *Dumêlang.* (to a group)
Hello!	*Ko ko!* (announcing arrival outside a yard or house)
Goodbye.	*Tsamaya sentle.* (said by person staying) *Sala sentle.* (said by person leaving)
Yes.	*Ee.*
No.	*Nnyaa.*
Please.	*Tsweetswee.*
Thank you.	*Kea leboga.*
Excuse me./Sorry.	*Intshwarele.*
Pardon me.	*Ke kopa tsela.*
No problem.	*Go siame.*
How are you?	*A o tsogile?* (in the morning)

How are you?	*O tlhotse jang?* (in the afternoon/evening)
I'm fine.	*Ke tlhotse sentle.* (pol) *Ke teng.* (inf)
How's it going?	*O kae?*
Are you well?	*A o sa tsogile sentle?*
Yes, I'm well.	*Ee, ke tsogile sentle.*
What's your name?	*Leina la gago ke mang?*
My name is ...	*Leina la me ke ...*
Where are you from?	*O tswa kae?*
I'm from ...	*Ke tswa kwa ...*
Where do you live?	*O nna kae?*
I live in ...	*Ke nna kwa ...*
Where are you going?	*O ya kae?*
Do you speak English?	*A o bua Sekgoa?*
Does anyone here speak English?	*A go na le o o bua Sekgoa?*
I don't understand.	*Ga ke tlhaloganye.*
Could you speak more slowly, please?	*A o ka bua ka bonya tswee-tswee?*

Accommodation

campsite	*lefelo la go robala mo tenteng*
guesthouse	*matlo a baeng*
hotel	*hotele*
youth hostel	*matlo a banana*

Where is a ... hotel?	*Hotele e e ... ko gae?*
cheap	*go tlase ka di tlotlwa*
good	*siame*

Do you have any rooms available?	*A go na le matlo?*

I'd like ...	*Ke batla ...*
a double room	*kamore tse pedi*
a room with a bathroom	*kamore e e nang le ntlwana ya go tlhapela*
a single room	*kamore e le mongwe*
to share a dorm	*go tlhakanela kamore*

How much is it ...?	*Ke bokae ...?*
for one night	*bosigo bo le bongwe*
for two nights	*masego a mated*
per person	*motho a le mongwe*

Eating & Drinking

What would you like?	O batla eng?
I'd like ...	Ke batla ...
I'm vegetarian.	Ke ja merogo fela.
Cheers!	Pula!
breakfast	sefitlholo
dinner	selaelo
lunch	dijo tsa motshegare
meals	dijo
menu	karate tsa dijo

beef	nama ya kgomo
bread	borotho
butter	mafura
chicken	koko
coffee	kofi
egg	mai
fish	tlhapi
fruit	leungo
goat	pudi
meat	nama
milk	mashi
mutton	nku
rice	raese
soft drink	sene tsididi
sugar	sukiri
tea	tee
vegetables	merogo
(boiled) water	metsi (a a bedileng)

Emergencies

Help!	Nthusa!
Leave me alone!	Ntlhogela!
Call a doctor!	Bitsa ngaka!
Call the police!	Bitsa mapodisi!
I'm lost.	Ke la tlhegile.
I'm ill.	Ke a lwala.
My friend is ill.	Tsala yame e a lwala.

Where is the ...?	E ko kae ...?
dentist	ngaka ya meno
doctor	ngaka
hospital	sepatela
pharmacy	khemesiti

aspirin	pilisi
condoms	dikausu
diarrhoea	letshololo
medicine	molemo
nausea	go feroga sebete
stomachache	mala a a botlhoko
syringe	mokento

Shopping & Services

I'm looking for a/the ...	Ke batla ...
bank	ntlo ya polokelo
city centre	toropo
market	mmaraka
museum	ntlo ya ditso
post office	poso
public toilet	matlwana a boitiketso
tourist office	ntlo ya bajanala

What time does it open/close?	Ke nako mang bula/tswala?
How much is it?	Ke bokae?
It's too expensive.	E a dura.
Can you lower the price?	Fokotsa tlhwatlhwa?

Time, Dates & Numbers

What time is it?	Ke nako mang?
afternoon	tshogololo
next week	beke e e tlang
night	bosigo
today	gompieno
tomorrow	ka moso
yesterday	maabane

Monday	mosupologo
Tuesday	labobedi
Wednesday	laboraro
Thursday	labone
Friday	latlhano
Saturday	matlhatso
Sunday	tshipi

1	bongwe
2	bobedi
3	borara

4	bone	**When is the ...?**	E ... goroga nako mung?
5	botlhano	**boat**	sekepe
6	borataro	**bus**	bese
7	bosupa	**canoe**	mokoro
8	borobabobedi	**train**	terena
9	boroba bongwe		
10	lesome	**I'd like ...**	Ke batla ...
20	masome a mabedi	**a one-way ticket**	karata ya go tsamaya fela
30	masome a mararo	**a return ticket**	karata ya go boa
40	masome a mane	**the first class**	ya ntlha
50	masome a matlhano	**the second class**	ya bobedi
60	masome amarataro		
70	masome a supa	**Which way is ...?**	Tsela ... e kae?
80	masome a a robang bobedi	**Where is the station/hotel?**	Seteseine/hotele se kae?
90	masome a a robang bongwe	**Can you show me on the map ...?**	A o mpotshe mo mepeng?
100	lekgolo	**Could you write the address?**	Nkwalele aterese?
1000	sekete	**Is it far?**	A go kgala?
		Go straight ahead.	Thlamalala.

Transport & Directions

		Turn left.	Chikela mo molemong.
Where is the ...?	E ko kae ...?	**Turn right.**	Chikela mo mojeng.
bus stop	maemelo a di bese	**near**	gaufi
train station	maemelo a terena	**far**	kgakala

GLOSSARY

ablutions block – camping-ground building with toilets, showers and a washing-up area

Afrikaans – language spoken in South Africa, which is a derivative of Dutch

ANC – African National Congress; ruling party in South Africa

apartheid – literally 'separate development of the races'; a political system in which people are officially segregated according to their race

ATVs – all-terrain vehicles

Bantu – the name used to describe over 400 ethnic groups in Africa united by a common language

barchan dunes – migrating crescent-shaped sand dunes

Basarwa – Batswana term for the San people; it means 'people of the sticks' and is considered pejorative

Batswana – Setswana name for the people of Botswana; adjective referring to anything of or from Botswana; also (confusingly) refers to people from the Batswana tribe; plural of *Motswana*

BDF – Botswana Defence Force; the Botswanan army

BDP – Botswana Democratic Party

Bechuanaland – the name given by the British to describe the Crown Colony they established in Botswana in 1885

Benguela current – the frigid current that flows northwards along the west African coast as far as Angola from Antarctica

boerewors – Afrikaner farmer's sausage

Boers – the Dutch word for 'farmer' which came to denote Afrikaans-speaking people

bogobe – sorghum porridge; a staple food

bojalwa – a popular and inexpensive sprouted-sorghum beer

bojazz – Botswana jazz

boomslang – dangerous and venomous tree-dwelling 2m-long snake

borankana – Setswana word meaning traditional entertainment

borehole – a deep well shaft in the ground used for the abstraction of water, oil or gas

braai – Afrikaans term for a barbecue featuring lots

of meat grilled on a special stand called a *braaivleis*

BSAC – British South Africa Company; late-19th-century company led by Cecil Rhodes

bushveld – flat grassy plain covered in thorn scrub

CDM – Consolidated Diamond Mines

Chibuku – *bojalwa* that is brewed commercially; the 'beer of good cheer' drunk in Zimbabwe and also in Botswana

CKGR – Central Kalahari Game Reserve

combi – usual term for 'minibus'

conflict diamonds – diamonds mined in conflict areas which are then sold illicitly

cuca shops – small bush shops of Northern Namibia; named for an Angolan beer that was once sold there

Debswana – De Beers Botswana Mining Company Ltd, partly owned by the Botswanan government, which mines, sorts and markets diamonds from Botswana

difaqane – forced migration or exodus by several Southern African tribes in the face of Zulu aggression in the 19th century

Ditshwanelo – the Botswana Centre for Human Rights

drift – river ford, mostly dry

DTA – Democratic Turnhalle Alliance

DWNP – Department of Wildlife and National Parks, which runs the Botswana government-owned national parks/reserves

elenga – village headman

euphorbia – several species of cactuslike succulents

FPK – First People of the Kalahari, a local advocacy organisation working for

the right of San who have been forcibly resettled from the Central Kalahari Game Reserve in the town of New Xade

Gemütlichkeit – a distinctively German atmosphere of comfort and hospitality

Gondwanaland – the prehistoric supercontinent which included most of the land masses in today's southern hemisphere

GPS – Global Positioning System

Great Zimbabwe – an ancient Southern African city located in modern Zimbabwe that was once the centre of a vast empire known as Monomotapa

guano – droppings from seabirds or bats which is harvested as a fertiliser

inselberg – isolated range or hill typical of the pro-Namib and Damaraland plains

karakul – variety of central Asian sheep, which produces high-grade wool and pelts

karata – phonecard; also ticket

kgosi – Setswana word for 'chief'

kgotla – traditionally constructed Batswana community affairs hall or open area used for meetings of the *dikgotla*

Khoisan – language grouping taking in all Southern African indigenous languages

kloof – ravine or small valley

koeksesters – small, gooey Afrikaner doughnuts, dripping in honey or sugar syrup

kokerboom – quiver tree; grows mainly in southern Namibia

konditorei – German pastry shop; found in larger Namibian towns

kopje – also *kopie;* small hill

kraal – Afrikaans version of the Portuguese word *'curral';* an enclosure for livestock or a hut village

lapa – circular area with a firepit, used for socialising

lediba – Setswana word for 'lagoon'; the singular of *madiba*

lekgapho – a unique Batswana design used to decorate *ntlo*

location – Namibian and South African name for township

mabele – Setswana word for sorghum, used to make *bogobe*

madiba – Setswana word for 'lagoons', plural of *lediba*

mahango – millet; a staple of the Owambo diet and used for brewing a favourite alcoholic beverage

marimba – African xylophone, made from strips of resonant wood with various-sized gourds for sound boxes

mbira – see *thumb piano*

mealie pap – Afrikaans name for maize-meal porridge; a staple food for most Namibians

MET – Namibia's Ministry of Environment & Tourism

Modimo – supreme being and creator of early Batswana tribal religion

mokolane – Setswana name for the palm *Hyphaene petersiana*

mokoro – traditional dugout canoe used in the Okavango Delta; plural *mekoro*

morama – an immense tuber, the pulp of which contains large quantities of water and serves as a source of liquid for desert dwellers

Motswana – one Tswana person, ie the singular of Batswana

!nara – type of melon that grows in the Namib Desert

NDF – Namibian Defence Forces, the Namibian military

Ndjambi – supernatural Herero being who represents good

ngashi – a pole made from the mogonono tree and used on a *mokoro*

NGO – nongovernmental organisation

N!odima – supernatural San being who represents good

n!oresi – traditional San lands; 'lands where one's heart is'

ntlo – round hut found in Batswana villages

NWR – Namibian Wildlife Resorts; semiprivate overseer of visitor facilities in Namibia's national parks

omiramba – fossil river channels in north and west Botswana; singular *omuramba*

oshana – dry river channel in Northern Namibia and Northwestern Botswana

oshikundu – alcoholic beverage made from *mahango*; popular throughout areas of Northern Namibia

pan – dry flat area of grassland or salt deposits, often a seasonal lake bed

panhandle – an informal geographic term used to describe an elongated protrusion of a geopolitical entity similar in shape to a peninsula and usually created by arbitrarily drawn international boundaries; in the case of Botswana and Namibia, this refers to the area of the Caprivi Strip

panveld – area containing many pans

pap – see *mealie pap*

participation safari – an inexpensive safari in which clients pitch their own tents, pack the vehicle and share cooking duties

pronking – four-legged leaping, as done by some antelopes (particularly springboks)

pula – the Botswana currency; 100 *thebe*; also Setswana word for 'rain'

quad bike – four-wheeled motorcycle often called an ATV (all-terrain vehicle)

robot – a traffic light

rondavel – a round hut which is often thatched

SACU – Southern African Customs Union, comprised of Botswana, South Africa, Lesotho, Namibia and Swaziland

San – a tribal group, which has inhabited Botswana for at least 30,000 years

sangoma – traditional Batswana doctor who believes that he/she is inhabited by spirits

savannah – grasslands with widely spaced trees

seif dunes – prominent linear sand dunes, as found in the Central Namib Desert

Setswana – language of the Batswana; the predominant language of Botswana

shebeen – illegal drinking establishment

shongololo – ubiquitous giant millipede

Sperrgebiet – 'forbidden area'; alluvial diamond region of southwestern Namibia

strandwolf – the Afrikaans name given to the Namib Desert brown hyena

Swapo – South-West Africa People's Organization; Namibia's liberation army and the ruling political party

thebe – one-hundredth of a *pula*; Setswana word for 'shield'

thumb piano – consists of narrow iron keys mounted in rows on a wooden sound board; the player plucks the ends of the keys with the thumbs; known as *mbira* in Tswana.

toktokkie – Afrikaans for the fog-basking tenebrionid beetle

township – indigenous suburb; generally a high-density black residential area

tsama – a desert melon historically eaten by the San people, and by livestock

Tswana – another word for *Batswana* or *Setswana*

Unita – National Union for the Total Independence of Angola

veld – open grassland, normally in plateau regions

Veterinary Cordon Fence a series of 1.5m-high, wire fences aimed at segregating wild and domestic animals

vlei – low-lying, marshy ground, covered with water during the rainy season

welwitschia – cone-bearing shrub native to the northern Namib plains

wildlife drive – a trip to spot wildlife, also known as a 'game drive'

WMA – Wildlife Management Area

behind the scenes

SEND US YOUR FEEDBACK

We love to hear from travellers – your comments keep us on our toes and help make our books better. Our well-travelled team reads every word on what you loved or loathed about this book. Although we cannot reply individually to postal submissions, we always guarantee that your feedback goes straight to the appropriate authors, in time for the next edition. Each person who sends us information is thanked in the next edition – the most useful submissions are rewarded with a selection of digital PDF chapters.

Visit **lonelyplanet.com/contact** to submit your updates and suggestions or to ask for help. Our award-winning website also features inspirational travel stories, news and discussions.

Note: We may edit, reproduce and incorporate your comments in Lonely Planet products such as guidebooks, websites and digital products, so let us know if you don't want your comments reproduced or your name acknowledged. For a copy of our privacy policy visit lonelyplanet.com/privacy.

OUR READERS

Many thanks to the travellers who used the last edition and wrote to us with helpful hints, useful advice and interesting anecdotes:

Dario Balboni, Jill Brinkman, Benjamin Burghart, James Carnegie, Lucy Chadwick, Nichola Cottis, Katy Eager, Hugo & Marieke Erken, Patricia Escher, Jacqui Fenwick, Joanne Hayes, Gisele Netto, Robert Newman, Tobias Schmidt Slordahl, Jan Skoglund, Astrid Stehouwer & Caspar Gooren, Zilke T'jonck, Regula Ziegler.

AUTHOR THANKS

Alan Murphy

A big thanks to my travel companion and friend Smitzy for his patience, advice and adventurous spirit (and for not getting further traffic infringements). Also I tip my hat to Anthony, my coauthor, for his professionalism. In Namibia there are too many to thank but special mention to Almuth Styles in Swakopmund whose assistance was much appreciated. And to the honorary consul in Windhoek for making me legal again after all my ID was stolen. To my gorgeous wife, Alison, who married me just before this research trip, you are my strength and my home.

Anthony Ham

Andy Raggett of Drive Botswana was an invaluable source of information at all stages of the journey. Thanks also to Mike Romeo of Explorer Safaris in Johannesburg, Will Gourlay for sending me here and Alan Murphy for coordinating the book with wisdom. Thanks also to Glyn Maude, Keitumetse Ngaka, Olefile Sebogiso, Nick Jacobsen, Monika Schiess and to Jan and Cleo in Khutse. Special thanks to Jan and Ron for their joyful spirit and utter integrity. To my three girls Marina, Carlota and Valentina: *Os quiero con todo mi corazon.*

Trent Holden & Kate Morgan

There are some HUGE thank yous to give out for the help we received while researching. First up thanks to Joy in Vic Falls and Kim in Livingstone for all your assistance in getting some of the nitty gritty stuff down pat. Thanks to the Seremwe brothers, James and George, for all their guidance and assistance, Sally Wynn for her unparalleled knowledge of Kariba and around, Choice Mushunje from Zimbabwe Parks, Gordon Adams, Ann Bruce and Jane High from the east, and Val from Bulawayo. Thanks also to all the travellers we met, including John and Linda Hutton for all the suggestions. Finally, huge thanks to the production team, particularly Will Gourlay, Glenn van der Knijff and coordinating author Alan Murphy.

ACKNOWLEDGMENTS

Climate Map Data Climate map data adapted from Peel MC, Finlayson BL & McMahon TA (2007) 'Updated World Map of the Köppen-Geiger Climate Classification', *Hydrology and Earth System Sciences*, 11, 163344.

Cover photograph: Gemsbok walking over sand dunes in the Naukluft National Park, Namibia, Frans Lanting / Corbis©.

This Book

This 3rd edition of Lonely Planet's *Botswana & Namibia* guidebook was researched and written by Alan Murphy, Anthony Ham, Trent Holden and Kate Morgan, and David Lukas wrote the text that formed the basis of the Wildlife section. The previous edition was written by Matthew D Firestone, Adam Karlin and Nicola Simmonds, with contributions from David Lukas and Mara Vorhees. The 1st edition was written by Paula Hardy and Matthew D Firestone, with contributions from Dr Caroline Evans, Ian Ketcheson, Fiona Watson and Elizabeth Bovair.

This guidebook was commissioned in Lonely Planet's Melbourne office, and produced by the following:

Commissioning Editors William Gourlay, Glenn van der Knijff

Coordinating Editor Tracy Whitmey

Coordinating Cartographer Andrew Smith

Coordinating Layout Designer Carol Jackson

Managing Editors Brigitte Ellemor, Martine Power

Managing Cartographers Alison Lyall, Adrian Persoglia

Managing Layout Designer Chris Girdler

Assisting Editors Janet Austin, Andrew Bain, Janice Bird, Kate James, Charlotte Orr

Cover & Internal Image Research Kylie McLaughlin

Language Content Branislava Vladisavljevic

Thanks to Dan Austin, Imogen Bannister, Yvonne Bischofberger, Frank Deim, Brendan Dempsey, Ryan Evans, Larissa Frost, James Hardy, Jane Hart, Genesys India, Jouve India, Asha Ioculari, Anne Mason, Annelies Mertens, Trent Paton, Kirsten Rawlings, Raphael Richards, Averil Robertson, Gerard Walker, Jeanette Wall, Wendy Wright.

index

NOTES

NOTES

how to use this book

These symbols will help you find the listings you want:

👁 Sights	👆 Tours	🍷 Drinking
🏊 Beaches	🎊 Festivals & Events	☆ Entertainment
🏃 Activities	🛏 Sleeping	🛍 Shopping
🎓 Courses	🍴 Eating	ℹ Information/Transport

Look out for these icons:

TOP CHOICE	Our author's recommendation
FREE	No payment required
🍃	A green or sustainable option

Our authors have nominated these places as demonstrating a strong commitment to sustainability – for example by supporting local communities and producers, operating in an environmentally friendly way, or supporting conservation projects.

These symbols give you the vital information for each listing:

📞 Telephone Numbers	📶 Wi-Fi Access	🚌 Bus
🕐 Opening Hours	🏊 Swimming Pool	⛴ Ferry
P Parking	🥗 Vegetarian Selection	M Metro
🚭 Nonsmoking	📋 English-Language Menu	S Subway
❄ Air-Conditioning	👪 Family-Friendly	🚋 Tram
@ Internet Access	🐾 Pet-Friendly	🚆 Train

Reviews are organised by author preference.

Map Legend

Sights
- 🏖 Beach
- ⛩ Buddhist
- 🏰 Castle
- ✝ Christian
- 🕉 Hindu
- ☪ Islamic
- ✡ Jewish
- 🗽 Monument
- 🏛 Museum/Gallery
- 🏚 Ruin
- 🍇 Winery/Vineyard
- 🐾 Zoo
- ⊙ Other Sight

Activities, Courses & Tours
- 🤿 Diving/Snorkelling
- 🛶 Canoeing/Kayaking
- ⛷ Skiing
- 🏄 Surfing
- 🏊 Swimming/Pool
- 🚶 Walking
- 🏄 Windsurfing
- ⊙ Other Activity/Course/Tour

Sleeping
- 🛏 Sleeping
- ⛺ Camping

Eating
- 🍴 Eating

Drinking
- ☕ Drinking
- ☕ Cafe

Entertainment
- 🎭 Entertainment

Shopping
- 🛍 Shopping

Information
- 💲 Bank
- 🏛 Embassy/Consulate
- ✚ Hospital/Medical
- @ Internet
- 👮 Police
- 📮 Post Office
- 📞 Telephone
- 🚻 Toilet
- ℹ Tourist Information
- ● Other Information

Transport
- ✈ Airport
- ⊗ Border Crossing
- 🚌 Bus
- Cable Car/Funicular
- Cycling
- Ferry
- Monorail
- P Parking
- Petrol Station
- Taxi
- Train/Railway
- Tram
- M Underground Train Station
- ● Other Transport

Routes
- Tollway
- Freeway
- Primary
- Secondary
- Tertiary
- Lane
- Unsealed Road
- Plaza/Mall
- Steps
- Tunnel
- Pedestrian Overpass
- Walking Tour
- Walking Tour Detour
- Path

Geographic
- 🏠 Hut/Shelter
- 🔦 Lighthouse
- 🔭 Lookout
- ▲ Mountain/Volcano
- 🌴 Oasis
- 🌲 Park
-)(Pass
- 🧺 Picnic Area
- 💧 Waterfall

Population
- ★ Capital (National)
- ◉ Capital (State/Province)
- ● City/Large Town
- ○ Town/Village

Boundaries
- International
- State/Province
- Disputed
- Regional/Suburb
- Marine Park
- Cliff
- Wall

Hydrography
- River, Creek
- Intermittent River
- Swamp/Mangrove
- Reef
- Canal
- Water
- Dry/Salt/Intermittent Lake
- Glacier

Areas
- Beach/Desert
- + + + Cemetery (Christian)
- × × × Cemetery (Other)
- Park/Forest
- Sportsground
- Sight (Building)
- Top Sight (Building)

Kate Morgan
Victoria Falls Having travelled in East and North Africa, Kate was keen to check out what the southern part of the continent had to offer. She was lucky enough to head off to Victoria Falls to stand in awe of the world's most impressive water-fall from both sides, in Zimbabwe and Zambia. Kate is a freelance writer based in Melbourne and has written for other Lonely Planet titles including *Japan* and *Phuket*. She's also compiled the music/travel anthology, *Song for the Road*.

Contributing Author
David Lukas teaches and writes about the natural world from his home on the edge of Yosemite National Park. He has contributed Environment and Wildlife chapters to more than 25 Lonely Planet guides, including *Tanzania, East Africa, South Africa, Lesotho & Swaziland* and *Botswana & Namibia*.

OUR STORY

A beat-up old car, a few dollars in the pocket and a sense of adventure. In 1972 that's all Tony and Maureen Wheeler needed for the trip of a lifetime – across Europe and Asia overland to Australia. It took several months, and at the end – broke but inspired – they sat at their kitchen table writing and stapling together their first travel guide, *Across Asia on the Cheap*. Within a week they'd sold 1500 copies. Lonely Planet was born.

Today, Lonely Planet has offices in Melbourne, London, Oakland and Delhi, with more than 600 staff and writers. We share Tony's belief that 'a great guidebook should do three things: inform, educate and amuse'.

OUR WRITERS

Alan Murphy

Coordinating Author, Namibia Alan remembers falling under Southern Africa's ambient spell after bouncing around in the rear of a bakkie on the way from Johannesburg airport in 1999. Since then he has been back numerous times for Lonely Planet, including this trip to Namibia. In particular, Alan finds wildlife watching exhilarating and although he can't compete with twitchers spending hours hiding in a bush waiting for a feathered discovery, he has certainly taken years off his life staking out waterholes. This was Alan's third time to Namibia, a country custom-built for road trips with landscapes that never cease to inspire. Alan lives with his wife in the Yarra Valley outside Melbourne, which he wishes was just a touch closer to Melbourne airport.

Anthony Ham

Botswana Anthony has been travelling around Africa for more than a decade, particularly the Sahara, Kenya and Botswana. A writer and photographer, he writes guidebooks about Africa – including *Kenya*, *Africa*, *Libya* and *West Africa* – and elsewhere for Lonely Planet. He also writes and photographs for magazines and newspapers around the world, among them *Travel Africa* and *Africa Geographic*. He counts among his passions conservation, wildlife, indigenous peoples and the wild places of Africa. He covered more than 8100km on his most recent trip to Botswana. When he's not in Africa, Anthony divides his time between Madrid and Melbourne, where he lives with his wife and two daughters.

Read more about Anthony at:
lonelyplanet.com/members/anthonyham

Trent Holden

Victoria Falls As a regular visitor to Africa, Trent rates the action at Victoria Falls up there with the best adventure destinations he's covered. As well as its thrills and spills, it's also a spot he loves for its good traveller vibes and fun, friendly locals. He currently resides in Melbourne, Australia and has worked on more than 15 books for Lonely Planet – most recently covering Uganda and parts of India. When not travelling he works as a freelance editor for Lonely Planet and writes about music and food.

OVER MORE
PAGE WRITERS

Published by Lonely Planet Publications Pty Ltd
ABN 36 005 607 983
3rd edition – Jun 2013
ISBN 978 1 74179 893 7
© Lonely Planet 2013   Photographs © as indicated 2013
10 9 8 7 6 5 4 3 2 1
Printed in China